The Golden Age Of
BRITISH
MOTORING

The Golden Age Of
BRITISH MOTORING

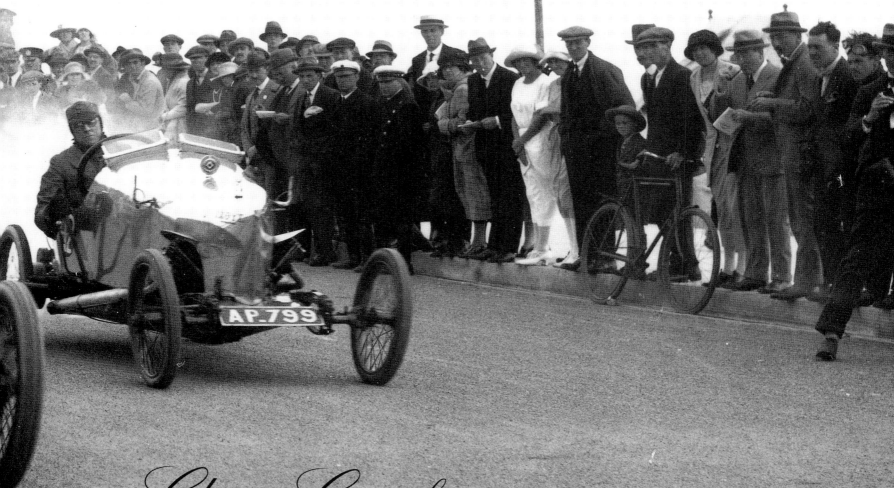

Classic Cars from 1900 to 1940

ROY BACON

on the work of

W J (BILL) BRUNELL

PRC

This edition first published in 1995 by
Promotional Reprint Company
Kiln House
210 New Kings Road
London SW6 4NZ
exclusively for Bookmart Ltd.
Desford Road
Enderby Leicester

Copyright
Text © Roy Bacon 1995
Photography © Beaulieu 1995
Design and layout © Promotional Reprint Company Ltd 1995

Designed by Blackjacks, London

ISBN 1 85648 315 0

Printed in Hong Kong

Reprinted 1996

W J BRUNELL
"artist with a camera"

Bill Brunell was a professional photographer all his adult life, concentrating on cars and related areas, but never shy of taking other subjects. Such a bald description does no justice to his abilities, and his own photographic albums were inscribed with "artist with a camera", which was no self-flattery, as these pages testify. As a Tony Hancock sketch put it, "He paints with light", and Bill did just that.

Born in May 1878, he was in his teens when a book called *How to Make a Box Camera for 3d* prompted him to construct his first camera. Problems in doing this led him to a local coach builder, and in turn to an introduction to motor vehicles. The home-made camera set his path for life, and it was soon replaced by a Thornton Piccard, which he used to take pictures of old London inns. Sales of these persuaded him that he had found his vocation.

This was emphasised when, early in 1901 and not yet 23, his pictures of Queen Victoria's funeral procession proved much better than those of the newspapers' photographers. Fleet Street beat a path to his door and he made more that day than his father could earn in three months. It also made his name and his work was then in constant demand.

He took to motorcycling and in 1913 was awarded a silver cigarette box for being the only entrant to climb Nailsworth Ladder and Warren Hill from the 170 who attempted them. He used a Douglas twin whose belt-and-pulley drive gave the effect of clutch slip so he could keep the engine speed up during the climbs.

Brunell was with Vickers at Brooklands at the start of the Great War but soon moved to the Ministry of Information, and worked for MI5 on assignment in Italy. Afterwards he had a couple of jobs before starting his own business as Pictorial Publicity. He had flair and good connections so was kept busy working for motoring magazines, especially *Autocar*, as well as taking pictures of stately home interiors, famous gardens and London scenes. His ability to take lovely photographs around the country shines out from the examples of his work included in this book.

Bill Brunell was a frequent rally and trial competitor. Perhaps the pinnacle of his achievements was to partner the Hon. Victor Bruce in 1926 when they became the first Englishmen to win the Monte Carlo Rally. This interest produced many of his fine pictures, taken at events over the years and across the country.

Brunell had a daughter, Kitty, who was as keen as her father to enter competition. At the early age of 16 she went on the 1928 Monte Carlo Rally with him, and in 1929 cajoled him into persuading Talbot to let her design a body for their 14/45hp chassis for her to drive in the Rally. This they did, and it became their Sportsman's Coupe! For 1930 they built another car for her, and this one was known as "Kitty II".

While Bill Brunell continued to drive his camera, Kitty drove in rallies and trials, often appearing in the resultant pictures. She met and married Ken Hutchinson, who raced at Donington Park in prewar days, and drove in trials and sprints. A wealthy director of Fry's Metal Works, he died in Italy in 1986, to be survived for a few years by Kitty.

Bill became a civilian photographer with the US Army during the Second World War – although by then of retirement age. He never stopped driving his camera and wrote on the back of a 1960 portrait, at 81, "Still doing a bit".

He spent his final years in semi-retirement with his second wife in a Surrey village near Dorking. He died on 23rd March 1965, aged 86, and left behind a remarkable record, not only of the sporting motoring scene between the wars, but also of the social and domestic life of that period.

We owe him a great debt and must be glad that he took up his camera.

Kitty Brunell and her father map out a trials course. The AA Road Book is a mine of information, while the cigarette box is for climbing Nailsworth Ladder on a Douglas in 1913.

The Brunell family out in their Clyno sidecar outfit, before the First World War. Kitty, Brunell's daughter, sits at the front, showing her early interest in powered transport.

Brunell combined transport and photography throughout his life as this early shot of two competitors in a motorcycle trial shows.

From the start, the ladies were keen to join in, and before 1914 most firms included models for them in their lists. Note the surface and spectators' clothing styles.

A sidecar outfit high on Rosedale Chimney in Yorkshire, the driver and passenger searching for grip on the poor surface while the spectators will them on.

Down at the Caerphilly Hill Climb in South Wales near Cardiff, this rider lacks helmet, cap, goggles or gloves as he tackles the ascent in pre First World War days.

A Humber taking part in the Caerphilly Hill Climb organised by the South Wales Auto Club. The conservative firm built this model type both before and after the First World War.

The scene is Snowdonia in North Wales, with a 10hp Singer, around 1920. One of several stretches of water in the area, each is still known as a 'Llyn'.

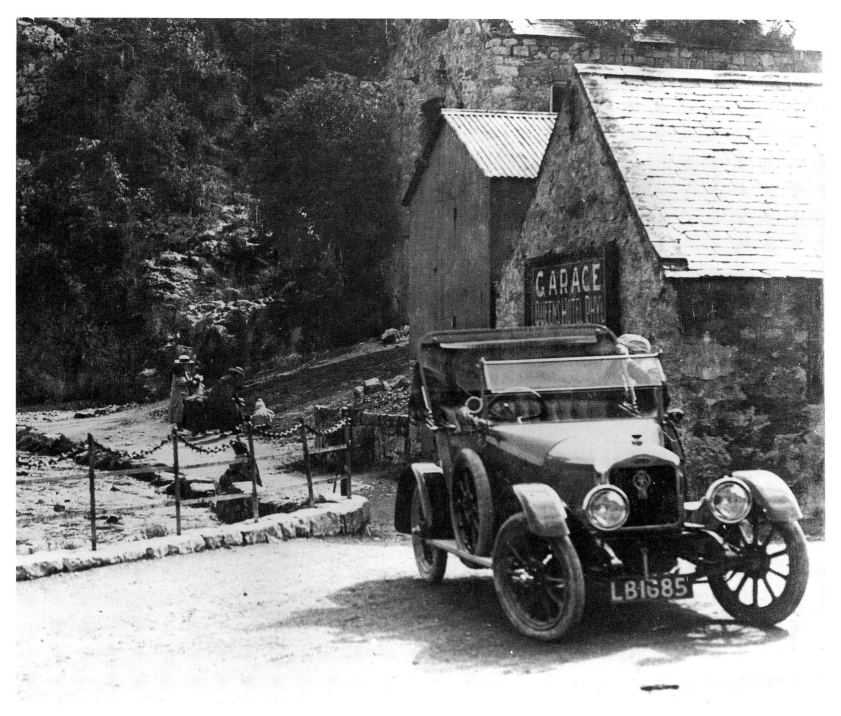

Dyserth Falls near Rhyl on the North Wales coast and the garage of the Queens Hotel, Rhyl, form the scenic backdrop for this 10hp Singer in the August sunshine of 1920.

Of these cars parked near the centre of Ludlow, Shropshire, in 1920, the front one is a 10hp Singer. The buildings remain virtually unchanged today.

The car is a 10hp Singer two-seater, seen here near Ludlow, Shropshire, in 1920. The castle and the church of this lovely town can be seen, too.

The house is timber framed and Tudor, the car is a 10hp Singer two-seater and the year is 1920, in the midst of peace after war, before the roaring twenties.

Seen here is an early Swift from a Coventry firm, which offered small cars of high quality. Unable to mass produce, they failed in 1931, having begun with bicycles and motorcycles.

This is a Swift from the early 1920s out on Dartmoor, in quite a lonely spot, although there is habitation in the valley below and another car lower on the hill.

A wonderful reflection at Aldbury in Hertfordshire on what must have been an exceptionally calm day; the car is a 1920 Standard.

For most drivers it was a long journey down to South Wales for the speed trials on the sands of Porthcawl, but worth the effort to run the cars.

A French Amilcar makes its way onto Porthcawl sands under the watchful eye of the police. The make was only built between the wars, and the1920s were its best years.

An array of competitors and officials collect on Porthcawl sands. The cars show a fine variety of body styles from racer to tourer, with preparations for the day underway.

Raymond Mays in his Brescia Bugatti on Porthcawl sands. He was a famous racing driver between the wars and associated with the postwar BRM in its early days.

An early Darracq halts to watch the progress of a sidecar competitor in a London to Edinburgh trial. The roads and traffic are typical of those times.

This Singer is parked close to Harlech Castle, North Wales, in the early 1920s. The Castle continues to dominate the skyline, though the roads are much altered.

An early Bullnose Morris motors out on the moors on a gated track. A helper to open and shut the barrier was always an asset.

The spirit of the 1920s embodied: a car, a narrow road approaching a bridge, and a wonderful view of the hills. The Lake District, Pennines, North Yorkshire and Scotland all offer this.

An HE steers between close-ranked spectators in July 1922 at the Shelsley Walsh hill climb esses. Herbert Engineering built these cars in Reading between 1920 and 1931.

Changing the coach horses outside the Crown Inn in Amersham High Street made for a tight squeeze for the Thornycroft bus, the car and the replacement horses.

A GWK tourer stops to check a signpost at Teddington in Gloucestershire. Built at Maidenhead, the marque used a friction disc to drive the rear axle and vary the gearing.

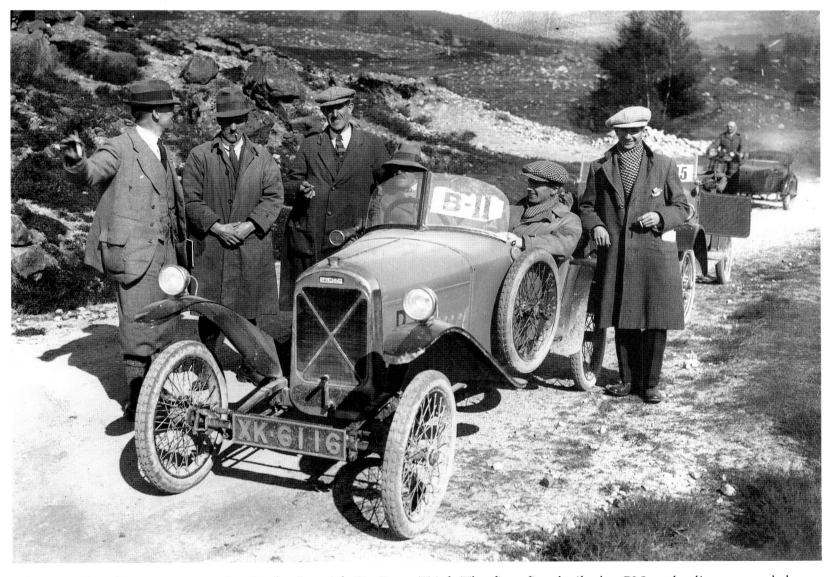

This French Salmson was running in the Scottish Six Days Trial. The firm first built the GN under licence, and the Salmson was launched in 1921.

Eric Longden campaigned his V-twin car at Brooklands, here at the Southsea Speed Trials, and elsewhere. Virtually a cyclecar, it ran under his name. An all-aluminium saloon body was also offered.

Raymond Mays in his Brescia Bugatti at the Southsea Speed Trials. Mays had many successes with this marque during the 1920s, moving on to others in the 1930s.

The Silver GNat of E G Sharp, on the left, and a Wolseley are poised on the start line at the Southsea Speed Trials, with another GN to follow.

A Bugatti just leads a GN away from the start line as both put the power down at the Southsea Speed Trials. The big V-twin engine and low weight of the GN made it highly competitive.

A competitor drives a 1928 French BNC in the Amersham hill climb, an event run by the Bugatti club. The firm's initials stood for Bollack, Netter et Cie.

A touch too wide on a bend in the Amersham Hill Climb but the bank saves the day for this Vernon-Derby (the name under which the French Derby was sold in Britain).

The thatch on the cottages and some of the wall plaster needs attention in this fine 1923 picture of a Morris Oxford tourer.

An open Riley, driven by C Montagu Johnston, taking part in the Brighton-Beer trial. The event was run for fun to test drivers' skills without damaging the car.

Seen here crossing Windsor Bridge, the Noma hailed from the USA – hence the left hand drive. Nomas were built from 1919 to 1923 using six-cylinder Continental engines.

This AC sports model dates from around 1922 so lacks front-wheel brakes. Its three-speed gearbox was built as a single unit with the worm-drive rear axle.

A Vauxhall slides from the first of the esses at Shelsley Walsh in 1923. The marque had many successes at this famous hill climb.

The Brunell family Morris Cowley at the Devil's Beef Tub, tours high in the hills at Ericstane Brae, a few miles north of Moffat, Dumfries, in the Scottish Lowlands.

This Morris Oxford features a second windscreen for the rear seat passengers when the top was down. The country scene of timber frame and thatch was typical in 1924.

This charming picture was taken in Richmond Park, Surrey. The car is a BSA of the early 1920s, the product of a firm best known for guns and motorcycles.

A 1924 Talbot 10/23 model parked at Chalgrove in the Chilterns. A popular model, the car ran well enough even when five up, as seen here.

Wantage in Berkshire, close by the Vale of the White Horse, is the country setting for this Calcott, the ladies and the young girls.

This GWK and its friction drive is in Frencham Pond during a car trial. The drive system worked well and the make was successful in both trials and record breaking.

Taken during the Scottish Six Days Trial, a Lagonda motors past a Calcott. Early Lagondas had advanced unit construction, while later they moved more to nice, but conventional, sports cars.

Mathis was an Alsace-based German firm, which after First World War border changes became French. This car is in the Scottish Six Days Trial.

This Belsize is at Bosham in Hampshire, close to Chichester. The Manchester-built marque failed in 1925, as its postwar products were too many and too costly to build.

An 8hp Talbot of the 1922-26 period motoring at Castle Coombe, Wiltshire. The village, which much later won prettiest in UK one year, had a postwar racing circuit close by.

Two Trojans seek grip on the Yorkshire Moors during a trial. Advertised as 'The simplest car in the world', Trojans used a two-stroke engine under the seat, two-speed epicyclic gearbox, chain drive to the rear axle and solid tyres. Eccentric!

Christ Church Gateway to Canterbury Cathedral, a shot taken around 1925. The centre car is an Austin Seven, and affluence on four wheels can be seen to the left.

Kirkstone Pass in the Lake District must have been quite an obstacle for the Vulcan, a marque which struggled through the postwar years to a 1928 end.

An 11hp Wolseley takes part in the 1926 Bognor Trial. Cars, motorcycles, the sidecar and peoples' apparel are all so typical of the 1920s.

A Vulcan Tourer, on trade plates, motors through Friday Street, a small village at the end of a lake surrounded by pine woods deep in the Surrey countryside.

The Windsor car was built from 1924 to 1927, had few bought-in parts and was better than most. Naturally it stands on Windsor Bridge with the Castle in the background.

The Windsor had front and rear brakes from the start, but their compensation was poor. This example is parked in the doorway of the Talbot Inn at Ripley in Surrey.

An Austin taking part in a trial run by the Brighton & Hove club over the South Downs. The trial was run for fun; there were few, if any, lady spectators on this occasion.

A parked Calcott and a sidecar outfit being passed by an AC and several other runners in a MCC London to Edinburgh Trial.

A Bugatti climbing Lynmouth Hill during a MCC London to Lands End Trial. It's a stiff climb even today, and was much worse in those days on the poor surface.

The Thames at Runnymead, site of the Magna Carta signing, appears peaceful with a swan, bicycles and a Calcott.

This fine Bentley stands beside the majestic King Alfred statue at the head of Winchester High Street, close to the River Itchen in Hampshire. This car is the third prototype: the time 1920.

A Coventry-built Calcott parked in Shrewsbury, Shropshire, a historic town nearly surrounded by the River Severn. The firm ran from 1913 until 1926, after which Singer took over the factory.

This Austin is parked at Bentley, Hampshire. Under the thatch is the Book of Bentley in stone which gives the village history and was donated by Lord Baden-Powell.

Typical motoring in the 1920s, when cars offered a real freedom to travel and the countryside was unspoiled. The car is a Calthorpe tourer.

A Calcott tourer seen close to Ludlow Castle in Shropshire, itself a centre of much history. The cars were described as dull but well made, and the stock colour was described as 'mole brown.'

Broadway is one of the loveliest of English villages with many fine buildings in Cotswold stone. The car is a Calthorpe of the early 1920s.

This Calthorpe stands by The Four Shire Stone on the Gloucestershire and Worcestershire border, close to Broadway in the Vale of Evesham.

A Bullnose Morris passes a parked Calthorpe by The Four Shire Stone on the county borders near Broadway. Calthorpe effectively ceased car production around 1924, but their motorcycles stayed to 1939.

The same Calthorpe checking the signposts near Broadway Hill. The steep drop with its bends was also known as Fish Hill, while the second sign is vague.

The Bullnose model enabled Morris to dominate the British market for many years. This one is at Exford in North Devon, about to cross the river Exe.

A typical four-seater touring car of the 1920s with its hood down and sidescreens stowed away. When up, the split windscreen opened for ventilation and forward vision.

Crossley supplied vehicles to the services in the First World War, so the company was soon back in civilian production. This tourer is passing under an inn sign which just has to be 'The Fox & Hounds'.

No telephone for a 999 call in Chipping Norton back in the 1920s; in case of fire you pulled the bell rope. The car is a Bullnose Morris.

Common enough at one time, if you travelled off the main roads you then expected a water splash, which had suited carts and horses for many a year. This is a Singer wading through the water.

AC used the same basic six-cylinder, overhead-camshaft engine from 1922 for some 40 years, concentrating on sports cars. This is a typical early Six.

A Morris Cowley stops at the sailor's grave at the Devil's Punch Bowl near Hindhead in Surrey. The driver has joined the party by the Ford Model T.

A quick stop to inspect the stone erected to commemorate the unknown sailor who was murdered by three tramps in 1786. The car is a Morris Cowley, and the scene is typical of the empty roads of the 1920s.

An old lychgate at Waltham St Lawrence between Reading and Maidenhead; the car is a Crossley.

A bleak road en-route to John O'Groats, one of the starting points of the 1926 Monte Carlo Rally. This AC Six is driven by the rally winner, the Hon Victor Bruce with his co-driver Bill Brunell.

Down in Monte Carlo at the end of the 1926 Rally, this Sunbeam is parked and ready for the final inspection. Excellent cars, but too many models spelt commercial disaster.

The Bugatti club comes out in force at Broadway in Worcestershire. From its earliest days, the marque was technically advanced, highly distinctive and very desirable.

The milestone (the shortest mile) at the junction of the Aylesbury road and the London to Oxford A40 just west of High Wycombe as it was in the 1920s. The car is a 1926 Lea-Francis fitted with a Cross & Ellis body.

A Buick parked outside the magnificent front of the Feathers Hotel, Ludlow. The Feathers is still one of England's finest for food, service and atmosphere, with some superb panelled rooms.

The Talbot 14/45 was a brilliant car, built for many years. This 1927 model is running in a Bournemouth Rally leaving a fine hotel behind it.

The gatehouse of Stokesey Castle at Ludlow, with its Norman keep, is steeped in history. The car is a tourer from Calcott, who also made motorcycles before the First World War.

A 1927 Talbot 14/45 seen on the packhorse bridge at Alternon, when such bridges were common around the country. The car's six-cylinder engine made for smooth running.

A 14/45 Talbot down in Devon at Newton St Cyres, just outside Exeter, among thatched roofs and white walled houses during the late 1920s.

A fine study of the Brunell's 1927 Talbot 14/45, seen in several of his photographs. Here he is out in the Southern England countryside, enjoying the sunshine.

The Brunell family 14/45 Talbot calling at a scenic spot on the Roman Causeway. The boat is named The Brownie.

A very English car, countryside and couple seen late in the 1920s. The car is the Brunell-owned Talbot 14/45 tourer with the top down. This large car performed well on its 1665cc.

Most Bentleys of the 1920s were like this one: large, expensive open sports cars in a mould that won five times at Le Mans.

The drive through Meonstoke on the A32 in the lovely Meon Valley is to this day one of the nicest in Hampshire. The Talbot Six, seen here in the late 1920s, is parked while passengers watch the trout.

Ringwood in Hampshire, on the edge of the New Forest by the River Avon, is a gracious place for a Morris Bullnose to stop for lunch or tea at 'The Old Cottage,' with the gift shop next door.

An 8hp Talbot of the 1920s with three ladies out to pick flowers. Talbot was associated with Darracq of France and Sunbeam. The 8hp model was a useful performer.

Taking the girls to school in a Morris Cowley of the late 1920s. 'Have you done your homework?'

This 1927 Morris Cowley is ready to transport madam to the black-tie dinner-dance or perhaps the theatre.

Doing the school run in the late 1920s, with mother, two daughters and a Morris Cowley. 'Be good and pull your socks up!'

The Morris Cowley out and about on its social duties, collecting friends from the local tennis club once the children were off hand for the day.

This is an 1898 6hp Daimler motoring through Reigate during the 1928 Brighton Pioneer run. Driver Doug Copley drove his car to and from his Birmingham home.

A 1901 Sunbeam Mabley with De Dion Bouton engine taking part in the 1928 Brighton Pioneer run. Described as a sofa on wheels, the driver sat behind the passenger while the driven rear wheel was offset from the front.

Even in 1928 this 1900 Benz 3.5hp dogcart and the others had to contend with a degree of traffic along the route.

Nearly there! A 1902 Renault passing the Pylons a few miles outside Brighton during the 1928 Brighton Pioneer run, with a fair selection of vehicles both parked and following.

Crowds of spectators lined up to watch the passing cars in the 1928 Brighton Pioneer run. Note the smart RAC patrolman's sidecar outfit, which could be in for a busy day.

Two official cars set about their duties in the 1928 Brighton Pioneer run, motoring past The Yorkshire Cafe. The lead car is a 1928 Alfa Romeo of 1500cc.

This is a 1902 7.5 hp Wolseley four-seater, rear-entrance model, passing the Plough Inn in the company of a cyclist and following vehicles.

The first Cadillac to come to Europe was this 1903 single-cylinder model, which ran in the RAC Reliability Trial of that year. Here it is well on its way to Brighton.

This car was entered in the 1928 London to Exeter trial as a Lea-Francis driven by H Stevens, but has a non-standard radiator grille. The trial was one of several long-distance events run by the MCC for many years.

Austin Sevens, one minus a front mudguard, during the 1928 London to Exeter trial, which was usually held in January, hence the dismal weather. The Seven was cheap, well made, classless and very popular.

A Bayliss Thomas storming up one of the sections during the 1928 London to Exeter trial. Traction in the muddy surface of these sections was often at a premium.

Raymond Mays, on the right, campaigned this car from 1928 to 1933 with much success. Based on a 1922 TT Vauxhall, it was supercharged by Amherst Villiers and much developed.

A nice Belgian Minerva seen at Boulogne during Bill Brunell's visit for the Coupe Boillot race meeting in 1928. Minerva built fine, but expensive, cars until 1939.

A massive Mercedes-Benz sits alongside a two-seat miniature form of powered transport for contrast, at Boulogne in 1928.

Kitty Brunell working on her father's Singer Junior entered for the 1928 Monte Carlo Rally. They started from John O'Groats but were forced to retire.

A Model A Ford crossing a tributary of the River Exe at Winsford in Somerset, with the Royal Oak inn behind. The A replaced the long-running T in 1928.

At the end of the 1928 Southport Rally the front is crowded with people, cars, motorcycles and a charabanc, with the fine pier in the background.

W Arnold's very smart 1926 37hp Bentley taking second prize in one of the many classes of the rally, despite its well-worn front tyres.

On the Bentley the running boards offered further storage space, as shown here.

The Bentley's boot and its fitted luggage being shown off by the owner – a smart way to travel.

Alvis used good parts and materials for their cars and kept the weight down, which resulted in a good performance and high reputation for both the sports cars and the tourers.

Neat seating for two in the dickey, although they sat out in the weather. The dickey seat was a common alternative to the car boot for many years. The car is being judged at the end of 1928 Southport Rally.

The Lanchester Straight Eight was only built for a short while, but always to the firm's high standards. The car had an overhead camshaft and delivered excellent performance.

The American Willys-Knight cars had six-cylinder, sleeve-valve engines, but were much cheaper than similar Daimlers. When the sleeves wore the car smoked badly.

F F Austin started from John O'Groats in this Morris Cowley and was the winner of the 1928 Southport Rally. For several years the Cowley was Britain's most popular car.

The famous flying stork on the bonnet shouts Hispano-Suiza, a Spanish car of which the best were built in France. This 1927 model is labelled Glissante on the bonnet side, had a Hopper body and was owned by Lt-Cdr Montague Graham White.

This 1928 Talbot 14/45 Sportsmans Coupe, with false dumb irons, appears at the finish of the Southport Rally and was among the prize winners.

This 1927 20.9hp car was built on a Darracq chassis and owned by E S Berry. It stands in the finishers' enclosure on the front at the end of the 1928 Southport Rally.

Mrs Kathleen May of Putney shows off her 1927 Marmon and the prizes she and it won in the 1928 Southport Rally. Hailing from the USA, the make offered plenty of car for the money.

This Austin has a highly desirable Swallow saloon body from William Lyons' firm, and is parked on the Southport sea front at the end of the 1928 rally.

The fitted tool-kit was one of the features of the Swallow-bodied Austin although the tools are hardly high-quality and the files lack handles.

This truly massive Daimler is at the end of the 1928 Southport Rally. The firm built expensive luxury cars which competed with the best, and were used by the royal family.

The Lanchester Straight Eight at the 1928 Southport Rally together with the trophies it had won for its proud owner.

A charming study of a 2-litre Ballot and its owner, taken at the end of the Southport Rally when it was time for a drink.

The final view of the front at Southport at the end of the rally. The cars are parked in the finishers' enclosure for inspection followed by the long trip home.

The French Amilcar was built between the wars, and offered attractive sports cars of good performance in the 1920s. This two-seater is running in an Ilkley Club trial.

A Yank at York. A Buick standing just outside Queen Margaretes Arch which straddles Gillygate, close by the magnificent Bootham Bar built into the York city walls.

The same American Buick passing close by Lincoln Cathedral and some of the town's fine old houses. The cars were a bargain to buy in the UK despite their 30hp road tax rating.

Deep in the English countryside, a Buick from the USA motoring at East Garston, north of Hungerford in Wiltshire, a byway little altered by the years.

Freddie Thatcher working on the twin carburettors of his well-appointed Triumph Super-Seven model; he later drove MGs at Brooklands with success.

Two Talbot Sixes in the 1929 Junior Car Club trial. To the left a 1926 18/55 and on the right Kitty Brunell with her 1928 14/45.

A 1928 Morris Oxford and others line up before continuing on their way in the 1929 JCC trial. Plus fours were common in those days!

A 1927 Standard 14/28 open tourer taking part in the Bognor Regis trial of 1929. Such events were popular and fun, and unlikely to harm the cars.

Working in the paddock prior to storming the Shelsley Walsh hill climb in May 1929. The car, the clothes and smoking on the job were all typical of the time.

This is the start of the Surbiton Grand Cup in 1929, outside the Talbot Inn at Ripley in Surrey, on the main London to Portsmouth road.

Kitty Brunell and her 14/45 Talbot Sportsman Coupe splash through a tributary of the River Exe at Winsford in Somerset, passing both church and chapel in the process.

A fine collection of MGs, a Riley and an Austin line up during the lunch stop at Launceston in Cornwall near the end of the London to Land's End trial.

More of the long line of London to Land's End trial competitors parked at Launceston while the drivers have their lunch. Austin, MG and Riley are among those on this damp day.

Storming up Hustyn Hill with a Frazer Nash during the London to Land's End trial, which was always a favourite with drivers and the massed spectators.

This American Gardner is climbing Beggars Roost in the London to Land's End trial. The car had a 4-litre, eight-cylinder engine, hydraulic brakes and central door locking.

Kitty Brunell drove this 14/45hp Talbot in the 1929 Monte Carlo Rally. She has her oilcan at the ready before changing the bald front tyres.

Kitty Brunell's 1665cc Talbot Sportsmans Coupe was one of only 24 finishers from 93 starters in the 1929 Monte Carlo Rally. It stands by the award presentation dais.

The front at Monte Carlo after the finish of the 1929 rally, with cars from many nations resting after their long journey.

At the end of the 1929 Monte Carlo Rally the finishing cars lined up outside the palace, where competitors exchanged stories of their adventures along the route.

A Riley taking part in a club trial during 1929, nothing too adventurous but a chance to visit some lovely countryside.

This Crossley tourer is being watched with interest as it goes through its paces during a typical club trial of the late 1920s. Crossleys were excellent and popular cars.

An Austin Seven takes part in a 1929 club trial. This model brought transport to many over a long time span, offering basic, albeit slow, motoring.

This well-timed photograph has caught the lady at the end of her well-judged swing while Brunell gets his clubs out of the family 14/45 Talbot.

Charles Mortimer raced motorcycles and cars at Brooklands, wrote some good books and dealt in fine cars such as this Speed Six Bentley. The car has a Barker boat-tailed, two-seater body, which was on their stand at the 1929 London Motor Show.

This fine Bentley pauses at St Albans in Hertfordshire to view Ye Old Fighting Cocks, previously the Round House, which was claimed to be the oldest inhabited house in England, having served monks as a boat house.

Taking in a fine view from Box Hill, Surrey, the Brunell 14/45 Talbot Coupe was a family favourite for several years.

A Triumph Super-Seven motors down at Dunster near Minehead on the North Somerset coast. Minehead is a charming village with castle, a watch tower and a long history.

Taken during the 1930 London to Edinburgh trial, this Austin saloon is climbing Park Rash, and making good headway despite its size.

Lower down Park Rash in the 1930 London to Edinburgh trial is this Lagonda. Park Rash was no easy climb for stock saloons.

Brunell kept his interest in motorcycles, and would certainly not have missed this chance to picture George Brough riding one of his delectable Brough Superior machines.

C H Lawford's Riley takes advantage of a helping hand on Ibberton Hill during the 1930 MCC London to Exeter trial.

High in the hills during the 1930 Monte Carlo Rally, Kitty Brunell and her 14/45 Talbot are seen here after they had climbed through those many hairpin bends on the road below.

Kitty motors down from the hills in the 1930 Monte Carlo Rally for a brief respite before the next icy mountain pass. Houses, hills and 'Cafe du Gard' are all typical of the country.

During the 1930 Monte Carlo Rally, the team takes a brief stop to view the vine terraces. The 14/45 Talbot is named Kitty II after Brunell's daughter, and is a big car for such an event.

During this Ilkley Club trial, lunch was taken at the Fleece Hotel in Thirsk in North Yorkshire.

Madeira Drive, Brighton, seen at the end of a rally. The drive is still the finish for the Pioneer Run and has been the scene of sprint races since Edwardian times.

Donald Healey seen with the Invicta he drove in a Brighton Rally. Healey won the 1931 Monte Carlo Rally in an Invicta and built desirable sports cars postwar.

Kitty Brunell leaving her Lea Francis 12/40 for a Blackburn Bluebird on a weekend trip in 1930. Not quite a 747, but still travelling in style.

The Austin Six was built for ten years from 1927 in various forms, and this saloon is at High Roding on the old Roman road, south of Great Dunmow in Essex.

Feeding the swans, sensibly from a distance, at the mill pond. The car is the Brunell's 1930 Talbot 75, a model developed from the 14/45 with a 2276cc engine.

Outside the Church House Inn with the Dart cafe behind, this Austin Six is in Old Stoke Gabriel, near the river Dart in Devon.

The Brunell family and their 1930 Talbot 75 are about to cross a small stream during a country drive. Originally listed as the 70, it was found to be 5mph faster.

Helmsdale Castle, dating from 1488, standing above the harbour and an Austin Six. The village is on the Scottish east coast in the far north.

This is Madeira Drive on the front at Brighton. The occasion is the RAC Rally, rather than the Pioneer Run or the kilometre sprint.

The magnificent castle at Hurstmonceux in Sussex, which dates from 1440 and the time of Henry VI. Various cars, including the Brunell's Austin in the car park.

This Singer saloon has a fine study of an ancient gateway at St Albans in Hertfordshire, a city with a long history stretching back to the Romans.

Two of the works Talbot 2.3-litre, six-cylinder cars seen at the 1930 Irish Grand Prix. Driven by Rose-Richards and the Hon Lewis, the cars were very quiet and nearly as fast as the Bentleys.

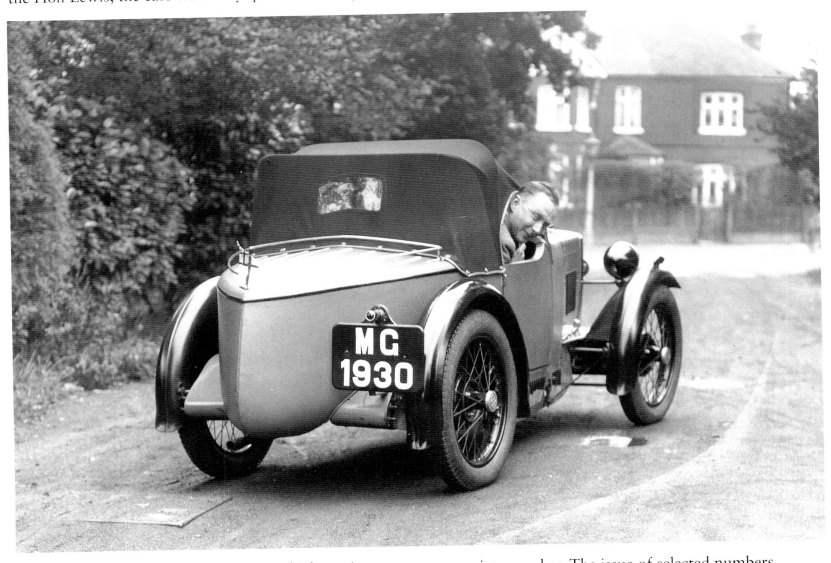

Charles Robinson seen with his MG, which carries a most appropriate number. The issue of selected numbers continued up to 1962; now they are just merchandise.

A Marmon from the USA, seen at Shottery, west of Stratford-upon-Avon, where Anne Hathaway's cottage is located.

This rare Ascot Six is a combination of an American engine and gearbox with a Letchworth-built body. Cyril Pullin, the instigator, also offered an unusual motorcycle, but both projects were short-lived, lasting from 1928-30.

The family 1930 Talbot 75 Fabric saloon, minus front number plate, enjoys the country air and sunshine.

The Brunell's 1930 Talbot 75 shows its fine lines while the family goes golfing in Worth Forest, near Crawley in Sussex.

Kitty Brunell shows off her Italian Bianchi. Their cars were undercut by Fiat on price so production ceased pre-Second World War, but the motorcycles continued into the 1960s.

A Singer Super Six passes a Morris Oxford and Austin 12 parked outside the Royal Oak, a 12th-century inn, by a charming village stream at Winsford in Somerset.

The Evans family, including dog, inspects one of the eight plugs from their delectable Bugatti. The alloy-spoked wheels were integral with the brake drums and were a feature for many years.

A Ford Model A stops on the way across Exmoor to check on the road to Cloutshaw. The Model A was first built for Britain at Cork and in Manchester.

The scene is Parkhurst on the Isle of Wight, but not the prison. The car is a Crossley, well made and a typical English tourer of the period.

This Ford is climbing New Mill Hill in a MCC London to Lands End Trial, a popular event for cars, motorcycles and sidecar outfits.

An American La Salle saloon parked outside the Abbey Gateway at Amesbury in Wiltshire, close to Stonehenge. The make was effectively a cheaper Cadillac.

Drivers wait to start in the 1930 MCC Buxton trial, with an Austin Seven ahead of a Standard Avon 9, and Fiat and Wolseley cars among others.

Taken during the 1930 MCC Buxton trial, a 1930 overhead-camshaft Morris Minor heads an MG Midget, which used the same engine, and an American De Soto, assembled at Kew.

Entitled 'A lane in February,' this picture shows a Lagonda out on a raw day but not stuck in snow. Most lanes were like this in those days.

Waving the family Morris Oxford out of its garage for the local runs to shops, school, station and social calls. The Oxford was better fitted out than the Cowley.

This 1930 Austin Seven driven by W G R Rushworth is on Nailsworth Ladder in a 1932 Bugatti Owners' Club event. From a standing start it was hard to find traction on the poor surface.

A Standard Swallow taking part in a JCC Half-day trial and checking just where it is in Bedfordshire. The car body is by William Lyons.

Roadside repairs being made on a Wolseley Hornet during a Brighton Rally. This popular model had a six-cylinder, overhead-camshaft engine, and was built from 1930 to 1936.

The gentleman is ready for his round of golf while the lady needs to organise tax and a number plate for the Singer 8 car. No doubt they were using trade plates.

This scene is typical of club trials between the wars when they were carefree events where competitors and spectators simply enjoyed their day out. The car is a Riley competing in the Beggers Roost Gold Award.

Guy Warburton thunders up Shelsley Walsh in a 3-litre Sunbeam in front of a good crowd. This was a very popular event for many years.

Earl Howe's big Mercedes-Benz, an Alfa Romeo and the 1.5-litre supercharged Delage seen at the 1931 Shelsley Walsh hill climb. The Delage had been a grand prix winner in the 1920s, and was later successfully raced by Dick Seaman.

This highly effective and dramatic photograph was taken at the sands on which the Skegness Speed Trials of 1931 were held. The car is an Austro-Daimler driven by Denis Conan Doyle.

Testing an MG on Tan Hill in the Pennines in April 1931, a pleasant way to pass a Spring day.

This is a water splash trial, the car a 1931 Austin Seven Ulster, and its future is in some doubt. A very English sport!

This Vauxhall, with its characteristic bonnet flutes, is being man-handled up a section in the 1931 Intervarsity Trial. Pushers preferred Austin Sevens!

Seen at the Brighton-Beer Trial, the MG just fits between the walls of the bridge. It is followed by a Norton sidecar outfit and others.

Both cars and motorcycles took part in the 1931 London to Barnstaple trial, which was typical of such events. This 346cc New Imperial was driven by Jessie Hole with her mother Rose in the sidecar.

A front-wheel drive BSA three-wheeler takes part in the 1931 London to Barnstaple trial. The vee windscreen marks it out as the sports version, its knobbly tyres changed for the event. An Austin Seven follows.

An Alfa Romeo, its badge somewhat awry, heads a line of cars running in the 1931 London to Barnstaple trial. The Alfa Romeo is one of the great sporting marques from Italy with a proud racing history.

An MG motors past that line of cars and the Alfa Romeo, leaving a trail of smoke in its rear. The octagon badge became famous for affordable sports cars.

The MG became very popular with enthusiasts, offering fun and enough performance to deal with sections such as this in the 1931 London to Barnstaple trial.

A sports Riley is readied on the starting line for the 1931 Lewes Speed Trials. A Bugatti is next up, with two saloons behind that.

The Bugatti driven by D G Evans leaving the 1931 Lewes Speed Trials start line and following in the wheel tracks of the Riley, as a Hotchkiss saloon rolls up to the line.

The same Bugatti with its fine array of club badges well down the Lewes Speed Trials course, which was the nearly straight, but steep and bumpy approach road to the Race Course.

The car is a racing Sunbeam from the 1920s, getting away well from the start line at the Lewes Speed Trials, with spectators nearly in the road. Around 25 seconds of excitement!

This single-seater racing car, seen at the Lewes Speed Trials, was based on a Frazer Nash, an excellent choice for such work.

Louis Chevrolet built this American Frontenac. Chevrolet also made special equipment for Fords, after leaving the firm bearing his name which was part of General Motors.

For 1931 the International Six Days Trial for motorcycles was held in the Italian Dolomites and centred on Merano. Italy won the Trophy while the scenery formed an impressive backdrop to the event.

A quintain post, believed to be the only one left in Britain, at Offhan, near Maidstone in Kent, all ready for lance practice. The car is an American Nash Eight.

The excellent Riley Nine was built from 1926 to 1937, and this one is parked among the boats on Mersea Island off the Essex coast near Colchester.

Maldon in Essex, and some fine timbered buildings form the backdrop for the same Riley Nine saloon. The model had a first-class engine, which made it a fine sporting car.

A Standard 16, mundane but well built and reliable, at Hambledon in Hampshire, a village famous in the annals of cricket.

The Triumph Super-Seven was well appointed and fitted with four-wheel hydraulic brakes. This one stands by a thatched house at Horley in Surrey.

Motoring between the wars was often like this: a drive out, a stop, and a picnic, even on a chilly day (hence the furs). The car is a Triumph Super Seven.

This Triumph Super-Seven is taking part in the Amersham Hill Climb run by the Middlesex club. Behind stands another runner, also due to be weighed.

An Alfa Romeo seen in the 1932 Oxford Speed Trials for cars and motorcycles held on the Eynsham By-pass just before it became a public road. It continues today as the A40, west of Oxford.

Rather than the 1932 Morris Oxford 6 Special Coupe, it is the gate that makes this picture. It is made from farm implements – but how many?

A crowd of small boys watch an Italian OM move off on Nailsworth Ladder in this 1932 Bugatti Owners Club event. A Bugatti is parked to the left.

For those who failed to climb Nailsworth Ladder, as has happened with this Austin, there was always a hard-working gang to pull the car out.

Long before the days of true car ferries, vehicles were craned on and off with a prayer for the slings to hold and minimal salt spray during the voyage.

A shot taken outside the Talbot Inn, the starting point for a motorcycle trial run by the Surbiton club. This would be a local event run for fun.

One family and their cars! An Italian Alfa Romeo with an American Chrysler behind it, a French Bugatti beside that, and yet another saloon bringing up the rear.

An official's Riley Nine follows a competitor's Morris through the water during the Brighton & Hove Barnstaple Trial. A horse and another Morris follow on.

Donington Park in March 1933, with Ken Hutchinson's Bugatti in the tree-lined section, raising some dust. Note that he carries a mechanic, even for this short race. Later he married Kitty Brunell.

This magnificent Delage is typical of that French firm's fine and elegant designs. It is leaving the Wykehurst Hotel at Bolney in Sussex, and Kitty Brunell is driving.

This Ford will have to reverse to complete its turn out of the track at the side. The shot was taken during an MCC Buxton Trial, among fine Derbyshire countryside.

The Experts Trial in Devon, with a Riley saloon tackling a section. It was a bleak post for the observer to man for much of the day, and these events depended on such stalwarts.

Kitty Brunell dealing with some essential maintenance for her immaculate MG, using one of the seat squabs as a kneeling pad.

Enough small boys for a football team admire Kitty Brunell and the different MG she drove in one of the Scottish Rallies.

Kitty Brunell and pioneer motorist S F Edge are deep in discussion. Edge won the 1902 Gordon Bennett Cup and set world records over 24 hours at Brooklands in 1907.

Kitty Brunell and her MG cross a remote plank bridge during a Scottish rally, which would have taken competitors through some fine scenery.

Kitty and the MG crossing a most impressive suspension bridge over the River Ness as they leave Inverness during a Scottish rally.

Kitty drove an Aston Martin in a Scottish rally one year, and has stopped here for her and friend to admire the view. Who can blame them?

A local well-wisher, complete with the national kilt and dirk, chatting to Kitty before the Aston Martin sets off in a Scottish rally.

Six club badges plus a horseshoe for luck in a Scottish rally for the Aston Martin, Kitty and friend.

Shelsley Walsh in September 1933 with the crowds watching a 3-litre Sunbeam tourer climbing the hill. Not as exciting as the racing cars but still effective.

Two sporting AC cars taking part in the RAC Hastings Rally. On the right is a 1933 model driven by Kitty Brunell.

A Crossley Ten from 1933 takes part in the Experts Trial for which its 1100cc four-cylinder engine with overhead inlet and side exhaust valves was hardly adequate.

A close-up look under the engine hood of the curious 1934 Crossley Burney model. Its six-cylinder, ohv engine and pre-selector gearbox were at the rear, it had all-round independent suspension, but only two dozen were built.

An MG negotiating the water splash part of the Fingle Bridge hill in the Brighton-Beer trial, under the watchful gaze of a local.

Two Rileys parked in Porlock village, Somerset, faced with climbing the famous hill – still a stiff challenge today. Even then, there was an easier road, with a toll, as an alternative.

An Armstrong-Siddeley saloon, the usual sphinx on the bonnet, about to start a hill climb. Armstrong-Siddeleys were a well-built, quality make, sold between the wars and after for a while.

An MG fights for grip on the New Mill Hill Climb during the London to Land's End Trial. It took skill and a careful approach to avoid wheelspin and surmount the obstacle.

An Alta tackling a section in the London to Land's End Trial. This rare marque was virtually hand-built by Geoffrey Taylor and his small team in a workshop close to the Kingston By-pass in Surrey.

Two Standards halted outside the Tors Hotel at Lynmouth on the North Devon coast. A 300-yard railway links to it twin, Lynton, some 500 feet above.

A highly-desirable Singer Le Mans carrying at least seven club badges and an MG Midget in the style it kept through to the 1950s. The event is the 1936 Rushmere hill climb.

Winners of a wet and windy Blackpool Rally seen on the deserted front at Blackpool. To the left is an Austin Seven, and to the right is a Fiat, both having come a long way from their Birmingham start point.

A fine pair of MGs, and others, seen at a Blackpool Rally where the marque had its own enclosure and tent for owners and their friends.

A Morris Six completes a special test on the front at the end of the Blackpool Rally, having come down from Glasgow.

There is no mistaking the Blackpool Tower further down the front from the parked cars. There are some fine models for visitors to inspect, with a SS Jaguar nearest and an Alvis beside it.

A fine SS Jaguar parked on the front at the end of the Blackpool Rally after its run up from London, being inspected by the judges.

This Flying Standard is seen departing from one of the oldest buildings in West Wycombe. The firm built this model type in a variety of sizes in the late 1930s.

An MG, the archetypal small British sports car, tackling a typical section in a club trial. The cars were cheap, charming, fun and very popular.

A nice Flying Standard crossing Aylesford Bridge over the Medway in Kent, just north of Maidstone, during a club trial, with another driver close behind.

This Talbot is seen at a stop-and-restart special test during the 1937 Welsh Rally, where cars had to halt and then move off without rolling back. This could be hard on the clutch and nerves.

A Triumph at the same test in the 1937 Welsh Rally. The firm began with bicycles and followed with motorcycles, but did not turn to four wheels until 1923, producing some attractive models in the 1930s.

This MG is leaving Cardiff at the start of the 1937 Welsh Rally under the watchful eye of the police and a large crowd of spectators.

A Cardiff starter in the 1937 Welsh Rally, driving a Singer Le Mans which was an excellent sports car of the time. Singer was a major firm in the 1920s, less so afterwards.

William Lyons progressed from sidecars to the Jaguar and during the 1930s built the archetypal sports car as the SS. These three won the team award in the 1937 Welsh Rally.

A Fiat 500, the *topolino,* which started from Swansea for the 1937 Welsh Rally. The four-cylinder engine sits ahead of its radiator under the small bonnet.

A 1936 Singer Nine Le Mans taking part in the 1937 Welsh Rally. Its fine overhead-camshaft engine made it a natural rival to the MG Midget.

By the 1930s, Rover had a name for producing good quality cars a little better than the average and this sports saloon is typical of those offered near the end of the decade.

Railton used a chassis and a big engine from the USA under British styling to offer inexpensive performance, so was always good value. The style was always very British and period.

This Austin was entered for the coachwork competition in the 1937 Welsh Rally and is from the late-1930s, complete with owner-driver. Note the interesting number plate.

The Jensen (on the left) is powered by an eight-cylinder engine from the USA. The Jensen and the SS Jaguar sports car are both fine examples of the British type, and were runners in the 1937 Welsh Rally.

Over the crest of one of the hills during the 1937 Welsh Rally goes a Dodge sedan from the USA. The firm became part of the Chrysler group in 1928 and is still going strong.

The model Y was the first true European Ford and was Britain's first £100 saloon. It sold in large numbers, and this one is taking a special test at the end of the 1937 Welsh Rally.

At the end of the 1937 Welsh Rally two Ford drivers enjoy a quiet smoke. These Fords, both Dagenham-built models, were typical of the late 1930s English style adopted by the firm.

This cairn and tablet on the Dumfries to Edinburgh road, south of Tweedsmuir, was erected in memory of the Edinburgh mail coach guard and driver who lost their lives in the 1831 snow storm. The car is a Standard Flying Six with an Avon body.

This Straker-Squire was built in the early 1920s, and is running in the 1937 Edinburgh Trial. Straker-Squires were well-made cars but of limited production.

Competing in a Watersplash trial, this Singer is near Chalfont St Giles in Buckinghamshire, the passenger driving his camera to record the recorder.

Taken during the 1937 MCC Torquay Rally, this Singer is undergoing one of the special tests. Very competitive on price, the car was fast and had excellent manners.

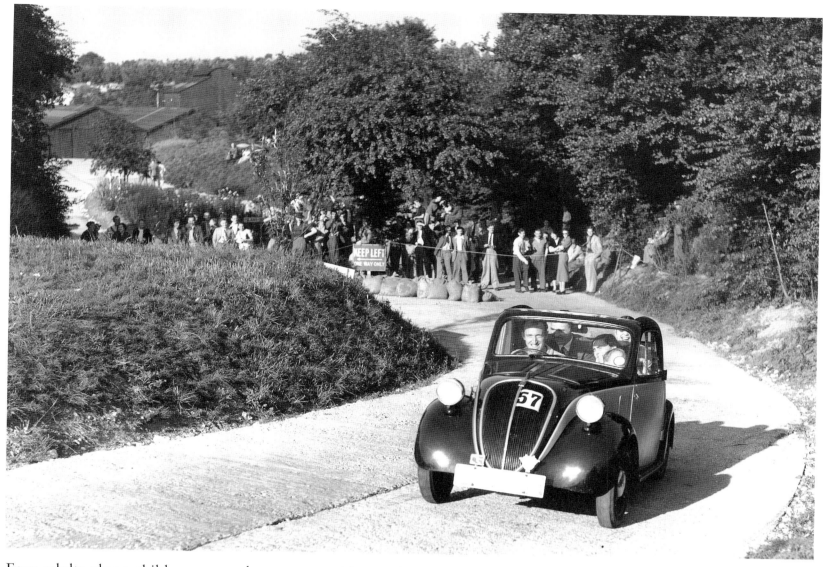

Four adults plus a child were somehow crammed into a tiny Fiat 500 to take part in a 1937 sprint event at the Autodrome School of Driving, South Croydon.

John Bolster campaigned his special, known as Bloody Mary, in the 1930s and postwar. Having little weight and two 1000cc V-twin JAP engines running on alcohol, its performance was always spectacular as this shot shows. He set fastest time of the day.

A Le Mans style start was commonly used for sports car races, but this one would seem to be a handicap event at Crystal Palace in 1937.

Seen at Crystal Palace in 1937, Watson's R-type MG is about to be lapped by Prince Bira and his 2.9-litre Maserati. Bira was a popular and highly successful driver in the 1930s and postwar.

Count Trossi and his Maserati lined up on the start line at the Crystal Palace October meeting in 1937. He won the second heat but retired in the final. The count's visit to England was mainly for the Grand Prix at Donington.

A works Mercedes-Benz driven by Lang at Donington, where it retired, demonstrated by Dick Seaman at Crystal Palace. The October 1937 event was the first motor race to be covered by television.

This veteran car race was held at one of the 1937 meetings at Crystal Palace. A Sunbeam is sandwiched between a Renault on the left and a Ford Model T special on the right.

This Lorraine Dietrich from pre-First World War days ran in the veteran race at Crystal Palace in 1937.

Prince Bira and his ERA seen hard at work in one of the events on the tight South London circuit. Bira raced from 1935 to around 1954 using ERA, Maserati, BMW and other marques.

The ERAs of Raymond Mays and Arthur Dobson fight for third place at Crystal Palace in 1937. The English Racing Automobiles cars were the backbone of voiturette racing for years.

This is one of the two massive Crystal Palace towers which dominated the intricate circuit. The towers were demolished early in the Second World War to prevent their use as landmarks. Postwar it was a simpler circuit.

Cars stand ready on the starting line for the veteran race at Crystal Palace.

Leslie Howard was a famous British film actor and this 1937 Bentley was his when Dominion and Cleveland sold petrol at 1s.5d. a gallon.

Taken at a Standard Car Club meeting, this lovely SS Jaguar produced by William Lyons had all the grace and pace of his later cars, even if not the space!

From 1907 to 1939 all manner of cars ran and raced at Brooklands from this Austin Seven to John Cobb's Napier-Railton, holder of the outright lap record.

Brooklands celebrations after a race in the late 1930s. The driver in the black shirt was band leader and postwar TV personality Billy Cotton; the car is a K3 type MG.

The field at Brooklands prepares for a race, with the Members banking in the distance. The front row has an R-type MG, Riley and ERA runners, while row two has another ERA and three Rileys.

Petite Kay Petre sprints to her Austin during the 1937 JCC Relay Race which the Austin team won at over 105mph. The supercharged 750cc cars used side valves at first but later adopted twin overhead camshafts.

This Morris 12, driven by P K Potter, has come rather unstuck in a section during the 1938 London to Edinburgh Trial. Sensibly, there is a tow chain fitted to the front bumper.

All hands to the rescue of J C Harris and his Morgan 4/4, which is in even more trouble on this sharp uphill hairpin bend during the 1938 London to Edinburgh Trial.

Earl Howe and his ERA lead Charles Mortimer in an Alta away from the start line of the Brighton Speed Trials of 1938. They took first and second places in the 1500cc supercharged racing class.

Anthony Heal's 1910 10-litre Fiat pulling away from Forrest Lycette's 1913 3.6-litre Hispano Suiza at the start of the kilometre run along the Madeira Drive in the 1938 Brighton Speed Trials.

This lovely 3.5-litre SS100 Jaguar is taking part in the 1938 MCC Torquay Rally. Its 100mph plus top speed was exceptional for the time and matched by gearbox, brakes, handling and looks.

The 1938 Welsh Rally MG team known as the Three Musketeers are neatly lined up outside an imposing park. From the left the bonnets are marked Porthos, Aramis and Athos.

This Allard Special is taking part in the 1939 Blackpool Rally, driven by Ken Hutchinson, with Kitty Brunell as a passenger. They are seen at the Trough of Bowland en route to Blackpool.

So evocative of the decade, this 1937 MG Midget TA is in trials trim with two spare wheels fitted with knobbly tyres. The driver is making last-minute adjustments.

Halted at a minor road junction in the byelanes to the west of Torbay in Devon, the driver of this 1935 Standard 10 enjoys a chat with a workman while his mate quenches his thirst.

This 1500cc Fiat six is taking part in the 1939 Abingdon Trial, at Bwlch-y-Groes in Wales. A car ahead of its time, the Fiat had independent front suspension, hydraulic brakes and a headlamp flasher.

These two MGs are high in the hills during the 1939 Abingdon Trial. The MGs were excellent cars, most suited to this type of event and very popular with club drivers. Look at the highly appropriate number for the second car.

The 1500cc Opel Olympia of M Truscott taking part in the London to Land's End Trial. The car was based on the Kadett but had overhead valves as well as unit construction, and offered good value for money.

The MCC catered for all in its trials. Competitors used cars, motorcycles, sidecar outfits and three-wheelers such as the front-wheel-drive BSA. The Morgan three-wheeler was rear-wheel driven.

This Lea-Francis is driven by H W Burman in the 1939 London to Land's End Trial. The firm offered this nice drophead coupe from 1937 after a company reformation. The 1628cc engine had its camshafts located high in the block.

Seen in the 1939 London to Land's End Trial, this Ford V-8 from the 1933-34 period shows its American origins. Various bodies were available, including this stylish coupe, and the series was a popular one.

C G Fitt and his 1911cc Frazer-Nash BMW tackle a typical section in the trial, a year when the weather was fine and conditions dry.

Congestion at Dartmeet in Devon offered good business for the Badgers Holt lunches and teas. There is a fine mix of prewar and early postwar vehicles in this picture.

Taken in 1960 when he was 81, Bill Brunell poses with his Attomjjan Anschutz camera with its Ross Lens, a typical pre-war professional camera, and a Standard car to match.

Index

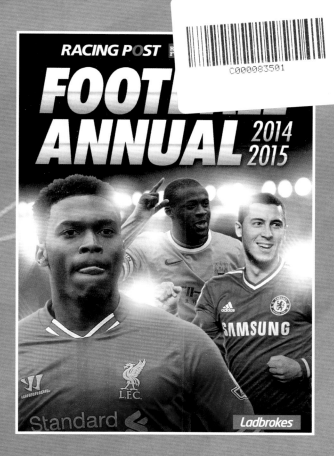

RACING POST

FOOTBALL ANNUAL 2014 2015

Ladbrokes

Edited by Dan Sait and Paul Charlton

Contributors *Paul Charlton, Dan Childs, Michael Cox, Alex Deacon, Andy Dietz, Danny Hayes, Dylan Hill, Glenn Jeffreys, Mark Langdon, Chris Mann, James Milton, Kevin Pullein, Dan Sait, Nigel Speight, Ian Wilkerson*

Cover designed by Jay Vincent

Published in 2014 by Racing Post Books, 27 Kingfisher Court, Hambridge Road, Newbury, Berkshire, RG14 5SJ

Copyright © 2014 Racing Post Books

A catalogue record for this book is available from the British Library.

ISBN 978-1-909471-31-3

Printed and bound in Great Britain by the Buxton Press

Liverpool fans in the main stand at Anfield

Last season will be hard to beat but 2014-15 could deliver a classic title race

So where do you start after a season like that? Manchester United's post-Sir Alex collapse? Liverpool's swashbuckling near-miss? A wonderful local lad done good story for Champions League winner Gareth Bale? Both Edinburgh clubs suffering relegation? A 100-1 winner in Spain's Primera Liga? Burnley's shoe-string success in the Championship? An absolute classic World Cup in Brazil?

There were simply too many great stories to pick out just one, but fans of the Premier League will be delighted to see England's top tier becoming a contest again. After the dreary United cakewalk in 2012-13, last season was a proper rollercoaster.

Brendan Rodgers deserves all the plaudits for taking 33-1 shots Liverpool not only back into the Champions League but also to the brink of the title. His side suffered an agonising slip in the final straight but Rodgers' rapid progress with a relatively low-budget, largely British squad suggests that spending big on imported talent needn't be the default approach from Premier League chairmen.

In the end, of course, money talked with big spending Manchester City taking the title. But it was far from straightforward for incoming manager Manuel Pellegrini, who started slowly in the Etihad hotseat and had to maintain his dignity in the face of growing criticism before the quality of his side finally shone through.

Another new face took a slightly different approach, as Jose Mourinho returned to Chelsea. The Happy One quickly became the Surly One and, with his former club Real Madrid storming to the Champions League while he suffered an underwhelming return to the Bridge, Mourinho has work to do to re-establish his Special One credentials.

Labelling his old adversary Arsene Wenger a 'specialist in failure' backfired as, although

Arsenal suffered yet another post-Christmas collapse in the league, the Gunners' FA Cup success finally ended their nine-year wait for silverware. Will a return to winning ways in the cup prove the catalyst for a change of league fortunes for an Arsenal team who looked imperious at times last term but incompetent at others? If it is, we could be on for another real treat of a title race.

Last season finished with just four points between the top three, while Everton, who showed great promise under Roberto Martinez, and Tottenham, who can only improve after another tumultuous campaign, finished within 17 points of City. And with United expecting to be reborn under the charismatic leadership of Louis van Gaal, we could be in for another belter.

In the Football League, the implementation of Financial Fair Play rules could be set to change the landscape altogether and we're also into unknown territory in Scotland, as both the Edinburgh giants and Rangers will be competing in the second tier.

It certainly doesn't lack for intrigue and you won't find more comprehensive betting coverage than in your daily Racing Post and weekly Racing & Football Outlook, out every Tuesday. Our unique stats, ratings, tips and analysis will help you'll find winners throughout the season and there are plenty of tools on soccerbase.com to keep you ahead of the game. Good luck for 2014-15!

Twists and turns look like the only certainty in the top flight

I t's been a while since we had five genuine contenders for the title all quoted in single figures, writes Figaro. The Premier League may not offer the best football but we can look forward to a season's worth of drama.

Look to lock in a profit by opening your Premier League portfolio with the title outsiders

There is little point making a big decision in August and sticking to it – pay close attention to fluctuations in the market and try to build up a portfolio where you can eventually lock in a profit.

The new season poses plenty of questions. Can Arsenal kick on from their FA Cup win – and can they can keep more of their players fit? How far will Manchester United bounce back under Louis van Gaal? Can Liverpool sustain their improvement by wisely investing the substantial fee they received for Luis Suarez?

So my tactic is to suggest backing the two outsiders of the five each-way. Between them, Arsenal and Chelsea gave us a good run for our money last season and had injuries not removed so many of the Gunners' key players from the scene for so long, you have to wonder if they might have clung on to top spot.

At least **Arsenal** ended the trophy drought and if they can get Theo Walcott and Alex Oxlade-Chamberlain back to their best early on and Aaron Ramsey and Jack Wilshere can continue to develop and deliver flair in

midfield, the Gunners must stand a chance.

Liverpool have lost Suarez but the Anfield giants have been very proactive, doing some good business early in the summer by investing in Southampton stars Rickie Lambert and Adam Lallana, and German Under-21 midfielder Emre Can. There are major targets like Swiss World Cup star Xherdan Shaqiri in the offing as well.

Van Gaal looks a great appointment for Manchester United, although he will only get his feet under the table in mid-July, when some of the summer transfer bargains will have been snapped up.

The bookmakers seem to have taken Jose Mourinho at his word when he promised that Chelsea would challenge for the title in his second season at Stamford Bridge.

Had the Blues not fired blanks against mediocre opponents at the death, the title would have been theirs. Diego Costa should solve their striker problem with Cesc Fabregas imported to maintain a steady supply of ammunition. It all looks good but

not good enough to justify prices under 2-1.

The relegation market is more interesting. **Southampton** have previously survived the sales of Theo Walcott, Alex Oxlade-Chamberlain and Gareth Bale, but losing three top players in Luke Shaw, Rickie Lambert and Adam Lallana, along with the manager and chairman all in one go is a different order of disruption.

Defender Dejan Lovren threatened to strike unless he got a move as well. There's plenty of cash in the coffers at Southampton but it remains to be seen if there is the will, skill and knowledge there to spend it quickly and blend a new team together.

If the Saints drop points early they'll be in trouble, because they meet four of the top five in the market between November 29 and December 28, and Ronald Koeman could have a tougher start to the Premier League than his compatriot at Old Trafford.

Derby were desperately unlucky to lose the Championship playoff final. They seem to have a far more settled leadership than

favourites Cardiff and appeal far more at best odds of 10-1 than the likes of Fulham, Norwich and Wigan at similar prices. Steve McClaren has got a great spirit going among a progressive group of youngsters.

Sheffield United are understandably favourites to win League 1. They made great strides under Nigel Clough last season but maybe not enough to warrant quotes as short as 4-1 in a section that has always been notoriously volatile.

This level has been an effective ceiling for relatively new league clubs in recent times, until Yeovil continued the upward journey into the Championship, although they lasted just one term. **Fleetwood** look like one of the best-run clubs of the lot though and they have the money for another promotion bid. Bet365's 8-1 about the Cod Army winning promotion could look generous by the spring.

Portsmouth are my main fancy for League 2. Although they ended last season with a run of seven games against teams no higher than ninth at the time, a return of W5, D2, L0 from those games was impressive.

Under new boss Andy Awford, they found their feet at their new level about seven months too late. There were six arrivals at Fratton Park in the early part of the summer, and now that the financial situation is more settled, their massive support should have plenty to cheer about.

In Scotland, all eyes are on the Championship where Rangers, Hearts and Hibernian do battle. In the Premiership, Aberdeen should hit the ground running after starting in the Europa League so early, so the 15-8 in the betting without Celtic might not last very long.

Dundee United have a windfall £3.2m to invest from the sale of Ryan Gauld so they could become real contenders too.

Recommended bets
Liverpool 5pts each-way,
Arsenal 5pts each-way,
Southampton 5pts to be relegated
Derby 5pts to win the Championship
Fleetwood 5pts League 1 promotion
Portsmouth 5pts to win League 2
Liverpool, Derby, Portsmouth, Grimsby to win, Southampton to be relegated, Fleetwood to be promoted 1pt Lucky 63

Premier League winner

	b365	BFred	Coral	Hills	Lads	Power
Chelsea	7-4	15-8	15-8	15-8	15-8	15-8
Man City	2	15-8	15-8	2	7-4	7-4
Man Utd	5	5	11-2	9-2	5	11-2
Arsenal	9	9	8	8	9	8
Liverpool	8	9	9	10	9	15-2
Tottenham	50	50	50	66	50	66
Everton	125	100	80	100	100	125
Newcastle	1000	1000	400	750	750	1000
Southampton	500	500	500	1250	500	500
Stoke	2000	2500	2000	750	2000	2500
Aston Villa	2000	2500	2000	4000	2000	2500
Swansea	2500	2500	2000	2500	2500	2500
Hull	5000	5000	5000	5000	4000	4000
Leicester	5000	5000	5000	5000	2500	3500
Sunderland	2500	5000	2500	2000	2000	3000
West Brom	4000	5000	5000	5000	4000	4000
West Ham	2500	5000	5000	1500	2500	3000
QPR	5000	5000	5000	7500	4000	4000
Burnley	7500	5000	5000	10000	5000	7500
C Palace	4000	5000	10000	7500	2500	4000

Win or each-way

Premier League relegation

	b365	BFred	Coral	Hills	Lads	Power
Burnley	4-7	4-7	4-7	1-2	8-15	4-7
QPR	15-8	2	2	2	2	7-4
Leicester	9-4	2	2	13-5	9-4	9-4
Hull	13-5	2	5-2	13-5	12-5	12-5
C Palace	5-2	5-2	2	9-4	11-4	9-4
West Brom	5-2	5-2	3	13-5	3	5-2
Aston Villa	3	7-2	3	11-4	3	3
Sunderland	9-2	4	9-2	5	5	9-2
Swansea	9-2	9-2	9-2	5	11-2	5
West Ham	6	11-2	9-2	6	9-2	6
Southampton	13-2	7	7	6	6	6
Newcastle	7	8	8	8	7	7
Stoke	9	7	7	9	8	8
Everton	200	100	150	100	80	200
Tottenham	500	150	275	250	100	500
Arsenal	1000	250	500	750	-	1000
Man Utd	1000	500	500	1000	-	1000
Liverpool	1000	500	500	750	-	1000
Man City	2000	1000	500	1500	-	2000
Chelsea	1500	1000	500	1500	-	2000

Win only

Championship winner

	b365	BFred	Coral	Hills	Lads	Power
Cardiff	8	7	7	15-2	7	7
Derby	10	9	15-2	9	9	8
Fulham	8	9	9	9	9	9
Norwich	8	10	9	11	10	10
Wigan	10	10	8	10	9	9
Nottm Forest	12	16	18	18	16	14
Reading	12	14	16	18	16	14
Watford	16	16	14	20	16	16
Blackburn	20	16	16	16	16	16
Wolves	16	20	16	16	16	16
Middlesbro	20	20	18	16	16	20
Brighton	18	16	16	18	16	12
Bolton	25	20	16	20	20	16
Bournemouth	25	20	20	22	16	20
Ipswich	25	20	18	22	20	20
Leeds	33	33	25	33	25	28
Sheff Weds	33	33	40	33	33	33
Brentford	40	40	40	50	33	40
Birmingham	66	40	40	50	50	50
Rotherham	66	50	50	40	50	50
Huddersfield	66	40	66	40	50	50
Charlton	66	50	40	50	66	40
Millwall	100	66	66	50	100	50
Blackpool	200	80	100	125	100	66

Win or each-way

League 1 winner

	b365	BFred	Coral	Hills	Lads	Power
Sheff Utd	11-2	11-2	5	6	11-2	5
Preston	9	9	9	15-2	9	9
Bristol C	15-2	9	8	8	8	9
Doncaster	11	10	10	12	11	10
Peterborough	12	9	11	12	11	12
Leyton Orient	9	14	12	12	14	14
Barnsley	18	14	14	16	14	14
MK Dons	16	14	14	18	14	16
Yeovil	20	16	14	20	16	14
Coventry	20	20	25	22	20	18
Swindon	25	25	25	25	20	20
Scunthorpe	25	25	25	25	20	25
Chesterfield	28	20	16	25	20	20
Fleetwood	25	22	16	22	20	20
Bradford	33	33	33	25	33	33
Walsall	40	33	25	33	25	33
Crawley	40	33	33	40	33	33
Oldham	50	40	40	33	40	33
Notts Co	50	33	33	33	33	25
Gillingham	50	50	66	40	50	50
Rochdale	66	33	33	40	33	40
Port Vale	66	40	40	66	50	50
Colchester	80	66	66	66	66	50
Crewe	80	50	66	80	66	66

Win or each-way

EXPERT FOOTBALL ADVICE EVERY DAY *RACING POST*

League 2 winner

	b365	BFred	Coral	Hills	Lads	Power
Luton	9	8	8	9	8	8
Bury	15-2	8	7	13-2	13-2	7
Portsmouth	10	9	9	9	9	9
Shrewsbury	8	9	9	11	11	10
Burton	12	14	16	16	14	16
Stevenage	16	14	14	14	14	16
Plymouth	16	16	14	14	16	16
York	18	18	14	16	16	16
Carlisle	16	16	16	20	16	16
Southend	20	16	16	16	16	16
Northampton	16	20	14	14	20	16
Oxford	16	16	20	22	20	16
Tranmere	25	18	14	25	16	16
Newport	25	25	25	28	25	25
Hartlepool	33	25	25	33	25	25
Cambridge	28	25	25	33	25	25
Cheltenham	33	28	20	33	25	25
Wimbledon	28	33	33	33	40	33
Mansfield	40	33	33	33	33	33
Dagenham	66	40	50	40	50	33
Wycombe	66	50	50	66	50	40
Accrington	80	40	50	50	50	50
Exeter	80	40	40	50	33	40
Morecambe	100	50	66	66	66	50

Win or each-way

Conference winner

	b365	BFred	Coral	Hills	Lads	Power
Bristol R	6	6	9-2	6	5	5
Forest Green	6	7	8	7	6	6
Eastleigh	9	10	11	11	10	10
Grimsby	11	9	10	15-2	9	10
Gateshead	12	12	14	10	9	11
Kidderminster	12	12	14	14	12	12
Halifax	16	16	16	16	16	14
Torquay	12	12	10	14	12	11
Wrexham	16	12	11	12	12	12
Barnet	12	16	14	20	16	20
Lincoln	20	18	20	18	20	18
Aldershot	25	20	20	25	25	22
Woking	25	25	25	20	25	22
Alfreton	33	33	40	40	33	33
Chester	33	25	30	40	33	28
Braintree	40	33	25	40	40	40
Telford	50	40	30	50	33	40
Dover	66	66	60	66	66	66
Macclesfield	66	50	30	66	66	40
Nuneaton	66	50	50	66	66	40
Altrincham	80	50	50	80	80	50
Southport	100	50	60	100	100	50
Welling	100	66	60	50	100	66
Dartford	150	100	100	100	150	100

Win or each-way

Scottish Premiership

	b365	BFred	Coral	Hills	Lads	Power
Celtic	1-66	1-66	1-50	1-50	1-40	1-40
Aberdeen	40	40	33	7-4	25	25
Motherwell	66	50	40	10-3	40	33
Dundee Utd	80	50	40	10-3	50	50
St Johnstone	100	150	150	11	125	125
Inverness	150	200	150	10	150	150
Kilmarnock	250	250	300	33	200	200
Ross County	300	300	300	25	250	250
Dundee	500	500	300	28	300	250
Partick	500	500	300	400	400	300
St Mirren	500	500	300	28	250	150
Hamilton	500	500	300	40	400	500

Win only

Scottish Championship

	b365	BFred	Coral	Hills	Lads	Power
Rangers	4-11	2-5	2-5	4-9	4-11	4-11
Hearts	3	10-3	4	11-4	7-2	3
Hibernian	6	11-2	5	6	5	11-2
Falkirk	40	25	33	22	25	20
Queen of Sth	66	40	50	40	33	33
Raith	150	80	100	80	66	66
Livingston	150	66	150	80	66	66
Dumbarton	200	150	250	150	250	100
Alloa	500	200	500	250	500	150
Cowdenbeath	500	400	500	300	500	150

Win or each-way

Scottish League One

	b365	BFred	Coral	Hills	Lads	Power
Dunfermline	Evs	Evs	Evs	10-11	11-10	Evs
Morton	11-2	5	5	5	9-2	5
Peterhead	9	9	9	9	9	8
Stranraer	10	9	11	11	9	8
Airdrieonians	10	10	14	14	10	10
Brechin	14	12	11	14	12	12
Ayr	14	12	12	20	12	9
Stenh'semuir	16	14	14	12	16	14
Forfar	20	20	20	22	20	18
Stirling	33	33	25	33	25	28

Win or each-way

Scottish League Two

	b365	BFred	Coral	Hills	Lads	Power
East Fife	5-2	5-2	11-4	5-2	5-2	12-5
Arbroath	4	5	7-2	9-2	4	7-2
Albion	5	9-2	5	5	9-2	5
Clyde	6	5	11-2	5	6	5
Annan	7	6	11-2	7	11-2	11-2
Berwick	7	8	9	15-2	8	8
Elgin	16	16	14	25	20	14
East Stirling	22	20	25	18	20	20
Montrose	25	20	25	25	20	18
Queen's Park	25	25	25	28	25	25

Win or each-way

Mark Langdon looks at the lessons from the last Premier League campaign

1 The Red Devils aren't nightmare opponents without Ferguson

It seems obvious now that Manchester United would struggle without Sir Alex Ferguson but 12 months ago the 2013 champions started the season as 5-2 second favourites to win the Premier League behind 23-10 market leaders Manchester City.

What followed was a great lesson for punters. Reputation counts for so much in football betting and it took several months before the prices started to reflect the carcrash which had quickly developed at Old Trafford under dethroned boss David Moyes.

The Red Devils won one match against the top eight, while four of the top six – City, Liverpool, Everton and Tottenham – all won at Old Trafford as the mental block teams had visiting the Theatre of Dreams quickly evaporated.

It could take some time for that fear factor to return even though Louis van Gaal looks an impressive replacement for Moyes.

2 Arsenal can win trophies

Sometimes the first one is the hardest. Andy Murray's Olympic success was the catalyst for US Open and Wimbledon glory; Atletico's 2013 Copa del Rey success at Real Madrid gave them the belief to win La Liga and it could be the same for Arsenal after their FA Cup triumph.

The Gunners spent 128 days at the Premier League summit last season before the almost inevitable collapse which has dogged them in recent campaigns.

However, coming from behind to beat Hull at Wembley should make them a stronger side for the challenges ahead this season.

3 Newcastle get an unfair bashing from the media

If you believe what you read in the the papers then Newcastle manager Alan Pardew is a terrible manager and Mike Ashley is a terrible owner, but the results don't suggest that is the case.

A recency bias means everyone only remembers the awful finish but Newcastle ended a respectable tenth last season. The season before they made the Europa League quarter-finals and the season before that nearly qualified for the Champions League.

4 Ashworth's absence was a huge blow for the Baggies

Losing a director of football is not usually seen as a disaster but West Brom looked rudderless the moment Dan Ashworth left his Hawthorns position to join the Football Association.

Pepe Mel had an horrific time as manager, the signings were poor and the club is heading in the wrong direction. They won only seven league matches last term and must be on the shortlist to suffer relegation this season.

5 Hughes has got his spark back

It was Stoke's first ever Premier League top-ten finish and the Potters deserve enormous credit for taking a chance on Mark Hughes following his shocking spell at QPR.

Sparky didn't cover himself in glory at Loftus Road but he showed tactical nous to land a number of telling blows, including home wins against Chelsea, Arsenal and United, while they also drew with champions Manchester City and fifth-placed Everton.

It was all achieved playing decent football and Hughes can be proud of his Britannia Stadium achievements with the potential for more of the same in 2014-15.

....

From top: Fergie sits in the directors' box now, Arsenal celebrate, Alan Pardew, Dan Ashworth in his new role, Sparky Hughes

AND FIVE THINGS WE WANT TO SEE IN 2014-15

1. A serious plan to improve the England national team

England's early World Cup exit will prompt yet another FA commission, which is 1-6 to conclude that there are too many foreign players in the Premier League. The real problem, of course, is too many English players in the England team.

2. Crystal Palace to continue making progress under Tony Pulis

Palace's form since Pulis arrived last November has been nothing short of remarkable. If they keep it up, they'll win the Premier League by 20 points and stroll to Champions League glory next season. By 2018, the Eagles will have been banned by Uefa for being too damn good and Dwight Gayle will become the world's first billion-pound footballer.

3. The end of Atletico Madrid's stranglehold on La Liga

Atletico's domination of Spanish football is inevitable given all the unfair advantages they have – talent, discipline, work ethic and team spirit, to name but a few. In contrast, Barcelona and Real Madrid must make do with Lionel Messi, Cristiano Ronaldo and a bit of creative accounting. Let's hope either of the plucky underdogs can end their long wait for the title this season.

Dan Ashworth

4. Goal-line technology ruling out any costly late equalisers

We've all been there – it's 4.53pm on a Saturday, every team in your acca is winning and Jeff Stelling cries: "There's been a goal!" Surely there's some technology that could ensure that – just occasionally – one of those 94th-minute goals goes in punters' favour? It is the 21st century, after all.

5. David Moyes to return to Old Trafford

When Louis van Gaal's Manchester United are trading at 1-250 for the title, having been awarded a record 28 penalties in their first dozen games, the rest of us will be desperate for some Moyes magic at Old Trafford.

James Milton

Van Gaal doesn't need to make wholesale changes to alter United's philosophy

While Louis van Gaal needs to strengthen Manchester United in terms of personnel, his most important task is introducing a new tactical identity, writes Michael Cox. It was difficult to deduce United's gameplan under David Moyes as the side slumped to seventh in the table last season, but they were tactically indistinct under Sir Alex Ferguson, too.

That might sound ludicrous given Ferguson's astonishing run of success at the club, but the characteristics associated with Ferguson's United were about determination, professionalism and a never-say-die spirit. That's not to say Ferguson was a poor strategist but it was always difficult to accurately sum up United's default gameplan, and his various assistants contributed heavily to tactical plans.

While Van Gaal shares many of Ferguson's qualities in terms of stern leadership, he's more of an ideologue. He's a proud Dutchman, and although his formations vary, he's likely to introduce energetic midfield pressing and good ball retention.

This is a contrast from United's general approach – they've always boasted talented passers but have rarely been a possession-orientated side, preferring to work the ball forward quickly from a solid defensive base.

Van Gaal's United should play much higher up the pitch. The key is the defence: the departures of Rio Ferdinand and Nemanja Vidic, once the best centre-back pairing in Europe, can only help this transition. Losing both in the same summer smacks of poor long-term planning, but both literally held back United over the past couple of seasons, with their declining mobility encouraging them to drop close to their own penalty box, preventing United from pressing. Van Gaal will encourage a more aggressive defensive line with younger, quicker centre-backs.

The Dutch coach will recruit new centre-backs but generally looks for young players with potential and might consider Chris Smalling and Phil Jones perfect for his new system. Neither has progressed as expected over the past couple of seasons but both might discover defending further away from goal is more suited to their skillset. Jonny

FACTFILE LOUIS VAN GAAL

Born Aloysius Paulus Maria van Gaal,
Amsterdam, August 8 1951
1972 Signs forms for Ajax
1973 Joins Royal Antwerp
1977 Joins Telstar
1978 Joins Sparta Rotterdam
1986 Joins AZ
1987 Retires from playing
1988 Ajax. Leo Beenhakker's No.2

Evans is a similar case – a calm defender who is better in terms of decision-making than making clearances, and capable of playing close to the halfway line.

This should transform the side overall. The idea that Manchester United require wholesale changes is completely untrue – a midfield of Juan Mata, Michael Carrick, Marouane Fellaini and Shinji Kagawa, plus Wayne Rooney and Robin van Persie further forward, is one of the best in the Premier League. They were simply mismanaged woefully last season.

For Fellaini and Mata, it was an extraordinarily difficult task to arrive at Old Trafford and be expected to lift a struggling, unmotivated side, and they should enjoy better second campaigns. Kagawa, meanwhile, could thrive under a manager who should appreciate his style, and Carrick would encourage United to play passing football. The front two remain among the best in the Premier League.

The attacking players don't need replacing, they simply need a kick up the backside, a new regime to get excited about, and be encouraged to play higher up the pitch. United's attackers are all extremely talented, but very selfless too, and intelligent in a positional sense – there's no reason they can't combine successfully, and bring some Total Football to Manchester.

Van Gaal is a in a fantastic situation at Manchester United. Succeeding Ferguson was a nightmare, but succeeding his successor is a brilliant opportunity to take charge of a huge club, and shape their philosophy. United simply need to push higher up the pitch, sign a couple of talented defenders and a midfielder, and Van Gaal might find transforming Manchester United's playing style is easier than many think.

1991 Ajax Head coach. Eredivisie 1994, 1995 and 1996, KNVB Cup 1993, Uefa Cup 1992, Champions League 1995, Uefa Super Cup 1995, Intercontinental Cup 1995, Champions League runners-up 1996

1997 Barcelona. Primera Liga 1998, 1999, Copa del Rey 1998, Uefa Super Cup 1997

2000 Holland national team. Fails to qualify for 2002 World Cup
2002 Barcelona
2004 Ajax technical director
2005 AZ head coach. Eredivisie 2009
2009 Bayern Munich. Bundesliga, DFB-Pokal, DFL-Supercup winners, Champions League runners-up 2010
2012 Holland national team. Leads them to third place at Brazil 2014

Last season's tables are a great pointer for ante-post punters

You don't have to look far down last season's league table to find the Premier League winners

T he higher a team finished in a division last season the more likely they are to win that division this season. And the more likely they are to be profitable to back.

The figures that follow come from a study of the Premier and Football Leagues over 19 seasons, 1995-96 to 2013-14. In that time there was no change in the size of the Premier League or any division of the Football League. There were 20 teams in the Premier League and 24 in the Championship, League 1 and League 2.

Let's begin with the most predictable competition, the Premier League. Only a very small number of teams ever had a realistic hope of becoming champions of England. Every year – 19 times out of 19 – the Premier League was won by a team who had finished in the top three the season before.

Backing all three ante-post every summer would have generated an extraordinary 26 per cent profit on turnover.

In the Football League, winners were drawn from a larger number of teams but it's still true to say that the higher a club finished in a division in one season the more likely they were to win that division in the next.

Let's separate Football League teams into groups according to where they finished in the previous season, and let's start with the

three highest placed teams in each division who did not win promotion in the previous season – the beaten playoff contestants who would have finished between third and sixth in the Championship and League 1 and between fourth and seventh in League 2.

Although there are four positions in each of those bands, for our purpose there were only ever three teams. The other team had won promotion through the playoffs and were now playing in another division.

Of the 171 teams who remained, 13 won promotion in the following season as champions – nearly eight per cent.

Now let's examine teams who finished in the next seven places, those who finished the previous season between seventh and 13th in the Championship and League 1 and between eighth and 14th in League 2. Of the 399 teams from those positions, 21 won promotion in the following season as champions – five per cent.

Finally, let's consider the other survivors, teams who were not relegated after finishing the previous season lower than 13th in the Championship and League 1 and lower than

14th in League 2. Of the 446 teams from those positions, only three won promotion in the following season as champions – less than one per cent.

You could nearly always discount nearly all such teams from your deliberation of ante-post betting markets. And that is a useful thing to be able to do – they account for almost a third of all competitors.

Anyone who did the opposite and backed all such teams ante-post every summer would have lost an astonishing 90 per cent of their total investment.

As the returns from these teams were so bad you might wonder whether better returns were available elsewhere. They were. Simply backing every other team that remained in the same division would have yielded a profit of 11 per cent on turnover. Bear in mind that professional gamblers rarely reach double figures for their career.

Teams promoted from the division below were also profitable to follow – 15 per cent surplus on turnover – but there were fewer of them and all the successes came in Leagues 1 and 2. No team finished top in their first season after promotion to the Championship.

Relegated teams, on the other hand, fared better in the Championship than in League 1 or League 2. However, they did not do as well as you might have anticipated.

The average finishing position of teams relegated from the Premier League to the Championship was eighth – outside the playoff places. The average number of points acquired by newly relegated teams in the Championship was 70, three fewer than the average number of points acquired by teams who finished in the lowest qualifying position for the playoffs.

Only six out of 58 relegated teams won the Championship, a strike rate of ten per cent. For all the buoyancy supposedly offered by parachute payments, relegated teams in the Championship tended to land harder than they – and many others – expected.

Anyone who backed all newly relegated teams ante-post every summer – in League 1 and League 2 as well as in the Championship – would have lost 35 per cent of their total investment. The teams most likely to reward you at the end of this season are elsewhere.

July 2014

Tuesday 1st-2nd	Champions League first qualifying round, first leg
Thursday 3rd	Europa League first qualifying round, first leg
Tuesday 8th-9th	Champions League first qualifying round, second leg
Thursday 10th	Europa League first qualifying round, second leg
Tuesday 15th-16th	Champions League second qualifying round, first leg
Thursday 17th	Europa League second qualifying round, first leg
Friday 18th	Champions League third qualifying round draw
	Europa League third qualifying round draw
Tuesday 22nd-23rd	Champions League second qualifying round, second leg
Thursday 24th	Europa League second qualifying round, second leg
Saturday 26th	Scottish Challenge Cup first round
Tuesday 29th-30th	Champions League third qualifying round, first leg
Thursday 31st	Europa League third qualifying round, first leg

August 2014

Friday 8th	Start of Dutch Eredivisie season
Saturday 2nd	Scottish League Cup first round
Saturday 9th	Start of Football League season
Tuesday 5th-6th	Champions League third qualifying round, second leg
Thursday 7th	Europa League third qualifying round, second leg
Friday 8th	Champions League playoff round draw
	Europa League playoff round draw
Saturday 9th	Start of Scottish Professional Football League season
	Start of French Ligue 1 season
	Start of Conference Premier season
	Start of Conference North-South season
Sunday 10th	FA Community Shield
	Arsenal v Manchester City
Monday 11th (week of)	League Cup first round
Tuesday 12th	Uefa Super Cup, Cardiff
	Real Madrid v Seville
Saturday 16th	Start of Premier League season
	FA Cup extra preliminary round
	Scottish Cup preliminary round
	Start of Portuguese Primeira Liga season
Tuesday 19th-20th	Champions League playoff round, first leg
	Scottish Challenge Cup second round
Thursday 21st	Europa League playoff round, first leg
Friday 22nd	Start of German Bundesliga season
Saturday 23rd	Start of Spanish Primera Liga season
Monday 25th (week of)	League Cup second round
Tuesday 26th-27th	Champions League playoff round, second leg
	Scottish League Cup second round
Thursday 28th	Champions League group stage draw
	Europa League playoff round, second leg
Friday 29th	Europa League group stage draw
Saturday 30th	FA Cup preliminary round
Sunday 31st	Start of Italian Serie A season

September 2014

Monday 1st (week of)	Football League Trophy first round
Wednesday 3rd	International friendly
	Republic of Ireland v Oman

Saturday 6th	FA Vase first qualifying round
	Scottish Challenge Cup quarter-finals
Sunday 7th	Euro 2016 qualifiers
	Germany v Scotland
	Georgia v Republic of Ireland
	Hungary v Northern Ireland
Monday 8th	Euro 2016 qualifiers
	Switzerland v England
Tuesday 9th	Euro 2016 qualifiers
	Andorra v Wales
Saturday 13th	FA Cup first qualifying round
	Scottish Cup first round
Tuesday 16th-17th	Champions League group stage, matchday one
Thursday 18th	Europa League group stage, matchday one
Monday 22nd (week of)	League Cup third round
Tuesday 23rd-24th	Scottish League Cup third round
Saturday 27th	FA Cup second qualifying round
Tuesday 30th	Champions League group stage, matchday two

October 2014

Wednesday 1st	Champions League group stage, matchday two
Thursday 2nd	Europa League group stage, matchday two
Saturday 4th	FA Vase second qualifying round
	Scottish Cup second round
Monday 6th (week of)	Football League Trophy second round
Thursday 9th	Euro 2016 qualifiers
	England v San Marino
Friday 10th	Euro 2016 qualifiers
	Wales v Bosnia-Hz
Saturday 11th	Euro 2016 qualifiers
	Scotland v Georgia
	Republic of Ireland v Gibraltar
	Northern Ireland v Faroe Islands
Sunday 12th	Euro 2016 qualifiers
	Estonia v England
Monday 13th	Euro 2016 qualifiers
	Wales v Cyprus
Tuesday 14th	Euro 2016 qualifiers
	Poland v Scotland
	Germany v Republic of Ireland
	Greece v Northern Ireland
Saturday 11th	FA Cup third qualifying round
Sunday 12th	Scottish Challenge Cup semi-finals
Saturday 18th	FA Trophy preliminary round
Tuesday 21st-22nd	Champions League group stage, matchday three
Thursday 23rd	Europa League group stage, matchday three
Saturday 25th	FA Cup fourth qualifying round
Monday 27th (week of)	League Cup fourth round
Tuesday 28th-29th	Scottish League Cup quarter-finals

November 2014

Saturday 1st	FA Trophy first qualifying round
	FA Vase first round
	Scottish Cup third round
Tuesday 4th-5th	Champions League group stage, matchday four
Thursday 6th	Europa League group stage, matchday four
Saturday 8th	FA Cup first round
Monday 10th (week of)	Football League Trophy area quarter-finals
Friday 14th	Euro 2016 qualifiers
	Scotland v Republic of Ireland
	Romania v Northern Ireland

Saturday 15th	Euro 2016 qualifiers
	England v Slovenia
	FA Trophy second qualifying round
Sunday 16th	Euro 2016 qualifiers
	Belgium v Wales
Saturday 22nd	FA Vase second round
Tuesday 18th	International friendly
	Scotland v England
Tuesday 25th-26th	Champions League group stage, matchday five
Thursday 27th	Europa League group stage, matchday five
Saturday 29th	Scottish Cup fourth round
	FA Trophy third qualifying round

December 2014

Monday 1st (week of)	League Cup fifth round
Saturday 6th	FA Cup second round
	FA Vase third round
Monday 8th (week of)	Football League Trophy area semi-finals
Tuesday 9th-10th	Champions League group stage, matchday six
Wednesday 10th	Fifa Club World Cup begins, Morocco
Thursday 11th	Europa League group stage, matchday six
Saturday 13th	FA Trophy first round
Monday 15th	Champions League last 16 draw
	Europa League last 32-last 16 draw
Saturday 20th	Fifa Club World Cup final, Marrakesh

January 2015

Saturday 3rd	FA Cup third round
Monday 5th (week of)	League Cup semi-finals, first leg
Saturday 10th	FA Trophy second round
Saturday 17th	2015 Africa Cup of Nations begins, Morocco
	FA Vase fourth round
Monday 12th (week of)	Football League Trophy area finals, first leg (subject to change)
Monday 19th (week of)	League Cup semi-finals, second leg
Saturday 24th	FA Cup fourth round
	FA Trophy third round
Saturday 31st	Scottish League Cup semi-finals

February 2015

Monday 2nd (week of)	Football League Trophy area finals, second leg (subject to change)
Saturday 7th	Scottish Cup fifth round
	FA Trophy fourth round
	FA Vase fifth round
Sunday 8th	2015 Africa Cup of Nations final, Marrakech
Saturday 14th	FA Cup fifth round
Tuesday 17th-18th	Champions League last 16, first leg
Thursday 19th	Europa League last 32, first leg
Saturday 21st	FA Trophy semi-finals, first leg
Tuesday 24th-25th	Champions League last 16, first leg
Thursday 26th	Europa League last 32, second leg
Saturday 28th	FA Trophy semi-finals, second leg
	FA Vase sixth round

March 2015

Sunday 1st	League Cup final
Saturday 7th	FA Cup sixth round
	Scottish Cup quarter-finals
Tuesday 10th-11th	Champions League last 16, second leg
Thursday 12th	Europa League last 16, first leg
Sunday 15th	Scottish League Cup final

Tuesday 17th-18th	Champions League last 16, second leg
Thursday 19th	Europa League last 16, second leg
Friday 20th	Champions League quarter-final draw
	Europa League quarter-final draw
Saturday 21st	FA Vase semi-finals, first leg
Sunday 22nd	Football League Trophy final
Friday 27th	Euro 2016 qualifiers
	England v Lithuania
Saturday 28th	Euro 2016 qualifiers
	Israel v Wales
	FA Vase semi-finals, second leg
Sunday 29th	Euro 2016 qualifiers Scotland v Gibraltar
	Republic of Ireland v Poland
	Northern Ireland v Finland
Sunday 29th	FA Trophy final

April 2015

Sunday 5th	Scottish Challenge Cup final
Sunday 12th	Scottish Premiership split
Tuesday 14th-15th	Champions League quarter-finals, first leg
Thursday 16th	Europa League quarter-finals, first leg
Saturday 18th-19th	FA Cup semi-finals
	Scottish Cup semi-finals
Tuesday 21st-22nd	Champions League quarter-finals, second leg
Thursday 23rd	Europa League quarter-finals, second leg
Friday 24th	Champions League semi-final draw
	Europa League semi-final draw

May 2015

Tuesday 5th-6th	Champions League semi-finals, first leg
Thursday 7th	Europa League semi-finals, first leg
Saturday 9th	FA Vase final
	Scottish Premiership playoffs begin
Tuesday 12th-13th	Champions League semi-finals, second leg
Thursday 14th	Europa League semi-finals, second leg
Sunday 17th	Conference playoff final
Saturday 23rd	League 2 playoff final
Sunday 24th	League 1 playoff final
Monday 25th	Championship playoff final
Wednesday 27th	Europa League final, Warsaw
Thursday 28th	Scottish Premiership playoff final, first leg
Saturday 30th	FA Cup final
	Scottish Cup final
Sunday 31st	Scottish Premiership playoff final, second leg

June 2015

Saturday 6th	Champions League final, Berlin
Sunday 7th	International friendly
	Republic of Ireland v England
Thursday 11th	2015 Copa America begins, Chile
Friday 12th	Euro 2016 qualifiers
	Wales v Belgium
Saturday 13th	Euro 2016 qualifiers
	Republic of Ireland v Scotland
	Northern Ireland v Romania
Sunday 14th	Euro 2016 qualifiers
	Slovenia v England

July 2015

Saturday 4	2015 Copa America final, Santiago

City look likely to be even better as they bid for a third title in four seasons

Manchester City made a sloppy start to 2013-14 and still forged their way to the top of the table, making it hard to look past them when assessing the 2014-15 title race, writes Dan Childs. Just seven points covered the top four and Liverpool, Chelsea and Arsenal will all be hopeful of bridging the small gap between themselves and domestic glory. However, it is City who have the most room for improvement.

There was a period at the start of last season when the Citizens and their new manager Manuel Pellegrini seemed to be going through a learning process and there were some tough lessons along the way – in their first six away games, City drew at Stoke (0-0) and lost to Cardiff (3-2), Aston Villa (3-2), Chelsea (2-1) and Sunderland (1-0).

As the season went on City's mistakes became fewer and the dominance of their midfield grew with Fernandinho and Yaya Toure becoming increasingly influential.

The worry for City's rivals is that 12 months on from Pellegrini's appointment, they are in a much better position to hit the ground running – if they take an early lead in the title race they may be impossible to stop.

The team best equipped to stay with them are Jose Mourinho's Chelsea, who have thrown down the gauntlet with the signings of Cesc Fabregas and Diego Costa – La Liga's third top scorer last season with 27 goals.

Costa's physical presence and eye for goal should ensure Chelsea's excellent approach play doesn't go to waste and there could be more goals to come from Eden Hazard, who has yet to repeat the prolific form he showed in French football with Lille.

However, more reinforcements may be needed if Chelsea are to get close to matching the firepower on show at City and Liverpool.

Last season, the partnership of Luis Suarez and Daniel Sturridge was a massive factor in taking Liverpool to the brink of the league title, but the Reds could suffer a dip in form this term.

The departure of Suarez to Barcelona deprives Brendan Rodgers of his main goalscoring threat and the Reds must also contend with the considerable extra workload of Champions League football, so they may have to take a couple of steps backwards before building on the amazing achievements of last season.

Arsenal, who have much more recent Champions League experience, look more likely to go close and will be on a high after the end of their nine-year trophy drought.

Arsene Wenger looks set to remain for the foreseeable future after signing a new contract and should have no problems steering them to a top-four finish but his team still look too lightweight to trust in the really big games and that may stop them from clinching a first league title in 11 years.

Manchester United are third in the betting but may struggle to finish higher than fifth in the first season under Louis van Gaal.

The Dutchman looks a sensible long-term appointment and has a proven track record at developing young talent. However, he has inherited an ageing squad and will need years not months to get the Red Devils back on their pedestal.

Key to the data

The table next to every team profile shows head-to-head data for every side they will have to play in the league this season.

1 Every team the club will play in the league in the order they finished last season

2 Results of last season's league meetings. **W** win **D** draw **L** loss. Where there was more than one league meeting, the latest is at the right. Regular season only

3 Head-to-head results over the last six seasons at the club's own ground. **P** games played **W** wins **D** draws **L** losses **OV** games with over 2.5 total goals **UN** games with under 2.5 total

goals **BS** games in which both teams scored **CS** number of clean sheets for the home side

4 Promoted and relegated teams shown in fawn in the order in which they finished last season

5 League finishes over the last three seasons

6 Over and under 2.5 and both sides to score stats, including rank in club's division last season. The bar chart shows, horizontally, from top to bottom and rounded to the nearest 5 per cent, the division high, the profiled club and the division low

Leading scorers Numbers in brackets show first goals then 'anytime' goals

ARSENAL

Nickname: The Gunners
Colours: Red and white
Ground: Emirates Stadium
Tel: 020-7704-4000

Capacity: 60,362
www.arsenal.com

Nothing much seems to change for Arsenal, who finished fourth again, but their FA Cup victory has taken some of the pressure off.

Having got that monkey off his back and signed a new contract, Arsene Wenger can prioritise Premier League points and ensuring the Gunners remain part of the Champions League furniture.

They finished just seven points off top spot but were often found wanting in the big games and suffered embarrassing losses at Anfield (5-1), the Etihad (6-3) and Stamford Bridge (6-0).

Adding some steel looks the obvious answer but Wenger has ignored the issue for years. The arrival of World Cup star Alexis Sanchez will help the Gunners to keep playing some of the best football in the league but third place looks the limit.

Longest run without a loss: 9
Longest run without a win: 4
Highest/lowest league position: 1/5
Clean sheets: 17
Yellow cards: 53 **Red cards:** 4
Average attendance: 60,013
Players used: 27
Leading scorer: O Giroud 16 (8,14)

	2013-14 H	A	Last six seasons at home P	W	D	L	OV	UN	BS	CS
Man City	D	L	6	2	3	1	0	6	1	4
Liverpool	W	L	6	2	3	1	1	5	3	2
Chelsea	D	L	6	1	2	3	4	2	3	2
Arsenal										
Everton	D	L	6	3	3	0	3	3	4	2
Tottenham	W	W	6	4	1	1	5	1	4	2
Man United	D	L	6	2	2	2	3	3	4	2
Southampton	W	D	2	2	0	0	1	1	1	1
Stoke	W	L	6	6	0	0	3	3	3	3
Newcastle	W	W	5	4	0	1	4	1	2	2
Crystal Palace	W	W	1	1	0	0	0	1	0	1
Swansea	D	W	3	1	1	1	1	2	1	1
West Ham	W	W	5	4	1	0	2	3	2	3
Sunderland	W	W	6	3	3	0	2	4	2	4
Aston Villa	L	W	6	3	0	3	5	1	3	2
Hull	W	W	3	2	0	1	2	1	1	2
West Brom	W	D	5	4	0	1	2	3	1	4
Leicester	-	-	-	-	-	-	-	-	-	-
Burnley			1	1	0	0	1	0	1	0
QPR			2	2	0	0	0	2	0	2

Season	Division	Pos	P	W	D	L	F	A	GD	Pts
2013-14	Premier League	4	38	24	7	7	68	41	+27	79
2012-13	Premier League	4	38	21	10	7	72	37	+35	73
2011-12	Premier League	3	38	21	7	10	74	49	+25	70

Over/Under 50%/50% 11th   **Both score** 45%/55% 12th

Key stat: The Emirates Stadium is close to assuming 'fortress' status with Arsenal unbeaten in their last 19 domestic home matches

2013-14 Premier League appearances

	P	G	Y	R
C Akpom	0 (1)	0	0	0
M Arteta	27 (4)	2	3	1
N Bendtner	1 (8)	2	0	0
S Cazorla	30 (1)	4	2	0
A Diaby	0 (1)	0	0	0
L Fabianski	1	0	0	0
M Flamini	18 (9)	2	8	1
K Gibbs	24 (4)	0	2	1
O Giroud	36	16	4	0
S Gnabry	5 (4)	1	0	0
C Jenkinson	7 (7)	1	1	0
K Kallstrom	1 (2)	0	1	0
L Koscielny	32	2	2	1
P Mertesacker	35	2	3	0
R Miyaichi	0 (1)	0	0	0
N Monreal	13 (10)	0	2	0
A O-Chamberlain	6 (8)	2	0	0
M Ozil	25 (1)	5	0	0
L Podolski	14 (6)	8	0	0
A Ramsey	20 (3)	10	3	0

	P	G	Y	R
T Rosicky	17 (10)	2	7	0
B Sagna	34 (1)	1	6	0
Y Sanogo	0 (8)	0	0	0
W Szczesny	37	0	2	0
T Vermaelen	7 (7)	0	0	0
T Walcott	9 (4)	5	1	0
J Wilshere	19 (5)	3	6	0

Olivier Giroud weighed in with 16 league goals

ASTON VILLA

Nickname: The Villans
Colours: Claret and blue
Ground: Villa Park
Tel: 0121-327-2299
Capacity: 42,785
www.avfc.co.uk

Aston Villa have flirted with relegation for the last three seasons and are in danger of finally dropping in May.

Randy Lerner has made no secret of his desire to sell a club that has been in decline for the past few seasons, and if the American does sell up there will be renewed uncertainty surrounding the future of manager Paul Lambert.

Another major concern is the fitness of star striker Christian Benteke, who will miss the start of the season with a long-term knee injury. Benteke has topped Villa's league scoring charts two seasons in a row, bagging 19 in 2012-13 and ten last season, and there hasn't been much of a supporting cast for the Belgian.

Goalkeeper Brad Guzan and centre-back Ron Vlaar are shining lights but the squad lacks quality.

Longest run without a loss: 5
Longest run without a win: 6
Highest/lowest league position: 9/16
Clean sheets: 9
Yellow cards: 78 **Red cards:** 0
Average attendance: 36,080
Players used: 26
Leading scorer: C Benteke 10 (1,8)

	2013-14		Last six seasons at home							
	H	A	P	W	D	L	OV	UN	BS	CS
Man City	W	L	6	3	1	2	2	4	3	1
Liverpool	L	D	6	1	1	4	1	5	1	2
Chelsea	W	L	6	2	1	3	3	3	3	2
Arsenal	L	W	6	0	3	3	4	2	4	2
Everton	L	L	6	1	3	2	3	3	4	1
Tottenham	L	L	6	0	2	4	3	3	4	0
Man United	L	L	6	0	3	3	3	3	3	1
Southampton	D	W	2	0	1	1	0	2	0	1
Stoke	L	L	6	1	4	1	2	4	4	2
Newcastle	L	L	5	2	1	2	2	3	3	2
Crystal Palace	L	L	1	0	0	1	0	1	0	0
Swansea	D	L	3	1	1	1	0	3	1	1
West Ham	L	D	5	2	2	1	2	3	2	2
Sunderland	D	W	6	2	3	1	2	4	3	2
Aston Villa										
Hull	W	D	3	3	0	0	2	1	1	2
West Brom	W	D	5	3	1	1	4	1	5	0
Leicester	-	-	-	-	-	-	-	-	-	-
Burnley			1	1	0	0	1	0	1	0
QPR			2	1	1	0	2	0	2	0

Season	Division	Pos	P	W	D	L	F	A	GD	Pts
2013-14	Premier League	15	38	10	8	20	39	61	-22	38
2012-13	Premier League	15	38	10	11	17	47	69	-22	41
2011-12	Premier League	16	38	7	17	14	37	53	-16	38

Over/Under 53%/47% 8th   **Both score** 47%/53% 7th

Key stat: Aston Villa have finished in the bottom six for three successive seasons – 16th in 2011-12, 15th in 2012-13 and 15th last term

2013-14 Premier League appearances

	P	G		Y	R
G Agbonlahor	29 (1)	4		7	0
M Albrighton	9 (10)	0		4	0
L Bacuna	28 (7)	5		6	0
N Baker	29 (1)	0		6	0
J Bennett	3 (2)	0		2	0
C Benteke	24 (2)	10		4	0
R Bertrand	16	0		3	0
J Bowery	2 (7)	0		0	0
C Clark	23 (4)	0		8	0
F Delph	33 (1)	3		7	0
K El Ahmadi	26 (5)	2		7	0
J Grealish	0 (1)	0		0	0
B Guzan	38	0		1	0
N Helenius	0 (3)	0		0	0
C Herd	2	0		2	0
G Holt	3 (7)	1		1	0
L Kozak	8 (6)	4		1	0
M Lowton	18 (5)	0		4	0
A Luna	16 (1)	1		2	0
J Okore	2 (1)	0		0	0

	P	G		Y	R
C Robinson	0 (4)	0		0	0
Y Sylla	5 (6)	0		1	0
A Tonev	6 (11)	0		0	0
R Vlaar	32	0		4	0
A Weimann	31 (6)	5		1	0
A Westwood	35	3		7	0

Christian Benteke misses the start of 2014-15

BURNLEY

Nickname: The Clarets
Colours: Claret and blue
Ground: Turf Moor **Capacity:** 21,940
Tel: 0871-221-1882 www.burnleyfootballclub.com

Crystal Palace adaped to Premier League life despite operating on the lowest budget but Burnley will struggle to follow in their footsteps.

They are superbly managed by Sean Dyche and should keep hold of top scorers Danny Ings and Sam Vokes. But they had luck with injuries last year, which is unlikely to be repeated, and their high pressing game could leave them exposed against top-class opponents.

The Clarets finished with the best defensive record in the Championship last season thanks largely to the centre-back partnership of Michael Duff and Jason Shackell, but Duff is 36 and may struggle to last the pace.

Survival isn't out of the question but Burnley are handicapped by their lack of finance and it could be a tough campaign.

Longest run without a loss: 16
Longest run without a win: 5
Highest/lowest league position: 1/3
Clean sheets: 19
Yellow cards: 51 **Red cards:** 2
Average attendance: 13,719
Players used: 23
Leading scorer: D Ings 21 (10,17)

	2013-14		Last six seasons at home							
	H	A	P	W	D	L	OV	UN	BS	CS
Man City			1	0	0	1	1	0	1	0
Liverpool			1	0	0	1	1	0	0	0
Chelsea			1	0	0	1	1	0	1	0
Arsenal			1	0	1	0	0	1	1	0
Everton			1	1	0	0	0	1	0	1
Tottenham			1	1	0	0	0	1	0	1
Man United			1	1	0	0	0	1	0	1
Southampton			2	1	1	0	1	1	2	0
Stoke			1	0	1	0	0	1	1	0
Newcastle			-	-	-	-	-	-	-	-
Crystal Palace			4	3	1	0	1	3	2	2
Swansea			2	1	0	1	1	1	1	0
West Ham			2	1	1	0	2	0	2	0
Sunderland			1	1	0	0	1	0	1	0
Aston Villa			1	0	1	0	0	1	1	0
Hull			4	3	0	1	1	3	0	3
West Brom			-	-	-	-	-	-	-	-
Leicester	L	D	4	1	0	3	2	2	1	1
Burnley										
QPR	W	D	3	2	1	0	0	3	0	3

Season	Division	Pos	P	W	D	L	F	A	GD	Pts
2013-14	Championship	2	46	26	15	5	72	37	+35	93
2012-13	Championship	11	46	16	13	17	62	60	+2	61
2011-12	Championship	13	46	17	11	18	61	58	+3	62

Over/Under 41%/59% 20th   **Both score** 50%/50% 16th

Key stat: Burnley are used to scoring goals on their travels. They have netted at least once in all of their last 12 away fixtures

2013-14 Premier League appearances

	P	G		Y	R
S Arfield	42 (3)	8		4	0
C Baird	5 (2)	0		0	0
A Barnes	11 (10)	3		1	0
A Cisak	0 (1)	0		0	0
M Duff	41	1		5	1
D Edgar	5 (12)	0		2	0
T Heaton	46	0		1	1
S Hewitt	0 (1)	0		0	0
D Ings	40	21		1	0
D Jones	46	1		9	0
M Kightly	32 (4)	5		1	0
D Lafferty	8 (2)	0		0	0
K Long	5 (2)	0		0	0
D Marney	38	3		10	0
B Mee	38	0		6	0
R Noble	0 (1)	0		0	0
J Shackell	46	2		4	0
J Stanislas	7 (20)	2		1	0
B Stock	2 (7)	0		1	0
K Treacy	9 (18)	2		1	0

	P	G		Y	R
K Trippier	41	1		1	0
S Vokes	39	20		2	0
R Wallace	5 (9)	0		1	0

Sean Dyche and Danny Ings celebrate promotion

CHELSEA

Nickname: The Blues
Colours: Blue
Ground: Stamford Bridge **Capacity:** 41,798
Tel: 0871-984-1955 www.chelseafc.com

Jose Mourinho reminded everyone of what a master tactician he is by steering Chelsea to victory in some massive games last season but his team made too many mistakes against lesser opposition and they must be more consistent if they are to finish top of the pile in 2014-15.

The lack of a prolific goalscorer was an obvious weakness, which Mourinho has addressed with the signing of Atletico Madrid forward Diego Costa.

But goals have gone out of the side with the departure of Frank Lampard and, given Costa's injury problems, Mourinho is likely to need more attacking reinforcements, although the capture of Cesc Fabregas could prove inspired.

The defence should remain strong and the Blues look by far the best bet to give Man City a run for their money.

Longest run without a loss: 14
Longest run without a win: 2
Highest/lowest league position: 1/4
Clean sheets: 18
Yellow cards: 59 **Red cards:** 3
Average attendance: 41,181
Players used: 29
Leading scorer: E Hazard 14 (3,10)

	2013-14		Last six seasons at home							
	H	A	P	W	D	L	OV	UN	BS	CS
Man City	W	W	6	4	1	1	3	3	3	3
Liverpool	W	W	6	2	1	3	2	4	3	1
Chelsea										
Arsenal	W	D	6	4	0	2	4	2	3	3
Everton	W	L	6	3	3	0	3	3	4	2
Tottenham	W	D	6	3	3	0	4	2	3	3
Man United	W	D	6	3	2	1	4	2	5	1
Southampton	W	W	2	1	1	0	2	0	2	0
Stoke	W	L	6	6	0	0	3	3	1	5
Newcastle	W	L	5	2	2	1	2	3	1	3
Crystal Palace	W	L	1	1	0	0	1	0	1	0
Swansea	W	W	3	3	0	0	1	2	1	2
West Ham	D	W	5	3	2	0	2	3	2	3
Sunderland	L	W	6	4	0	2	5	1	3	2
Aston Villa	W	L	6	4	1	1	5	1	4	2
Hull	W	W	3	2	1	0	1	2	1	2
West Brom	D	D	5	4	1	0	3	2	2	3
Leicester	-	-	-	-	-	-	-	-	-	-
Burnley			1	1	0	0	1	0	0	1
QPR			2	1	0	1	1	1	1	0

Season	Division	Pos	P	W	D	L	F	A	GD	Pts
2013-14	Premier League	3	38	25	7	6	71	27	+44	82
2012-13	Premier League	3	38	22	9	7	75	39	+36	75
2011-12	Premier League	6	38	18	10	10	65	46	+19	64

Over/Under 53%/47% 8th   **Both score** 42%/58% 13th

Key stat: Chelsea had the best defensive record in the league last season and kept at least one clean sheet against all the top ten teams

2013-14 Premier League appearances

	P	G		Y	R
N Ake	0 (1)	0		0	0
C Azpilicueta	26 (3)	0		1	0
D Ba	5 (14)	5		0	0
R Bertrand	1	0		0	0
G Cahill	29 (1)	1		2	0
P Cech	34	0		0	0
A Cole	15 (2)	0		1	0
K De Bruyne	2 (1)	0		1	0
M Essien	2 (3)	0		3	0
S Eto'o	16 (5)	9		1	0
E Hazard	32 (3)	14		2	0
B Ivanovic	36	3		8	0
T Kalas	2	0		0	0
F Lampard	20 (6)	6		4	0
D Luiz	15 (4)	0		6	0
R Lukaku	0 (2)	0		0	0
J Mata	11 (2)	0		0	0
N Matic	15 (2)	0		3	0
J Mikel	11 (13)	1		3	0
Oscar	24 (9)	8		4	0

	P	G		Y	R
Ramires	29 (1)	1		8	1
M Salah	6 (4)	2		1	0
A Schurrle	15 (15)	8		1	0
M Schwarzer	4	0		0	0
J Swift	0 (1)	0		0	0
J Terry	34	2		3	0
F Torres	16 (12)	5		4	1
Willian	18 (7)	4		4	1
M van Ginkel	0 (2)	0		0	0

Eden Hazard's 14 goals included four penalties

Nickname: The Eagles
Colours: Red and blue
Ground: Selhurst Park
Tel: 020-8768-6000

Capacity: 26,225
www.cpfc.co.uk

Plenty of teams have suffered from second-season syndrome but Palace look well equipped to avoid that fate.

Tony Pulis was named manager of the year last term and it was well deserved after leading the Eagles from second bottom to 11th after his appointment in late November.

Only Cardiff and Norwich scored fewer top-flight goals, but Palace did pose an attacking threat under Pulis and the improvement in form of Dwight Gayle and Jason Puncheon offers encouragement.

The squad needs a few additions but a decent spine is already in place. Mile Jedinak provides midfield power, Damien Delaney is a solid central defender and Julian Speroni excelled in goal. And with the excellent Pulis in the dugout, Palace should continue to move forward.

Longest run without a loss: 5
Longest run without a win: 8
Highest/lowest league position: 11/20
Clean sheets: 12
Yellow cards: 58 **Red cards:** 2
Average attendance: 24,114 **Players used:** 31
Leading scorer: J Puncheon 7 (5,6) D Gayle 7 (2,5)

	2013-14		Last six seasons at home							
	H	A	P	W	D	L	OV	UN	BS	CS
Man City	L	L	1	0	0	1	0	1	0	0
Liverpool	D	L	1	0	1	0	1	0	0	0
Chelsea	W	L	1	1	0	0	0	1	0	1
Arsenal	L	L	1	0	0	1	0	1	0	0
Everton	D	W	1	0	1	0	0	1	0	1
Tottenham	L	L	1	0	0	1	0	1	0	0
Man United	L	L	1	0	0	1	0	1	0	0
Southampton	L	L	3	1	0	2	1	2	0	1
Stoke	W	L	1	1	0	0	0	1	0	1
Newcastle	L	L	2	0	0	2	1	1	0	0
Crystal Palace										
Swansea	L	D	4	1	0	3	1	3	0	1
West Ham	W	W	2	1	0	1	1	1	1	1
Sunderland	W	D	1	1	0	0	1	0	1	0
Aston Villa	W	W	1	1	0	0	0	1	0	1
Hull	W	W	4	2	2	0	1	3	1	3
West Brom	W	L	2	1	1	0	1	1	2	0
Leicester			4	1	1	2	3	1	3	0
Burnley			4	2	2	0	1	3	1	3
QPR			3	0	1	2	1	2	1	1

Season	Division	Pos	P	W	D	L	F	A	GD	Pts
2013-14	Premier League	11	38	13	6	19	33	48	-15	45
2012-13	Championship	5	46	19	15	12	73	62	+11	72
2011-12	Championship	17	46	13	17	16	46	51	-5	56

Over/Under 29%/71% 20th   **Both score** 29%/71% 20th

Key stat: Eight of Crystal Palace's 13 league wins last season were by a 1-0 scoreline

2013-14 Premier League appearances

	P	G		Y	R
B Bannan	13 (2)	1		1	0
Y Bolasie	23 (6)	0		1	1
M Chamakh	27 (5)	5		9	0
S Dann	14	1		4	0
D Delaney	37	1		9	0
K Dikgacoi	25 (1)	0		3	1
S Dobbie	1	0		0	0
D Gabbidon	22 (1)	1		0	0
O Garvan	1 (1)	0		0	0
D Gayle	8 (15)	7		1	0
J Gomez Campana	4 (2)	0		0	0
A Guedioura	4 (4)	0		0	0
W Hennessey	1	0		0	0
T Ince	5 (3)	1		0	0
M Jedinak	38	1		7	0
C Jerome	20 (8)	2		4	0
J Kebe	2 (4)	0		0	0
J Ledley	14	2		1	0
A Mariappa	23 (1)	1		6	0
P McCarthy	0 (1)	0		0	0

	P	G		Y	R
D Moxey	18 (2)	0		2	0
G Murray	3 (11)	1		1	0
S O'Keefe	2 (10)	1		2	0
J Parr	7 (8)	0		0	0
K Phillips	0 (4)	0		0	0
J Puncheon	29 (5)	7		2	0
J Speroni	37	0		0	0
J Thomas	3 (6)	0		2	0
J Ward	36	0		3	0
A Wilbraham	1 (3)	0		0	0
J Williams	0 (9)	0		0	0

Dwight Gayle finished with four goals in two games

EVERTON

Nickname: The Toffees
Colours: Blue and white
Ground: Goodison Park
Tel: 0870-442-1878

Capacity: 39,571
www.evertonfc.com

That Everton fans were disappointed to miss out on Champions League football says everything about the fantastic job Roberto Martinez did for them last term.

Three defeats in the last five games left them seven points adrift of Arsenal but they finished three points above Tottenham and eight clear of Man United.

By overachieving, Martinez has sent expectation levels through the roof and another push for the top four will be the aim. However, Romelu Lukaku looks unlikely to return and there is bound to be interest in star midfielder Ross Barkley, who seems to improve with every game.

Everton will continue to play silky, attacking football under Martinez, but he may struggle to assemble such a strong squad as last time and a slight drop off in performance is to be expected.

Longest run without a loss: 10
Longest run without a win: 3
Highest/lowest league position: 4/7
Clean sheets: 15
Yellow cards: 55 **Red cards:** 1
Average attendance: 37,731
Players used: 28
Leading scorer: R Lukaku 15 (4,13)

	2013-14		Last six seasons at home							
	H	A	P	W	D	L	OV	UN	BS	CS
Man City	L	L	6	4	0	2	3	3	3	3
Liverpool	D	L	6	1	2	3	2	4	2	1
Chelsea	W	L	6	4	1	1	2	4	2	4
Arsenal	W	D	6	1	2	3	3	3	4	1
Everton										
Tottenham	D	L	6	3	3	0	3	3	3	3
Man United	W	W	6	3	2	1	2	4	3	2
Southampton	W	L	2	2	0	0	2	0	2	0
Stoke	W	D	6	4	1	1	2	4	2	3
Newcastle	W	W	5	2	2	1	4	1	4	0
Crystal Palace	L	D	1	0	0	1	1	0	1	0
Swansea	W	W	3	2	1	0	1	2	1	2
West Ham	W	W	5	3	2	0	3	2	3	2
Sunderland	L	W	6	5	0	1	3	3	1	4
Aston Villa	W	W	6	1	4	1	5	1	6	0
Hull	W	W	3	3	0	0	2	1	2	1
West Brom	D	D	5	3	1	1	2	3	2	3
Leicester	-	-	-	-	-	-	-	-	-	-
Burnley			1	1	0	0	0	1	0	1
QPR			2	1	0	1	0	2	0	1

Season	Division	Pos	P	W	D	L	F	A	GD	Pts
2013-14	Premier League	5	38	21	9	8	61	39	+22	72
2012-13	Premier League	6	38	16	15	7	55	40	+15	63
2011-12	Premier League	7	38	15	11	12	50	40	+10	56

Over/Under 50%/50% 11th   **Both score** 47%/53% 7th

Key stat: Everton played some thrilling attacking football towards the end of the campaign and scored at least two goals in nine of their last 11 matches

2013-14 Premier League appearances

	P	G		Y	R
A Alcaraz	5 (1)	0		0	0
V Anichebe	0	0		0	0
L Baines	32	5		6	0
R Barkley	25 (9)	6		5	0
G Barry	32	3		10	0
S Coleman	36	6		3	0
G Deulofeu	9 (16)	3		1	0
S Distin	33	0		3	0
M Fellaini	3	0		0	0
L Garbutt	0 (1)	0		0	0
D Gibson	0 (1)	0		0	0
J Heitinga	1 (1)	0		0	0
T Hibbert	0 (1)	0		0	0
T Howard	37	0		4	1
P Jagielka	26	0		2	0
N Jelavic	5 (4)	0		0	0
A Kone	0 (5)	0		0	0
R Lukaku	29 (2)	15		1	0
J McCarthy	31 (3)	1		5	0
A McGeady	4 (12)	0		0	0

	P	G		Y	R
K Mirallas	28 (4)	8		6	0
S Naismith	13 (18)	5		1	0
L Osman	27 (11)	3		4	0
B Oviedo	8 (1)	2		1	0
S Pienaar	19 (4)	1		2	0
J Robles	1 (1)	0		0	0
J Stones	15 (6)	0		1	0
L Traore	0 (1)	0		0	0

Ross Barkley got Everton's first goal of 2013-14

HULL CITY

1904

Nickname: The Tigers
Colours: Amber and black
Ground: The KC Stadium
Tel: 0870-837-0003

Capacity: 25,404
www.hullcitytigers.com

Hull became distracted by their run to the FA Cup final and finished only four points above the relegation zone in 16th place.

However, they never looked in serious danger of being relegated and should have few problems extending their stay in the division to a third successive season.

The row over the proposed name change rumbles on but there seems no immediate danger of chairman Assem Allam pulling the plug on his investment, which has allowed Steve Bruce to put together a highly competitive squad.

Nikica Jelavic and Shane Long did okay after arriving in January but could make an even bigger impact given a full pre-season at the club.

Defensively Hull look solid and the distraction of the Europa League needn't stop them putting a solid season together.

Longest run without a loss: 4
Longest run without a win: 5
Highest/lowest league position: 8/16
Clean sheets: 10
Yellow cards: 54 **Red cards:** 4
Average attendance: 24,116
Players used: 27
Leading scorer: S Long 4 (2,4) N Jelavic 4 (0,3)

	2013-14		Last six seasons at home							
	H	A	P	W	D	L	OV	UN	BS	CS
Man City	L	L	3	1	1	1	2	1	2	0
Liverpool	W	L	3	1	1	1	2	1	2	1
Chelsea	L	L	3	0	1	2	1	2	1	0
Arsenal	L	L	3	0	0	3	3	0	2	0
Everton	L	L	3	1	1	1	2	1	2	0
Tottenham	D	L	3	0	1	2	1	3	0	0
Man United	L	L	3	0	0	3	2	1	2	0
Southampton	L	L	2	0	0	2	0	2	0	0
Stoke	D	L	3	1	1	1	2	1	2	1
Newcastle	L	W	2	0	1	1	1	1	2	0
Crystal Palace	L	L	4	0	2	2	0	4	1	1
Swansea	W	D	2	2	0	0	0	2	0	2
West Ham	W	L	4	2	1	1	1	3	1	2
Sunderland	W	W	3	1	0	2	1	2	1	1
Aston Villa	D	L	3	0	1	2	0	3	0	1
Hull										
West Brom	W	D	2	1	1	0	1	1	1	1
Leicester			3	1	1	1	1	2	1	1
Burnley			4	0	0	4	2	2	2	0
QPR			1	0	1	0	0	1	0	1

Season	Division	Pos	P	W	D	L	F	A	GD	Pts
2013-14	Premier League	16	38	10	7	21	38	53	-15	37
2012-13	Championship	2	46	24	7	15	61	52	+9	79
2011-12	Championship	8	46	19	11	16	47	44	+3	68

Over/Under 34%/66% 19th   **Both score** 37%/63% 16th

Key stat: Hull have conceded two goals or more in each of their last seven matches

---

2013-14 Premier League appearances

	P	G	Y	R		P	G	Y	R
S Aluko	10 (7)	1	1	0	A McLean	0 (1)	0	0	0
G Boyd	9 (20)	2	2	0	P McShane	9 (1)	0	0	0
R Brady	11 (5)	3	2	0	D Meyler	27 (3)	2	8	0
A Bruce	19 (1)	0	2	0	N Proschwitz	0 (2)	0	0	0
J Chester	22 (2)	1	0	0	S Quinn	4 (11)	0	0	0
C Davies	37	2	6	0	L Rosenior	22 (7)	1	5	0
A Elmohamady	38	2	3	0	Y Sagbo	16 (12)	2	2	1
A Faye	3	0	0	0					
M Figueroa	31 (1)	0	6	0					
M Fryatt	0 (10)	2	0	0					
Gedo	0 (2)	0	0	0					
D Graham	12 (6)	1	1	0					
S Harper	11 (2)	0	1	0					
T Huddlestone	35 (1)	2	5	1					
E Jakupovic	1	0	0	0					
N Jelavic	16	4	3	0					
R Koren	10 (12)	2	1	0					
J Livermore	34 (2)	3	6	0					
S Long	15	4	0	0					
A McGregor	26	0	0	2					

Nikica Jelavic scored five after his January move

LEICESTER CITY

Nickname: The Foxes
Colours: Blue
Ground: King Power Stadium **Capacity:** 32,312
Tel: 0844-815-6000 www.lcfc.com

A sizeable gap still exists between the top two divisions, but Leicester won the Championship in such impressive style that it is hard to imagine them failing to consolidate their top-flight status.

Nigel Pearson will keep faith with most of his squad but was quick to sign Marc Albrighton, who will fit perfectly into the Foxes' 4-4-2 system, and their energetic, attacking approach will cause problems for many Premier League opponents.

They may have to adapt against the top sides but strikers Dave Nugent and Jamie Vardy are assured of some decent service and should score enough goals to keep Leicester's heads above water.

Defensively they rely a lot on powerful centre-back Wes Morgan although the signing of Matthew Upson will add experience and knowhow.

Longest run without a loss: 21
Longest run without a win: 3
Highest/lowest league position: 1/3
Clean sheets: 18
Yellow cards: 52 **Red cards:** 2
Average attendance: 24,994
Players used: 23
Leading scorer: D Nugent 20 (8,17)

	2013-14		Last six seasons at home							
	H	A	P	W	D	L	OV	UN	BS	CS
Man City			-	-	-	-	-	-	-	-
Liverpool			-	-	-	-	-	-	-	-
Chelsea			-	-	-	-	-	-	-	-
Arsenal			-	-	-	-	-	-	-	-
Everton			-	-	-	-	-	-	-	-
Tottenham			-	-	-	-	-	-	-	-
Man United			-	-	-	-	-	-	-	-
Southampton			1	1	0	0	1	0	1	0
Stoke			-	-	-	-	-	-	-	-
Newcastle			1	0	1	0	0	1	0	1
Crystal Palace			4	2	1	1	2	2	2	2
Swansea			2	2	0	0	2	0	2	0
West Ham			1	0	0	1	1	0	1	0
Sunderland			-	-	-	-	-	-	-	-
Aston Villa			-	-	-	-	-	-	-	-
Hull			3	2	1	0	2	1	3	0
West Brom			1	0	0	1	1	0	1	0
Leicester										
Burnley	D	W	4	2	2	0	2	2	2	2
QPR	W	W	3	2	0	1	1	2	0	2

Season	Division	Pos	P	W	D	L	F	A	GD	Pts
2013-14	Championship	1	46	31	9	6	83	43	+40	102
2012-13	Championship	6	46	19	11	16	71	48	+23	68
2011-12	Championship	9	46	18	12	16	66	55	+11	66

Over/Under 59%/41% 1st   **Both score** 57%/43% 6th

Key stat: Leicester, who were the second highest scorers in the Championship last season, have scored in each of their last 33 matches

2013-14 Premier League appearances

	P	G		Y	R
D Drinkwater	43 (2)	7		3	0
L Dyer	31 (9)	7		0	0
D Hammond	7 (22)	1		3	0
M James	28 (7)	1		4	1
A King	24 (6)	4		1	0
A Knockaert	36 (6)	5		6	0
P Konchesky	31	1		2	1
R Mahrez	12 (7)	3		0	0
I Miquel	6 (1)	0		1	0
L Moore	26 (4)	1		2	0
W Morgan	45	2		3	0
D Nugent	44 (2)	20		2	0
K Phillips	2 (10)	2		0	0
J Schlupp	15 (11)	1		1	0
K Schmeichel	46	0		2	0
S St. Ledger	1	0		0	0
G Taylor-Fletcher	2 (19)	3		1	0
J Vardy	36 (1)	16		8	0
M Waghorn	0 (2)	0		0	0
M Wasilewski	26 (5)	0		6	0

	P	G		Y	R
Z Whitbread	3	0		1	0
C Wood	7 (19)	4		0	0
R de Laet	35 (1)	2		6	0

Dave Nugent bagged 20 Championship goals

LIVERPOOL

Nickname: The Reds
Colours: Red
Ground: Anfield
Tel: 0151-263-2361

Capacity: 45,276
www.liverpoolfc.com

It may be some time before Liverpool get a better chance to win the Premier League title than they had last season but they are moving in the right direction.

The demands of Champions League football will be a tough for a squad high on quality but short on numbers and it may be even tougher for Brendan Rodgers to achieve another top-two finish.

The Reds have plenty of money to spend after the sale of Premier League golden boot Luis Suarez to Barcelona, but despite some high quality arrivals at Anfield over the summer the loss of such a world-class talent – even one with a significant downside – will come as a blow to Rodgers' ambitions.

Avoiding injuries is key but Liverpool play with pace and creativity, and have the quality to retain their top-four status.

Longest run without a loss: 16
Longest run without a win: 2
Highest/lowest league position: 1/5
Clean sheets: 10
Yellow cards: 54 **Red cards:** 1
Average attendance: 44,671
Players used: 25
Leading scorer: L Suarez 31 (6,18)

	2013-14		Last six seasons at home							
	H	A	P	W	D	L	OV	UN	BS	CS
Man City	W	L	6	2	4	0	4	2	5	1
Liverpool										
Chelsea	L	L	6	3	1	2	2	4	2	2
Arsenal	W	L	6	1	2	3	4	2	5	0
Everton	W	D	6	3	3	0	3	3	2	4
Tottenham	W	W	6	4	1	1	3	3	2	3
Man United	W	W	6	4	1	1	3	3	4	2
Southampton	L	W	2	1	0	1	0	2	0	1
Stoke	W	W	6	3	3	0	1	5	0	6
Newcastle	W	D	5	4	1	0	4	1	3	2
Crystal Palace	W	D	1	1	0	0	1	0	1	0
Swansea	W	D	3	2	1	0	2	1	1	2
West Ham	W	W	5	3	2	0	3	2	1	4
Sunderland	W	W	6	4	2	0	4	2	3	3
Aston Villa	D	W	6	2	2	2	5	1	4	2
Hull	W	L	3	2	1	0	2	1	2	1
West Brom	W	D	5	3	0	2	2	3	1	2
Leicester			-	-	-	-	-	-	-	-
Burnley			1	1	0	0	1	0	0	1
QPR			2	2	0	0	0	2	0	2

Season	Division	Pos	P	W	D	L	F	A	GD	Pts
2013-14	Premier League	2	38	26	6	6	101	50	+51	84
2012-13	Premier League	7	38	16	13	9	71	43	+28	61
2011-12	Premier League	8	38	14	10	14	47	40	+7	52

Over/Under 79%/21% 1st   **Both score** 66%/34% 1st

Key stat: Liverpool have scored two goals or more in 17 of their last 19 Premier League fixtures

2013-14 Premier League appearances

	P	G		Y	R
D Agger	16 (4)	2		0	0
J Allen	15 (9)	1		4	0
I Aspas	5 (9)	0		3	0
A Cissokho	12 (3)	0		2	0
P Coutinho	28 (5)	5		1	0
J Enrique	6 (2)	0		0	0
J Flanagan	23	1		3	0
S Gerrard	33 (1)	13		7	0
J Henderson	35	4		4	1
J Ibe	0 (1)	0		0	0
Joao Teixeira	0 (1)	0		0	0
G Johnson	29	0		3	0
M Kelly	0 (5)	0		0	0
Lucas	20 (7)	0		6	0
Luis Alberto	0 (9)	0		0	0
S Mignolet	38	0		0	0
V Moses	6 (13)	1		1	0
M Sakho	17 (1)	1		0	0
M Skrtel	36	7		6	0
B Smith	0 (1)	0		0	0

	P	G		Y	R
R Sterling	24 (9)	9		3	0
D Sturridge	26 (3)	21		2	0
L Suarez	33	31		6	0
K Toure	15 (5)	0		2	0
A Wisdom	1 (1)	0		1	0

Premier League golden boot Luis Suarez

MANCHESTER CITY

Nickname: The Citizens
Colours: Sky blue and white
Ground: Etihad Stadium
Tel: 0870-062-1894

Capacity: 47,405
www.mcfc.co.uk

Financial Fair Play may impact on Man City's Champions League hopes – their squad will be restricted to 21 players – but it's unlikely to prevent them from sealing a third Premier League title in four years.

It can be dangerous to stand still – and City are unlikely to make many squad improvements while Uefa continue to take a dim view over their accounts – but with such a strong squad, it's hard to see Manuel Pellegrini's side being usurped.

They will be even stronger if Sergio Aguero has an injury-free campaign and Spain's decision to omit Javier Garcia and Alvaro Negredo from their World Cup squad means the pair will be fresh.

Yaya Toure made some odd comments early in the summer but may struggle to force a move and could once again be the driving force for the defending champs.

Longest run without a loss: 12
Longest run without a win: 2
Highest/lowest league position: 1/8
Clean sheets: 16
Yellow cards: 72 **Red cards:** 1
Average attendance: 47,080
Players used: 23
Leading scorer: Y Toure 20 (5,17)

Man City	2013-14 H	2013-14 A	Last six seasons at home P	W	D	L	OV	UN	BS	CS
Liverpool	W	L	6	3	2	1	5	1	3	3
Chelsea	L	L	6	4	0	2	3	3	3	2
Arsenal	W	D	6	4	1	1	4	2	3	2
Everton	W	W	6	2	1	3	2	4	3	1
Tottenham	W	W	6	4	0	2	4	2	3	2
Man United	W	W	6	2	1	3	2	4	2	2
Southampton	W	D	2	2	0	0	2	0	2	0
Stoke	W	D	6	6	0	0	4	2	0	6
Newcastle	W	W	5	5	0	0	5	0	3	2
Crystal Palace	W	W	1	1	0	0	0	1	0	1
Swansea	W	W	3	3	0	0	2	1	0	3
West Ham	W	W	5	5	0	0	4	1	3	2
Sunderland	D	L	6	4	2	0	5	1	3	3
Aston Villa	W	L	6	6	0	0	5	1	2	4
Hull	W	W	3	2	1	0	1	2	2	1
West Brom	W	W	5	5	0	0	4	1	2	3
Leicester			-	-	-	-	-	-	-	-
Burnley		1	0	1	0	1	0	1	0
QPR		2	2	0	0	2	0	2	0

Season	Division	Pos	P	W	D	L	F	A	GD	Pts
2013-14	Premier League	1	38	27	5	6	102	37	+65	86
2012-13	Premier League	2	38	23	9	6	66	34	+32	78
2011-12	Premier League	1	38	28	5	5	93	29	+64	89

Over/Under 66%/34% 3rd   **Both score** 53%/47% 4th

Key stat: Man City scored two goals or more in 11 of their final 12 matches and scored 63 home league goals – an average of 3.32 per game

2013-14 Premier League appearances

	P	G		Y	R
S Aguero	20 (3)	17		4	0
D Boyata	1	0		0	0
G Clichy	18 (2)	0		1	0
M Demichelis	27	2		6	0
E Dzeko	23 (8)	16		4	0
Fernandinho	29 (4)	5		8	0
J Hart	31	0		1	0
Javi Garcia	14 (15)	0		7	0
S Jovetic	2 (11)	3		1	0
A Kolarov	21 (9)	1		2	0
V Kompany	28	4		6	1
J Lescott	8 (2)	0		0	0
J Milner	12 (19)	1		3	0
S Nasri	29 (5)	7		3	0
M Nastasic	11 (2)	1		4	0
J Navas	18 (14)	4		0	0
A Negredo	21 (11)	9		1	0
C Pantilimon	7	0		1	0
M Richards	2	0		0	0
J Rodwell	1 (4)	0		0	0

	P	G		Y	R
D Silva	26 (1)	7		5	0
Y Toure	35	20		4	0
P Zabaleta	34 (1)	1		11	0

Sergio Aguero got 17 goals in 23 appearances

MANCHESTER UNITED

Nickname: The Red Devils
Colours: Red and white
Ground: Old Trafford
Tel: 0870-442-1994

Capacity: 75,765
www.manutd.com

Man United are likely to improve under Louis van Gaal but not to the degree that the markets expect.

The Dutchman inherits a side that finished 15 points outside of the top four last season and whose key attacking components – Wayne Rooney and Robin van Persie – are past their best.

A massive overhaul has begun and further cuts will be needed as United prepare for a season without any European football. They will need a lean, quality squad of around 20 players to avoid dressing room unrest but getting under-performing players off the Old Trafford wage bill will be a tough task.

Van Gaal's side could be back in Europe this time next year but qualification for the Europa League looks the most likely route.

Longest run without a loss: 7
Longest run without a win: 4
Highest/lowest league position: 5/10
Clean sheets: 13
Yellow cards: 68 **Red cards:** 3
Average attendance: 75,206
Players used: 30
Leading scorer: W Rooney 17 (3,13)

	2013-14		Last six seasons at home							
	H	A	P	W	D	L	OV	UN	BS	CS
Man City	L	L	6	3	0	3	5	1	4	1
Liverpool	L	L	6	4	0	2	6	0	5	0
Chelsea	D	L	6	3	1	2	4	2	3	2
Arsenal	W	D	6	5	1	0	3	3	3	3
Everton	L	L	6	4	1	1	2	4	1	4
Tottenham	L	D	6	4	0	2	5	1	4	2
Man United										
Southampton	D	D	2	1	1	0	1	1	2	0
Stoke	W	L	6	6	0	0	5	1	3	3
Newcastle	L	W	5	2	2	1	2	3	3	1
Crystal Palace	W	W	1	1	0	0	0	1	0	1
Swansea	W	W	3	3	0	0	1	2	1	2
West Ham	W	W	5	5	0	0	3	2	1	4
Sunderland	L	W	6	4	1	1	2	4	2	3
Aston Villa	W	W	6	5	0	1	5	1	3	2
Hull	W	W	3	3	0	0	3	0	2	1
West Brom	L	W	5	3	1	1	3	2	2	3
Leicester	-	-	-	-	-	-	-	-	-	-
Burnley			1	1	0	0	1	0	0	1
QPR			2	2	0	0	1	1	1	1

Season	Division	Pos	P	W	D	L	F	A	GD	Pts
2013-14	Premier League	7	38	19	7	12	64	43	+21	64
2012-13	Premier League	1	38	28	5	5	86	43	+43	89
2011-12	Premier League	2	38	28	5	5	89	33	+56	89

Over/Under 58%/42% 5th

Both score 47%/53% 7th

Key stat: Man United won just one of their 14 matches against teams which finished in the top eight last season

2013-14 Premier League appearances

	P	G	Y	R
Anderson	2 (2)	0	0	0
A Buttner	5 (3)	0	2	0
M Carrick	26 (3)	1	5	0
T Cleverley	18 (4)	1	3	0
J Evans	17	0	0	0
P Evra	33	1	2	0
Fabio Da Silva	1	0	0	0
M Fellaini	12 (4)	0	2	0
R Ferdinand	12 (2)	0	0	0
D Fletcher	9 (3)	0	0	0
R Giggs	6 (6)	0	3	0
J Hernandez	6 (18)	4	2	0
A Januzaj	15 (12)	4	7	0
P Jones	26	1	5	0
S Kagawa	14 (4)	0	0	0
T Lawrence	1	0	0	0
A Lindegaard	1	0	0	0
J Mata	14 (1)	6	0	0
Nani	7 (4)	0	0	0
Rafael Da Silva	18 (1)	0	5	0

	P	G	Y	R
W Rooney	27 (2)	17	8	0
C Smalling	21 (4)	1	2	0
L Valencia	20 (9)	2	7	1
N Vidic	23 (2)	0	6	2
D Welbeck	15 (10)	9	0	0
J Wilson	1	2	0	0
A Young	13 (7)	2	4	0
W Zaha	0 (2)	0	0	0
D de Gea	37	0	1	0
R van Persie	18 (3)	12	2	0

England's most undervalued goal machine?

NEWCASTLE UNITED

Nickname: The Magpies
Colours: Black and white
Ground: St James' Park **Capacity:** 52,405
Tel: 0191-201-8400 www.nufc.co.uk

Newcastle showed relegation form in the second half of last season, losing 14 of their last 20 league games, and they need to be careful to avoid being dragged into a dogfight this season.

They have retained a manager, Alan Pardew, who is unpopular with a large section of the supporters and they look a much weaker team without Loic Remy, who bagged 14 top flight goals last term.

The midfield has lacked quality since Yohan Cabaye left in the summer and star quality is thin on the ground with goalkeeper Tim Krul looking like the club's most prized asset.

Pardew will try to bring in fresh talent but a high turnover of players will make it difficult to make a fast start and he could be in the frame to be the season's first managerial casualty.

Longest run without a loss: 4
Longest run without a win: 6
Highest/lowest league position: 6/11
Clean sheets: 10
Yellow cards: 53 **Red cards:** 5
Average attendance: 50,395
Players used: 26
Leading scorer: L Remy 14 (5,11)

	2013-14		Last six seasons at home							
	H	A	P	W	D	L	OV	UN	BS	CS
Man City	L	L	5	0	1	4	3	2	3	0
Liverpool	D	L	5	2	1	2	4	1	3	1
Chelsea	W	L	5	2	1	2	2	3	2	1
Arsenal	L	L	5	0	2	3	2	3	2	1
Everton	L	L	5	1	1	3	4	1	3	1
Tottenham	L	W	5	2	2	1	4	1	4	0
Man United	L	W	5	1	1	3	4	1	1	2
Southampton	D	L	2	1	1	0	1	1	2	0
Stoke	W	L	5	3	1	1	5	0	4	1
Newcastle										
Crystal Palace	W	W	2	2	0	0	0	2	0	2
Swansea	L	L	4	1	1	2	3	1	2	2
West Ham	D	W	4	1	2	1	2	2	1	2
Sunderland	L	L	5	1	2	2	3	2	3	0
Aston Villa	W	W	5	4	1	0	2	3	2	3
Hull	L	W	2	0	0	2	2	0	2	0
West Brom	W	L	6	3	2	1	6	0	6	0
Leicester			1	1	0	0	0	1	0	1
Burnley			-	-	-	-	-	-	-	-
QPR			3	2	1	0	0	3	1	2

Season	Division	Pos	P	W	D	L	F	A	GD	Pts
2013-14	Premier League	10	38	15	4	19	43	59	-16	49
2012-13	Premier League	16	38	11	8	19	45	68	-23	41
2011-12	Premier League	5	38	19	8	11	56	51	+5	65

Over/Under 63%/37% 4th   **Both score** 37%/63% 16th

Key stat: Newcastle have scored fewer than two goals in 14 of their last 16 matches

2013-14 Premier League appearances

	P	G	Y	R		P	G	Y	R
Sammy Ameobi	4 (6)	0	1	0	M Sissoko	35	3	8	0
Shola Ameobi	14 (12)	2	1	1	S Taylor	9 (1)	1	0	1
V Anita	28 (6)	1	2	0	C Tiote	31 (2)	0	10	0
A Armstrong	0 (4)	0	0	0	M Williamson	32 (1)	0	0	0
H Ben Arfa	13 (14)	3	1	0	M Yanga-Mbiwa	17 (6)	0	5	1
Y Cabaye	17 (2)	7	5	0	L de Jong	8 (4)	0	0	0
P Cisse	15 (9)	2	0	0					
F Coloccini	27	0	2	0					
M Debuchy	28 (1)	1	7	1					
P Dummett	11 (7)	1	1	1					
R Elliot	2	0	0	0					
D Gosling	4 (4)	0	1	0					
Y Gouffran	31 (4)	6	3	0					
J Gutierrez	1 (1)	0	0	0					
M Haidara	3 (8)	0	2	0					
T Krul	36	0	0	0					
S Marveaux	2 (7)	0	0	0					
G Obertan	0 (3)	0	0	0					
L Remy	24 (2)	14	2	1					
D Santon	26 (1)	0	1	0					

Loic Remy grabbed 14 goals on loan from QPR

QUEENS PARK RANGERS

Nickname: The R's
Colours: Blue and white
Ground: Loftus Road
Tel: 020-8743-0262

Capacity: 18,439
www.qpr.co.uk

Harry Redknapp was relieved to see his side sneak back into the big time after being outplayed in the playoff final but it will be a massive job to keep QPR up.

Rangers' huge debt places a question mark over how much money chairman Tony Fernandes can commit to revamping an ageing squad.

There is plenty of top-flight experience on hand, including centre-back Richard Dunne, who was superb throughout last season. However, he's had injury problems in the past and should they return QPR may struggle to replace him.

Charlie Austin will be relied upon to get the goals and looks to have the right qualities to make an impact in his first top-flight campaign. But QPR are likely to be in the thick of the relegation battle and survival could be a close-run thing.

Longest run without a loss: 11
Longest run without a win: 5
Highest/lowest league position: 1/4
Clean sheets: 17
Yellow cards: 64 **Red cards:** 4
Average attendance: 16,655
Players used: 35
Leading scorer: C Austin 17 (10,15)

	2013-14		Last six seasons at home							
	H	A	P	W	D	L	OV	UN	BS	CS
Man City			2	0	1	1	1	1	1	1
Liverpool			2	1	0	1	2	0	1	0
Chelsea			2	1	1	0	0	2	0	2
Arsenal			2	1	0	1	1	1	1	0
Everton			2	0	2	0	0	2	2	0
Tottenham			2	1	1	0	0	2	0	2
Man United			2	0	0	2	0	2	0	0
Southampton			2	1	0	1	2	0	2	0
Stoke			2	1	0	1	0	2	0	1
Newcastle			3	0	1	2	1	2	1	1
Crystal Palace			3	1	2	0	1	2	2	1
Swansea			5	3	1	1	3	2	1	3
West Ham			1	0	0	1	1	0	1	0
Sunderland			2	1	0	1	2	0	2	0
Aston Villa			2	0	2	0	0	2	2	0
Hull			1	0	1	0	0	1	1	0
West Brom			3	1	1	1	2	1	3	0
Leicester	**L**	**L**	3	1	0	2	1	2	1	1
Burnley	**D**	**L**	3	0	2	1	2	1	3	0
QPR										

Season	Division	Pos	P	W	D	L	F	A	GD	Pts
2013-14	Championship	4	46	23	11	12	60	44	+16	80
2012-13	Premier League	20	38	4	13	21	30	60	-30	25
2011-12	Premier League	17	38	10	7	21	43	66	-23	37

Over/Under 39%/61% 22nd   **Both score** 43%/57% 20th

Key stat: QPR are unbeaten in their last eight matches at Loftus Road

2013-14 Premier League appearances

	P	G	Y	R
B Assou-Ekotto	30 (1)	0	5	1
C Austin	28 (3)	17	3	0
J Barton	33 (1)	3	12	1
Y Benayoun	10 (6)	3	1	1
T Carroll	23 (3)	0	2	0
J Chevanton	0 (2)	0	0	0
C Donaldson	1	0	0	0
K Doyle	8 (1)	2	1	0
R Dunne	41	0	6	1
M Ehmer	0 (1)	0	0	0
A Faurlin	5 (2)	0	1	0
E Granero	1	0	1	0
R Green	45	0	0	0
K Henry	17 (10)	1	2	0
C Hill	40	2	4	0

	P	G	Y	R
T Hitchcock	0 (1)	1	0	0
D Hoilett	23 (12)	4	3	0
A Hughes	11	0	0	0
J Jenas	15 (10)	2	2	0
A Johnson	10 (7)	2	2	0
W Keane	6 (4)	0	0	0
N Kranjcar	21 (8)	2	4	0
M Maiga	2 (6)	1	0	0
R Morrison	14 (1)	6	3	0
B Murphy	1 (1)	0	0	0
G O'Neil	23 (6)	1	5	0
N Onuoha	24 (2)	2	2	0
M Petrasso	0 (1)	0	0	0
M Phillips	13 (8)	3	1	0
D Simpson	32 (1)	0	4	0
A Traore	13 (9)	2	0	0
S Wright-Phillips	4 (7)	0	0	0
L Young	1	0	0	0
Yun Suk-Young	4 (3)	1	0	0
B Zamora	7 (10)	3	0	0

SOUTHAMPTON

Nickname: The Saints
Colours: Red and white
Ground: St Mary's Stadium
Tel: 0845-688-9448

Capacity: 32,689
www.saintsfc.co.uk

Mauricio Pochettino led Southampton to eighth place last season but his departure – along with the exodus of key players – will be bitterly disappointing.

Had they kept their team and manager together, Southampton could have looked forward to finishing no lower than eighth and might have pushed the likes of Everton, Tottenham and Man United in the battle for Europa League places.

But Rickie Lambert, Adam Lallana and Luke Shaw have left and this could be a transitional season.

There should be plenty of funds to bring in fresh talent and highly rated youngsters James Ward-Prowse, Calum Chambers and Sam Gallagher are likely to get better. But Saints are likely to regress from last season and will have done well if they post a top-half finish.

Longest run without a loss: 8
Longest run without a win: 6
Highest/lowest league position: 3/9
Clean sheets: 15
Yellow cards: 60 **Red cards:** 0
Average attendance: 30,211
Players used: 24
Leading scorer: J Rodriguez 15 (6,13)

	2013-14		Last six seasons at home							
	H	A	P	W	D	L	OV	UN	BS	CS
Man City	D	L	2	1	1	0	1	1	2	0
Liverpool	L	W	2	1	0	1	2	0	1	0
Chelsea	L	L	2	1	0	1	2	0	1	0
Arsenal	D	L	2	0	2	0	1	1	2	0
Everton	W	L	2	1	1	0	0	2	0	2
Tottenham	L	L	2	0	0	2	2	0	2	0
Man United	D	D	2	0	1	1	1	1	2	0
Southampton										
Stoke	D	D	2	0	2	0	1	1	2	0
Newcastle	W	D	2	2	0	0	1	1	0	2
Crystal Palace	W	W	3	3	0	0	0	3	0	3
Swansea	W	W	3	1	2	0	1	2	2	1
West Ham	D	L	3	1	2	0	0	3	1	2
Sunderland	D	D	2	0	1	1	0	2	1	0
Aston Villa	L	D	2	1	0	1	2	0	2	0
Hull	W	W	2	2	0	0	2	0	2	0
West Brom	W	W	2	1	0	1	1	1	0	1
Leicester			1	0	0	1	0	1	0	0
Burnley			2	1	1	0	1	1	1	1
QPR			2	0	1	1	1	1	1	1

Season	Division	Pos	P	W	D	L	F	A	GD	Pts
2013-14	Premier League	8	38	15	11	12	54	46	+8	56
2012-13	Premier League	14	38	9	14	15	49	60	-11	41
2011-12	Championship	2	46	26	10	10	85	46	+39	88

Over/Under 45%/55% 15th   **Both score** 47%/53% 7th

Key stat: Southampton were positive at St Mary's and on their travels last season and have scored in 12 of their last 13 away matches

2013-14 Premier League appearances

	P	G	Y	R		P	G	Y	R
A Boruc	29	0	0	0	L Shaw	35	0	4	0
C Chambers	18 (4)	0	0	0	V Wanyama	19 (4)	0	7	0
N Clyne	20 (5)	0	3	0	J Ward-Prowse	16 (18)	0	3	0
J Cork	21 (7)	0	5	0	M Yoshida	7 (1)	1	0	0
K Davis	2	0	0	0					
S Davis	28 (6)	2	3	0					
G Do Prado	0 (9)	0	0	0					
J Fonte	35 (1)	3	7	0					
D Fox	3	0	0	0					
S Gallagher	3 (15)	1	0	0					
P Gazzaniga	7 (1)	0	0	0					
J Hooiveld	3	0	1	0					
A Lallana	37 (1)	9	3	0					
R Lambert	31 (6)	13	2	0					
D Lovren	31	2	7	0					
P Osvaldo	9 (4)	3	3	0					
G Ramirez	3 (15)	1	2	0					
H Reed	0 (4)	0	0	0					
J Rodriguez	30 (3)	15	3	0					
M Schneiderlin	31 (2)	2	8	0					

The England contingent impressed at St Mary's

STOKE CITY

Nickname: The Potters
Colours: Red and white
Ground: Britannia Stadium **Capacity:** 27,740
Tel: 0871-663-2008 www.stokecityfc.com

Mark Hughes impressed in his first year at Stoke, modifying their long-ball style of play and leading them to ninth place. That was their highest finish since 1975, but it may be that Hughes has found Stoke's ceiling at his first attempt.

There are significant challenges on the horizon with key centre-back Ryan Shawcross attracting interest from rival clubs and attackers Peter Crouch, Peter Odemwingie and Jon Walters all the wrong side of 30.

However, Stoke are likely to remain tough to beat and a force to be reckoned with at the Britannia Stadium where they lost just three league games last season.

Without significant investment a push for a European place looks beyond them but a mid-table finish and a decent cup run looks well within their capability.

Longest run without a loss: 5
Longest run without a win: 8
Highest/lowest league position: 9/17
Clean sheets: 9
Yellow cards: 75 **Red cards:** 5
Average attendance: 26,137
Players used: 26
Leading scorer: P Crouch 8 (2,8)

	2013-14 H	A	Last six seasons at home P	W	D	L	OV	UN	BS	CS
Man City	D	L	6	1	5	0	0	6	4	2
Liverpool	L	L	6	3	2	1	2	4	3	3
Chelsea	W	L	6	1	2	3	3	3	3	1
Arsenal	W	L	6	3	2	1	3	3	4	2
Everton	D	L	6	1	4	1	1	5	4	2
Tottenham	L	L	6	2	0	4	5	1	5	0
Man United	W	L	6	1	1	4	2	4	3	0
Southampton	D	D	2	0	2	0	1	1	2	0
Stoke										
Newcastle	W	L	5	3	1	1	3	2	3	2
Crystal Palace	W	L	1	1	0	0	1	0	1	0
Swansea	D	D	3	2	1	0	0	3	1	2
West Ham	W	W	5	2	1	2	2	3	3	0
Sunderland	W	L	6	4	1	1	1	5	1	4
Aston Villa	W	W	6	3	2	1	4	2	4	2
Hull	W	D	3	2	1	0	0	3	1	2
West Brom	D	W	5	1	3	1	1	4	2	3
Leicester	-	-	-	-	-	-	-	-	-	-
Burnley			1	1	0	0	0	1	0	1
QPR			2	1	0	1	1	1	1	1

Season	Division	Pos	P	W	D	L	F	A	GD	Pts
2013-14	Premier League	9	38	13	11	14	45	52	-7	50
2012-13	Premier League	13	38	9	15	14	34	45	-11	42
2011-12	Premier League	14	38	11	12	15	36	53	-17	45

Over/Under 45%/55% 15th **Both score** 50%/50% 6th

Key stat: Stoke retain the solid defensive core they possessed under Tony Pulis and have conceded more than one goal in just one of their last 13 games

2013-14 Premier League appearances

	P	G		Y	R		P	G		Y	R
C Adam	20 (11)	7		6	0	B Shea	0 (1)	0		0	0
M Arnautovic	27 (3)	4		3	0	T Sorensen	4	0		0	0
O Assaidi	12 (7)	4		1	0	J Walters	27 (5)	5		8	1
A Begovic	32	1		1	0	G Whelan	28 (4)	0		5	1
J Butland	2 (1)	0		0	0	A Wilkinson	2 (3)	0		1	0
G Cameron	37	2		7	0	M Wilson	30 (3)	0		6	1
P Crouch	30 (4)	8		7	0						
M Etherington	5 (6)	0		0	0						
J Guidetti	0 (6)	0		0	0						
R Huth	12	0		4	0						
S Ireland	14 (11)	2		3	0						
C Jerome	0 (1)	0		0	0						
K Jones	4 (3)	0		0	0						
M Muniesa	7 (6)	0		0	0						
S Nzonzi	34 (2)	2		5	1						
P Odemwingie	15	6		3	0						
W Palacios	5 (11)	0		3	0						
J Pennant	0 (8)	1		1	0						
E Pieters	34 (2)	1		5	0						
R Shawcross	37	1		6	1						

The sleeves never fit but the goals keep coming

SUNDERLAND

Nickname: Mackems/The Black Cats
Colours: Red and white
Ground: Stadium of Light
Capacity: 48,707
Tel: 0191-551-5000
www.safc.com

Sunderland could be a team to watch as they embark on their first full campaign under Gus Poyet.

They had two purple patches last term, winning six games out of eight between early January and early February and taking 13 points from 15 from mid-April to early May. The second of those runs featured three amazing results – a 2-2 draw at Man City, a 2-1 win at Chelsea and a 1-0 victory at Man United – that took them from the foot of the table to safety in the final weeks of the season.

Poyet's challenge is to get those sort of performances out of the players more regularly. Losing energetic midfielder Jack Colback to Newcastle is a blow but the best is yet to come from powerful striker Connor Wickham, who could be a key man for them this season and beyond.

Longest run without a loss: 5
Longest run without a win: 9
Highest/lowest league position: 14/20
Clean sheets: 11
Yellow cards: 70 **Red cards:** 7
Average attendance: 41,089
Players used: 31
Leading scorer: A Johnson 8 (3,6)

	2013-14		Last six seasons at home							
	H	**A**	**P**	**W**	**D**	**L**	**OV**	**UN**	**BS**	**CS**
Man City	W	D	6	4	1	1	1	5	1	4
Liverpool	L	L	6	2	1	3	1	5	2	2
Chelsea	L	W	6	0	0	6	6	0	6	0
Arsenal	L	L	6	1	2	3	2	4	4	1
Everton	L	W	6	1	3	2	1	5	3	1
Tottenham	L	L	6	1	2	3	4	2	5	1
Man United	L	W	6	0	1	5	2	4	2	1
Southampton	D	D	2	0	2	0	1	1	2	0
Stoke	W	L	6	4	2	0	1	5	1	5
Newcastle	W	W	5	2	2	1	2	3	4	0
Crystal Palace	D	L	1	0	1	0	0	1	0	1
Swansea	L	L	3	1	1	1	1	2	1	2
West Ham	L	D	5	2	1	2	3	2	2	2
Sunderland										
Aston Villa	L	D	6	1	1	4	2	4	2	1
Hull	L	L	3	2	0	1	1	2	1	1
West Brom	W	L	5	2	1	2	4	1	3	2
Leicester	-	-	-	-	-	-	-	-	-	-
Burnley			1	1	0	0	1	0	1	0
QPR			2	1	1	0	1	1	1	1

Season	Division	Pos	P	W	D	L	F	A	GD	Pts
2013-14	Premier League	14	38	10	8	20	41	60	-19	38
2012-13	Premier League	17	38	9	12	17	41	54	-13	39
2011-12	Premier League	13	38	11	12	15	45	46	-1	45

Over/Under 55%/45% 6th   **Both score** 47%/53% 7th

Key stat: Sunderland haven't featured in a 1-1 draw in 37 games stretching back to the second game of 2013-14 when they bagged a point at Southampton

2013-14 Premier League appearances

	P	G		Y	R
M Alonso	16	0		5	1
J Altidore	19 (12)	1		3	0
E Ba	0 (1)	0		0	0
P Bardsley	26	2		9	0
F Borini	25 (7)	7		6	0
L Bridcutt	9 (3)	0		4	0
W Brown	24 (1)	0		2	3
A Cabral	1	0		1	0
L Cattermole	21 (3)	1		5	1
O Celustka	14 (7)	0		1	0
J Colback	28 (5)	3		6	0
C Cuellar	4	0		0	0
M Diakite	7	0		0	0
A Dossena	6 (1)	0		1	1
S Fletcher	13 (7)	3		1	0
C Gardner	7 (11)	2		5	0
E Giaccherini	16 (8)	4		4	0
Ji Dong-Won	2 (3)	0		0	0
A Johnson	28 (8)	8		2	0
S Ki	25 (2)	3		3	0

	P	G		Y	R
S Larsson	24 (7)	1		6	0
V Mannone	28 (1)	0		0	0
C Mavrias	1 (3)	0		0	0
J O'Shea	33	1		2	1
V Roberge	7 (2)	0		1	0
I Scocco	0 (6)	0		0	0
S Sessegnon	2	0		0	0
D Vaughan	2 (1)	0		0	0
S Vergini	10 (1)	0		2	0
K Westwood	10	0		0	0
C Wickham	10 (5)	5		1	0

Connor Wickham was unstoppable in April

SWANSEA CITY

Nickname: The Swans
Colours: White
Ground: Liberty Stadium
Tel: 01792-616-600

Capacity: 20,745
www.swanseacity.net

A few eyebrows were raised when Garry Monk replaced Michael Laudrup in the Swansea dugout but he steered them to safety and can guide them into the top half in his first full season at the helm.

The Swans ended up 12th, which was a decent achievement considering the injury problems of key striker Michu.

Wilfried Bony had an impressive first season in England, scoring 16 goals, and if they can hold onto him, the Ivorian could form a potent partnership with the Spaniard.

Swansea played some great football in the Europa League and were unlucky to lose to Napoli in the round of 32.

However, the absence of further European action should help them focus more on the league and facilitate an improvement in their finishing position.

Longest run without a loss: 3
Longest run without a win: 8
Highest/lowest league position: 9/15
Clean sheets: 8
Yellow cards: 56 **Red cards:** 3
Average attendance: 20,406
Players used: 27
Leading scorer: W Bony 16 (2,12)

	2013-14 H	A	Last six seasons at home P	W	D	L	OV	UN	BS	CS
Man City	L	L	3	1	1	1	1	2	1	2
Liverpool	D	L	3	1	2	0	1	2	1	2
Chelsea	L	L	3	0	2	1	0	3	2	0
Arsenal	L	D	3	1	0	2	2	1	2	0
Everton	L	L	3	0	0	3	2	1	1	0
Tottenham	L	L	3	0	1	2	2	1	3	0
Man United	L	L	3	0	1	2	1	2	2	0
Southampton	L	L	3	1	1	1	1	2	0	2
Stoke	D	D	3	2	1	0	2	1	2	1
Newcastle	W	W	4	2	1	1	1	3	1	2
Crystal Palace	D	W	4	1	2	1	2	2	2	2
Swansea										
West Ham	D	L	2	1	1	0	1	1	0	2
Sunderland	W	W	3	1	2	0	2	1	1	2
Aston Villa	W	D	3	1	2	0	2	1	2	1
Hull	D	L	2	0	2	0	0	2	2	0
West Brom	L	W	4	2	0	2	3	1	2	1
Leicester			2	2	0	0	0	2	0	2
Burnley			2	1	1	0	0	2	1	1
QPR			5	2	3	0	1	4	2	3

Season	Division	Pos	P	W	D	L	F	A	GD	Pts
2013-14	Premier League	12	38	11	9	18	54	54	0	42
2012-13	Premier League	9	38	11	13	14	47	51	-4	46
2011-12	Premier League	11	38	12	11	15	44	51	-7	47

Over/Under 53%/47% 8th

Both score 53%/47% 4th

Key stat: Swansea tightened up defensively towards the end of the season and conceded fewer than two goals in their last seven matches

2013-14 Premier League appearances

	P	G	Y	R
Alvaro Vazquez	5 (7)	0	0	0
J Amat	13 (4)	0	3	0
K Bartley	1 (1)	0	0	0
W Bony	27 (7)	16	4	0
L Britton	23 (2)	0	2	0
J Canas	19 (4)	0	5	0
Chico	30 (1)	3	6	2
B Davies	32 (2)	2	3	0
N Dyer	19 (8)	6	1	0
M Emnes	2 (5)	1	2	0
J Fulton	1 (1)	0	1	0
P Hernandez	17 (10)	2	2	0
S Ki	0 (1)	0	0	0
R Lamah	4 (5)	2	1	0
L Lita	0 (2)	0	0	0
Michu	15 (2)	2	2	0
D Ngog	0 (3)	0	0	0
A Pozuelo	7 (15)	0	1	0
A Rangel	29 (1)	0	8	0
W Routledge	32 (3)	2	2	0

	P	G	Y	R
J Shelvey	29 (3)	6	4	0
N Taylor	6 (4)	0	1	0
D Tiendalli	9 (1)	0	0	0
G Tremmel	12	0	0	0
M Vorm	26	0	2	1
A Williams	34	1	5	0
J de Guzman	26 (8)	4	1	0

Wilfried Bony led defences a merry dance

TOTTENHAM HOTSPUR

Nickname: Spurs
Colours: White and navy blue
Ground: White Hart Lane
Tel: 0870-420-5000
Capacity: 36,284
www.tottenhamhotspur.com

Mauricio Pochettino is the latest man to walk through White Hart Lane's revolving door but he may struggle to improve on the combined efforts of Andre Villas-Boas and Tim Sherwood.

The race for the top four is sure to be hugely competitive. Liverpool will be flush with Champions League cash while Man United are set to improve and even if Pochettino improves Spurs, it may not be enough for a Champions League place.

Hugo Lloris, Christian Eriksen and Emmanuel Adebayor look like being key players and there are hopes that Pochettino could be the man to get the best out of compatriot Erik Lamela, who was a huge disappointment last season.

However, most of the Gareth Bale money has been spent, so little more than steady improvement can be expected.

Longest run without a loss: 6
Longest run without a win: 4
Highest/lowest league position: 4/9
Clean sheets: 14
Yellow cards: 66 **Red cards:** 4
Average attendance: 35,808
Players used: 28
Leading scorer: E Adebayor 11 (4,7)

	2013-14		Last six seasons at home							
	H	A	P	W	D	L	OV	UN	BS	CS
Man City	L	L	6	3	1	2	5	1	4	2
Liverpool	L	L	6	5	0	1	6	0	4	1
Chelsea	D	L	6	2	3	1	2	4	5	1
Arsenal	L	L	6	3	2	1	4	2	4	1
Everton	W	D	6	3	2	1	2	4	3	2
Tottenham										
Man United	D	W	6	0	4	2	3	3	4	2
Southampton	W	W	2	2	0	0	1	1	1	1
Stoke	W	W	6	3	2	1	3	3	3	2
Newcastle	L	W	5	4	0	1	2	3	1	3
Crystal Palace	W	W	1	1	0	0	0	1	0	1
Swansea	W	W	3	3	0	0	1	2	1	2
West Ham	L	L	5	3	1	1	2	3	1	3
Sunderland	W	W	6	4	1	1	2	4	3	3
Aston Villa	W	W	6	4	1	1	3	3	2	4
Hull	W	D	3	1	1	1	3	0	2	2
West Brom	D	D	5	2	3	0	1	4	3	2
Leicester	-	-	-	-	-	-	-	-	-	-
Burnley	W		1	1	0	0	1	0	0	1
QPR	W	W	2	2	0	0	2	0	2	0

Season	Division	Pos	P	W	D	L	F	A	GD	Pts
2013-14	Premier League	6	38	21	6	11	55	51	+4	69
2012-13	Premier League	5	38	21	9	8	66	46	+20	72
2011-12	Premier League	4	38	20	9	9	66	41	+25	69

Over/Under 50%/50% 11th   **Both score** 37%/63% 16th

Key stat: Tottenham secured just one point from a possible 24 against the top four last season

2013-14 Premier League appearances

	P	G	Y	R
E Adebayor	20 (1)	11	0	0
N Bentaleb	11 (4)	0	2	0
E Capoue	8 (4)	1	1	0
N Chadli	15 (9)	1	1	0
V Chiriches	16 (1)	1	1	0
M Dawson	31 (1)	0	7	0
J Defoe	3 (11)	1	1	0
M Dembele	22 (6)	1	5	0
C Eriksen	23 (2)	7	3	0
B Friedel	1	0	0	0
E Fryers	3 (4)	0	0	0
L Holtby	6 (7)	1	1	0
Y Kaboul	11 (2)	1	1	2
H Kane	6 (4)	3	0	0
E Lamela	3 (6)	0	1	0
A Lennon	26 (1)	1	1	0
H Lloris	37	0	2	0
K Naughton	19 (3)	0	6	0
Paulinho	28 (2)	6	4	1
A Pritchard	0 (1)	0	0	0

	P	G	Y	R
D Rose	22	1	4	1
Sandro	10 (7)	1	6	0
G Sigurdsson	14 (11)	5	2	0
R Soldado	22 (6)	6	6	0
A Townsend	12 (13)	1	2	0
M Veljkovic	0 (2)	0	0	0
J Vertonghen	23	0	4	0
K Walker	26	1	5	0

Emmanuel Adebayor grabbed 11 goals last term

WEST BROMWICH ALBION

Nickname: The Baggies/Throstles/Albion
Colours: Navy blue and white
Ground: The Hawthorns **Capacity:** 26,445
Tel: 0871-271-1100 www.wba.co.uk

West Brom have struggled for stability since the dismissal of Steve Clarke last December and will be hoping things settle down under new boss Alan Irvine.

Their tally of seven league wins was the joint-lowest in the division and included only four victories at the Hawthorns.

They spread their 43 goals around, with Saido Berahino and Stephane Sessegnon joint-top scorers with just five goals and the acquisition of a regular goalscorer will surely be a priority.

Albion conceded far too many goals during Pepe Mel's ill-fated reign but have decent players in midfield and centre-backs Gareth McAuley and Jonas Olsson are a solid, well-established partnership.

They also have a top-class goalkeeper in Ben Foster and the signing of Joleon Lescott adds further defensive strength.

Longest run without a loss: 5
Longest run without a win: 9
Highest/lowest league position: 10/18
Clean sheets: 7
Yellow cards: 67 **Red cards:** 0
Average attendance: 25,193 **Players used:** 28
Leading scorer: S Sessegnon 5 (1,5)
S Berahino 5 (3,5)

| | 2013-14 | | Last six seasons at home | | | | | | | |
	H	A	P	W	D	L	OV	UN	BS	CS
Man City	L	L	5	1	1	3	3	2	3	1
Liverpool	D	L	5	2	1	2	2	3	2	1
Chelsea	D	D	5	2	1	2	3	2	3	1
Arsenal	D	L	5	0	2	3	4	1	5	0
Everton	D	D	5	2	1	2	1	4	2	2
Tottenham	D	D	5	1	2	2	2	3	3	1
Man United	L	W	5	0	1	4	5	0	3	0
Southampton	L	L	2	1	0	1	0	2	0	1
Stoke	L	D	5	0	0	5	2	3	1	0
Newcastle	W	L	6	2	2	2	3	3	5	1
Crystal Palace	W	L	2	1	0	1	0	2	0	1
Swansea	L	W	4	1	0	3	2	2	2	0
West Ham	W	D	4	2	2	0	2	2	2	2
Sunderland	W	L	5	5	0	0	4	1	1	4
Aston Villa	D	L	5	1	3	1	4	1	4	1
Hull	D	L	2	0	1	1	1	1	1	0
West Brom										
Leicester			1	1	0	0	1	0	0	1
Burnley			-	-	-	-	-	-	-	-
QPR			3	2	1	0	2	1	2	1

Season	Division	Pos	P	W	D	L	F	A	GD	Pts
2013-14	Premier League	17	38	7	15	16	43	59	-16	36
2012-13	Premier League	8	38	14	7	17	53	57	-4	49
2011-12	Premier League	10	38	13	8	17	45	52	-7	47

Over/Under 42%/58% 17th **Both score** 58%/42% 3rd

Key stat: Seven of West Brom's last nine home fixtures have featured goals for both teams

2013-14 Premier League appearances

	P	G		Y	R
M Amalfitano	26 (2)	4		3	0
N Anelka	11 (1)	2		0	0
V Anichebe	11 (13)	3		3	0
S Berahino	11 (21)	5		0	0
C Brunt	25 (3)	3		7	0
L Daniels	0 (1)	0		0	0
C Dawson	10 (2)	0		1	0
G Dorrans	12 (2)	2		4	0
B Foster	24			1	0
Z Gera	5 (9)	0		1	0
B Jones	21			5	0
S Long	12 (4)	3		2	0
D Lugano	7 (2)	1		2	0
G McAuley	32	2		4	0
J Morrison	23 (9)	1		1	0
Y Mulumbu	33 (4)	2		7	0
B Myhill	14	0		0	0
L O'Neil	0 (3)	0		0	0
J Olsson	32	1		10	0
G Popov	1 (1)	0		0	0

	P	G		Y	R
S Reid	16	0		3	0
L Ridgewell	33	1		6	0
M Rosenberg	1 (3)	0		0	0
S Sessegnon	23 (3)	5		0	0
S Sinclair	4 (4)	0		0	0
Thievy	3 (3)	2		0	0
M Vydra	7 (16)	3		0	0
C Yacob	22 (5)	1		7	0

Saido Berahino enjoyed a decent debut season

WEST HAM UNITED

Nickname: The Hammers/Irons
Colours: Claret and blue
Ground: Boleyn Ground
Tel: 020-8548-2748

Capacity: 35,016
www.whufc.com

West Ham's owners kept Sam Allardyce on as they thought he was the man most likely to preserve Premier League status, but their confidence may be misplaced.

Allardyce's relationship with the fans deteriorated during last season and the fallout had a negative impact on results.

The Hammers are usually strong on home soil but lost nine of 19 matches at Upton Park, where the atmosphere was often laced with anxiety and discontent.

A more entertaining brand of football has been promised but Allardyce knows only one way to play and will rely heavily on injury-prone striker Andy Carroll.

New signing Enner Valencia impressed at the World Cup but there are signs that opposition teams are getting better at negating Allardyce's tactics and another difficult season is in prospect.

Longest run without a loss: 5
Longest run without a win: 7
Highest/lowest league position: 10/19
Clean sheets: 14
Yellow cards: 64 **Red cards:** 5
Average attendance: 34,196
Players used: 29
Leading scorer: K Nolan 7 (2,5)

	2013-14		Last six seasons at home							
	H	A	P	W	D	L	OV	UN	BS	CS
Man City	L	L	5	1	2	2	2	3	3	2
Liverpool	L	L	5	1	0	4	5	0	4	0
Chelsea	L	D	5	1	1	3	3	2	3	0
Arsenal	L	L	5	0	1	4	4	1	3	0
Everton	L	L	5	0	1	4	4	1	5	0
Tottenham	W	W	5	2	0	3	2	3	2	2
Man United	L	L	5	0	1	4	3	2	2	0
Southampton	W	D	3	2	1	0	2	1	3	0
Stoke	L	L	5	2	1	2	2	3	2	1
Newcastle	L	D	4	1	1	2	3	1	3	1
Crystal Palace	L	L	2	0	1	1	0	2	0	1
Swansea	W	D	2	2	0	0	0	2	0	2
West Ham										
Sunderland	D	W	5	2	2	1	1	4	1	3
Aston Villa	D	W	5	2	1	2	2	3	2	2
Hull	W	L	4	4	0	0	3	1	2	2
West Brom	D	L	4	1	3	0	3	1	3	1
Leicester			1	1	0	0	1	0	1	0
Burnley			2	1	0	1	2	0	2	0
QPR			1	0	1	0	0	1	1	0

Season	Division	Pos	P	W	D	L	F	A	GD	Pts
2013-14	Premier League	13	38	11	7	20	40	51	-11	40
2012-13	Premier League	10	38	12	10	16	45	53	-8	46
2011-12	Championship	3	46	24	14	8	81	48	+33	86

Over/Under 47%/53% 14th   **Both score** 39%/61% 15th

Key stat: Andy Carroll has scored just two goals in his last 19 appearances

---

2013-14 Premier League appearances

	P	G	Y	R
Adrian	20	0	2	0
P Armero	3 (2)	0	2	0
M Borriello	0 (2)	0	0	0
A Carroll	12 (3)	2	0	1
C Cole	9 (17)	5	1	0
J Cole	6 (14)	3	2	0
J Collins	22 (2)	1	6	0
J Collison	6 (4)	0	0	0
G Demel	30 (2)	1	3	0
M Diame	29 (6)	4	4	0
A Diarra	1 (2)	0	1	0
S Downing	29 (3)	1	0	0
J Jaaskelainen	18	0	0	0
M Jarvis	23 (9)	2	1	0
R Johnson	2 (2)	0	1	0
E Lee	0 (1)	0	0	0
M Maiga	11 (3)	1	0	0
G McCartney	20 (2)	0	4	0
R Morrison	12 (4)	3	5	0
M Noble	38	3	7	1

	P	G	Y	R
A Nocerino	2 (8)	0	3	0
K Nolan	33	7	7	2
J O'Brien	13 (4)	0	4	0
M Petric	0 (3)	0	0	0
R Rat	11 (4)	0	1	0
W Reid	18 (4)	1	2	0
M Taylor	16 (4)	0	3	0
J Tomkins	31	0	6	1
R Vaz Te	3 (5)	2	0	0

Kevin Nolan performed seven chicken dances

Premier League stats 2013-14

Key Points in all tables (except the league table) do not include any deductions imposed by the league.
POS H A Overall league position, rank from home games only, rank from away games only **Sup** Average match supremacy **GFA** Goals For Average **GAA** Goals Against Average **PGA** Points Gained Average

Pos	H	A	League table 2013-14	P	Home W	D	L	F	A	Away W	D	L	F	A	GD	Pts
1	1	3	Man City	38	17	1	1	63	13	10	4	5	39	24	+65	86 (C)
2	2	1	Liverpool	38	16	1	2	53	18	10	5	4	48	32	+51	84
3	3	5	Chelsea	38	15	3	1	43	11	10	4	5	28	16	+44	82
4	4	2	Arsenal	38	13	5	1	36	11	11	2	6	32	30	+27	79
5	5	7	Everton	38	13	3	3	38	19	8	6	5	23	20	+22	72
6	7	6	Tottenham	38	11	3	5	30	23	10	3	6	25	28	+4	69
7	9	4	Man Utd	38	9	3	7	29	21	10	4	5	35	22	+21	64
8	8	8	Southampton	38	8	6	5	32	23	7	5	7	22	23	+8	56
9	6	16	Stoke	38	10	6	3	27	17	3	5	11	18	35	-7	50
10	10	9	Newcastle	38	8	3	8	23	28	7	1	11	20	31	-16	49
11	11	12	C Palace	38	8	3	8	18	23	5	3	11	15	25	-15	45
12	15	11	Swansea	38	6	5	8	33	26	5	4	10	21	28	0	42
13	13	14	West Ham	38	7	3	9	25	26	4	4	11	15	25	-11	40
14	19	10	Sunderland	38	5	3	11	21	27	5	5	9	20	33	-19	38
15	17	13	Aston Villa	38	6	3	10	22	29	4	5	10	17	32	-22	38
16	12	18	Hull	38	7	4	8	20	21	3	3	13	18	32	-15	37
17	16	15	West Brom	38	4	9	6	24	27	3	6	10	19	32	-16	36
18	14	20	Norwich	38	6	6	7	17	18	2	3	14	11	44	-34	33 (R)
19	20	17	Fulham	38	5	3	11	24	38	4	2	13	16	47	-45	32 (R)
20	18	19	Cardiff	38	5	5	9	20	35	2	4	13	12	39	-42	30 (R)

Best attack

		GF	GFA
1	Man City	102	2.68
2	Liverpool	101	2.66
3	Chelsea	71	1.87
4	Arsenal	68	1.79
5	Man Utd	64	1.68
6	Everton	61	1.61
7	Tottenham	55	1.45
8	Southampton	54	1.42
9	Swansea	54	1.42
10	Stoke	45	1.18
11	Newcastle	43	1.13
12	West Brom	43	1.13
13	Sunderland	41	1.08
14	West Ham	40	1.05
15	Fulham	40	1.05
16	Aston Villa	39	1.03
17	Hull	38	1.00
18	C Palace	33	0.87
19	Cardiff	32	0.84
20	Norwich	28	0.74

Best defence

		GA	GAA
1	Chelsea	27	0.71
2	Man City	37	0.97
3	Everton	39	1.03
4	Arsenal	41	1.08
5	Man Utd	43	1.13
6	Southampton	46	1.21
7	C Palace	48	1.26
8	Liverpool	50	1.32
9	Tottenham	51	1.34
10	West Ham	51	1.34
11	Stoke	52	1.37
12	Hull	53	1.39
13	Swansea	54	1.42
14	Newcastle	59	1.55
15	West Brom	59	1.55
16	Sunderland	60	1.58
17	Aston Villa	61	1.61
18	Norwich	62	1.63
19	Cardiff	74	1.95
20	Fulham	85	2.24

Top scorers

	Team	Goals scored	
L Suarez	Liverpool	31	
D Sturridge	Liverpool	21	
Y Toure	Man City	20	
S Aguero	Man City	17	
W Rooney	Man Utd	17	
W Bony	Swansea	16	
E Dzeko	Man City	16	
O Giroud	Arsenal	16	
R Lukaku	Everton	15	
J Rodriguez	Southampton	15	

Ian Rush was the last Liverpool man to score 30

Over 2.5 goals

	H	A	%
Liverpool	14	16	79%
Fulham	14	12	68%
Man City	14	11	66%
Newcastle	11	13	63%
Man United	10	12	58%

Under 2.5 goals

	H	A	%
C Palace	14	13	71%
Hull	14	11	66%
Norwich	14	10	63%
West Brom	12	10	58%
Southampton, Stoke			55%

Both to score

	H	A	%
Liverpool	11	14	66%
Fulham	14	9	61%
West Brom	11	11	58%
Swansea	11	9	53%
Man City	8	12	53%

Both not to score

	H	A	%
C Palace	14	13	71%
Hull	14	10	63%
Norwich	12	12	63%
Tottenham	12	12	63%
Newcastle	12	12	63%

Results 2013-14

	Arsenal	Aston Villa	Cardiff	Chelsea	C Palace	Everton	Fulham	Hull	Liverpool	Man City	Man Utd	Newcastle	Norwich	Southampton	Stoke	Sunderland	Swansea	Tottenham	West Brom	West Ham
Arsenal		1-3	2-0	0-0	2-0	1-1	2-0	2-0	2-0	1-1	0-0	3-0	4-1	2-0	3-1	4-1	2-2	1-0	1-0	3-1
Aston Villa	1-2		2-0	1-0	0-1	0-2	1-2	3-1	0-1	3-2	0-3	1-2	4-1	0-0	1-4	0-0	1-1	0-2	4-3	0-2
Cardiff	0-3	0-0		1-2	0-3	0-0	3-1	0-4	3-6	3-2	2-2	1-2	2-1	0-3	1-1	2-2	1-0	0-1	1-0	0-2
Chelsea	6-0	2-1	4-1		2-1	1-0	2-0	2-0	2-1	2-1	3-1	3-0	0-0	3-1	3-0	1-2	1-0	4-0	2-2	0-0
C Palace	0-2	1-0	2-0	1-0		0-0	1-4	1-0	3-3	0-2	0-2	0-3	1-1	0-1	1-0	3-1	0-2	0-1	3-1	1-0
Everton	3-0	2-1	2-1	1-0	2-3		4-1	2-1	3-3	2-3	2-0	3-2	2-0	2-1	4-0	0-1	3-2	0-0	0-0	1-0
Fulham	1-3	2-0	1-2	1-3	2-2	1-3		2-2	2-3	2-4	1-3	1-0	1-0	0-3	1-0	1-4	1-2	1-2	1-1	2-1
Hull	0-3	0-0	1-1	0-2	0-1	0-2	6-0		3-1	0-2	2-3	1-4	1-0	0-1	0-0	1-0	1-0	1-1	2-0	1-0
Liverpool	5-1	2-2	3-1	0-2	3-1	4-0	4-0	2-0		3-2	1-0	2-1	5-1	0-1	1-0	2-1	4-3	4-0	4-1	4-1
Man City	6-3	4-0	4-2	0-1	1-0	3-1	5-0	2-0	2-1		4-1	4-0	7-0	4-1	1-0	2-2	3-0	6-0	3-1	2-0
Man Utd	1-0	4-1	2-0	0-0	2-0	0-1	2-2	3-1	0-3	0-3		0-1	4-0	1-1	3-2	0-1	2-0	1-2	1-2	3-1
Newcastle	0-1	1-0	3-0	2-0	1-0	0-3	1-0	2-3	2-2	0-2	0-4		2-1	1-1	5-1	0-3	1-2	0-4	2-1	0-0
Norwich	0-2	0-1	0-0	1-3	1-0	2-2	1-2	1-0	2-3	0-0	0-1	0-0		1-0	1-1	2-0	1-1	1-0	0-1	3-1
Southampton	2-2	2-3	0-1	0-3	2-0	2-0	2-0	4-1	0-3	1-1	1-1	4-0	4-2		2-2	1-1	2-0	2-3	1-0	0-0
Stoke	1-0	2-1	0-0	3-2	2-1	1-1	4-1	1-0	3-5	0-0	2-1	1-0	0-1	1-1		2-0	1-1	0-1	0-0	3-1
Sunderland	1-3	0-1	4-0	3-4	0-0	0-1	0-1	0-2	1-3	1-0	1-2	2-1	0-0	2-2	1-0		1-3	1-2	2-0	1-2
Swansea	1-2	4-1	3-0	0-1	1-1	1-2	2-0	1-1	2-2	2-3	1-4	3-0	3-0	0-1	3-3	4-0		1-3	1-2	0-0
Tottenham	0-1	3-0	1-0	1-1	2-0	1-0	3-1	1-0	0-5	1-5	2-2	0-1	2-0	3-2	3-0	5-1	1-0		1-1	0-3
West Brom	1-1	2-2	3-3	1-1	2-0	1-1	1-1	1-1	1-1	2-3	0-3	1-0	0-2	0-1	1-2	3-0	0-2	3-3		1-0
West Ham	1-3	0-0	2-0	0-3	0-1	2-3	3-0	2-1	1-2	1-3	0-2	1-3	2-0	3-1	0-1	0-0	2-0	2-0	3-3	

Record when first to score

		P	W	D	L	F	A	Sup	PGA	Pts
1	Man City	29	24	3	2	91	26	+2.24	2.6	75
2	Liverpool	28	23	3	2	83	30	+1.89	2.6	72
3	Arsenal	24	22	1	1	52	11	+1.71	2.8	67
4	Chelsea	24	20	2	2	55	14	+1.71	2.6	62
5	Everton	22	19	1	2	47	17	+1.36	2.6	58
6	Tottenham	19	16	3	0	35	7	+1.47	2.7	51
7	Southampton	23	15	4	4	45	22	+1.00	2.1	49
8	Man Utd	17	15	2	0	42	7	+2.06	2.8	47
9	Newcastle	19	14	2	3	35	16	+1.00	2.3	44
10	C Palace	16	13	1	2	26	12	+0.88	2.5	40
11	Swansea	15	10	4	1	35	11	+1.60	2.3	34
12	Stoke	16	9	5	2	26	19	+0.44	2.0	32
13	Hull	14	9	4	1	27	8	+1.36	2.2	31
14	West Ham	17	10	1	6	32	22	+0.59	1.8	31
15	Sunderland	14	9	1	4	26	16	+0.71	2.0	28
16	Norwich	13	7	3	3	16	12	+0.31	1.8	24
17	West Brom	11	6	4	1	22	14	+0.73	2.0	22
18	Fulham	12	6	4	2	17	12	+0.42	1.8	22
19	Aston Villa	11	6	2	3	17	16	+0.09	1.8	20
20	Cardiff	9	5	1	3	15	16	-0.11	1.8	16

Record when keeping a clean sheet

		P	W	D	F	Sup	PGA	Pts
1	Liverpool	10	10	0	28	+2.80	3.0	30
2	Fulham	5	5	0	6	+1.20	3.0	15
3	Tottenham	14	13	1	23	+1.64	2.9	40
4	Arsenal	17	15	2	29	+1.71	2.8	47
5	Man City	16	14	2	44	+2.75	2.8	44
6	Swansea	8	7	1	19	+2.38	2.8	22
7	Southampton	15	13	2	24	+1.60	2.7	41
8	Man Utd	13	11	2	26	+2.00	2.7	35
9	C Palace	12	10	2	13	+1.08	2.7	32
10	Chelsea	18	14	4	34	+1.89	2.6	46
11	Hull	10	8	2	18	+1.80	2.6	26
12	Newcastle	10	8	2	13	+1.30	2.6	26
13	Everton	15	11	4	22	+1.47	2.5	37
14	West Brom	7	5	2	8	+1.14	2.4	17
15	Sunderland	11	7	4	13	+1.18	2.3	25
16	Norwich	12	7	5	9	+0.75	2.2	26
17	West Ham	14	8	6	18	+1.29	2.1	30
18	Stoke	9	5	4	6	+0.67	2.1	19
19	Aston Villa	9	4	5	5	+0.56	1.9	17
20	Cardiff	7	3	4	3	+0.43	1.9	13

McClaren's progressive young Rams can recover from playoff heartbreak

The Championship has long been considered a punters' graveyard, and the implementation of Financial Fair Play rules looks set to make life even harder, writes Dan Sait. No longer is it just panicky chairmen, volatile managers, season-altering loan signings and surprise sugar daddies we have to account for – now we must predict which clubs will cut their cloth to suit, and which will defy the rule makers and spend their way out of the division.

But the truth is that until we've seen at least a full season of FFP in action, we can't be sure how well it will be either implemented or navigated. And if last season told us anything, it's that there's more than one way to escape this league – Leicester bought their way out, Burnley did it on a shoestring, and Tony Fernandes arguably gambled QPR's future on promotion and got lucky.

For now, it's best to focus on known facts, and that means being wary of the favourites. QPR's failure to oblige at 9-2 last term made it 13 years since a favourite won in the second tier and 8-1 Cardiff don't look the most likely team to buck that trend this season.

There is quality in the team and money in the coffers, but relative rookie manager Ole Gunnar Solskjaer won just three of 18 league games as Cardiff boss last season and Vincent Tan is an unpredictable boardroom presence.

Fulham look the best equipped to bounce straight back up but are also a short price and it's worth noting that in the last seven seasons only Newcastle have recovered from relegation to win the Championship.

Derby look the pick of last term's second-tier sides. They finished 12 points clear of the next closest non-promoted team and, after Steve McClaren had settled in, took 2.06 points per game from their final 32 matches.

They aren't a huge at 10-1 but four of the last seven Championship winners were teams who failed in the playoffs the year before and McClaren has a talented young squad who are now battle-hardened at this level.

At bigger prices, **Blackburn** are tasty at 20-1 for the title or 13-2 for promotion. There are lots of goals in the team and while the club may well fall foul of FFP rules, the squad looks strong enough to ride a transfer embargo. The defence needs work but Gary Bowyer has impressed so far and can sort it.

At the wrong end of the table, it's hard to argue with **Blackpool** as favourites for the drop and even at 13-8 I'm interested. They look a club heading only one direction under the unambitious ownership of Karl Oyston, who again has a new manager in the dugout.

Those immediately behind Blackpool all have fair reasons to believe they can stay up though, and I don't fancy Millwall, Charlton, Rotherham or Huddersfield at short prices.

But next in line are 9-2 pair **Birmingham** and **Brentford**, who both look too big. Blues are hoping for new investment but, as they know, these things can take time. They again went backwards last term to finish 21st, and manager Lee Clark struggled with both the pressure and lack of quality players available.

And while Brentford won 19 League 1 home games last term, they lost at home to each of the rest of the top four and had only the fifth-best away record – form that hints at a struggle against higher quality opposition.

Derby celebrate Craig Bryson's penalty against Nottingham Forest

BIRMINGHAM

Nickname: Blues
Colours: Blue
Ground: St Andrew's (29,409)
Tel: 0844-557-1875   www.bcfc.com

Paul Caddis's 93rd-minute goal on the final day kept Blues up and sparked riotous celebrations but they looked a beaten side for much of the run-in and manager Lee Clark needs to regroup if he's to avoid another nervous campaign.

Clark will have benefitted from the experience of a relegation near-miss but while old hand Paul Robinson stood tall as captain, too many of those around him wilted under the pressure. More goals are needed and more belief, too.

Longest run without win/loss: 6/10
High/low league position: 15/22
Clean sheets: 7 **Yellows:** 80 **Reds:** 2
Avg attendance: 17,659 **Players used:** 39
Leading scorer: F Macheda 10 (1,6)
Key stat: Birmingham won all seven games away from home against sides in the bottom eight, but just one of seven at home

	2013-14 H	A	Last six seasons at home P	W	D	L	OV	UN	BS	CS
Norwich			1	0	1	0	0	1	1	0
Fulham			2	1	0	1	0	2	0	1
Cardiff			3	0	2	1	0	3	2	0
Derby	D	D	4	2	2	0	3	1	3	1
Wigan	L	D	3	1	1	1	0	3	0	2
Brighton	L	L	3	0	2	1	1	2	1	1
Reading	L	L	3	1	0	2	2	1	2	1
Blackburn	L	W	4	2	1	1	3	1	4	0
Ipswich	D	L	4	2	1	1	2	2	3	0
Bournemouth	L	W	1	0	0	1	1	0	1	0
Nottm Forest	D	L	4	2	1	1	2	2	2	2
Middlesbro	D	L	3	2	1	0	3	0	2	1
Watford	L	L	4	2	0	2	3	1	1	1
Bolton	L	D	4	2	0	2	4	0	4	0
Leeds	L	L	3	2	0	1	1	2	1	2
Sheff Wed	W	L	3	2	1	0	2	1	2	1
Huddersfield	L	W	2	0	0	2	1	1	1	0
Charlton	L	W	3	1	1	1	1	2	2	0
Millwall	W	W	3	2	1	0	2	1	1	2
Blackpool	D	W	5	2	2	1	1	4	2	2
Birmingham										
Wolves			4	2	1	1	2	2	3	1
Brentford			-	-	-	-	-	-	-	-
Rotherham			-	-	-	-	-	-	-	-

Season	Division	Pos	P	W	D	L	F	A	GD	Pts
2013-14	Championship	21	46	11	11	24	58	74	-16	44
2012-13	Championship	12	46	15	16	15	63	69	-6	61
2011-12	Championship	4	46	20	16	10	78	51	+27	76

Over/Under 52%/48% 4th   **Both score** 54%/46% 10th

BLACKBURN

Nickname: Rovers
Colours: Blue and white
Ground: Ewood Park (31,154)
Tel: 0871-702-1875   www.rovers.co.uk

Sanity seems to be breaking out at Ewood Park with a manager lasting a full season, sensible signings arriving and owners Venky's keeping a low profile.

Gary Bowyer stopped the club sliding into the third tier upon his arrival in March 2013 and he made big strides last term, remoulding an unbalanced unit into a strong second-tier squad.

Jordan Rhodes remains a huge asset, and January signings Craig Conway and Rudy Gestede add further attacking class.

Longest run without win/loss: 4/12
High/low league position: 8/15
Clean sheets: 15 **Yellows:** 75 **Reds:** 4
Avg attendance: 16,640 **Players used:** 32
Leading scorer: J Rhodes 25 (9,18)
Key stat: Blackburn had a win percentage of just 31 without January signings Conway and Gestede – it rose to 54 when they both played

	2013-14 H	A	Last six seasons at home P	W	D	L	OV	UN	BS	CS
Norwich			1	1	0	0	0	1	0	1
Fulham			4	3	1	0	1	3	2	2
Cardiff			1	0	0	1	1	0	1	0
Derby	D	D	2	1	1	0	0	2	1	1
Wigan	W	L	5	4	0	1	3	2	3	1
Brighton	D	L	2	0	2	0	1	1	0	1
Reading	D	W	1	0	1	0	0	1	0	1
Blackburn										
Ipswich	W	L	2	2	0	0	0	2	0	2
Bournemouth	L	W	1	0	0	1	1	0	0	0
Nottm Forest	L	L	2	1	0	1	1	1	0	1
Middlesbro	W	D	3	1	1	1	1	2	2	1
Watford	W	D	2	2	0	0	0	2	0	2
Bolton	W	L	6	3	1	2	5	1	4	2
Leeds	W	W	2	1	1	0	0	2	0	2
Sheff Wed	D	D	2	1	1	0	0	2	0	2
Huddersfield	D	W	2	1	1	0	0	2	0	2
Charlton	L	W	2	0	0	2	1	1	1	0
Millwall	W	D	2	1	0	1	1	1	1	0
Blackpool	W	D	3	1	2	0	1	2	2	1
Birmingham	L	W	4	1	1	2	2	2	2	0
Wolves			4	2	0	2	3	1	2	1
Brentford			-	-	-	-	-	-	-	-
Rotherham			-	-	-	-	-	-	-	-

Season	Division	Pos	P	W	D	L	F	A	GD	Pts
2013-14	Championship	8	46	18	16	12	70	62	+8	70
2012-13	Championship	17	46	14	16	16	55	62	-7	58
2011-12	Premier League	19	38	8	7	23	48	78	-30	31

Over/Under 50%/50% 9th   **Both score** 54%/46% 10th

BLACKPOOL

Nickname: The Seasiders
Colours: Tangerine and white
Ground: Bloomfield Road (17,338)
Tel: 0870-443-1953   www.blackpoolfc.co.uk

The lack of investment is catching up with Blackpool and the club will continue to struggle under Karl Oyston's ownership.

Paul Ince's unhappy 11 months as manager was ended by text message, star man Tom Ince was farmed out on loan and Blackpool fell from fifth in December to a survival scrap on the final day.

Caretaker manager Barry Ferguson was the latest disenchanted boss to walk out and it's hard to see what the attraction was for incoming incumbent Jose Riga.

Longest run without win/loss: 17/7
High/low league position: 4/22
Clean sheets: 12 **Yellows:** 83 **Reds:** 10
Avg attendance: 15,153 **Players used:** 38
Leading scorer: T Ince 7 (4,7)
Key stat: Blackpool won just three of their last 30 games of the 2013-14 season

	2013-14 H	A	Last six seasons at home P	W	D	L	OV	UN	BS	CS
Norwich			1	1	0	0	0	1	0	1
Fulham			1	0	1	0	0	1	0	
Cardiff			4	0	3	1	1	3	4	0
Derby	L	L	5	2	1	2	3	2	3	1
Wigan	W	W	2	1	0	1	1	1	1	1
Brighton	L	D	3	1	1	1	1	2	2	0
Reading	W	L	4	3	1	0	1	3	1	3
Blackburn	D	L	3	1	1	1	2	1	2	1
Ipswich	L	D	5	3	0	2	2	3	1	3
Bournemouth	L	W	1	0	0	1	0	1	0	0
Nottm Forest	D	W	5	1	3	1	3	2	5	0
Middlesbro	L	D	4	3	0	1	2	2	1	2
Watford	W	L	5	2	2	1	2	3	2	2
Bolton	D	L	3	1	2	0	2	1	2	1
Leeds	D	L	3	2	1	0	1	2	2	1
Sheff Wed	W	L	4	1	1	2	1	3	1	2
Huddersfield	W	D	2	1	0	1	1	1	1	1
Charlton	L	D	3	1	0	2	1	2	0	1
Millwall	W	L	3	3	0	0	1	2	1	2
Blackpool										
Birmingham	L	D	5	1	2	2	3	2	4	1
Wolves			3	1	1	1	3	0	3	0
Brentford			-	-	-	-	-	-	-	-
Rotherham			-	-	-	-	-	-	-	-

Season	Division	Pos	P	W	D	L	F	A	GD	Pts
2013-14	Championship	20	46	11	13	22	38	66	-28	46
2012-13	Championship	15	46	14	17	15	62	63	-1	59
2011-12	Championship	5	46	20	15	11	79	59	+20	75

Over/Under 33%/67% 23rd   **Both score** 46%/54% 19th

BOLTON

Nickname: The Trotters
Colours: White and blue
Ground: The Reebok Stadium (28,100)
Tel: 01204-673-673   www.bwfc.co.uk

Bolton's promotion bid was over before it started, as they failed to maintain their fine end-of-season 2012-13 form and began 2013-14 without a win in ten.

And while Dougie Freedman did eventually manage to address that slide and move Bolton into a comfortable mid-table position, the club's financial figures give Trotters fans reason to worry.

With Bolton's debt now up around the £164m mark, the belt tightening must surely begin in earnest.

Longest run without win/loss: 10/8
High/low league position: 14/24
Clean sheets: 12 **Yellows:** 70 **Reds:** 2
Avg attendance: 15,821 **Players used:** 34
Leading scorer: J Beckford 7 (4,7)
L Jutkiewicz 7 (3,7)
Key stat: After a dire first ten matches, Bolton averaged 1.5 points a game – top-ten form

	2013-14 H	A	Last six seasons at home P	W	D	L	OV	UN	BS	CS
Norwich			1	0	0	1	1	0	1	0
Fulham			4	0	2	2	2	1	2	
Cardiff			1	1	0	0	1	0	1	0
Derby	D	D	2	1	1	0	1	1	1	1
Wigan	D	L	5	1	2	2	3	3	3	1
Brighton	L	L	2	1	0	1	0	2	0	1
Reading	D	L	1	0	1	0	0	1	1	0
Blackburn	W	L	6	4	1	1	3	3	2	3
Ipswich	D	L	2	0	1	1	1	1	2	0
Bournemouth	D	W	1	0	1	0	1	0	1	0
Nottm Forest	D	L	2	0	2	0	1	1	2	0
Middlesbro	D	L	3	2	1	0	3	0	3	0
Watford	W	W	2	2	0	0	1	1	1	1
Bolton										
Leeds	L	W	2	0	1	1	1	1	1	0
Sheff Wed	D	W	2	0	1	1	0	2	1	0
Huddersfield	L	W	2	1	0	1	0	2	0	1
Charlton	D	D	2	1	1	0	0	2	1	1
Millwall	W	W	2	1	1	0	1	1	2	0
Blackpool	D	W	3	1	2	0	2	1	2	1
Birmingham	D	W	4	2	2	0	4	0	4	0
Wolves			4	3	1	0	0	4	1	3
Brentford			-	-	-	-	-	-	-	-
Rotherham			-	-	-	-	-	-	-	-

Season	Division	Pos	P	W	D	L	F	A	GD	Pts
2013-14	Championship	14	46	14	17	15	59	60	-1	59
2012-13	Championship	7	46	18	14	14	69	61	+8	68
2011-12	Premier League	18	38	10	6	22	46	77	-31	36

Over/Under 41%/59% 20th   **Both score** 54%/46% 10th

BOURNEMOUTH

Nickname: The Cherries
Colours: Red and black
Ground: Goldsands Stadium (9,287)
Tel: 01202-726-300   www.afcb.co.uk

Upon his return to Dean Court in 2012-13, Eddie Howe lifted Bournemouth from fourth bottom of League 1 to automatic promotion in just six months. But he bettered even that last year, leading the club to their highest ever league finish.

Bournemouth struggled to adapt to life at a higher level early in the season, losing their first two away games 6-1 and 5-1, but they gradually settled and a run of eight wins in ten briefly had the Cherries flirting with the playoff places.

Longest run without win/loss: 7/6
High/low league position: 8/17
Clean sheets: 9 **Yellows:** 68 **Reds:** 4
Avg attendance: 13,259 **Players used:** 27
Leading scorer: L Grabban 22 (7,18)
Key stat: Only Leicester and Blackburn took more shots than Bournemouth last season

	2013-14 H	A	Last six seasons at home P	W	D	L	OV	UN	BS	CS
Norwich			-	-	-	-	-	-	-	-
Fulham			-	-	-	-	-	-	-	-
Cardiff			-	-	-	-	-	-	-	-
Derby	L	L	1	0	0	1	0	1	0	0
Wigan	W	L	1	1	0	0	0	1	0	1
Brighton	D	D	2	1	1	0	0	2	1	1
Reading	W	W	1	1	0	0	1	0	1	0
Blackburn	L	W	1	0	0	1	1	0	1	0
Ipswich	D	D	1	0	1	0	0	1	1	0
Bournemouth										
Nottm Forest	W	D	1	1	0	0	1	0	1	0
Middlesbro	D	D	1	0	1	0	0	1	0	1
Watford	D	L	1	0	1	0	0	1	1	0
Bolton	L	L	1	0	0	1	0	1	0	0
Leeds	W	L	1	1	0	0	1	0	1	0
Sheff Wed	L	W	3	1	1	1	1	2	1	2
Huddersfield	W	L	3	2	1	0	1	2	2	1
Charlton	W	L	3	1	1	1	2	1	2	0
Millwall	W	L	1	1	0	0	1	0	1	0
Blackpool	L	W	1	0	0	1	1	0	1	0
Birmingham	L	W	1	0	0	1	0	1	0	0
Wolves			-	-	-	-	-	-	-	-
Brentford			4	2	1	1	2	2	2	1
Rotherham			2	1	1	0	0	2	0	2

Season	Division	Pos	P	W	D	L	F	A	GD	Pts
2013-14	Championship	10	46	18	12	16	67	66	+1	66
2012-13	League 1	2	46	24	11	11	76	53	+23	83
2011-12	League 1	11	46	15	13	18	48	52	-4	58

Over/Under 52%/48% 4th   **Both score** 61%/39% 2nd

BRENTFORD

Nickname: The Bees
Colours: Red
Ground: Griffin Park (12,763)
Tel: 0845-3456-442   www.brentfordfc.co.uk

Brentford suffered an agonising finale in 2012-13, losing to a 94th-minute goal after a missing a potentially promotion-sealing penalty, so many neutrals were cheering the Bees on last season.

Fears that their form would suffer after manager Uwe Rosler left in December proved unfounded, as replacement Mark Warburton – a former City trader – began his reign with six consecutive wins and guided the club to promotion with three games to spare.

Longest run without win/loss: 3/19
High/low league position: 1/12
Clean sheets: 20 **Yellows:** 76 **Reds:** 4
Avg attendance: 6,455 **Players used:** 34
Leading scorer: C Donaldson 17 (6,15)
Key stat: Brentford lost all three home games against the other sides in the final top four of League 1 last term

	2013-14 H	A	Last six seasons at home P	W	D	L	OV	UN	BS	CS
Norwich			1	1	0	0	1	0	1	0
Fulham			-	-	-	-	-	-	-	-
Cardiff			-	-	-	-	-	-	-	-
Derby			-	-	-	-	-	-	-	-
Wigan			-	-	-	-	-	-	-	-
Brighton			2	0	1	1	0	2	0	1
Reading			-	-	-	-	-	-	-	-
Blackburn			-	-	-	-	-	-	-	-
Ipswich			-	-	-	-	-	-	-	-
Bournemouth			4	1	3	0	0	4	2	2
Nottm Forest			-	-	-	-	-	-	-	-
Middlesbro			-	-	-	-	-	-	-	-
Watford			-	-	-	-	-	-	-	-
Bolton			-	-	-	-	-	-	-	-
Leeds			1	0	1	0	0	1	0	1
Sheff Wed			2	1	0	1	1	1	1	1
Huddersfield			3	1	0	2	2	1	0	1
Charlton			3	1	1	1	2	2	2	0
Millwall			1	0	1	0	1	0	1	0
Blackpool			-	-	-	-	-	-	-	-
Birmingham			-	-	-	-	-	-	-	-
Wolves	L	D	1	0	0	1	1	0	0	0
Brentford										
Rotherham	L	L	2	0	1	1	0	2	0	1

Season	Division	Pos	P	W	D	L	F	A	GD	Pts
2013-14	League 1	2	46	28	10	8	72	43	+29	94
2012-13	League 1	3	46	21	16	9	62	47	+15	79
2011-12	League 1	9	46	18	13	15	63	52	+11	67

Over/Under 46%/54% 14th   **Both score** 43%/57% 22nd

BRIGHTON

Nickname: The Seagulls
Colours: Blue and white
Ground: AmEx Stadium (30,750)
Tel: 01273-695-400   www.seagulls.co.uk

Oscar Garcia's resignation was a surprise as he delivered free-flowing football and a place in the playoffs. And replacing him with Sami Hyypia seems a bit of a punt, as the Finn was sacked after just nine months in sole charge at Leverkusen.

Hyypia will do well to retain Brighton's attractive style but must address their conversion rate, as the Seagulls tended to dominate possession but only six Championship sides scored fewer goals. Even Yeovil had more shots on target.

Longest run without win/loss: 5/8
High/low league position: 6/16
Clean sheets: 20 **Yellows:** 75 **Reds:** 2
Avg attendance: 21,389 **Players used:** 33
Leading scorer: L Ulloa 14 (6,12)
Key stat: Only promoted Burnley had a better defensive record in last season's Championship than Brighton

	2013-14 H	A	Last six seasons at home P	W	D	L	OV	UN	BS	CS
Norwich			1	0	0	1	1	0	1	0
Fulham			-	-	-	-	-	-	-	-
Cardiff			2	0	2	0	1	1	1	1
Derby	L	L	3	2	0	1	2	1	2	1
Wigan	L	W	1	0	0	1	1	0	1	0
Brighton										
Reading	D	D	2	0	1	1	0	2	1	0
Blackburn	W	D	2	1	1	0	1	1	1	1
Ipswich	L	L	3	1	1	1	1	2	1	1
Bournemouth	D	D	2	0	2	0	0	2	2	0
Nottm Forest	L	W	3	1	1	1	1	2	1	2
Middlesbro	L	W	3	0	1	2	0	3	1	0
Watford	D	L	3	0	2	1	2	1	3	0
Bolton	W	W	2	1	1	0	1	1	2	0
Leeds	W	L	5	1	2	2	3	2	2	1
Sheff Wed	D	L	3	2	1	0	1	2	1	2
Huddersfield	D	D	5	1	2	2	2	3	2	2
Charlton	W	L	4	1	2	1	1	3	1	2
Millwall	D	W	5	1	3	1	3	2	4	0
Blackpool	D	W	3	1	2	0	2	1	3	0
Birmingham	W	W	3	1	1	1	0	3	1	1
Wolves			1	1	0	0	0	1	0	1
Brentford			2	2	0	0	1	1	0	2
Rotherham			-	-	-	-	-	-	-	-

Season	Division	Pos	P	W	D	L	F	A	GD	Pts
2013-14	Championship	6	46	19	15	12	55	40	+15	72
2012-13	Championship	4	46	19	18	9	69	43	+26	75
2011-12	Championship	10	46	17	15	14	52	52	0	66

Over/Under 30%/70% 24th   **Both score** 43%/57% 20th

CARDIFF

Nickname: The Bluebirds
Colours: Red
Ground: Cardiff City Stadium (33,000)
Tel: 02920-221-001   www.cardiffcityfc.co.uk

Owner Vincent Tan moved through his repertoire last year, replacing respected head of recruitment Iain Moody with a work experience kid, poking his nose into the dressing room and then delivering the punchline by sacking Malky Mackay – the man who had gained promotion for Cardiff in 2013 and had lifted them a point and two places clear of relegation.

Tan continues to pour money into the club but it's hard to know what the Bluebirds' erratic owner will do next.

Longest run without win/loss: 7/3
High/low league position: 12/20
Clean sheets: 7 **Yellows:** 49 **Reds:** 1
Avg attendance: 32,206 **Players used:** 32
Leading scorer: J Mutch 7 (3,6)
Key stat: Cardiff's points per game slumped from 1.06 before Mackay's resignation ultimatum to 0.59 for the final 22 games

	2013-14 H	A	Last six seasons at home P	W	D	L	OV	UN	BS	CS
Norwich	W	D	3	2	1	0	3	0	3	0
Fulham	W	W	1	1	0	0	1	0	1	0
Cardiff										
Derby			5	4	1	0	3	2	4	1
Wigan			-	-	-	-	-	-	-	-
Brighton			2	0	0	2	1	1	1	0
Reading			4	1	3	0	3	1	3	1
Blackburn			1	1	0	0	1	0	0	1
Ipswich			5	0	2	3	3	2	2	1
Bournemouth			-	-	-	-	-	-	-	-
Nottm Forest			5	3	1	1	1	4	1	3
Middlesbro			4	2	0	2	2	2	1	2
Watford			5	4	1	0	4	1	5	0
Bolton			1	0	1	0	0	1	1	0
Leeds			3	2	1	0	2	1	3	0
Sheff Wed			3	3	0	0	1	2	1	2
Huddersfield			1	1	0	0	0	1	0	1
Charlton			2	1	1	0	0	2	0	2
Millwall			3	2	1	0	1	2	1	2
Blackpool			4	2	1	1	2	2	2	2
Birmingham			3	2	0	1	2	1	2	1
Wolves	W		2	1	0	1	2	0	2	0
Brentford			-	-	-	-	-	-	-	-
Rotherham			-	-	-	-	-	-	-	-

Season	Division	Pos	P	W	D	L	F	A	GD	Pts
2013-14	Premier League	20	38	7	9	22	32	74	-42	30
2012-13	Championship	1	46	25	12	9	72	45	+27	87
2011-12	Championship	6	46	19	18	9	66	53	+13	75

Over/Under 55%/45% 6th   **Both score** 42%/58% 13th

CHARLTON

Nickname: Addicks
Colours: Red and white
Ground: The Valley (27,111)
Tel: 020-8333-4000   www.cafc.co.uk

Chris Powell's side impressed upon their return to the second tier in 2012-13 but started slowly last term, and Powell was under pressure as soon as Belgian Roland Duchatelet took over. With Charlton still struggling in March, Powell was replaced by Belgian manager Jose Riga.

Riga did produce, getting the Addicks out of the bottom three, but has now been replaced himself by another Belgian, Bob Peeters. Charlton fans look set for a rollercoaster ride under Duchatelet.

Longest run without win/loss: 6/5
High/low league position: 17/24
Clean sheets: 13 **Yellows:** 58 **Reds:** 4
Avg attendance: 15,995 **Players used:** 35
Leading scorer: M Sordell 7 (1,5)
Key stat: Only Blackpool and Doncaster scored fewer Championship goals than Charlton last term

	2013-14 H	A	Last six seasons at home P	W	D	L	OV	UN	BS	CS
Norwich			2	1	0	1	1	1	1	0
Fulham			-	-	-	-	-	-	-	-
Cardiff			2	1	1	0	2	0	2	0
Derby	L	L	3	0	2	1	1	2	2	0
Wigan	D	L	1	0	1	0	0	1	0	1
Brighton	W	L	4	1	1	2	4	0	3	0
Reading	L	L	2	1	0	1	1	1	1	0
Blackburn	L	W	2	0	1	1	1	1	2	0
Ipswich	L	D	3	1	0	2	2	1	2	0
Bournemouth	W	L	3	3	0	0	1	2	0	3
Nottm Forest	D	W	3	0	1	2	0	3	1	0
Middlesbro	L	L	2	0	0	2	1	1	1	0
Watford	W	D	3	1	0	2	3	0	3	0
Bolton	D	D	2	1	1	0	1	1	1	1
Leeds	L	W	3	2	0	1	2	1	2	1
Sheff Wed	D	W	5	1	2	2	2	3	4	1
Huddersfield	D	L	5	2	2	1	1	4	2	2
Charlton										
Millwall	L	D	3	0	1	2	1	2	1	0
Blackpool	D	W	3	1	2	0	2	1	2	1
Birmingham	L	W	3	0	2	1	0	3	1	1
Wolves			2	1	0	1	2	0	2	0
Brentford			3	2	0	1	0	3	0	2
Rotherham			-	-	-	-	-	-	-	-

Season	Division	Pos	P	W	D	L	F	A	GD	Pts
2013-14	Championship	18	46	13	12	21	41	61	-20	51
2012-13	Championship	9	46	17	14	15	65	59	+6	65
2011-12	League 1	1	46	30	11	5	82	36	+46	101

Over/Under 43%/57% 17th   **Both score** 39%/61% 23rd

DERBY

Nickname: The Rams
Colours: White and black
Ground: Pride Park Stadium (33,502)
Tel: 0871-472-1884   www.dcfc.co.uk

There was more pain in the Wembley rain for Steve McClaren as his Derby side lost a playoff final in which their opponents, QPR, had just one shot on target.

That the Rams could dominate so totally and fail to score was a bitter irony for the Championship's top scorers but McClaren's young side showed over the course of the season that they have the quality to bounce back, if they can show the mental toughness to recover from such a disappointing finale.

Longest run without win/loss: 4/9
High/low league position: 2/14
Clean sheets: 13 **Yellows:** 74 **Reds:** 2
Avg attendance: 20,279 **Players used:** 27
Leading scorer: C Martin 20 (4,16)
Key stat: Derby's average points per game shot up from 1.2 to 2.0 after McClaren took charge

	2013-14 H	A	Last six seasons at home P	W	D	L	OV	UN	BS	CS
Norwich			2	1	0	1	2	0	2	0
Fulham			-	-	-	-	-	-	-	-
Cardiff			5	1	2	2	2	3	3	1
Derby										
Wigan	L	W	1	0	0	1	0	1	0	0
Brighton	W	W	3	1	1	1	0	3	0	2
Reading	L	D	5	1	0	4	3	2	3	0
Blackburn	D	D	2	0	2	0	0	2	2	0
Ipswich	D	L	6	0	2	4	3	3	3	1
Bournemouth	W	W	1	1	0	0	0	1	0	1
Nottm Forest	W	L	6	3	2	1	1	5	2	3
Middlesbro	W	L	5	3	1	1	4	1	4	0
Watford	W	W	6	5	0	1	4	2	4	2
Bolton	D	D	2	0	2	0	0	2	1	1
Leeds	W	D	4	4	0	0	3	1	3	1
Sheff Wed	W	W	4	3	1	0	4	0	1	3
Huddersfield	W	D	2	2	0	0	2	0	1	1
Charlton	W	W	3	3	0	0	1	1	1	2
Millwall	L	W	4	2	1	1	1	3	0	3
Blackpool	W	W	5	4	0	1	4	1	4	0
Birmingham	D	D	4	2	2	0	2	2	4	0
Wolves			2	0	1	1	1	1	1	1
Brentford			-	-	-	-	-	-	-	-
Rotherham			-	-	-	-	-	-	-	-

Season	Division	Pos	P	W	D	L	F	A	GD	Pts
2013-14	Championship	3	46	25	10	11	84	52	+32	85
2012-13	Championship	10	46	16	13	17	65	62	+3	61
2011-12	Championship	12	46	18	10	18	50	58	-8	64

Over/Under 57%/43% 2nd   **Both score** 57%/43% 6th

FULHAM

Nickname: The Cottagers
Colours: White and black
Ground: Craven Cottage (25,700)
Tel: 0870-442-1222   www.fulhamfc.com

Fulham's ownership changed hands last summer and the instability created seems to have played a part in their relegation.

Shahid Khan sacked two managers and while neither Martin Jol nor his replacement, Rene Meulensteen, can claim to have covered themselves in glory, the lack of permanence seemed to affect morale and confidence.

Felix Magath will hope that a more settled campaign will help him get a better response from a strong squad.

Longest run without win/loss: 9/2
High/low league position: 14/20
Clean sheets: 5 **Yellows:** 58 **Reds:** 1
Avg attendance: 30,565 **Players used:** 39
Leading scorer: S Sidwell 7 (3,7)
Key stat: Fulham took just one point from a possible 48 against sides finishing in the Premier League's top eight

| | 2013-14 | | Last six seasons at home | | | | | | | |
	H	A	P	W	D	L	OV	UN	BS	CS
Norwich	W	W	3	3	0	0	2	1	1	2
Fulham			-	-	-	-	-	-	-	-
Cardiff	L	L	1	0	0	1	1	0	1	0
Derby			-	-	-	-	-	-	-	-
Wigan			5	4	1	0	2	3	3	2
Brighton			-	-	-	-	-	-	-	-
Reading			1	0	0	1	1	0	1	0
Blackburn			4	2	1	1	3	1	3	1
Ipswich			-	-	-	-	-	-	-	-
Bournemouth			-	-	-	-	-	-	-	-
Nottm Forest			-	-	-	-	-	-	-	-
Middlesbro			1	1	0	0	1	0	0	1
Watford			-	-	-	-	-	-	-	-
Bolton			4	3	1	0	2	2	2	2
Leeds			-	-	-	-	-	-	-	-
Sheff Wed			-	-	-	-	-	-	-	-
Huddersfield			-	-	-	-	-	-	-	-
Charlton			-	-	-	-	-	-	-	-
Millwall			-	-	-	-	-	-	-	-
Blackpool			1	1	0	0	1	0	0	1
Birmingham			2	1	1	0	1	1	2	0
Wolves			3	2	1	0	2	1	1	2
Brentford			-	-	-	-	-	-	-	-
Rotherham			-	-	-	-	-	-	-	-

Season	Division	Pos	P	W	D	L	F	A	GD	Pts
2013-14	Premier League	19	38	9	5	24	40	85	-45	32
2012-13	Premier League	12	38	11	10	17	50	60	-10	43
2011-12	Premier League	9	38	14	10	14	48	51	-3	52

Over/Under 68%/32% 2nd   **Both score** 61%/39% 2nd

HUDDERSFIELD

Nickname: The Terriers
Colours: Blue and white
Ground: John Smith's Stadium (24,554)
Tel: 01484-484-100   www.htafc.com

The Terriers enjoyed a stress-free season after a nailbiting 2012-13 and manager Mark Robins can take plenty of the credit.

His signings have paid off more often than not, with James Vaughan rattling in the goals before injury, January signing Nahki Wells dealing well with the step up and Adam Hammill leading the assists.

Robins continues to build for the future and will approach his second full season at the club in optimistic mood given the steady nature of board and dugout.

Longest run without win/loss: 10/5
High/low league position: 8/17
Clean sheets: 9 **Yellows:** 71 **Reds:** 4
Avg attendance: 14,990 **Players used:** 29
Leading scorer: Vaughan 10 (4,8) Ward 10 (3,7)
Key stat: Huddersfield were the 17th-best home side, the 17th-best away side and they finished in 17th place

| | 2013-14 | | Last six seasons at home | | | | | | | |
	H	A	P	W	D	L	OV	UN	BS	CS
Norwich			1	0	0	1	1	0	1	0
Fulham			-	-	-	-	-	-	-	-
Cardiff			1	0	1	0	0	1	0	1
Derby	D	L	2	1	1	0	0	2	1	1
Wigan	W	L	1	1	0	0	0	1	0	1
Brighton	D	D	5	2	2	1	4	1	5	0
Reading	L	D	1	0	0	1	0	1	0	0
Blackburn	L	D	2	0	1	1	2	0	2	0
Ipswich	L	L	2	0	1	1	0	2	0	1
Bournemouth	W	L	3	1	1	1	2	1	2	0
Nottm Forest	L	L	2	0	1	1	1	1	1	0
Middlesbro	D	D	2	1	1	0	2	0	2	0
Watford	L	W	2	0	0	2	2	0	2	0
Bolton	L	W	2	0	1	1	1	1	1	0
Leeds	W	L	4	2	1	1	3	1	3	1
Sheff Wed	L	W	4	1	1	2	0	4	0	2
Huddersfield			-	-	-	-	-	-	-	-
Charlton	W	D	5	3	1	1	2	3	3	1
Millwall	W	W	4	3	0	1	2	2	1	3
Blackpool	D	L	2	0	2	0	0	2	2	0
Birmingham	L	W	2	0	1	1	1	1	2	0
Wolves			1	1	0	0	1	0	1	0
Brentford			3	1	2	0	2	1	2	1
Rotherham			-	-	-	-	-	-	-	-

Season	Division	Pos	P	W	D	L	F	A	GD	Pts
2013-14	Championship	17	46	14	11	21	58	65	-7	53
2012-13	Championship	19	46	15	13	18	53	73	-20	58
2011-12	League 1	4	46	21	18	7	79	47	+32	81

Over/Under 52%/48% 4th   **Both score** 61%/39% 2nd

IPSWICH

Nickname: Town/Tractor Boys
Colours: Blue and white
Ground: Portman Road (30,311)
Tel: 01473-400-500   www.itfc.co.uk

Mick McCarthy rarely disappoints at this level and he did well to keep Ipswich in playoff contention for most of 2013-14.

That was some achievement given his budget and all the more so considering he lost key striker David McGoldrick to injury in February.

McGoldrick should be fit for the start of 2014-15 but Ipswich's real weakness is a lack of midfield flair to create chances for him. And unfortunately for McCarthy, serious guile doesn't tend to come cheap.

Longest run without win/loss: 5/8
High/low league position: 6/14
Clean sheets: 12 **Yellows:** 54 **Reds:** 1
Avg attendance: 16,285 **Players used:** 26
Leading scorer: D McGoldrick 14 (7,11)
Key stat: While left-back Aaron Cresswell provided 13 assists last season, no Ipswich midfielder created more than three goals

	2013-14 H	A	Last six seasons at home P	W	D	L	OV	UN	BS	CS
Norwich			2	1	0	1	2	0	2	0
Fulham			-	-	-	-	-	-	-	-
Cardiff			5	3	0	2	3	2	2	3
Derby	W	D	6	4	0	2	2	4	2	3
Wigan	L	L	1	0	0	1	1	0	1	0
Brighton	W	W	3	2	0	1	2	1	1	1
Reading	W	L	5	3	0	2	3	2	3	2
Blackburn	W	L	2	1	1	0	1	1	2	0
Ipswich										
Bournemouth	D	D	1	0	1	0	1	0	1	0
Nottm Forest	D	D	6	2	2	2	3	3	5	0
Middlesbro	W	L	5	2	3	0	3	2	4	1
Watford	D	L	6	0	3	3	2	4	3	1
Bolton	W	D	2	2	0	0	0	2	0	2
Leeds	L	D	4	3	0	1	4	0	3	1
Sheff Wed	W	D	4	1	2	1	2	2	2	1
Huddersfield	W	W	2	1	1	0	2	0	2	0
Charlton	D	D	3	0	2	1	1	2	3	0
Millwall	W	L	4	3	0	1	3	1	0	3
Blackpool	D	W	5	2	3	0	2	3	3	2
Birmingham	W	D	4	2	1	1	1	3	2	1
Wolves			2	0	0	2	0	2	0	0
Brentford			-	-	-	-	-	-	-	-
Rotherham			-	-	-	-	-	-	-	-

Season	Division	Pos	P	W	D	L	F	A	GD	Pts
2013-14	Championship	9	46	18	14	14	60	54	+6	68
2012-13	Championship	14	46	16	12	18	48	61	-13	60
2011-12	Championship	15	46	17	10	19	69	77	-8	61

Over/Under 43%/57% 17th   **Both score** 57%/43% 6th

LEEDS

Nickname: United
Colours: White
Ground: Elland Road (37,914)
Tel: 0113-367-6000   www.leedsunited.com

Massimo Cellino completed his takeover in March after winning an appeal against a Football League veto, and forking out huge sums to keep Leeds afloat.

United fans will be tired of off-field antics like the bizarre on-off sacking of Brian McDermott – who did eventually depart in May – but an ageing team lacking pace and creativity won't offer much relief. Championship top scorer Ross McCormack carried the team at times and his sale leaves a huge hole.

Longest run without win/loss: 7/5
High/low league position: 5/16
Clean sheets: 10 **Yellows:** 71 **Reds:** 2
Avg attendance: 19,945 **Players used:** 29
Leading scorer: R McCormack 28 (9,21)
Key stat: McCormack scored or assisted 63 per cent of Leeds' league goals in 2013-14

	2013-14 H	A	Last six seasons at home P	W	D	L	OV	UN	BS	CS
Norwich			2	1	1	0	2	0	2	0
Fulham			-	-	-	-	-	-	-	-
Cardiff			3	0	1	2	1	2	1	0
Derby	D	L	4	0	1	3	2	2	3	0
Wigan	W	L	1	1	0	0	0	1	0	1
Brighton	W	L	5	2	1	2	4	1	5	0
Reading	L	L	3	0	1	2	1	2	1	1
Blackburn	L	L	2	0	1	1	2	0	2	0
Ipswich	D	W	4	2	2	0	1	3	2	2
Bournemouth	W	L	1	1	0	0	1	0	1	0
Nottm Forest	L	L	4	2	0	2	3	1	3	0
Middlesbro	W	D	4	2	1	1	2	2	3	0
Watford	D	L	4	0	2	2	3	1	3	0
Bolton	L	W	2	1	0	1	1	1	1	1
Leeds										
Sheff Wed	D	L	2	1	1	0	1	1	2	0
Huddersfield	W	L	4	1	1	2	4	0	4	0
Charlton	L	W	3	0	2	1	0	3	1	1
Millwall	W	L	6	5	0	1	2	4	2	3
Blackpool	W	D	3	2	0	1	1	2	0	2
Birmingham	W	W	3	1	0	2	2	1	1	1
Wolves			1	1	0	0	0	1	0	1
Brentford			1	0	1	0	0	1	1	0
Rotherham			-	-	-	-	-	-	-	-

Season	Division	Pos	P	W	D	L	F	A	GD	Pts
2013-14	Championship	15	46	16	9	21	59	67	-8	57
2012-13	Championship	13	46	17	10	19	57	66	-9	61
2011-12	Championship	14	46	17	10	19	65	68	-3	61

Over/Under 52%/48% 4th   **Both score** 54%/46% 10th

MIDDLESBRO

Nickname: Boro
Colours: Red and white
Ground: Riverside Stadium (34,998)
Tel: 0844-499-6789   www.mfc.co.uk

Boro had suffered two late slumps under Tony Mowbray in 2011-12 and 2012-13, so when they made a slow start last term it was no great surprise to see him depart.

The team improved immediately after Mowbray's departure, with caretaker boss Mark Venus ringing the changes and being rewarded with a 4-0 win over Doncaster. Aitor Karanka's arrival in the dugout heralded further improvement, with Boro signing off with six wins in their final eight games.

Longest run without win/loss: 8/6
High/low league position: 9/19
Clean sheets: 17 **Yellows:** 81 **Reds:** 8
Avg attendance: 15,906 **Players used:** 35
Leading scorer: A Adomah 12 (5,9)
Key stat: Middlesbro averaged 1.55 points a game under Karanka – form to put them on the fringes of the playoffs

	2013-14 H	A	Last six seasons at home P	W	D	L	OV	UN	BS	CS
Norwich			1	0	1	0	0	1	1	0
Fulham			1	0	1	0	0	1	0	1
Cardiff			4	2	0	2	1	3	1	1
Derby	W	L	5	4	1	0	2	3	2	3
Wigan	D	D	2	0	2	0	0	2	0	2
Brighton	L	W	3	1	0	2	0	3	0	1
Reading	W	L	4	2	1	1	2	2	2	1
Blackburn	D	L	3	1	2	0	0	3	0	3
Ipswich	W	L	5	3	1	1	2	3	2	3
Bournemouth	D	D	1	0	1	0	1	0	1	0
Nottm Forest	D	D	5	2	3	0	1	4	4	1
Middlesbro										
Watford	D	L	5	2	1	2	3	2	3	1
Bolton	W	D	3	2	0	1	2	1	2	1
Leeds	D	L	4	1	1	2	1	3	1	2
Sheff Wed	D	L	3	2	1	0	1	2	2	1
Huddersfield	D	D	2	1	1	0	1	1	1	1
Charlton	W	W	2	1	1	0	1	1	1	1
Millwall	L	W	4	0	1	3	2	2	3	0
Blackpool	D	W	4	1	2	1	3	1	3	0
Birmingham	W	D	3	2	0	1	2	1	2	0
Wolves			1	1	0	0	0	1	0	1
Brentford			-	-	-	-	-	-	-	-
Rotherham			-	-	-	-	-	-	-	-

Season	Division	Pos	P	W	D	L	F	A	GD	Pts
2013-14	Championship	12	46	16	16	14	62	50	+12	64
2012-13	Championship	16	46	18	5	23	61	70	-9	59
2011-12	Championship	7	46	18	16	12	52	51	+1	70

Over/Under 43%/57% 17th   **Both score** 48%/52% 18th

MILLWALL

Nickname: The Lions
Colours: Blue and white
Ground: The Den (19,734)
Tel: 020-7232-1222   www.millwallfc.co.uk

Ian Holloway's January arrival revived a side going backwards under Steve Lomas, and he helped the Lions sign off in style with an eight-match unbeaten run.

Holloway struggled in the top flight but he remains a fine manager at this level and has achieved promotion to the Premier League with similarly unfashionable sides, Blackpool and Crystal Palace.

A repeat is highly unlikely but, given a summer to organise and repair, Holloway should keep Millwall moving forward.

Longest run without win/loss: 7/8
High/low league position: 16/23
Clean sheets: 10 **Yellows:** 87 **Reds:** 6
Avg attendance: 11,396 **Players used:** 40
Leading scorer: S Morison 8 (3,8)
Key stat: Millwall's points-per-game tally rose from 0.92 before Holloway arrived to 1.18 after he took charge

	2013-14 H	A	Last six seasons at home P	W	D	L	OV	UN	BS	CS
Norwich			2	1	1	0	1	1	2	0
Fulham			-	-	-	-	-	-	-	-
Cardiff			3	0	2	1	1	2	1	1
Derby	L	W	4	2	1	1	2	2	2	2
Wigan	W	W	1	1	0	0	1	0	1	0
Brighton	L	D	5	0	2	3	1	4	3	0
Reading	L	D	3	0	1	2	2	1	1	1
Blackburn	D	L	2	0	1	1	2	0	2	0
Ipswich	W	L	4	3	1	0	2	2	2	2
Bournemouth	W	L	1	1	0	0	0	1	0	1
Nottm Forest	D	W	4	1	2	1	1	3	1	2
Middlesbro	L	W	4	1	0	3	3	1	3	0
Watford	D	L	4	1	1	2	2	2	2	1
Bolton	D	L	2	1	1	0	1	1	2	0
Leeds	W	L	6	5	0	1	3	3	3	2
Sheff Wed	D	D	2	0	1	1	1	1	2	0
Huddersfield	L	L	4	3	0	1	3	1	2	1
Charlton	D	W	3	1	2	0	1	2	0	3
Millwall										
Blackpool	W	L	3	1	1	1	2	1	2	0
Birmingham	L	L	3	0	1	2	3	0	2	0
Wolves	L		1	0	0	1	0	1	0	0
Brentford			1	0	1	0	0	1	1	0
Rotherham			-	-	-	-	-	-	-	-

Season	Division	Pos	P	W	D	L	F	A	GD	Pts
2013-14	Championship	19	46	11	15	20	46	74	-28	48
2012-13	Championship	20	46	15	11	20	51	62	-11	56
2011-12	Championship	16	46	15	12	19	55	57	-2	57

Over/Under 50%/50% 9th   **Both score** 52%/48% 15th

NORWICH

Nickname: The Canaries
Colours: Yellow and green
Ground: Carrow Road (27,224)
Tel: 01603-760-760   www.canaries.co.uk

The Canaries' summer spending backfired spectacularly, with strike duo Ricky van Wolfswinkel and Gary Hooper – bought at a combined £13.5m – returning just seven league goals between them.

But the entire squad disappointed last season and Chris Hughton's conservative tactics didn't help the team either.

His replacement, rookie manager Neil Adams, is likely to face a huge rebuilding job as the club is likely to sell key players in the wake of their costly relegation.

Longest run without win/loss: 7/3
High/low league position: 12/18
Clean sheets: 12 **Yellows:** 63 **Reds:** 2
Avg attendance: 31,181 **Players used:** 25
Leading scorer: Snodgrass 6 (3,6) Hooper 6 (3,6)
Key stat: No side has scored fewer than Norwich's 28 goals in a Premier League season since Derby in 2007-08

	2013-14 H	A	Last six seasons at home P	W	D	L	OV	UN	BS	CS
Norwich										
Fulham	L	L	3	0	2	1	1	2	2	1
Cardiff	D	L	3	1	2	0	0	3	1	2
Derby			2	1	0	1	2	0	2	0
Wigan			2	1	1	0	1	1	2	0
Brighton			1	1	0	0	1	0	1	0
Reading			3	2	0	1	2	1	2	0
Blackburn			1	0	1	0	1	0	1	0
Ipswich			2	2	0	0	1	1	1	1
Bournemouth			-	-	-	-	-	-	-	-
Nottm Forest			2	1	0	1	2	0	2	0
Middlesbro			1	1	0	0	0	1	0	1
Watford			2	1	0	1	1	1	1	1
Bolton			1	1	0	0	0	1	0	1
Leeds			2	1	1	0	0	2	1	1
Sheff Wed			1	0	0	1	0	1	0	0
Huddersfield			1	1	0	0	1	0	0	1
Charlton			2	1	1	0	1	1	1	1
Millwall			2	2	0	0	1	1	1	1
Blackpool			1	0	1	0	0	1	1	0
Birmingham			1	0	1	0	0	1	1	0
Wolves			2	2	0	0	2	0	2	0
Brentford			1	1	0	0	0	1	0	1
Rotherham			-	-	-	-	-	-	-	-

Season	Division	Pos	P	W	D	L	F	A	GD	Pts
2013-14	Premier League	18	38	8	9	21	28	62	-34	33
2012-13	Premier League	11	38	10	14	14	41	58	-17	44
2011-12	Premier League	12	38	12	11	15	52	66	-14	47

Over/Under 37%/63% 18th   **Both score** 37%/63% 16th

NOTTM FOREST

Nickname: Forest
Colours: Red and white
Ground: City Ground (30,540)
Tel: 0115-982-4444 www.nottinghamforest.co.uk

Forest got within touching distance of the playoffs before blowing it once again, and that isn't the only worrying pattern emerging at the City Ground.

Since buying the club in July 2012, Fawaz Al-Hasawi has fired four managers and the appointment of Forest legend Stuart Pearce looks a risky choice.

Al-Hasawi's investment offers the club security but until he steps back and allows his managers to manage, it's hard to see him getting the most from his money.

Longest run without win/loss: 12/14
High/low league position: 4/11
Clean sheets: 13 **Yellows:** 91 **Reds:** 4
Avg attendance: 19,249 **Players used:** 36
Leading scorer: A Reid 9 (3,9)
Key stat: Forest averaged 1.54 points per game under Billy Davies and just 0.89 after he was sacked

	2013-14 H	A	Last six seasons at home P	W	D	L	OV	UN	BS	CS
Norwich			2	0	1	1	1	1	2	0
Fulham			-	-	-	-	-	-	-	-
Cardiff			5	2	1	2	2	3	2	1
Derby	W	L	6	3	0	3	4	2	4	1
Wigan	L	L	1	0	0	1	1	0	1	0
Brighton	L	W	3	0	2	1	2	1	3	0
Reading	L	D	5	2	1	2	3	2	3	2
Blackburn	W	W	2	1	1	0	1	1	1	1
Ipswich	D	D	6	4	2	0	2	4	2	4
Bournemouth	D	L	1	0	1	0	0	1	1	0
Nottm Forest										
Middlesbro	D	D	5	3	2	0	1	4	1	4
Watford	W	D	6	3	1	2	4	2	4	1
Bolton	W	D	2	1	1	0	1	1	1	1
Leeds	W	W	4	2	1	1	3	1	3	0
Sheff Wed	D	W	4	3	1	0	3	1	3	1
Huddersfield	W	W	2	2	0	0	1	1	1	1
Charlton	L	D	3	1	1	1	1	2	1	1
Millwall	L	D	4	1	1	2	3	1	4	0
Blackpool	L	D	5	0	3	2	0	5	1	2
Birmingham	W	D	4	1	2	1	2	2	3	1
Wolves			2	1	0	1	1	1	1	0
Brentford			-	-	-	-	-	-	-	-
Rotherham			-	-	-	-	-	-	-	-

Season	Division	Pos	P	W	D	L	F	A	GD	Pts
2013-14	Championship	11	46	16	17	13	67	64	+3	65
2012-13	Championship	8	46	17	16	13	63	59	+4	67
2011-12	Championship	19	46	14	8	24	48	63	-15	50

Over/Under 50%/50% 9th   **Both score** 63%/37% 1st

READING

Nickname: The Royals
Colours: Blue and white
Ground: Madejski Stadium (24,197)
Tel: 0118-968-1100   www.readingfc.co.uk

Reading suffered final day heartbreak, slipping out of the playoff places having been in the top six for most of the season.

And while the Royals provided plenty of entertaining football, the fact that co-owners Anton Zingarevich and John Madejski have been trying but failing to sell the club for so long must be a concern.

Nigel Adkins is a capable manager but the boardroom stalemate delayed his summer rebuilding plans and he may be playing catchup by the start of 2014-15.

Longest run without win/loss: 4/6
High/low league position: 5/9
Clean sheets: 12 **Yellows:** 76 **Reds:** 6
Avg attendance: 16,823 **Players used:** 26
Leading scorer: A Le Fondre 15 (6,11)
Key stat: Reading failed to win any of their home games against the top eight last season

	2013-14 H	A	Last six seasons at home P	W	D	L	OV	UN	BS	CS
Norwich			3	1	2	0	1	2	1	2
Fulham			1	0	1	0	1	0	1	0
Cardiff			4	0	2	2	1	3	3	0
Derby	D	W	5	3	2	0	4	1	3	2
Wigan	L	L	2	0	0	2	2	0	1	0
Brighton	D	D	2	1	1	0	1	1	0	2
Reading										
Blackburn	L	D	1	0	0	1	0	1	0	0
Ipswich	W	L	5	3	1	1	1	4	2	2
Bournemouth	L	L	1	0	0	1	1	0	1	0
Nottm Forest	D	W	5	1	3	1	0	5	2	2
Middlesbro	W	L	4	2	1	1	1	3	1	2
Watford	D	W	5	1	3	1	2	3	3	1
Bolton	W	D	1	1	0	0	1	0	1	0
Leeds	W	W	3	2	1	0	0	3	0	3
Sheff Wed	L	L	3	2	0	1	2	1	0	2
Huddersfield	D	W	1	0	1	0	0	1	1	0
Charlton	W	W	2	1	1	0	1	1	1	1
Millwall	D	W	3	1	2	0	2	1	3	0
Blackpool	W	L	4	4	0	0	3	1	3	1
Birmingham	W	W	3	2	0	1	1	2	1	2
Wolves			1	1	0	0	0	1	0	1
Brentford			-	-	-	-	-	-	-	-
Rotherham			-	-	-	-	-	-	-	-

Season	Division	Pos	P	W	D	L	F	A	GD	Pts
2013-14	Championship	7	46	19	14	13	70	56	+14	71
2012-13	Premier League	19	38	6	10	22	43	73	-30	28
2011-12	Championship	1	46	27	8	11	69	41	+28	89

Over/Under 46%/54% 15th   **Both score** 59%/41% 4th

ROTHERHAM

Nickname: The Millers
Colours: Red and white
Ground: New York Stadium (12,009)
Tel: 08444-140-733   www.themillers.co.uk

Steve Evans isn't everyone's cup of tea but he's earned promotion in each of his last four seasons, first taking Crawley from the Conference to League 1 and now leading Rotherham into the second tier.

His Millers play attractive football, too, pressing high and commiting plenty of players to attack. He might come unstuck trying that at a higher level but there's certainly no lack of ambition from him or owner Tony Stewart, with both talking of pushing on to the Premier League.

Longest run without win/loss: 5/16
High/low league position: 3/11
Clean sheets: 15 **Yellows:** 73 **Reds:** 5
Avg attendance: 8,061 **Players used:** 30
Leading scorer: K Agard 21 (7,17)
Key stat: Rotherham had the second-best goalscoring record but only the ninth-best defence in League 1 last term

	2013-14 H	A	Last six seasons at home P	W	D	L	OV	UN	BS	CS
Norwich			-	-	-	-	-	-	-	-
Fulham			-	-	-	-	-	-	-	-
Cardiff			-	-	-	-	-	-	-	-
Derby			-	-	-	-	-	-	-	-
Wigan			-	-	-	-	-	-	-	-
Brighton			-	-	-	-	-	-	-	-
Reading			-	-	-	-	-	-	-	-
Blackburn			-	-	-	-	-	-	-	-
Ipswich			-	-	-	-	-	-	-	-
Bournemouth			2	1	0	1	1	1	1	1
Nottm Forest			-	-	-	-	-	-	-	-
Middlesbro			-	-	-	-	-	-	-	-
Watford			-	-	-	-	-	-	-	-
Bolton			-	-	-	-	-	-	-	-
Leeds			-	-	-	-	-	-	-	-
Sheff Wed			-	-	-	-	-	-	-	-
Huddersfield			-	-	-	-	-	-	-	-
Charlton			-	-	-	-	-	-	-	-
Millwall			-	-	-	-	-	-	-	-
Blackpool			-	-	-	-	-	-	-	-
Birmingham			-	-	-	-	-	-	-	-
Wolves	D	L	1	0	1	0	1	0	1	0
Brentford	W	W	2	1	1	0	1	1	0	2
Rotherham										

Season	Division	Pos	P	W	D	L	F	A	GD	Pts
2013-14	League 1	4	46	24	14	8	86	58	+28	86
2012-13	League 2	2	46	24	7	15	74	59	+15	79
2011-12	League 2	10	46	18	13	15	67	63	+4	67

Over/Under 63%/37% 2nd   **Both score** 57%/43% 6th

SHEFFIELD WED

Nickname: The Owls
Colours: Blue and white
Ground: Hillsborough (39,732)
Tel: 0870-999-1867   www.swfc.co.uk

Wednesday again started horribly last term but this time the board wasn't so patient with Dave Jones, sacking him after the team won just one of their first 16 games.

Stuart Gray took over as caretaker for a 12-game run that saw the Owls reach the fifth round of the FA Cup as well as beating Leicester, drawing with Burnley and thrashing Leeds 6-0 en route to taking 15 points from 27. Unsurprisingly, Gray was offered the full-time gig.

Longest run without win/loss: 12/8
High/low league position: 14/24
Clean sheets: 10 **Yellows:** 93 **Reds:** 5
Avg attendance: 19,704 **Players used:** 39
Leading scorer: C Maguire 9 (4,9)
Key stat: Wednesday beat four of the top seven on home soil

	2013-14		Last six seasons at home							
	H	A	P	W	D	L	OV	UN	BS	CS
Norwich			1	1	0	0	1	0	1	0
Fulham	-	-	-	-	-	-	-	-	-	-
Cardiff			3	2	0	1	1	2	1	1
Derby	L	L	4	0	2	2	1	3	1	1
Wigan	L	L	1	0	0	1	1	0	0	0
Brighton	W	D	3	3	0	0	1	2	1	2
Reading	W	W	3	1	0	2	2	1	2	0
Blackburn	D	D	2	1	1	0	2	0	2	0
Ipswich	D	L	4	0	3	1	0	4	2	1
Bournemouth	L	W	3	1	1	1	2	1	2	1
Nottm Forest	L	D	4	1	1	2	0	4	1	1
Middlesbro	W	D	3	2	0	1	2	1	2	2
Watford	L	W	4	2	0	2	3	1	3	1
Bolton	L	L	2	0	0	2	2	0	2	0
Leeds	W	D	2	1	1	0	1	1	1	1
Sheff Wed										
Huddersfield	L	W	4	0	1	3	3	1	3	0
Charlton	L	L	5	2	1	2	3	2	3	1
Millwall	D	D	2	1	1	0	2	0	2	0
Blackpool	W	L	4	2	1	1	0	4	1	2
Birmingham	W	L	3	2	1	0	2	1	3	0
Wolves			2	0	1	0	2	0	0	1
Brentford			2	0	1	1	1	1	1	1
Rotherham	-	-	-	-	-	-	-	-	-	-

Season	Division	Pos	P	W	D	L	F	A	GD	Pts
2013-14	Championship	16	46	13	14	19	63	65	-2	53
2012-13	Championship	18	46	16	10	20	53	61	-8	58
2011-12	League 1	2	46	28	9	9	81	48	+33	93

Over/Under 46%/54% 15th   **Both score** 59%/41% 4th

WATFORD

Nickname: The Hornets
Colours: Yellow and red
Ground: Vicarage Road (17,477)
Tel: 0845-442-1881   www.watfordfc.co.uk

Watford kept most of their 2012-13 loanees but the departures of 20-goal Matej Vydra – back for next season – and Nathaniel Chalobah seemed to undermine a side who were third in 2013.

They started brightly enough, taking 21 points from the first 11 games, but the nine-match winless streak that followed cost Gianfranco Zola his job.

Beppe Sannino got 35 points from his first 22 games in charge, but the Hornets were marooned in mid-table by then.

Longest run without win/loss: 10/6
High/low league position: 4/15
Clean sheets: 12 **Yellows:** 10 **Reds:** 6
Avg attendance: 14,459 **Players used:** 38
Leading scorer: T Deeney 24 (8,19)
Key stat: Only Derby and Leicester scored more goals than Watford last season

	2013-14		Last six seasons at home							
	H	A	P	W	D	L	OV	UN	BS	CS
Norwich			2	1	1	0	2	0	2	0
Fulham	-	-	-	-	-	-	-	-	-	-
Cardiff			5	1	3	1	3	2	3	1
Derby	L	L	6	3	0	3	4	2	3	1
Wigan	W	L	1	1	0	0	0	1	0	1
Brighton	W	D	3	2	0	1	0	3	0	2
Reading	L	D	5	1	2	2	3	2	3	1
Blackburn	D	L	2	1	1	0	2	0	1	1
Ipswich	W	D	6	5	0	1	5	1	5	0
Bournemouth	W	D	1	1	0	0	1	0	1	0
Nottm Forest	D	L	6	2	3	1	1	5	3	2
Middlesbro	W	D	5	3	1	1	3	2	4	1
Watford										
Bolton	L	L	2	1	0	1	1	1	1	0
Leeds	W	D	4	1	1	2	2	2	2	1
Sheff Wed	L	W	4	2	1	1	3	1	3	0
Huddersfield	L	W	2	1	0	1	2	0	1	1
Charlton	D	L	3	1	1	1	1	2	2	1
Millwall	W	D	4	3	1	0	2	2	1	3
Blackpool	W	L	5	1	1	3	4	1	3	1
Birmingham	W	W	4	2	1	1	3	1	2	1
Wolves			2	1	0	1	2	0	2	0
Brentford	-	-	-	-	-	-	-	-	-	-
Rotherham	-	-	-	-	-	-	-	-	-	-

Season	Division	Pos	P	W	D	L	F	A	GD	Pts
2013-14	Championship	13	46	15	15	16	74	64	+10	60
2012-13	Championship	3	46	23	8	15	85	58	+27	77
2011-12	Championship	11	46	16	16	14	56	64	-8	64

Over/Under 57%/43% 2nd   **Both score** 57%/43% 6th

WIGAN

Nickname: The Latics
Colours: Blue and white
Ground: DW Stadium (25,133)
Tel: 01942-774-000   www.wiganlatics.co.uk

Owen Coyle's appointment always felt like a risk and so it proved, with a slow start under the Scot scuppering Wigan's chances of finishing in the top two.

There was still a lot to like about the Latics' campaign, though, as they rallied under Uwe Rosler to reach the playoffs, where they lost to QPR. In the FA Cup they won away at Man City and only lost a semi-final against Arsenal on penalties. Wigan didn't embarrass themselves in Europe either, losing just three games.

Longest run without win/loss: 4/8
High/low league position: 5/14
Clean sheets: 16 **Yellows:** 74 **Reds:** 2
Avg attendance: 16,062 **Players used:** 34
Leading scorer: J Gomez 7 (2,7)
N Powell 7 (1, 7)
Key stat: The Latics averaged 1.22 points before Rosler arrived but 1.82 under him

WOLVES

Nickname: Wolves
Colours: Gold and black
Ground: Molineux Stadium (30,852)
Tel: 0871-880-8442   www.wolves.co.uk

Wolves bounced back from successive relegations in style, taking the League 1 title with a record tally of 103 points.

Kenny Jackett deserves credit for reshaping a creaking squad and instilling a winning mentality upon his arrival last summer. And while a club the size of Wolves would be expected to go well in the third tier, the chaos at Molineux in the years prior to Jackett's arrive suggests it was no mean feat making them look a proper team once again.

Longest run without win/loss: 3/11
High/low league position: 1/3
Clean sheets: 25 **Yellows:** 64 **Reds:** 1
Avg attendance: 15,107 **Players used:** 28
Leading scorer: N Dicko 13 (2,8)
Key stat: Four different players scored ten or more league goals for Wolves last season

	2013-14 H	A	Last six seasons at home P	W	D	L	OV	UN	BS	CS
Norwich			2	1	1	0	0	2	1	1
Fulham			5	0	3	2	1	4	3	1
Cardiff			-	-	-	-	-	-	-	-
Derby	L	W	1	0	0	1	1	0	1	0
Wigan										
Brighton	L	W	1	0	0	1	0	1	0	0
Reading	W	W	2	2	0	0	2	0	1	1
Blackburn	W	L	5	3	2	0	4	1	4	1
Ipswich	W	W	1	1	0	0	0	1	0	1
Bournemouth	W	L	1	1	0	0	1	0	0	1
Nottm Forest	W	W	1	1	0	0	1	0	1	0
Middlesbro	D	D	2	0	1	1	1	1	1	0
Watford	W	L	1	1	0	0	0	1	0	0
Bolton	W	D	5	1	3	1	2	3	3	2
Leeds	W	L	1	1	0	0	0	1	0	1
Sheff Wed	W	W	1	1	0	0	0	1	0	1
Huddersfield	W	L	1	1	0	0	1	0	1	0
Charlton	W	D	1	1	0	0	1	0	1	0
Millwall	L	L	1	0	0	1	0	1	0	0
Blackpool	L	L	2	0	0	2	1	1	0	0
Birmingham	D	W	3	1	1	1	2	1	2	1
Wolves			3	2	0	1	1	2	1	1
Brentford			-	-	-	-	-	-	-	-
Rotherham			-	-	-	-	-	-	-	-

Season	Division	Pos	P	W	D	L	F	A	GD	Pts
2013-14	Championship	5	46	21	10	15	61	48	+13	73
2012-13	Premier League	18	38	9	9	20	47	73	-26	36
2011-12	Premier League	15	38	11	10	17	42	62	-20	43

Over/Under 48%/52% 13th   **Both score** 39%/61% 23rd

	2013-14 H	A	Last six seasons at home P	W	D	L	OV	UN	BS	CS
Norwich			2	0	2	0	2	0	2	0
Fulham			3	2	1	0	1	2	2	1
Cardiff			2	0	1	1	2	0	2	0
Derby			2	1	1	0	1	1	1	1
Wigan			3	1	0	2	2	1	2	0
Brighton			1	0	1	0	1	0	1	0
Reading			1	0	0	1	1	0	0	0
Blackburn			4	0	2	2	1	3	3	0
Ipswich			2	0	1	1	0	2	0	1
Bournemouth			-	-	-	-	-	-	-	-
Nottm Forest			2	1	0	1	2	0	2	0
Middlesbro			1	1	0	0	1	0	1	0
Watford			2	1	1	0	1	1	2	0
Bolton			4	1	1	2	4	0	4	0
Leeds			1	0	1	0	1	0	1	0
Sheff Wed			2	2	0	0	1	1	1	1
Huddersfield			1	0	0	1	1	0	1	0
Charlton			2	1	1	0	1	1	2	0
Millwall			1	0	0	1	0	1	0	0
Blackpool			3	2	0	1	2	1	1	2
Birmingham			4	2	1	1	0	4	1	2
Wolves										
Brentford	D	W	1	0	1	0	0	1	0	1
Rotherham	W	D	1	1	0	0	1	0	1	0

Season	Division	Pos	P	W	D	L	F	A	GD	Pts
2013-14	League 1	1	46	31	10	5	89	31	+58	103
2012-13	Championship	23	46	14	9	23	55	69	-14	51
2011-12	Premier League	20	38	5	10	23	40	82	-42	25

Over/Under 43%/57% 18th   **Both score** 37%/63% 24th

Key Points in all tables (except the league table) do not include any deductions imposed by the league. **POS H A** Overall league position, rank from home games only, rank from away games only **Sup** Average match supremacy **GFA** Goals For Average **GAA** Goals Against Average **PGA** Points Gained Average

League table 2013-14

Pos	H	A		P	Home W	D	L	F	A	Away W	D	L	F	A	GD	Pts
1	1	1	Leicester	46	17	4	2	46	22	14	5	4	37	21	+40	102 (C)
2	2	2	Burnley	46	15	6	2	37	14	11	9	3	35	23	+35	93 (P)
3	4	3	Derby	46	14	4	5	46	25	11	6	6	38	27	+32	85
4	3	10	QPR	46	15	6	2	38	18	8	5	10	22	26	+16	80 (P)
5	5	6	Wigan	46	12	7	4	35	23	9	3	11	26	25	+13	73
6	11	5	Brighton	46	10	7	6	31	21	9	8	6	24	19	+15	72
7	13	4	Reading	46	8	10	5	38	25	11	4	8	32	31	+14	71
8	7	7	Blackburn	46	11	7	5	34	21	7	9	7	36	41	+8	70
9	6	13	Ipswich	46	12	6	5	35	24	6	8	9	25	30	+6	68
10	10	12	Bournemouth	46	11	5	7	40	27	7	7	9	27	39	+1	66
11	12	11	Nottm Forest	46	10	7	6	38	29	6	10	7	29	35	+3	65
12	8	14	Middlesbro	46	10	9	4	35	20	6	7	10	27	30	+12	64
13	9	18	Watford	46	11	5	7	39	25	4	10	9	35	35	+10	60
14	18	9	Bolton	46	6	11	6	29	23	8	6	9	30	37	-1	59
15	14	15	Leeds	46	9	5	9	35	31	7	4	12	24	36	-8	57
16	15	19	Sheff Wed	46	9	4	10	39	33	4	10	9	24	32	-2	53
17	17	17	Huddersfield	46	8	6	9	34	32	6	5	12	24	33	-7	53
18	20	16	Charlton	46	7	6	10	21	28	6	6	11	20	33	-20	51
19	19	20	Millwall	46	6	9	8	26	33	5	6	12	20	41	-28	48
20	21	22	Blackpool	46	7	6	10	20	27	4	7	12	18	39	-28	46
21	24	8	Birmingham	46	2	8	13	29	40	9	3	11	29	34	-16	44
22	16	24	Doncaster	46	9	4	10	27	32	2	7	14	12	38	-31	44 (R)
23	22	23	Barnsley	46	5	8	10	22	36	4	4	15	22	41	-33	39 (R)
24	23	21	Yeovil	46	4	6	13	19	32	4	7	12	25	43	-31	37 (R)

Best attack

		GF	GFA
1	Derby	84	1.83
2	Leicester	83	1.80
3	Watford	74	1.61
4	Burnley	72	1.57
5	Reading	70	1.52
6	Blackburn	70	1.52
7	Bournemouth	67	1.46
8	Nottm Forest	67	1.46
9	Sheff Wed	63	1.37
10	Middlesbro	62	1.35
11	Wigan	61	1.33
12	QPR	60	1.30
13	Ipswich	60	1.30
14	Bolton	59	1.28
15	Leeds	59	1.28
16	Huddersfield	58	1.26
17	Birmingham	58	1.26
18	Brighton	55	1.20
19	Millwall	46	1.00
20	Barnsley	44	0.96
21	Yeovil	44	0.96
22	Charlton	41	0.89
23	Doncaster	39	0.85
24	Blackpool	38	0.83

Best defence

		GA	GAA
1	Burnley	37	0.80
2	Brighton	40	0.87
3	Leicester	43	0.93
4	QPR	44	0.96
5	Wigan	48	1.04
6	Middlesbro	50	1.09
7	Derby	52	1.13
8	Ipswich	54	1.17
9	Reading	56	1.22
10	Bolton	60	1.30
11	Charlton	61	1.33
12	Blackburn	62	1.35
13	Nottm Forest	64	1.39
14	Watford	64	1.39
15	Sheff Wed	65	1.41
16	Huddersfield	65	1.41
17	Bournemouth	66	1.43
18	Blackpool	66	1.43
19	Leeds	67	1.46
20	Doncaster	70	1.52
21	Millwall	74	1.61
22	Birmingham	74	1.61
23	Yeovil	75	1.63
24	Barnsley	77	1.67

Top scorers

		Team	Goals scored	
R McCormack	Leeds	28	||||||||||||||||||||||||||||
J Rhodes	Blackburn	25	|||||||||||||||||||||||||
T Deeney	Watford	24	||||||||||||||||||||||||
L Grabban	Bournemouth	22	||||||||||||||||||||||
D Ings	Burnley	21	|||||||||||||||||||||

Over 2.5 goals

	H	A	%
Leicester	14	13	59%
Derby	14	12	57%
Watford	12	14	57%
Birmingham,			52%
Bournemouth, Doncaster, Huddersfield, Leeds			

Under 2.5 goals

	H	A	%
Brighton	15	17	70%
Blackpool	16	15	67%
QPR	12	16	61%
Bolton	16	11	59%
Burnley	15	12	59%

Both to score

	H	A	%
Nottm Forest	14	15	63%
Bournemouth	14	14	61%
Huddersfield	13	15	61%
Reading	15	12	59%
Sheff Wed	13	14	59%

Both not to score

	H	A	%
Charlton	14	14	61%
Wigan	12	16	61%
Doncaster	13	14	59%
Brighton	11	15	57%
QPR	11	15	57%

SOCCERBASE.COM

Results 2013-14

	Barnsley	Birmingham	Blackburn	Blackpool	Bolton	Bournemouth	Brighton	Burnley	Charlton	Derby	Doncaster	Huddersfield	Ipswich	Leeds	Leicester	Middlesbrough	Millwall	Nottm Forest	QPR	Reading	Sheff Wed	Watford	Wigan	Yeovil
Barnsley		0-3	2-2	2-0	0-1	0-1	0-0	0-1	2-2	1-2	0-0	2-1	2-2	0-1	0-3	3-2	1-0	1-0	2-3	1-1	1-1	1-5	0-4	1-1
Birmingham	1-1		2-4	1-1	1-2	2-4	0-1	3-3	0-1	3-3	1-1	1-2	1-1	1-3	1-2	2-2	4-0	0-0	0-2	1-2	4-1	0-1	0-1	0-2
Blackburn	5-2	2-3		2-0	4-1	0-1	3-3	1-2	0-1	1-1	1-0	0-0	2-0	1-0	1-1	1-0	3-2	0-1	2-0	0-0	0-0	1-0	4-3	0-0
Blackpool	1-0	1-2	2-2		0-0	0-1	0-1	0-1	0-3	1-3	1-1	1-0	2-3	1-1	2-2	0-2	1-0	1-1	0-2	1-0	2-0	1-0	1-0	1-2
Bolton	1-0	2-2	4-0	1-0		2-2	0-2	0-1	1-1	2-2	3-0	0-1	1-1	0-1	0-1	2-2	3-1	1-1	0-1	1-1	1-1	2-0	1-1	1-1
Bournemouth	1-0	0-2	1-3	1-2	0-2		1-1	1-1	2-1	0-1	5-0	2-1	1-1	4-1	0-1	0-0	5-2	4-1	2-1	3-1	2-4	1-1	1-0	3-0
Brighton	1-2	1-0	3-0	1-1	3-1	1-1		2-0	3-0	1-2	1-0	0-0	0-1	3-1	0-2	1-1	1-3	2-0	1-1	1-1	1-1	1-1	1-2	2-0
Burnley	1-0	3-0	1-1	2-1	1-1	1-1	0-0		3-0	2-0	2-0	3-2	1-0	2-1	0-2	0-1	3-1	3-1	2-0	2-1	1-1	0-0	2-0	2-0
Charlton	1-2	0-2	1-3	0-0	0-0	1-0	3-2	0-3		0-2	2-0	0-0	0-1	2-4	2-1	0-1	0-1	1-1	1-0	0-1	1-1	3-1	0-0	3-2
Derby	2-1	1-1	1-1	5-1	0-0	1-0	1-0	0-3	3-0		3-1	3-1	4-4	3-1	0-1	2-1	0-1	5-0	1-0	1-3	3-0	4-2	0-1	3-2
Doncaster	2-2	1-3	2-0	1-3	1-2	0-1	1-3	0-2	3-0	0-2		2-0	0-3	0-3	1-0	0-0	0-0	2-2	2-1	1-3	1-0	2-1	3-0	2-1
Huddersfield	5-0	1-3	2-4	1-1	0-1	5-1	1-1	2-1	2-1	1-1	0-0		0-3	3-2	0-2	2-2	1-0	0-3	1-1	0-1	0-2	1-2	1-0	5-1
Ipswich	1-1	1-0	3-1	0-0	1-0	2-2	2-0	0-1	1-1	2-1	2-1	2-1		1-2	1-2	3-1	3-0	1-1	1-3	2-0	2-1	1-1	1-3	2-1
Leeds	0-0	4-0	1-2	2-0	1-5	2-1	2-1	1-2	0-1	1-1	1-2	5-1	1-1		0-1	2-1	2-1	0-2	0-1	2-4	1-1	3-3	2-0	2-0
Leicester	2-1	3-2	2-1	3-1	5-3	2-1	1-4	1-1	3-0	4-1	1-0	2-1	3-0	0-0		2-0	3-0	0-2	1-0	1-0	2-1	2-2	2-0	1-1
Middlesbrough	3-1	3-1	0-0	1-1	1-0	3-3	0-1	1-0	1-0	1-0	4-0	1-1	2-0	0-0	1-2		1-2	1-1	1-3	3-0	1-1	2-2	0-0	4-1
Millwall	1-0	2-3	2-2	3-1	1-1	1-0	0-1	2-2	0-1	1-5	0-0	0-1	1-0	2-0	1-3	0-2		2-2	2-2	0-3	1-1	2-2	2-1	0-1
Nottm Forest	3-2	1-0	4-1	0-1	3-0	1-1	1-2	1-1	0-1	1-0	0-0	1-0	0-0	2-1	2-2	2-2	1-2		2-0	2-3	3-3	4-2	1-4	3-1
QPR	2-0	1-0	0-0	1-1	2-1	3-0	0-0	3-3	1-0	2-1	2-1	1-1	0-1	2-0	1-1	5-2				1-3	2-1	2-1	1-0	3-0
Reading	1-3	2-0	0-1	5-1	7-1	1-2	0-0	2-2	1-0	0-0	4-1	1-1	2-1	1-0	2-0	1-1	1-1				0-2	3-3	1-2	1-1
Sheff Wed	1-0	4-1	3-3	2-0	1-3	1-2	1-0	1-2	2-3	0-1	0-1	1-2	1-1	6-0	2-1	1-0	2-2	0-1	3-0	5-2		1-4	0-3	1-1
Watford	3-0	1-0	3-3	4-0	0-1	6-1	2-0	1-1	1-1	2-3	2-1	1-4	3-1	3-0	0-3	1-0	4-0	1-1	0-0	0-1	0-1		1-0	0-3
Wigan	2-0	0-0	2-1	0-2	3-2	3-0	0-1	0-0	2-1	1-3	2-2	2-1	2-0	1-0	2-2	2-2	0-1	2-1	0-0	3-0	1-0	2-1		3-3
Yeovil	1-4	0-1	0-1	1-0	2-2	1-1	0-0	1-2	2-2	0-3	1-0	1-2	0-1	1-2	1-2	1-4	1-1	3-1	0-1	0-1	2-0	0-0	0-1	

Record when first to score

		P	W	D	L	F	A	Sup	PGA	Pts
1	Leicester	31	27	3	1	62	18	+1.42	2.7	84
2	Burnley	28	23	5	0	53	15	+1.36	2.6	74
3	Derby	24	19	4	1	51	15	+1.50	2.5	61
4	QPR	23	19	3	1	45	16	+1.26	2.6	60
5	Reading	23	17	6	0	53	19	+1.48	2.5	57
6	Bournemouth	22	17	5	0	46	17	+1.32	2.5	56
7	Brighton	24	17	3	4	42	18	+1.00	2.3	54
8	Blackburn	21	17	2	2	45	21	+1.14	2.5	53
9	Wigan	19	16	3	0	42	13	+1.53	2.7	51
10	Bolton	23	14	8	1	43	19	+1.04	2.2	50
11	Nottm Forest	23	14	7	2	38	16	+0.96	2.1	49
12	Watford	25	14	7	4	59	30	+1.16	2.0	49
13	Ipswich	26	13	9	4	42	25	+0.65	1.8	48
14	Middlesbro	22	14	5	3	40	19	+0.95	2.1	47
15	Sheff Wed	20	12	6	2	43	18	+1.25	2.1	42
16	Huddersfield	21	12	5	4	38	25	+0.62	2.0	41
17	Blackpool	23	11	6	6	31	29	+0.09	1.7	39
18	Leeds	16	12	2	2	33	13	+1.25	2.4	38
19	Charlton	16	11	4	1	25	11	+0.88	2.3	37
20	Millwall	17	10	5	2	26	20	+0.35	2.1	35
21	Doncaster	15	10	2	3	26	15	+0.73	2.1	32
22	Barnsley	16	9	5	2	32	24	+0.50	2.0	32
23	Birmingham	14	9	4	1	33	15	+1.29	2.2	31
24	Yeovil	20	8	7	5	29	26	+0.15	1.6	31

Record when keeping a clean sheet

		P	W	D	F	Sup	PGA	Pts
1	Leicester	18	17	1	31	+1.72	2.9	52
2	Sheff Wed	10	9	1	19	+1.90	2.8	28
3	Bournemouth	9	8	1	14	+1.56	2.8	25
4	Burnley	19	16	3	30	+1.58	2.7	51
5	Derby	13	11	2	23	+1.77	2.7	35
6	Ipswich	12	10	2	18	+1.50	2.7	32
7	QPR	17	13	4	21	+1.24	2.5	43
8	Nottm Forest	13	10	3	17	+1.31	2.5	33
9	Bolton	12	9	3	16	+1.33	2.5	30
10	Reading	12	9	3	13	+1.08	2.5	30
11	Watford	12	9	3	20	+1.67	2.5	30
12	Blackpool	12	9	3	11	+0.92	2.5	30
13	Brighton	20	14	6	22	+1.10	2.4	48
14	Middlesbro	17	12	5	21	+1.24	2.4	41
15	Wigan	16	11	5	22	+1.38	2.4	38
16	Leeds	10	7	3	15	+1.50	2.4	24
17	Millwall	10	7	3	8	+0.80	2.4	24
18	Birmingham	7	5	2	12	+1.71	2.4	17
19	Yeovil	9	6	3	10	+1.11	2.3	21
20	Blackburn	15	9	6	12	+0.80	2.2	33
21	Charlton	13	8	5	11	+0.85	2.2	29
22	Doncaster	13	7	6	13	+1.00	2.1	27
23	Huddersfield	9	5	4	9	+1.00	2.1	19
24	Barnsley	6	3	3	4	+0.67	2.0	12

Simon Grayson can work his promotion magic on North End nearly men

Preston and Leyton Orient finished at least 18 points ahead of any non-promoted League 1 side bar Peterborough last season, and that gives them a big edge in the promotion battle, writes Dylan Hill. And it's **Preston** who make the most appeal at a general 9-1 as Orient, playoff final losers on penalties to Rotherham, won just three of their final ten league matches of the regular campaign and owed much to their early form.

In contrast, Preston were strong throughout the season and managed to turn around their moderate home form with six wins in the last seven, the only exception being a 0-0 draw with Sheffield United in which they couldn't make their clear superiority count.

North End have since raided Orient to take Jamie Jones, who was one of the best goalkeepers in the division last season.

Apart from Jones, adding the pace and creativity that was the only thing missing against the Blades has been Preston's priority, with strikers Andy Little and Jordan Hugill bought from Rangers and Port Vale respectively. And there should also be more to come from Joe Garner, whose increasing confidence was shown by his stunning strike against Rotherham in the playoffs.

Manager Simon Grayson certainly has the record to suggest he can get Preston up. Grayson has won League 1 promotion with Blackpool, Leeds a nd Huddersfield, and Leeds' success in 2010 also followed playoff disappointment the previous season.

Favourites Sheffield United are just about the most likely to team to go up automatically alongside Preston, but are no value to do so.

Nigel Clough did an outstanding job after replacing David Weir, but the Blades did things the hard way – they scored more than twice on just three occasions and failed to win a single match in which they conceded more than one goal. Clough didn't get the best of what has proved to be an outstanding Derby team during a long spell at Pride Park and Rams fans have pointed to his negativity as the reason for his failure. Unless Clough learns to take the handbrake off, Sheffield United may lack the firepower normally associated with champions.

Instead **Scunthorpe** look a fair each-way bet at a general 25-1. The Iron were sensational after Russ Wilcox arrived last November and better teams brought out the best in them – they averaged 1.58 points per game against sides in the bottom half but that rose to 1.95 against top-half teams.

Striker **Paddy Madden** scored 22 goals in this division for Yeovil two seasons ago before things went sour in Somerset and he could be ready to make an impact after scoring five goals following his move to Scunthorpe in January. His odds will be well worth looking out for when bookmakers price up the top-scorer market.

It's hard to argue with the identity of those shortest in the market for relegation as the likes of Crewe, Gillingham and Colchester face a tough scrap to survive, but there's no way **Walsall** should be so much bigger.

Walsall finished on a run of just two wins in 18 matches and have lost captain Andy Butler and top scorer Craig Westcarr. They are massive at 7-1 to go down.

Joe Garner enjoys the moment after scoring a screamer against Rotherham in the playoffs

BARNSLEY

Nickname: Tykes
Colours: Red and white
Ground: Oakwell (23,287)
Tel: 01226-211-211   www.barnsleyfc.co.uk

For a second successive season Barnsley sacked their manager after a poor start, but while David Flitcroft had managed to drag the club to safety in 2013, Danny Wilson couldn't pull off the same miracle.

Wilson managed only 24 points from his 26 matches at the helm and it's a further worry that he has a history of struggling to maintain initial success at his previous clubs.

Holding on to top scorer Chris O'Grady could prove vital to the Tykes' chances.

Longest run without win/loss: 6/4
High/low league position: 22/24
Clean sheets: 6 **Yellows:** 67 **Reds:** 6
Avg attendance: 13,445 **Players used:** 36
Leading scorer: C O'Grady 15 (5,10)
Key stat: No side in the Championship failed to score on more occasions than Barnsley, who blanked 20 times

	2013-14 H	A	Last six seasons at home P	W	D	L	OV	UN	BS	CS
Doncaster	D	D	5	2	2	1	2	3	2	2
Barnsley										
Yeovil	D	W	1	0	1	0	0	1	1	0
Leyton Orient			-	-	-	-	-	-	-	-
Preston			3	1	1	1	1	2	1	1
Peterborough			3	1	1	1	1	2	1	1
Sheffield United			3	1	1	1	2	1	2	1
Swindon			-	-	-	-	-	-	-	-
Port Vale			-	-	-	-	-	-	-	-
MK Dons			-	-	-	-	-	-	-	-
Bradford			-	-	-	-	-	-	-	-
Bristol City			5	2	1	2	3	2	3	2
Walsall			-	-	-	-	-	-	-	-
Crawley Town			-	-	-	-	-	-	-	-
Oldham			-	-	-	-	-	-	-	-
Colchester			-	-	-	-	-	-	-	-
Gillingham			-	-	-	-	-	-	-	-
Coventry			4	2	0	2	2	2	2	1
Crewe			-	-	-	-	-	-	-	-
Notts County			-	-	-	-	-	-	-	-
Chesterfield			-	-	-	-	-	-	-	-
Scunthorpe			2	1	1	0	1	1	2	0
Rochdale			-	-	-	-	-	-	-	-
Fleetwood Town			-	-	-	-	-	-	-	-

Season	Division	Pos	P	W	D	L	F	A	GD	Pts
2013-14	Championship	23	46	9	12	25	44	77	-33	39
2012-13	Championship	21	46	14	13	19	56	70	-14	55
2011-12	Championship	21	46	13	9	24	49	74	-25	48

Over/Under 50%/50% 9th   **Both score** 50%/50% 16th

BRADFORD

Nickname: The Bantams
Colours: Amber and claret
Ground: Coral Windows Stadium (25,136)
Tel: 01274-773-355   www.bradfordcityfc.co.uk

Bradford came up through the playoffs in 2012-13 but had big ambitions after reaching the 2013 League Cup final.

They did end up in the top half but any hopes for a top-six finish were dampened by the January sale of prolific striker Nahki Wells for £1.5m.

Replacement Aaron McLean took time to find his feet but he scored in each of the Bantams' last two games and Bradford have enough quality and resources to enjoy another decent campaign.

Longest run without win/loss: 13/7
High/low league position: 4/15
Clean sheets: 14 **Yellows:** 56 **Reds:** 2
Avg attendance: 10,731 **Players used:** 32
Leading scorer: N Wells 14 (4,10)
Key stat: Bradford were the only League 1 team to lose fewer than half of the matches in which they trailed at half-time last season

	2013-14 H	A	Last six seasons at home P	W	D	L	OV	UN	BS	CS
Doncaster			-	-	-	-	-	-	-	-
Barnsley			-	-	-	-	-	-	-	-
Yeovil			-	-	-	-	-	-	-	-
Leyton Orient	D	W	1	0	1	0	0	1	1	0
Preston	D	D	1	0	1	0	0	1	0	1
Peterborough	W	L	1	1	0	0	0	1	0	1
Sheffield United	W	D	1	1	0	0	0	1	0	1
Swindon	D	L	2	0	2	0	0	2	1	1
Port Vale	W	L	6	1	2	3	0	6	1	2
MK Dons	W	W	1	1	0	0	0	1	0	1
Bradford										
Bristol City	D	D	1	0	1	0	0	1	1	0
Walsall	L	W	1	0	0	1	0	1	0	0
Crawley Town	W	L	2	1	0	1	2	0	2	0
Oldham	L	D	1	0	0	1	1	0	1	0
Colchester	D	W	1	0	1	0	1	0	1	0
Gillingham	D	W	5	1	3	1	2	3	3	1
Coventry	D	D	1	0	1	0	1	0	1	0
Crewe	D	D	4	1	1	2	4	0	3	1
Notts County	D	L	3	1	2	0	1	2	2	1
Chesterfield			4	2	1	1	2	2	1	2
Scunthorpe			-	-	-	-	-	-	-	-
Rochdale			3	1	0	2	2	1	1	1
Fleetwood Town			1	1	0	0	0	1	0	1

Season	Division	Pos	P	W	D	L	F	A	GD	Pts
2013-14	League 1	11	46	14	17	15	57	54	+3	59
2012-13	League 2	7	46	18	15	13	63	52	+11	69
2011-12	League 2	18	46	12	14	20	54	59	-5	50

Over/Under 41%/59% 19th   **Both score** 50%/50% 16th

BRISTOL CITY

Nickname: The Robins
Colours: Red and white
Ground: Ashton Gate (21,804)
Tel: 0871-222-666   www.bcfc.co.uk

Surprisingly, Bristol City spent much of last season battling to avoid successive relegations as the loss of a number of key players led to a terrible start.

However, they eventually recovered from their post-relegation slump and did well over the second half of the campaign, picking up 42 points from their final 25 matches of the season.

Korey Smith, Luke Freeman and Mark Little are good signings and the Robins look like promotion contenders.

Longest run without win/loss: 12/6
High/low league position: 13/24
Clean sheets: 6 **Yellows:** 66 **Reds:** 2
Avg attendance: 9,521 **Players used:** 34
Leading scorer: S Baldock 24 (10,18)
Key stat: Bristol City conceded the most first-half goals in League 1 at 37 but shipped just 30 in the second half

	2013-14 H	A	Last six seasons at home P	W	D	L	OV	UN	BS	CS
Doncaster			4	3	0	1	3	1	3	1
Barnsley			5	4	1	0	3	2	3	2
Yeovil			-	-	-	-	-	-	-	-
Leyton Orient	D	W	1	0	1	0	1	0	1	0
Preston	D	L	4	1	3	0	1	3	4	0
Peterborough	L	W	4	1	1	2	3	1	3	0
Sheffield United	L	L	4	1	1	2	2	2	1	2
Swindon	D	L	1	0	1	0	0	1	0	1
Port Vale	W	D	1	1	0	0	1	0	0	1
MK Dons	D	D	1	0	1	0	1	0	1	0
Bradford	D	D	1	0	1	0	1	0	1	0
Bristol City										
Walsall	W	W	1	1	0	0	0	1	0	1
Crawley Town	W	D	1	1	0	0	0	1	0	1
Oldham	D	D	1	0	1	0	0	1	1	0
Colchester	D	D	1	0	1	0	0	1	1	0
Gillingham	W	D	1	1	0	0	1	0	1	0
Coventry	L	L	5	2	1	2	3	2	4	1
Crewe	D	L	1	0	1	0	0	1	0	1
Notts County	W	D	1	1	0	0	1	0	1	0
Chesterfield										
Scunthorpe			2	1	1	0	0	2	1	1
Rochdale			-	-	-	-	-	-	-	-
Fleetwood Town			-	-	-	-	-	-	-	-

Season	Division	Pos	P	W	D	L	F	A	GD	Pts
2013-14	League 1	12	46	13	19	14	70	67	+3	58
2012-13	Championship	24	46	11	8	27	59	84	-25	41
2011-12	Championship	20	46	12	13	21	44	68	-24	49

Over/Under 59%/41% 5th   **Both score** 76%/24% 1st

CHESTERFIELD

Nickname: Spireites
Colours: Blue and white
Ground: The Proact Stadium (10,300)
Tel: 01246-209-765   www.chesterfield-fc.co.uk

Chesterfield came up as League 2 champions three years ago only to be relegated immediately, but a repeat seems most unlikely.

The Spireites have recovered superbly under Paul Cook, who built their success on a mean defence – only Southend could beat their record of 40 goals conceded.

While no Chesterfield player scored more than 11 league goals, it bodes well that goals came from all over the pitch – five players contributed at least seven.

Longest run without win/loss: 7/8
High/low league position: 1/5
Clean sheets: 20 **Yellows:** 63 **Reds:** 7
Avg attendance: 5,141 **Players used:** 26
Leading scorer: G Roberts 11 (5,10) E Doyle 11 (3, 10)
Key stat: Chesterfield didn't lose any of the 19 games in which they were level at half-time

	2013-14 H	A	Last six seasons at home P	W	D	L	OV	UN	BS	CS
Doncaster			-	-	-	-	-	-	-	-
Barnsley			-	-	-	-	-	-	-	-
Yeovil			1	0	1	0	1	0	1	0
Leyton Orient			1	0	1	0	0	1	0	1
Preston			1	0	0	1	0	1	0	0
Peterborough			-	-	-	-	-	-	-	-
Sheffield United			1	0	0	1	0	1	0	0
Swindon			-	-	-	-	-	-	-	-
Port Vale			4	2	1	1	3	1	2	1
MK Dons			1	0	1	0	0	1	1	0
Bradford			4	0	3	1	2	2	3	0
Bristol City			-	-	-	-	-	-	-	-
Walsall			1	0	1	0	0	1	1	0
Crawley Town			-	-	-	-	-	-	-	-
Oldham			1	0	1	0	0	1	1	0
Colchester			1	0	0	1	0	1	0	0
Gillingham			3	1	0	2	1	2	1	0
Coventry			-	-	-	-	-	-	-	-
Crewe			2	0	1	1	2	0	2	0
Notts County			3	2	0	1	3	0	3	0
Chesterfield										
Scunthorpe	D	D	2	0	1	1	1	1	2	0
Rochdale	D	D	5	3	2	0	3	2	3	2
Fleetwood Town	W	D	2	1	0	1	2	0	2	0

Season	Division	Pos	P	W	D	L	F	A	GD	Pts
2013-14	League 2	1	46	23	15	8	71	40	+31	84
2012-13	League 2	8	46	18	13	15	60	45	+15	67
2011-12	League 1	22	46	10	12	24	56	81	-25	42

Over/Under 37%/63% 19th   **Both score** 48%/52% 13th

COLCHESTER

Nickname: The U's
Colours: Blue and white
Ground: Colchester Community Stadium (10,105)
Tel: 01206-508-800   www.cu-fc.com

The U's have been struggling to keep their heads above water for some time, both in terms of finance and avoiding relegation.

At least Colchester secured safety with a game to spare last season rather than enduring the final-day drama of 2012-13.

But things are getting even tougher for Joe Dunne and captain Brian Wilson was among the players that the U's couldn't afford to keep this summer. Unless they can find new investment the club looks to be facing a bleak future.

Longest run without win/loss: 11/4
High/low league position: 12/19
Clean sheets: 12 **Yellows:** 70 **Reds:** 2
Avg attendance: 4,709 **Players used:** 36
Leading scorer: F Sears 12 (4,10)
Key stat: Only Preston produced more than Colchester's nine draws against teams from the top half of League 1 last season

	2013-14 H	2013-14 A	Last six seasons at home P	W	D	L	OV	UN	BS	CS
Doncaster	-	-	1	0	0	1	1	0	1	0
Barnsley	-	-	-	-	-	-	-	-	-	-
Yeovil			5	3	2	0	2	3	2	3
Leyton Orient	L	L	6	4	1	1	3	3	4	2
Preston	L	D	3	2	0	1	2	1	1	2
Peterborough	W	L	3	2	0	1	1	2	1	1
Sheffield United	L	D	3	0	2	1	0	3	2	0
Swindon	L	D	5	3	0	2	4	1	3	1
Port Vale	W	L	1	1	0	0	0	1	0	1
MK Dons	W	D	6	2	0	4	4	2	3	1
Bradford	L	D	1	0	0	1	0	1	0	0
Bristol City	D	D	1	0	1	0	1	0	1	0
Walsall	D	W	6	4	1	1	1	5	2	3
Crawley Town	D	L	2	0	2	0	0	2	2	0
Oldham	L	W	6	3	1	2	2	4	2	2
Colchester										
Gillingham	W	W	2	2	0	0	2	0	1	1
Coventry	W	L	2	1	0	1	2	0	2	0
Crewe	L	D	3	0	0	3	2	1	2	0
Notts County	L	L	4	2	0	2	3	1	2	0
Chesterfield			1	0	0	1	1	0	1	0
Scunthorpe			3	0	2	1	1	2	2	1
Rochdale			2	1	1	0	0	2	0	2
Fleetwood Town	-	-	-	-	-	-	-	-	-	-

Season	Division	Pos	P	W	D	L	F	A	GD	Pts
2013-14	League 1	16	46	13	14	19	53	61	-8	53
2012-13	League 1	20	46	14	9	23	47	68	-21	51
2011-12	League 1	10	46	13	20	13	61	66	-5	59

Over/Under 46%/54% 14th   **Both score** 52%/48% 12th

COVENTRY

Nickname: The Sky Blues
Colours: Sky blue
Ground: Sixfields Stadium (7,300)
Tel: 0870-421-1987   www.ccfc.co.uk

It shows how well Coventry started last season that a ten-point deduction never looked likely to relegate them, but the Sky Blues didn't have much to spare after a closing run of four wins in 22 matches.

That dispels any notion that Coventry should finally be looking upwards now that they start the season on a level footing.

Continuing to play their home matches at Northampton won't help and they must keep young hotshot Callum Wilson.

Longest run without win/loss: 7/7
High/low league position: 4/11
Clean sheets: 9 **Yellows:** 74 **Reds:** 1
Avg attendance: 6,769 **Players used:** 32
Leading scorer: C Wilson 21 (6,17)
Key stat: Coventry's 24 matches against top-half teams in League 1 last season produced 88 goals – an average of 3.67 per game

	2013-14 H	2013-14 A	Last six seasons at home P	W	D	L	OV	UN	BS	CS
Doncaster			5	4	0	1	4	1	4	3
Barnsley			4	3	1	0	2	2	2	2
Yeovil			1	0	0	1	0	1	0	0
Leyton Orient	W	L	2	1	0	1	1	1	1	0
Preston	D	D	5	0	4	1	2	3	4	1
Peterborough	W	L	3	2	1	0	3	0	3	0
Sheffield United	W	L	5	2	2	1	3	2	4	1
Swindon	L	L	2	0	0	2	2	0	2	0
Port Vale	D	L	1	0	1	0	1	0	1	0
MK Dons	L	W	2	0	1	1	1	1	2	0
Bradford	D	D	1	0	1	0	0	1	0	1
Bristol City	W	W	5	2	1	2	3	2	3	1
Walsall	W	W	2	2	0	0	2	0	2	0
Crawley Town	D	L	2	1	1	0	2	0	2	0
Oldham	D	D	2	1	1	0	1	1	2	0
Colchester	W	L	2	1	1	0	1	1	1	1
Gillingham	W	L	1	1	0	0	1	0	1	0
Coventry										
Crewe	D	W	2	0	1	1	2	0	2	0
Notts County	W	L	2	1	0	1	2	0	1	1
Chesterfield			-	-	-	-	-	-	-	-
Scunthorpe			3	1	1	1	2	1	3	0
Rochdale			-	-	-	-	-	-	-	-
Fleetwood Town	-	-	-	-	-	-	-	-	-	-

Season	Division	Pos	P	W	D	L	F	A	GD	Pts
2013-14	League 1	18	46	16	13	17	74	77	-3	51
2012-13	League 1	15	46	18	11	17	66	59	+7	55
2011-12	Championship	23	46	9	13	24	41	65	-24	40

Over/Under 67%/33% 1st   **Both score** 70%/30% 2nd

CRAWLEY

Nickname: The Red Devils
Colours: Red and white
Ground: Broadfield Stadium (5,973)
Tel: 01293-410-002   www.crawleytownfc.com

Crawley punched above their weight financially to gain successive promotions into League 1 and they've done well to twice finish in mid-table.

That seemed some way off when Richie Barker was sacked in November, but the Red Devils lost just two of the first 14 matches under John Gregory.

Worryingly, though, Gregory's initial impact wore off as they lost eight of the last 13, with just three wins in that time, and he is braced for further budget cuts.

Longest run without win/loss: 9/7
High/low league position: 9/19
Clean sheets: 11 **Yellows:** 59 **Reds:** 5
Avg attendance: 4,599 **Players used:** 27
Leading scorer: M Tubbs 8 (4,7)
Key stat: Crawley failed to score in 15 matches last season – more than any side in League 1 outside the bottom six

	2013-14 H	A	Last six seasons at home P	W	D	L	OV	UN	BS	CS
Doncaster			1	0	1	0	0	1	1	0
Barnsley			-	-	-	-	-	-	-	-
Yeovil			1	0	0	1	0	1	0	0
Leyton Orient	W	W	2	2	0	0	1	1	1	1
Preston	D	L	2	1	1	0	1	1	1	1
Peterborough	W	W	1	1	0	0	0	1	0	1
Sheffield United	L	D	2	0	0	2	0	2	0	0
Swindon	D	D	3	0	2	1	2	1	1	1
Port Vale	L	L	2	1	0	1	2	0	1	0
MK Dons	L	W	2	1	0	1	0	2	0	1
Bradford	W	L	2	2	0	0	1	1	1	1
Bristol City	D	L	1	0	1	0	0	1	1	0
Walsall	D	W	2	0	2	0	1	1	1	1
Crawley Town										
Oldham	W	L	2	1	1	0	2	0	1	1
Colchester	W	D	2	2	0	0	1	1	0	2
Gillingham	W	L	2	1	0	1	2	0	2	0
Coventry	W	D	2	2	0	0	1	1	1	1
Crewe	L	L	3	1	1	1	1	2	2	1
Notts County	W	L	2	1	1	0	0	2	0	2
Chesterfield			-	-	-	-	-	-	-	-
Scunthorpe			1	1	0	0	1	0	0	1
Rochdale			-	-	-	-	-	-	-	-
Fleetwood Town			1	0	1	0	0	1	1	0

Season	Division	Pos	P	W	D	L	F	A	GD	Pts
2013-14	League 1	14	46	14	15	17	48	54	-6	57
2012-13	League 1	10	46	18	14	14	59	58	+1	68
2011-12	League 2	3	46	23	15	8	76	54	+22	84

Over/Under 35%/65% 21st   **Both score** 50%/50% 16th

CREWE

Nickname: The Railwaymen
Colours: Red and white
Ground: The Alexandra Stadium (10,109)
Tel: 01270-213-014   www.crewealex.net

Another struggle lies ahead for Crewe, who scraped to safety despite racking up a woeful -26 goal difference. That figure was a result of 14 of their 21 defeats coming by at least two goals, and they relied on some tight wins to stay up.

Improvement is needed, particularly with top scorer Chuks Aneke having signed for Belgian side Zulte Waregem.

As usual Crewe's famous academy has produced many young first-team players who should progress – but how quickly?

Longest run without win/loss: 7/4
High/low league position: 17/23
Clean sheets: 8 **Yellows:** 55 **Reds:** 3
Avg attendance: 5,244 **Players used:** 33
Leading scorer: C Aneke 14 (7,11)
Key stat: Crewe picked up just six points after falling behind last season, the lowest total in League 1

	2013-14 H	A	Last six seasons at home P	W	D	L	OV	UN	BS	CS
Doncaster			1	0	0	1	1	0	1	0
Barnsley			-	-	-	-	-	-	-	-
Yeovil			2	1	0	1	0	2	0	1
Leyton Orient	L	L	3	0	1	2	1	2	2	0
Preston	W	W	2	2	0	0	1	1	1	1
Peterborough	D	L	2	0	2	0	1	1	2	0
Sheffield United	W	L	2	2	0	0	1	1	0	2
Swindon	D	L	4	3	1	0	1	3	2	2
Port Vale	L	W	4	1	1	2	3	1	4	0
MK Dons	W	L	3	2	1	0	2	1	2	1
Bradford	D	D	4	2	1	1	1	3	1	2
Bristol City	W	D	1	1	0	0	0	1	0	1
Walsall	L	D	3	2	0	1	2	1	1	1
Crawley Town	W	W	3	2	1	0	0	3	1	2
Oldham	D	D	3	0	1	2	1	2	1	0
Colchester	D	W	3	2	1	0	1	2	1	2
Gillingham	L	W	3	1	0	2	2	1	2	0
Coventry	L	D	2	1	0	1	1	1	1	1
Crewe										
Notts County	L	L	3	0	0	3	2	1	2	0
Chesterfield			2	1	0	1	0	2	0	1
Scunthorpe			2	2	0	0	1	1	1	1
Rochdale			1	0	1	0	1	0	1	0
Fleetwood Town			-	-	-	-	-	-	-	-

Season	Division	Pos	P	W	D	L	F	A	GD	Pts
2013-14	League 1	19	46	13	12	21	54	80	-26	51
2012-13	League 1	13	46	18	10	18	54	62	-8	64
2011-12	League 2	7	46	20	12	14	67	59	+8	72

Over/Under 61%/39% 3rd   **Both score** 57%/43% 6th

DONCASTER

Nickname: Rovers
Colours: Red and white
Ground: Keepmoat Stadium (15,231)
Tel: 01302-764-664   www.doncasterroversfc.co.uk

Doncaster suffered final-day heartbreak last season, as a stoppage-time goal for Birmingham saw them relegated.

Still, it's hard to have a lot of sympathy when they lost seven of their last eight matches and that run of form hints at a tough task for Paul Dickov in 2014-15.

Yet the fact that Rovers bounced straight back up to the Championship when relegated in 2012 at least suggests they are well equipped to deal with being a yo-yo club.

Longest run without win/loss: 8/4
High/low league position: 17/22
Clean sheets: 13 **Yellows:** 71 **Reds:** 3
Avg attendance: 12,765 **Players used:** 33
Leading scorer: C Brown 9 (3,8)
Key stat: Doncaster played out six goalless draws last season – no Championship side was involved in more

	2013-14 H	A	Last six seasons at home P	W	D	L	OV	UN	BS	CS
Doncaster										
Barnsley	D	D	5	1	1	3	1	4	1	1
Yeovil	W	L	2	1	1	0	1	1	2	0
Leyton Orient			1	1	0	0	0	1	0	1
Preston			4	0	2	2	1	3	3	0
Peterborough			2	1	1	0	1	1	2	0
Sheffield United			4	1	2	1	1	3	2	1
Swindon			1	1	0	0	0	1	0	1
Port Vale			-	-	-	-	-	-	-	-
MK Dons			1	0	1	0	0	1	0	1
Bradford			-	-	-	-	-	-	-	-
Bristol City			4	2	2	0	0	4	2	2
Walsall			1	0	0	1	1	0	1	0
Crawley Town			1	0	0	1	0	1	0	0
Oldham			1	1	0	0	0	1	0	1
Colchester			1	1	0	0	0	1	0	1
Gillingham			-	-	-	-	-	-	-	-
Coventry			5	1	3	1	1	4	3	2
Crewe			1	0	0	1	0	1	0	0
Notts County			1	0	0	1	0	1	0	0
Chesterfield			-	-	-	-	-	-	-	-
Scunthorpe			3	3	0	0	3	0	1	2
Rochdale			-	-	-	-	-	-	-	-
Fleetwood Town			-	-	-	-	-	-	-	-

Season	Division	Pos	P	W	D	L	F	A	GD	Pts
2013-14	Championship	22	46	11	11	24	39	70	-31	44
2012-13	League 1	1	46	25	9	12	62	44	+18	84
2011-12	Championship	24	46	8	12	26	43	80	-37	36

Over/Under 52%/48% 4th   **Both score** 41%/59% 22nd

FLEETWOOD

Nickname: The Cod Army
Colours: Red and white
Ground: Highbury Stadium (5,092)
Tel: 01253 770702 www.fleetwoodtownfc.com

Few clubs have ever enjoyed such a rapid rise as Fleetwood, whose victory in the League 2 playoff final in just their second season as a Football League club made it six promotions in ten seasons.

There was no fluke about it either, as Fleetwood finished a clear fourth and caught the eye with their attractive style.

The Cod Army have been given significant financial backing all the way and have the spending power to excel in the third tier.

Longest run without win/loss: 4/7
High/low league position: 1/8
Clean sheets: 14 **Yellows:** 61 **Reds:** 1
Avg attendance: 3,477 **Players used:** 32
Leading scorer: A Sarcevic 13 (5,10)
Key stat: Fleetwood scored the first goal and went on to win 20 matches last season – the most in League 2

	2013-14 H	A	Last six seasons at home P	W	D	L	OV	UN	BS	CS
Doncaster			-	-	-	-	-	-	-	-
Barnsley			-	-	-	-	-	-	-	-
Yeovil			-	-	-	-	-	-	-	-
Leyton Orient			-	-	-	-	-	-	-	-
Preston			-	-	-	-	-	-	-	-
Peterborough			-	-	-	-	-	-	-	-
Sheffield United			-	-	-	-	-	-	-	-
Swindon			-	-	-	-	-	-	-	-
Port Vale			1	0	0	1	1	0	1	0
MK Dons			-	-	-	-	-	-	-	-
Bradford			1	0	1	0	1	0	1	0
Bristol City			-	-	-	-	-	-	-	-
Walsall			-	-	-	-	-	-	-	-
Crawley Town			1	0	0	1	1	0	1	0
Oldham			-	-	-	-	-	-	-	-
Colchester			-	-	-	-	-	-	-	-
Gillingham			1	0	1	0	1	0	1	0
Coventry			-	-	-	-	-	-	-	-
Crewe			-	-	-	-	-	-	-	-
Notts County			-	-	-	-	-	-	-	-
Chesterfield	D	L	2	0	1	1	1	1	2	0
Scunthorpe	L	D	1	0	0	1	0	1	0	0
Rochdale	D	W	2	0	1	1	1	1	0	1
Fleetwood Town										

Season	Division	Pos	P	W	D	L	F	A	GD	Pts
2013-14	League 2	4	46	22	10	14	66	52	+14	76
2012-13	League 2	13	46	15	15	16	55	57	-2	60
2011-12	Conference	1	46	31	10	5	102	48	+54	103

Over/Under 43%/57% 10th   **Both score** 48%/52% 13th

GILLINGHAM

Nickname: The Gills
Colours: Blue and white
Ground: Priestfield Stadium (11,440)
Tel: 01634-300-000 www.gillinghamfootballclub.com

Last season was a relentless battle against the drop for Gillingham after they failed to win any of their first eight matches.

The Gills traded the more brash management style of Martin Allen for the seemingly safer hands of Peter Taylor in October and there was enough initial improvement to keep them up, with Taylor winning 11 of his first 25 matches in charge, but the fact that they won just two of their final ten matches will be a concern.

Longest run without win/loss: 8/3
High/low league position: 12/24
Clean sheets: 7 **Yellows:** 57 **Reds:** 3
Avg attendance: 6,216 **Players used:** 33
Leading scorer: C McDonald 17 (3,16)
Key stat: Gillingham were the only team in League 1 last season not to have a single goalless draw

	2013-14 H	A	Last six seasons at home P	W	D	L	OV	UN	BS	CS
Doncaster			-	-	-	-	-	-	-	-
Barnsley			-	-	-	-	-	-	-	-
Yeovil			1	1	0	0	0	1	0	1
Leyton Orient	L	L	2	0	1	1	1	1	2	0
Preston	L	L	1	0	0	1	1	0	1	0
Peterborough	D	L	1	0	1	0	1	0	1	0
Sheffield United	L	W	1	0	0	1	0	1	0	0
Swindon	W	D	3	3	0	0	2	1	1	2
Port Vale	W	L	5	3	1	1	3	2	3	2
MK Dons	W	W	2	1	1	0	2	0	2	0
Bradford	L	D	5	2	1	2	1	4	1	2
Bristol City	D	L	1	0	1	0	0	1	1	0
Walsall	D	D	2	0	2	0	1	1	1	1
Crawley Town	W	L	2	1	0	1	0	2	0	1
Oldham	L	L	2	1	0	1	0	2	0	1
Colchester	L	L	2	0	1	1	0	2	0	1
Gillingham										
Coventry	W	L	1	1	0	0	1	0	1	0
Crewe	L	W	3	0	0	3	3	0	3	0
Notts County	W	L	2	1	1	0	2	0	2	0
Chesterfield			3	1	1	1	1	2	2	0
Scunthorpe			-	-	-	-	-	-	-	-
Rochdale			2	0	1	1	1	1	2	0
Fleetwood Town			1	0	1	0	1	0	1	0

Season	Division	Pos	P	W	D	L	F	A	GD	Pts
2013-14	League 1	17	46	15	8	23	60	79	-19	53
2012-13	League 2	1	46	23	14	9	66	39	+27	83
2011-12	League 2	8	46	20	10	16	79	62	+17	70

Over/Under 61%/39% 3rd   **Both score** 65%/35% 3rd

LEYTON ORIENT

Nickname: The O's
Colours: Red
Ground: Matchroom Stadium (9,311)
Tel: 0871-310-1881   www.leytonorient.com

The O's set the pace for much of the season in League 1 but fell agonisingly short of promotion, losing to Rotherham on penalties in the playoff final.

A vibrant attack was the key to their season, with Russell Slade's men getting shut out just four times in 46 games. And Orient continue to punch above their weight financially, having also finished seventh in two of the last three seasons.

That said, they couldn't exploit a great start and may just have missed the boat.

Longest run without win/loss: 5/12
High/low league position: 1/5
Clean sheets: 14 **Yellows:** 77 **Reds:** 1
Avg attendance: 5,605 **Players used:** 28
Leading scorer: D Mooney 19 (8,15)
Key stat: Leyton Orient won six matches after falling behind last season, the most in League 1

	2013-14 H	A	Last six seasons at home P	W	D	L	OV	UN	BS	CS
Doncaster			1	0	0	1	0	1	0	0
Barnsley			-	-	-	-	-	-	-	-
Yeovil			5	2	1	2	3	2	3	1
Leyton Orient										
Preston	L	D	3	2	0	1	1	2	1	1
Peterborough	L	W	3	1	0	2	3	0	3	0
Sheffield United	D	D	3	0	2	1	0	3	2	0
Swindon	W	W	5	2	2	1	2	3	1	4
Port Vale	W	W	1	1	0	0	1	0	1	0
MK Dons	W	W	6	2	1	3	5	1	4	1
Bradford	L	D	1	0	0	1	0	1	0	0
Bristol City	L	D	1	0	0	1	1	0	1	0
Walsall	D	D	6	2	3	1	1	5	3	2
Crawley Town	L	L	2	0	0	2	1	1	1	0
Oldham	D	D	6	2	2	2	3	3	5	1
Colchester	W	W	6	3	0	3	3	3	3	0
Gillingham	W	W	2	2	0	0	2	0	2	0
Coventry	W	L	2	1	0	1	0	2	0	1
Crewe	W	W	3	2	1	0	0	3	1	2
Notts County	W	D	4	3	0	1	3	1	2	1
Chesterfield			1	0	1	0	0	1	1	0
Scunthorpe			3	0	1	2	3	0	3	0
Rochdale			2	2	0	0	2	0	2	0
Fleetwood Town			-	-	-	-	-	-	-	-

Season	Division	Pos	P	W	D	L	F	A	GD	Pts
2013-14	League 1	3	46	25	11	10	85	45	+40	86
2012-13	League 1	7	46	21	8	17	55	48	+7	71
2011-12	League 1	20	46	13	9	24	48	75	-27	50

Over/Under 50%/50% 11th   **Both score** 63%/37% 4th

MK DONS

Nickname: The Dons
Colours: White
Ground: stadium:mk (30,500)
Tel: 01908-622-922   www.mkdons.co.uk

The Dons have disappointed in the last two campaigns, falling well short of the playoffs despite being well fancied on the back of their three top-five finishes in the previous four years.

One win in their last eight matches saw them slide to tenth last term, but manager Karl Robinson has claimed that as a major achievement given his team's chronic luck with injuries.

Robinson has also been promised a significant budget to put things right.

Longest run without win/loss: 5/7
High/low league position: 6/12
Clean sheets: 10 **Yellows:** 73 **Reds:** 3
Avg attendance: 6,901 **Players used:** 34
Leading scorer: P Bamford 14 (4,12)
Key stat: MK Dons failed to win just four of the games in which they took the lead – fewer than every League 1 side bar Tranmere

	2013-14 H	A	Last six seasons at home P	W	D	L	OV	UN	BS	CS
Doncaster			1	1	0	0	1	0	0	1
Barnsley			-	-	-	-	-	-	-	-
Yeovil			5	3	1	1	3	2	2	2
Leyton Orient	L	L	6	3	0	3	4	2	4	2
Preston	D	D	3	0	2	1	0	3	1	1
Peterborough	L	L	3	1	0	2	1	2	1	1
Sheffield United	L	W	3	2	0	1	0	3	0	2
Swindon	D	W	5	3	1	1	3	2	4	1
Port Vale	W	L	1	1	0	0	1	0	0	1
MK Dons										
Bradford	L	L	1	0	0	1	1	0	1	0
Bristol City	D	D	1	0	1	0	1	0	1	0
Walsall	W	W	6	2	1	3	1	5	2	2
Crawley Town	L	W	2	0	1	1	0	2	0	1
Oldham	W	W	6	4	2	0	3	3	2	4
Colchester	D	L	6	3	3	0	2	4	4	2
Gillingham	L	L	2	1	0	1	0	2	0	1
Coventry	L	W	2	0	0	2	2	0	2	0
Crewe	W	L	3	2	1	0	1	2	1	2
Notts County	W	W	4	3	1	0	3	1	3	1
Chesterfield			1	1	0	0	1	0	1	0
Scunthorpe			3	0	1	2	0	3	0	1
Rochdale			2	1	1	0	1	1	2	0
Fleetwood Town			-	-	-	-	-	-	-	-

Season	Division	Pos	P	W	D	L	F	A	GD	Pts
2013-14	League 1	10	46	17	9	20	63	65	-2	60
2012-13	League 1	8	46	19	13	14	62	45	+17	70
2011-12	League 1	5	46	22	14	10	84	47	+37	80

Over/Under 59%/41% 5th   **Both score** 54%/46% 10th

NOTTS COUNTY

Nickname: The Magpies
Colours: Black and white
Ground: Meadow Lane (20,280)
Tel: 0115-952-9000   www.nottscountyfc.co.uk

County defied the odds by dragging themselves to safety last season, winning six of their last nine matches as Shaun Derry turned things around after a disastrous start under Chris Kiwomya.

That should be the springboard to a better season, but it's worth noting how often County have flattered to deceive, often improving for a change in manager before falling into a fresh slump.

Incredibly, Derry is their ninth permanent gaffer since October 2009.

Longest run without win/loss: 7/3
High/low league position: 16/24
Clean sheets: 10 **Yellows:** 88 **Reds:** 7
Avg attendance: 5,684 **Players used:** 41
Leading scorer: C McGregor 12 (3,10)
Key stat: Notts County had the worst away record in League 1 last season, collecting just 12 points on their travels

	2013-14 H	A	Last six seasons at home P	W	D	L	OV	UN	BS	CS
Doncaster			1	0	0	1	0	1	0	0
Barnsley			-	-	-	-	-	-	-	-
Yeovil			3	2	0	1	3	0	2	1
Leyton Orient	D	L	4	1	2	1	2	2	3	1
Preston	L	L	3	0	1	2	0	3	0	1
Peterborough	L	L	2	0	0	2	1	1	1	0
Sheffield United	W	L	3	1	1	1	2	1	3	0
Swindon	W	L	3	3	0	0	0	3	0	3
Port Vale	W	L	3	3	0	0	3	0	3	0
MK Dons	L	L	4	1	1	2	2	2	3	1
Bradford	W	D	3	3	0	0	3	0	1	2
Bristol City	D	L	1	0	1	0	0	1	1	0
Walsall	L	D	4	1	1	2	2	2	3	0
Crawley Town	W	L	2	1	1	0	0	2	1	1
Oldham	W	D	4	3	0	1	1	3	1	2
Colchester	W	W	4	4	0	0	2	2	2	2
Gillingham	W	L	2	1	0	1	1	1	1	0
Coventry	W	L	2	1	1	0	2	0	1	1
Crewe	W	W	3	2	1	0	1	2	1	2
Notts County										
Chesterfield			3	2	0	1	0	3	0	2
Scunthorpe			2	2	0	0	1	1	1	1
Rochdale			4	2	0	2	2	2	2	2
Fleetwood Town			-	-	-	-	-	-	-	-

Season	Division	Pos	P	W	D	L	F	A	GD	Pts
2013-14	League 1	20	46	15	5	26	64	77	-13	50
2012-13	League 1	12	46	16	17	13	61	49	+12	65
2011-12	League 1	7	46	21	10	15	75	63	+12	73

Over/Under 57%/43% 7th   **Both score** 52%/48% 12th

OLDHAM

Nickname: The Latics
Colours: Blue
Ground: Boundary Park (10,850)
Tel: 08712-262-235 www.oldhamathletic.co.uk

Oldham did well to haul themselves towards a mid-table finish last season, going unbeaten in their last ten matches.

They should be capable of progressing again as their impressive manager Lee Johnson – the youngest in the Football League – is learning his trade all the time and will focus on finding a regular scorer after Jonson Clarke-Harris topped last season's charts with just six league goals.

But it won't be easy on the tight budget that currently limits Oldham's ambitions.

Longest run without win/loss: 6/10
High/low league position: 14/19
Clean sheets: 10 **Yellows:** 71 **Reds:** 5
Avg attendance: 5,106 **Players used:** 37
Leading scorer: J Clarke-Harris 6 (2,5)
Key stat: Oldham scored exactly one goal in 25 games last term, with eight 1-0 wins and 11 1-1 draws

	2013-14 H	A	Last six seasons at home P	W	D	L	OV	UN	BS	CS
Doncaster			1	0	0	1	1	0	1	0
Barnsley			-	-	-	-	-	-	-	-
Yeovil			5	1	2	2	1	4	1	3
Leyton Orient	D	D	6	2	3	1	0	6	3	2
Preston	L	L	3	1	1	1	2	1	3	0
Peterborough	W	L	3	1	0	2	3	0	2	0
Sheffield United	D	D	3	0	1	2	0	3	1	0
Swindon	W	W	5	2	2	1	2	3	2	2
Port Vale	W	L	1	1	0	0	1	0	1	0
MK Dons	L	L	6	4	0	2	5	1	5	1
Bradford	D	W	1	0	1	0	0	1	1	0
Bristol City	D	D	1	0	1	0	0	1	1	0
Walsall	L	L	6	3	2	1	2	4	4	1
Crawley Town	W	L	2	2	0	0	1	1	1	1
Oldham										
Colchester	L	W	6	0	4	2	1	5	3	1
Gillingham	W	W	2	2	0	0	0	2	0	2
Coventry	D	D	2	0	1	1	0	2	0	1
Crewe	D	D	3	0	2	1	1	2	3	0
Notts County	D	L	4	2	2	0	3	1	3	1
Chesterfield			1	1	0	0	1	0	1	0
Scunthorpe			3	1	1	1	2	1	2	1
Rochdale			2	1	0	1	1	1	1	1
Fleetwood Town			-	-	-	-	-	-	-	-

Season	Division	Pos	P	W	D	L	F	A	GD	Pts
2013-14	League 1	15	46	14	14	18	50	59	-9	56
2012-13	League 1	19	46	14	9	23	46	59	-13	51
2011-12	League 1	16	46	14	12	20	50	66	-16	54

Over/Under 35%/65% 21st   **Both score** 57%/43% 6th

PETERBOROUGH

Nickname: The Posh
Colours: Blue
Ground: London Road (14,640)
Tel: 01733-563 947   www.theposh.com

Relegated from the Championship in 2013 despite getting 54 points, Peterborough fully expected to go straight back up. But chairman Darragh MacAnthony described it as an "epic failure" to finish a distant sixth before losing in the playoffs.

Posh should improve, especially if they hang on to Britt Assombalonga, but they couldn't adapt when the goals dried up, twice suffering losing streaks of at least four games – a common problem for Darren Ferguson's teams.

Longest run without win/loss: 6/8
High/low league position: 2/7
Clean sheets: 17 **Yellows:** 63 **Reds:** 8
Avg attendance: 6,781 **Players used:** 34
Leading scorer: B Assombalonga 23 (7,18)
Key stat: Peterborough scored four goals or more seven times last season

	2013-14 H	A	Last six seasons at home P	W	D	L	OV	UN	BS	CS
Doncaster			2	0	0	2	2	0	2	0
Barnsley			3	1	0	2	3	0	3	0
Yeovil			2	0	1	1	2	0	2	0
Leyton Orient	L	W	3	1	1	1	3	0	2	1
Preston	W	L	2	1	0	1	0	2	0	1
Peterborough										
Sheffield United	D	L	2	1	1	0	0	2	0	2
Swindon	W	L	3	2	1	0	2	1	2	1
Port Vale	D	W	1	0	1	0	0	1	0	1
MK Dons	W	W	3	2	1	0	2	1	2	1
Bradford	W	L	1	1	0	0	1	0	1	0
Bristol City	L	W	4	1	0	3	3	1	2	1
Walsall	D	L	3	2	1	0	1	2	1	2
Crawley Town	L	L	1	0	0	1	0	1	0	0
Oldham	W	L	3	2	1	0	3	0	3	0
Colchester	W	L	3	2	1	0	1	2	2	1
Gillingham	W	D	1	1	0	0	1	0	1	0
Coventry	W	L	3	2	0	1	0	3	0	2
Crewe	W	D	2	2	0	0	2	0	2	0
Notts County	W	W	2	1	0	1	2	0	2	0
Chesterfield			-	-	-	-	-	-	-	-
Scunthorpe			2	2	0	0	2	0	1	1
Rochdale			1	1	0	0	1	0	1	0
Fleetwood Town			-	-	-	-	-	-	-	-

Season	Division	Pos	P	W	D	L	F	A	GD	Pts
2013-14	League 1	6	46	23	5	18	72	58	+14	74
2012-13	Championship	22	46	15	9	22	66	75	-9	54
2011-12	Championship	18	46	13	11	22	67	77	-10	50

Over/Under 50%/50% 11th   **Both score** 43%/57% 22nd

PORT VALE

Nickname: The Valiants
Colours: White and black
Ground: Vale Park (19,148)
Tel: 01782-655-800   www.port-vale.co.uk

Ninth place was a great achievement for Vale last season in their first campaign after promotion from League 2.

Micky Adams' side built their success on being ruthless against the lesser lights, with 15 of their 18 wins coming against bottom-half teams.

However, the Valiants are unlikely to do anywhere near as well this term. Only two teams outside the bottom four had a worse goal difference in 2013-14, as Vale relied on a string of single-goal victories.

Longest run without win/loss: 4/3
High/low league position: 8/15
Clean sheets: 11 **Yellows:** 82 **Reds:** 3
Avg attendance: 6,851 **Players used:** 27
Leading scorer: T Pope 12 (4,12)
Key stat: Port Vale won four matches in which they trailed at half-time last season – more than any other club in League 1

	2013-14 H	A	Last six seasons at home P	W	D	L	OV	UN	BS	CS
Doncaster			-	-	-	-	-	-	-	-
Barnsley			-	-	-	-	-	-	-	-
Yeovil			-	-	-	-	-	-	-	-
Leyton Orient	L	L	1	0	0	1	0	1	0	0
Preston	L	L	1	0	0	1	0	1	0	0
Peterborough	L	D	1	0	0	1	0	1	0	0
Sheffield United	L	L	1	0	0	1	1	0	1	0
Swindon	L	L	2	0	0	2	1	1	1	0
Port Vale										
MK Dons	W	L	1	1	0	0	0	1	0	1
Bradford	W	L	6	4	1	1	4	2	4	1
Bristol City	D	L	1	0	1	0	0	1	1	0
Walsall	W	W	1	1	0	0	0	1	0	1
Crawley Town	W	W	2	1	1	0	2	0	2	0
Oldham	W	L	1	1	0	0	0	1	0	1
Colchester	W	L	1	1	0	0	0	1	0	1
Gillingham	W	L	5	2	1	2	3	2	3	1
Coventry	W	D	1	1	0	0	1	0	1	0
Crewe	L	W	4	1	1	2	2	2	3	0
Notts County	W	L	3	2	0	1	3	0	3	0
Chesterfield			4	0	1	3	1	3	2	0
Scunthorpe			-	-	-	-	-	-	-	-
Rochdale			3	1	2	0	2	1	3	0
Fleetwood Town			1	0	0	1	0	1	0	0

Season	Division	Pos	P	W	D	L	F	A	GD	Pts
2013-14	League 1	9	46	18	7	21	59	73	-14	61
2012-13	League 2	3	46	21	15	10	87	52	+35	78
2011-12	League 2	12	46	20	9	17	68	60	+8	59

Over/Under 57%/43% 7th   **Both score** 54%/46% 10th

PRESTON

Nickname: The Lilywhites/North End
Colours: White and navy blue
Ground: Deepdale (23,404)
Tel: 0870-442-1964   www.pnefc.co.uk

Preston struggled against the best teams, winning just twice in ten matches against other top-six sides, and that weakness proved their undoing in the playoffs.

Otherwise it was an excellent season for North End, who moved into the top six in early September and never relinquished it, despite never quite threatening the automatic promotion places.

Simon Grayson – promoted from League 1 with three previous clubs – should be just the man to put that right.

Longest run without win/loss: 4/12
High/low league position: 3/6
Clean sheets: 16 **Yellows:** 76 **Reds:** 4
Avg attendance: 6,623 **Players used:** 26
Leading scorer: J Garner 18 (6,13)
Key stat: Preston didn't lose a single match after taking the lead last season – the only team in League 1 to achieve such a record

	2013-14 H	A	Last six seasons at home P	W	D	L	OV	UN	BS	CS
Doncaster			4	1	1	2	1	3	1	1
Barnsley			3	1	0	2	3	0	3	0
Yeovil			2	2	0	0	2	0	2	0
Leyton Orient	D	W	3	0	2	1	0	3	1	1
Preston										
Peterborough	W	L	2	2	0	0	1	1	1	1
Sheffield United	D	W	6	2	2	2	3	3	3	2
Swindon	W	L	2	2	0	0	2	0	2	0
Port Vale	W	W	1	1	0	0	1	0	1	0
MK Dons	D	D	3	0	3	0	1	2	2	1
Bradford	D	D	1	0	1	0	1	0	1	0
Bristol City	W	D	4	2	1	1	2	2	1	2
Walsall	W	W	3	1	1	1	2	1	2	1
Crawley Town	W	D	2	1	0	1	1	1	1	1
Oldham	W	W	3	2	1	0	2	1	2	1
Colchester	D	W	3	0	2	1	1	2	2	1
Gillingham	W	W	1	1	0	0	1	0	1	0
Coventry	D	D	5	3	2	0	4	1	5	0
Crewe	L	L	2	0	0	2	1	1	1	0
Notts County	W	W	3	2	1	0	0	3	0	3
Chesterfield			1	0	1	0	0	1	0	1
Scunthorpe			4	2	1	1	3	1	2	2
Rochdale			1	0	0	1	0	1	0	0
Fleetwood Town			-	-	-	-	-	-	-	-

Season	Division	Pos	P	W	D	L	F	A	GD	Pts
2013-14	League 1	5	46	23	16	7	72	46	+26	85
2012-13	League 1	14	46	14	17	15	54	49	+5	59
2011-12	League 1	15	46	13	15	18	54	60	-14	54

Over/Under 46%/54% 14th   **Both score** 52%/48% 12th

ROCHDALE

Nickname: The Dale
Colours: Blue and black
Ground: Spotland Stadium (10,037)
Tel: 0870-822-1907   www.rochdaleafc.co.uk

Keith Hill again worked his magic at Spotland last season. The first Rochdale boss to gain promotion in 41 years when he took the club into the third tier in 2010, Hill repeated the trick in the first full season of his second stint at the club.

Dale finished ninth after promotion in 2010-11, but mere survival would be a big achievement this time around.

They won just four matches against top-half teams last season, which doesn't bode well for competing at a higher level.

Longest run without win/loss: 4/6
High/low league position: 1/9
Clean sheets: 19 **Yellows:** 70 **Reds:** 9
Avg attendance: 3,519 **Players used:** 29
Leading scorer: S Hogan 17 (7,12)
Key stat: Rochdale won 13 of the 14 matches in which they led at half-time last season

	2013-14 H	A	Last six seasons at home P	W	D	L	OV	UN	BS	CS
Doncaster			-	-	-	-	-	-	-	-
Barnsley			-	-	-	-	-	-	-	-
Yeovil			2	0	1	1	0	2	0	1
Leyton Orient			2	0	1	1	0	2	1	0
Preston			1	0	1	0	0	1	1	0
Peterborough			1	0	1	0	1	0	1	0
Sheffield United			1	0	0	1	1	0	1	0
Swindon			1	0	1	0	1	0	1	0
Port Vale			3	1	2	0	1	2	1	2
MK Dons			2	0	0	2	2	0	2	0
Bradford			3	1	1	1	2	1	1	2
Bristol City			-	-	-	-	-	-	-	-
Walsall			2	1	1	0	2	0	2	0
Crawley Town			-	-	-	-	-	-	-	-
Oldham			2	1	1	0	1	1	2	0
Colchester			2	0	1	1	2	0	2	0
Gillingham			2	0	1	1	0	2	1	0
Coventry			-	-	-	-	-	-	-	-
Crewe			1	1	0	0	0	1	0	1
Notts County			4	3	0	1	2	2	1	2
Chesterfield	D	D	5	1	3	1	3	2	5	0
Scunthorpe	L	L	2	1	0	1	1	1	0	1
Rochdale										
Fleetwood Town	L	D	2	0	1	1	1	1	1	1

Season	Division	Pos	P	W	D	L	F	A	GD	Pts
2013-14	League 2	3	46	24	9	13	69	48	+21	81
2012-13	League 2	12	46	16	13	17	68	70	-2	61
2011-12	League 1	24	46	8	14	24	47	81	-34	38

Over/Under 65%/35% 1st   **Both score** 41%/59% 22nd

SCUNTHORPE

Nickname: The Iron
Colours: Claret and blue
Ground: Glanford Park (9,144)
Tel: 01724-848 077   www.scunthorpe-united.co.uk

Russ Wilcox made an astonishing impact at Scunthorpe last season to lead the club to promotion from League 2.

Stepping up from assistant in December, Wilcox broke the Football League record for the longest unbeaten run at the start of a managerial reign and ended up with just one defeat in 30 matches, albeit with 15 draws.

Scunthorpe also performed a lot better against teams in the top half, suggesting they could thrive at a higher level.

Longest run without win/loss: 5/28
High/low league position: 1/13
Clean sheets: 21 **Yellows:** 49 **Reds:** 2
Avg attendance: 4,109 **Players used:** 30
Leading scorer: S Winnall 23 (12,20)
Key stat: Scunthorpe led at half-time in 19 matches last season, two more than any other League 2 team

	2013-14 H	A	Last six seasons at home P	W	D	L	OV	UN	BS	CS
Doncaster			3	0	1	2	3	0	3	0
Barnsley			2	1	1	0	1	1	1	1
Yeovil			3	2	0	1	2	1	1	1
Leyton Orient			3	2	0	1	3	0	3	0
Preston			4	1	1	2	3	1	3	0
Peterborough			2	2	0	0	1	1	0	2
Sheffield United			4	2	2	0	2	2	4	0
Swindon			2	1	1	0	2	0	2	0
Port Vale			-	-	-	-	-	-	-	-
MK Dons			3	0	0	3	2	1	0	0
Bradford			-	-	-	-	-	-	-	-
Bristol City			2	1	0	1	1	1	0	1
Walsall			3	0	2	1	0	3	2	0
Crawley Town			1	1	0	0	1	0	1	0
Oldham			3	1	1	2	1	2	2	1
Colchester			3	2	1	0	1	2	1	2
Gillingham			-	-	-	-	-	-	-	-
Coventry			3	1	0	2	1	2	1	1
Crewe			2	1	0	1	2	0	1	1
Notts County			2	0	2	0	1	1	1	1
Chesterfield	D	D	2	0	2	0	1	1	2	0
Scunthorpe										
Rochdale	W	W	2	2	0	0	1	1	0	2
Fleetwood Town	D	W	1	0	1	0	0	1	0	1

Season	Division	Pos	P	W	D	L	F	A	GD	Pts
2013-14	League 2	2	46	20	21	5	68	44	+24	81
2012-13	League 1	21	46	13	9	24	49	73	-24	48
2011-12	League 1	18	46	10	22	14	55	59	-4	52

Over/Under 35%/65% 21st   **Both score** 48%/52% 13th

SHEFFIELD UTD

Nickname: The Blades
Colours: Red and white
Ground: Bramall Lane (32,609)
Tel: 0871-222-1899   www.sufc.co.uk

United start 2014-15 as title favourites following a remarkable transformation under Nigel Clough last season.

The Blades had taken just nine points from 13 matches when Clough replaced David Weir, but they steadily picked up to finish seventh, reaching the semi-finals of the FA Cup and ending the campaign unbeaten in eight in the league.

The worry is they still don't score many goals, but even so they will surely be in the thick of the promotion battle.

Longest run without win/loss: 10/8
High/low league position: 7/24
Clean sheets: 17 **Yellows:** 55 **Reds:** 2
Avg attendance: 11,842 **Players used:** 39
Leading scorer: C Porter 7 (3,7)
Key stat: Sheffield United lost 12 of the 13 games in which they conceded more than one goal last term

	2013-14 H	A	Last six seasons at home P	W	D	L	OV	UN	BS	CS
Doncaster			4	0	3	1	1	3	2	1
Barnsley			3	1	2	0	2	1	2	1
Yeovil			2	1	0	1	1	1	0	1
Leyton Orient	D	D	3	1	2	0	1	2	2	1
Preston	L	D	6	4	1	1	1	5	1	4
Peterborough	W	D	2	2	0	0	0	2	0	2
Sheffield United										
Swindon	W	L	2	2	0	0	0	2	0	2
Port Vale	W	W	1	1	0	0	1	0	1	0
MK Dons	L	W	3	1	1	1	1	2	1	1
Bradford	D	L	1	0	1	0	1	0	1	0
Bristol City	W	W	4	4	0	0	3	1	1	3
Walsall	D	L	3	2	1	0	1	2	2	1
Crawley Town	D	W	2	0	1	0	2	1	0	0
Oldham	D	D	3	0	2	1	1	2	3	0
Colchester	D	W	3	2	1	0	2	1	1	2
Gillingham	L	L	1	0	0	1	1	0	1	0
Coventry	W	L	5	2	1	2	2	3	3	1
Crewe	W	L	2	1	1	0	2	0	2	0
Notts County	W	L	3	2	1	0	2	1	3	0
Chesterfield			1	1	0	0	1	0	1	0
Scunthorpe			4	2	0	2	3	1	1	1
Rochdale			1	1	0	0	1	0	0	1
Fleetwood Town										

Season	Division	Pos	P	W	D	L	F	A	GD	Pts
2013-14	League 1	7	46	18	13	15	48	46	+2	67
2012-13	League 1	5	46	19	18	9	56	42	+14	75
2011-12	League 1	3	46	27	9	10	92	51	+41	90

Over/Under 35%/65% 21st   **Both score** 46%/54% 20th

SWINDON

Nickname: The Robins
Colours: Red and white
Ground: County Ground (14,983)
Tel: 0871-423-6433 www.swindontownfc.co.uk

Few clubs have suffered greater upheaval off the pitch than Swindon in the last 18 months and this summer saw a courtroom battle to decide on the club's ownership.

Through it all, Mark Cooper, who only became manager last July, did a superb job to steer Swindon to eighth, helped by six wins in their last nine matches.

However, the end of a link-up with Tottenham that came about through Tim Sherwood means they are unlikely to do so well in the loan market.

Longest run without win/loss: 7/4
High/low league position: 7/13
Clean sheets: 11 **Yellows:** 88 **Reds:** 7
Avg attendance: 7,497 **Players used:** 34
Leading scorer: D N'Guessan 8 (2,8)
N Ranger 8 (3, 8)
Key stat: Swindon got a greater proportion of their goals last season against top-half teams

	2013-14 H	A	Last six seasons at home P	W	D	L	OV	UN	BS	CS
Doncaster			1	0	1	0	0	1	1	0
Barnsley			-	-	-	-	-	-	-	-
Yeovil			4	2	0	2	3	1	3	0
Leyton Orient	L	L	5	1	1	3	3	2	3	0
Preston	W	L	2	1	1	0	0	2	1	1
Peterborough	W	L	3	1	2	0	2	1	3	0
Sheffield United	W	L	2	1	1	0	1	1	1	1
Swindon										
Port Vale	W	W	2	2	0	0	2	0	1	1
MK Dons	L	D	5	1	2	2	1	4	2	2
Bradford	W	D	1	1	0	0	2	0	2	0
Bristol City	W	D	1	1	0	0	1	0	2	0
Walsall	L	D	5	1	3	1	3	2	4	1
Crawley Town	D	D	3	2	1	0	2	1	1	2
Oldham	L	L	5	1	2	1	2	1	4	2
Colchester	D	W	5	1	2	2	2	3	3	1
Gillingham	D	L	3	2	1	0	2	1	2	1
Coventry	W	W	2	1	1	0	2	0	2	0
Crewe	W	D	4	3	1	0	3	1	1	3
Notts County	W	L	3	1	1	1	1	2	1	2
Chesterfield			-	-	-	-	-	-	-	-
Scunthorpe			2	1	1	0	1	1	2	0
Rochdale			1	0	1	0	0	1	1	0
Fleetwood Town			-	-	-	-	-	-	-	-

Season	Division	Pos	P	W	D	L	F	A	GD	Pts
2013-14	League 1	8	46	19	9	18	63	59	+4	66
2012-13	League 1	6	46	20	14	12	72	39	+33	74
2011-12	League 2	1	46	29	6	11	75	32	+43	90

Over/Under 50%/50% 11th   **Both score** 57%/43% 6th

WALSALL

Nickname: The Saddlers
Colours: Red and white
Ground: Banks's Stadium (10,989)
Tel: 0871-221-0442   www.saddlers.co.uk

Walsall have flourished under Dean Smith, but there will always be limits for a club of their modest means and so it proved last season.

Finishing ninth in 2013 put Walsall's players in the shop window, and it proved impossible to replace the 31 goals of strike pair Will Grigg and Jamie Paterson, who both left last summer.

They finished on a run of just two wins in 18 matches and a difficult summer suggests they face a relegation scrap.

Longest run without win/loss: 10/7
High/low league position: 6/14
Clean sheets: 11 **Yellows:** 41 **Reds:** 5
Avg attendance: 5,181 **Players used:** 22
Leading scorer: C Westcarr 14 (4,11)
Key stat: Walsall were unbeaten in 19 matches in which they scored the first goal last season

	2013-14 H	A	Last six seasons at home P	W	D	L	OV	UN	BS	CS
Doncaster			1	0	0	1	1	0	0	0
Barnsley			-	-	-	-	-	-	-	-
Yeovil			5	1	2	2	1	4	2	1
Leyton Orient	D	D	6	1	2	3	2	4	3	1
Preston	L	L	3	2	0	1	2	1	1	1
Peterborough	W	D	3	1	0	2	2	1	2	1
Sheffield United	W	D	3	2	1	0	2	1	3	0
Swindon	D	W	5	1	2	2	2	3	4	0
Port Vale	L	L	1	0	0	1	0	1	0	0
MK Dons	L	L	6	2	0	4	4	2	2	1
Bradford	L	W	1	0	0	1	0	1	0	0
Bristol City	L	L	1	0	0	1	0	1	0	0
Walsall										
Crawley Town	L	D	2	0	1	1	2	0	2	0
Oldham	W	W	6	3	1	2	3	3	3	2
Colchester	L	D	6	4	0	2	1	5	1	3
Gillingham	D	D	2	0	2	0	0	2	1	1
Coventry	L	L	2	1	0	1	1	1	0	1
Crewe	D	W	3	0	3	0	1	2	3	0
Notts County	D	W	4	0	2	2	1	3	2	0
Chesterfield			1	1	0	0	1	0	1	0
Scunthorpe			3	1	1	1	3	0	3	0
Rochdale			2	0	2	0	0	2	0	2
Fleetwood Town			-	-	-	-	-	-	-	-

Season	Division	Pos	P	W	D	L	F	A	GD	Pts
2013-14	League 1	13	46	14	16	16	49	49	0	58
2012-13	League 1	9	46	17	17	12	65	58	+7	68
2011-12	League 1	19	46	10	20	16	51	57	-6	50

Over/Under 30%/70% 24th   **Both score** 50%/50% 16th

YEOVIL

Nickname: The Glovers
Colours: Green and white
Ground: Huish Park (9,565)
Tel: 01935-423-662   www.ytfc.net

Playoff winners in 2013, Yeovil were well out of their depth in the Championship.

A falling out with Paddy Madden, whose goals had earned promotion, didn't help and the Glovers finished with one win in their last 13 games.

Only seven teams in the last 21 years have gone down from the Championship with fewer than Yeovil's 37 points and, as the average finishing position of all relegated teams has been 11th in that time, they'll do well to hold their own.

Longest run without win/loss: 11/5
High/low league position: 21/24
Clean sheets: 9 **Yellows:** 84 **Reds:** 4
Avg attendance: 11,470 **Players used:** 35
Leading scorer: I Miller 10 (4,8)
Key stat: Yeovil picked up just three points after conceding the first goal last season, the poorest return of any Championship club

	2013-14 H	A	Last six seasons at home P	W	D	L	OV	UN	BS	CS
Doncaster	W	L	2	2	0	0	1	1	1	1
Barnsley	L	D	1	0	0	1	1	0	1	0
Yeovil										
Leyton Orient			5	2	3	0	4	1	3	2
Preston			2	2	0	0	2	0	2	0
Peterborough			2	0	0	2	0	2	0	0
Sheffield United			2	0	0	2	0	2	0	0
Swindon			4	1	1	2	1	3	1	1
Port Vale			-	-	-	-	-	-	-	-
MK Dons			5	3	1	1	1	4	1	3
Bradford			-	-	-	-	-	-	-	-
Bristol City			-	-	-	-	-	-	-	-
Walsall			5	1	3	1	2	3	4	1
Crawley Town			1	0	1	0	1	0	1	0
Oldham			5	3	2	0	4	1	4	1
Colchester			5	3	0	2	3	2	3	0
Gillingham			1	0	1	0	0	1	0	1
Coventry			1	0	1	0	0	1	1	0
Crewe			2	2	0	0	1	1	1	1
Notts County			3	2	1	0	1	2	1	2
Chesterfield			1	1	0	0	1	0	1	0
Scunthorpe			3	1	1	1	3	0	2	1
Rochdale			2	1	0	1	1	1	1	0
Fleetwood Town			-	-	-	-	-	-	-	-

Season	Division	Pos	P	W	D	L	F	A	GD	Pts
2013-14	Championship	24	46	8	13	25	44	75	-31	37
2012-13	League 1	4	46	23	8	15	71	56	+15	77
2011-12	League 1	17	46	14	12	20	59	80	-21	54

Over/Under 48%/52% 13th   **Both score** 54%/46% 10th

League 1 stats 2013-14

Key Points in all tables (except the league table) do not include any deductions imposed by the league.
POS H A Overall league position, rank from home games only, rank from away games only **Sup** Average match supremacy **GFA** Goals For Average **GAA** Goals Against Average **PGA** Points Gained Average

League table 2013-14

Pos	H	A		P	Home W	D	L	F	A	Away W	D	L	F	A	GD	Pts
1	2	1	Wolves	46	17	4	2	48	15	14	6	3	41	16	+58	103 (C)
2	1	5	Brentford	46	19	1	3	44	17	9	9	5	28	26	+29	94 (P)
3	7	3	Leyton Orient	46	13	3	7	43	23	12	8	3	42	22	+40	86
4	9	2	Rotherham	46	10	10	3	44	30	14	4	5	42	28	+28	86 (P)
5	3	4	Preston	46	12	9	2	44	26	11	7	5	28	20	+26	85
6	5	8	Peterborough	46	14	3	6	34	21	9	2	12	38	37	+14	74
7	6	14	Sheff Utd	46	12	7	4	31	18	6	6	11	17	28	+2	67
8	4	16	Swindon	46	14	3	6	40	27	5	6	12	23	32	+4	66
9	8	19	Port Vale	46	13	3	7	35	30	5	4	14	24	43	-14	61
10	18	6	MK Dons	46	8	5	10	29	30	9	4	10	34	35	-2	60
11	14	12	Bradford	46	8	9	6	35	27	6	8	9	22	27	+3	59
12	15	9	Bristol C	46	7	10	6	34	28	6	9	8	36	39	+3	58
13	20	7	Walsall	46	7	7	9	21	28	7	9	7	28	21	0	58
14	11	18	Crawley	46	10	7	6	24	23	4	8	11	24	31	-6	57
15	19	10	Oldham	46	7	8	8	23	28	7	6	10	27	31	-9	56
16	17	13	Colchester	46	8	5	10	29	29	5	9	9	24	32	-8	53
17	12	20	Gillingham	46	10	5	8	35	31	5	3	15	25	48	-19	53
18	13	11	Coventry	46	9	8	6	41	39	7	5	11	33	38	-3	51
19	21	15	Crewe	46	7	7	9	26	34	6	5	12	28	46	-26	51
20	10	24	Notts Co	46	12	2	9	40	28	3	3	17	24	49	-13	50
21	23	17	Tranmere	46	6	8	9	30	39	6	3	14	22	40	-27	47 (R)
22	16	23	Carlisle	46	8	6	9	27	32	3	6	14	16	44	-33	45 (R)
23	24	21	Shrewsbury	46	6	7	10	22	28	3	8	12	22	37	-21	42 (R)
24	22	22	Stevenage	46	7	5	11	29	34	4	4	15	17	38	-26	42 (R)

Coventry deducted 10pts

Best attack

		GF	GFA
1	Wolves	89	1.93
2	Rotherham	86	1.87
3	Leyton Orient	85	1.85
4	Coventry	74	1.61
5	Brentford	72	1.57
6	Preston	72	1.57
7	Peterborough	72	1.57
8	Bristol C	70	1.52
9	Notts Co	64	1.39
10	Swindon	63	1.37
11	MK Dons	63	1.37
12	Gillingham	60	1.30
13	Port Vale	59	1.28
14	Bradford	57	1.24
15	Crewe	54	1.17
16	Colchester	53	1.15
17	Tranmere	52	1.13
18	Oldham	50	1.09
19	Walsall	49	1.07
20	Sheff Utd	48	1.04
21	Crawley	48	1.04
22	Stevenage	46	1.00
23	Shrewsbury	44	0.96
24	Carlisle	43	0.93

Best defence

		GA	GAA
1	Wolves	31	0.67
2	Brentford	43	0.93
3	Leyton Orient	45	0.98
4	Preston	46	1.00
5	Sheff Utd	46	1.00
6	Walsall	49	1.07
7	Bradford	54	1.17
8	Crawley	54	1.17
9	Rotherham	58	1.26
10	Peterborough	58	1.26
11	Swindon	59	1.28
12	Oldham	59	1.28
13	Colchester	61	1.33
14	MK Dons	65	1.41
15	Shrewsbury	65	1.41
16	Bristol C	67	1.46
17	Stevenage	72	1.57
18	Port Vale	73	1.59
19	Carlisle	76	1.65
20	Coventry	77	1.67
21	Notts Co	77	1.67
22	Gillingham	79	1.72
23	Tranmere	79	1.72
24	Crewe	80	1.74

Top scorers

	Team	Goals scored	
S Baldock	Bristol C	24	IIIIIIIIIIIIIIIIIIIIIIII
B Assombalonga	Peterborough	23	IIIIIIIIIIIIIIIIIIIIIII
K Agard	Rotherham	21	IIIIIIIIIIIIIIIIIIIII
C Wilson	Coventry	21	IIIIIIIIIIIIIIIIIIIII
R Lowe	Tranmere	19	IIIIIIIIIIIIIIIIIII
D Mooney	Leyton Orient	19	IIIIIIIIIIIIIIIIIII

Over 2.5 goals

	H	A	%
Coventry	16	15	67%
Rotherham	16	13	63%
Crewe	14	14	61%
Gillingham	11	17	61%
Bristol C, MK Dons			59%

Under 2.5 goals

	H	A	%
Walsall	16	16	70%
Crawley Town	15	15	65%
Oldham	16	14	65%
Sheff Utd	15	15	65%
Shrewsbury	16	12	61%

Both to score

	H	A	%
Bristol C	16	19	76%
Coventry	16	16	70%
Gillingham	14	16	65%
Leyton Orient	12	17	63%
Tranmere	16	11	59%

Both not to score

	H	A	%
Wolves	16	13	63%
Brentford	14	12	57%
Peterborough	14	12	57%
Sheff Utd	11	14	54%
Stevenage	10	15	54%

Results 2013-14

	Bradford	Brentford	Bristol C	Carlisle	Colchester	Coventry	Crawley	Crewe	Gillingham	Leyton Orient	MK Dons	Notts Co	Oldham	Peterborough	Port Vale	Preston	Rotherham	Sheff Utd	Shrewsbury	Stevenage	Swindon	Tranmere	Walsall	Wolves
Bradford		4-0	1-1	4-0	2-2	3-3	2-1	3-3	1-1	1-1	1-0	1-1	2-3	1-0	1-0	0-0	0-1	2-0	2-1	2-3	1-1	0-1	0-2	1-2
Brentford	2-0		3-1	0-0	3-1	3-1	1-0	5-0	2-1	0-2	3-1	3-1	1-0	3-2	2-0	1-0	0-1	3-1	1-0	2-0	3-2	2-0	1-0	0-3
Bristol C	2-2	1-2		2-1	1-1	1-2	2-0	0-0	2-1	2-2	2-2	2-1	1-1	0-3	5-0	1-1	1-2	0-1	1-1	4-1	0-0	2-2	1-0	1-2
Carlisle	1-0	0-0	2-4		2-4	0-4	1-1	2-1	1-2	1-5	3-0	2-1	0-1	2-1	0-1	0-1	1-2	1-0	0-0	0-0	1-0	4-1	1-1	2-2
Colchester	0-2	4-1	2-2	1-1		2-1	1-1	1-2	3-0	1-2	3-1	0-4	0-1	1-0	1-0	1-2	0-0	0-1	1-0	4-0	1-2	1-2	1-1	0-3
Coventry	0-0	0-2	5-4	1-2	2-0		2-2	2-2	2-1	3-1	1-2	3-0	1-1	4-2	2-2	4-4	0-3	3-2	0-0	1-0	1-2	1-5	2-1	1-1
Crawley	1-0	0-1	1-1	0-0	1-0	3-2		1-2	3-2	2-1	0-2	1-0	1-0	1-0	0-3	2-2	1-2	0-2	1-1	1-1	0-0	2-0	0-0	2-1
Crewe	0-0	1-3	1-0	2-1	0-0	1-2	1-0		0-3	1-2	2-0	1-3	1-1	2-2	1-2	2-1	3-3	3-0	1-1	0-3	1-1	2-0	1-0	0-2
Gillingham	0-1	1-1	1-1	1-0	0-1	4-2	1-0	1-3		1-2	3-2	2-1	0-1	2-2	3-2	1-2	3-4	0-1	1-1	3-2	2-0	2-0	2-2	1-0
Leyton Orient	0-1	0-1	1-3	4-0	2-1	2-0	2-3	2-0	5-1		2-1	5-1	1-1	1-2	3-2	0-1	1-0	1-1	3-0	2-0	2-0	2-0	1-1	1-3
MK Dons	2-3	2-2	2-2	0-1	0-0	1-3	0-2	1-0	0-1	1-3		3-1	2-1	0-2	3-0	0-0	3-2	0-1	3-2	4-1	1-1	0-1	1-0	0-1
Notts Co	3-0	0-1	1-1	4-1	2-0	3-0	1-0	4-0	3-1	0-0	1-3		3-2	2-4	4-2	0-1	0-1	2-1	2-3	0-1	2-0	2-0	1-5	0-1
Oldham	1-1	0-0	1-1	1-0	0-2	0-0	1-0	1-1	1-1	1-2	1-1	1-1		5-4	3-1	1-3	0-2	1-1	1-2	1-0	2-1	0-1	0-1	0-3
Peterborough	2-1	1-3	1-2	4-1	2-0	1-0	0-2	4-2	2-0	1-3	2-1	4-3	2-1		0-0	2-0	0-0	0-0	1-0	0-1	1-0	3-0	0-0	1-0
Port Vale	2-1	1-1	1-1	2-1	2-0	3-2	2-1	1-3	2-1	0-2	1-0	2-1	1-0	0-1		0-2	2-0	1-2	3-1	2-2	2-3	3-2	1-0	1-3
Preston	2-2	0-3	1-0	6-1	1-1	1-1	1-0	0-2	3-1	1-1	2-2	2-0	2-1	3-1	3-2		3-3	0-0	5-2	3-0	2-1	1-1	2-1	0-0
Rotherham	0-0	3-0	2-1	0-0	2-2	1-3	2-2	4-2	4-1	2-1	2-2	6-0	3-2	0-1	1-0	0-0		3-1	2-2	2-1	0-4	1-1	1-1	3-3
Sheff Utd	2-2	0-0	3-0	1-0	1-1	2-1	1-1	3-1	1-2	1-1	0-1	2-1	1-1	2-0	2-1	0-1	1-0		2-0	1-0	1-0	3-1	1-1	0-2
Shrewsbury	2-1	1-1	2-2	1-0	1-1	1-1	1-3	2-0	0-0	0-1	1-2	2-4	0-0	0-1	0-3	2-0	1-0	2-0		0-1	1-0	0-1		
Stevenage	1-1	2-1	1-3	1-3	2-3	0-1	2-0	1-0	3-1	2-1	0-1	2-3	0-1	3-4	0-1	1-1	1-1	0-3	0-0		1-3	2-0	3-1	3-2
Swindon	1-0	1-0	3-2	3-1	0-0	2-1	1-1	5-0	2-2	1-3	1-2	2-0	0-1	2-1	5-2	1-0	1-2	2-1	3-1	1-0		1-0	1-3	1-4
Tranmere	1-2	3-4	1-1	0-0	2-1	3-1	3-3	1-0	1-2	0-4	3-2	3-2	2-2	0-5	0-1	1-2	1-2	0-0	2-1	0-0	1-2		1-1	1-1
Walsall	0-2	1-1	0-1	2-0	0-1	0-1	1-2	1-1	1-1	1-1	0-3	1-1	1-0	2-0	0-2	0-3	1-1	2-1	1-0	2-1	1-1	3-1		0-3
Wolves	2-0	0-0	3-1	3-0	4-2	1-1	2-1	2-0	4-0	1-1	0-2	2-0	2-0	2-0	3-0	2-0	6-4	2-0	0-0	2-0	3-2	2-0	0-1	

Record when first to score

		P	W	D	L	F	A	Sup	PGA	Pts
1	Wolves	35	29	5	1	80	20	+1.71	2.6	92
2	Brentford	30	25	4	1	61	20	+1.37	2.6	79
3	Preston	29	22	7	0	61	25	+1.24	2.5	73
4	Rotherham	26	21	3	2	60	27	+1.27	2.5	66
5	Leyton Orient	27	19	6	2	61	18	+1.59	2.3	63
6	Peterborough	24	18	1	5	47	23	+1.00	2.3	55
7	Swindon	23	16	4	3	46	22	+1.04	2.3	52
8	Sheff Utd	22	16	3	3	34	15	+0.86	2.3	51
9	Gillingham	21	14	4	3	38	22	+0.76	2.2	46
10	Walsall	19	13	6	0	33	10	+1.21	2.4	45
11	MK Dons	18	14	2	2	39	18	+1.17	2.4	44
12	Crewe	23	12	7	4	45	32	+0.57	1.9	43
13	Port Vale	20	13	3	4	36	22	+0.70	2.1	42
14	Bradford	21	12	6	3	36	18	+0.86	2.0	42
15	Coventry	21	13	3	5	43	29	+0.67	2.0	42
16	Colchester	19	12	5	2	35	16	+1.00	2.2	41
17	Bristol C	20	11	8	1	42	23	+0.95	2.1	41
18	Oldham	20	11	8	1	26	15	+0.55	2.1	41
19	Notts Co	19	13	1	5	46	22	+1.26	2.1	40
20	Crawley	18	11	5	2	28	16	+0.67	2.1	38
21	Tranmere	14	11	2	1	25	11	+1.00	2.5	35
22	Stevenage	16	9	2	5	31	22	+0.56	1.8	29
23	Carlisle	14	8	3	3	23	14	+0.64	1.9	27
24	Shrewsbury	14	6	5	3	21	16	+0.36	1.6	23

Record when keeping a clean sheet

		P	W	D	F	Sup	PGA	Pts
1	Gillingham	7	7	0	11	+1.57	3.0	21
2	Leyton Orient	14	13	1	29	+2.07	2.9	40
3	Notts Co	10	9	1	22	+2.20	2.8	28
4	Wolves	25	21	4	47	+1.88	2.7	67
5	Peterborough	17	14	3	26	+1.53	2.6	45
6	Walsall	11	9	2	14	+1.27	2.6	29
7	Port Vale	11	9	2	14	+1.27	2.6	29
8	Oldham	10	8	2	8	+0.80	2.6	26
9	Brentford	20	15	5	26	+1.30	2.5	50
10	Rotherham	15	11	4	25	+1.67	2.5	37
11	Swindon	11	8	3	16	+1.45	2.5	27
12	Crawley	11	8	3	11	+1.00	2.5	27
13	Sheff Utd	17	12	5	17	+1.00	2.4	41
14	Preston	16	11	5	17	+1.06	2.4	38
15	Bradford	14	10	4	19	+1.36	2.4	34
16	MK Dons	10	7	3	13	+1.30	2.4	24
17	Colchester	12	8	4	14	+1.17	2.3	28
18	Coventry	9	6	3	12	+1.33	2.3	21
19	Crewe	8	5	3	9	+1.13	2.3	18
20	Tranmere	8	5	3	5	+0.63	2.3	18
21	Bristol C	6	4	2	9	+1.50	2.3	14
22	Stevenage	10	6	4	10	+1.00	2.2	22
23	Shrewsbury	10	5	5	8	+0.80	2.0	20
24	Carlisle	12	5	7	7	+0.58	1.8	22

Bury possess the creative talents to make their mark on the League 2 title picture

Promotion from the Conference ended five years of pain for Luton and they will be hoping that last season's success proves the catalyst for a climb back up the league ladder, writes Andy Dietz. Having spent 20 years in the top flight, Luton's decline, which was accelerated by points deductions due to financial problems, has been well documented, but the state of depression at Kenilworth Road has been replaced by a tide of optimism.

The bookmakers have earmarked the Hatters as one of the division's front-runners and the omens are good as three teams coming up from the Conference in the last six seasons have gained back-to-back promotions.

Manager John Still has proven pedigree at this level and Luton should be in the mix, but it might be best to look elsewhere for the title winners.

Portsmouth and **Bury** are also prominent in the betting and, while Bury are a small club in comparison to their main market rivals, they have attracted some big names at this level.

The return of fan favourite Ryan Lowe, who smashed 19 goals for relegated Tranmere in League 1 last season, is the marquee signing that shows they mean business.

The Shakers already have an impressive supply line – they had three of the top ten players with the most assists in League 2 last season – but they have bolstered it still further by securing loan star Danny Mayor on a permanent basis and enticing back another former favourite in Nicky Adams, who can be a real creative force.

Defenders Pablo Mills and Jim McNulty have experience at a higher level, as does manager David Flitcroft, who did a solid enough job in the Championship with Barnsley before being shown the door at Oakwell.

Having taken over in December, Flitcroft turned around Bury's fortunes and made them a tough proposition – they are unbeaten in their last 16 home games.

Another progressive side to consider are **Plymouth**, who could be worth backing on the handicaps.

The Pilgrims were the division's biggest risers last term and, after suffering their fair share of off-the-field problems, they now appear a more settled outfit.

The continued stability should see them improve again and, with average crowds in excess of 7,000, they could start to fulfil their potential.

The relegation betting is wide open with half the league quoted at single-digit prices.

While a case can be made for usual suspects Morecambe and Wycombe, who will be operating on meagre budgets, the value lies with **Hartlepool** at any double-figure prices you can find.

Pools were on the fringes of the playoffs in March but only avoided relegation by three points following an alarming end-of-season slump during which they lost seven of their final nine games.

Manager Colin Cooper refused to attribute the poor finish to the loss of his assistant Craig Hignett but he is going to need all the help he can get in what he describes as a make or break campaign.

Danny Mayor – eight assists last season – has turned his loan from Sheffield Wednesday into a permanent move

ACCRINGTON

Nickname: Stanley
Colours: Red
Ground: Crown Ground (5,070)
Tel: 01254-356-950 www.accringtonstanley.co.uk

A shocking start to the season nearly cost Stanley dear but first-season manager James Beattie settled into the role and got his side out of trouble.

Having taken two points from their first ten games, the board could have been forgiven for panicking but their patience in Beattie ensured a much stronger finish.

Accrington's first league win came as late as October 22, so it was some turnaround by the former England striker and he should benefit for the experience.

Longest run without win/loss: 12/8
High/low league position: 14/24
Clean sheets: 11 **Yellows:** 66 **Reds:** 4
Avg attendance: 2,926 **Players used:** 29
Leading scorer: K Naismith 10 (1,8)
Key stat: Stanley were drawing 23 league games at half-time but converted only four of them into wins

	2013-14 H	A	P	W	D	L	OV	UN	BS	CS
							Last six seasons at home			
Tranmere			-	-	-	-	-	-	-	-
Carlisle			-	-	-	-	-	-	-	-
Shrewsbury			4	1	1	2	3	1	4	0
Stevenage			1	1	0	0	0	1	0	1
Southend	D	L	4	1	2	1	2	2	4	0
Burton	L	L	5	2	1	2	3	2	3	0
York	D	D	2	0	1	1	0	2	1	0
Oxford	D	W	4	0	2	2	1	3	0	2
Dag & Red	L	D	5	1	1	3	2	3	1	2
Plymouth	D	D	3	0	2	1	1	2	2	0
Mansfield	D	W	1	0	1	0	0	1	1	0
Bury	D	L	4	1	1	2	2	2	2	2
Portsmouth	D	L	1	0	1	0	1	0	1	0
Newport Co	D	L	1	0	1	0	1	0	1	0
Accrington										
Exeter	L	W	3	1	0	2	3	0	2	0
Cheltenham	L	W	5	1	1	3	3	2	2	1
Morecambe	W	W	6	4	2	0	2	4	4	2
Hartlepool	D	L	1	0	1	0	0	1	0	1
AFC Wimbledon	W	D	3	3	0	0	3	0	2	1
Northampton	L	L	5	2	0	3	4	1	3	0
Wycombe	D	D	4	0	2	2	0	4	2	0
Luton			1	0	1	0	0	1	0	1
Cambridge U			-	-	-	-	-	-	-	-

Season	Division	Pos	P	W	D	L	F	A	GD	Pts
2013-14	League 2	15	46	14	15	17	54	56	-2	57
2012-13	League 2	18	46	14	12	20	51	68	-17	54
2011-12	League 2	14	46	14	15	17	54	66	-12	57

Over/Under 46%/54% 7th   **Both score** 59%/41% 1st

AFC WIMBLEDON

Nickname: The Dons
Colours: Blue and yellow
Ground: Cherry Red Records Stadium (4,850)
Tel: 0208-547-3528   www.afcwimbledon.co.uk

Although well clear of the relegation places, the Dons suffered an almighty scare towards the end of last season as a points deduction hung over them.

In the end, the Football League's decision to take three points off their tally for fielding an ineligible player did not threaten their league status.

Wimbledon started quickly but their form tailed off and manager Neal Ardley has opted to freshen up his squad by releasing some of his established players.

Longest run without win/loss: 7/4
High/low league position: 3/17
Clean sheets: 10 **Yellows:** 73 **Reds:** 4
Avg attendance: 4,207 **Players used:** 30
Leading scorer: M Smith 9 (3,8)
Key stat: Wimbledon gained 30 points from losing positions last season, the second-highest in League 2

	2013-14 H	A	P	W	D	L	OV	UN	BS	CS
							Last six seasons at home			
Tranmere			-	-	-	-	-	-	-	-
Carlisle			-	-	-	-	-	-	-	-
Shrewsbury			1	1	0	0	1	0	1	0
Stevenage			1	0	0	1	1	0	0	0
Southend	L	W	3	0	0	3	2	1	1	0
Burton	W	D	3	2	1	0	2	1	2	1
York	L	W	4	2	0	2	1	3	1	1
Oxford	L	L	4	0	0	4	1	3	0	0
Dag & Red	D	L	3	1	2	0	2	1	3	0
Plymouth	D	W	3	0	2	1	1	2	3	0
Mansfield	D	L	3	2	1	0	1	2	1	2
Bury	L	D	1	0	0	1	0	1	0	0
Portsmouth	W	L	1	1	0	0	1	0	0	1
Newport Co	D	W	2	0	2	0	2	0	2	0
Accrington	D	L	3	0	1	2	1	2	2	0
Exeter	W	L	2	1	1	0	2	0	2	0
Cheltenham	W	L	3	2	1	0	1	3	0	0
Morecambe	L	D	3	1	1	1	1	2	1	1
Hartlepool	W	L	1	1	0	0	1	0	1	0
AFC Wimbledon										
Northampton	L	D	3	0	1	2	1	2	1	0
Wycombe	W	W	2	1	1	0	1	1	1	1
Luton			2	0	2	0	0	2	1	1
Cambridge U			2	1	1	0	1	1	0	2

Season	Division	Pos	P	W	D	L	F	A	GD	Pts
2013-14	League 2	20	46	14	14	18	49	57	-8	53
2012-13	League 2	20	46	14	11	21	54	76	-22	54
2011-12	League 2	16	46	15	9	22	62	78	-16	54

Over/Under 39%/61% 19th   **Both score** 46%/54% 18th

BURTON

Nickname: The Brewers
Colours: Yellow and black
Ground: Pirelli Stadium (6,912)
Tel: 01283-565938   www.burtonalbionfc.co.uk

Another season of admirable consistency returned the Brewers to the playoffs and they went one better than in 2012-13 by reaching the final before falling short.

Manager Gary Rowett is confident the pain of going so close will act as the catalyst to spur his players on this term.

However, having solved his side's defensive issues – the goals against column went down to 42 from 65 in the previous campaign – Rowett now needs to address a chronic lack of goals.

Longest run without win/loss: 4/10
High/low league position: 2/14
Clean sheets: 18 **Yellows:** 59 **Reds:** 5
Avg attendance: 3,558 **Players used:** 29
Leading scorer: B Kee 12 (7,10)
Key stat: No team in League 2 put more shots off target than Burton and only the bottom four scored fewer goals than their 47

	2013-14 H	A	Last six seasons at home P	W	D	L	OV	UN	BS	CS
Tranmere			-	-	-	-	-	-	-	-
Carlisle			-	-	-	-	-	-	-	-
Shrewsbury			3	0	3	0	0	3	2	1
Stevenage			2	1	0	1	0	2	0	1
Southend	**L**	**L**	4	2	0	2	1	3	1	1
Burton										
York	**D**	**D**	3	2	1	0	2	1	3	0
Oxford	**L**	**W**	5	1	2	2	1	4	1	2
Dag & Red	**D**	**L**	4	2	1	1	1	3	3	0
Plymouth	**W**	**W**	3	3	0	0	1	2	1	2
Mansfield	**W**	**D**	2	2	0	0	0	2	0	2
Bury	**D**	**D**	3	0	2	1	2	1	2	1
Portsmouth	**L**	**D**	1	0	0	1	1	0	1	0
Newport Co	**W**	**D**	1	1	0	0	0	1	0	1
Accrington	**W**	**W**	5	2	1	2	1	4	2	1
Exeter	**D**	**W**	2	1	1	0	1	1	2	0
Cheltenham	**W**	**D**	5	3	0	2	3	2	3	1
Morecambe	**L**	**W**	5	4	0	1	4	1	4	0
Hartlepool	**W**	**D**	1	1	0	0	1	0	0	1
AFC Wimbledon	**D**	**L**	3	2	1	0	2	1	3	0
Northampton	**W**	**L**	5	2	2	1	2	3	3	1
Wycombe	**W**	**W**	3	2	0	1	1	2	1	2
Luton			-	-	-	-	-	-	-	-
Cambridge U			1	1	0	0	1	0	1	0

Season	Division	Pos	P	W	D	L	F	A	GD	Pts
2013-14	League 2	6	46	19	15	12	47	42	+5	72
2012-13	League 2	4	46	22	11	13	71	65	+6	76
2011-12	League 2	17	46	14	12	20	54	81	-27	54

Over/Under 26%/74% 26th   **Both score** 41%/59% 23rd

BURY

Nickname: The Shakers
Colours: White and blue
Ground: Gigg Lane (11,313)
Tel: 0161-764-4881   www.buryfc.co.uk

Appointed midway through the season, David Flitcroft oversaw a major upturn in Bury's fortunes as they rose from the relegation places to mid-table.

Some 47 players represented Bury in the league as Flitcroft overhauled his squad, but progress was made and they were unbeaten at home under the new manager.

Bury were the country's most active club in the transfer market last term but it's been quality over quantity this summer.

Longest run without win/loss: 8/7
High/low league position: 10/23
Clean sheets: 16 **Yellows:** 50 **Reds:** 3
Avg attendance: 3,751 **Players used:** 47
Leading scorer: D Nardiello 11 (3,8)
Key stat: Bury had three of the top ten players with the most assists in League 2 last season

	2013-14 H	A	Last six seasons at home P	W	D	L	OV	UN	BS	CS
Tranmere			2	1	0	1	0	2	0	1
Carlisle			2	0	1	1	0	2	1	0
Shrewsbury			4	3	1	0	2	2	2	2
Stevenage			3	2	0	1	2	1	1	2
Southend	**D**	**D**	2	1	1	0	0	2	1	1
Burton	**D**	**D**	3	2	1	0	1	2	0	3
York	**W**	**L**	1	1	0	0	1	0	1	0
Oxford	**D**	**L**	2	1	1	0	1	1	1	1
Dag & Red	**D**	**L**	3	0	3	0	1	2	2	1
Plymouth	**W**	**L**	1	1	0	0	1	0	0	1
Mansfield	**D**	**W**	1	0	1	0	0	1	0	1
Bury										
Portsmouth	**D**	**L**	2	1	1	0	1	1	1	1
Newport Co	**D**	**D**	1	0	1	0	0	1	0	1
Accrington	**W**	**D**	4	3	0	1	2	2	0	3
Exeter	**W**	**D**	3	2	0	1	0	3	0	2
Cheltenham	**W**	**L**	3	1	0	2	2	1	2	0
Morecambe	**L**	**D**	4	2	1	1	1	3	1	2
Hartlepool	**W**	**W**	3	2	0	1	2	1	2	1
AFC Wimbledon	**D**	**W**	1	0	1	0	0	1	1	0
Northampton	**D**	**W**	3	0	3	0	1	2	3	0
Wycombe	**W**	**W**	4	1	1	2	2	2	2	2
Luton			1	0	0	1	1	0	1	0
Cambridge U			-	-	-	-	-	-	-	-

Season	Division	Pos	P	W	D	L	F	A	GD	Pts
2013-14	League 2	12	46	13	20	13	59	51	+8	59
2012-13	League 1	22	46	9	14	23	45	73	-28	41
2011-12	League 1	14	46	15	11	20	60	79	-19	56

Over/Under 50%/50% 2nd   **Both score** 52%/48% 8th

CAMBRIDGE

Nickname: The U's
Colours: Yellow and black
Ground: Abbey Stadium (10,847)
Tel: 01223-566-500   www.cambridge-united.co.uk

Victory over Gateshead in the Conference playoff final returned Cambridge to the Football League after a nine-year exile.

Richard Money's side enjoyed two Wembley wins last term, as they lifted the FA Trophy two months earlier, but it is the second success than means the most.

After starting the campaign unbeaten in 16 games, they nearly blew it with some disappointing end-of-season form but the U's got back on track when it mattered.

Longest run without win/loss: 8/9
High/low league position: 7/20
Clean sheets: 12 **Yellows:** 52 **Reds:** 3
Avg attendance: 2,003 **Players used:** 39
Leading scorer: T Elliott 15 (7,12)
Key stat: Cambridge failed to score in five of their last seven games last season

	2013-14 H	A	Last six seasons at home P	W	D	L	OV	UN	BS	CS
Tranmere			-	-	-	-	-	-	-	-
Carlisle			-	-	-	-	-	-	-	-
Shrewsbury			-	-	-	-	-	-	-	-
Stevenage			2	0	1	1	1	1	2	0
Southend			-	-	-	-	-	-	-	-
Burton			1	1	0	0	0	1	0	1
York			4	2	0	2	1	3	1	1
Oxford			2	0	2	0	0	2	2	0
Dag & Red			-	-	-	-	-	-	-	-
Plymouth			-	-	-	-	-	-	-	-
Mansfield			5	3	0	2	5	0	5	0
Bury			-	-	-	-	-	-	-	-
Portsmouth			-	-	-	-	-	-	-	-
Newport Co			3	0	2	1	0	3	1	1
Accrington			-	-	-	-	-	-	-	-
Exeter			-	-	-	-	-	-	-	-
Cheltenham			-	-	-	-	-	-	-	-
Morecambe			-	-	-	-	-	-	-	-
Hartlepool			-	-	-	-	-	-	-	-
AFC Wimbledon			2	0	1	1	2	0	2	0
Northampton			-	-	-	-	-	-	-	-
Wycombe			-	-	-	-	-	-	-	-
Luton	D	D	5	0	4	1	2	3	4	1
Cambridge U										

Season	Division	Pos	P	W	D	L	F	A	GD	Pts
2013-14	Conference	2	46	23	13	10	72	35	+37	82
2012-13	Conference	14	46	15	14	17	68	69	-1	59
2011-12	Conference	9	46	19	14	13	57	41	+16	71

Over/Under 37%/63% 22nd   **Both score** 37%/63% 22nd

CARLISLE

Nickname: Cumbrians/The Blues
Colours: Blue
Ground: Brunton Park (18,202)
Tel: 01228-526-237   www.carlisleunited.co.uk

Cumbria's only professional club crashed down to the bottom tier for the first time in nine years after a miserable campaign.

Positives are hard to find, particularly when you consider Carlisle capitulated at the business end of the season – they won just one of their final 15 games, none of their closing six and failed to score in their last three.

There was also a notable lack of continuity in the squad as they used the highest number of players in League 1.

Longest run without win/loss: 8/4
High/low league position: 13/22
Clean sheets: 12 **Yellows:** 73 **Reds:** 5
Avg attendance: 5,316 **Players used:** 47
Leading scorer: D Amoo 8 (0,7)
Key stat: Carlisle's 'goals for' tally of 43 was the worst in League 1 last season

	2013-14 H	A	Last six seasons at home P	W	D	L	OV	UN	BS	CS
Tranmere	W	D	6	3	1	2	4	2	2	3
Carlisle										
Shrewsbury	D	D	2	0	2	0	1	1	1	1
Stevenage	D	W	3	2	1	0	1	2	1	2
Southend			2	2	0	0	2	0	2	0
Burton			-	-	-	-	-	-	-	-
York			-	-	-	-	-	-	-	-
Oxford			-	-	-	-	-	-	-	-
Dag & Red			1	0	0	1	0	1	0	0
Plymouth			1	0	1	0	0	1	1	0
Mansfield			-	-	-	-	-	-	-	-
Bury			2	2	0	0	2	0	2	0
Portsmouth			1	1	0	0	1	0	1	0
Newport Co			-	-	-	-	-	-	-	-
Accrington			-	-	-	-	-	-	-	-
Exeter			3	1	1	1	2	1	2	0
Cheltenham			1	1	0	0	0	1	0	1
Morecambe			-	-	-	-	-	-	-	-
Hartlepool			5	3	0	2	3	2	2	2
AFC Wimbledon			-	-	-	-	-	-	-	-
Northampton			1	0	1	0	0	1	1	0
Wycombe			2	1	1	0	1	1	1	1
Luton			-	-	-	-	-	-	-	-
Cambridge U			-	-	-	-	-	-	-	-

Season	Division	Pos	P	W	D	L	F	A	GD	Pts
2013-14	League 1	22	46	11	12	23	43	76	-33	45
2012-13	League 1	17	46	14	13	19	56	77	-21	55
2011-12	League 1	8	46	18	15	13	65	66	-1	69

Over/Under 54%/46% 9th   **Both score** 50%/50% 16th

CHELTENHAM

Nickname: The Robins
Colours: Red and white
Ground: The Abbey Business Stadium (7,133)
Tel: 01242-573-558   www.ctfc.com

The Robins suffered an alarming decline last season, tumbling down the league having contested the playoffs in the previous two campaigns.

No League 2 side lost more points from winning positions, and a wretched season reached a nadir in April when two players admitted to manager Mark Yates in training that they had "not been trying".

It looks a big challenge for Yates to address the issues within his squad and rediscover his side's consistency.

Longest run without win/loss: 7/11
High/low league position: 10/22
Clean sheets: 14 **Yellows:** 55 **Reds:** 0
Avg attendance: 3,412 **Players used:** 30
Leading scorer: B Harrison 13 (7,13)
Key stat: Cheltenham lost a staggering seven league games from a winning position

	2013-14 H	A	Last six seasons at home P	W	D	L	OV	UN	BS	CS
Tranmere			1	1	0	0	0	1	0	1
Carlisle			1	0	1	0	0	1	1	0
Shrewsbury			3	0	1	2	1	2	1	1
Stevenage			1	1	0	0	0	1	0	1
Southend	L	D	5	1	1	3	3	2	2	2
Burton	D	L	5	3	1	1	2	3	2	2
York	D	L	2	0	2	0	1	1	2	0
Oxford	D	D	4	1	3	0	2	2	3	1
Dag & Red	L	W	4	2	1	1	2	2	3	1
Plymouth	L	D	3	2	0	1	3	0	3	0
Mansfield	L	W	1	0	0	1	1	0	1	0
Bury	W	L	3	2	0	1	2	1	2	0
Portsmouth	D	D	1	0	1	0	1	0	1	0
Newport Co	D	W	1	0	1	0	0	1	0	1
Accrington	L	W	5	1	1	3	4	1	4	0
Exeter	W	D	2	2	0	0	1	1	0	2
Cheltenham										
Morecambe	W	W	5	3	1	1	2	3	2	3
Hartlepool	D	W	2	1	1	0	1	1	1	1
AFC Wimbledon	W	L	3	2	1	0	1	2	1	2
Northampton	D	D	6	2	3	1	2	4	3	2
Wycombe	D	W	3	1	1	1	2	1	2	1
Luton			-	-	-	-	-	-	-	-
Cambridge U			-	-	-	-	-	-	-	-

Season	Division	Pos	P	W	D	L	F	A	GD	Pts
2013-14	League 2	17	46	13	16	17	53	63	-10	55
2012-13	League 2	5	46	20	15	11	58	51	+7	75
2011-12	League 2	6	46	23	8	15	66	50	+16	77

Over/Under 46%/54% 7th   **Both score** 59%/41% 1st

DAG & RED

Nickname: Daggers
Colours: Red and white
Ground: LB of Barking & Dag Stadium (6,070)
Tel: 020-8592-1549   www.daggers.co.uk

A top-ten finish represents significant improvement for the Daggers after two seasons flirting with relegation.

With the second-lowest crowds in League 2 and an inexperienced manager at the helm, there was a palpable sense of anxiety going into the season.

However, Wayne Burnett reversed a poor set of results as interim boss and brought a fresh approach in his first full season, and Dagenham achieved their third-best Football League points tally.

Longest run without win/loss: 5/8
High/low league position: 7/15
Clean sheets: 11 **Yellows:** 67 **Reds:** 3
Avg attendance: 2,975 **Players used:** 31
Leading scorer: R Murphy 13 (4,13)
Key stat: The Daggers did not lose a league game when they scored first last season, winning 13 and drawing four

	2013-14 H	A	Last six seasons at home P	W	D	L	OV	UN	BS	CS
Tranmere			1	0	1	0	1	0	1	0
Carlisle			1	1	0	0	1	0	0	1
Shrewsbury			3	1	0	2	2	1	1	1
Stevenage			-	-	-	-	-	-	-	-
Southend	D	W	3	0	1	2	2	1	2	0
Burton	W	D	4	2	2	0	1	3	3	1
York	W	L	2	1	0	1	0	2	0	1
Oxford	W	L	3	1	0	2	0	3	0	1
Dag & Red										
Plymouth	L	L	4	0	1	3	2	2	2	1
Mansfield	D	L	1	0	1	0	0	1	0	1
Bury	W	D	3	2	0	1	3	0	3	0
Portsmouth	L	L	1	0	0	1	1	0	1	0
Newport Co	D	W	1	0	1	0	0	1	1	0
Accrington	D	W	5	2	3	0	2	3	3	2
Exeter	D	D	4	0	3	1	1	3	4	0
Cheltenham	L	W	4	1	0	3	2	2	1	1
Morecambe	D	D	5	0	2	3	2	3	4	0
Hartlepool	L	L	2	0	1	1	0	2	1	0
AFC Wimbledon	W	D	3	1	0	2	0	3	0	1
Northampton	L	D	4	0	0	4	1	3	0	0
Wycombe	W	L	3	2	0	1	1	2	0	2
Luton			1	1	0	0	0	1	0	1
Cambridge U			-	-	-	-	-	-	-	-

Season	Division	Pos	P	W	D	L	F	A	GD	Pts
2013-14	League 2	9	46	15	15	16	53	59	-6	60
2012-13	League 2	22	46	13	12	21	55	62	-7	51
2011-12	League 2	19	46	14	8	24	50	72	-22	50

Over/Under 43%/57% 9th   **Both score** 59%/41% 1st

EXETER

Nickname: The Grecians
Colours: Red, white and black
Ground: St James' Park (8,830)
Tel: 0871-855-1904   www.exetercityfc.co.uk

After eight years at Exeter, Paul Tisdale is now second only to Arsene Wenger as the longest-serving league manager. But last term was tough for him as, after a bright start, his men battled relegation for the second half of the season, only securing survival in their penultimate match.

There could be another tough year ahead as Tisdale, who blooded plenty of youngsters last season, will not be able to sign any players until August as the club is under a transfer embargo.

Longest run without win/loss: 7/5
High/low league position: 3/21
Clean sheets: 8 **Yellows:** 40 **Reds:** 1
Avg attendance: 4,223 **Players used:** 27
Leading scorer: A Gow 7 (0,6)
Key stat: Exeter gained seven more points on the road than they did at home last season

	2013-14 H	A	Last six seasons at home P	W	D	L	OV	UN	BS	CS
Tranmere			3	2	1	0	2	1	2	1
Carlisle			3	1	1	1	2	1	2	1
Shrewsbury			1	0	0	1	0	1	0	0
Stevenage			1	0	1	0	0	1	1	0
Southend	L	W	3	2	0	1	1	2	0	2
Burton	L	D	2	1	0	1	1	1	0	1
York	W	L	2	1	1	0	1	1	2	0
Oxford	D	D	2	0	1	1	1	1	1	1
Dag & Red	D	D	4	2	1	1	3	1	3	0
Plymouth	W	W	3	2	1	0	1	2	2	1
Mansfield	L	D	1	0	0	1	0	1	0	0
Bury	D	L	3	1	2	0	2	1	2	1
Portsmouth	D	L	1	0	1	0	0	1	1	0
Newport Co	L	D	1	0	0	1	0	1	0	0
Accrington	L	W	3	2	0	1	1	2	1	1
Exeter										
Cheltenham	D	L	2	0	1	1	0	2	1	0
Morecambe	D	L	3	0	2	1	2	1	2	0
Hartlepool	L	W	4	1	1	2	3	1	2	1
AFC Wimbledon	W	L	2	2	0	0	0	2	0	2
Northampton	L	W	2	1	0	1	1	1	0	1
Wycombe	L	D	5	2	1	2	2	3	3	1
Luton			1	0	0	1	0	1	0	0
Cambridge U			-	-	-	-	-	-	-	-

Season	Division	Pos	P	W	D	L	F	A	GD	Pts
2013-14	League 2	16	46	14	13	19	54	57	-3	55
2012-13	League 2	10	46	18	10	18	63	62	+1	64
2011-12	League 1	23	46	10	12	24	46	75	-29	42

Over/Under 43%/57% 9th   **Both score** 54%/46% 7th

HARTLEPOOL

Nickname: Pools
Colours: White and blue
Ground: Victoria Park (7,856)
Tel: 01429-272-584 www.hartlepoolunited.co.uk

Having been within striking distance of the playoffs in March, Pools finished just three points above the bottom two.

The alarming slump followed the exit of assistant manager Craig Hignett to Middlesbrough, with Colin Cooper's side losing seven of their last nine matches.

Cooper has played down the significance of the departure but has readily admitted he is set for a make-or-break campaign in first full-time role as a manager.

Longest run without win/loss: 6/5
High/low league position: 8/22
Clean sheets: 13 **Yellows:** 69 **Reds:** 6
Avg attendance: 3,912 **Players used:** 30
Leading scorer: L James 13 (6,12)
Key stat: Hartlepool gained 20 points on their travels, which was the second-lowest total in League 2

	2013-14 H	A	Last six seasons at home P	W	D	L	OV	UN	BS	CS
Tranmere			5	2	1	2	1	4	2	1
Carlisle			5	2	1	2	5	0	3	1
Shrewsbury			1	0	1	0	1	0	1	0
Stevenage			2	0	1	1	0	2	0	1
Southend	L	D	3	2	0	1	2	1	0	2
Burton	D	L	1	0	1	0	0	1	1	0
York	W	D	1	1	0	0	0	1	0	1
Oxford	L	L	1	0	0	1	1	0	1	0
Dag & Red	W	W	2	1	0	1	1	1	1	0
Plymouth	W	D	2	2	0	0	0	2	0	2
Mansfield	L	W	1	0	0	1	0	1	0	0
Bury	L	L	3	2	0	1	2	1	0	2
Portsmouth	D	L	2	0	2	0	0	2	0	2
Newport Co	W	L	1	1	0	0	1	0	0	1
Accrington	W	D	1	1	0	0	1	0	1	0
Exeter	L	W	4	1	1	2	1	3	2	1
Cheltenham	L	D	2	1	0	1	1	1	1	0
Morecambe	W	W	1	1	0	0	1	0	1	0
Hartlepool										
AFC Wimbledon	W	L	1	1	0	0	1	0	1	0
Northampton	W	L	2	2	0	0	0	2	0	2
Wycombe	L	L	3	0	1	2	2	1	3	0
Luton			-	-	-	-	-	-	-	-
Cambridge U			-	-	-	-	-	-	-	-

Season	Division	Pos	P	W	D	L	F	A	GD	Pts
2013-14	League 2	19	46	14	11	21	50	56	-6	53
2012-13	League 1	23	46	9	14	23	39	67	-28	41
2011-12	League 1	13	46	14	14	18	50	55	-5	56

Over/Under 48%/52% 5th   **Both score** 39%/61% 25th

LUTON

Nickname: The Hatters
Colours: Orange, white and black
Ground: Kenilworth Road (10,226)
Tel: 01582 411 622   www.lutontown.co.uk

The dark cloud hanging over Kenilworth Road has finally lifted, with the Hatters at last escaping the Conference last April.

Five years of pain – exacerbated by a sense of injustice regarding the total of 40 points deducted that saw Luton crash out of the Football League – are at last behind them.

Manager John Still played a pivotal role as his side broke through the 100-point barrier and his knowledge of League 2 is a definite plus.

Longest run without win/loss: 7/5
High/low league position: 2/11
Clean sheets: 12 **Yellows:** 65 **Reds:** 5
Avg attendance: 3,914 **Players used:** 32
Leading scorer: A Gray 17 (3,14)
Key stat: Not only did Luton exceed 100 points last season but they also smashed in 102 goals

MANSFIELD

Nickname: The Stags
Colours: Yellow and blue
Ground: One Call Stadium (8,186)
Tel: 01623-482 482   www.mansfieldtown.net

The Field Mill faithful will be satisfied with their first season back in the Football League but there must be some supporters wondering what might have been. Were it not for a 13-match winless run at the end of 2013, the Stags would have finished a lot higher than the 11th place they eventually secured.

A strong finish offers encouragement, although they need to buck up their ideas on their own patch as only four teams picked up fewer points at home.

Longest run without win/loss: 13/8
High/low league position: 3/20
Clean sheets: 17 **Yellows:** 90 **Reds:** 8
Avg attendance: 3,806 **Players used:** 34
Leading scorer: S Clucas 8 (2,8)
Key stat: Mansfield came back to win just one of the 17 games in which the opposition scored first

	2013-14 H	A	Last six seasons at home P	W	D	L	OV	UN	BS	CS
Tranmere			-	-	-	-	-	-	-	-
Carlisle			-	-	-	-	-	-	-	-
Shrewsbury			1	1	0	0	1	0	1	0
Stevenage			1	0	0	1	0	1	0	0
Southend			-	-	-	-	-	-	-	-
Burton			-	-	-	-	-	-	-	-
York			3	1	1	1	2	1	2	1
Oxford			1	1	0	0	1	0	1	0
Dag & Red			1	1	0	0	1	0	1	0
Plymouth			-	-	-	-	-	-	-	-
Mansfield			4	2	1	1	2	2	2	2
Bury			1	0	0	1	1	0	1	0
Portsmouth			-	-	-	-	-	-	-	-
Newport Co			3	1	2	0	1	2	2	1
Accrington			1	0	0	1	1	0	1	0
Exeter			1	0	0	1	1	0	1	0
Cheltenham			-	-	-	-	-	-	-	-
Morecambe			1	0	1	0	0	1	1	0
Hartlepool			-	-	-	-	-	-	-	-
AFC Wimbledon			2	1	0	1	2	0	1	1
Northampton			-	-	-	-	-	-	-	-
Wycombe			1	0	0	1	0	1	0	0
Luton										
Cambridge U	D	D	5	2	2	1	2	3	2	2

Season	Division	Pos	P	W	D	L	F	A	GD	Pts
2013-14	Conference	1	46	30	11	5	102	35	+67	101
2012-13	Conference	7	46	18	13	15	70	62	+8	67
2011-12	Conference	5	46	22	15	9	78	42	+36	81

Over/Under 59%/41% 4th   **Both score** 41%/59% 21st

	2013-14 H	A	Last six seasons at home P	W	D	L	OV	UN	BS	CS
Tranmere			-	-	-	-	-	-	-	-
Carlisle			-	-	-	-	-	-	-	-
Shrewsbury			-	-	-	-	-	-	-	-
Stevenage			2	1	0	1	2	0	2	0
Southend	W	L	1	1	0	0	1	0	1	0
Burton	D	L	2	0	1	1	0	2	0	1
York	L	W	5	2	1	2	1	4	1	2
Oxford	L	L	3	1	0	2	3	0	3	0
Dag & Red	W	D	1	1	0	0	1	0	0	1
Plymouth	L	D	1	0	0	1	0	1	0	0
Mansfield										
Bury	L	D	1	0	0	1	1	0	1	0
Portsmouth	D	D	1	0	1	0	1	0	1	0
Newport Co	W	D	4	2	1	1	4	0	3	1
Accrington	L	D	1	0	0	1	1	0	1	0
Exeter	D	W	1	0	1	0	0	1	0	1
Cheltenham	L	W	1	0	0	1	0	1	0	0
Morecambe	L	W	1	0	0	1	1	0	1	0
Hartlepool	L	W	1	0	0	1	1	0	1	0
AFC Wimbledon	W	D	3	1	0	2	1	2	1	1
Northampton	W	D	1	1	0	0	1	0	0	1
Wycombe	D	W	1	0	1	0	1	0	1	0
Luton			4	0	4	0	1	3	2	2
Cambridge U			5	3	1	1	3	2	4	1

Season	Division	Pos	P	W	D	L	F	A	GD	Pts
2013-14	League 2	11	46	15	15	16	49	58	-9	60
2012-13	Conference	1	46	30	5	11	92	52	+40	95
2011-12	Conference	3	46	25	14	7	87	48	+39	89

Over/Under 43%/57% 9th   **Both score** 43%/57% 19th

MORECAMBE

Nickname: The Shrimps
Colours: Red and white
Ground: The Globe Arena (6,400)
Tel: 01524-411-797   www.morecambefc.com

The Shrimps begin their eighth consecutive League 2 season with the primary goal of making it nine next May.

That was the objective last term and although a fast start promised more, Morecambe were dragged into a relegation fight, securing safety with victory in their penultimate game.

No side had a poorer record against teams in the bottom half, so it's no wonder manager Jim Bentley described the season as his hardest yet.

Longest run without win/loss: 10/9
High/low league position: 4/19
Clean sheets: 8 **Yellows:** 75 **Reds:** 5
Avg attendance: 2,964 **Players used:** 25
Leading scorer: P Amond 11 (1,11)
Key stat: Morecambe conceded first in 34 of their 46 league games last season

	2013-14 H	A	Last six seasons at home P	W	D	L	OV	UN	BS	CS
Tranmere			-	-	-	-	-	-	-	-
Carlisle			-	-	-	-	-	-	-	-
Shrewsbury			4	2	1	1	0	4	1	2
Stevenage			1	0	1	0	0	1	0	1
Southend	W	W	4	4	0	0	2	2	2	2
Burton	L	W	5	2	2	1	3	2	3	1
York	D	L	2	0	2	0	1	1	1	1
Oxford	D	L	4	0	3	1	1	3	2	1
Dag & Red	D	D	5	2	1	2	4	1	4	1
Plymouth	W	L	3	1	1	1	3	0	3	0
Mansfield	L	W	1	0	0	1	0	1	0	0
Bury	D	W	4	1	2	1	2	2	1	3
Portsmouth	D	L	1	0	1	0	1	0	1	0
Newport Co	W	W	1	1	0	0	1	0	1	0
Accrington	L	L	6	0	2	4	4	2	5	1
Exeter	W	D	3	1	1	1	1	2	1	1
Cheltenham	L	L	5	2	2	1	4	2	4	2
Morecambe										
Hartlepool	L	L	1	0	0	1	1	0	1	0
AFC Wimbledon	D	W	3	1	1	1	2	1	3	0
Northampton	D	D	5	0	2	3	3	2	5	0
Wycombe	D	L	4	0	2	2	1	3	1	1
Luton			1	0	0	1	1	0	1	0
Cambridge U										

Season	Division	Pos	P	W	D	L	F	A	GD	Pts
2013-14	League 2	18	46	13	15	18	52	64	-12	54
2012-13	League 2	16	46	15	13	18	55	61	-6	58
2011-12	League 2	15	46	14	14	18	63	57	+6	56

Over/Under 48%/52% 5th   **Both score** 57%/43% 5th

NEWPORT COUNTY

Nickname: The Exiles
Colours: Yellow and black
Ground: Rodney Parade (7,850)
Tel: 01633-670-690   www.newport-county.co.uk

Under the astute guidance of Justin Edinburgh, the Exiles took the step up to League 2 in their stride.

Edinburgh has a win ratio of 42 per cent in the last five years and he will have spent the backend of 2013-14 planning for the new campaign, as his side never looked likely to move out of mid-table.

While County racked up the points at home, they struggled when crossing the Welsh border – only Bristol Rovers and Hartlepool fared worse on their travels.

Longest run without win/loss: 8/6
High/low league position: 4/15
Clean sheets: 15 **Yellows:** 75 **Reds:** 7
Avg attendance: 3,834 **Players used:** 32
Leading scorer: C Zebroski 12 (5,11)
Key stat: Only relegated Bristol Rovers won fewer games on the road than Newport

	2013-14 H	A	Last six seasons at home P	W	D	L	OV	UN	BS	CS
Tranmere			-	-	-	-	-	-	-	-
Carlisle			-	-	-	-	-	-	-	-
Shrewsbury			-	-	-	-	-	-	-	-
Stevenage			-	-	-	-	-	-	-	-
Southend	W	D	1	1	0	0	1	0	1	0
Burton	D	L	1	0	1	0	0	1	1	0
York	W	L	3	3	0	0	3	0	1	2
Oxford	W	D	1	1	0	0	1	0	1	0
Dag & Red	L	D	1	0	0	1	1	0	1	0
Plymouth	L	D	1	0	0	1	1	0	1	0
Mansfield	D	L	4	3	1	0	0	4	1	3
Bury	D	D	1	0	1	0	0	1	0	1
Portsmouth	L	W	1	0	0	1	1	0	1	0
Newport Co										
Accrington	W	D	1	1	0	0	1	0	1	0
Exeter	D	W	1	0	1	0	0	1	0	1
Cheltenham	L	D	1	0	0	1	0	1	0	0
Morecambe	L	L	1	0	0	1	1	0	1	0
Hartlepool	W	L	1	1	0	0	1	0	0	1
AFC Wimbledon	L	D	2	0	1	1	2	0	2	0
Northampton	L	L	1	0	0	1	1	0	1	0
Wycombe	W	W	1	1	0	0	0	1	0	1
Luton			3	1	1	1	2	2	2	0
Cambridge U			3	1	1	1	1	2	2	0

Season	Division	Pos	P	W	D	L	F	A	GD	Pts
2013-14	League 2	14	46	14	16	16	56	59	-3	58
2012-13	Conference	3	46	25	10	11	85	60	+25	85
2011-12	Conference	19	46	11	14	21	53	65	-12	47

Over/Under 50%/50% 2nd   **Both score** 57%/43% 5th

NORTHAMPTON

Nickname: The Cobblers
Colours: Claret and white
Ground: Sixfields Stadium (7,300)
Tel: 01604-683-700   www.ntfc.co.uk

From just missing out on promotion in 2013 to staying up on a crazy final day, it's been a year of contrast at Sixfields.

A season of underachievement almost reached breaking point as the Cobblers trailed in their must-win final match, but they kept their composure to pull off the great escape.

They spent 217 days in the bottom two but Chris Wilder's arrival proved the turning point, as the former Oxford boss took 31 points from the last 20 games.

Longest run without win/loss: 7/6
High/low league position: 21/24
Clean sheets: 12 **Yellows:** 74 **Reds:** 4
Avg attendance: 4,541 **Players used:** 41
Leading scorer: D Carter 5 (1,4)
Key stat: Northampton put the fewest shots on target in League 2 and midfielder Darren Carter was their top scorer with just five goals

	2013-14		Last six seasons at home							
	H	A	P	W	D	L	OV	UN	BS	CS
Tranmere			1	0	1	0	0	1	1	0
Carlisle			1	1	0	0	0	1	0	1
Shrewsbury			3	1	0	2	2	1	2	1
Stevenage			1	1	0	0	0	1	0	1
Southend	W	L	5	2	1	2	5	0	5	0
Burton	W	L	5	2	1	2	2	3	3	2
York	L	L	2	0	0	2	0	2	0	0
Oxford	W	L	4	4	0	0	3	1	3	1
Dag & Red	D	W	4	3	1	0	3	1	3	1
Plymouth	L	L	3	1	1	1	0	3	0	2
Mansfield	D	L	1	0	1	0	0	1	1	0
Bury	L	D	3	0	1	2	2	1	2	0
Portsmouth	L	D	1	0	0	1	0	0	0	0
Newport Co	W	W	1	1	0	0	1	0	1	0
Accrington	W	W	5	3	2	0	1	4	0	5
Exeter	L	W	2	1	0	1	2	0	1	1
Cheltenham	D	D	6	2	2	2	4	2	6	0
Morecambe	D	D	5	2	2	1	2	3	1	3
Hartlepool	W	L	2	2	0	0	0	2	0	2
AFC Wimbledon	D	W	3	2	1	0	1	2	1	2
Northampton										
Wycombe	L	D	3	1	1	1	2	1	3	0
Luton			-	-	-	-	-	-	-	-
Cambridge U			-	-	-	-	-	-	-	-

Season	Division	Pos	P	W	D	L	F	A	GD	Pts
2013-14	League 2	21	46	13	14	19	42	57	-15	53
2012-13	League 2	6	46	21	10	15	64	55	+9	73
2011-12	League 2	20	46	12	12	22	56	79	-23	48

Over/Under 35%/65% 22nd   **Both score** 43%/57% 19th

OXFORD

Nickname: The U's
Colours: Yellow
Ground: The Kassam Stadium (12,500)
Tel: 01865-337533   www.oufc.co.uk

Oxford have certainly been consistent since returning to the Football League in 2010. In four League 2 seasons, they've finished 12th, ninth, ninth and eighth, but fans have become frustrated at their inability to secure a playoff spot.

The U's have blown chances before but their latest capitulation was hard to take. Oxford had a 13-point cushion on those outside the top seven as late as February, but they missed out on the playoffs after losing ten of their last 13 games.

Longest run without win/loss: 6/8
High/low league position: 1/8
Clean sheets: 15 **Yellows:** 67 **Reds:** 5
Avg attendance: 5,197 **Players used:** 23
Leading scorer: J Constable 10 (7,10)
Key stat: In five of the past seven seasons, the team that finished in Oxford's position of eighth have been promoted the following year

	2013-14		Last six seasons at home							
	H	A	P	W	D	L	OV	UN	BS	CS
Tranmere			-	-	-	-	-	-	-	-
Carlisle			-	-	-	-	-	-	-	-
Shrewsbury			2	2	0	0	1	1	1	1
Stevenage			3	1	1	1	2	1	3	0
Southend	L	L	4	1	0	3	0	4	0	1
Burton	L	W	5	2	2	1	4	1	4	1
York	L	D	4	2	1	1	1	3	1	2
Oxford										
Dag & Red	W	L	3	2	0	1	3	0	3	0
Plymouth	L	W	3	2	0	1	3	0	3	0
Mansfield	W	W	3	3	0	0	1	2	0	3
Bury	W	D	2	1	0	1	2	0	2	0
Portsmouth	D	W	1	0	1	0	0	1	0	1
Newport Co	D	L	1	0	1	0	0	1	0	1
Accrington	L	D	4	1	2	1	2	2	2	2
Exeter	D	D	2	0	1	1	1	1	1	1
Cheltenham	D	D	4	1	2	1	3	3	3	1
Morecambe	W	D	4	2	1	1	3	1	2	2
Hartlepool	W	W	1	1	0	0	0	1	0	1
AFC Wimbledon	W	W	4	4	0	0	2	2	2	2
Northampton	W	L	4	4	0	0	2	2	2	2
Wycombe	D	W	3	0	2	1	2	1	2	0
Luton			1	1	0	0	0	1	0	1
Cambridge U			2	1	1	0	1	1	1	1

Season	Division	Pos	P	W	D	L	F	A	GD	Pts
2013-14	League 2	8	46	16	14	16	53	50	+3	62
2012-13	League 2	9	46	19	8	19	60	61	-1	65
2011-12	League 2	9	46	17	17	12	59	48	+11	68

Over/Under 41%/59% 16th   **Both score** 43%/57% 19th

PLYMOUTH

Nickname: The Pilgrims
Colours: Green and white
Ground: Home Park (16,388)
Tel: 01752-562-561   www.pafc.co.uk

Plymouth were the section's big movers last season, jumping up 11 places to tenth following a much-improved campaign.

The Devonshire club are investing in the future, too, submitting plans for a new grandstand to help encourage the expansion of an already healthy fanbase.

Stability off the pitch has obviously had an effect on it, but long-standing defensive problems still need addressing as their goals against and clean sheet records are obvious areas for improvement.

Longest run without win/loss: 7/6
High/low league position: 8/19
Clean sheets: 11 **Yellows:** 60 **Reds:** 3
Avg attendance: 5,896 **Players used:** 29
Leading scorer: R Reid 17 (10,15)
Key stat: Plymouth did not come back to win any of the 21 league games when the opposition scored first

	2013-14 H	A	Last six seasons at home P	W	D	L	OV	UN	BS	CS
Tranmere			1	0	0	1	1	0	1	0
Carlisle			1	0	1	0	0	1	1	0
Shrewsbury			1	1	0	0	0	1	0	1
Stevenage			-	-	-	-	-	-	-	-
Southend	D	L	3	0	3	0	1	2	3	0
Burton	L	L	3	1	0	2	2	1	2	0
York	L	D	2	1	0	1	1	1	0	1
Oxford	L	W	3	0	1	2	0	3	1	0
Dag & Red	W	W	4	2	2	0	2	2	2	2
Plymouth										
Mansfield	D	W	1	0	1	0	0	1	1	0
Bury	W	L	1	1	0	0	1	0	1	0
Portsmouth	D	D	1	0	1	0	0	1	1	0
Newport Co	D	W	1	0	1	0	0	1	0	1
Accrington	D	D	3	0	3	0	1	2	1	2
Exeter	L	L	3	2	0	1	1	2	1	2
Cheltenham	D	W	3	1	1	1	1	2	2	1
Morecambe	W	L	3	2	1	0	2	1	0	1
Hartlepool	D	L	2	0	1	1	0	2	1	0
AFC Wimbledon	L	D	3	0	0	3	2	1	2	0
Northampton	W	W	3	3	0	0	2	1	2	1
Wycombe	L	W	2	0	0	2	1	1	0	0
Luton			-	-	-	-	-	-	-	-
Cambridge U			-	-	-	-	-	-	-	-

Season	Division	Pos	P	W	D	L	F	A	GD	Pts
2013-14	League 2	10	46	16	12	18	51	58	-7	60
2012-13	League 2	21	46	13	13	20	46	55	-9	52
2011-12	League 2	21	46	10	16	20	47	64	-17	46

Over/Under 41%/59% 16th   **Both score** 48%/52% 13th

PORTSMOUTH

Nickname: Pompey
Colours: Blue and white
Ground: Fratton Park (21,178)
Tel: 023-9273-1204   www.portsmouthfc.co.uk

It was far from the season Pompey's huge support hoped for, but it would have been a lot worse had Andy Awford not steered the club to safety in the final games.

Former manager Richie Barker was sacked with just seven games left and his side just two points above relegation.

But Awford oversaw a strong finish, with Portsmouth winning five and drawing two under the caretaker manager, a run that led to the ex-player being handed a 12-month rolling contract.

Longest run without win/loss: 7/7
High/low league position: 11/22
Clean sheets: 15 **Yellows:** 64 **Reds:** 4
Avg attendance: 10,062 **Players used:** 39
Leading scorer: J Wallace 7 (2,7)
Key stat: Pompey shared League 2's worst defensive record with bottom-placed Torquay as both sides shipped 66 goals

	2013-14 H	A	Last six seasons at home P	W	D	L	OV	UN	BS	CS
Tranmere			1	1	0	0	0	1	0	1
Carlisle			1	0	1	0	0	1	1	0
Shrewsbury			1	1	0	0	1	0	1	0
Stevenage			1	0	1	0	0	1	0	1
Southend	L	L	1	0	0	1	1	0	1	0
Burton	D	W	1	0	1	0	0	1	0	1
York	L	L	1	0	0	1	0	1	0	0
Oxford	L	D	1	0	0	1	1	0	1	0
Dag & Red	W	W	1	1	0	0	0	1	0	1
Plymouth	D	D	1	0	1	0	1	0	1	0
Mansfield	D	D	1	0	1	0	0	1	1	0
Bury	W	D	2	2	0	0	0	2	0	2
Portsmouth										
Newport Co	L	W	1	0	0	1	0	1	0	0
Accrington	W	D	1	1	0	0	0	1	0	1
Exeter	W	D	1	1	0	0	1	0	1	0
Cheltenham	D	D	1	0	1	0	0	1	0	1
Morecambe	W	D	1	1	0	0	1	0	0	1
Hartlepool	W	D	2	1	0	1	1	1	1	1
AFC Wimbledon	W	L	1	1	0	0	0	1	0	1
Northampton	D	W	1	0	1	0	0	1	0	1
Wycombe	D	W	1	0	1	0	1	0	1	0
Luton			-	-	-	-	-	-	-	-
Cambridge U			-	-	-	-	-	-	-	-

Season	Division	Pos	P	W	D	L	F	A	GD	Pts
2013-14	League 2	13	46	14	17	15	56	66	-10	59
2012-13	League 1	24	46	10	12	24	51	69	-18	32
2011-12	Championship	22	46	13	11	22	50	59	-9	40

Over/Under 50%/50% 2nd   **Both score** 50%/50% 10th

SHREWSBURY

Nickname: The Shrews
Colours: Blue and amber
Ground: Greenhous Meadow (9,875)
Tel: 0871-811-8800   www.shrewsburytown.com

Shrewsbury have made big changes as they look to bounce back from relegation.

Micky Mellon has been appointed as manager, there have been changes in the boardroom and the playing squad is undergoing a transformation.

The slate has been wiped clean and that's probably just what the club needed – they collapsed in January following Graham Turner's decision to end his 35-year managerial career, winning just three of 19 games after he departed.

Longest run without win/loss: 7/5
High/low league position: 13/24
Clean sheets: 10 **Yellows:** 46 **Reds:** 4
Avg attendance: 6,160 **Players used:** 38
Leading scorer: J Taylor 9 (5,8)
Key stat: Shrewsbury scored first in just 14 of their 46 League 1 matches last term

	2013-14 H	A	Last six seasons at home P	W	D	L	OV	UN	BS	CS
Tranmere	L	L	2	0	1	1	0	2	1	0
Carlisle	D	D	2	1	1	0	2	0	2	0
Shrewsbury										
Stevenage	W	W	3	3	0	0	1	2	1	2
Southend			2	1	1	0	1	1	2	0
Burton			3	3	0	0	2	1	1	2
York			-	-	-	-	-	-	-	-
Oxford			2	1	1	0	2	0	1	1
Dag & Red			3	3	0	0	2	1	2	1
Plymouth			1	0	1	0	0	1	1	0
Mansfield			-	-	-	-	-	-	-	-
Bury			4	1	2	1	1	3	1	2
Portsmouth			1	1	0	0	1	0	1	0
Newport Co			-	-	-	-	-	-	-	-
Accrington			4	2	1	1	0	4	0	3
Exeter			1	0	1	0	0	1	1	0
Cheltenham			3	1	2	0	0	3	1	2
Morecambe			4	1	1	2	2	2	2	2
Hartlepool			1	0	1	0	0	1	1	0
AFC Wimbledon			1	0	1	0	0	1	0	1
Northampton			3	2	1	0	2	1	2	1
Wycombe			2	0	1	1	0	2	1	0
Luton			1	1	0	0	1	0	0	1
Cambridge U			-	-	-	-	-	-	-	-

Season	Division	Pos	P	W	D	L	F	A	GD	Pts
2013-14	League 1	23	46	9	15	22	44	65	-21	42
2012-13	League 1	16	46	13	16	17	54	60	-6	55
2011-12	League 2	2	46	26	10	10	66	41	+25	88

Over/Under 39%/61% 20th   **Both score** 52%/48% 12th

SOUTHEND

Nickname: The Shrimpers
Colours: Blue
Ground: Roots Hall (11,927)
Tel: 01702-304-050   www.southendunited.co.uk

Once the disappointment of their playoff semi-final defeat subsides, the Shrimpers can draw plenty of positives from a rock-solid campaign.

Manager Phil Brown should be satisfied with his first full season in charge after a run of six wins in the last eight matches propelled his side to a fifth-place finish.

The club remain frustrated by the lack of progress over their plans for a new stadium but there are grounds for optimism about progress on the pitch.

Longest run without win/loss: 12/8
High/low league position: 3/14
Clean sheets: 19 **Yellows:** 58 **Reds:** 8
Avg attendance: 4,735 **Players used:** 30
Leading scorer: B Corr 12 (7,11)
Key stat: Southend had the meanest defence in League 2 last season, conceding just 39 goals

	2013-14 H	A	Last six seasons at home P	W	D	L	OV	UN	BS	CS
Tranmere			2	1	1	0	1	1	2	0
Carlisle			2	1	1	0	2	0	1	1
Shrewsbury			2	1	0	1	1	1	0	1
Stevenage			1	1	0	0	0	1	0	1
Southend										
Burton	W	W	4	1	1	2	0	4	1	1
York	W	D	2	1	1	0	1	1	1	1
Oxford	W	W	4	4	0	0	3	1	2	2
Dag & Red	L	D	3	1	1	1	1	2	2	0
Plymouth	W	D	3	2	0	1	0	3	0	2
Mansfield	W	L	1	1	0	0	1	0	0	1
Bury	D	D	2	0	2	0	0	2	1	1
Portsmouth	W	W	1	1	0	0	1	0	1	0
Newport Co	D	L	1	0	1	0	0	1	0	1
Accrington	W	D	4	1	2	1	1	3	2	1
Exeter	L	W	3	1	1	1	2	1	2	1
Cheltenham	D	W	5	2	1	2	3	2	3	2
Morecambe	L	L	4	0	1	3	2	2	3	0
Hartlepool	D	W	3	2	1	0	2	1	3	0
AFC Wimbledon	L	W	3	1	0	2	1	2	1	1
Northampton	W	L	5	2	2	1	2	3	3	2
Wycombe	D	L	4	2	2	0	1	3	3	1
Luton			-	-	-	-	-	-	-	-
Cambridge U			-	-	-	-	-	-	-	-

Season	Division	Pos	P	W	D	L	F	A	GD	Pts
2013-14	League 2	5	46	19	15	12	56	39	+17	72
2012-13	League 2	11	46	16	13	17	61	55	+6	61
2011-12	League 2	4	46	25	8	13	77	48	+29	83

Over/Under 37%/63% 20th   **Both score** 50%/50% 10th

STEVENAGE

Nickname: The Boro
Colours: White and red
Ground: Lamex Stadium (6,722)
Tel: 01438-223223   www.stevenagefc.com

Not even the return of the club's most successful manager could inspire Boro, as they crashed to rock bottom in League 1.

Graham Westley led the club into the third tier for the first time following back-to-back promotions three years ago, but he endured a frustrating season and his charges won once in their last 12 games.

And once relegation had become an inevitability, the outspoken manager claimed he "hadn't enjoyed working with the group". Expect wholesale changes.

Longest run without win/loss: 10/6
High/low league position: 17/24
Clean sheets: 10 **Yellows:** 89 **Reds:** 5
Avg attendance: 4,191 **Players used:** 39
Leading scorer: F Zoko 10 (3,9)
Key stat: Stevenage gained just six points from their last 14 away league games

	2013-14		Last six seasons at home							
	H	A	P	W	D	L	OV	UN	BS	CS
Tranmere	W	D	3	2	1	0	2	1	3	0
Carlisle	L	D	3	1	1	1	1	2	2	1
Shrewsbury	L	L	3	0	2	1	1	2	3	0
Stevenage										
Southend			1	0	1	0	0	1	1	0
Burton			2	2	0	0	2	0	2	0
York			2	1	1	0	1	1	1	1
Oxford			3	1	2	0	0	3	1	2
Dag & Red			-	-	-	-	-	-	-	-
Plymouth			-	-	-	-	-	-	-	-
Mansfield			2	2	0	0	2	0	2	0
Bury			3	1	2	0	3	0	2	1
Portsmouth			1	1	0	0	1	0	1	0
Newport Co			-	-	-	-	-	-	-	-
Accrington			1	0	1	0	1	0	1	0
Exeter			1	0	1	0	0	1	0	1
Cheltenham			1	1	0	0	1	0	0	1
Morecambe			1	1	0	0	1	0	0	1
Hartlepool			2	1	1	0	1	1	1	1
AFC Wimbledon			1	0	1	0	0	1	0	1
Northampton			1	0	0	1	0	1	0	0
Wycombe			2	0	1	1	0	2	1	0
Luton			1	0	0	1	0	1	0	0
Cambridge U			2	2	0	0	2	0	2	0

Season	Division	Pos	P	W	D	L	F	A	GD	Pts
2013-14	League 1	24	46	11	9	26	46	72	-26	42
2012-13	League 1	18	46	15	9	22	47	64	-17	54
2011-12	League 1	6	46	18	19	9	69	44	+25	73

Over/Under 46%/54% 14th   **Both score** 46%/54% 20th

TRANMERE

Nickname: The Rovers
Colours: White
Ground: Prenton Park (16,151)
Tel: 0871 221 2001 www.tranmererovers.co.uk

A turbulent three months ended with Rovers relegated to the bottom tier for the first time since the 1988-89 campaign.

An investigation by the FA into manager Ronnie Moore, who was suspended in February and sacked in April after pleading guilty to breaching betting rules, cast a shadow over Prenton Park.

The board moved quickly to install a new face in the dugout, placing their trust in novice Rob Edwards, who steps up from the role as assistant at Exeter.

Longest run without win/loss: 5/5
High/low league position: 17/24
Clean sheets: 8 **Yellows:** 84 **Reds:** 8
Avg attendance: 4,914 **Players used:** 34
Leading scorer: R Lowe 19 (8,15)
Key stat: Tranmere conceded three goals or more in ten league games, which contributed to a goals-against average of 1.71 per game

	2013-14		Last six seasons at home							
	H	A	P	W	D	L	OV	UN	BS	CS
Tranmere										
Carlisle	D	L	6	2	2	2	3	3	3	2
Shrewsbury	W	W	2	1	0	1	1	1	1	0
Stevenage	D	L	3	2	1	0	2	1	1	2
Southend			2	1	1	0	1	1	1	1
Burton			-	-	-	-	-	-	-	-
York			-	-	-	-	-	-	-	-
Oxford			-	-	-	-	-	-	-	-
Dag & Red			1	1	0	0	0	1	0	1
Plymouth			1	1	0	0	0	1	0	1
Mansfield			-	-	-	-	-	-	-	-
Bury			2	2	0	0	1	1	0	2
Portsmouth			1	0	1	0	1	0	1	0
Newport Co			-	-	-	-	-	-	-	-
Accrington			-	-	-	-	-	-	-	-
Exeter			3	3	0	0	2	1	1	2
Cheltenham			1	1	0	0	0	1	0	1
Morecambe			-	-	-	-	-	-	-	-
Hartlepool			5	1	2	2	0	5	1	2
AFC Wimbledon			-	-	-	-	-	-	-	-
Northampton			1	1	0	0	1	0	1	0
Wycombe			2	1	0	1	1	1	0	1
Luton			-	-	-	-	-	-	-	-
Cambridge U			-	-	-	-	-	-	-	-

Season	Division	Pos	P	W	D	L	F	A	GD	Pts
2013-14	League 1	21	46	12	11	23	52	79	-27	47
2012-13	League 1	11	46	19	10	17	58	48	+10	67
2011-12	League 1	12	46	14	14	18	49	53	-4	56

Over/Under 54%/46% 9th   **Both score** 59%/41% 5th

Nickname: The Chairboys
Colours: Sky and navy blue
Ground: Adams Park (10,000)
Tel: 01494-472-100   www.wwfc.com

Wycombe stayed up on goal difference following a nail-biting final day, and the odds were heavily stacked against Gareth Ainsworth's men as they had to win their last game and hope Bristol Rovers lost.

Results went Wycombe's way but the drama did not end there. Rovers appealed their relegation, claiming the Chairboys' breach of the FA rules on third party ownership should have resulted in a points deduction. But Wycombe survived the enquiry and stay in the fourth tier.

Longest run without win/loss: 9/6
High/low league position: 5/23
Clean sheets: 9 **Yellows:** 74 **Reds:** 9
Avg attendance: 3,922 **Players used:** 29
Leading scorer: D Morgan 8 (2,7)
Key stat: Wycombe had the worst second-half record in League 2 last season

	2013-14 H	A	P	W	D	L	OV	UN	BS	CS
Tranmere			2	1	0	1	1	1	1	0
Carlisle			2	0	0	2	0	2	1	1
Shrewsbury			2	0	2	0	1	1	2	0
Stevenage			2	0	0	2	0	2	0	0
Southend	W	D	4	2	1	1	3	1	4	0
Burton	L	L	3	2	0	1	3	0	2	1
York	D	L	2	1	1	0	1	1	1	1
Oxford	L	D	3	0	1	2	1	2	1	1
Dag & Red	W	L	3	3	0	0	1	2	1	2
Plymouth	L	W	2	0	1	1	0	2	1	0
Mansfield	L	D	1	0	0	1	0	1	0	0
Bury	L	L	4	2	0	2	2	2	2	1
Portsmouth	L	D	1	0	0	1	0	1	0	0
Newport Co	L	L	1	0	0	1	0	1	0	0
Accrington	D	D	4	1	1	2	2	2	2	1
Exeter	D	W	5	1	3	1	2	3	4	0
Cheltenham	L	D	3	1	1	1	2	1	3	0
Morecambe	W	D	4	2	2	0	1	3	2	2
Hartlepool	W	W	3	3	0	0	2	1	1	2
AFC Wimbledon	L	L	2	0	0	2	1	1	0	0
Northampton	D	W	3	0	3	0	1	2	2	1
Wycombe										
Luton			1	0	1	0	0	1	0	1
Cambridge U			-	-	-	-	-	-	-	-

Season	Division	Pos	P	W	D	L	F	A	GD	Pts
2013-14	League 2	22	46	12	14	20	46	54	-8	50
2012-13	League 2	15	46	17	9	20	50	60	-10	60
2011-12	League 1	21	46	11	10	25	65	88	-23	43

Over/Under 35%/65% 22nd   **Both score** 48%/52% 13th

Nickname: Minstermen
Colours: Red, white and blue
Ground: Bootham Crescent (8,105)
Tel: 01904-624447 www.yorkcityfootballclub.co.uk

Their promotion dreams may have been dashed by Fleetwood in the playoff semi-finals but the Minstermen's form in 2014 bodes well for the future.

At the end of December, York were only out of the relegation places on goal difference but the turn of the year heralded a dramatic turnaround.

Nigel Worthington's men were hugely impressive during an unbeaten run in the last 17 games as they won 11 matches, keeping 13 clean sheets along the way.

Longest run without win/loss: 9/17
High/low league position: 6/23
Clean sheets: 22 **Yellows:** 73 **Reds:** 3
Avg attendance: 4,171 **Players used:** 33
Leading scorer: W Fletcher 10 (4,8)
Key stat: Half of York's 18 league victories came courtesy of a 1-0 scoreline

	2013-14 H	A	P	W	D	L	OV	UN	BS	CS
Tranmere			-	-	-	-	-	-	-	-
Carlisle			-	-	-	-	-	-	-	-
Shrewsbury			-	-	-	-	-	-	-	-
Stevenage			2	0	1	1	0	2	1	0
Southend	D	L	2	1	1	0	1	1	1	1
Burton	D	D	3	1	1	1	2	1	1	2
York										
Oxford	D	W	4	1	3	0	1	3	2	2
Dag & Red	W	L	2	2	0	0	2	0	2	0
Plymouth	D	W	2	1	1	0	0	2	1	1
Mansfield	L	W	5	2	2	1	4	1	4	1
Bury	W	L	1	1	0	0	0	1	0	1
Portsmouth	W	W	1	1	0	0	1	0	1	0
Newport Co	W	L	3	2	1	0	1	2	2	1
Accrington	D	D	2	0	2	0	0	2	2	0
Exeter	W	L	2	1	0	1	2	0	2	0
Cheltenham	D	D	2	0	2	0	0	2	0	2
Morecambe	D	D	2	1	0	1	1	1	1	1
Hartlepool	D	L	1	0	1	0	0	1	0	1
AFC Wimbledon	L	W	4	2	0	2	3	1	1	1
Northampton	W	W	2	1	1	0	0	2	1	1
Wycombe	W	D	2	1	0	1	1	1	1	1
Luton			3	2	1	0	1	2	0	3
Cambridge U			4	0	4	0	2	2	2	2

Season	Division	Pos	P	W	D	L	F	A	GD	Pts
2013-14	League 2	7	46	18	17	11	52	41	+11	71
2012-13	League 2	17	46	12	19	15	50	60	-10	55
2011-12	Conference	4	46	23	14	9	81	45	+36	83

Over/Under 35%/65% 22nd   **Both score** 39%/61% 25th

League 2 stats 2013-14

Key Points in all tables (except the league table) do not include any deductions imposed by the league.
POS H A Overall league position, rank from home games only, rank from away games only **Sup** Average match supremacy **GFA** Goals For Average **GAA** Goals Against Average **PGA** Points Gained Average

League table 2013-14

Pos	H	A		P	Home W	D	L	F	A	Away W	D	L	F	A	GD	Pts
1	2	2	Chesterfield	46	12	9	2	36	16	11	6	6	35	24	+31	84 (C)
2	3	1	Scunthorpe	46	10	11	2	32	19	10	10	3	36	25	+24	81 (P)
3	1	4	Rochdale	46	15	3	5	42	22	9	6	8	27	26	+21	81 (P)
4	5	3	Fleetwood	46	11	6	6	41	30	11	4	8	25	22	+14	76 (P)
5	4	7	Southend	46	11	7	5	29	16	8	8	7	27	23	+17	72
6	7	5	Burton	46	11	6	6	27	22	8	9	6	20	20	+5	72
7	6	8	York	46	10	9	4	23	15	8	8	7	29	26	+11	71
8	17	9	Oxford	46	8	6	9	24	23	8	8	7	29	27	+3	62
9	14	13	Dag & Red	46	8	7	8	25	25	7	8	8	28	34	-6	60
10	16	12	Plymouth	46	8	7	8	23	26	8	5	10	28	32	-7	60
11	20	6	Mansfield	46	7	6	10	27	32	9	6	6	22	26	-9	60
12	9	20	Bury	46	8	12	3	33	23	5	8	10	26	28	+8	59
13	12	16	Portsmouth	46	9	6	8	26	25	5	11	7	30	41	-10	59
14	8	22	Newport Co	46	10	6	7	37	27	4	10	9	19	32	-3	58
15	18	14	Accrington	46	6	10	7	33	29	8	5	10	21	27	-2	57
16	21	10	Exeter	46	6	6	11	22	27	8	7	8	32	30	-3	55
17	22	11	Cheltenham	46	5	9	9	29	35	8	7	8	24	28	-10	55
18	13	21	Morecambe	46	7	10	6	30	26	6	5	12	22	38	-12	54
19	11	23	Hartlepool	46	10	3	10	30	27	4	8	11	20	29	-6	53
20	15	17	AFC W'bledon	46	8	7	8	27	29	6	7	10	22	28	-8	53
21	19	18	Northampton	46	7	7	9	24	32	6	7	10	18	25	-15	53
22	23	15	Wycombe	46	6	6	11	20	27	6	8	9	26	27	-8	50
23	10	24	Bristol R	46	10	6	7	28	21	2	8	13	15	33	-11	50 (R)
24	24	19	Torquay	46	4	8	11	18	31	8	1	14	24	35	-24	45 (R)

Best attack

		GF	GFA
1	Chesterfield	71	1.54
2	Rochdale	69	1.50
3	Scunthorpe	68	1.48
4	Fleetwood	66	1.43
5	Bury	59	1.28
6	Southend	56	1.22
7	Portsmouth	56	1.22
8	Newport Co	56	1.22
9	Accrington	54	1.17
10	Exeter	54	1.17
11	Oxford	53	1.15
12	Dag & Red	53	1.15
13	Cheltenham	53	1.15
14	York	52	1.13
15	Morecambe	52	1.13
16	Plymouth	51	1.11
17	Hartlepool	50	1.09
18	Mansfield	49	1.07
19	AFC W'bledon	49	1.07
20	Burton	47	1.02
21	Wycombe	46	1.00
22	Bristol R	43	0.93
23	Northampton	42	0.91
24	Torquay	42	0.91

Best defence

		GA	GAA
1	Southend	39	0.85
2	Chesterfield	40	0.87
3	York	41	0.89
4	Burton	42	0.91
5	Scunthorpe	44	0.96
6	Rochdale	48	1.04
7	Oxford	50	1.09
8	Bury	51	1.11
9	Fleetwood	52	1.13
10	Wycombe	54	1.17
11	Bristol R	54	1.17
12	Accrington	56	1.22
13	Hartlepool	56	1.22
14	AFC W'bledon	57	1.24
15	Exeter	57	1.24
16	Northampton	57	1.24
17	Plymouth	58	1.26
18	Mansfield	58	1.26
19	Dag & Red	59	1.28
20	Newport Co	59	1.28
21	Cheltenham	63	1.37
22	Morecambe	64	1.39
23	Portsmouth	66	1.43
24	Torquay	66	1.43

Top scorers

	Team	Goals scored	
S Winnall	Scunthorpe	23	▏▏▏▏▏▏▏▏▏▏▏▏▏▏▏▏▏▏▏▏▏▏▏
S Hogan	Rochdale	17	▏▏▏▏▏▏▏▏▏▏▏▏▏▏▏▏▏
R Reid	Plymouth	17	▏▏▏▏▏▏▏▏▏▏▏▏▏▏▏▏▏
B Harrison	Cheltenham	13	▏▏▏▏▏▏▏▏▏▏▏▏▏
L James	Hartlepool	13	▏▏▏▏▏▏▏▏▏▏▏▏▏
R Murphy	Dag & Red	13	▏▏▏▏▏▏▏▏▏▏▏▏▏
J O'Toole	Bristol R	13	▏▏▏▏▏▏▏▏▏▏▏▏▏
A Sarcevic	Fleetwood	13	▏▏▏▏▏▏▏▏▏▏▏▏▏

Over 2.5 goals

	H	A	%
Rochdale	16	14	65%
Bury	9	14	50%
Newport Co	14	9	50%
Portsmouth	9	14	50%
Hartlepool, Morecambe			48%

Under 2.5 goals

	H	A	%
Burton	16	18	74%
Northampton	12	18	65%
Scunthorpe	16	14	65%
Wycombe	15	15	65%
York	18	12	65%

Both to score

	H	A	%
Dag & Red	10	17	59%
Accrington	16	11	59%
Cheltenham	16	11	59%
Morecambe	16	10	57%
Newport Co	16	10	57%

Both not to score

	H	A	%
York	16	12	61%
Hartlepool	14	14	61%
Burton	13	14	59%
Rochdale	14	13	59%
Northampton, Oxford, Mansfield			57%

	Accrington	AFC W'bledon	Bristol R	Burton	Bury	Cheltenham	Chesterfield	Dag & Red	Exeter	Fleetwood	Hartlepool	Mansfield	Morecambe	Newport Co	Northampton	Oxford	Plymouth	Portsmouth	Rochdale	Scunthorpe	Southend	Torquay	Wycombe	York
Accrington		3-2	2-1	0-1	0-0	0-1	3-1	1-2	2-3	2-0	0-0	1-1	5-1	3-3	0-1	0-0	1-1	2-2	1-2	2-3	1-1	2-1	1-1	1-1
AFC W'bledon	1-1		0-0	3-1	0-1	4-3	1-1	1-1	2-1	2-0	2-1	0-0	0-3	2-2	0-2	0-2	1-1	4-0	0-3	3-2	0-1	0-2	1-0	0-1
Bristol R	0-1	3-0		2-0	1-1	1-0	0-0	1-2	2-1	1-3	2-2	0-1	1-0	3-1	1-0	1-1	2-1	2-0	1-2	0-0	0-0	1-2	0-1	3-2
Burton	2-1	1-1	1-0		2-2	2-1	0-2	1-1	1-1	2-4	3-0	1-0	0-1	1-0	1-0	0-2	1-0	1-2	1-0	2-2	0-1	2-0	1-0	1-1
Bury	3-0	1-1	2-1	0-0		4-1	0-2	1-1	2-0	2-2	1-0	0-0	0-2	0-0	1-1	1-1	4-0	4-4	0-0	2-2	1-1	1-3	1-0	2-1
Cheltenham	1-2	1-0	0-0	2-2	2-1		1-4	2-3	1-0	1-2	2-2	1-2	3-0	0-0	1-1	2-2	1-3	2-2	1-2	0-2	1-2	1-0	1-1	2-2
Chesterfield	1-0	2-0	3-1	0-2	4-0	2-0		1-1	1-1	2-1	1-1	0-1	1-0	1-1	0-0	3-0	2-0	0-0	2-2	1-1	2-1	3-1	2-0	2-2
Dag & Red	0-0	1-0	2-0	2-0	2-1	1-2	0-1		1-1	0-1	0-2	0-0	1-1	1-1	0-3	1-0	1-2	1-4	3-1	3-1	0-1	1-0	2-0	2-0
Exeter	0-1	2-0	2-1	0-1	2-2	1-1	0-2	2-2		3-0	0-3	0-1	1-1	0-2	0-1	0-0	3-1	1-1	0-1	2-0	0-2	1-2	0-1	2-1
Fleetwood	3-1	0-0	3-1	2-3	2-1	0-2	1-1	3-1	1-2		2-0	5-4	2-2	4-1	2-0	1-1	0-4	3-1	0-0	0-1	1-1	4-1	1-0	1-2
Hartlepool	2-1	3-1	4-0	1-1	0-3	0-1	1-2	2-1	0-2	0-1		2-4	2-1	3-0	2-0	1-3	1-0	0-0	0-3	0-0	0-1	3-0	1-2	2-0
Mansfield	2-3	1-0	1-1	0-0	1-4	0-2	0-0	3-0	0-0	1-0	1-4		1-2	2-1	3-0	1-3	0-1	2-2	3-0	0-2	2-1	1-3	2-2	0-1
Morecambe	1-2	1-1	2-1	0-1	0-0	0-1	4-3	2-2	2-0	1-0	1-2	0-1		4-1	1-1	1-1	2-2	1-2	1-1	2-1	1-1	1-1	1-1	0-0
Newport Co	4-1	1-2	1-0	1-1	0-0	0-1	3-2	1-2	1-1	0-0	2-0	1-1	2-3		1-2	3-2	1-2	1-2	2-2	3-1	2-1	2-0	3-0	
Northampton	1-0	2-2	0-0	1-0	0-3	1-1	1-3	2-2	1-2	1-0	2-0	1-1	0-0	3-1		3-1	0-2	0-1	0-3	1-1	2-1	1-2	1-4	2-0
Oxford	1-2	2-1	0-1	1-2	2-1	1-1	0-1	2-1	0-0	0-2	1-0	3-0	3-0	0-0	2-0		2-3	0-0	1-1	0-2	0-2	1-0	2-2	0-1
Plymouth	0-0	1-2	1-0	0-1	2-1	1-1	2-1	2-1	1-2	0-2	1-1	1-1	5-0	0-0	1-0	0-2		1-1	1-0	0-2	1-1	2-0	0-3	0-4
Portsmouth	1-0	1-0	3-2	0-0	1-0	0-0	0-2	1-0	3-2	0-1	1-0	1-1	3-0	0-2	0-0	1-4	3-3		3-0	1-2	1-2	0-1	2-2	0-1
Rochdale	2-1	1-2	2-0	1-1	1-0	2-0	2-0	2-1	3-1	1-2	3-0	3-0	2-1	3-0	3-2	3-0	3-0	3-0		0-4	0-3	1-0	3-2	0-0
Scunthorpe	0-2	0-0	1-1	1-0	2-2	2-0	1-1	1-1	0-4	0-0	1-0	2-0	2-0	1-1	1-1	1-0	5-1	3-0			2-2	3-1	0-0	2-2
Southend	1-0	0-1	1-1	1-0	0-0	1-1	3-0	0-1	2-3	2-0	1-3	0-0	2-0	3-0	1-0	2-1	1-1	0-1				1-0	1-1	2-1
Torquay	0-1	1-1	1-1	1-1	2-1	4-2	0-2	0-1	1-3	0-1	0-0	0-0	1-1	0-1	1-2	1-3	1-1	1-1	2-1	0-1	1-0		0-3	0-3
Wycombe	0-0	0-3	1-2	1-2	1-2	1-2	1-0	2-0	1-1	1-1	2-1	0-1	1-0	0-1	1-1	0-1	0-1	0-1	0-2	1-1	2-1	3-2		1-1
York	1-1	0-2	0-0	0-0	1-0	0-0	0-2	3-1	2-1	0-2	0-0	1-2	1-0	1-0	1-0	0-0	1-1	4-2	0-0	4-1	0-0	1-0	2-0	

Record when first to score

		P	W	D	L	F	A	Sup	PGA	Pts
1	Scunthorpe	32	18	13	1	57	24	+1.03	2.1	67
2	Fleetwood	26	20	4	2	57	24	+1.27	2.5	64
3	Chesterfield	27	19	7	1	52	16	+1.33	2.4	64
4	York	26	18	6	2	44	17	+1.04	2.3	60
5	Burton	24	18	5	1	34	14	+0.83	2.5	59
6	Rochdale	22	19	1	2	49	10	+1.77	2.6	58
7	Southend	23	16	5	2	36	11	+1.09	2.3	53
8	Plymouth	23	16	4	3	41	18	+1.00	2.3	52
9	Oxford	21	15	4	2	39	16	+1.10	2.3	49
10	Mansfield	22	14	6	2	36	17	+0.86	2.2	48
11	Portsmouth	22	14	4	4	39	25	+0.64	2.1	46
12	Cheltenham	27	12	8	7	40	33	+0.26	1.6	44
13	Dag & Red	17	13	4	0	27	9	+1.06	2.5	43
14	Newport Co	21	12	6	3	40	24	+0.76	2.0	42
15	Bury	20	11	7	2	40	19	+1.05	2.0	40
16	Hartlepool	16	13	0	3	36	11	+1.56	2.4	39
17	Northampton	19	12	3	4	30	18	+0.63	2.1	39
18	Wycombe	18	10	7	1	31	15	+0.89	2.1	37
19	Accrington	16	11	3	2	31	16	+0.94	2.3	36
20	Bristol R	18	11	3	4	29	17	+0.67	2.0	36
21	Exeter	19	10	6	3	37	20	+0.89	1.9	36
22	Torquay	17	10	4	3	29	19	+0.59	2.0	34
23	AFC W'bledon	11	6	5	0	19	6	+1.18	2.1	23
24	Morecambe	9	5	2	2	13	6	+0.78	1.9	17

Record when keeping a clean sheet

		P	W	D	F	Sup	PGA	Pts
1	Chesterfield	20	16	4	31	+1.55	2.6	52
2	Rochdale	19	15	4	36	+1.89	2.6	49
3	Southend	19	15	4	27	+1.42	2.6	49
4	Burton	18	14	4	18	+1.00	2.6	46
5	Plymouth	11	9	2	18	+1.64	2.6	29
6	Dag & Red	11	9	2	13	+1.18	2.6	29
7	Wycombe	9	7	2	12	+1.33	2.6	23
8	Scunthorpe	21	16	5	28	+1.33	2.5	53
9	Fleetwood	14	10	4	15	+1.07	2.4	34
10	Cheltenham	14	10	4	14	+1.00	2.4	34
11	Northampton	12	8	4	12	+1.00	2.3	28
12	Exeter	8	5	3	13	+1.63	2.3	18
13	Morecambe	8	5	3	9	+1.13	2.3	18
14	Torquay	6	4	2	5	+0.83	2.3	14
15	York	22	13	9	20	+0.91	2.2	48
16	Mansfield	17	10	7	16	+0.94	2.2	37
17	Oxford	15	9	6	17	+1.13	2.2	33
18	Portsmouth	15	9	6	13	+0.87	2.2	33
19	Hartlepool	13	8	5	20	+1.54	2.2	29
20	AFC W'bledon	10	6	4	13	+1.30	2.2	22
21	Newport Co	15	8	7	14	+0.93	2.1	31
22	Bury	16	8	8	18	+1.13	2.0	32
23	Bristol R	14	7	7	11	+0.79	2.0	28
24	Accrington	11	5	6	7	+0.64	1.9	21

Back Harriers to fly again in the Conference after finding the right manager

L uton walked to the title last season, but behind them very little separated the sides in the Conference Premier and the market suggests it could be a similar scenario this year, writes Danny Hayes. Bristol Rovers are sure to be popular as they bid to make an immediate return to League 2 but, like many sides who drop out of the Football League, they are by no means guaranteed to live up to those expectations.

The Gas have flirted with relegation to the Conference for a few years and a woeful end to last season saw them slip out of the league for the first time since the 1920s. The loss of Football League finances has been offset by a sell-on fee for former striker Rickie Lambert, but they have lost key personnel, namely John-Joe O'Toole, and it may take a season for them to adapt to life at this level.

The other relegated side, Torquay, are more familiar with non-league football, but they may also need a year of consolidation as the squad is set for a huge overhaul.

Gateshead and Grimsby, both beaten in the playoffs, are sure to figure prominently again. Gateshead enjoyed their best ever finish and won plenty of plaudits for their playing style, before coming unstuck against Cambridge in the playoff final.

With a strong following and the majority of the squad still intact, there's no reason why they shouldn't again aim for the top five.

Grimsby were beaten in the playoffs for the second season in succession but it was worrying how they were outplayed by Gateshead. They could only muster 65 goals last year and will need to add a more potent goal threat if they are to push for the title.

One side who did not struggle for goals was Halifax. The part-time outfit excelled themselves to finish fifth in their first season in the Conference as FC Halifax, largely thanks to the exploits of foward Lee Gregory. However, Gregory is expected to depart and that won't help the Shaymen.

With no outstanding candidate it could pay to look further down last season's table, with **Kidderminster** fitting the bill nicely.

The Harriers finished second two years ago but things fell apart last season, with three different managers taking charge at various points in the campaign. Their form deteriorated when Steve Burr left for talks with Forest Green in November, and, after he was eventually sacked, Andy Thorn only lasted two months. But Gary Whild came in to steady the ship and a fine end to the season saw them just miss out on the playoffs.

With a strong and experienced squad in place and the addition of forward Craig Reid, who enjoyed a prolific campaign at this level two seasons ago, Kidderminster look well placed to put last season behind them and push for promotion.

Barnet, Forest Green and Eastleigh are others in with a shout of making the playoffs, with the Spitfires the most interesting of the trio, after signing Football League strikers James Constable and Jake Midson. If they hit it off instantly, Eastleigh's stay at this level may not be a long one.

At the other end of the table, the harsh realities of football finances were again evident, when both Hereford and Salisbury

Kidderminster's top scorer, 11-goal Michael Gash, in FA Cup fourth-round action against Sunderland

were expelled from the league.

Chester and Dartford were thus granted a reprieve from relegation but are likely to struggle again, along with promoted clubs Telford, Altrincham and Dover.

But, at bigger prices, **Nuneaton** should be backed for the drop. They finished 13th last season but results tailed off dramatically in the second half of campaign and didn't improve when Kevin Wilkin left to take over at Wrexham. His replacement, Brian Reid, did well in five seasons in charge of Ayr but has no experience at this level. If Nuneaton start this campaign as they ended the last, they could struggle to turn things round.

In the Conference South, it's difficult to look past **Bromley**. They were the front-runners for much of 2013-14 but wilted in the latter stages. However, the Ravens have strengthened and they look the strongest outfit in the South.

In the North, **Barrow** could be the most interesting. The league was very close last year but, under new ownership, the Bluebirds have invested significantly in their squad and look well placed to push for the title.

Conference table 2013-14

Pos	H	A		P	Home W	D	L	F	A	Away W	D	L	F	A	GD	Pts
1	1	1	Luton	46	18	3	2	64	16	12	8	3	38	19	+67	101 (C)
2	3	2	Cambridge U	46	16	4	3	49	14	7	9	7	23	21	+37	82 (P)
3	9	3	Gateshead	46	12	7	4	42	24	10	6	7	30	26	+22	79
4	10	4	Grimsby	46	11	7	5	40	26	11	5	7	25	20	+19	78
5	2	5	Halifax	46	16	6	1	55	19	6	5	12	30	39	+27	77
6	11	6	Braintree	46	12	4	7	27	18	9	7	7	30	21	+18	74
7	4	7	Kidderminster	46	15	4	4	45	22	5	8	10	21	37	+7	72
8	14	8	Barnet	46	11	6	6	30	26	8	7	8	28	27	+5	70
9	18	9	Woking	46	11	4	8	32	30	9	4	10	34	39	-3	68
10	5	10	Forest Green	46	13	6	4	47	22	6	4	13	33	44	+14	67
11	7	11	Alfreton	46	13	6	4	45	33	8	1	14	24	41	-5	67
12	6	12	Salisbury	46	13	6	4	34	21	6	4	13	24	42	-5	67
13	12	13	Nuneaton	46	12	4	7	29	25	6	8	9	25	35	-6	66
14	17	14	Lincoln	46	10	7	6	30	19	7	7	9	30	40	+1	65
15	16	15	Macclesfield	46	11	5	7	35	27	7	2	14	27	36	-1	61
16	19	16	Welling	46	10	5	8	31	24	6	7	10	28	37	-2	60
17	15	17	Wrexham	46	11	5	7	31	21	5	6	12	30	40	0	59
18	8	18	Southport	46	13	5	5	33	23	1	6	16	20	48	-18	53
19	13	19	Aldershot	46	11	6	6	48	32	5	7	11	21	30	+7	51
20	20	20	Hereford	46	9	6	8	24	24	4	6	13	20	39	-19	51
21	22	21	Chester FC	46	5	12	6	26	30	7	3	13	23	40	-21	51 (R)
22	21	22	Dartford	46	8	3	12	32	35	4	5	14	17	39	-25	44 (R)
23	23	23	Tamworth	46	6	7	10	25	31	4	2	17	18	50	-38	39 (R)
24	24	24	Hyde	46	0	3	20	18	57	1	4	18	20	62	-81	10 (R)

Aldershot deducted 10pts, Alfreton deducted 3pts

Conference results 2013-14

	Aldershot	Alfreton	Barnet	Braintree	Cambridge U	Chester FC	Dartford	Forest Green	Gateshead	Grimsby	Halifax	Hereford	Hyde	Kidderminster	Lincoln	Luton	Macclesfield	Nuneaton	Salisbury	Southport	Tamworth	Welling	Woking	Wrexham
Aldershot		2-3	3-3	2-1	0-1	2-0	3-0	2-2	1-2	0-3	2-2	1-2	1-0	0-0	2-3	3-3	1-0	2-2	3-2	5-1	6-0	3-1	2-1	2-0
Alfreton	1-4		3-1	3-1	1-1	0-1	2-1	3-2	1-1	3-3	3-0	2-1	3-0	3-1	1-1	0-5	0-1	1-1	3-2	2-1	4-2	2-2	3-1	1-0
Barnet	1-3	1-0		1-1	2-2	3-0	1-0	2-1	0-1	2-1	0-4	2-0	3-2	1-0	1-1	1-2	1-2	1-1	1-3	1-0	1-0	0-0	1-3	1-1
Braintree	1-0	3-1	0-3		1-0	3-0	1-0	1-1	0-0	0-0	1-1	0-1	0-2	1-2	0-1	1-1	1-0	2-2	2-3	2-3	2-0	2-3	2-0	3-0
Cambridge U	4-0	0-1	1-1	1-0		0-1	1-1	2-1	1-0	1-2	5-1	1-0	7-2	5-1	1-0	1-1	3-0	3-0	2-0	3-1	3-0	2-1	2-0	0-0
Chester FC	1-1	0-1	2-1	0-2	0-0		0-0	1-2	1-1	0-0	2-1	0-2	3-2	0-0	3-3	1-1	2-1	3-3	2-2	2-2	2-0	1-3	0-2	0-0
Dartford	1-1	1-0	0-2	0-2	3-3	0-1		0-1	0-1	1-0	1-2	2-0	4-3	3-0	1-2	1-2	2-1	1-2	1-1	1-0	2-3	1-2	5-1	1-5
Forest Green	3-1	3-1	1-2	0-2	3-2	3-0	1-0		1-0	2-1	2-1	1-1	8-0	1-1	4-1	0-0	2-3	1-0	4-0	3-1	1-2	0-0	2-2	1-1
Gateshead	0-0	3-0	1-2	1-0	2-0	3-2	2-0	1-1		1-2	1-1	2-1	4-0	3-1	3-1	0-0	2-2	2-1	3-2	2-2	5-0	1-1	0-2	0-3
Grimsby	1-1	3-1	2-1	1-0	0-1	2-1	5-2	3-1	2-2		0-1	1-1	3-1	1-1	1-2	2-3	1-2	2-0	0-0	3-1	1-1	2-2	3-1	3-1
Halifax	4-0	2-0	2-1	0-0	1-1	2-1	2-0	1-0	3-3	4-0		1-1	4-0	1-1	5-1	2-0	2-1	2-2	5-1	1-0	2-0	3-0	3-4	3-2
Hereford	0-2	3-2	0-1	1-1	1-0	2-2	2-2	1-0	0-1	0-1	3-2		0-0	1-1	1-0	0-0	1-2	0-1	1-0	4-1	1-0	2-1	0-2	0-2
Hyde	2-2	1-2	0-1	0-3	0-1	1-2	0-2	2-6	0-2	0-1	1-5	2-2		1-3	3-4	0-1	0-3	2-2	0-2	1-2	0-3	0-1	0-2	2-5
Kidderminster	0-0	1-3	1-0	2-2	2-0	3-1	1-2	4-1	3-1	0-1	2-0	2-1	2-1		4-1	0-2	2-1	0-0	3-0	1-1	5-3	2-0	2-0	3-1
Lincoln	0-1	4-1	3-3	2-0	1-0	1-1	0-0	2-1	0-1	0-2	3-1	1-1	3-0	2-0		0-0	1-0	1-2	0-1	1-0	0-0	1-2	2-2	2-0
Luton	1-0	3-0	2-1	2-3	0-0	3-0	3-0	4-1	4-2	0-0	4-3	7-0	4-1	6-0	3-2		3-1	3-0	2-0	0-2	3-1	0-1	0-1	5-0
Macclesfield	1-1	0-1	2-0	0-1	0-1	3-2	3-1	1-2	0-2	1-1	2-2	1-0	3-0	1-1	3-1	1-2		0-1	1-0	2-2	2-1	2-1	3-2	2-2
Nuneaton	2-1	3-0	0-1	1-1	0-0	1-0	3-1	1-1	1-4	0-1	0-1	2-1	1-0	2-1	2-2	0-5	1-0		1-2	3-1	1-0	2-0	0-2	2-2
Salisbury	1-0	0-0	2-1	1-1	0-3	3-1	1-0	1-4	0-0	1-0	3-1	4-1	2-0	1-1	1-2	0-0	3-2	2-1		1-1	0-1	3-0	2-0	2-1
Southport	1-0	2-1	1-1	0-4	1-0	0-0	3-0	2-0	2-1	2-1	2-1	0-3	1-1	1-2	0-1	1-0	4-1	1-0	3-1		2-0	2-2	1-1	1-2
Tamworth	1-0	1-0	0-0	0-0	0-1	3-4	0-2	1-2	0-1	0-2	2-0	1-0	1-1	0-3	0-0	3-4	1-0	1-1	1-2	4-1		1-1	2-4	2-2
Welling	1-0	1-2	1-1	0-2	2-2	2-0	1-1	5-2	2-0	1-0	0-1	0-1	0-2	1-2	1-0	1-2	1-0	1-2	0-0	4-3	2-0		3-0	1-1
Woking	1-2	2-1	0-0	1-0	0-3	0-1	3-0	2-1	1-2	1-2	0-0	3-0	3-2	1-0	0-0	0-4	3-2	2-0	1-3	2-0	2-2	2-4		2-1
Wrexham	2-1	2-3	0-1	2-3	1-1	0-2	1-2	2-0	3-2	0-1	0-0	2-0	2-2	0-0	0-1	2-0	1-0	3-0	1-1	1-0	2-0	2-1	2-0	

Luton captain Ronnie Henry lifts the trophy as Steve McNulty sprays the bubbly

Conference North table 2013-14

Pos	H	A		P	Home					Away					GD	Pts
					W	D	L	F	A	W	D	L	F	A		
1	1	1	Telford	42	16	2	3	46	20	9	8	4	36	33	+29	85 (C)
2	4	2	Nth Ferriby	42	13	6	2	47	25	11	4	6	33	26	+29	82
3	5	3	Altrincham	42	13	5	3	47	21	11	4	6	48	30	+44	81 (P)
4	3	4	Hednesford	42	14	3	4	52	27	10	3	8	35	38	+22	78
5	6	5	Guiseley	42	14	2	5	35	20	9	7	5	43	36	+22	78
6	2	6	Boston Utd	42	15	4	2	54	21	5	8	8	31	39	+25	72
7	10	7	Brackley	42	8	8	5	30	23	9	8	4	36	22	+21	67
8	12	8	Solihull Moors	42	7	9	5	29	27	10	5	6	34	25	+11	65
9	7	9	Harrogate T	42	12	6	3	47	24	7	3	11	28	35	+16	63
10	15	10	Bradford PA	42	7	7	7	36	36	8	5	8	30	34	-4	57
11	18	11	Barrow	42	6	8	7	20	28	8	6	7	30	28	-6	56
12	19	12	Colwyn Bay	42	5	9	7	26	32	9	4	8	37	35	-4	55
13	9	13	Leamington	42	10	3	8	26	19	3	10	8	28	34	+1	52
14	8	14	Stockport	42	9	7	5	40	27	3	7	11	18	30	+1	50
15	11	15	Worcester	42	8	6	7	26	22	5	5	11	14	31	-13	50
16	14	16	Gainsborough	42	8	4	9	41	40	5	2	14	26	46	-19	45
17	17	17	Gloucester	42	7	6	8	36	34	4	5	12	28	43	-13	44
18	13	18	Vauxhall M	42	9	3	9	27	36	3	5	13	16	38	-31	44
19	20	19	Stalybridge	42	6	6	9	34	45	4	3	14	23	43	-31	39
20	16	20	Oxford C	42	7	6	8	29	26	2	7	12	21	44	-20	37 (R)
21	22	21	Histon	42	5	5	11	23	37	2	6	13	19	39	-34	32 (R)
22	21	22	Workington	42	6	5	10	25	38	0	5	16	14	47	-46	28 (R)

Harrogate deducted 3pts, Oxford C deducted 3pts

Conference North results 2013-14

	Altrincham	Barrow	Boston Utd	Brackley	Bradford PA	Colwyn Bay	Gainsboro	Gloucester	Guiseley	Harrogate T	Hednesford	Histon	Leamington	Nth Ferriby	Oxford C	Solihull M	Stalybridge	Stockport	Telford	Vauxhall M	Worcester	Workington
Altrincham		2-1	0-0	1-0	4-1	3-1	3-0	2-0	4-1	1-3	1-3	2-2	3-2	1-1	2-2	1-0	5-0	3-0	1-1	5-1	1-2	2-0
Barrow	1-1		4-4	0-1	0-1	1-1	0-6	0-0	1-0	1-0	1-0	2-1	0-0	2-0	1-1	0-2	1-1	2-4	0-3	1-1	0-1	2-0
Boston Utd	3-2	1-0		1-2	2-3	2-1	6-0	2-0	3-0	3-3	4-0	0-0	2-0	2-0	2-1	4-1	4-1	0-0	1-1	5-2	2-1	5-3
Brackley	1-2	1-2	3-2		0-1	2-2	3-1	1-3	1-2	2-2	1-0	3-0	1-1	1-1	2-1	1-0	3-0	0-0	1-1	2-1	0-0	1-1
Bradford PA	2-4	2-2	1-1	0-5		1-2	4-0	3-1	0-3	0-0	1-2	3-0	3-2	0-4	3-3	2-2	1-1	0-2	3-1	0-0	6-1	1-0
Colwyn Bay	1-3	1-2	3-3	2-2	2-2		0-2	1-1	2-2	2-1	1-3	1-0	1-1	0-3	1-1	3-1	1-2	0-0	0-1	1-0	0-0	3-2
Gainsborough	5-4	2-1	0-1	2-2	4-2	0-2		3-3	1-2	2-0	1-2	3-1	1-1	1-4	6-0	2-3	0-2	1-5	1-3	1-1	2-1	3-0
Gloucester	2-0	1-3	1-3	2-2	2-3	2-3	0-1		1-1	5-2	5-1	2-0	3-3	1-1	0-2	0-3	1-0	2-0	1-2	2-2	2-1	1-1
Guiseley	2-2	2-1	1-0	0-2	0-2	2-1	3-1	3-1		2-0	1-2	1-1	2-1	1-0	2-0	0-3	3-1	2-0	6-1	1-0	0-1	1-0
Harrogate T	3-2	3-1	4-0	0-1	1-1	2-2	1-1	4-2	2-3		3-1	0-1	1-1	5-0	3-2	2-1	2-1	3-1	2-2	1-1	1-2	3-0
Hednesford	1-1	3-1	4-2	2-2	2-0	2-1	1-3	4-1	3-2	1-3		2-1	3-2	0-1	3-0	1-2	4-1	3-1	3-3	2-0	4-0	4-0
Histon	0-5	0-0	1-2	3-3	1-0	3-1	2-0	1-3	1-1	0-1	0-1		1-1	0-3	2-2	0-3	1-4	2-1	0-1	1-2	1-2	3-1
Leamington	0-1	1-1	0-0	3-1	2-0	2-1	0-1	0-1	2-3	1-2	2-1	1-0		0-2	4-0	0-1	1-0	2-1	2-2	0-1	1-0	2-0
Nth Ferriby	2-1	2-2	3-0	1-1	2-1	2-3	2-0	3-1	2-3	3-2	3-0	4-4	4-1		2-1	1-1	2-0	0-0	2-2	2-0	2-1	3-1
Oxford C	1-2	0-1	1-1	0-1	1-1	1-2	1-0	1-0	3-3	1-2	1-2	2-1	2-2	2-3		0-2	2-1	4-1	2-0	3-0	0-0	1-1
Solihull Moors	0-1	0-2	1-2	1-0	2-2	2-2	3-2	2-1	0-3	3-0	2-3	0-0	0-0	2-0	2-2		3-3	1-0	2-1	1-1	1-1	2-0
Stalybridge	0-5	1-3	3-3	1-1	2-2	2-3	2-2	3-3	2-3	3-2	0-4	2-1	1-1	2-3	1-1	2-3		0-0	0-2	3-2	1-2	2-0
Stockport	0-0	2-2	1-4	0-2	4-1	0-1	3-1	2-2	3-3	3-1	0-1	1-0	1-1	1-2	2-0	2-2	2-0		4-2	4-1	4-0	1-1
Telford	3-1	0-1	2-1	2-1	2-1	4-1	3-0	2-1	4-2	0-1	5-3	3-2	1-2	2-0	4-0	1-1	3-1	2-0		1-0	0-0	2-1
Vauxhall M	1-2	1-1	2-2	0-3	0-2	0-3	2-1	3-2	0-5	1-0	2-2	4-0	2-1	0-1	1-0	0-2	1-3	2-1	2-4		1-0	2-1
Worcester	1-3	1-0	3-0	1-1	1-2	2-1	2-2	0-1	0-0	1-1	0-2	1-1	0-3	0-1	0-2	3-1	2-1	0-0	0-1	2-0		4-0
Workington	1-6	2-3	1-0	0-3	0-2	0-3	4-2	4-2	1-1	0-3	2-2	2-3	1-2	3-3	1-0	0-0	1-0	1-1	0-1	0-1	1-0	

Conference South table 2013-14

Pos	H	A		P	Home					Away					GD	Pts
					W	D	L	F	A	W	D	L	F	A		
1	1	1	Eastleigh	42	17	2	2	40	16	9	6	6	31	24	+31	86 (C)
2	2	2	Sutton Utd	42	15	3	3	44	16	8	9	4	33	23	+38	81
3	3	3	Bromley	42	15	2	4	54	26	10	3	8	28	24	+32	80
4	4	4	Ebbsfleet	42	13	5	3	34	14	8	6	7	33	26	+27	74
5	15	5	Dover	42	7	6	8	22	19	13	3	5	41	19	+25	69 (P)
6	6	6	Havant & W	42	13	2	6	36	23	6	10	5	21	20	+14	69
7	7	7	Bath City	42	11	6	4	38	26	7	6	8	26	26	+12	66
8	5	8	Staines	42	13	5	3	33	22	5	4	12	23	35	-1	63
9	16	9	Concord R	42	7	5	9	33	34	10	5	6	25	25	-1	61
10	10	10	Eastbourne	42	10	5	6	34	27	6	5	10	21	32	-4	58
11	8	11	Weston S-M.	42	11	4	6	31	25	5	5	11	19	30	-5	57
12	13	12	Gosport Bor	42	9	4	8	25	22	7	3	11	21	29	-5	55
13	18	13	Boreham W	42	6	7	8	36	34	8	4	9	29	21	+10	53
14	14	14	Basingstoke	42	8	5	8	26	22	7	3	11	29	34	-1	53
15	12	15	Bishop's St.	42	8	7	6	31	27	5	6	10	32	41	-5	52
16	9	16	Farnborough	42	11	2	8	37	29	4	3	14	25	49	-16	50
17	11	17	Chelmsford	42	10	4	7	32	30	4	3	14	25	47	-20	49
18	21	18	Maidenhead	42	5	4	12	23	35	7	6	8	32	34	-14	46
19	19	19	Whitehawk	42	5	8	8	25	34	7	2	12	31	37	-15	46
20	20	20	Hayes & Y	42	6	3	12	23	25	7	3	11	22	27	-7	45 (R)
21	17	21	Tonbridge	42	6	8	7	24	30	3	5	13	19	47	-34	40 (R)
22	22	22	Dorchester	42	4	5	12	18	45	4	2	15	15	49	-61	31 (R)

Conference South results 2013-14

	Basingstoke	Bath City	Bishops St.	Boreham W	Bromley	Chelmsford	Concord R	Dorchester	Dover	Eastbourne	Eastleigh	Ebbsfleet	Farnborough	Gosport Bor	Havant & W	Hayes & Y	Maidenhead	Staines	Sutton Utd	Tonbridge	Weston S-M.	Whitehawk
Basingstoke		0-0	0-0	1-0	0-1	2-3	0-1	2-1	2-0	1-2	2-0	2-2	4-0	2-1	0-1	0-1	2-2	2-1	0-1	0-0	3-2	1-3
Bath City	0-1		2-1	2-2	1-2	4-1	3-1	1-0	0-2	2-1	0-1	2-2	4-2	1-1	3-1	3-2	1-0	1-1	2-2	2-2	1-0	3-1
Bishops St.	5-3	1-2		1-3	1-0	1-1	0-1	1-1	2-2	1-0	2-2	3-2	1-3	4-0	2-1	0-0	1-1	1-0	1-2	2-1	0-0	1-2
Boreham W	1-1	0-1	2-2		1-1	4-3	0-2	5-0	2-2	3-1	0-3	2-1	1-1	2-0	0-2	1-3	2-2	0-2	1-3	7-0	1-1	1-3
Bromley	3-2	2-2	3-2	2-1		5-0	1-2	4-1	0-4	2-1	1-2	0-0	3-0	2-1	2-0	2-1	6-1	3-0	2-4	5-1	2-1	4-0
Chelmsford	1-0	1-0	2-1	0-6	3-1		2-2	4-1	0-4	3-0	0-0	1-2	3-1	1-0	0-0	0-0	0-3	3-2	0-2	7-1	1-2	0-2
Concord R	1-2	0-2	0-2	0-4	2-3	1-3		1-0	1-2	1-1	3-2	1-2	5-0	0-2	3-3	3-1	4-1	2-1	0-0	2-2	2-0	1-1
Dorchester	0-4	0-2	1-3	1-4	3-2	2-0	2-2		0-4	0-0	1-2	1-3	1-0	1-1	0-2	0-2	0-3	1-1	0-0	2-1	0-3	2-6
Dover	1-1	2-0	2-3	0-0	0-2	2-2	0-1	1-0		0-0	1-2	2-1	0-1	3-0	0-0	2-0	1-0	0-1	3-1	1-2	1-1	
Eastbourne	1-3	3-2	4-1	1-0	1-1	4-2	0-0	0-1	0-4		1-1	1-1	5-2	1-3	0-1	3-1	2-0	2-0	1-1	2-1	2-0	0-2
Eastleigh	2-1	2-1	4-2	0-1	2-1	1-0	1-1	6-0	1-0	2-0		3-1	1-0	2-1	0-0	1-0	3-2	1-0	1-0	1-2	3-1	3-2
Ebbsfleet	1-0	1-1	2-1	0-0	1-3	0-2	4-0	4-0	0-2	1-0	3-1		3-0	2-1	0-0	1-0	1-1	3-0	2-0	1-0	1-1	3-1
Farnborough	0-3	2-4	4-2	2-0	2-1	2-0	0-2	3-2	1-0	3-3	0-1	0-1		1-0	2-2	1-2	3-0	1-2	1-2	3-2	4-0	2-0
Gosport Bor	2-0	3-1	2-1	2-1	1-2	2-1	1-2	1-1	0-1	1-2	0-2	0-2	1-0		0-0	3-0	0-2	2-0	2-2	2-0	0-0	0-2
Havant & W	4-1	1-0	2-0	1-1	1-0	3-0	1-0	5-1	3-4	1-1	1-0	1-0	2-1	3-0		1-2	1-3	0-2	0-5	1-2	2-0	2-0
Hayes & Y	0-0	0-2	2-3	1-0	0-2	4-0	1-0	2-0	1-0	0-1	1-1	1-2	0-0	0-1			1-2	1-2	0-0	0-3	1-2	3-2
Maidenhead	0-1	0-1	2-2	0-1	1-1	1-3	1-3	1-2	2-3	1-0	2-2	1-2	1-3	2-1				3-1	3-2	0-0	0-3	1-0
Staines	4-5	1-0	2-0	3-1	2-1	3-1	0-1	1-0	2-2	2-1	0-0	1-1	3-2	0-3	1-0	2-1	0-0		2-1	0-0	2-1	2-1
Sutton Utd	4-0	2-2	1-2	1-0	1-0	2-0	1-0	0-1	1-0	4-0	1-1	3-1	3-3	2-0	3-1	2-0	3-2	4-1		1-2	3-0	2-0
Tonbridge	2-1	1-1	1-1	0-2	1-1	2-1	2-2	1-2	0-2	2-1	2-1	0-2	1-3	0-2	0-0	1-1	2-4	1-1	1-1		1-0	3-1
Weston S-M.	1-0	2-0	2-2	3-0	0-1	2-0	5-0	3-0	2-1	0-1	3-2	0-6	2-1	0-1	1-1	0-3	0-0	0-3	1-1	2-1		2-1
Whitehawk	1-0	2-2	1-1	0-2	1-2	0-4	0-2	3-0	0-1	1-2	1-4	1-1	3-1	1-1	2-2	1-0	0-3	3-3	3-3	1-0	0-0	

An early start in Europe should help the Dons get off to a flyer at home

There must be a tinge of concern for any manager heading into a new job this summer, but it's pretty safe to say that Ronny Deila's worries should be minimal, writes Ian Wilkerson. As Neil Lennon's replacement at Celtic, he inherits a team who won the Scottish Premiership by 29 points last season and have been as short as 1-66 this summer to retain their title.

The Norwegian joined Celtic from Stromsgodset and has been compared to Dortmund's Jurgen Klopp because of his attacking philosophy – it could be fun to watch him work with a team who scored 102 goals last term.

However, as another domestic triumph seems inevitable, it will be in Europe where he is tested. So, for the third season since Rangers' demotion to the basement, the most interesting market is who will provide Celtic's toughest challenge this season.

Motherwell pipped Aberdeen to second spot on the final day last term and it would be no surprise if they were battling it out again.

The Dons were reborn after four successive finishes in the bottom half of the table and winning the League Cup gave them an additional boost. Returning to training in early June because of their Europa League commitments could help them make a good start and Aberdeen appear to be on the up under Derek McInnes.

Dundee United could put up a decent challenge but with star midfielder Ryan Gauld having left for Sporting Lisbon and concerns about Andy Robertson's future, they might have plenty to do.

The innovation of a playoff place at the bottom of the table was a big success last season and there will be plenty of teams with concerns about avoiding the drop.

Partick, Kilmarnock and St Mirren will have to improve while new boys Dundee and Hamilton would be happy to consolidate.

Rangers are one step away from being back in the top division and Ally McCoist has rolled back the years by signing former favourites Kris Boyd and Kenny Miller to try and get them there.

But they face Edinburgh duo Hibernian and Hearts in the second tier and punters should keep an eye on the Jambos – with their financial problems seemingly behind them after a takeover and the appointment of former Scotland manager Craig Levein, they could push the Gers all the way.

After falling short in the playoffs to get back into the Championship, Dunfermline, who were the second-best team in League One are fancied to get over the line this year.

Pars boss Jim Jefferies has signed Ayr striker Michael Moffat, and Dunfermline look ready to go. But it would be no surprise if Peterhead, having finally got out of the basement, run them closest.

Relegated pair East Fife and Arbroath lead the field in League Two, but neither spark much enthusiasm in what looks an open section, so look out for Clyde under the stewardship of former Rangers midfielder Barry Ferguson – the Bully Wee were unlucky to lose to East Fife on penalties in the playoff semi-finals last term.

*Niall McGinn fired 14 goals
for Aberdeen last season*

ABERDEEN

Nickname: The Dons
Colours: Red
Ground: Pittodrie (21,421)
Tel: 01224 650-400   www.afc.co.uk

Having finished in the bottom half for the last four seasons, there was at last some joy to be had at Pittodrie, as they celebrated a Scottish League Cup final win over Inverness and only missed out on second place by conceding with virtually the last kick of their final game.

That's given the Dons something to build on and, boosted by the addition of striker Adam Rooney, who has already had half a season under Derek McInnes, they should challenge for second again.

Longest run without win/loss: 3/9
High/low league position: 2/5
Clean sheets: 15 **Yellows:** 53 **Reds:** 4
Avg attendance: 8,886 **Players used:** 26
Leading scorer: N McGinn 13 (3,10)
Key stat: Aberdeen lost just one of the 19 games in which they scored the first goal

	2013-14 H	A	Last six seasons at home P	W	D	L	OV	UN	BS	CS
Celtic	L W	L L	10	2	2	6	6	4	6	0
Motherwell	L L	W D	9	1	3	5	4	5	3	3
Aberdeen										
Dundee Utd	W D	W W	10	3	5	2	5	5	7	1
Inverness CT	W L	W D	9	4	0	5	3	6	3	3
St Johnstone	D W D	W	10	3	4	3	2	8	3	5
Ross County	W	L D	3	1	1	1	0	3	0	2
St Mirren	W	D W	10	5	4	1	2	8	2	7
Kilmarnock	W W	W	12	6	3	3	5	7	4	6
Partick	W	W L	1	1	0	0	1	0	0	1
Dundee			2	2	0	0	0	2	0	2
Hamilton			6	3	0	3	4	2	3	3

Season	Division	Pos	P	W	D	L	F	A	GD	Pts
2013-14	Premiership	3	38	20	8	10	53	38	+15	68
2012-13	Premiership	8	38	11	15	12	41	43	-2	48
2011-12	Premiership	9	38	9	14	15	36	44	-8	41

Over/Under 39%/61% 10th   **Both score** 47%/53% 7th

Top scorers	P	G		Y	R
N McGinn	35 (1)	13		1	0
A Rooney	13	7		2	0
S Vernon	14 (11)	6		2	0
P Pawlett	33 (2)	5		5	0
B Robson	20 (8)	4		4	1
W Flood	31 (2)	3		4	0
C Zola	11 (9)	3		1	0
J Hayes	28 (3)	2		5	0
R Jack	34	2		6	0
M Reynolds	37	2		0	0

CELTIC

Nickname: The Bhoys
Colours: Green and white
Ground: Celtic Park (60,355)
Tel: 0871-226-1888   www.celticfc.net

The continued absence of Rangers from the top flight means that Celtic again go off at a very short price to retain the title.

It is difficult to see anyone challenging them in the league but the Bhoys will look to address their cup form after failing to get their hands on either trophy last term.

Neil Lennon departed in the summer and while incoming manager Ronny Deila has enjoyed success in Norway with Stromsgodset, he remains a relatively inexperienced coach.

Longest run without win/loss: 1/26
High/low league position: 1/2
Clean sheets: 21 **Yellows:** 44 **Reds:** 2
Avg attendance: 15,230 **Players used:** 31
Leading scorer: K Commons 27 (11,19)
Key stat: Celtic found the net in all 38 Premiership matches

	2013-14 H	A	Last six seasons at home P	W	D	L	OV	UN	BS	CS
Celtic										
Motherwell	W W	W D	11	10	1	0	5	6	1	10
Aberdeen	W W	W L	10	10	0	0	7	3	5	5
Dundee Utd	D W	W W	12	8	4	0	8	4	10	2
Inverness CT	D W	W W	9	6	2	1	5	4	3	5
St Johnstone	W W	W D	10	8	1	1	5	5	3	6
Ross County	W D	W	3	2	1	0	2	1	2	1
St Mirren	W W	W	9	9	0	0	5	4	1	8
Kilmarnock	W	W W	8	6	1	1	6	2	4	3
Partick	W	W W	1	1	0	0	0	1	0	1
Dundee			2	2	0	0	1	1	0	2
Hamilton			5	5	0	0	3	2	1	4

Season	Division	Pos	P	W	D	L	F	A	GD	Pts
2013-14	Premiership	1	38	31	6	1	102	25	+77	99
2012-13	Premiership	1	38	24	7	7	92	35	+57	79
2011-12	Premiership	1	38	30	3	5	84	21	+63	93

Over/Under 63%/37% 2nd   **Both score** 45%/55% 8th

Top scorers	P	G		Y	R
K Commons	32 (2)	27		1	0
A Stokes	30 (3)	20		2	1
L Griffiths	11 (2)	7		3	0
T Pukki	13 (12)	7		2	0
G Samaras	10 (10)	7		3	0
C Mulgrew	27 (1)	6		5	0
V van Dijk	35 (1)	5		2	1
J Forrest	10 (6)	4		1	0
J Ledley	18 (2)	4		1	0
A Balde	3 (17)	3		3	0

DUNDEE

Nickname: The Dark Blues
Colours: Blue and white
Ground: Dens Park (11,506)
Tel: 01382-889966   www.dundeefc.co.uk

The Championship winners bounced straight back into the top flight thanks in large part to a solid defence that conceded just 26 goals.

Paul Hartley arrived at Dens Park in February and helped them over the line and it will be interesting to see how he does in the top flight after learning the ropes at Alloa. And while Dundee face a real battle to stay up, former Rangers midfielder Kevin Thomson will bring a great deal of experience.

Longest run without win/loss: 3/5
High/low league position: 1/4
Clean sheets: 19 **Yellows:** 48 **Reds:** 2
Avg attendance: 3,511 **Players used:** 27
Leading scorer: P MacDonald 17 (8,14)
Key stat: The Dark Blues took 32 points from their 18 Championship away matches

| | 2013-14 | | Last six seasons at home | | | | | | | |
	H	A	P	W	D	L	OV	UN	BS	CS
Celtic			1	0	0	1	0	1	0	0
Motherwell			2	0	0	2	2	0	1	0
Aberdeen			2	0	1	1	1	1	2	0
Dundee Utd			1	0	0	1	0	0	0	0
Inverness CT			4	0	3	1	3	1	4	0
St Johnstone			4	0	2	2	2	2	3	0
Ross County			10	3	2	5	2	8	3	4
St Mirren			2	1	0	1	1	1	1	0
Kilmarnock			2	0	1	1	1	1	1	1
Partick			8	5	1	2	4	4	2	4
Dundee										
Hamilton	D W	W D	4	1	2	1	1	3	1	2

Season	Division	Pos	P	W	D	L	F	A	GD	Pts
2013-14	Championship	1	36	21	6	9	54	26	+28	69
2012-13	Premiership	12	38	7	9	22	28	66	-38	30
2011-12	Championship	2	36	15	10	11	53	43	+10	55

Over/Under 39%/61% 9th   **Both score** 33%/67% 10th

Top league scorers	P	G		Y	R
P MacDonald	33 (2)	17		5	0
R Conroy	20 (12)	7		0	0
C Beattie	8 (10)	5		1	0
M Boyle	18 (11)	4		3	0
D Gallagher	36	4		5	0
J McAlister	36	4		2	0
I Davidson	25 (1)	3		6	1
C Nade	6 (7)	3		1	0
K McBride	19 (6)	2		4	0
C Wighton	7 (6)	2		0	0

DUNDEE UNITED

Nickname: The Terrors
Colours: Orange and black
Ground: Tannadice Park (14,223)
Tel: 01382-833-166 www.dundeeunitedfc.co.uk

While a talented bunch, United suffered with inconsistency last term and slumped to a seven-match winless run from Boxing Day which went a long way to denying them a place in the Europa League.

They also suffered the disappointment of losing to St Johnstone in the Scottish Cup final but the young talent at Tannadice still makes for exciting times.

Ryan Gauld's departure is a blow, but United can make progress in Jackie McNamara's second full season.

Longest run without win/loss: 7/7
High/low league position: 2/6
Clean sheets: 7 **Yellows:** 49 **Reds:** 3
Avg attendance: 7,323 **Players used:** 26
Leading scorer: N Ciftci 11 (4,9)
Key stat: Dundee United scored just six goals in the opening 15 minutes of their matches

| | 2013-14 | | Last six seasons at home | | | | | | | |
	H	A	P	W	D	L	OV	UN	BS	CS
Celtic	L L	D L	12	2	3	7	6	6	6	1
Motherwell	D W	W W	12	5	2	5	9	3	7	3
Aberdeen	L L	L D	10	4	2	4	6	4	8	1
Dundee Utd										
Inverness CT	L W	D D	9	5	2	2	6	3	5	2
St Johnstone	W L	L L	8	3	3	2	2	6	2	4
Ross County	W	W L	3	1	2	0	0	3	1	2
St Mirren	W W	L	9	5	2	2	6	3	6	3
Kilmarnock	W W	W	10	4	5	1	4	6	5	4
Partick	W	D D	1	1	0	0	1	0	1	1
Dundee			2	1	1	0	1	1	1	1
Hamilton			4	1	2	1	1	3	3	0

Season	Division	Pos	P	W	D	L	F	A	GD	Pts
2013-14	Premiership	4	38	16	10	12	65	50	+15	58
2012-13	Premiership	6	38	11	14	13	51	62	-11	47
2011-12	Premiership	4	38	16	11	11	62	50	+12	59

Over/Under 58%/42% 5th   **Both score** 61%/39% 2nd

Top scorers	P	G		Y	R
N Ciftci	27 (5)	11		6	0
S Armstrong	32 (4)	8		2	0
G Mackay-Steven	27 (8)	7		3	0
R Gauld	21 (10)	6		1	0
B Graham	11 (19)	6		0	0
F El Alagui	4 (9)	3		0	0
D Goodwillie	9 (10)	3		1	0

R Dow, G Gunning, J Rankin, A Robertson, K Watson all 3 goals

HAMILTON

Nickname: The Accies
Colours: Red and white
Ground: New Douglas Park (6,078)
Tel: 01698-368-652   www.acciesfc.co.uk

	2013-14 H	A	Last six seasons at home P	W	D	L	OV	UN	BS	CS
Celtic			4	0	1	3	2	2	3	0
Motherwell			5	1	3	1	2	3	1	3
Aberdeen			5	1	2	2	1	4	2	1
Dundee Utd			5	1	1	3	1	4	2	0
Inverness CT			3	1	0	2	2	1	2	1
St Johnstone			4	1	1	2	1	3	1	2
Ross County			2	1	0	1	1	1	1	0
St Mirren			5	1	3	1	1	4	1	4
Kilmarnock			6	3	3	0	3	3	3	3
Partick			4	2	1	1	1	3	1	2
Dundee	L D	D L	4	1	1	2	3	1	3	0
Hamilton										

Season	Division	Pos	P	W	D	L	F	A	GD	Pts
2013-14	Championship	2	36	19	10	7	68	41	+27	67
2012-13	Championship	5	36	14	9	13	52	45	+7	51
2011-12	Championship	4	36	14	7	15	55	56	-1	49

Over/Under 44%/56% 7th   **Both score** 56%/44% 3rd

Hamilton will go into the season still buzzing from their unlikely playoff success over Hibernian after they had lost the first leg 2-0 at New Douglas Park.

Young manager Alex Neil will be aiming to keep the Accies out of the bottom two and will probably put his faith in the young talent that the club have been so good at developing in recent years.

They finished bottom by seven points the last time they were in the top flight, but they should improve upon that.

Longest run without win/loss: 4/11
High/low league position: 1/3
Clean sheets: 12 **Yellows:** 68 **Reds:** 5
Avg attendance: 1,529 **Players used:** 27
Leading scorer: J Keatings 13 (5,10)
A Andreu 13 (3, 9)
Key stat: Hamilton won 13 and drew two of the 15 games they were winning at half-time

Top league scorers	P	G	Y	R
A Andreu	28 (7)	13	3	0
J Keatings	29 (1)	13	1	0
M Antoine-Curier	17 (12)	12	3	0
L Longridge	17 (10)	8	0	0
J Scotland	14 (1)	8	3	0
D MacKinnon	30 (1)	3	11	0
A Crawford	33 (3)	2	5	0
Z Gordon	34	2	8	1
A Ryan	1 (18)	2	1	0

M Canning, M Devlin, G Gillespie, J Tena all 1 goal

INVERNESS CT

Nickname: Caley
Colours: Blue and red
Ground: Caledonian Stadium (7,750)
Tel: 01463-222-880   www.ictfc.com

	2013-14 H	A	Last six seasons at home P	W	D	L	OV	UN	BS	CS
Celtic	L D	L L	8	1	1	6	4	4	4	1
Motherwell	W L	L L	9	3	0	6	8	1	7	2
Aberdeen	L D	L W	9	3	2	4	4	5	3	3
Dundee Utd	D D	W L	8	1	3	4	4	4	5	2
Inverness CT										
St Johnstone	W W	L W	7	3	3	1	0	7	2	4
Ross County	L	W W	5	3	0	2	5	0	4	1
St Mirren	W D	D	9	4	3	2	7	2	6	3
Kilmarnock	W	W L	8	4	3	1	5	3	8	0
Partick	L W	D	4	2	0	2	3	1	3	1
Dundee			3	2	1	0	1	2	2	1
Hamilton			5	0	3	2	0	5	3	0

Season	Division	Pos	P	W	D	L	F	A	GD	Pts
2013-14	Premiership	5	38	16	9	13	44	44	0	57
2012-13	Premiership	4	38	13	15	10	64	60	+4	54
2011-12	Premiership	10	38	10	9	19	42	60	-18	39

Over/Under 45%/55% 9th   **Both score** 34%/66% 11th

Thistle got off to a rip-roaring start, winning ten of their first 15 games, but they were unable to stay with the pace.

In light of that start, finishing fifth might be regarded as a disappointment, but Terry Butcher's departure midway through the season upset their rhythm.

However, John Hughes is a good replacement and that's two successive seasons that Inverness have finished in the top six. Anything less than that would now be regarded as a disappointment.

Longest run without win/loss: 5/6
High/low league position: 1/5
Clean sheets: 18 **Yellows:** 57 **Reds:** 2
Avg attendance: 5,876 **Players used:** 22
Leading scorer: B McKay 18 (7,14)
Key stat: Inverness took just one point from the 14 games in which their opponents scored first

Top scorers	P	G	Y	R
B McKay	38	18	1	0
A Doran	33	5	3	0
R Foran	23 (1)	4	7	0
R Christie	3 (12)	3	1	0
G Shinnie	36	3	6	0
G Tansey	15 (1)	2	3	0
G Warren	34	2	7	0

R Draper, L Polworth, D Raven, N Ross, J Vincent, M Watkins, D Williams all 1 goal

KILMARNOCK

Nickname: Killie
Colours: Blue and white
Ground: Rugby Park (18,128)
Tel: 01563 545-300   www.kilmarnockfc.co.uk

Killie must regard last season as a lucky escape as they needed a final day goal from Kris Boyd to ensure they didn't finish in the new playoff place.

Two wins in their final two matches ultimately spared them, but Allan Johnston has work to do this season.

Boyd scored 22 of Kilmarnock's 45 goals last season but opted to return to Rangers after his contract expired in the summer and it's pretty obvious what has to be Johnston's main concern.

Longest run without win/loss: 9/2
High/low league position: 8/12
Clean sheets: 7 **Yellows:** 61 **Reds:** 5
Avg attendance: 5,202 **Players used:** 33
Leading scorer: K Boyd 22 (7,18)
Key stat: Kilmarnock won just two of the 13 league games they were drawing at half-time

	2013-14		Last six seasons at home							
	H	A	P	W	D	L	OV	UN	BS	CS
Celtic	L L	L	11	1	1	9	9	2	6	1
Motherwell	L	L W	10	4	2	4	3	7	2	5
Aberdeen	L	L L	9	3	3	3	2	7	5	3
Dundee Utd	L	L L	9	2	3	4	5	4	7	1
Inverness CT	L W	L	9	3	1	5	6	3	7	2
St Johnstone	D L	L	9	2	3	4	6	3	7	2
Ross County	W D	W L	3	2	1	0	2	1	1	2
St Mirren	W W	D L	13	7	2	4	7	6	9	2
Kilmarnock										
Partick	W L	D D	2	1	0	1	0	2	2	0
Dundee			2	0	1	1	1	1	1	1
Hamilton			5	3	0	2	3	2	1	3

Season	Division	Pos	P	W	D	L	F	A	GD	Pts
2013-14	Premiership	9	38	11	6	21	45	66	-21	39
2012-13	Premiership	9	38	11	12	15	52	53	-1	45
2011-12	Premiership	7	38	11	14	13	44	61	-17	47

Over/Under 63%/37% 2nd   **Both score** 61%/39% 2nd

Top league scorers	P	G		Y	R
K Boyd	35 (1)	22		1	1
R McKenzie	28 (5)	4		2	0
C Johnston	15 (6)	3		3	0
D Barr	12	2		3	1
S Clohessy	24	2		5	0
R Muirhead	10 (11)	2		1	0
B Nicholson	14 (9)	2		0	0

L Ashcroft, S Clingan, A Eremenko, M Gardyne, J Irvine, V Maksimenko, C Slater all 1 goal

MOTHERWELL

Nickname: The Well/The Steelmen
Colours: Amber and claret
Ground: Fir Park (13,677)
Tel: 01698-333-333   www.motherwellfc.co.uk

Motherwell again claimed second place in 2014, thanks to their late winner against Aberdeen in their final game.

They finished strongly by winning their final three games and improved in the second half of the campaign after disappointing cup exits at the hands of Albion Rovers and ten-man Aberdeen.

However, they need to shore things up at the back. Well kept just two clean sheets in their final 17 games, but should challenge again to be best of the rest.

Longest run without win/loss: 3/6
High/low league position: 2/5
Clean sheets: 11 **Yellows:** 59 **Reds:** 2
Avg attendance: 6,456 **Players used:** 25
Leading scorer: J Sutton 22 (9,18)
Key stat: Just eight of Motherwell's 38 league games were goalless at half-time

	2013-14		Last six seasons at home							
	H	A	P	W	D	L	OV	UN	BS	CS
Celtic	L D	L L	12	3	2	7	8	4	7	1
Motherwell										
Aberdeen	L D	W W	10	4	4	2	4	6	7	2
Dundee Utd	L	D L L	11	3	3	5	6	5	6	1
Inverness CT	W W	L W	9	6	2	1	6	3	4	4
St Johnstone	W W	L L	9	6	1	2	8	1	6	2
Ross County	W W	W	4	4	0	0	3	1	3	1
St Mirren	W	W L	9	4	3	2	4	5	5	2
Kilmarnock	W L	W	10	3	3	4	5	5	6	2
Partick	W W	W	2	2	0	0	1	1	1	1
Dundee			1	0	1	0	0	1	1	0
Hamilton			5	4	0	1	0	5	0	4

Season	Division	Pos	P	W	D	L	F	A	GD	Pts
2013-14	Premiership	2	38	22	4	12	64	60	+4	70
2012-13	Premiership	2	38	18	9	11	67	51	+16	63
2011-12	Premiership	3	38	18	8	12	49	44	+5	62

Over/Under 68%/32% 1st   **Both score** 53%/47% 6th

Top league scorers	P	G		Y	R
J Sutton	37 (1)	22		2	0
L Ainsworth	22 (7)	11		1	0
H Anier	19 (14)	9		1	0
J McFadden	21 (6)	4		1	0
S McManus	37	4		5	0
I Vigurs	33 (3)	4		7	0
Z Francis-Angol	21 (12)	3		0	0
K Lasley	37	2		7	0

S Hutchinson, R McHugh, C Moore, C Reid all 1 goal

PARTICK

Nickname: The Jags
Colours: Yellow and red
Ground: Firhill Stadium (10,915)
Tel: 0141-579-1971   www.ptfc.co.uk

There were encouraging signs for Partick in their first season back in the top flight and avoiding the relegation playoff meant that their initial target was achieved. However, their home form was desperately poor and is an obvious place to start when looking for improvements.

Claiming just eight wins all season meant they scraped home and they should be able to better that total this season, but it's difficult to see them challenging for a place in the top six.

Longest run without win/loss: 9/4
High/low league position: 7/11
Clean sheets: 4 **Yellows:** 70 **Reds:** 5
Avg attendance: 6,905 **Players used:** 26
Leading scorer: K Doohlan 11 (7,10)
Key stat: Partick won just two of their 19 home matches last season

	2013-14 H	A	Last six seasons at home P	W	D	L	OV	UN	BS	CS
Celtic	L L	L	2	0	0	2	2	0	2	0
Motherwell	L	L L	1	0	0	1	1	0	1	0
Aberdeen	L W	L	2	1	0	1	2	0	1	0
Dundee Utd	D D	L	2	0	2	0	0	2	1	1
Inverness CT	D	W L	3	1	1	1	1	2	1	1
St Johnstone	L	D D	3	1	1	1	1	2	0	2
Ross County	D L	W D	10	1	4	5	3	7	5	1
St Mirren	L D	W D	2	0	1	1	1	1	1	0
Kilmarnock	D D	L W	2	0	2	0	0	2	2	0
Partick										
Dundee			8	1	4	3	0	8	1	4
Hamilton			4	3	1	0	1	3	1	3

Season	Division	Pos	P	W	D	L	F	A	GD	Pts
2013-14	Premiership	10	38	8	14	16	46	65	-19	38
2012-13	Championship	1	36	23	9	4	76	28	+48	78
2011-12	Championship	6	36	12	11	13	50	39	+11	47

Over/Under 50%/50% 6th   **Both score** 68%/32% 1st

Top league scorers	P	G		Y	R
K Doohlan	22 (14)	11		3	0
K Higginbotham	33 (3)	8		10	0
L Taylor	17 (3)	7		2	0
S Lawless	17 (11)	4		0	0
A Muirhead	18 (2)	3		3	0
C Erskine	14 (1)	2		3	0
G Fraser	18 (1)	2		1	0
L Mair	17	2		2	0
A Sinclair	36	2		5	1

C Balatoni, C Elliott, R Forbes, J McMillan, G Moncur all 1 goal

ROSS COUNTY

Nickname: County
Colours: Blue, red and white
Ground: Victoria Park (6,541)
Tel: 01349-860860   rosscountyfootballclub.co.uk

Ross County will probably be encouraged by the fact that they endured a nine-match run in which they claimed just one point and still managed to finish at the top of the bottom half of the split.

They won three of their final four games to avoid any flirtation with the playoff spot and it seems likely that they will have a similar season this term.

County could do with an outlet up front, though, as they scored more than once in just eight of their final 31 games.

Longest run without win/loss: 9/4
High/low league position: 7/12
Clean sheets: 7 **Yellows:** 68 **Reds:** 5
Avg attendance: 5,750 **Players used:** 29
Leading scorer: M De Leeuw 9 (4,9)
Key stat: Ross County conceded at least two goals in 21 of their 38 league matches

	2013-14 H	A	Last six seasons at home P	W	D	L	OV	UN	BS	CS
Celtic	L	L D	4	1	2	1	2	2	4	0
Motherwell	L	L L	3	1	1	1	2	1	2	1
Aberdeen	W D	L	3	2	1	0	1	2	2	1
Dundee Utd	L W	L	4	2	0	2	3	1	2	2
Inverness CT	L L	W	6	2	2	2	3	3	2	3
St Johnstone	W	L W	5	2	1	2	3	2	3	2
Ross County										
St Mirren	W W	L L	3	2	1	0	2	1	1	2
Kilmarnock	L W	L D	4	1	1	2	2	2	2	1
Partick	L D	D W	10	2	4	4	5	5	5	3
Dundee			9	1	4	4	3	6	5	1
Hamilton			2	2	0	0	1	1	1	1

Season	Division	Pos	P	W	D	L	F	A	GD	Pts
2013-14	Premiership	7	38	11	7	20	44	62	-18	40
2012-13	Premiership	5	38	13	14	11	47	48	-1	53
2011-12	Championship	1	36	22	13	1	72	32	+40	79

Over/Under 63%/37% 2nd   **Both score** 61%/39% 2nd

Top league scorers	P	G		Y	R
M De Leeuw	19 (14)	9		6	0
R Brittain	34	7		6	1
F Kiss	17	6		6	1
Y Arquin	14 (2)	4		3	0
G Carey	31 (5)	3		7	0
Y Songo'o	17	3		2	0
S Kettlewell	22 (3)	2		6	1
R Quinn	20 (9)	2		5	0
I Sproule	7 (3)	2		0	1

Boyd, Cooper, Gordon, Maatsen, Saunders, Slew all 1 goal

ST JOHNSTONE

Nickname: The Saints
Colours: Blue and white
Ground: McDiarmid Park (10,673)
Tel: 01738-459090 www.perthstjohnstonefc.co.uk

It was a campaign to remember at McDiarmid Park as St Johnstone not only achieved a top-six finish with plenty in hand but also enjoyed a Scottish Cup final win over Dundee United, which ended their 130-year wait for silverware.

Stevie May played a huge part with 27 goals in all competitions, and keeping hold of him will be crucial if St Johnstone are to enjoy more success this term. If they can hold him to his contract, which expires next summer, Saints can push on.

Longest run without win/loss: 5/6
High/low league position: 5/8
Clean sheets: 16 **Yellows:** 62 **Reds:** 6
Avg attendance: 4,720 **Players used:** 28
Leading scorer: S May 20 (10,15)
Key stat: St Johnstone scored just 13 away goals last season

ST MIRREN

Nickname: The Saints
Colours: Black and white
Ground: St Mirren Park (8,029)
Tel: 0141-889-2558 www.saintmirren.net

St Mirren were always playing catch-up after claiming just two points from their first seven games and they won just twice in 15 league games from December 29. However, they were another team to stage a late rally and avoid the playoffs.

The Buddies relied heavily on 35-year-old striker Steven Thompson for goals and if the years begin to catch up with him it's difficult to be optimistic about St Mirren's chances of avoiding another season of looking over their shoulders.

Longest run without win/loss: 7/5
High/low league position: 7/12
Clean sheets: 8 **Yellows:** 50 **Reds:** 4
Avg attendance: 5,729 **Players used:** 27
Leading scorer: S Thompson 13 (6,10)
Key stat: St Mirren took just 11 points from their 19 away games

	2013-14 H	A	Last six seasons at home P	W	D	L	OV	UN	BS	CS
Celtic	L D	L L	8	1	2	5	4	4	4	0
Motherwell	W W	L L	9	4	1	4	5	4	3	4
Aberdeen	L D	D L D	8	2	2	4	3	5	4	2
Dundee Utd	W W	L W	10	2	4	4	4	6	4	4
Inverness CT	W L	L L	8	4	2	2	2	6	0	6
St Johnstone										
Ross County	W L	L	6	2	3	1	3	3	3	2
St Mirren	W	L W	8	5	2	1	3	5	3	4
Kilmarnock	W	D W	7	4	1	2	3	4	2	3
Partick	D D	W	4	1	3	0	1	3	3	1
Dundee			3	2	1	0	0	3	0	3
Hamilton			4	2	1	1	1	3	2	2

Season	Division	Pos	P	W	D	L	F	A	GD	Pts
2013-14	Premiership	6	38	15	8	15	48	42	+6	53
2012-13	Premiership	3	38	14	14	10	45	44	+1	56
2011-12	Premiership	6	38	14	8	16	43	50	-7	50

Over/Under 39%/61% 10th   **Both score** 29%/71% 12th

Top league scorers	P	G		Y	R
S May	34 (4)	20		4	0
S MacLean	18 (3)	8		3	1
N Hasselbaink	20 (10)	5		3	0
D MacKay	36	3		5	0
S Anderson	29	2		4	1

S Brown, L Caddis, T Clancy, M Davidson, R Fallon, G Miller, M O'Halloran, D Wotherspoon, F Wright all 1 goal

	2013-14 H	A	Last six seasons at home P	W	D	L	OV	UN	BS	CS
Celtic	L	L L	9	1	1	7	4	5	2	1
Motherwell	L W	L	10	2	5	3	4	5	5	3
Aberdeen	D L	L	12	4	4	4	3	9	6	3
Dundee Utd	W	L L	9	1	5	3	3	6	5	2
Inverness CT	D	L D	9	2	3	4	6	3	6	2
St Johnstone	W L	L	9	1	5	3	3	6	5	2
Ross County	W W	L L	4	3	0	1	3	1	3	1
St Mirren										
Kilmarnock	D W	L L	10	5	4	1	2	8	4	5
Partick	L D	W D	2	0	1	1	1	1	1	1
Dundee			2	1	0	1	2	0	2	0
Hamilton			7	2	3	2	5	2	2	2

Season	Division	Pos	P	W	D	L	F	A	GD	Pts
2013-14	Premiership	8	38	10	9	19	39	58	-19	39
2012-13	Premiership	11	38	9	14	15	47	60	-13	41
2011-12	Premiership	8	38	9	16	13	39	51	-12	43

Over/Under 47%/53% 8th   **Both score** 42%/58% 9th

Top league scorers	P	G		Y	R
S Thompson	37	13		5	0
K McLean	28 (2)	7		2	0
P McGowan	33 (3)	4		4	0
C Newton	36 (1)	4		3	0
J McGinn	31 (4)	3		7	0
A Campbell	7 (4)	2		1	0
J Naismith	26 (1)	2		3	0
G Wylde	6 (11)	2		0	0
G Harkins	7 (8)	1		0	0
S Kelly	32 (1)	1		1	0

Scottish Premiership stats 2013-14

Key Points in all tables (except the league table) do not include any deductions imposed by the league.
POS H A Overall league position, rank from home games only, rank from away games only **Sup** Average match supremacy **GFA** Goals For Average **GAA** Goals Against Average **PGA** Points Gained Average

League table 2013-14

Pos	H	A		P	Home W	D	L	F	A	Away W	D	L	F	A	GD	Pts
1	1	1	Celtic	38	16	3	0	50	10	15	3	1	52	15	+77	99 (C)
2	2	3	Motherwell	38	13	2	4	39	29	9	2	8	25	31	+4	70
3	5	2	Aberdeen	38	10	3	5	20	13	10	5	5	33	25	+15	68
4	3	6	Dundee Utd	38	11	2	6	40	23	5	8	6	25	27	+15	58
5	6	4	Inverness CT	38	8	6	5	26	16	8	3	8	18	28	0	57
6	4	7	St Johnstone	38	10	4	5	35	16	5	4	10	13	26	+6	53
7	8	11	Ross County	38	8	2	9	25	29	3	5	11	19	33	-18	40
8	7	12	St Mirren	38	7	7	5	23	20	3	2	14	16	38	-19	39
9	9	10	Kilmarnock	38	7	3	9	25	30	4	3	12	20	36	-21	39
10	12	5	Partick	38	2	8	9	21	37	6	6	7	25	28	-19	38
11	11	9	Hibernian	38	4	7	9	20	29	4	4	10	11	22	-20	35 (R)
12	10	8	Hearts	38	6	3	10	21	29	4	5	10	24	36	-20	23 (R)

Hearts deducted 15pts

Best attack

		GF	GFA
1	Celtic	102	2.68
2	Dundee Utd	65	1.71
3	Motherwell	64	1.68
4	Aberdeen	53	1.39
5	St Johnstone	48	1.26
6	Partick	46	1.21
7	Kilmarnock	45	1.18
8	Hearts	45	1.18
9	Inverness CT	44	1.16
10	Ross County	44	1.16
11	St Mirren	39	1.03
12	Hibernian	31	0.82

Best defence

		GA	GAA
1	Celtic	25	0.66
2	Aberdeen	38	1.00
3	St Johnstone	42	1.11
4	Inverness CT	44	1.16
5	Dundee Utd	50	1.32
6	Hibernian	51	1.34
7	St Mirren	58	1.53
8	Motherwell	60	1.58
9	Ross County	62	1.63
10	Hearts	65	1.71
11	Partick	65	1.71
12	Kilmarnock	66	1.74

Top scorers

	Team	Goals scored	
K Commons	Celtic	27	▌▌▌▌▌▌▌▌▌▌▌▌▌▌
K Boyd	Kilmarnock	22	▌▌▌▌▌▌▌▌▌▌▌
J Sutton	Motherwell	22	▌▌▌▌▌▌▌▌▌▌▌
S May	St Johnstone	20	▌▌▌▌▌▌▌▌▌▌
A Stokes	Celtic	20	▌▌▌▌▌▌▌▌▌▌

SOCCERBASE.COM SMARTERBETTING

Record when first to score

		P	W	D	L	F	A	Sup	PGA	Pts
1	Celtic	30	30	0	0	88	11	+2.57	3.0	90
2	Motherwell	24	17	4	3	46	24	+0.92	2.3	55
3	Aberdeen	19	17	1	1	35	10	+1.32	2.7	52
4	Inverness CT	19	16	3	0	34	7	+1.42	2.7	51
5	Dundee Utd	20	15	4	1	53	18	+1.75	2.5	49
6	St Johnstone	19	14	4	1	40	11	+1.53	2.4	46
7	Ross County	17	10	5	2	30	19	+0.65	2.1	35
8	St Mirren	17	9	4	4	33	21	+0.71	1.8	31
9	Kilmarnock	16	9	2	5	27	16	+0.69	1.8	29
10	Partick	16	5	8	3	27	25	+0.13	1.4	23
11	Hearts	10	7	0	3	20	11	+0.90	2.1	21
12	Hibernian	8	6	2	0	15	5	+1.25	2.5	20

Record when keeping a clean sheet

		P	W	D	F	Sup	PGA	Pts
1	Celtic	21	21	0	56	+2.67	3.0	63
2	Motherwell	11	11	0	18	+1.64	3.0	33
3	Aberdeen	15	13	2	22	+1.47	2.7	41
4	Kilmarnock	7	6	1	12	+1.71	2.7	19
5	Ross County	7	6	1	10	+1.43	2.7	19
6	St Johnstone	16	13	3	28	+1.75	2.6	42
7	Inverness CT	18	13	5	24	+1.33	2.4	44
8	Dundee Utd	7	5	2	14	+2.00	2.4	17
9	St Mirren	8	5	3	10	+1.25	2.3	18
10	Hearts	6	4	2	10	+1.67	2.3	14
11	Hibernian	8	4	4	8	+1.00	2.0	16
12	Partick	4	1	3	2	+0.50	1.5	6

Over 2.5 goals

		H	A	%
	Motherwell	16	10	68%
	Celtic	12	12	63%
	Kilmarnock	11	13	63%
	Ross County	13	11	63%
	Dundee Utd	13	9	58%

Under 2.5 goals

		H	A	%
	Hibernian	12	13	66%
	Aberdeen	13	10	61%
	St Johnstone	11	12	61%
	Inverness CT	11	10	55%
	St Mirren	13	7	53%

Both to score

		H	A	%
	Partick	13	13	68%
	Dundee Utd	11	12	61%
	Kilmarnock	11	12	61%
	Ross County	12	11	61%
	Hearts	7	14	55%

Both not to score

		H	A	%
	St Johnstone	13	14	71%
	Inverness CT	11	14	66%
	Hibernian	10	13	61%
	St Mirren	10	12	58%
	Celtic	11	10	55%

Results 2013-14

	Aberdeen	Celtic	Dundee United	Hearts	Hibernian	Inverness CT	Kilmarnock	Motherwell	Partick	Ross County	St Johnstone	St Mirren
Aberdeen		0-2/2-1	1-0/1-1	1-3	1-0	1-0/0-1	2-1/2-1	0-1/0-1	4-0	1-0	0-0/1-0/1-1	2-0
Celtic	3-1/5-2		1-1/3-1	2-0	1-0	2-2/5-0/6-0	4-0	2-0/3-0	1-0	2-1/1-1	2-1/3-0	1-0/3-0
Dundee United	1-2/1-3	0-1/0-2		4-1	2-2	0-1/2-1	1-0/3-2	2-2/3-1/5-1	4-1	1-0	4-0/0-1	4-0/3-2
Hearts	2-1/1-1	1-3/0-2	0-0/1-2		1-0/2-0	0-2	0-4/5-0	0-1	0-2/2-4	2-2/2-0	0-2	0-2/2-1
Hibernian	0-2/0-2	1-1/0-4	1-1/1-3	2-1/1-2		0-2	3-0/0-1	0-1/3-3	1-1/1-1	0-0/2-1	0-0	2-0/2-3
Inverness CT	3-4/0-0	0-1	1-1/1-1	2-0/0-0	3-0/0-0		2-1	2-0/1-2	1-2/1-0	1-2	1-0/2-0	3-0/2-2
Kilmarnock	0-1	2-5/0-3	1-4	2-0/4-2	1-2/1-1	1-2/2-0		0-2	2-1/1-2	2-0/2-2	0-0/1-2	2-1/1-0
Motherwell	1-3/2-2	0-5/3-3	0-4	2-1/4-1	1-0	2-0/2-1	2-1/1-2		1-0/4-3	3-1/2-1	4-0/2-1	3-0
Partick	0-3/3-1	1-2/1-5	0-0/1-1	1-1/2-4	0-1/3-1	0-0	1-1/1-1	1-5		3-3/2-3	0-1	0-3/1-1
Ross County	1-0/1-1	1-4	2-4/3-0	2-1/1-2	0-2/1-0	0-3/1-2	1-2/2-1	1-2	1-3/1-1		1-0	3-0/2-1
St Johnstone	0-2	0-1/3-3	3-0/2-0	1-0/3-3	1-2/2-0	4-0/0-1	3-1	2-0/3-0	1-1/1-1	4-0/0-1		2-0
St Mirren	1-1/0-1	0-4	4-1	1-1/1-1	0-0/2-0	0-0	1-1/2-0	0-1/3-2	1-2/0-0	2-1/1-0	4-3/0-1	

Kris Commons scored 27 goals in 34 Premiership appearances

ALLOA

Nickname: The Wasps   **Ground:** Recreation Park
Web: www.alloaathletic.co.uk

It was always going to be tough for Alloa after successive promotions, and they just avoided the relegation playoffs. Manager Paul Hartley left midway though 2013-14 and it looks a tougher division this season, so the Wasps may find things tough again.

	2013-14 H	A	P	W	D	L	OV	UN	BS	CS
Hibernian			-	-	-	-	-	-	-	-
Hearts			-	-	-	-	-	-	-	-
Falkirk	D W	D L	2	1	1	0	1	1	0	2
Queen of Sth	L L	D L	4	1	0	3	2	2	1	1
Dumbarton	L L	D L	6	0	1	5	5	1	5	1
Livingston	W L	L L	4	1	1	2	3	1	2	1
Raith	W L	L D	4	1	2	1	0	4	1	2
Alloa										
Cowdenbeath	W L	W D	4	3	0	1	3	1	3	0
Rangers										

Season	Division	Pos	P	W	D	L	F	A	GD	Pts
2013-14	Championship	8	36	11	7	18	34	51	-17	40
2012-13	League One	2	36	20	7	9	62	35	+27	67
2011-12	League Two	1	36	23	8	5	70	39	+31	77

Over/Under 42%/58% 8th   **Both score** 36%/64% 9th

COWDENBEATH

Nickname: The Blue Brazil   **Ground:** Central Park
Web: www.cowdenbeathfc.com

Cowdenbeath did well to avoid relegation in the playoffs and showed they can live with the best teams in the section by beating promoted pair Dundee and Hamilton. However, Jimmy Nicholl must replace key strikers Greg Stewart and Kane Hemmings.

	2013-14 H	A	P	W	D	L	OV	UN	BS	CS
Hibernian			-	-	-	-	-	-	-	-
Hearts			-	-	-	-	-	-	-	-
Falkirk	W L	L L	6	2	2	2	4	3	2	
Queen of Sth	L D	D L	4	0	2	2	2	2	3	0
Dumbarton	W L	D L	10	4	3	3	5	5	5	4
Livingston	L W	L W	4	1	2	1	3	1	3	1
Raith	L W	D W	6	1	2	3	4	2	4	1
Alloa	L D	L W	4	0	3	1	1	3	3	0
Cowdenbeath										
Rangers										

Season	Division	Pos	P	W	D	L	F	A	GD	Pts
2013-14	Championship	9	36	11	7	18	50	72	-22	40
2012-13	Championship	8	36	8	12	16	51	65	-14	36
2011-12	League One	1	36	20	11	5	68	29	+39	71

Over/Under 56%/44% 2nd   **Both score** 53%/47% 4th

DUMBARTON

Nickname: The Sons   **Ground:** Bet Butler Stadium
Web: www.dumbartonfootballclub.com

It was a great achievement for the part-time Sons to finish fifth last season and score the second- highest number of goals in the division. However, their flimsy defence is likely to face tougher tests this time, so it would be no surprise to see them slip back.

	2013-14 H	A	P	W	D	L	OV	UN	BS	CS
Hibernian			-	-	-	-	-	-	-	-
Hearts			-	-	-	-	-	-	-	-
Falkirk	D W	W L	4	1	1	2	1	3	2	0
Queen of Sth	L L	W L	2	0	0	2	1	1	0	0
Dumbarton										
Livingston	L D	W W	6	0	1	5	6	0	4	0
Raith	L D	L W	4	1	1	2	4	0	4	0
Alloa	D W	W W	6	3	2	1	5	1	6	0
Cowdenbeath	D W	L W	10	3	3	4	7	3	5	1
Rangers										

Season	Division	Pos	P	W	D	L	F	A	GD	Pts
2013-14	Championship	5	36	15	6	15	65	64	+1	51
2012-13	Championship	7	36	13	4	19	58	83	-25	43
2011-12	League One	4	36	17	7	12	61	61	0	58

Over/Under 78%/22% 1st   **Both score** 75%/25% 1st

FALKIRK

Nickname: The Bairns   **Ground:** Falkirk Stadium
Web: www.falkirkfc.co.uk

Falkirk were challenging for promotion for most of the season but just couldn't get over the line. Manager Gary Holt has moved on and stability could be the name of the game for the Bairns. They could be more likely to make a challenge in 2015-16.

	2013-14 H	A	P	W	D	L	OV	UN	BS	CS
Hibernian			3	0	1	2	2	1	3	0
Hearts			3	1	1	1	1	2	1	1
Falkirk										
Queen of Sth	W W	L W	6	5	0	1	4	2	2	3
Dumbarton	L W	D L	4	1	0	3	3	1	3	1
Livingston	W D	W W	6	3	1	2	4	2	5	1
Raith	W W	D W	8	4	2	2	4	4	5	2
Alloa	D W	D L	2	1	1	0	1	1	1	1
Cowdenbeath	W W	L W	6	6	0	0	4	2	1	5
Rangers			3	0	0	3	1	2	1	0

Season	Division	Pos	P	W	D	L	F	A	GD	Pts
2013-14	Championship	3	36	19	9	8	59	33	+26	66
2012-13	Championship	3	36	18	8	13	52	48	+4	53
2011-12	Championship	3	36	13	13	10	53	48	+5	52

Over/Under 47%/53% 5th   **Both score** 53%/47% 4th

HEARTS

Nickname: Jambos   **Ground:** Tynecastle
Web: www.heartsfc.co.uk

Hearts have had a dismal time but start afresh under new ownership and with former Scotland boss Craig Levein in charge. Despite their relegation, Hearts finished 2013-14 in fine fettle and could make a swift return to the top flight.

	2013-14 H	A	Last six seasons at home P	W	D	L	OV	UN	BS	CS
Hibernian	W W	L W	11	6	3	2	2	9	2	8
Hearts										
Falkirk			3	2	1	0	2	1	2	1
Queen of Sth			-	-	-	-	-	-	-	-
Dumbarton			-	-	-	-	-	-	-	-
Livingston			-	-	-	-	-	-	-	-
Raith			-	-	-	-	-	-	-	-
Alloa			-	-	-	-	-	-	-	-
Cowdenbeath			-	-	-	-	-	-	-	-
Rangers			7	2	0	5	5	2	4	1

Season	Division	Pos	P	W	D	L	F	A	GD	Pts
2013-14	Premiership	12	38	10	8	20	45	65	-20	23
2012-13	Premiership	10	38	11	11	16	40	49	-9	44
2011-12	Premiership	5	38	15	7	16	45	43	+2	52

Over/Under 50%/50% 6th   **Both score** 55%/45% 5th

HIBERNIAN

Nickname: The Hibees   **Ground:** Easter Road
Web: www.hibernianfc.co.uk

Last season was a disaster at Easter Road as Hibs conspired to get themselves relegated through the playoffs. Terry Butcher was appointed in November but sacked by June, and there's no certainly guarantee a side in turmoil will bounce straight back.

	2013-14 H	A	Last six seasons at home P	W	D	L	OV	UN	BS	CS
Hibernian										
Hearts	W L	L L	11	2	5	4	5	6	8	2
Falkirk			3	2	1	0	1	2	1	2
Queen of Sth			-	-	-	-	-	-	-	-
Dumbarton			-	-	-	-	-	-	-	-
Livingston			-	-	-	-	-	-	-	-
Raith			-	-	-	-	-	-	-	-
Alloa			-	-	-	-	-	-	-	-
Cowdenbeath			-	-	-	-	-	-	-	-
Rangers			8	0	1	7	4	4	3	0

Season	Division	Pos	P	W	D	L	F	A	GD	Pts
2013-14	Premiership	11	38	8	11	19	31	51	-20	35
2012-13	Premiership	7	38	13	12	13	49	52	-3	51
2011-12	Premiership	11	38	8	9	21	40	67	-27	33

Over/Under 34%/66% 12th   **Both score** 39%/61% 10th

LIVINGSTON

Nickname: Livi Lions   **Ground:** Almondvale
Web: www.livingstonfc.co.uk

Livi never really got going last season and will have to cope with the loss of top goalscorer Marc McNulty, which could be a difficult task for experienced manager John McGlynn. Avoiding a relegation scrap could be the priority this term.

	2013-14 H	A	Last six seasons at home P	W	D	L	OV	UN	BS	CS
Hibernian			-	-	-	-	-	-	-	-
Hearts			-	-	-	-	-	-	-	-
Falkirk	L L	L D	6	1	1	4	4	2	4	0
Queen of Sth	D L	D L	6	1	4	1	5	1	5	1
Dumbarton	L L	W D	6	2	1	3	4	2	4	2
Livingston										
Raith	W W	L W	6	4	1	1	4	2	3	3
Alloa	W W	L W	4	3	1	0	3	1	2	2
Cowdenbeath	W W	W L	4	3	1	0	2	2	2	2
Rangers										

Season	Division	Pos	P	W	D	L	F	A	GD	Pts
2013-14	Championship	6	36	13	7	16	51	56	-5	46
2012-13	Championship	4	36	14	10	12	58	56	+2	52
2011-12	Championship	5	36	13	9	14	56	54	+2	48

Over/Under 56%/44% 2nd   **Both score** 47%/53% 7th

QUEEN OF THE SOUTH

Nickname: Doonhamers **Ground:** Palmerston Park
Web: www.qosfc.com

The Doonhamers had a decent campaign after storming to the Division Two title in 2013, and fourth place last term was a good finish. It will be difficult to maintain that trajectory, but they've shown that they can surprise more illustrious opponents.

	2013-14 H	A	Last six seasons at home P	W	D	L	OV	UN	BS	CS
Hibernian			-	-	-	-	-	-	-	-
Hearts			-	-	-	-	-	-	-	-
Falkirk	W L	L L	6	1	1	4	3	3	3	2
Queen of Sth										
Dumbarton	L W	W W	2	1	0	1	2	0	2	0
Livingston	D W	D W	6	2	2	2	4	2	3	1
Raith	L W	L L	8	3	1	4	3	5	3	3
Alloa	D W	W W	4	2	2	0	1	3	1	3
Cowdenbeath	D W	W D	4	2	2	0	3	1	3	1
Rangers										

Season	Division	Pos	P	W	D	L	F	A	GD	Pts
2013-14	Championship	4	36	16	7	13	53	39	+14	55
2012-13	League One	1	36	29	5	2	92	23	+69	92
2011-12	Championship	10	36	7	11	18	38	64	-26	32

Over/Under 47%/53% 5th   **Both score** 50%/50% 6th

RAITH

Nickname: The Rovers **Ground:** Stark's Park
Web: www.raithrovers.net

Beating Rangers in the Ramsdens Cup final papered over the cracks of a poor season for the men from Kirkcaldy. They won just three of their final 20 matches and it's difficult to see them making much of an impression in a tougher section this season.

	2013-14 H	A	P	W	D	L	OV	UN	BS	CS
Hibernian			-	-	-	-	-	-	-	-
Hearts			-	-	-	-	-	-	-	-
Falkirk	D L	L L	8	3	3	2	5	3	6	2
Queen of Sth	W W	W L	8	4	1	3	3	5	3	2
Dumbarton	W L	W D	4	2	1	1	4	0	4	0
Livingston	W L	L L	6	1	1	4	2	4	1	2
Raith										
Alloa	W D	L W	4	3	1	0	3	1	4	0
Cowdenbeath	D L	W L	6	1	3	2	5	1	5	0
Rangers										

Season	Division	Pos	P	W	D	L	F	A	GD	Pts
2013-14	Championship	7	36	11	9	16	48	61	-13	42
2012-13	Championship	6	36	11	13	12	45	48	-3	46
2011-12	Championship	7	36	11	11	14	46	49	-3	44

Over/Under 53%/47% 4th **Both score** 61%/39% 2nd

RANGERS

Nickname: The Gers **Ground:** Ibrox Stadium
Web: www.rangers.co.uk

The Gers cruised to League One success last term but should find what is expected to be their final campaign outside the top flight much tougher. Their off-the-field issues look far from resolved and Rangers winning the title is not the formality it was last year.

	2013-14 H	A	P	W	D	L	OV	UN	BS	CS
Hibernian			6	4	1	1	3	3	1	4
Hearts			9	5	3	1	3	6	4	5
Falkirk			3	3	0	0	3	0	2	1
Queen of Sth			-	-	-	-	-	-	-	-
Dumbarton			-	-	-	-	-	-	-	-
Livingston			-	-	-	-	-	-	-	-
Raith			-	-	-	-	-	-	-	-
Alloa			-	-	-	-	-	-	-	-
Cowdenbeath			-	-	-	-	-	-	-	-
Rangers										

Season	Division	Pos	P	W	D	L	F	A	GD	Pts
2013-14	League One	1	36	33	3	0	106	18	+88	102
2012-13	League Two	1	36	25	8	3	87	29	+58	83
2011-12	Premiership	2	38	26	5	7	77	28	+49	73

Over/Under 64%/36% 6th **Both score** 36%/64% 11th

Rangers last met Hearts in the SPL back in 2012

Results 2013-14

	Alloa	Cowdenbeath	Dumbarton	Dundee	Falkirk	Hamilton	Livingston	Morton	Queen of Sth	Raith
Alloa		3-1/0-1	1-2/1-5	0-1/0-3	0-0/3-0	1-0/0-3	1-0/0-3	2-0/2-0	0-3/0-1	1-0/0-1
Cowdenbeath	0-2/2-2		3-2/2-4	0-2/2-0	1-0/0-2	2-4/1-1	2-3/4-0	5-1/3-0	0-2/1-1	3-4/1-0
Dumbarton	1-1/4-1	0-0/5-1		1-4/0-1	1-1/2-1	2-1/4-1	1-2/2-2	3-1/2-0	0-1/0-3	2-4/3-3
Dundee	1-0/1-1	1-2/4-0	3-0/2-1		1-1/0-1	0-0/1-0	3-0/0-1	3-1/2-0	2-1/1-0	2-0/0-0
Falkirk	0-0/3-1	4-0/5-0	1-2/2-0	3-1/2-0		1-2/0-0	4-1/1-1	3-1/1-1	2-1/1-0	3-1/2-1
Hamilton	0-1/2-1	1-0/3-4	4-1/3-3	0-3/1-1	2-0/3-1		2-0/2-0	1-0/10-2	2-0/3-1	1-1/3-2
Livingston	3-2/2-0	5-1/1-0	1-3/1-2	2-1/0-2	0-3/0-1	0-0/1-1		2-2/0-1	3-3/1-2	3-0/2-0
Morton	0-2/0-1	2-0/1-1	2-0/3-0	1-2/1-0	0-2/1-1	1-1/3-4	1-5/2-0		0-2/1-1	1-1/0-0
Queen of Sth	0-0/3-1	1-1/2-1	1-2/3-1	4-3/0-1	2-0/1-2	0-1/1-1	2-2/2-0	2-0/3-0		0-1/1-0
Raith	4-2/1-1	3-3/1-2	2-1/1-3	0-0/0-2	1-1/2-4	0-1/2-4	1-0/2-4	2-1/2-1	2-1/3-2	

League table 2013-14

Pos	H	A		P	Home W	D	L	F	A	Away W	D	L	F	A	GD	Pts
1	3	1	Dundee	36	11	4	3	27	9	10	2	6	27	17	+28	69 (C)
2	2	2	Hamilton	36	12	3	3	43	21	7	7	4	25	20	+27	67 (P)
3	1	3	Falkirk	36	12	4	2	38	13	7	5	6	21	20	+26	66
4	4	5	Queen of Sth	36	9	4	5	28	17	7	3	8	25	22	+14	55
5	5	4	Dumbarton	36	7	5	6	33	28	8	1	9	32	36	+1	51
6	6	6	Livingston	36	7	4	7	27	24	6	3	9	24	32	-5	46
7	7	8	Raith	36	7	4	7	29	33	4	5	9	19	28	-13	42
8	9	7	Alloa	36	7	1	10	15	24	4	6	8	19	27	-17	40
9	8	9	Cowdenbeath	36	7	3	8	32	30	4	4	10	18	42	-22	40
10	10	10	Morton	36	5	6	7	20	23	1	2	15	12	48	-39	26 (R)

Best attack

		GF	GFA
1	Hamilton	68	1.89
2	Dumbarton	65	1.81
3	Falkirk	59	1.64
4	Dundee	54	1.50
5	Queen of Sth	53	1.47
6	Livingston	51	1.42
7	Cowdenbeath	50	1.39
8	Raith	48	1.33
9	Alloa	34	0.94
10	Morton	32	0.89

Best defence

		GA	GAA
1	Dundee	26	0.72
2	Falkirk	33	0.92
3	Queen of Sth	39	1.08
4	Hamilton	41	1.14
5	Alloa	51	1.42
6	Livingston	56	1.56
7	Raith	61	1.69
8	Dumbarton	64	1.78
9	Morton	71	1.97
10	Cowdenbeath	72	2.00

Top scorers

		Team	Goals scored
R Loy		Falkirk	20
K Hemmings		Cowdenbeath	18
P MacDonald		Dundee	17
M McNulty		Livingston	17
A Andreu		Hamilton	13
J Keatings		Hamilton	13
I Russell		Queen of Sth	13

Key POS H A Position, home/away rank **Sup** Avg supremacy
GFA/GAA Goals For/Against Avg **PGA** Pts Gained Avg

Record when first to score

		P	W	D	L	F	A	Sup	PGA	Pts
1	Dundee	25	20	3	2	49	13	+1.44	2.5	63
2	Falkirk	24	19	3	2	54	17	+1.54	2.5	60
3	Hamilton	20	16	4	0	51	17	+1.70	2.6	52
4	Queen of Sth	16	14	1	1	32	6	+1.63	2.7	43
5	Cowdenbeath	19	11	4	4	41	30	+0.58	1.9	37
6	Alloa	15	11	1	3	25	9	+1.07	2.4	36
7	Dumbarton	13	11	1	1	38	15	+1.77	2.6	34
8	Livingston	18	9	6	3	38	23	+0.83	1.8	33
9	Raith	10	8	1	1	21	13	+0.80	2.5	25
10	Morton	9	6	1	2	14	6	+0.89	2.1	19

Record when keeping a clean sheet

		P	W	D	F	Sup	PGA	Pts
1	Queen of Sth	12	11	1	22	+1.83	2.8	34
2	Dundee	19	16	3	32	+1.68	2.7	51
3	Morton	7	6	1	11	+1.57	2.7	19
4	Livingston	7	6	1	12	+1.71	2.7	19
5	Cowdenbeath	7	6	1	12	+1.71	2.7	19
6	Alloa	13	10	3	16	+1.23	2.5	33
7	Falkirk	13	10	3	23	+1.77	2.5	33
8	Hamilton	12	9	3	15	+1.25	2.5	30
9	Raith	6	3	3	3	+0.50	2.0	12
10	Dumbarton	2	1	1	2	+1.00	2.0	4

Over 2.5 goals

	H	A	%
Dumbarton	12	16	78%
Cowdenbeath	9	11	56%
Livingston	10	10	56%

Under 2.5 goals

	H	A	%
Dundee	11	11	61%
Morton	14	8	61%
Alloa	10	11	58%

Both to score

	H	A	%
Dumbarton	13	14	75%
Raith	14	8	61%
Hamilton	10	10	56%

Both not to score

	H	A	%
Dundee	12	12	67%
Alloa	15	8	64%
Morton, Livingston			53%

AIRDRIEONIANS

Nickname: Diamonds **Ground:** Excelsior Stadium
Web: www.airdriefc.com

Airdrieonians looked doomed after winning just three of their first 20 games, but they recovered well after Gary Bollan joined as manager. They showed promotion form in the rest of the season to finish sixth and shouldn't flirt with relegation this time.

	2013-14 H	A	Last six seasons at home P	W	D	L	OV	UN	BS	CS
Morton			6	3	0	3	5	1	2	3
Dunfermline	L W	L W	8	1	3	4	4	4	5	1
Stranraer	W D	L D	2	1	1	0	1	1	2	0
Ayr	L W	D L	6	2	2	2	4	2	3	1
Stenhousemuir	L D	D W	6	2	2	2	3	3	3	1
Airdrieonians										
Forfar	L W	D D	6	4	1	1	4	2	3	2
Brechin	W W	L D	6	3	2	1	5	1	6	0
Peterhead			2	1	1	0	1	1	1	1
Stirling			2	1	1	0	1	1	2	0

Season	Division	Pos	P	W	D	L	F	A	GD	Pts
2013-14	League One	6	36	12	9	15	47	57	-10	45
2012-13	Championship	10	36	5	7	24	41	89	-48	22
2011-12	League One	4	36	14	10	12	68	60	+8	52

Over/Under 53%/47% 11th **Both score** 56%/44% 9th

AYR

Nickname: Honest Men **Ground:** Somerset Park
Web: www.ayrunitedfc.co.uk

Ayr were the third-highest scorers in the division after Rangers and Dunfermline, which helped the Honest Men squeeze into the playoffs. However, the defence needs work if they're to improve on fourth place as they conceded 66 goals in 36 games.

	2013-14 H	A	Last six seasons at home P	W	D	L	OV	UN	BS	CS
Morton			4	1	1	2	0	4	0	2
Dunfermline	L D	L L	4	1	1	2	2	2	3	1
Stranraer	L W	D L	6	5	0	1	6	0	4	2
Ayr										
Stenhousemuir	W L	D D	6	3	1	2	4	2	5	1
Airdrieonians	D W	W L	6	3	2	1	4	2	4	2
Forfar	W L	W L	6	3	0	3	4	2	4	1
Brechin	D L	D L	8	3	2	3	5	3	5	2
Peterhead			4	1	3	0	1	3	2	2
Stirling			2	1	1	0	1	1	2	0

Season	Division	Pos	P	W	D	L	F	A	GD	Pts
2013-14	League One	4	36	14	7	15	65	66	-1	49
2012-13	League One	7	36	12	5	19	53	65	-12	41
2011-12	Championship	9	36	9	11	16	44	67	-23	38

Over/Under 67%/33% 4th **Both score** 58%/42% 6th

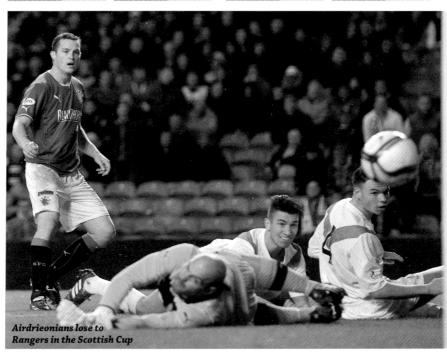

Airdrieonians lose to Rangers in the Scottish Cup

BRECHIN

Nickname: The City   **Ground:** Glebe Park
Web: www.brechincity.com

City were highly fancied but failed to make much of an impression and were never really in the running for a playoff place. However, they won three and drew one of their last five games, so there is hope if manager Ray McKinnon can keep his squad fit.

	2013-14 H A		Last six seasons at home P	W	D	L	OV	UN	BS	CS
Morton			-	-	-	-	-	-	-	-
Dunfermline	D W	L L	2	1	1	0	1	1	2	0
Stranraer	D L	L W	6	3	2	1	4	2	4	2
Ayr	D W	D W	8	5	1	2	4	4	4	2
Stenhousemuir	L L	L L	10	5	2	3	5	5	5	4
Airdrieonians	W D	L L	6	2	3	1	3	3	6	0
Forfar	W L	L D	8	3	1	4	5	3	5	1
Brechin										
Peterhead			6	3	2	1	5	1	5	1
Stirling			6	2	1	3	4	2	5	1

Season	Division	Pos	P	W	D	L	F	A	GD	Pts
2013-14	League One	8	36	12	6	18	57	71	-14	42
2012-13	League One	3	36	19	4	13	72	59	+13	61
2011-12	League One	8	36	10	11	15	47	62	-15	41

Over/Under 75%/25% 2nd   **Both score** 83%/17% 1st

DUNFERMLINE

Nickname: The Pars   **Ground:** East End Park
Web: www.dafc.co.uk

The Pars were expected to provide Rangers with their biggest challenge and while they were clearly the second best team in the division, they failed to navigate the play offs. The experience of boss Jim Jefferies should help them make another bold challenge.

	2013-14 H A		Last six seasons at home P	W	D	L	OV	UN	BS	CS
Morton			8	4	1	3	6	2	6	1
Dunfermline										
Stranraer	W W	W L	2	2	0	0	2	0	2	0
Ayr	W W	W D	4	3	0	1	3	1	2	1
Stenhousemuir	W D	W W	2	1	1	0	1	1	1	1
Airdrieonians	W L	W L	8	3	2	3	3	5	4	3
Forfar	D D	L W	2	0	2	0	0	2	1	1
Brechin	W W	D L	2	2	0	0	2	0	2	0
Peterhead			-	-	-	-	-	-	-	-
Stirling			2	2	0	0	2	0	1	1

Season	Division	Pos	P	W	D	L	F	A	GD	Pts
2013-14	League One	2	36	19	6	11	68	54	+14	63
2012-13	Championship	9	36	14	7	15	62	59	+3	34
2011-12	Premiership	12	38	5	10	23	40	82	-42	25

Over/Under 72%/28% 3rd   **Both score** 67%/33% 4th

FORFAR

Nickname: The Loons   **Ground:** Station Park
Web: www.forfarathletic.co.uk

The Loons got off to a poor start and didn't set the world alight at the end of the season either, so a mid-table finish was probably fair. It will be interesting to see how manager Dick Campbell gets on now that his twin brother Ian is no longer his assistant.

	2013-14 H A		Last six seasons at home P	W	D	L	OV	UN	BS	CS
Morton			-	-	-	-	-	-	-	-
Dunfermline	W L	D D	2	1	0	1	2	0	1	1
Stranraer	L W	W L	6	5	0	1	3	3	2	4
Ayr	L W	L W	6	5	0	1	5	1	5	0
Stenhousemuir	L W	D L	10	4	3	3	7	3	7	3
Airdrieonians	D D	W L	6	1	2	3	5	1	6	0
Forfar										
Brechin	W D	L W	8	4	3	1	3	5	5	3
Peterhead			2	1	1	0	1	1	2	0
Stirling			2	1	1	0	2	0	2	0

Season	Division	Pos	P	W	D	L	F	A	GD	Pts
2013-14	League One	7	36	12	7	17	55	62	-7	43
2012-13	League One	4	36	17	3	16	67	74	-7	54
2011-12	League One	7	36	11	9	16	59	72	-13	42

Over/Under 58%/42% 6th   **Both score** 58%/42% 6th

MORTON

Nickname: The Ton   **Ground:** Cappielow Park
Web: www.gmfc.net

Morton had a dismal season in the second tier as the club was hit by financial problems and they need to pick themselves up from a 10-2 thumping by Hamilton on the final day of the season. Arresting the slide would probably be enough for them.

	2013-14 H A		Last six seasons at home P	W	D	L	OV	UN	BS	CS
Morton										
Dunfermline			8	3	1	4	4	4	5	0
Stranraer			-	-	-	-	-	-	-	-
Ayr			4	4	0	0	3	1	3	1
Stenhousemuir			-	-	-	-	-	-	-	-
Airdrieonians			6	5	1	0	2	4	2	4
Forfar			-	-	-	-	-	-	-	-
Brechin			-	-	-	-	-	-	-	-
Peterhead			-	-	-	-	-	-	-	-
Stirling			2	1	1	0	0	2	0	2

Season	Division	Pos	P	W	D	L	F	A	GD	Pts
2013-14	Championship	10	36	6	8	22	32	71	-39	26
2012-13	Championship	2	36	20	7	9	73	47	+26	67
2011-12	Championship	8	36	10	12	14	40	55	-15	42

Over/Under 39%/61% 9th   **Both score** 47%/53% 7th

PETERHEAD

Nickname: The Blue Toon **Ground:** Balmoor
Web: www.peterheadfc.com

The Blue Toon were able to recover from a sluggish start and were worthy champions in League Two, inspired once again by goal machine Rory McAllister. It would be no surprise if they made another bold challenge now they are finally out of the basement.

	2013-14		Last six seasons at home							
	H	A	P	W	D	L	OV	UN	BS	CS
Morton			-	-	-	-	-	-	-	-
Dunfermline			-	-	-	-	-	-	-	-
Stranraer			4	2	1	1	2	2	2	2
Ayr			4	1	0	3	4	0	3	1
Stenhousemuir			4	0	2	2	3	1	2	0
Airdrieonians			2	1	0	1	2	0	2	0
Forfar			2	0	1	1	1	1	2	0
Brechin			6	2	1	3	3	3	2	1
Peterhead										
Stirling	W L	L W	8	2	5	1	4	4	6	1

Season	Division	Pos	P	W	D	L	F	A	GD	Pts
2013-14	League Two	1	36	23	7	6	74	38	+36	76
2012-13	League Two	2	36	17	8	11	52	28	+24	59
2011-12	League Two	5	36	15	6	15	51	53	-2	51

Over/Under 64%/36% 2nd   **Both score** 58%/42% 4th

STENHOUSEMUIR

Nickname: Warriors **Ground:** Ochilview Park
Web: www.stenhousemuirfc.com

The Warriors waited a full month to replace manager Martyn Corrigan with Scott Booth and that indecision probably cost them a top-four place. With the team now settled, they look likely to make another push for the playoffs at least.

	2013-14		Last six seasons at home							
	H	A	P	W	D	L	OV	UN	BS	CS
Morton			-	-	-	-	-	-	-	-
Dunfermline	L L	L D	2	0	0	2	2	0	2	0
Stranraer	W D	L D	4	1	2	1	1	3	2	2
Ayr	D D	L W	6	3	3	0	3	3	5	1
Stenhousemuir										
Airdrieonians	D L	W D	6	1	2	3	3	3	4	1
Forfar	D W	W L	10	3	2	5	5	5	5	2
Brechin	W W	W W	10	4	4	2	7	3	9	1
Peterhead			4	3	1	0	2	2	3	1
Stirling			4	2	0	2	4	0	2	2

Season	Division	Pos	P	W	D	L	F	A	GD	Pts
2013-14	League One	5	36	12	12	12	57	66	-9	48
2012-13	League One	6	36	12	13	11	59	59	0	49
2011-12	League One	5	36	15	6	15	54	49	+5	51

Over/Under 56%/44% 10th   **Both score** 72%/28% 2nd

STIRLING

Nickname: The Binos **Ground:** Forthbank Stadium
Web: www.stirlingalbionfc.co.uk

The Binos came up through the playoffs by hitting form at just the right time, winning eight of their final ten matches of 2013-14. If the spirit of that run can be maintained they could go well, but gaining a foothold at a higher level has to be the priority.

	2013-14		Last six seasons at home							
	H	A	P	W	D	L	OV	UN	BS	CS
Morton			2	1	0	1	1	1	1	0
Dunfermline			2	0	1	1	0	2	0	0
Stranraer			2	1	0	1	2	0	2	0
Ayr			2	1	1	0	1	1	1	1
Stenhousemuir			4	1	3	0	2	2	3	1
Airdrieonians			2	0	0	2	1	1	1	0
Forfar			2	0	1	1	2	0	2	0
Brechin			6	3	0	3	4	2	4	2
Peterhead	W L	L W	8	5	1	2	3	5	3	4
Stirling										

Season	Division	Pos	P	W	D	L	F	A	GD	Pts
2013-14	League Two	3	36	16	10	10	60	50	+10	58
2012-13	League Two	7	36	12	9	15	59	58	+1	45
2011-12	League One	10	36	12	6	18	46	70	-24	34

Over/Under 64%/36% 2nd   **Both score** 64%/36% 3rd

STRANRAER

Nickname: The Blues **Ground:** Stair Park
Web: www.stranraerfc.org

Victory on the final day of the regular season ended a run of nine games without a win for Stranraer. Their poor form caught up with them in the playoffs as they flopped in the semi-finals, but another top-four finish looks a reasonable aim this season.

	2013-14		Last six seasons at home							
	H	A	P	W	D	L	OV	UN	BS	CS
Morton			-	-	-	-	-	-	-	-
Dunfermline	L W	L L	2	1	0	1	2	0	2	0
Stranraer										
Ayr	D W	W L	6	2	1	3	3	3	3	2
Stenhousemuir	W D	L D	4	1	3	0	0	4	2	3
Airdrieonians	W D	L D	2	1	1	0	1	1	2	0
Forfar	L W	W L	6	4	0	2	4	2	2	2
Brechin	W L	D W	6	2	0	4	5	1	3	1
Peterhead			4	1	0	3	3	1	1	0
Stirling			2	1	0	1	1	1	1	1

Season	Division	Pos	P	W	D	L	F	A	GD	Pts
2013-14	League One	3	36	14	9	13	57	57	0	51
2012-13	League One	8	36	10	7	19	43	71	-28	37
2011-12	League Two	3	36	17	7	12	77	57	+20	58

Over/Under 58%/42% 6th   **Both score** 67%/33% 4th

Results 2013-14

	Airdrieonians	Arbroath	Ayr	Brechin	Dunfermline	East Fife	Forfar	Rangers	Stenh'semuir	Stranraer
Airdrieonians		2-1/2-0	0-1/3-0	3-1/2-1	0-3/2-0	1-3/2-1	0-2/5-1	0-6/0-1	0-1/1-1	3-2/1-1
Arbroath	3-2/0-1		0-3/2-3	2-1/0-1	0-3/1-2	2-2/2-1	3-0/2-3	0-3/1-2	3-4/2-1	1-2/4-2
Ayr	2-2/3-0	2-0/2-1		2-2/1-3	2-4/1-1	2-0/4-1	2-0/2-3	0-2/0-2	4-3/2-3	3-6/5-0
Brechin	4-3/1-1	3-1/2-4	1-1/2-1		1-1/3-2	2-0/3-0	2-1/1-5	3-4/1-2	0-1/1-3	1-1/1-3
Dunfermline	2-1/0-1	2-3/3-0	5-1/3-0	3-1/2-1		1-2/1-2	1-1/0-0	0-4/1-1	3-2/0-0	3-1/3-2
East Fife	1-0/0-0	2-1/1-0	1-4/0-5	1-3/1-2	0-1/1-3		1-3/2-1	0-4/0-1	1-0/1-2	1-2/1-1
Forfar	3-3/1-1	1-1/0-2	0-1/4-2	2-0/1-1	4-0/2-4	2-0/1-2		0-1/0-2	1-2/3-0	1-2/1-0
Rangers	2-0/3-0	5-1/3-2	3-0/2-1	4-1/2-1	3-1/2-0	5-0/2-0	6-1/3-0		8-0/3-3	1-1/3-0
Stenh'semuir	1-1/1-2	3-2/2-2	1-1/1-1	3-2/4-2	4-5/1-2	1-1/1-1	1-1/4-1	0-2/0-4		1-0/1-1
Stranraer	3-1/1-1	3-2/1-1	1-1/4-0	3-0/1-2	1-2/3-1	2-0/2-0	0-4/3-1	0-3/0-2	1-0/1-1	

League table 2013-14

Pos	H	A		P	W	D	L	F	A	W	D	L	F	A	GD	Pts
						Home					Away					
1	1	1	Rangers	36	16	2	0	60	12	17	1	0	46	6	+88	102 (C)
2	2	2	Dunfermline	36	9	4	5	33	23	10	2	6	35	31	+14	63
3	3	6	Stranraer	36	9	4	5	30	22	5	5	8	27	35	0	51
4	5	4	Ayr	36	8	3	7	39	33	6	4	8	26	33	-1	49
5	7	3	Stenh'semuir	36	5	8	5	30	31	7	4	7	27	35	-9	48
6	4	8	Airdrieonians	36	9	2	7	27	26	3	7	8	20	31	-10	45
7	8	5	Forfar	36	6	4	8	27	24	6	3	9	28	38	-7	43
8	6	7	Brechin	36	7	4	7	32	34	5	2	11	25	37	-14	42
9	10	9	East Fife	36	5	2	11	15	33	4	3	11	16	36	-38	32 (R)
10	9	10	Arbroath	36	6	1	11	28	36	3	3	12	24	39	-23	31 (R)

Best attack

		GF	GFA
1	Rangers	106	2.94
2	Dunfermline	68	1.89
3	Ayr	65	1.81
4	Stranraer	57	1.58
5	Stenh'semuir	57	1.58
6	Brechin	57	1.58
7	Forfar	55	1.53
8	Arbroath	52	1.44
9	Airdrieonians	47	1.31
10	East Fife	31	0.86

Best defence

		GA	GAA
1	Rangers	18	0.50
2	Dunfermline	54	1.50
3	Stranraer	57	1.58
4	Airdrieonians	57	1.58
5	Forfar	62	1.72
6	Ayr	66	1.83
7	Stenh'semuir	66	1.83
8	East Fife	69	1.92
9	Brechin	71	1.97
10	Arbroath	75	2.08

Top scorers

	Team	Goals scored
M Moffat	Ayr	26
J Daly	Rangers	18
L McCulloch	Rangers	17
J Longworth	Stranraer	14
M Grehan	Stranraer	13

Key Points in all tables (except the league table) do not include any deductions imposed by the league. **POS H A** Overall league position, rank from home games only, rank from away games only **Sup** Average match supremacy **GFA** Goals For Average **GAA** Goals Against Average **PGA** Points Gained Average

Record when first to score

		P	W	D	L	F	A	Sup	PGA	Pts
1	Rangers	32	30	2	0	91	9	+2.56	2.9	92
2	Ayr	20	14	4	2	49	22	+1.35	2.3	46
3	Forfar	21	12	5	4	47	24	+1.10	2.0	41
4	Stranraer	19	12	4	3	42	22	+1.05	2.1	40
5	Dunfermline	17	12	2	3	37	17	+1.18	2.2	38
6	Airdrieonians	16	10	5	1	31	15	+1.00	2.2	35
7	Brechin	15	11	1	3	34	20	+0.93	2.3	34
8	Stenh'semuir	16	10	3	3	38	27	+0.69	2.1	33
9	Arbroath	13	7	3	3	30	24	+0.46	1.8	24
10	East Fife	8	4	2	2	9	7	+0.25	1.8	14

Record when keeping a clean sheet

		P	W	D	F	Sup	PGA	Pts
1	Rangers	23	23	0	68	+2.96	3.0	69
2	Ayr	9	9	0	24	+2.67	3.0	27
3	Stranraer	5	5	0	12	+2.40	3.0	15
4	Brechin	3	3	0	6	+2.00	3.0	9
5	Arbroath	2	2	0	5	+2.50	3.0	6
6	Forfar	8	7	1	18	+2.25	2.8	22
7	Airdrieonians	6	5	1	9	+1.50	2.7	16
8	East Fife	4	3	1	3	+0.75	2.5	10
9	Stenh'semuir	4	3	1	3	+0.75	2.5	10
10	Dunfermline	7	5	2	13	+1.86	2.4	17

Over 2.5 goals

	H	A	%
Arbroath	16	12	78%
Brechin	12	15	75%
Dunfermline	13	13	72%

Under 2.5 goals

	H	A	%
Airdrieonians	8	9	47%
Stenh'semuir	9	7	44%
East Fife, Forfar, Stranraer			42%

Both to score

	H	A	%
Brechin	15	15	83%
Stenhousemuir	15	11	72%
Arbroath	12	13	69%

Both not to score

	H	A	%
Rangers	9	14	64%
Airdrieonians	9	7	44%
East Fife	8	8	44%

ALBION

Nickname: The Wee Rovers **Ground:** Cliftonhill
Web: www.albionroversfc.com

Albion had a run to the quarter-finals of the Scottish Cup, taking Rangers to a replay and beating Motherwell, but their league exploits were less auspicious. They won only two away games and need to improve to force their way into the playoff picture.

	2013-14 H A	Last six seasons at home P W D L OV UN BS CS							
East Fife		4	0	2	2	2	2	2	0
Arbroath		6	3	1	2	2	4	1	3
Annan	W L D L	8	3	3	2	1	7	1	5
Clyde	W W D L	4	3	1	0	2	2	2	2
Berwick	L L L L	8	4	1	3	5	3	4	1
Montrose	L W L L	8	3	1	4	1	7	1	3
Albion									
East Stirling	W W W D	8	6	0	2	4	4	3	3
Elgin	D W W D	8	4	2	2	5	3	5	2
Queen's Park	W W D L	6	4	0	2	3	3	3	2

Season	Division	Pos	P	W	D	L	F	A	GD	Pts
2013-14	League Two	7	36	12	8	16	41	54	-13	44
2012-13	League One	10	36	7	3	26	45	82	-37	24
2011-12	League One	9	36	10	7	19	43	66	-23	37

Over/Under 50%/50% 10th   **Both score** 53%/47% 6th

ANNAN

Nickname: Galabankies **Ground:** Galabank
Web: www.annanathleticfc.com

Annan made big strides and were second for much of the campaign before being beaten in the playoffs by in-form Stirling. Manager Jim Chapman should help them continue to make progress in his second full season in the dugout.

	2013-14 H A	Last six seasons at home P W D L OV UN BS CS							
East Fife		-	-	-	-	-	-	-	-
Arbroath		2	1	0	1	2	0	1	1
Annan									
Clyde	L L L W	8	3	0	5	2	6	2	3
Berwick	W W L W	12	3	6	3	7	5	10	1
Montrose	W W W L	12	7	3	2	8	4	9	3
Albion	D W L W	8	2	4	2	4	4	6	2
East Stirling	L L D L	12	7	1	4	10	2	8	3
Elgin	W W W W	12	5	5	2	6	6	6	4
Queen's Park	W D W W	10	5	1	4	7	3	8	1

Season	Division	Pos	P	W	D	L	F	A	GD	Pts
2013-14	League Two	2	36	19	6	11	69	49	+20	63
2012-13	League Two	8	36	11	10	15	54	65	-11	43
2011-12	League Two	6	36	13	10	13	53	53	0	49

Over/Under 61%/39% 4th   **Both score** 67%/33% 1st

ARBROATH

Nickname: Red Lichties **Ground:** Gayfield Park
Web: www.arbroathfc.co.uk

Arbroath had a season to forget and manager Gary Sheerin departed to coach the kids at Aberdeen in the summer. A playoff bid is realistic but defensive reinforcements are required, as the Red Lichties conceded at least twice in 26 of their 36 league games.

	2013-14 H A	Last six seasons at home P W D L OV UN BS CS							
East Fife	D W L L	10	4	3	3	5	5	4	3
Arbroath									
Annan		2	1	0	1	1	1	1	0
Clyde		4	3	0	1	2	2	1	2
Berwick		2	2	0	0	2	0	2	0
Montrose		2	2	0	0	2	0	1	1
Albion		6	5	1	0	5	1	5	1
East Stirling		2	1	0	1	1	1	1	1
Elgin		2	1	0	1	1	1	1	1
Queen's Park		4	2	2	0	2	2	2	2

Season	Division	Pos	P	W	D	L	F	A	GD	Pts
2013-14	League One	10	36	9	4	23	52	75	-23	31
2012-13	League One	5	36	15	7	14	47	57	-10	52
2011-12	League One	7	36	17	12	7	76	51	+25	63

Over/Under 78%/22% 1st   **Both score** 69%/31% 3rd

BERWICK

Nickname: The Borderers **Ground:** Shielfield Park
Web: www.berwickrangersfc.co.uk

The Borderers improved in the second half of the season after the appointment of manager Colin Cameron and were unfortunate not to sneak into the playoffs. The former Wolves midfielder can also still play so they should be able to threaten again.

	2013-14 H A	Last six seasons at home P W D L OV UN BS CS							
East Fife		-	-	-	-	-	-	-	-
Arbroath		2	1	0	1	2	0	1	0
Annan	W L L L	12	4	2	6	8	4	8	1
Clyde	L W L D	8	4	2	2	5	3	4	2
Berwick									
Montrose	D W D D	12	5	2	5	6	6	5	4
Albion	W W W W	8	3	2	3	6	2	6	1
East Stirling	W W L D	12	7	2	3	6	6	5	5
Elgin	L L L W	12	6	4	2	8	4	9	3
Queen's Park	W W W W	10	7	2	1	4	6	5	5

Season	Division	Pos	P	W	D	L	F	A	GD	Pts
2013-14	League Two	5	36	15	7	14	63	49	+14	52
2012-13	League Two	4	36	14	7	15	59	55	+4	48
2011-12	League Two	7	36	12	12	12	61	58	+3	48

Over/Under 61%/39% 4th   **Both score** 53%/47% 6th

CLYDE

Nickname: The Bully Wee   **Ground:** Broadwood
Web: www.clydefc.co.uk

Clyde were unlucky not to reach the playoff final, losing on penalties in the semis. They blew hot and cold at the end of the season but will have gained confidence from coming so close. The appointment of Barry Ferguson looks an interesting move, too.

	2013-14		Last six seasons at home							
	H	A	P	W	D	L	OV	UN	BS	CS
East Fife			2	1	0	1	2	0	2	0
Arbroath			4	1	1	2	1	3	1	1
Annan	W L	W W	8	2	2	4	4	4	4	1
Clyde										
Berwick	W D	W L	8	4	2	2	6	2	6	2
Montrose	L D	W W	8	3	2	3	3	5	4	3
Albion	D W	L L	4	1	1	2	3	1	2	1
East Stirling	L W	W W	8	6	0	2	5	3	4	4
Elgin	W W	L L	8	2	4	2	5	3	6	1
Queen's Park	W L	D W	8	1	0	7	6	2	4	1

Season	Division	Pos	P	W	D	L	F	A	GD	Pts
2013-14	League Two	4	36	17	6	13	50	48	+2	57
2012-13	League Two	9	36	12	4	20	42	66	-24	40
2011-12	League Two	9	36	8	11	17	35	50	-15	35

Over/Under 56%/44% 6th   **Both score** 47%/53% 10th

EAST FIFE

Nickname: The Fifers   **Ground:** Bayview
Web: www.eastfifefc.info

East Fife had high hopes following a summer of change off the pitch last year, but it didn't materialise and they were eventually sunk by Stirling in the playoffs. That could be a wake-up call but don't expect them to storm the bottom division as they did in 2008.

	2013-14		Last six seasons at home							
	H	A	P	W	D	L	OV	UN	BS	CS
East Fife										
Arbroath	W W	D L	10	5	3	2	6	4	7	2
Annan			-	-	-	-	-	-	-	-
Clyde			2	1	1	0	0	2	1	1
Berwick			-	-	-	-	-	-	-	-
Montrose			-	-	-	-	-	-	-	-
Albion			4	2	0	2	2	2	2	2
East Stirling			-	-	-	-	-	-	-	-
Elgin			-	-	-	-	-	-	-	-
Queen's Park			2	1	0	1	2	0	2	0

Season	Division	Pos	P	W	D	L	F	A	GD	Pts
2013-14	League One	9	36	9	5	22	31	69	-38	32
2012-13	League One	9	36	8	8	20	50	65	-15	32
2011-12	League One	6	36	14	6	16	55	57	-2	48

Over/Under 58%/42% 6th   **Both score** 56%/44% 9th

EAST STIRLING

Nickname: The Shire   **Ground:** Ochilview Park
Web: www.eaststirlingshirefc.co.uk

The perennial strugglers had a sniff of a place in the playoffs but tailed off badly, losing seven of their last eight games to eventually finish eighth. New boss Craig Tully would be content to improve on that placing after taking the reins.

	2013-14		Last six seasons at home							
	H	A	P	W	D	L	OV	UN	BS	CS
East Fife			-	-	-	-	-	-	-	-
Arbroath			2	0	0	2	2	0	2	0
Annan	D W	W W	12	5	3	4	8	4	9	2
Clyde	L L	W L	8	3	2	3	3	5	2	4
Berwick	W D	L L	12	6	2	4	5	7	4	5
Montrose	D L	L L	12	6	2	4	10	2	9	3
Albion	L D	L L	8	3	2	3	3	5	4	3
East Stirling										
Elgin	W W	W L	12	7	3	2	7	5	7	4
Queen's Park	D L	W D	10	2	1	7	5	5	5	1

Season	Division	Pos	P	W	D	L	F	A	GD	Pts
2013-14	League Two	8	36	12	8	16	45	59	-14	44
2012-13	League Two	10	36	8	5	23	49	97	-48	29
2011-12	League Two	10	36	6	6	24	38	88	-50	24

Over/Under 56%/44% 6th   **Both score** 58%/42% 4th

ELGIN

Nickname: Black & Whites   **Ground:** Borough Briggs
Web: www.elgincity.co.uk

City finished ninth despite scoring 62 goals last term and the defence will have to be shored up if they are to improve on that next season. Barry Wilson takes the reins for his first full campaign in 2014-15 and it would be no surprise if Elgin struggled again.

	2013-14		Last six seasons at home							
	H	A	P	W	D	L	OV	UN	BS	CS
East Fife			-	-	-	-	-	-	-	-
Arbroath			2	1	0	1	2	0	2	0
Annan	L L	L L	12	4	2	6	8	4	8	3
Clyde	W W	L L	8	4	1	3	4	4	4	1
Berwick	W L	W W	12	6	1	5	9	3	8	3
Montrose	D L	D W	12	8	1	3	9	3	9	2
Albion	L D	D L	8	2	3	3	4	4	6	1
East Stirling	L W	L L	12	5	0	7	6	6	4	3
Elgin										
Queen's Park	W D	D L	10	3	2	5	4	6	5	1

Season	Division	Pos	P	W	D	L	F	A	GD	Pts
2013-14	League Two	9	36	9	9	18	62	73	-11	36
2012-13	League Two	5	36	13	10	13	67	69	-2	49
2011-12	League Two	4	36	16	6	8	60	68	+8	57

Over/Under 75%/25% 1st   **Both score** 67%/33% 1st

MONTROSE

Nickname: Gable Endies **Ground:** Links Park
Web: www.montrosefc.co.uk

It was a scruffy season for Montrose and the Gable Endies never really looked like getting into the playoff picture. They have finished in the top four just once in the last 18 campaigns and it's difficult to see them doing so this time.

	2013-14 H	A	P	W	D	L	OV	UN	BS	CS
East Fife			-	-	-	-	-	-	-	-
Arbroath			2	1	0	1	2	0	0	1
Annan	L W	L L	12	2	5	5	5	7	7	2
Clyde	L L	W D	8	4	1	3	5	3	4	2
Berwick	D D	D L	12	1	8	3	4	8	11	1
Montrose										
Albion	W W	W L	8	3	2	3	3	5	3	3
East Stirling	W W	D W	12	7	1	4	7	5	4	4
Elgin	D L	D W	12	5	3	4	8	4	6	3
Queen's Park	L W	W D	10	2	1	7	6	4	7	1

Season	Division	Pos	P	W	D	L	F	A	GD	Pts
2013-14	League Two	6	36	12	10	14	44	56	-12	46
2012-13	League Two	6	36	12	11	13	60	68	-8	47
2011-12	League Two	8	36	11	5	20	58	75	-17	38

Over/Under 56%/44% 6th **Both score** 53%/47% 6th

QUEEN'S PARK

Nickname: The Spiders **Ground:** Hampden Park
Web: www.queensparkfc.co.uk

The Spiders endured a dismal campaign and were rooted to the bottom of the table throughout. They were required to field a very young side for most of the season, and while the squad should have benefited from the experience, it's a long road to recovery.

	2013-14 H	A	P	W	D	L	OV	UN	BS	CS
East Fife			2	1	1	0	1	1	1	1
Arbroath			4	1	1	2	2	2	3	0
Annan	L L	L D	10	3	4	3	5	5	4	4
Clyde	D L	L W	8	5	1	2	5	3	3	4
Berwick	L L	L L	10	3	3	4	5	5	6	2
Montrose	L D	W L	10	6	2	2	7	3	6	3
Albion	D W	L L	6	3	1	2	2	4	2	2
East Stirling	L D	D W	10	7	1	2	4	6	4	6
Elgin	D W	L D	10	3	3	4	4	6	4	3
Queen's Park										

Season	Division	Pos	P	W	D	L	F	A	GD	Pts
2013-14	League Two	10	36	5	9	22	36	68	-32	24
2012-13	League Two	3	36	16	8	12	60	54	+6	56
2011-12	League Two	2	36	19	6	11	70	48	+22	63

Over/Under 53%/47% 9th **Both score** 53%/47% 6th

TV cameras at Arbroath's Gayfield Park

Results 2013-14

	Albion	Annan	Berwick	Clyde	East Stirling	Elgin City	Montrose	Peterhead	Queen's Park	Stirling
Albion		2-0/0-2	0-2/0-3	3-0/1-0	3-2/2-1	0-0/5-2	0-2/1-0	1-2/0-0	2-1/1-0	2-1/0-2
Annan	1-1/2-0		3-2/4-0	1-2/0-1	1-2/2-3	2-1/2-0	2-1/1-0	2-0/2-1	3-2/1-1	4-4/1-2
Berwick	2-1/3-1	4-2/1-4		0-1/3-0	2-0/1-0	2-3/2-3	1-1/5-0	1-3/1-2	4-0/1-0	1-1/4-0
Clyde	2-2/4-0	2-1/0-3	1-0/3-3		1-2/1-0	2-1/4-0	0-3/1-1	1-3/0-2	3-0/1-2	2-1/1-0
East Stirling	1-4/1-1	1-1/2-1	1-0/1-1	0-1/2-4		3-0/3-0	2-2/1-2	1-4/2-0	1-1/1-4	2-2/1-0
Elgin City	1-2/1-1	2-3/2-3	2-0/1-3	1-0/3-1	0-1/5-0		3-3/2-3	2-4/2-3	3-2/1-1	4-0/2-3
Montrose	2-1/2-1	0-2/2-1	1-1/0-0	0-2/0-2	2-0/2-0	3-3/0-3		2-1/2-3	1-2/1-0	1-2/0-0
Peterhead	1-1/2-0	0-2/2-1	1-1/0-0	1-1/3-0	1-1/2-0	1-1/4-0	2-2/2-1		2-1/1-0	3-1/0-4
Queen's Park	1-1/4-0	2-5/0-1	0-4/1-3	1-1/1-3	1-3/0-0	3-3/2-0	0-1/1-1	0-5/0-2		0-2/0-1
Stirling	2-1/2-0	0-2/1-1	3-1/2-1	1-1/4-1	1-3/2-1	1-1/2-2	3-1/2-2	2-0/1-2	3-0/2-2	

League table 2013-14

Pos	H	A		P	W (Home)	D	L	F	A	W (Away)	D	L	F	A	GD	Pts
1	1	1	Peterhead	36	11	6	1	37	16	12	1	5	37	22	+36	76 (C)
2	3	2	Annan	36	10	3	5	34	23	9	3	6	35	26	+20	63
3	2	4	Stirling	36	9	6	3	34	22	7	4	7	26	28	+10	58 (P)
4	6	3	Clyde	36	9	3	6	29	24	8	3	7	21	24	+2	57
5	4	6	Berwick	36	10	2	6	38	22	5	5	8	25	27	+14	52
6	7	5	Montrose	36	7	4	7	21	24	5	6	7	23	32	-12	46
7	5	10	Albion	36	10	2	6	23	20	2	6	10	18	34	-13	44
8	8	7	East Stirling	36	6	6	6	26	28	6	2	10	19	31	-14	44
9	9	8	Elgin City	36	6	3	9	37	33	3	6	9	25	40	-11	36
10	10	9	Queen's Park	36	2	5	11	17	36	3	4	11	19	32	-32	24

Best attack

		GF	GFA
1	Peterhead	74	2.06
2	Annan	69	1.92
3	Berwick	63	1.75
4	Elgin City	62	1.72
5	Stirling	60	1.67
6	Clyde	50	1.39
7	East Stirling	45	1.25
8	Montrose	44	1.22
9	Albion	41	1.14
10	Queen's Park	36	1.00

Best defence

		GA	GAA
1	Peterhead	38	1.06
2	Clyde	48	1.33
3	Annan	49	1.36
4	Berwick	49	1.36
5	Stirling	50	1.39
6	Albion	54	1.50
7	Montrose	56	1.56
8	East Stirling	59	1.64
9	Queen's Park	68	1.89
10	Elgin City	73	2.03

Top scorers

	Team	Goals scored
R McAllister	Peterhead	32 ▮▮▮▮▮▮▮▮▮▮▮▮▮▮▮▮▮▮▮▮▮▮▮▮▮▮▮▮▮▮▮▮
L Currie	Berwick	17 ▮▮▮▮▮▮▮▮▮▮▮▮▮▮▮▮▮
C Gunn	Elgin City	15 ▮▮▮▮▮▮▮▮▮▮▮▮▮▮▮
D Lavery	Berwick	15 ▮▮▮▮▮▮▮▮▮▮▮▮▮▮▮
J White	Stirling	15 ▮▮▮▮▮▮▮▮▮▮▮▮▮▮▮

Key Points in all tables (except the league table) do not include any deductions imposed by the league. **POS H A** Overall league position, rank from home games only, rank from away games only **Sup** Average match supremacy **GFA** Goals For Average **GAA** Goals Against Average **PGA** Points Gained Average

Record when first to score

		P	W	D	L	F	A	Sup	PGA	Pts
1	Peterhead	21	17	2	2	52	14	+1.81	2.5	53
2	Clyde	20	16	3	1	38	11	+1.35	2.6	51
3	Annan	22	15	5	2	49	21	+1.27	2.3	50
4	Stirling	17	13	4	0	38	12	+1.53	2.5	43
5	Berwick	20	13	4	3	48	17	+1.55	2.2	43
6	Albion	18	12	5	1	35	17	+1.00	2.3	41
7	East Stirling	16	11	2	3	30	19	+0.69	2.2	35
8	Montrose	13	10	2	1	26	12	+1.08	2.5	32
9	Elgin City	17	7	4	6	40	29	+0.65	1.5	25
10	Queen's Park	11	3	4	4	19	17	+0.18	1.2	13

Record when keeping a clean sheet

		P	W	D	F	Sup	PGA	Pts
1	Clyde	11	11	0	21	+1.91	3.0	33
2	Annan	10	10	0	21	+2.10	3.0	30
3	Berwick	11	11	1	29	+2.64	2.8	31
4	Peterhead	11	10	1	28	+2.55	2.8	31
5	Stirling	8	7	1	16	+2.00	2.8	22
6	East Stirling	7	6	1	11	+1.57	2.7	19
7	Elgin City	6	5	1	15	+2.50	2.7	16
8	Montrose	8	6	2	11	+1.38	2.5	20
9	Albion	7	5	2	8	+1.14	2.4	17
10	Queen's Park	3	2	1	6	+2.00	2.3	7

Over 2.5 goals

	H	A	%
Elgin	13	14	75%
Peterhead	11	12	64%
Stirling	12	11	64%

Under 2.5 goals

	H	A	%
Albion	10	8	50%
Queens Park	10	7	47%
E Stirling, Montrose, Clyde			44%

Both to score

	H	A	%
Annan	12	12	67%
Elgin	13	11	67%
Stirling	14	9	64%

Both not to score

	H	A	%
Clyde	9	10	53%
Albion, Queen's Park, Montrose, Berwick			47%

Law change means value may now lie in looking long and hard at bookies' offers

T he coming season might appear to be more of the same from a betting perspective, but things are set to change in ways that simply haven't been picked up by many outside of the bookmakers and trade pages, writes Alex Deacon. As the changes relate to the taxation on bookmakers' profits, on first inspection they might appear to have little to do with the punter. But, in reality, they will have a profound impact.

In many ways the perception of the bookmaking world is light years behind the thinking of the biggest operators, especially those with a strong online-only presence.

You might read about this or that bookie winning or losing eye-watering amounts of money but in truth that is an antiquated view of the world – what really counts is acquiring the customer in the first place. Whether they win or lose will be resolved in the long-term. Losing money on an individual event or market is not such a big deal to the large-scale bookmaker in the second decade of the 21st century. Losses that are reported as big wins for the punters are now little more than good PR stories.

Historically, new customers have been acquired by offering free bets and the like and it is these offers that will be affected, with the change in taxation law intended to rein in those operators who take bets from the UK but who are registered offshore.

Now for the bit where this is relevant to the value-conscious punter. Once upon a time, value for football bettors came from comparing 12X prices and I'm sure many punters think that's where the major differentiation between the bookies lies.

False.

In truth, the difference between prices is generally so small that it's of little use when the bookies market their wares. The real value is found by digging down into the various offers and promotions to pull out the real price differences – it's not easy.

If, for example, one firm is offering free bets for a market and another is offering cash back, it's hard to factor both in to obtain a true picture of pricing, particularly when the coupon prices will have very little difference between them.

Where punters can take advantage as this law change approaches is by realising that layers will be commercially forced to change the way they offer promotions. Free bets, in particular, will, at least in the way they are currently offered, incur a substantial incremental cost for bookmakers as they too will now be registered as actual bets. They might once have been 'free' to both customer and, to a large extent, bookmaker, but now the operator will pay tax on these offers.

As operators adjust to this change and seek to make competitive offers and promotions, mistakes will be made. And mistakes in bookmaking are, aside from luck and/or hard work, where punters can profit.

These changes won't happen until the end of this calendar year. But it's almost certain that with the shift of emphasis there will be times when, in a bid to make competitive standout offers, bookies get it wrong, in the same way that once upon a time we used to see genuine mistakes in pricing.

About the Outlook Index

Our unique ratings give an objective view of every club. Each team has a rating, roughly on a scale of 0 to 1,000, which goes up or down with league results and takes into account the relative strength of opposition. The tables show each team's overall rating, plus ratings for home and away form (a separate ratings sytem) and a Trend rating (-20 to +20). The bars show the Trend, based on the last 60 matches but weighted towards more recent games, to help identify the teams in form. The tables show final ratings for 2013-14.

Premier League 2013-14

	Current	H	A		Trend
Man City	972	1000	941		+5
Chelsea	963	992	940		-2
Liverpool	962	962	929		+6
Arsenal	953	966	939		+1
Everton	936	950	905		-2
Tottenham	932	941	926		-4
Man Utd	929	955	948		-5
Southampton	906	892	875		+4
Stoke	899	921	862		+8
Crystal Palace	887	880	835		+13
Sunderland	881	858	878		+5
Swansea	876	881	866		+3
West Ham	874	889	859		0
Newcastle	874	890	875		-10
WBA	865	884	863		-3
Aston Villa	864	868	871		-6
Fulham	862	864	856		+4
Norwich	855	887	833		-8
Hull	852	860	837		-8
Cardiff	851	860	836		-3

Championship 2013-14

	Current	H	A		Trend
Leicester	888	879	863		+4
Burnley	874	861	846		+3
Derby	860	856	827		+4
Reading	853	848	852		+4
Blackburn	852	852	831		+9
Wigan	851	867	846		-8
Brighton	847	842	843		+2
QPR	846	880	820		0
Middlesbro	842	842	805		+5
Bolton	840	852	829		+6
Ipswich	836	854	815		+3
Bournemouth	835	829	798		+1
Charlton	824	811	823		+6
Watford	823	839	810		-8
Millwall	820	813	808		+13
Nottm Forest	819	825	826		-10
Sheff Wed	818	814	812		-7
Leeds	811	816	801		0
Huddersfield	810	812	800		0
Doncaster	798	791	784		-5
Barnsley	795	804	783		-6
Birmingham	793	790	831		-10
Blackpool	786	804	796		-4
Yeovil	785	781	762		-3

GET THE OUTLOOK INDEX EVERY TUESDAY IN THE RACING & FOOTBALL OUTLOOK

Crystal Palace finished 2013-14 with a healthy +13 Trend figure

Oxford, pictured losing away to Newport, finished with League 2's worst Outlook Index rating

League 1 2013-14

	Current	H	A		Trend
Wolves	**828**	832	816	ⅡⅢⅢⅢ	+6
Rotherham	**800**	773	782	ⅠⅢⅢⅢ	+5
Brentford	**799**	828	766	ⅢⅢⅢⅢ	-7
Sheff Utd	**789**	802	758	ⅠⅢⅢⅢⅢ	+9
Preston	**788**	796	769	ⅡⅠ	-2
Leyton Orient	**780**	772	777	ⅢⅢⅠ	-4
Peterborough	**776**	811	759	ⅠⅠ	-1
Bristol City	**768**	780	765	ⅠⅢⅢⅢ	+6
Swindon	**768**	794	742	ⅠⅡ	+2
Oldham	**764**	750	752	ⅠⅢⅢⅢⅢ	+9
Notts Co	**756**	774	722	ⅠⅢⅢⅢⅢ	+10
Bradford	**753**	747	730	ⅠⅢⅢⅢ	+6
Crewe	**751**	743	742	ⅠⅢⅢⅢ	+5
Colchester	**750**	753	745	ⅠⅢⅠ	+3
MK Dons	**748**	747	775	ⅢⅢⅠ	-4
Crawley	**746**	765	729	ⅢⅢⅠ	-4
Port Vale	**743**	762	717		0
Coventry	**742**	762	743	ⅢⅢⅢⅠ	-7
Carlisle	**738**	753	720	ⅡⅠ	-2
Gillingham	**737**	758	713	ⅡⅠ	-2
Walsall	**735**	753	754	ⅢⅢⅢⅢⅢⅢ	-13
Tranmere	**729**	749	726	ⅢⅢⅢⅢ	-8
Stevenage	**725**	738	719	ⅢⅢⅠ	-3
Shrewsbury	**721**	739	725	ⅢⅢⅢⅠ	-6

League 2 2013-14

	Current	H	A		Trend
Scunthorpe	**748**	755	743	ⅠⅠ	-1
York	**746**	729	736	ⅠⅢⅢⅢⅢ	+10
Chesterfield	**744**	750	732	ⅠⅢⅢⅢ	+6
Southend	**737**	723	719	ⅠⅢⅢⅢⅢ	+11
Rochdale	**731**	744	719	ⅢⅢⅠ	-4
Fleetwood	**727**	723	718	ⅠⅡ	+2
Bury	**724**	739	712	ⅠⅡ	+2
Accrington	**724**	715	708	ⅠⅢⅢⅠ	+5
Portsmouth	**721**	735	721	ⅠⅢⅢⅢ	+6
Burton	**720**	744	704	ⅢⅢⅢⅢ	-7
Mansfield	**717**	707	723	ⅠⅢⅠ	+4
Northampton	**713**	712	700	ⅠⅢⅠ	+4
Dag & Red	**706**	687	711		0
Exeter	**706**	693	714	ⅠⅢⅢⅠ	+5
Newport Co	**704**	706	683	ⅠⅢⅠ	+4
Plymouth	**700**	700	709	ⅢⅢⅢⅢ	-9
Morecambe	**700**	712	693	ⅠⅠ	+1
Wimbledon	**700**	688	697		0
Wycombe	**697**	700	699	ⅡⅠ	-2
Hartlepool	**691**	717	698	ⅠⅢⅢⅢⅢ	-10
Cheltenham	**691**	702	710	ⅢⅢⅢⅠ	-8
Bristol Rovers	**688**	726	677	ⅢⅢⅢⅢ	-10
Torquay	**687**	686	697	ⅠⅠ	-1
Oxford Utd	**685**	704	701	ⅢⅢⅢⅢⅢⅠ	-13

Conference 2013-14

	Current	H	A		Trend
Luton	**720**	718	700	ⅠⅠ	+1
Gateshead	**694**	684	665	ⅠⅢⅢⅢⅢ	+9
Halifax	**690**	720	622	ⅠⅢⅢⅢ	+8
Grimsby	**682**	682	685	ⅢⅠ	-2
Braintree	**681**	671	678	ⅠⅢ	+2
Woking	**677**	671	653	ⅠⅢⅢⅢ	+7
Lincoln	**676**	666	661	ⅠⅢⅢⅢⅢ	+12
Barnet	**674**	689	662	ⅠⅠ	-1
Kidderminster	**672**	708	667	ⅠⅠ	+1
Forest Green	**671**	668	644	ⅠⅠ	+1
Cambridge	**667**	692	655	ⅠⅢⅢⅠ	-7
Aldershot	**664**	687	667	ⅢⅠ	+2
Wrexham	**660**	678	654	ⅢⅠ	-2
Salisbury	**658**	682	642	ⅠⅢⅢ	-6
Nuneaton	**657**	667	642	ⅠⅢⅢ	-5
Chester	**655**	650	644	ⅠⅢⅢ	+5
Southport	**654**	664	620	ⅠⅢⅢⅢ	+7
Welling	**651**	646	644	ⅠⅢⅢ	-6
Alfreton	**650**	674	642	ⅠⅢⅢⅢⅢⅢ	-13
Macclesfield	**649**	669	638	ⅠⅢⅢ	-4
Hereford	**642**	649	656	ⅢⅠ	-2
Dartford	**633**	638	625	ⅢⅠ	-3
Tamworth	**618**	644	605	ⅢⅠ	-2
Hyde	**570**	581	600	ⅠⅢⅢⅢ	-6

Scottish Premiership 2013-14

	Current	H	A		Trend
Celtic	**921**	963	883		0
Motherwell	**860**	862	828	ⅠⅢⅢ	+4
Aberdeen	**846**	833	826	ⅢⅠ	-3
St Johnstone	**837**	847	804	ⅠⅢⅢ	+3
Inverness CT	**836**	828	819	ⅠⅠ	+1
Dundee Utd	**834**	837	819	ⅢⅠ	-2
Ross County	**809**	817	782	ⅠⅢⅢ	+4
Hearts	**806**	808	793	ⅠⅢⅢⅢ	+6
St Mirren	**802**	822	770	ⅠⅠ	+1
Partick	**802**	782	789	ⅢⅠ	+2
Kilmarnock	**797**	795	790	ⅠⅠ	-1
Hibernian	**782**	786	786	ⅠⅢⅢⅢⅢⅢⅢ	-16

Scottish Championship 2013-14

	Current	H	A		Trend
Dundee	**778**	787	761	ⅠⅠ	-1
Falkirk	**770**	776	747	ⅠⅢⅢⅢ	+6
Hamilton	**766**	770	752	ⅠⅡ	+2
Queen Of Sth	**750**	761	730	ⅠⅠ	+1
Dumbarton	**735**	720	726	ⅠⅡ	+2
Livingston	**732**	734	736	ⅢⅢⅠ	-3
Cowdenbeath	**729**	730	696	ⅠⅢⅢⅢ	+8
Raith	**713**	733	712	ⅢⅢⅢⅢⅢ	-11
Morton	**710**	736	690	ⅠⅢⅠ	+3
Alloa	**702**	696	698	ⅠⅢⅢⅢⅠ	-9

Scottish League One 2013-14

	Current	H	A	Trend
Rangers	**864**	919	866	0
Dunfermline	**712**	718	737	-4
Airdrieonians	**690**	692	678	+16
Stenhsemuir	**682**	670	679	+6
Brechin	**672**	684	667	+1
Ayr	**670**	692	665	-3
Forfar	**666**	671	668	-6
Stranraer	**664**	683	642	-7
Arbroath	**644**	660	652	+1
East Fife	**639**	645	646	-6

Scottish League Two 2013-14

	Current	H	A	Trend
Peterhead	**679**	673	673	+4
Stirling	**647**	668	633	+9
Annan	**638**	638	641	-1
Clyde	**620**	631	619	+1
Berwick	**618**	648	608	+1
Montrose	**616**	622	611	+1
Elgin	**602**	622	606	+1
Albion	**601**	648	586	-5
East Stirling	**591**	613	576	-9
Queen's Park	**585**	591	616	-3

Italian Serie A 2013-14

	Current	H	A	Trend
Juventus	**997**	1012	994	+4
Napoli	**949**	981	947	+2
Roma	**945**	979	944	-5
Milan	**922**	964	927	+4
Torino	**915**	913	902	+7
Fiorentina	**913**	928	942	-5
Parma	**910**	941	902	0
Lazio	**902**	949	898	+1
Inter	**900**	941	916	+1
Atalanta	**890**	924	872	-2
Udinese	**886**	951	891	-2
Sampdoria	**884**	902	890	-4
Verona	**884**	896	866	+4
Genoa	**878**	909	853	-3
Sassuolo	**875**	875	898	+7
Catania	**871**	936	830	+8
Chievo	**870**	879	892	0
Cagliari	**870**	907	872	-5
Bologna	**859**	876	881	-7
Livorno	**835**	873	835	-9

German Bundesliga 2013-14

	Current	H	A	Trend
B Munich	**1012**	1010	997	-3
Dortmund	**973**	960	967	+8
Schalke	**945**	959	918	0
Leverkusen	**940**	950	935	+1
Wolfsburg	**938**	929	916	+7
Augsburg	**922**	919	902	+6
Mainz	**921**	926	897	+1
B M'gladbach	**921**	949	894	0
Hoffenheim	**904**	913	878	+3
Hannover	**900**	942	864	+6
Werder Bremen	**897**	900	881	+4
Freiburg	**896**	906	884	+1
Frankfurt	**889**	900	886	-5
H Berlin	**888**	879	900	-5
Stuttgart	**887**	890	889	+2
Hamburg	**872**	890	876	-8
Nuremburg	**870**	883	878	-14
Braunschweig	**869**	893	862	-5

Spanish Primera Liga 2013-14

	Current	H	A	Trend
Barcelona	**1006**	1068	998	-6
Atl Madrid	**1005**	1012	982	+1
Real Madrid	**1005**	1041	992	-8
Ath Bilbao	**960**	971	943	+1
Seville	**959**	971	925	+2
Real Sociedad	**953**	971	934	-5
Villarreal	**945**	970	923	+3
Celta Vigo	**939**	933	912	+10
Valencia	**932**	973	924	-3
Malaga	**927**	938	926	0
Levante	**922**	924	922	+2
Getafe	**920**	923	907	+9
Rayo Vallecano	**920**	918	926	+1
Elche	**920**	929	910	+1
Almeria	**916**	923	883	+6
Osasuna	**914**	930	904	0
Real Valladolid	**911**	930	888	-3
Espanyol	**910**	919	907	-6
Granada	**909**	911	914	-2
Real Betis	**886**	909	891	-5

French Ligue 1 2013-14

	Current	H	A	Trend
Paris St-G	**944**	956	940	-2
Monaco	**922**	916	918	+2
St Etienne	**910**	919	895	+7
Lille	**909**	943	906	+2
Lyon	**891**	911	907	-1
Marseille	**889**	908	896	+2
Lens	**871**	880	854	-4
Lorient	**871**	897	848	+2
Sochaux	**869**	888	841	+14
Rennes	**869**	857	884	+8
Bordeaux	**866**	914	870	-1
Toulouse	**866**	876	874	-4
Evian TG	**866**	868	848	+5
Bastia	**860**	901	825	+2
Montpellier	**859**	896	864	-4
Nantes	**858**	875	859	-1
Nice	**847**	893	836	-7
Guingamp	**847**	881	852	-5
Valenciennes	**827**	852	824	-12
Ajaccio	**824**	842	813	0

Money talks for top-rated PSG in French Ligue 1

Pools draws chart 2013-14   X score-draw, 0 goalless draw

Pools No.	Aug 3 10 17 24 31	Sept 7 14 21 28	Oct 5 12 19 26	Nov 2 9 16 23 30	Dec 7 14 21 28	Jan 4 11 18 25	Feb 1 8 15 22	Mar 1 8 15 22 29	Apr 5 12 19 26	May 3	X	0
1	- - - - -	- - - -	- - - X	- 0 X - -	X X - -	- - - X	- - - -	- - X - -	- 0 - -	-	6	2
2	- - - - 0	X - - -	- 0 - -	- X - X -	- - - X	- - - -	- - - -	- - - - -	- X - -	-	5	2
3	- - - 0	- X - -	- 0 - -	- 0 0 X -	- - - -	- - - -	- - - X	- - - - -	- - X 0	-	4	5
4	X X - - -	X - - X	- - - -	- - - - -	- - - -	- - X X	- - - -	- - - - -	- X - -	-	7	0
5	X - - - -	0 - - -	X 0 - -	- - 0 0 -	- - X X	- - - -	- - X X	- - - - -	- - X -	-	4	4
6	- - X - -	X 0 - -	0 - - -	- X - X -	- - - 0	- 0 - -	- - - -	- - - - -	- - - -	-	4	4
7	- X - 0	- - X -	X - - -	- X 0 - -	- - X -	- - - X	- - 0 -	- - - - -	- - - -	-	5	3
8	- - - X	- X - -	0 - - -	- X X - -	- 0 - -	- - - -	- - 0 -	- - - - -	- - - -	-	4	2
9	- 0 - -	- - - X	X - - 0	X - X X -	0 - - -	- X - X	X - - -	- - - - -	- - - -	-	8	3
10	- - - 0	- - - X	- - 0 -	0 - X - -	0 - - 0	- - - -	- - - -	- X - X -	- - - -	-	4	4
11	- X - X	- 0 - -	X X - 0	- - X X -	- X 0 X X	- - - -	- 0 - -	- - - - -	- - - -	-	9	4
12	- - - -	0 0 - -	- - X -	- - X X -	- - 0 -	X - X -	- - - -	- - - - -	- - - -	-	7	3
13	X - - -	X - X -	0 X - 0	- - - 0 -	X - X -	- X - X	- X - -	- 0 - - -	- - - -	-	8	4
14	- - - X	- - - -	X 0 - -	- - X - -	- 0 - -	- - - -	- - - -	- - - - -	- - X -	-	4	2
15	- - - X	- - X -	- X - X	- X - 0 -	X - 0 -	0 - - -	- - - -	- - - - -	- - - -	-	5	3
16	X - 0 -	- X - -	X X X -	0 0 - X -	- X - X	- X - -	- - - -	- - - - -	- - - -	-	9	3
17	- - X -	0 - - -	- X - -	X - X - -	X - - X	- 0 - -	- X - -	- - - - -	- - - -	-	5	2
18	- - X -	X X X -	0 - - -	X X - 0 -	- 0 - X	0 0 - -	- - - -	- - - - -	- - - -	-	8	4
19	X - - X	X X X -	X X 0 -	- 0 - - -	X X - X	- - - -	- - - -	- - - - -	- - - -	-	11	2
20	0 - - X	- X - -	- - X -	0 X 0 X X	0 - X - -	X X - -	- - - -	- - - - -	- - - -	-	10	5
21	0 0 - -	X - - -	X - 0 -	X 0 0 - X	- X - X	- X - -	X - - -	- - - - -	- - - -	-	10	5
22	0 - X -	0 - X -	- X - -	X X - 0 -	- X X -	- - - -	- - - -	- - - - -	- - - -	-	5	3
23	- X - -	- - - -	X - X -	X - X X -	- X X -	- X - -	- - - -	- - - - -	- - - -	-	8	0
24	- - - X	- X - 0	- X - X	- 0 - 0 -	X - 0 - -	0 - - -	X - - 0	- - - - -	0 X 6 4	-	6	4
25	- - 0 -	X X 0 -	X - X 0	- 0 - 0 0	- 0 - -	- X X X	- - - -	- - - - -	- - - -	-	8	6
26	X X X -	- - - -	0 - X -	- - X X -	X 0 X - -	X - X -	- X - X	- - - - -	- - - -	-	11	3
27	- 0 X -	0 - X -	- 0 - -	X - X - -	X - 0 - -	X - - -	- - - -	- - - - -	- - - -	-	6	4
28	- - X -	X X - X	- - 0 X	X X - X -	X - X - -	- - - -	- - - -	- - - - -	- - - -	-	10	1
29	- - - X	- X - X	- 0 - X	- X - X -	X - X - -	- 0 - 0	- - - -	- - - - -	- - - -	-	5	2
30	- X - X	- - - -	0 - X -	X - X - -	0 - X - -	0 - 7 3	- - - -	- - - - -	- - - -	-	7	3
31	- X X X	- - - X	0 0 - -	X - 0 X -	- 0 - -	- - - -	- - - -	- - - - -	- - - -	-	6	4
32	- 0 - X	- X X -	X - 0 -	X X - 0 -	X X - X -	- - - -	- - - -	- - - - -	- - - -	-	10	3
33	- X - -	X - - 0	- X X -	X X - X -	- - - -	- - - -	- - - -	- - - - -	- - - -	-	9	0
34	X - X -	0 - - 0	- 0 - X	X - 0 - -	0 - - 0	- X - -	- - - -	- - - - -	- - - -	-	5	5
35	- - - X	- 0 - -	X - X X	- X 0 - -	0 X X -	0 - X -	- - - -	- - - - -	- - - -	-	8	4
36	- - 0 X	0 X - X	X X X X	X - X - -	X X - -	X - - -	- - - -	- - - - -	- - - -	-	12	2
37	- X - -	X X - 0	X - X X	- - - -	- - - -	- - - -	- - - -	- - - - -	- - - -	-	7	1
38	- - 0 -	X X - -	X 0 X X	0 0 X X -	- - - -	- - - -	- - - -	- - - - -	- - - -	-	8	5
39	0 - X -	X 0 - X	0 X X 0	X 0 - 0 -	- - - -	- - - -	- - - -	- - - - -	- - - -	-	6	5
40	- - - -	X - - -	X - - -	0 X - X 0	4 2 - -	- - - -	- - - -	- - - - -	- - - -	-	4	2
41	0 - X X	X - - 0	X - X -	0 - 0 - X	- X - 7 4	- - - -	- - - -	- - - - -	- - - -	-	7	4
42	- X - -	0 - - X	- X - 0	X 0 - X -	5 3 - -	- - - -	- - - -	- - - - -	- - - -	-	5	3
43	0 X - -	X - X -	X - 0 X	0 X 0 - 0	X X 105 -	- - - -	- - - -	- - - - -	- - - -	-	10	5
44	- X 0 -	X - - X	- 0 - X	0 X 0 - X	7 4 - -	- - - -	- - - -	- - - - -	- - - -	-	7	4
45	- - X -	X - X X	X 0 - 0	0 X - X 0	8 6 - -	- - - -	- - - -	- - - - -	- - - -	-	8	6
46	- 0 X 0	- X - X	X X - 0	0 X 6 4 -	- - - -	- - - -	- - - -	- - - - -	- - - -	-	6	4
47	0 - - X	- X - X	X 0 - 0	X 0 - X 6 3	- - - -	- - - -	- - - -	- - - - -	- - - -	-	6	3
48	- X 0 - 0	- X 0 X	X X 0 X	0 X 6 4 -	- - - -	- - - -	- - - -	- - - - -	- - - -	-	6	4
49	- - X - X	0 0 0 X	X 3 4 3	- - - - -	- - - -	- - - -	- - - -	- - - - -	- - - -	-	4	3
X	7 6 12 13 8	10 8 12 5	5 11 8 6	9 7 9 6 6	11 13 10 12	7 7 10 11	10 12 5 3	7 8 8 7 12	4 8 7 8	9	**337**	
0	6 5 2 3 5	4 5 1 4	3 4 4 5	4 3 0 5 3	3 4 6 4	3 4 4 7	4 6 3 3	5 6 10 2 4	4 1 4 3	3		**159**

British weekend results only

BRITISH CUP RESULTS 2013-14

CAPITAL ONE CUP

First round

Monday August 5 2013
Preston ....(0) 1-0 (0)..... Blackpool

Tuesday August 6 2013
Barnsley........(0) 0-0 (0)... Scunthorpe
AET 0-0 90 mins, Barnsley 5-4 pens
Birmingham..(0) 3-2 (0)......Plymouth
AET 2-2 90 mins
Bournemouth(0) 1-0 (0)...Portsmouth
Brentford ......(0) 3-2 (1)....Dag & Red
Brighton ....(1) 1-3 (0)..Newport Co
AET 1-1 90 mins
Bristol R........(1) 1-3 (3)........Watford
Bury..............(2) 3-2 (1).......... Crewe
Charlton ....(1) 4-0 (0)..........Oxford
Cheltenham ..(1) 4-3 (1)........Crawley
AET 3-3 90 mins
Colchester.....(0) 1-5 (1)Peterborough
Doncaster .....(0) 1-0 (0)..... Rochdale
Exeter ....(0) 0-2 (1).............QPR
Gillingham....(0) 0-2 (1)....... Bristol C
Huddersfield .(1) 2-1 (0)....... Bradford
Leyton Orient(2) 3-2 (1)...... Coventry
Middlesbro ...(1) 1-2 (1)....Accrington
Millwall ....(0) 2-1 (0) AFC W'bledon
Morecambe ..(0) 1-0 (0)......... Wolves
Northampton(0) 1-2 (1)...... MK Dons
Nottm Forest.(1) 3-1 (0)...... Hartlepool
Oldham ....(0) 0-1 (1).......... Derby
Port Vale ....(0) 1-2 (1)......... Walsall
Rotherham....(2) 2-1 (1).... Sheff Wed
Sheff Utd ......(0) 1-2 (0).......... Burton
Shrewsbury ..(1) 1-3 (2)......... Bolton
Southend ......(0) 0-1 (1).......... Yeovil
Stevenage.....(0) 2-0 (0)....... Ipswich
Swindon ....(0) 1-0 (0)....... Torquay
Tranmere .....(2) 2-0 (0)..... Mansfield
Wycombe .....(1) 1-2 (1)......Leicester
York ....(0) 0-4 (1)........Burnley

Wednesday August 7 2013
Carlisle ....(1) 3-3 (0)....Blackburn
AET 2-2 90 mins, Carlisle 4-3 pens
Leeds............(2) 2-1 (1)..Chesterfield
Notts Co ....(2) 3-2 (1).... Fleetwood

Second round

Tuesday September 27 2013
Barnsley........(0) 1-5 (1)Southampton
Bristol C........(2) 2-1 (0)..... C Palace
Burnley.........(2) 2-0 (0)........Preston
Burton ....(0) 2-2 (1)........Fulham
AET 1-1 90 mins, Fulham 5-4 pens
Carlisle ....(1) 2-5 (1)......Leicester
Derby ....(3) 5-0 (0)......Brentford
Doncaster .....(0) 1-3 (1).......... Leeds
Huddersfield .(1) 3-2 (1)...... Charlton
Leyton Orient(0) 0-1 (0).............. Hull
AET 0-0 90 mins

Liverpool ......(2) 4-2 (0).......Notts Co
AET 2-2 90 mins
Norwich........(2) 6-3 (0)............. Bury
Peterborough(3) 6-0 (0)........Reading
QPR ....(0) 0-2 (1)......Swindon
Sunderland ...(0) 4-2 (1)...... MK Dons
Tranmere ......(1) 1-1 (0).......... Bolton
AET 1-1 90 mins, Tranmere 4-2 pens
West Brom.....(3) 3-0 (0)..Newport Co
West Ham.....(1) 2-1 (0)..Cheltenham
Yeovil............(1) 3-3 (2) . Birmingham
AET 2-2 90 mins, Birmingham 3-2 pens

Wednesday September 28 2013
Accrington ....(0) 0-2 (0)..........Cardiff
Aston Villa ....(2) 3-0 (0)... Rotherham
Everton ....(1) 2-1 (1).... Stevenage
AET 1-1 90 mins
Morecambe ..(0) 0-2 (0).... Newcastle
Nottm Forest.(0) 2-1 (0)........Millwall
AET 1-1 90 mins
Stoke ....(2) 3-1 (0)........Walsall
Watford ....(1) 2-0 (0)Bournemouth

Third round

Tuesday September 24 2013
Aston Villa ....(0) 0-4 (1)....Tottenham
Burnley ....(1) 2-1 (1) Nottm Forest
Fulham ....(0) 2-1 (1)........ Everton
Hull ....(0) 1-0 (0).Huddersfield
Leicester ....(0) 2-1 (1).......... Derby
Man City.......(1) 5-0 (0).......... Wigan
Southampton(1) 2-0 (0)...... Bristol C
Sunderland ...(1) 2-0 (0)Peterborough
Swindon ....(0) 0-2 (2)........Chelsea
Watford ....(1) 2-3 (0)....... Norwich
AET 2-2 90 mins
West Ham.....(2) 3-2 (1).........Cardiff

Wednesday September 25 2013
Birmingham..(0) 3-1 (0)...... Swansea
Man Utd ....(0) 1-0 (0)...... Liverpool
Newcastle.....(1) 2-0 (0).......... Leeds
Tranmere ......(0) 0-2 (1)............Stoke
West Brom....(0) 1-1 (0).........Arsenal
AET 1-1 90 mins, Arsenal 4-3 pens

Fourth round

Tuesday October 29 2013
Arsenal ....(0) 0-2 (1)........ Chelsea
Birmingham..(1) 4-4 (1)............Stoke
AET 3-3 90 mins, Stoke 4-2 pens
Burnley ....(0) 0-2 (0).... West Ham
Leicester ....(2) 4-3 (1)........ Fulham
Man Utd ....(1) 4-0 (0)...... Norwich

Wednesday October 30 2013
Newcastle.....(0) 0-2 (0)...... Man City
AET 0-0 90 mins
Tottenham ....(1) 2-2 (0).............. Hull
AET 1-1 90 mins, Tottenham 8-7 pens

Wednesday November 6 2013
Sunderland ...(0) 2-1 (0)Southampton

Quarter-finals

Tuesday December 17 2013
Leicester ....(0) 1-3 (2)...... Man City
Sunderland ...(0) 2-1 (0)........ Chelsea
AET 1-1 90 mins

Wednesday December 18 2013
Stoke ....(0) 0-2 (0).......Man Utd
Tottenham ....(0) 1-2 (0).... West Ham

Semi-finals

Tuesday January 7 2014
Sunderland ...(1) 2-1 (0).......Man Utd

Wednesday January 8 2014
Man City.......(3) 6-0 (0).... West Ham

Tuesday January 21 2014
West Ham.....(0) 0-3 (2)...... Man City
Agg. 9-0 Man City

Wednesday January 22 2014
Man Utd ....(1) 2-1 (0)...Sunderland
AET 1-0 90 mins. 3-3 agg. Sunderland
2-1 pens

Final

Sunday March 2 2014
Man City.......(0) 3-1 (1)...Sunderland

City's scorers – Navas, Toure and Nasri – pose with the trophy

SCOTTISH LEAGUE CUP

First round

Saturday August 3 2013

Airdrieonians (3) 4-3 (2) Stenh'semuir
Arbroath .... (0) 0-1 (0) ..... Montrose
Berwick .... (0) 0-5 (2)Cowdenbeath
Dumbarton ...(1) 1-0 (0) .... Albion
East Fife .... (0) 2-6 (0) .... Morton
     AET 2-2 90 mins
East Stirling ..(0) 0-2 (1) . Dunfermline
Elgin City ...... (1) 1-3 (2) .... Livingston
Falkirk .... (0) 3-0 (0) .... Clyde
Forfar .... (1) 2-1 (0) .... Rangers
     AET 1-1 90 mins
Peterhead ..... (0) 0-2 (0) .... Alloa
Queen of Sth.(0) 3-0 (0) .... Annan
Raith .... (2) 6-0 (0) Queen's Park
Stirling .... (0) 0-3 (2) ..... Hamilton
Stranraer .... (3) 4-3 (0) .... Brechin

Tuesday August 6 2013

Partick .... (1) 2-1 (0) .... Ayr

Second round

Tuesday August 27 2013

Aberdeen ...... (0) 0-0 (0) .... Alloa
     AET 0-0 90 mins, Aberdeen 6-5 pens
Airdrieonians (0) 0-2 (1) .... Livingston
Dundee ....(0) 2-1 (1) .... Forfar
     AET 1-1 90 mins
Falkirk .... (2) 2-1 (1) . Dunfermline
Kilmarnock .....(0) 0-1 (1) ...... Hamilton
Morton .... (0) 4-0 (0) ...... Montrose
Partick .... (0) 3-1 (0) .Cowdenbeath
     AET 0-0 90 mins
Queen of Sth.(0) 2-1 (0) ...... St Mirren
     AET 0-0 90 mins
Raith .... (0) 1-1 (0) .... Hearts
     AET 1-1 90 mins, Hearts 5-4 pens
Stranraer .... (0) 3-2 (1) . Ross County

Wednesday August 28 2013

Dumbarton ...(1) 2-3 (0) ..Dundee Utd

Third round

Tuesday September 24 2013

Celtic .... (0) 0-1 (0) .... Morton
     AET 0-0 90 mins
Dundee ....(0) 0-1 (1) .Inverness CT
Hamilton .... (0) 3-0 (1) .St Johnstone
Hibernian ...... (3) 5-3 (1) ...... Stranraer

Wednesday September 25 2013

Dundee Utd ..(2) 4-1 (0) .... Partick
Falkirk .... (0) 0-5 (2) ..... Aberdeen
Hearts .... (1) 3-3 (1) Queen of Sth
     AET 2-2 90 mins, Hearts 4-2 pens
Livingston ..... (0) 1-2 (1) .. Motherwell

Quarter-finals

Tuesday October 29 2013

Inverness CT .(0) 2-1 (1) ..Dundee Utd
     AET 1-1 90 mins

Wednesday October 30 2013

Hibernian ...... (0) 0-1 (1) .... Hearts

Morton .... (0) 0-1 (0) .St Johnstone
Motherwell ...(0) 0-2 (0) ..... Aberdeen

Semi-finals

Saturday February 1 2014

Aberdeen .... (2) 4-0 (0) .St Johnstone

Sunday February 2 2014

Hearts .... (0) 2-2 (0) .Inverness CT
     AET 2-2 90 mins, Inverness CT 4-2 pens

Final

Sunday March 16 2014

Aberdeen ...... (0) 0-0 (0) .Inverness CT
     AET 0-0 90 mins, Aberdeen 4-2 pens

FA TROPHY

First round

Saturday November 30 2013

Aldershot	1-1	.. Weston S-M.
Alfreton	0-1	.... Nuneaton
Altrincham	1-2	.... Leek
Arlesey	1-5	.....Whitehawk
Basingstoke ...	0-0	.......Havant & W
Bradford PA ...	2-1	.Kidderminster
Braintree	0-0	.... Welling
Bury Town	0-3	.... Eastleigh
Chester FC	1-2	.... Barrow
Chorley	2-1	Curzon Ashton
Coalville	1-1	.... Grimsby
Dartford	1-1	....Forest Green
Daventry Town	0-1	...Maidenhead
E Thurrock	1-1	.... Dover
Ebbsfleet	3-0	.... Gloucester
Gateshead	4-1	...... Hednesford
Gosport Bor ...	1-0	...... Concord R
Halifax	0-1	.... Guiseley
Hayes & Y	0-1	.... Barnet
Hereford	0-3	.... Woking
Hungerford T...	2-0	........Chesham
Hyde	1-2	.... Nth Ferriby
Leamington ...	0-0	.... Northwich
Lincoln............	5-1	.....Stalybridge
Salisbury.........	0-1	.. Cambridge U
Southport	1-2	..... Boston Utd
Staines............	0-0	.... Luton
Tamworth	2-0	... Macclesfield
Tonbridge	0-0	........St Albans
Worcester	0-0	............Telford
Wrexham	2-1	Gresley Rovers

Sunday December 1 2013

Hendon .... 1-2 ......Whitehawk

First round replays

Tuesday December 3 2013

Dover	3-1	...... E Thurrock
Forest Green ...	1-0	.... Dartford
Grimsby	3-0	.... Coalville
Havant & W	1-0	....Basingstoke
Luton	2-0	.... Staines
Northwich.......	0-1	.... Leamington
St Albans	4-0	......Tonbridge
Telford	0-3	.... Worcester
Weston S-M....	2-5	.... Aldershot

Second round

Saturday December 14 2013

Aldershot........	4-1	.......Worcester
Barnet............	1-2	.......Grimsby
Barrow............	0-2	...Maidenhead
Braintree.........	1-3	.... Lincoln
Chorley...........	0-0	....Forest Green
Dover	2-0	....Leamington
Eastleigh.........	2-0	....Gateshead
Gosport Bor	0-0	.......Nuneaton
Guiseley..........	3-0	....Bradford PA
Leek................	0-1	..Hungerford T
Luton	2-0	.......Wrexham
Nth Ferriby......	4-0	.... Woking
St Albans	1-2	..Cambridge U
Tamworth........	2-0	..... Boston Utd
Whitehawk......	1-1	....Havant & W
Whitstable	1-2	.... Ebbsfleet

Second round replays

Monday December 16 2013

Havant & W .... 3-1 .....Whitehawk

Tuesday December 17 2013

Forest Green ... 0-0 ....Chorley
     AET 0-0 90 mins, Chorley 3-1 pens
Nuneaton .... 0-0 ....Gosport Bor
     AET 0-0 90 mins, Gosport Bor 4-3 pens

Third round

Saturday January 11 2014

Aldershot........	3-0	.... Guiseley
Cambridge U ..	2-2	.... Luton
Eastleigh.........	3-2	.... Dover
Grimsby..........	2-1	...Maidenhead
Havant & W	1-0	.... Ebbsfleet
Hungerford T ..	0-1	....Gosport Bor
Lincoln............	0-4	..... Nth Ferriby
Tamworth	1-1	...........Chorley

Third round replays

Tuesday January 14 2014

Chorley........... 2-2 ....Tamworth
     AET 2-2 90 mins, Tamworth 6-5 pens
Luton .... 0-1 .. Cambridge U

Quarter-finals

Saturday February 1 2014

Eastleigh......... 0-1 .. Cambridge U
Grimsby........... 4-1 ....Tamworth
Nth Ferriby...... 1-2 ....Gosport Bor

Tuesday February 4 2014

Havant & W .... 4-1 .... Aldershot

Semi-finals

Saturday February 15 2014

Cambridge U .. 2-1 ....Grimsby

Monday February 17 2014

Havant & W .... 1-1 ....Gosport Bor

Saturday February 22 2014

Gosport Bor .... 2-0 ....Havant & W
     Agg. 3-1 Gosport Bor
Grimsby........... 1-1 ..Cambridge U
     Agg 3-2 Cambridge

Peterborough celebrate winning the Johnstone's Paint Trophy

Final

Sunday March 23 2014
Cambridge U .. 4-0   ....Gosport Bor

JOHNSTONE'S PAINT TROPHY

Southern Area first round
Tuesday September 3
Brentford ......(1) 5-3 (0) AFC W'bledon
Cheltenham ..(1) 3-3 (2)......Plymouth
AET, Plymouth 5-4 pens
Dag & Red ....(0) 4-1 (1).... Colchester
Exeter ....(0) 0-2 (1).....Wycombe
Gillingham....(0) 1-3 (2)Leyton Orient
MK Dons.......(0) 2-0 (0)Northampton
Torquay ....(0) 0-0 (0)...Portsmouth
AET, Portsmouth 5-3 pens
Wednesday September 4 2013
Bristol C........(1) 2-1 (0)........Bristol R

Northern Area first round
Tuesday September 3
Crewe...........(0) 1-0 (0)....Accrington
Hartlepool.....(1) 5-0 (0).......Bradford
Notts Co ....(1) 1-0 (0)..........Burton
Port Vale ....(0) 2-1 (0)............ Bury
Scunthorpe ...(0) 0-0 (0)......Sheff Utd
AET, Sheff Utd 5-3 pens
Shrewsbury ..(1) 1-4 (3)........Oldham
Tranmere ......(1) 2-0 (1).....Fleetwood
Wolves ....(1) 2-2 (0).........Walsall
AET, Wolves 4-2 pens

Southern Area second round
Tuesday October 8 2013
Crawley ....(2) 2-3 (1)..Newport Co
Leyton Orient(0) 0-0 (0)...... Coventry
AET, Leyton Orient 4-2 pens
Oxford ....(0) 1-2 (0)...Portsmouth
Peterborough(1) 2-1 (0)......Brentford
Southend......(0) 2-5 (1)...Dag & Red
Stevenage.....(0) 2-1 (1)...... MK Dons
Swindon ....(0) 2-1 (1)......Plymouth
Wycombe .....(2) 2-1 (0)....... Bristol C

Northern Area second round
Tuesday October 8 2013
Fleetwood ....(2) 4-0 (0).......... Crewe

Mansfield .....(0) 0-1 (0)..Chesterfield
Morecambe ..(0) 0-0 (0).........Carlisle
AET, Carlisle 4-3 pens
Port Vale ....(0) 0-1 (1)......Rochdale
Preston ....(0) 0-2 (2).........Oldham
Sheff Utd ......(0) 0-1 (1)....Hartlepool
Wolves ....(0) 0-0 (0)......Notts Co
AET, Notts Co 3-1 pens
York ....(0) 0-3 (1)... Rotherham

Southern Area quarter-finals
Tuesday November 12 2013
Newport Co ..(2) 3-0 (0)...Portsmouth
Peterborough(0) 1-0 (0)....Dag & Red
Stevenage.....(3) 3-2 (2)Leyton Orient
Swindon ....(0) 2-1 (1).....Wycombe

Northern Area quarter-finals
Tuesday November 12 2013
Chesterfield ..(1) 3-0 (0)......Rochdale
Hartlepool.....(1) 1-2 (2)... Rotherham
Oldham ....(2) 5-1 (1).......Notts Co
Wednesday November 13 2013
Fleetwood ....(1) 2-0 (0).........Carlisle

Southern Area semi-finals
Tuesday December 10 2013
Newport Co ..(0) 0-3 (1)Peterborough
Swindon ....(1) 1-1 (0).... Stevenage
AET, Swindon 3-1 pens

Northern Area semi-finals
Tuesday December 10 2013
Fleetwood ....(1) 2-1 (0)... Rotherham
Oldham ....(1) 1-1 (1)..Chesterfield
AET, Chesterfield 6-5 pens

Southern Area final
Wednesday February 5 2014
Peterborough(2) 2-2 (2).......Swindon
Monday February 17 2014
Swindon ....(1) 1-1 (0)Peterborough
AET 1-1 90 mins, 3-3 agg. Peterboro 4-3 pens

Northern Area final
Tuesday February 4 2014
Fleetwood ....(1) 1-3 (2)..Chesterfield

Tuesday February 18 2014
Chesterfield ..(0) 0-1 (0).... Fleetwood
Agg. 3-2 Chesterfield

Final

Sunday March 30 2014
Chesterfield ..(0) 1-3 (2)Peterborough

SCOTTISH CHALLENGE CUP

Preliminary round
Saturday July 13 2013
Spartans ....(0) 4-2 (0) Threave Rvrs
Saturday July 20 2013
Threave Rvrs.(0) 1-0 (0).......Spartans
Agg: Spartans 4-3

First round
Saturday July 27 2013
Airdrieonians(1) 2-1 (1)...... Hamilton
Alloa.............(0) 0-1 (0)........ Dundee
Annan............(0) 1-0 (0).........Morton
Berwick ....(1) 3-2 (0).... Livingston
AET 1-1 90 mins
Clyde ....(0) 1-2 (0).......... Falkirk
Cowdenbeath(1) 1-3 (1). Dunfermline
Elgin City ......(0) 2-0 (0)...... Montrose
Forfar ....(2) 2-1 (1)....... East Fife
Formartine Utd(2) 2-0 (0)..East Stirling
Peterhead .....(1) 2-1 (1).......Brechin
Queen of Sth.(3) 4-0 (0).......Spartans
Queen's Park.(1) 1-2 (0).............. Ayr
Raith.............(0) 2-1 (0)........ Stirling
Stenh'semuir.(1) 4-4 (2).......Arbroath
AET 2-2 90 mins
Stranraer.......(1) 4-2 (2)...Dumbarton
Sunday July 28 2013
Albion...........(0) 0-4 (2)........Rangers

Second round
Tuesday August 13 2013
Airdrieonians(0) 0-2 (1) Queen of Sth
Ayr ....(1) 1-2 (0).......... Falkirk
AET 1-1 90 mins
Dundee.........(0) 3-1 (0)...........Forfar
AET 1-1 90 mins
Dunfermline..(0) 0-2 (1)........... Raith
Peterhead .....(1) 1-3 (0) Stenh'semuir
AET 1-1 90 mins
Stranraer.......(1) 2-3 (2).......... Annan
Wednesday August 21 2013
Formartine Utd(1) 5-1 (1)......Elgin City
Tuesday August 27 2013
Rangers ....(0) 2-0 (0).......Berwick

Quarter-finals
Saturday September 7 2013
Annan...........(0) 4-0 (0)Formartine Utd
Dundee.........(0) 1-1 (0) Stenh'semuir
AET 1-1 90 mins, Stenh'semuir 5-4 pens
Raith.............(0) 1-0 (0).......... Falkirk
Tuesday September 17 2013
Queen of Sth.(0) 0-3 (1)........Rangers

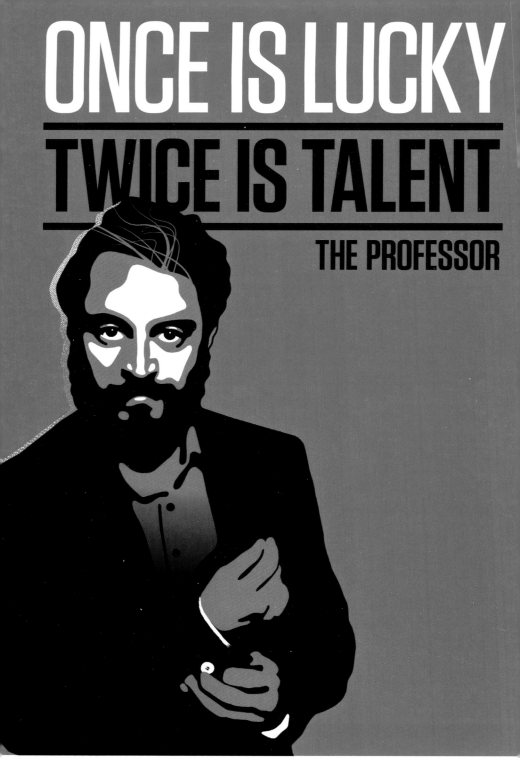

WHEN YOU KNOW

YOU KNOW YOU KNOW

GUT TRUSTER

THIS IS THE
Ladbrokes
LIFE

Semi-finals

Sunday October 13 2013
Raith............(1) 3-0 (0).........Annan

Tuesday October 29 2013
Stenh'semuir.(0) 0-1 (0)........Rangers

Final

Sunday April 6 2014
Raith............(0) 1-0 (0)........Rangers
AET 0-0 90 mins

SCOTTISH CUP

First round

Saturday September 14 2013
Brora Rangers .(0) 1-0 (0)Vale of Leithen
Coldstream ...(0) 0-6 (2) Wick Academy
Deveronvale .(2) 5-0 (0) Clachnacuddin
Edinburgh U .(0) 0-2 (2).......Spartans
Forres M ....(3) 4-5 (2)..........Keith
Fort William ..(0) 0-0 (0).....Newton S
Fraserburgh ..(0) 4-0 (0)Civil Service S
Gala F...........(1) 3-1 (1)... Glasgow U
Girvan ....(0) 1-5 (2)....Auchinleck
Golspie S ......(0) 0-4 (2). Edinburgh C
Hawick Royal (0) 0-1 (1) St Cuthbert's
Huntly...........(2) 3-4 (0). Preston Ath.
Inverurie L ...(1) 3-0 (0)...Burntisland
Linlithgow R .(1) 2-0 (0) Nairn County
Lossiemouth .(0) 0-0 (0)..........Culter
Selkirk...........(0) 1-3 (1).......Turriff U
Threave Rvrs .(0) 3-0 (0)..........Rothes
Wigtown & B (0) 3-4 (3)Buckie Thistle

First round replays

Saturday September 21 2013
Culter ....(0) 3-1 (0)..Lossiemouth
Newton S......(0) 3-1 (0)..Fort William

Second round

Saturday October 5 2013
Albion...........(0) 1-0 (0)......Spartans
Auchinleck ....(3) 4-0 (0) St Cuthbert's
Berwick ....(0) 2-1 (1).....Peterhead
Brora Rangers (1) 1-1 (1)Cove Rangers
Buckie Thistle(0) 0-0 (0)..........Annan
Dalbeattie Star(0)0-1 (0).....Montrose
Deveronvale .(0) 2-2 (1). Linlithgow R
Edinburgh C..(1) 4-4 (2).. Fraserburgh
Formartine Utd(0) 0-2 (2)Inverurie Locos
Gala Fairydean(0) 0-3 (0)............Clyde
Keith.............(0) 0-4 (0)......Elgin City
Newton S......(0) 0-6 (1)..........Culter
Queen's Park..(1) 2-0 (0). Preston Ath.
Stirling..........(1) 2-2 (1)..Whitehill W
Turriff U ....(2) 4-2 (0) Wick Academy

Sunday October 6 2013
East Stirling ..(2) 6-0 (0)Threave Rovers

Second round replays

Saturday October 12 2013
Cove Rangers(0) 0-3 (1). Brora Rangers
Fraserburgh ..(0) 2-0 (0). Edinburgh C

Linlithgow Rose(1) 1-3 (1).Deveronvale
Preston Ath...(0) 1-2 (2) Queen's Park
Whitehill W ..(1) 1-2 (1)........ Stirling

Saturday October 19 2013
Annan...........(3) 4-0 (0)Buckie Thistle

Third round

Friday November 1 2013
Rangers ....(0) 3-0 (0) Airdrieonians

Saturday November 2 2013
Albion...........(0) 1-0 (0). Deveronvale
Alloa.............(0) 3-0 (0)Inverurie Locos
Arbroath ....(0) 0-2 (0).........Brechin
Ayr ....(1) 3-2 (1) Queen's Park
Clyde ....(1) 2-1 (1). Brora Rangers
Culter ....(0) 1-1 (0)........ Berwick
Dumbarton ...(1) 2-1 (0)Cowdenbeath
Elgin City ......(1) 3-5 (2). Dunfermline
Forfar ....(1) 2-1 (0)...... East Fife
Fraserburgh ..(0) 2-1 (1).... Montrose
Queen of Sth.(0) 1-0 (0)...... Hamilton
Stenh'semuir.(0) 2-2 (1)..........Annan
Stranraer.......(1) 2-2 (2)....Auchinleck
Turriff U ....(0) 0-3 (2).......... Stirling

Sunday November 3 2013
East Stirling ..(0) 0-2 (0)............ Raith

Third round replays

Saturday November 9 2013
Auchinleck ....(0) 2-3 (1)...... Stranraer
Berwick ....(1) 3-1 (0)..........Culter

Tuesday November 12 2013
Annan...........(1) 2-4 (0) Stenh'semuir
AET 2-2 90 mins

Fourth round

Friday November 29 2013
Dundee Utd ..(1) 5-2 (0)... Kilmarnock

Saturday November 30 2013
Albion...........(0) 1-0 (0).. Motherwell
Alloa.............(0) 3-2 (1).........Stirling
Ayr ....(0) 1-1 (1). Dunfermline
Berwick ....(1) 1-3 (2)...Dumbarton
Brechin ....(0) 1-1 (0)...........Forfar
Clyde ....(1) 1-1 (1)...... Stranraer
Dundee.........(0) 0-1 (1)...........Raith
Falkirk...........(0) 0-2 (0)........Rangers
Inverurie CT .(1) 4-0 (0).........Morton
Queen of Sth.(2) 2-2 (1)...... St Mirren
Ross County..(0) 0-1 (1)..... Hibernian
St Johnstone.(1) 2-0 (0).... Livingston
Stenh'semuir.(0) 3-0 (0).. Fraserburgh

Sunday December 1 2013
Hearts...........(0) 0-7 (5)...........Celtic
Partick ....(0) 0-1 (1)..... Aberdeen

Fourth round replays

Wednesday December 4 2013
Dunfermline..(0) 1-0 (0)..............Ayr

Tuesday December 10 2013
Forfar ....(1) 3-3 (1).........Brechin
AET 2-2 90 mins, Forfar 4-3 pens
St Mirren ......(1) 3-0 (0) Queen of Sth
Stranraer.......(0) 4-1 (0)............Clyde

St Johnstone's Steven Anderson scores in the final

Fifth round

Friday February 7 2014
Rangers ....(3) 4-0 (0). Dunfermline

Saturday February 8 2014
Albion...........(1) 2-0 (0) Stenh'semuir
Alloa.............(0) 0-1 (1)...Dumbarton
Celtic ....(1) 1-2 (1)..... Aberdeen
Forfar ....(0) 0-4 (2).St Johnstone
Hibernian......(2) 2-3 (2)............ Raith
Stranraer.......(1) 2-2 (1).Inverness CT

Sunday February 9 2014
Dundee Utd ..(1) 2-1 (1)...... St Mirren

Fifth round replay

Tuesday February 18 2014
Inverness CT .(1) 2-0 (0)..... Stranraer

Sixth round

Saturday March 8 2014
Aberdeen......(0) 1-0 (0)...Dumbarton
Raith.............(1) 1-3 (1).St Johnstone

Sunday March 9 2014
Inverness CT .(0) 0-5 (3)..Dundee Utd
Rangers ....(0) 1-1 (1)..........Albion

Sixth round replay

Monday March 17 2014
Albion...........(0) 0-2 (1)........Rangers

Semi-finals

Saturday April 12 2014
Rangers ....(1) 1-3 (2)..Dundee Utd

Sunday April 13 2014
St Johnstone .(0) 2-1 (1) ..... Aberdeen

Final

Saturday May 17 2014
St Johnstone .(1) 2-0 (0) ..Dundee Utd

FA CUP

First round proper

Friday November 8 2013
AFC W'bledon.(0) 1-3 (0) ...... Coventry
Bristol R........(1) 3-3 (2) ....York

Saturday November 9 2013
Accrington ....(0) 0-1 (0) ..... Tranmere
Boreham W ..(0) 0-0 (0) .... Carlisle
Braintree.......(1) 1-1 (0) ..Newport Co
Brentford ......(3) 5-0 (0) .... Staines
Bristol C........(1) 3-0 (0) ..... Dag & Red
Chesterfield ..(0) 2-0 (0)Daventry Town
Colchester.....(0) 2-3 (2) ..... Sheff Utd
Corby............(0) 1-2 (0) .... Dover
Gillingham ....(0) 1-1 (0) .... Brackley
Gloucester ....(0) 0-2 (1) ..... Fleetwood
Grimsby ....(0) 0-0 (0) ...Scunthorpe
Hartlepool.....(2) 3-2 (1)......Notts Co
Hednesford ...(0) 1-2 (0)......Crawley
Kidderminster(2) 4-1 (1)....Sutton Utd
Leyton Orient(3) 5-2 (1) ..... Southport
Lincoln..........(0) 0-0 (0) ..... Plymouth
MK Dons.......(1) 4-1 (0) .... Halifax
Macclesfield..(1) 4-0 (0) .... Swindon
Morecambe ..(0) 3-3 (2) .... Southend
Oldham ....(1) 1-1 (1) .... Wolves
Oxford ....(0) 2-2 (1)......Gateshead
Peterborough(0) 2-0 (0) ....Exeter

Preston ....(3) 6-0 (0) .... Barnet
Rotherham....(1) 3-0 (0) .... Bradford
Salisbury.......(3) 4-2 (0) .... Dartford
St Albans ......(1) 1-8 (2) ..... Mansfield
Stevenage.....(2) 2-1 (0) ...Portsmouth
Stourbridge...(2) 4-1 (1) Biggleswade T
Tamworth .....(1) 1-0 (0)...Cheltenham
Torquay ....(0) 0-2 (0) ..... Rochdale
Walsall ....(1) 3-0 (0)..Shrewsbury
Welling ....(2) 2-1 (0) .... Luton
Wrexham......(1) 3-1 (0) ....Alfreton
Wycombe .....(1) 1-1 (1) .... Crewe

Sunday November 10 2013
Bishop's St....(0) 1-2 (0)Northampton
Burton ....(1) 2-0 (0) .... Hereford

Monday November 11 2013
Shortwood....(0) 0-4 (2).......Port Vale

Tuesday November 19 2013
Bury..............(0) 0-0 (0) Cambridge U

First round replays

Monday November 18 2013
Brackley........(1) 1-0 (0)... Gillingham

Tuesday November 19 2013
Carlisle ....(0) 2-1 (1) .. Boreham W
Crewe............(0) 0-2 (0) ..... Wycombe
Newport Co ..(1) 1-0 (0) ...... Braintree
Scunthorpe ...(0) 1-2 (1)........Grimsby
Wolves ....(0) 1-2 (1)........Oldham
York..............(0) 2-3 (2)........Bristol R

Wednesday November 20 2013
Plymouth ......(4) 5-0 (0) .... Lincoln

Tuesday December 3 2013
Cambridge U (0) 2-1 (0) .... Bury

Second round

Friday December 6 2013
Port Vale ....(1) 4-1 (0) ...... Salisbury

Saturday December 7 2013
Bristol R........(0) 0-0 (0) ....Crawley
Carlisle ....(1) 3-2 (0) ......Brentford
Chesterfield ..(1) 1-3 (2) ......Southend
Fleetwood ....(0) 1-1 (0) ....Burton
Grimsby ....(0) 2-0 (0)Northampton
Hartlepool.....(0) 1-1 (1) ...... Coventry
Kidderminster(3) 0-2 (0)..Newport Co
Leyton Orient(1) 1-0 (0) .... Walsall
MK Dons.......(0) 1-0 (0) ....Dover
Macclesfield..(1) 3-2 (0) .... Brackley
Oldham ....(1) 1-1 (1)...... Mansfield
Peterborough(2) 5-0 (0) ...... Tranmere
Plymouth ......(3) 3-1 (0) ...... Welling
Rotherham....(1) 1-2 (0) ...... Rochdale
Stevenage.....(1) 4-0 (0) .. Stourbridge
Wycombe .....(0) 0-1 (1).........Preston

Sunday December 8 2013
Cambridge U (0) 0-2 (1) ...... Sheff Utd
Tamworth .....(0) 1-2 (1)....... Bristol C

Monday December 9 2013
Wrexham......(1) 1-2 (0) ....Oxford

Second round replays

Tuesday December 17 2013
Burton ....(1) 1-0 (0) ....Fleetwood
Coventry.......(1) 2-1 (0) ....Hartlepool
Mansfield .....(1) 1-4 (0) ....Oldham

Wednesday January 8 2014
Crawley ....(1) 1-2 (0) ....Bristol R

Third round

Saturday January 4 2014
Arsenal ....(1) 2-0 (0).... Tottenham
Aston Villa ....(0) 1-2 (1)...... Sheff Utd
Barnsley........(1) 1-2 (0)...... Coventry
Blackburn .....(0) 1-1 (1)...... Man City
Bolton...........(1) 2-1 (1).... Blackpool
Brighton ....(1) 1-0 (0)........Reading
Bristol C........(0) 1-1 (0)........Watford
Doncaster .....(0) 2-3 (0).... Stevenage
Everton ....(2) 4-0 (0).............QPR
Grimsby ....(1) 2-3 (0).Huddersfield
Ipswich ....(1) 1-1 (1).........Preston
Kidderminster(0) 0-0 (0)Peterborough
Macclesfield..(0) 1-1 (1).... Sheff Wed
Middlesbro ...(0) 0-2 (1).............. Hull
Newcastle.....(0) 1-2 (0)......... Cardiff
Norwich........(1) 1-1 (1).........Fulham
Rochdale ......(1) 2-0 (0)........... Leeds
Southampton(2) 4-3 (0)........Burnley
Southend......(2) 4-1 (0).......Millwall
Stoke ....(1) 2-1 (0)......Leicester
West Brom....(0) 0-2 (1)...... C Palace
Wigan...........(2) 3-3 (2)...... MK Dons
Yeovil............(1) 4-0 (0)Leyton Orient

Sunday January 5 2014
Derby ....(0) 0-2 (0)........ Chelsea
Liverpool ......(0) 2-0 (0)........ Oldham
Man Utd ....(1) 1-2 (1)...... Swansea
Nottm Forest.(1) 5-0 (0).... West Ham
Port Vale ....(2) 2-2 (0)......Plymouth
Sunderland ...(1) 3-1 (1)......... Carlisle

Tuesday January 14 2014
Birmingham ..(1) 3-0 (0)........Bristol R
Bournemouth(2) 4-1 (1)..........Burton
Charlton ....(0) 2-2 (2).........Oxford

Third round replays

Tuesday January 14 2014
Fulham ....(2) 3-0 (0)....... Norwich
MK Dons.......(1) 1-3 (0).......... Wigan
AET 1-1 90 mins
Peterborough(1) 2-3 (0)Kidderminster
Plymouth ......(2) 2-3 (1).......Port Vale
Preston ....(0) 3-2 (0)........ Ipswich
Sheff Wed.....(1) 4-1 (0). Macclesfield
Watford ....(1) 2-0 (0)....... Bristol C

Wednesday January 15 2014
Man City.......(1) 5-0 (0).....Blackburn

Tuesday January 21 2014
Oxford ....(0) 0-3 (2)....... Charlton

Fourth round

Friday January 24 2014
Arsenal ....(2) 4-0 (0)...... Coventry
Nottm Forest.(0) 0-0 (0).........Preston

Saturday January 25 2014
Birmingham ..(1) 1-2 (0)...... Swansea
Bolton...........(0) 0-1 (0).......... Cardiff
Bournemouth(0) 0-2 (1)...... Liverpool

Huddersfield .(0) 0-1 (0)....... Charlton
Man City.......(0) 4-2 (2).......Watford
Port Vale ....(1) 1-3 (2)....... Brighton
Rochdale ......(0) 1-2 (0).... Sheff Wed
Southampton(1) 2-0 (0)............. Yeovil
Southend......(0) 0-2 (0).............. Hull
Stevenage.....(0) 0-4 (2)....... Everton
Sunderland ...(1) 1-0 (0)Kidderminster
Wigan...........(1) 2-1 (0)....... C Palace

Sunday January 26 2014
Chelsea.........(1) 1-0 (0)...........Stoke
Sheff Utd ......(1) 1-1 (0).........Fulham

Fourth round replays

Tuesday February 4 2014
Fulham ....(0) 0-1 (0)...... Sheff Utd
AET 0-0 90 mins

Wednesday February 5 2014
Preston ....(0) 0-2 (1) Nottm Forest

Fifth round

Saturday February 15 2014
Cardiff ....(1) 1-2 (2).......... Wigan
Man City.......(1) 2-0 (0)........ Chelsea
Sunderland ...(0) 1-0 (0)Southampton

Sunday February 16 2014
Arsenal ....(1) 2-1 (0)...... Liverpool
Everton ....(1) 3-1 (1)...... Swansea
Sheff Utd ......(0) 3-1 (1) Nottm Forest

Monday February 17 2014
Brighton ....(1) 1-1 (0).............. Hull

Monday February 24 2014
Sheff Wed.....(0) 1-2 (1)....... Charlton

Fifth round replay

Monday February 24 2014
Hull ....(2) 2-1 (0)....... Brighton

Sixth round

Saturday March 8 2014
Arsenal ....(1) 4-1 (1)........ Everton

Sunday March 9 2014
Hull ....(0) 3-0 (0)...Sunderland
Man City.......(0) 1-2 (1).......... Wigan
Sheff Utd ......(0) 2-0 (0)....... Charlton

Semi-finals

Saturday April 12 2014
Wigan...........(0) 1-1 (0).........Arsenal
AET 1-1 90 mins, Arsenal 4-2 pens

Sunday April 13 2014
Hull ....(1) 5-3 (2)...... Sheff Utd

Final

Saturday May 17 2014
Arsenal ....(1) 3-2 (2).............. Hull
AET 2-2 90 mins

....

Arsenal supporters capture
the moment as their trophy
drought comes to an end

Expect a return to business as usual in Spain after last term's 100-1 shock winners

A tletico Madrid provided the biggest story in European football last season, breaking the Barcelona-Real Madrid duopoly at the top of La Liga at odds of 100-1 to become the first team other than Spain's big two to win the title since Valencia in 2004, writes Paul Charlton. It was a huge upset, especially in the context of the Spanish top flight, but overall shocks were thin on the ground.

Atletico were the only champions in the top 16 European leagues on Uefa's country coefficients – which are used to decide the seedings for the Champions League and Europa League – not to have finished in the top two in 2012-13. And 12 of the 16 champions in that campaign had been first or second the previous year, too, with only Austria Vienna, fourth in 2011-12, out of the top three.

You don't have to look far down the league tables to put together a shortlist for the champions of Europe's major domestic leagues, and even some of those which had been reliably unpredictable in recent years – France, for example – look easier to call than they used to be. The relatively light sanctions imposed by Uefa for breaches of the Financial Fair Play regulations by Paris Saint-Germain and Manchester City don't look likely to change things any time soon but that doesn't mean that punters aren't faced with some interesting questions ahead of the new season.

Turning back to Spain, Atletico look unlikely to retain the title. Diego Costa was the summer's first high-profile departure, and while the club has a superb record of polishing strikers, having had Fernando Torres and Radamel Falcao on the books in recent seasons, Diego Simeone would have to be a miracle worker to repeat last season's extraordinary achievements – although last season did suggest he might be.

The real question is probably whether Barcelona's new coach, Luis Enrique, can lead them to the title, or if we should be backing Champions League winners Real Madrid at odds-on.

Enrique, a former Barcelona captain and coach of Barca B, took Celta Vigo from a point above the relegation zone in 2013 to a place in the top ten last term, beating Real Madrid along the way. And, although his new side have lost some of their lustre, Barcelona don't require the same anything like the same level of improvement.

The Catalans finished with their lowest points total and goal difference since 2008-09 – the club's first campaign under Pep Guardiola, during which they won the Copa del Rey, Primera Liga and Champions League treble – but they still finished with 87 points and a goal difference of +67 under Gerardo Martinez and went into the final day of the season with a chance to win the title.

At odds-against with most firms at the time of writing, Barcelona represent the value in the Spanish title race and exchange players will surely find opportunities to trade Spain's big two over the course of the season.

It cannot, however, be overemphasised what an important transfer window this is for Barcelona. The 14-month transfer ban imposed by Fifa is on hold pending an appeal to the Court of Arbitration for Sport. But that

The big prizes ended up in Madrid last term but Barcelona still have plenty of world-class talent

is likely to be resolved before the January transfer window meaning that there is a chance that the Catalan giants won't be able to top up the playing staff at the midpoint of the campaign.

That said, it's been a busy summer and Luis Suarez looks a good fit once he has served his suspension for biting Italy's Giorgio Chiellini at the World Cup.

Barcelona's former manager, Pep Guardiola, kept Bayern Munich at the top of the tree in the Bundesliga, with the German champions finishing 19 points clear of second-placed Borussia Dortmund.

At the bottom of the table, Hamburg, one of the founder members of the Bundesliga, came closer than ever to being relegated from Germany's top flight, finishing a point

clear of 17th place and beating Greuther Furth in the playoff.

However, Paderborn, who are about to embark on their first ever season in the Bundesliga, look more likely candidates to finish in the bottom two, while the value may be with Hertha Berlin to go down.

They finished a very respectable 11th in their first season back in the top flight but that was all down to a terrific start to the campaign. Jos Luhukay's side took just 13 points from 17 games over the second half of the season and top scorer Adrian Ramos, who grabbed 16 of Hertha's 40 league goals, will be playing his football for Borussia Dortmund in 2014-15. Only the bottom two, Nuremburg and Braunschweig, scored fewer goals in the Bundesliga than Hertha.

ATALANTA

Atleti Azzurri d'Italia — www.atalanta.it

	2013-14 H	A	Last six seasons at home P	W	D	L	OV	UN	BS	CS
Juventus	L	L	5	0	0	5	3	2	3	0
Roma	D	L	5	2	1	2	4	1	4	1
Napoli	W	L	5	3	1	1	2	3	2	2
Fiorentina	L	L	5	2	0	3	2	3	2	1
Inter	D	W	5	2	3	0	2	3	5	0
Parma	L	L	4	2	1	1	3	1	3	0
Torino	W	L	4	3	0	1	2	2	2	2
Milan	W	L	5	1	1	3	1	4	2	0
Lazio	W	L	5	3	0	2	2	3	1	2
Verona	L	L	1	0	0	1	0	1	0	0
Atalanta										
Sampdoria	W	L	4	2	1	1	2	2	1	2
Udinese	W	L	5	2	3	0	1	4	1	4
Genoa	D	D	5	1	2	2	0	5	2	1
Cagliari	W	L	5	4	1	0	1	4	2	3
Chievo	W	W	5	2	1	2	2	3	2	1
Sassuolo	L	L	2	1	0	1	0	2	0	1
Palermo			4	2	1	1	2	2	2	2
Empoli			1	0	0	1	1	0	1	0
Cesena			1	1	0	0	1	0	1	0

Season	Division	Pos	P	W	D	L	F	A	GD	Pts
2013-14	Serie A	11	38	15	5	18	43	51	-8	50
2012-13	Serie A	15	38	11	9	18	39	56	-17	40
2011-12	Serie A	12	38	13	13	12	41	43	-2	46

Over/Under 45%/55% 15th **Both score** 47%/53% 11th

CAGLIARI

Is Arenas — www.cagliaricalcio.net

	2013-14 H	A	Last six seasons at home P	W	D	L	OV	UN	BS	CS
Juventus	L	L	6	1	0	5	3	3	3	1
Roma	L	D	6	2	2	2	6	0	5	0
Napoli	D	L	6	1	3	2	1	5	2	2
Fiorentina	W	D	6	3	2	1	3	3	3	3
Inter	D	D	6	2	2	2	3	3	4	1
Parma	W	D	5	2	2	1	0	5	1	3
Torino	W	L	3	2	1	0	2	1	2	1
Milan	L	L	6	0	2	4	2	4	3	1
Lazio	L	L	6	2	0	4	2	4	1	2
Verona	W	L	1	1	0	0	1	0	1	1
Atalanta	W	L	5	3	1	1	2	2	2	2
Sampdoria	D	L	5	3	2	0	2	3	2	3
Udinese	W	L	6	2	2	2	3	3	1	3
Genoa	W	W	6	4	0	2	4	2	3	1
Cagliari										
Chievo	L	D	6	2	1	3	2	4	2	2
Sassuolo	D	D	1	0	1	0	1	0	1	0
Palermo			5	3	2	0	3	2	4	1
Empoli			-	-	-	-	-	-	-	-
Cesena			2	1	0	1	1	0	1	1

Season	Division	Pos	P	W	D	L	F	A	GD	Pts
2013-14	Serie A	15	38	9	12	17	34	53	-19	39
2012-13	Serie A	11	38	12	11	15	43	55	-12	47
2011-12	Serie A	15	38	10	13	15	37	46	-9	43

Over/Under 47%/53% 11th **Both score** 55%/45% 3rd

CESENA

Dino Manuzzi — www.cesenacalcio.it

	2013-14 H	A	Last six seasons at home P	W	D	L	OV	UN	BS	CS
Juventus			2	0	1	1	1	1	1	0
Roma			2	0	0	2	1	1	1	0
Napoli			2	0	0	2	2	0	2	0
Fiorentina			2	0	2	0	1	1	1	1
Inter			2	0	0	2	1	1	1	1
Parma			2	0	2	0	1	1	2	0
Torino			1	0	1	0	0	1	1	0
Milan			2	1	0	1	1	1	1	1
Lazio			2	1	0	1	1	1	1	1
Verona			1	0	1	0	0	1	0	1
Atalanta			1	0	0	1	0	1	0	0
Sampdoria			1	0	0	1	0	1	0	0
Udinese			2	0	0	2	1	1	0	0
Genoa			2	1	1	0	0	2	0	2
Cagliari			2	1	1	0	0	2	1	1
Chievo			2	1	1	0	0	2	0	2
Sassuolo			2	0	0	2	1	1	0	0
Palermo	D	L	3	0	2	1	2	1	2	1
Empoli	W	D	3	1	0	2	2	1	2	1
Cesena										

Season	Division	Pos	P	W	D	L	F	A	GD	Pts
2013-14	Serie B	4	42	17	15	10	45	35	+10	66
2012-13	Serie B	14	42	12	14	16	46	59	-13	50
2011-12	Serie A	20	38	4	10	24	24	60	-36	22

Over/Under 31%/69% 21st **Both score** 43%/57% 21st

CHIEVO

Marc'Antonio Bentegodi — www.chievoverona.tv

	2013-14 H	A	Last six seasons at home P	W	D	L	OV	UN	BS	CS
Juventus	L	L	6	1	2	3	2	4	3	2
Roma	L	L	6	1	2	3	1	5	1	2
Napoli	L	D	6	4	0	2	3	3	3	3
Fiorentina	L	L	6	2	1	3	2	4	3	1
Inter	W	D	6	2	1	3	3	3	3	0
Parma	L	D	5	0	3	2	2	3	3	2
Torino	L	L	3	0	2	1	0	3	2	0
Milan	D	L	6	0	1	5	2	4	2	1
Lazio	L	L	6	0	0	6	4	2	3	0
Verona	L	W	1	0	0	1	0	1	0	0
Atalanta	L	L	5	1	3	1	0	5	2	2
Sampdoria	L	L	5	1	2	2	2	3	3	1
Udinese	W	L	6	1	3	2	3	3	4	1
Genoa	W	L	6	3	1	2	3	3	3	1
Cagliari	D	W	6	2	4	0	1	5	2	4
Chievo										
Sassuolo	L	W	1	0	0	1	0	1	0	0
Palermo			5	3	2	0	0	5	1	4
Empoli			-	-	-	-	-	-	-	-
Cesena			2	2	0	0	1	1	1	1

Season	Division	Pos	P	W	D	L	F	A	GD	Pts
2013-14	Serie A	16	38	10	6	22	34	54	-20	36
2012-13	Serie A	12	38	12	9	17	37	52	-15	45
2011-12	Serie A	10	38	12	13	13	35	45	-10	49

Over/Under 50%/50% 6th **Both score** 42%/58% 17th

EMPOLI

Carlo Castellani — www.empolicalcio.it

	2013-14 H	A	P	W	D	L	OV	UN	BS	CS
Juventus			-	-	-	-	-	-	-	-
Roma			-	-	-	-	-	-	-	-
Napoli			-	-	-	-	-	-	-	-
Fiorentina			-	-	-	-	-	-	-	-
Inter			-	-	-	-	-	-	-	-
Parma			1	0	0	1	1	0	1	0
Torino			3	1	2	0	0	3	1	2
Milan			-	-	-	-	-	-	-	-
Lazio			-	-	-	-	-	-	-	-
Verona			2	0	1	1	1	1	2	0
Atalanta			1	1	0	0	1	0	0	1
Sampdoria			1	0	0	1	1	0	1	0
Udinese			-	-	-	-	-	-	-	-
Genoa			-	-	-	-	-	-	-	-
Cagliari			-	-	-	-	-	-	-	-
Chievo			-	-	-	-	-	-	-	-
Sassuolo			5	1	2	2	2	3	3	0
Palermo	D	W	1	0	1	0	0	1	1	0
Empoli										
Cesena	D	L	3	2	1	0	0	3	0	3

Season	Division	Pos	P	W	D	L	F	A	GD	Pts
2013-14	Serie B	2	42	20	12	10	59	35	+24	72
2012-13	Serie B	4	42	20	13	9	69	51	+18	73
2011-12	Serie B	18	42	12	11	19	48	59	-11	47

Over/Under 43%/57% 13th **Both score** 50%/50% 13th

FIORENTINA

Artemio Franchi — www.violachannel.tv

	2013-14 H	A	P	W	D	L	OV	UN	BS	CS
Juventus	W	L	6	1	3	2	3	3	3	2
Roma	L	L	6	2	1	3	3	3	2	1
Napoli	L	W	6	1	2	3	3	3	4	0
Fiorentina										
Inter	L	L	6	1	3	2	4	2	4	2
Parma	D	D	5	3	1	1	3	2	2	3
Torino	D	D	3	2	1	0	2	1	2	1
Milan	L	W	6	0	2	4	3	3	3	1
Lazio	L	D	6	2	1	3	2	4	2	3
Verona	W	W	1	1	0	0	1	0	1	0
Atalanta	W	W	5	4	1	0	3	2	3	2
Sampdoria	W	D	5	3	2	0	2	3	2	3
Udinese	W	L	6	6	0	0	6	0	6	0
Genoa	D	W	6	5	1	0	3	3	3	2
Cagliari	D	L	6	4	2	0	2	4	3	3
Chievo	W	W	6	4	0	2	4	2	4	1
Sassuolo	L	W	1	0	0	1	1	0	1	0
Palermo			5	2	1	2	1	4	1	3
Empoli										
Cesena			2	2	0	0	0	2	0	2

Season	Division	Pos	P	W	D	L	F	A	GD	Pts
2013-14	Serie A	4	38	19	8	11	65	44	+21	65
2012-13	Serie A	4	38	21	7	10	72	44	+28	70
2011-12	Serie A	13	38	11	13	14	37	43	-6	46

Over/Under 55%/45% 2nd **Both score** 50%/50% 8th

GENOA

Luigi Ferraris — www.genoafc.it

	2013-14 H	A	P	W	D	L	OV	UN	BS	CS
Juventus	L	L	6	1	2	3	3	3	3	1
Roma	W	L	6	5	0	1	5	1	5	1
Napoli	L	D	6	3	0	3	4	2	4	0
Fiorentina	L	D	6	1	3	2	4	2	5	0
Inter	W	L	6	1	1	4	1	5	0	2
Parma	W	D	5	2	3	0	3	2	4	1
Torino	D	L	3	1	2	0	1	2	2	1
Milan	L	D	6	2	1	3	1	5	2	2
Lazio	W	W	6	3	1	2	3	3	3	2
Verona	W	L	1	1	0	0	0	1	0	1
Atalanta	D	D	5	1	4	0	1	4	4	1
Sampdoria	L	W	5	3	1	1	3	2	3	1
Udinese	D	L	6	4	1	1	4	2	3	3
Genoa										
Cagliari	L	L	6	4	0	2	4	2	4	1
Chievo	W	L	6	2	1	3	4	2	4	1
Sassuolo	W	L	1	1	0	0	0	1	0	1
Palermo			5	3	2	0	1	4	2	3
Empoli										
Cesena			2	1	1	0	1	1	2	0

Season	Division	Pos	P	W	D	L	F	A	GD	Pts
2013-14	Serie A	14	38	11	11	16	41	50	-9	44
2012-13	Serie A	17	38	8	14	16	38	52	-14	38
2011-12	Serie A	17	38	11	9	18	50	69	-19	42

Over/Under 34%/66% 20th **Both score** 45%/55% 14th

HELLAS VERONA

Stadio Marc'Antonio Bentegodi — www.hellasverona.it

	2013-14 H	A	P	W	D	L	OV	UN	BS	CS
Juventus	D	L	1	0	1	0	1	0	1	0
Roma	L	L	1	0	0	1	1	0	0	1
Napoli	L	L	1	0	0	1	1	0	0	0
Fiorentina	L	L	1	0	0	1	1	0	1	0
Inter	L	L	1	0	0	1	0	1	0	0
Parma	W	L	1	1	0	0	1	0	0	0
Torino	L	D	2	0	0	2	2	0	2	0
Milan	W	L	1	1	0	0	1	0	1	0
Lazio	W	D	1	1	0	0	1	0	0	0
Verona										
Atalanta	W	W	1	1	0	0	1	0	0	1
Sampdoria	W	L	2	1	1	0	0	2	1	1
Udinese	D	W	1	0	1	0	1	0	1	0
Genoa	W	L	1	1	0	0	1	0	0	1
Cagliari	W	L	1	1	0	0	1	0	1	0
Chievo	L	W	1	0	0	1	0	1	0	0
Sassuolo	W	W	3	3	0	0	0	3	0	3
Palermo										
Empoli			2	0	2	0	0	2	0	2
Cesena			2	0	2	0	0	2	0	2

Season	Division	Pos	P	W	D	L	F	A	GD	Pts
2013-14	Serie A	10	38	16	6	16	62	68	-6	54
2012-13	Serie B	2	42	23	13	6	67	32	+35	82
2011-12	Serie B	4	42	23	9	10	60	41	+19	78

Over/Under 71%/29% 1st **Both score** 58%/42% 2nd

INTER

San Siro www.inter.it

2013-14	H	A	Last six seasons at home							
			P	W	D	L	OV	UN	BS	CS
Juventus	D	L	6	2	2	2	2	4	3	3
Roma	L	D	6	1	3	2	4	2	4	1
Napoli	D	L	6	4	1	1	5	1	4	1
Fiorentina	W	W	6	6	0	0	3	3	3	3
Inter										
Parma	D	W	5	4	1	0	3	2	2	3
Torino	W	D	3	1	2	0	1	2	2	1
Milan	W	L	6	4	1	1	2	4	3	2
Lazio	W	L	6	5	0	1	4	2	4	2
Verona	W	W	1	1	0	0	1	0	1	0
Atalanta	L	D	5	2	1	2	4	1	4	1
Sampdoria	D	W	5	2	3	0	1	4	3	2
Udinese	D	W	6	3	1	2	3	3	3	2
Genoa	W	L	6	3	3	0	2	4	3	3
Cagliari	D	D	6	3	3	0	3	3	4	2
Chievo	D	L	6	5	1	0	3	3	4	2
Sassuolo	W	W	1	1	0	0	1	0	1	0
Palermo			5	3	2	0	4	1	4	1
Empoli			-	-	-	-	-	-	-	-
Cesena			2	2	0	0	2	0	2	0

Season	Division	Pos	P	W	D	L	F	A	GD	Pts
2013-14	Serie A	5	38	15	15	8	62	39	+23	60
2012-13	Serie A	9	38	16	6	16	55	57	-2	54
2011-12	Serie A	6	38	17	7	14	58	55	+3	58

Over/Under 45%/55% 15th **Both score** 50%/50% 8th

JUVENTUS

Juventus Stadium www.juventus.com

2013-14	H	A	Last six seasons at home							
			P	W	D	L	OV	UN	BS	CS
Juventus										
Roma	W	W	6	4	1	1	4	2	3	3
Napoli	W	L	6	4	1	1	4	2	2	4
Fiorentina	W	L	6	4	2	0	1	5	3	3
Inter	W	D	6	4	1	1	3	3	4	2
Parma	W	W	5	3	0	2	4	1	4	1
Torino	W	W	3	3	0	0	1	2	0	3
Milan	W	W	6	4	0	2	3	3	2	2
Lazio	W	D	6	4	2	0	3	3	4	2
Verona	W	D	1	1	0	0	1	0	1	0
Atalanta	W	W	5	4	1	0	4	1	3	2
Sampdoria	W	W	5	2	2	1	4	1	5	0
Udinese	W	W	6	5	0	1	3	3	2	4
Genoa	W	W	6	4	2	0	4	2	5	1
Cagliari	W	W	6	3	2	1	3	4	2	2
Chievo	W	W	6	3	3	0	3	3	4	2
Sassuolo	W	W	1	1	0	0	1	0	0	1
Palermo			5	2	0	3	3	2	2	2
Empoli			-	-	-	-	-	-	-	-
Cesena			2	2	0	0	1	1	1	1

Season	Division	Pos	P	W	D	L	F	A	GD	Pts
2013-14	Serie A	1	38	33	3	2	80	23	+57	102
2012-13	Serie A	1	38	27	6	5	71	24	+47	87
2011-12	Serie A	1	38	23	15	0	68	20	+48	84

Over/Under 47%/53% 11th **Both score** 39%/61% 19th

LAZIO

Olimpico www.sslazio.it

2013-14	H	A	Last six seasons at home							
			P	W	D	L	OV	UN	BS	CS
Juventus	D	L	6	0	2	4	0	6	2	0
Roma	D	L	6	3	1	2	4	2	4	1
Napoli	L	L	6	2	2	2	4	4	4	1
Fiorentina	D	W	6	3	2	1	1	5	1	4
Inter	W	L	6	4	0	3	3	2	3	2
Parma	W	D	5	4	0	1	3	2	3	2
Torino	D	L	3	0	3	0	1	2	3	0
Milan	D	D	6	2	2	2	3	3	4	1
Lazio										
Verona	D	L	1	0	1	0	1	0	1	0
Atalanta	L	L	5	3	0	2	0	5	0	3
Sampdoria	W	D	5	4	1	0	0	5	1	4
Udinese	W	W	6	4	1	1	6	0	5	1
Genoa	L	L	6	2	1	3	2	4	3	1
Cagliari	W	W	6	4	0	2	3	3	3	2
Chievo	W	W	6	1	3	2	2	4	2	2
Sassuolo	W	D	1	1	0	0	1	0	1	0
Palermo			5	3	2	0	1	4	1	4
Empoli			-	-	-	-	-	-	-	-
Cesena			2	2	0	0	1	1	1	1

Season	Division	Pos	P	W	D	L	F	A	GD	Pts
2013-14	Serie A	9	38	15	11	12	54	54	0	56
2012-13	Serie A	7	38	18	7	13	51	42	+9	61
2011-12	Serie A	4	38	18	8	12	56	47	+9	62

Over/Under 42%/58% 19th **Both score** 53%/47% 6th

MILAN

San Siro www.acmilan.com

2013-14	H	A	Last six seasons at home							
			P	W	D	L	OV	UN	BS	CS
Juventus	L	L	6	2	2	2	2	4	3	2
Roma	D	L	6	2	2	2	4	2	4	1
Napoli	L	L	6	2	3	1	2	4	3	3
Fiorentina	L	W	6	3	0	3	2	4	2	3
Inter	W	L	6	3	0	3	2	4	0	3
Parma	L	L	5	4	0	1	4	1	3	2
Torino	D	D	3	2	1	0	1	2	2	1
Milan										
Lazio	D	D	6	2	4	0	3	3	4	2
Verona	W	L	1	1	0	0	0	1	0	1
Atalanta	W	L	5	4	0	1	3	2	1	3
Sampdoria	W	W	5	4	0	1	3	2	0	4
Udinese	W	L	6	4	2	0	4	2	5	1
Genoa	D	W	6	4	2	0	1	5	3	3
Cagliari	W	W	6	6	0	0	4	2	3	3
Chievo	W	W	6	6	0	0	4	2	2	4
Sassuolo	W	L	1	1	0	0	1	0	1	0
Palermo			5	4	0	1	3	2	1	3
Empoli			-	-	-	-	-	-	-	-
Cesena			2	2	0	0	0	2	0	2

Season	Division	Pos	P	W	D	L	F	A	GD	Pts
2013-14	Serie A	8	38	16	9	13	57	49	+8	57
2012-13	Serie A	3	38	21	9	8	67	39	+28	72
2011-12	Serie A	2	38	24	8	6	74	33	+41	80

Over/Under 53%/47% 5th **Both score** 55%/45% 3rd

NAPOLI

San Paolo — www.ssnapoli.it

	2013-14 H	A	Last six seasons at home P	W	D	L	OV	UN	BS	CS
Juventus	W	L	6	4	2	0	4	2	4	2
Roma	W	L	6	3	1	2	4	2	3	2
Napoli										
Fiorentina	L	W	6	2	2	2	3	3	3	2
Inter	W	D	6	4	2	0	2	4	3	3
Parma	L	L	5	2	0	3	3	2	3	1
Torino	W	W	3	1	1	1	1	2	2	1
Milan	W	W	6	2	3	1	5	1	5	1
Lazio	W	W	6	3	2	1	3	3	2	3
Verona	W	W	1	1	0	0	1	0	1	0
Atalanta	W	L	5	3	1	1	2	3	2	3
Sampdoria	W	W	5	4	1	0	1	4	0	5
Udinese	D	D	6	2	3	1	4	2	4	2
Genoa	D	W	6	3	2	1	1	5	2	3
Cagliari	W	D	6	4	2	0	5	1	4	2
Chievo	D	W	6	4	1	1	2	4	2	4
Sassuolo	D	W	1	0	1	0	0	1	1	0
Palermo			5	4	1	0	2	3	1	4
Empoli			-	-	-	-	-	-	-	-
Cesena			2	1	1	0	0	2	0	2

Season	Division	Pos	P	W	D	L	F	A	GD	Pts
2013-14	Serie A	3	38	23	9	6	77	39	+38	78
2012-13	Serie A	2	38	23	9	6	73	36	+37	78
2011-12	Serie A	5	38	16	13	9	66	46	+20	61

Over/Under 50%/50% 6th   **Both score** 50%/50% 8th

PALERMO

Renzo Barbera — www.palermocalcio.it

	2013-14 H	A	Last six seasons at home P	W	D	L	OV	UN	BS	CS
Juventus			5	2	0	3	1	4	1	1
Roma			5	3	1	1	3	2	3	1
Napoli			5	3	0	2	5	0	4	0
Fiorentina			5	2	0	3	4	1	2	2
Inter			5	2	1	2	2	3	3	1
Parma			4	2	0	2	4	0	4	0
Torino			2	1	1	0	0	2	0	2
Milan			5	3	1	1	4	1	3	1
Lazio			5	3	1	1	3	2	3	1
Verona			-	-	-	-	-	-	-	-
Atalanta			4	3	0	1	3	1	3	1
Sampdoria			4	2	2	0	2	2	2	2
Udinese			5	2	1	2	3	2	3	1
Genoa			5	3	2	0	3	2	3	3
Cagliari			5	3	2	0	3	2	4	1
Chievo			5	3	1	1	5	0	4	1
Sassuolo			-	-	-	-	-	-	-	-
Palermo										
Empoli	L	D	1	0	0	1	1	0	1	0
Cesena	W	D	3	1	1	1	2	1	2	0

Season	Division	Pos	P	W	D	L	F	A	GD	Pts
2013-14	Serie B	1	42	25	11	6	62	28	+34	86
2012-13	Serie A	18	38	6	14	18	34	54	-20	32
2011-12	Serie A	16	38	11	10	17	52	62	-10	43

Over/Under 43%/57% 13th   **Both score** 50%/50% 13th

PARMA

Ennio Tardini — www.fcparma.com

	2013-14 H	A	Last six seasons at home P	W	D	L	OV	UN	BS	CS
Juventus	L	L	5	1	2	2	1	4	2	2
Roma	L	L	5	1	1	3	3	2	3	1
Napoli	W	W	5	1	1	3	3	2	4	1
Fiorentina	D	D	5	0	5	0	2	3	5	0
Inter	L	D	5	3	1	1	1	4	2	2
Parma										
Torino	W	D	2	2	0	0	2	0	2	0
Milan	W	W	5	2	1	2	1	4	2	1
Lazio	D	L	5	1	3	1	1	4	3	1
Verona	W	L	1	1	0	0	0	1	0	1
Atalanta	W	W	4	3	0	1	2	2	2	2
Sampdoria	W	D	4	4	0	0	1	3	1	3
Udinese	W	L	5	3	1	1	2	3	1	3
Genoa	D	L	5	1	3	1	2	3	4	1
Cagliari	D	L	5	2	1	2	3	2	2	2
Chievo	D	W	5	3	2	0	1	4	1	4
Sassuolo	W	W	2	1	1	0	1	1	2	0
Palermo			4	3	1	0	2	2	2	2
Empoli			1	1	0	0	0	1	0	1
Cesena			2	1	1	0	1	1	1	1

Season	Division	Pos	P	W	D	L	F	A	GD	Pts
2013-14	Serie A	6	38	15	13	10	58	46	+12	58
2012-13	Serie A	10	38	13	10	15	45	46	-1	49
2011-12	Serie A	8	38	15	11	12	54	53	+1	56

Over/Under 45%/55% 15th   **Both score** 55%/45% 3rd

ROMA

Olimpico — www.asroma.it

	2013-14 H	A	Last six seasons at home P	W	D	L	OV	UN	BS	CS
Juventus	L	L	6	1	1	4	2	4	3	1
Roma										
Napoli	W	L	6	3	2	1	3	3	4	1
Fiorentina	W	W	6	5	0	1	5	1	5	1
Inter	D	W	6	3	2	1	3	3	2	3
Parma	W	W	5	4	1	0	2	3	2	3
Torino	W	D	3	3	0	0	2	1	2	1
Milan	W	D	6	2	3	1	3	3	3	3
Lazio	W	D	6	4	1	1	1	5	2	4
Verona	W	W	1	1	0	0	1	0	0	1
Atalanta	W	W	5	5	0	0	3	2	3	2
Sampdoria	W	W	5	3	1	1	3	2	3	2
Udinese	W	L	6	4	1	1	4	2	5	1
Genoa	W	L	6	6	0	0	5	1	2	4
Cagliari	D	W	6	3	1	2	5	1	4	2
Chievo	W	W	6	4	1	1	0	6	0	5
Sassuolo	D	W	1	0	1	0	0	1	1	0
Palermo			5	4	0	1	4	1	4	1
Empoli			-	-	-	-	-	-	-	-
Cesena			2	1	1	0	1	1	1	1

Season	Division	Pos	P	W	D	L	F	A	GD	Pts
2013-14	Serie A	2	38	26	7	5	72	25	+47	85
2012-13	Serie A	6	38	18	8	12	71	56	+15	62
2011-12	Serie A	7	38	16	8	14	60	54	+6	56

Over/Under 47%/53% 11th   **Both score** 34%/66% 20th

SAMPDORIA

Luigi Ferraris — www.sampdoria.it

	2013-14 H	A	Last six seasons at home P	W	D	L	OV	UN	BS	CS
Juventus	L	L	5	2	2	1	1	4	1	3
Roma	L	L	5	2	2	1	3	2	3	1
Napoli	L	L	5	1	1	3	3	2	3	1
Fiorentina	D	L	5	2	1	2	2	3	1	2
Inter	L	D	5	1	1	3	1	4	1	1
Parma	D	L	4	1	2	1	0	4	2	1
Torino	D	W	4	1	2	1	0	4	2	1
Milan	L	L	5	2	2	1	2	3	3	1
Lazio	D	L	5	3	1	1	2	3	3	1
Verona	W	L	2	2	0	0	1	1	0	2
Atalanta	W	L	4	3	0	1	1	3	1	3
Sampdoria										
Udinese	W	D	5	2	2	1	3	2	2	2
Genoa	L	W	5	2	0	3	2	3	1	1
Cagliari	W	D	5	1	2	2	1	4	2	1
Chievo	W	W	5	3	2	0	2	3	3	2
Sassuolo	L	W	2	0	1	1	1	1	2	0
Palermo			4	0	1	3	2	2	3	0
Empoli			1	1	0	0	0	1	0	1
Cesena			1	1	0	0	1	1	0	1

Season	Division	Pos	P	W	D	L	F	A	GD	Pts
2013-14	Serie A	12	38	12	9	17	48	62	-14	45
2012-13	Serie A	14	38	11	10	17	43	51	-8	42
2011-12	Serie B	6	42	17	16	9	53	34	+19	67

Over/Under 50%/50% 6th **Both score** 45%/55% 14th

SASSUOLO

Stadio Citta del Tricolore — www.sassuolocalcio.it

	2013-14 H	A	Last six seasons at home P	W	D	L	OV	UN	BS	CS
Juventus	L	L	1	0	0	1	1	0	1	0
Roma	L	D	1	0	0	1	0	1	0	0
Napoli	L	D	1	0	0	1	0	1	0	0
Fiorentina	L	W	1	0	0	1	0	1	0	0
Inter	L	L	1	0	0	1	1	0	0	0
Parma	L	L	2	0	1	1	1	1	1	0
Torino	L	L	4	0	1	3	2	2	2	1
Milan	W	L	1	1	0	0	1	0	1	0
Lazio	D	L	1	0	1	0	1	0	1	0
Verona	L	L	3	1	1	1	1	2	2	1
Atalanta	W	W	2	1	0	1	1	1	2	1
Sampdoria	L	W	2	0	1	1	1	1	1	1
Udinese	L	L	1	0	0	1	0	1	0	0
Genoa	W	L	1	1	0	0	1	0	1	0
Cagliari	D	D	1	0	1	0	0	1	0	0
Chievo	L	W	1	0	0	1	0	1	0	0
Sassuolo										
Palermo			-	-	-	-	-	-	-	-
Empoli			5	3	1	1	2	3	2	2
Cesena			2	1	1	0	1	1	1	1

Season	Division	Pos	P	W	D	L	F	A	GD	Pts
2013-14	Serie A	17	38	9	7	22	43	72	-29	34
2012-13	Serie B	1	42	25	10	7	78	40	+38	85
2011-12	Serie B	3	42	22	14	6	57	33	+24	80

Over/Under 50%/50% 6th **Both score** 53%/47% 6th

TORINO

Olimpico di Torino — www.torino.it

	2013-14 H	A	Last six seasons at home P	W	D	L	OV	UN	BS	CS
Juventus	L	L	3	0	0	3	0	3	0	0
Roma	D	L	3	0	1	2	1	2	1	1
Napoli	L	L	3	1	0	2	1	2	1	1
Fiorentina	D	D	3	0	2	1	2	1	2	1
Inter	D	L	3	0	1	2	2	1	2	0
Parma	D	L	2	0	1	1	1	1	2	0
Torino										
Milan	D	D	3	0	2	1	3	0	3	0
Lazio	W	D	3	2	0	1	1	2	1	0
Verona	D	W	2	0	1	1	2	0	2	0
Atalanta	W	L	4	3	0	1	3	1	3	1
Sampdoria	L	D	4	1	1	2	2	2	2	1
Udinese	W	W	3	2	1	0	0	3	0	3
Genoa	W	D	3	1	1	1	2	1	2	1
Cagliari	W	L	3	1	0	2	1	2	1	0
Chievo	W	W	3	2	1	0	1	2	2	1
Sassuolo	W	W	4	2	0	2	2	2	1	2
Palermo			2	1	1	0	0	2	0	2
Empoli			3	3	0	0	3	0	2	1
Cesena			1	0	1	0	0	1	1	1

Season	Division	Pos	P	W	D	L	F	A	GD	Pts
2013-14	Serie A	7	38	15	12	11	58	48	+10	57
2012-13	Serie A	16	38	8	16	14	46	55	-9	39
2011-12	Serie B	2	38	22	14	11	57	28	+29	83

Over/Under 50%/50% 6th **Both score** 61%/39% 1st

UDINESE

Friuli — www.udinese.it

	2013-14 H	A	Last six seasons at home P	W	D	L	OV	UN	BS	CS
Juventus	L	L	6	2	1	3	4	2	2	2
Roma	L	L	6	3	1	2	3	3	4	1
Napoli	D	D	6	2	4	0	3	4	4	2
Fiorentina	W	L	6	5	0	1	3	3	3	2
Inter	L	D	6	2	0	4	5	1	3	1
Parma	W	L	5	2	2	1	4	1	4	0
Torino	L	L	3	2	0	1	0	3	0	2
Milan	W	L	6	4	1	1	3	3	3	3
Lazio	L	L	6	3	2	1	3	3	4	2
Verona	L	D	1	0	0	1	1	0	1	0
Atalanta	D	L	5	2	2	1	3	2	3	2
Sampdoria	D	L	5	2	2	1	3	2	4	1
Udinese										
Genoa	W	D	6	3	2	1	1	5	1	4
Cagliari	W	L	6	4	2	0	3	3	4	2
Chievo	W	L	6	4	1	1	3	3	2	3
Sassuolo	W	W	1	1	0	0	1	0	1	0
Palermo			5	4	1	0	3	2	4	1
Empoli			-	-	-	-	-	-	-	-
Cesena			2	2	0	0	1	1	1	1

Season	Division	Pos	P	W	D	L	F	A	GD	Pts
2013-14	Serie A	13	38	12	8	18	46	57	-11	44
2012-13	Serie A	5	38	18	12	8	59	45	+14	66
2011-12	Serie A	3	38	18	10	10	52	35	+17	64

Over/Under 47%/53% 11th **Both score** 45%/55% 14th

League table 2013-14

Pos	H	A		P	Home					Away					GD	Pts
					W	D	L	F	A	W	D	L	F	A		
1	1	1	Juventus	38	19	0	0	47	9	14	3	2	33	14	+57	102 (C)
2	2	2	Roma	38	15	3	1	44	9	11	4	4	28	16	+47	85
3	3	3	Napoli	38	13	4	2	43	15	10	5	4	34	24	+38	78
4	11	4	Fiorentina	38	9	4	6	36	29	10	4	5	29	15	+21	65
5	9	5	Inter	38	8	9	2	27	18	7	6	6	35	21	+23	60
6	7	6	Parma	38	9	7	3	27	18	6	6	7	31	28	+12	58
7	8	7	Torino	38	9	6	4	31	20	6	6	7	27	28	+10	57
8	4	9	Milan	38	11	4	4	28	17	5	5	9	29	32	+8	57
9	5	10	Lazio	38	10	6	3	32	21	5	5	9	22	33	0	56
10	10	8	Verona	38	10	3	6	35	28	6	3	10	27	40	-6	54
11	6	15	Atalanta	38	11	3	5	28	22	4	2	13	15	29	-8	50
12	16	11	Sampdoria	38	7	5	7	28	29	5	4	10	20	33	-14	45
13	12	16	Udinese	38	9	4	6	27	24	3	4	12	19	33	-11	44
14	13	14	Genoa	38	8	5	6	22	19	3	6	10	19	31	-9	44
15	14	18	Cagliari	38	8	4	7	24	27	1	8	10	10	26	-19	39
16	17	13	Chievo	38	6	2	11	19	22	4	4	11	15	32	-20	36
17	20	12	Sassuolo	38	5	2	12	23	39	4	5	10	20	33	-29	34
18	15	20	Catania	38	7	6	6	25	25	1	2	16	9	41	-32	32 (R)
19	19	17	Bologna	38	3	8	8	15	27	2	6	11	13	31	-30	29 (R)
20	18	19	Livorno	38	4	5	10	23	33	2	2	15	16	44	-38	25 (R)

Results 2013-14

	Atalanta	Bologna	Cagliari	Catania	Chievo	Fiorentina	Genoa	Verona	Inter	Juventus	Lazio	Livorno	Milan	Napoli	Parma	Roma	Sampdoria	Sassuolo	Torino	Udinese
Atalanta		2-1	1-0	2-1	2-1	0-2	1-1	1-2	1-1	1-4	2-1	2-0	2-1	3-0	0-4	1-1	3-0	0-2	2-0	2-0
Bologna	0-2		1-0	1-2	0-0	0-3	1-0	1-4	1-1	0-2	0-0	1-0	3-3	2-2	1-1	0-1	2-2	0-0	1-2	0-2
Cagliari	2-1	0-3		2-1	0-1	1-0	2-1	1-0	1-1	1-4	0-2	1-2	1-2	1-1	1-0	1-3	2-2	2-2	2-1	3-0
Catania	2-1	2-0	1-1		2-0	0-3	1-1	0-0	0-3	0-1	3-1	3-3	1-3	2-4	0-0	4-1	2-1	0-0	1-2	1-0
Chievo	0-1	3-0	0-0	2-0		1-2	2-1	0-1	2-1	1-2	0-2	3-0	0-0	2-4	1-2	0-2	0-1	0-1	0-1	2-1
Fiorentina	2-0	3-0	1-1	2-1	3-1		3-3	4-3	1-2	4-2	0-1	1-0	0-2	1-2	2-2	0-1	2-1	3-4	2-2	2-1
Genoa	1-1	0-0	1-2	2-0	2-1	2-5		2-0	1-0	0-1	2-0	0-0	1-2	0-2	1-0	1-0	0-1	2-0	1-1	3-3
Verona	2-1	0-0	2-1	4-0	0-1	3-5	3-0		0-2	2-2	4-1	2-1	2-1	0-3	3-2	1-3	2-0	2-0	1-3	2-2
Inter	1-2	2-2	1-1	0-0	1-1	2-1	2-0	4-2		1-1	4-1	2-0	1-0	0-0	3-3	0-3	1-1	1-0	1-0	0-0
Juventus	1-0	1-0	3-0	4-0	3-1	1-0	2-0	2-1	3-1		4-1	2-0	3-2	3-0	2-1	3-0	4-2	4-0	1-0	1-0
Lazio	0-1	1-0	2-0	3-1	3-0	0-0	0-2	3-3	1-0	1-1		2-0	1-1	2-4	3-2	0-0	2-0	3-2	3-3	2-1
Livorno	1-0	2-1	1-1	2-0	2-4	0-1	0-1	2-3	2-2	0-2	0-2		2-2	1-1	0-3	0-2	1-2	3-1	3-3	1-2
Milan	3-0	1-0	3-1	1-0	3-0	0-2	1-1	1-0	0-2	1-1	3-0		1-2	2-4	2-2	1-0	2-1	1-1	1-1	1-0
Napoli	2-0	3-0	3-0	2-1	1-1	0-1	1-1	5-1	4-2	2-0	4-2	4-0	3-1		0-1	1-0	2-0	1-1	2-0	3-3
Parma	4-3	1-1	0-0	0-0	0-0	2-2	1-1	2-0	0-2	0-1	1-1	2-0	3-2	1-0		1-3	2-0	3-1	3-1	1-0
Roma	3-1	5-0	0-0	4-0	1-0	2-1	4-0	3-0	0-0	0-1	2-0	3-0	2-0	2-0	4-2		3-0	1-1	2-1	3-2
Sampdoria	1-0	1-1	1-0	2-0	2-1	0-0	0-3	5-0	0-4	0-1	1-1	4-2	0-2	2-5	1-1	0-2		3-4	2-2	3-0
Sassuolo	2-0	2-1	1-1	3-1	0-1	0-1	4-2	1-2	0-7	1-3	2-2	1-4	4-3	0-2	0-1	0-2	1-2		0-2	1-2
Torino	1-0	1-2	2-1	4-1	4-1	0-0	2-1	2-2	3-3	0-1	1-0	3-1	2-2	0-1	1-1	1-1	0-2	2-0		2-0
Udinese	1-1	1-1	2-0	1-0	3-0	1-0	1-0	1-3	0-3	0-2	2-3	5-3	1-0	1-1	3-1	0-1	3-3	1-0	0-2	

Over 2.5 goals top five

	H	A	%
Verona	14	13	71%
Catania	10	11	55%
Fiorentina	13	8	55%
Livorno	10	11	55%
Milan	8	12	53%

Under 2.5 goals top five

	H	A	%
Genoa	14	11	66%
Lazio	11	11	58%
Atalanta	9	12	55%
Bologna	12	9	55%
Inter	12	9	55%
Parma	13	8	55%

Both to score top five

	H	A	%
Torino	11	12	61%
Verona	11	11	58%
Parma	9	12	55%
Cagliari	12	9	55%
Milan	8	13	55%

Both not to score top five

	H	A	%
Roma	13	12	66%
Juventus	12	11	61%
Bologna	11	11	58%
Chievo	12	10	58%
Genoa, Udinese, Sampdoria			55%

AUGSBURG

SGL arena   www.fcaugsburg.de

	2013-14 H	A	P	W	D	L	OV	UN	BS	CS
B Munich										
B Munich	W	L	3	1	0	2	1	2	1	1
B Dortmund	L	D	3	0	1	2	2	1	1	1
Schalke	L	L	3	0	2	1	1	2	2	1
B Leverkusen	L	L	3	0	0	3	3	0	3	0
Wolfsburg	L	D	3	1	1	1	1	2	1	2
M'gladbach	D	W	3	1	2	0	1	2	2	1
Mainz	W	L	4	2	1	1	2	2	3	0
Augsburg										
Hoffenheim	W	L	3	2	0	1	1	2	1	1
Hannover	D	L	3	0	2	1	0	3	1	1
Hertha Berlin	D	D	3	1	2	0	1	2	1	2
W Bremen	W	L	3	2	1	0	2	1	3	0
E Frankfurt	W	D	2	2	0	0	1	1	1	1
Freiburg	W	W	4	1	2	1	3	1	4	0
Stuttgart	W	W	3	2	0	1	3	0	2	1
Hamburg	W	W	3	2	0	1	1	2	1	1
Cologne			1	1	0	0	1	0	1	0
Paderborn			2	2	0	0	1	1	0	2

Season	Division	Pos	P	W	D	L	F	A	GD	Pts
2013-14	Bundesliga	8	34	15	7	12	47	47	0	52
2012-13	Bundesliga	15	34	8	9	17	33	51	-18	33
2011-12	Bundesliga	14	34	8	14	12	36	49	-13	38

Over/Under 62%/38% 5th   **Both score** 62%/38% 5th

BAYERN MUNICH

Allianz Arena   www.fcbayern.de

	2013-14 H	A	P	W	D	L	OV	UN	BS	CS
B Munich										
B Dortmund	L	W	6	2	1	3	4	2	4	0
Schalke	W	W	6	4	1	1	3	3	3	2
B Leverkusen	W	D	6	4	1	1	5	1	4	2
Wolfsburg	W	W	6	6	0	0	4	2	2	4
M'gladbach	W	W	6	4	1	1	3	3	4	1
Mainz	W	W	5	3	1	1	4	1	3	2
Augsburg	W	L	3	3	0	0	3	0	1	2
Hoffenheim	D	W	6	5	1	0	4	2	3	3
Hannover	W	W	6	6	0	0	5	1	2	4
Hertha Berlin	W	W	4	4	0	0	4	0	3	1
W Bremen	W	W	6	3	2	1	4	2	5	1
E Frankfurt	W	W	5	5	0	0	4	1	2	3
Freiburg	W	D	5	5	0	0	4	1	2	3
Stuttgart	W	W	6	5	0	1	4	2	4	2
Hamburg	W	W	6	5	1	0	5	1	3	3
Cologne			4	1	2	1	2	2	1	3
Paderborn			-	-	-	-	-	-	-	-

Season	Division	Pos	P	W	D	L	F	A	GD	Pts
2013-14	Bundesliga	1	34	29	3	2	94	23	+71	90
2012-13	Bundesliga	1	34	29	4	1	98	18	+80	91
2011-12	Bundesliga	2	34	23	4	7	77	22	+55	73

Over/Under 62%/38% 5th   **Both score** 44%/56% 17th

COLOGNE

RheinEnergieStadion   www.fc-koeln.de

	2013-14 H	A	P	W	D	L	OV	UN	BS	CS
B Munich			4	1	1	2	3	1	3	0
B Dortmund			4	0	0	4	3	1	3	0
Schalke			4	2	0	2	3	1	3	1
B Leverkusen			4	1	0	3	0	4	0	1
Wolfsburg			4	0	2	2	2	2	3	0
M'gladbach			4	0	1	3	3	1	2	0
Mainz			3	2	1	0	1	2	2	1
Augsburg			1	1	0	0	1	0	0	1
Hoffenheim			4	1	1	2	2	2	2	1
Hannover			4	3	0	1	2	2	1	2
Hertha Berlin			4	1	0	3	3	1	2	1
W Bremen			4	2	2	0	1	3	1	3
E Frankfurt			3	1	2	0	0	3	1	2
Freiburg			3	2	1	0	2	1	1	2
Stuttgart			4	0	1	3	3	1	3	0
Hamburg			4	1	1	2	3	1	3	0
Cologne										
Paderborn	L	D	2	1	0	1	1	1	0	1

Season	Division	Pos	P	W	D	L	F	A	GD	Pts
2013-14	2.Bundesliga	1	34	19	11	4	53	20	+33	68
2012-13	2.Bundesliga	5	34	14	12	8	43	33	+10	54
2011-12	Bundesliga	17	34	8	6	20	39	75	-36	30

Over/Under 35%/65% 18th   **Both score** 38%/62% 17th

Dortmund had to play second fiddle to Bayern again

DORTMUND

Westfalenstadion   www.bvb.de

	2013-14 H	A	Last six seasons at home P	W	D	L	OV	UN	BS	CS
B Munich	L	W	6	2	2	2	2	4	3	2
B Dortmund										
Schalke	D	W	6	1	3	2	2	4	2	3
B Leverkusen	L	D	6	3	1	2	2	4	1	3
Wolfsburg	W	W	6	3	2	1	3	3	4	2
M'gladbach	L	L	6	5	0	1	5	1	3	3
Mainz	W	W	5	3	2	0	2	3	3	2
Augsburg	D	W	3	2	1	0	3	0	2	1
Hoffenheim	W	D	6	2	3	1	3	3	5	1
Hannover	W	W	6	5	1	0	4	2	5	1
Hertha Berlin	L	W	4	1	1	2	2	2	3	1
W Bremen	W	W	6	6	0	0	2	4	2	4
E Frankfurt	W	W	5	4	0	1	5	0	2	3
Freiburg	W	W	5	5	0	0	4	1	1	4
Stuttgart	W	W	6	2	4	0	3	3	4	2
Hamburg	W	L	6	5	0	1	3	3	3	3
Cologne			4	4	0	0	2	2	1	3
Paderborn			-	-	-	-	-	-	-	-

Season	Division	Pos	P	W	D	L	F	A	GD	Pts
2013-14	Bundesliga	2	34	22	5	7	80	38	+42	71
2012-13	Bundesliga	2	34	19	9	6	81	42	+39	66
2011-12	Bundesliga	1	34	25	6	3	80	25	+55	81

Over/Under 79%/21% 2nd   **Both score** 56%/44% 8th

EINTRACHT FRANKFURT

Commerzbank-Arena   www.eintracht.de

	2013-14 H	A	Last six seasons at home P	W	D	L	OV	UN	BS	CS
B Munich	L	L	5	1	1	3	2	3	3	0
B Dortmund	L	L	5	1	2	2	2	3	3	1
Schalke	D	L	5	1	2	2	3	2	3	2
B Leverkusen	L	W	5	2	0	3	3	2	2	0
Wolfsburg	L	L	5	1	2	2	4	1	4	0
M'gladbach	W	L	5	2	0	3	2	3	2	1
Mainz	W	L	4	3	0	1	2	2	2	2
Augsburg	L	L	2	1	1	0	1	1	2	0
Hoffenheim	L	D	5	1	1	3	4	1	4	0
Hannover	L	L	5	3	0	2	5	0	3	1
Hertha Berlin	W	L	3	1	1	1	1	2	1	1
W Bremen	D	W	5	2	2	1	2	3	2	2
E Frankfurt										
Freiburg	L	D	4	2	0	2	3	1	3	0
Stuttgart	W	D	5	1	1	3	4	1	3	0
Hamburg	D	D	5	1	2	2	4	1	5	0
Cologne			3	0	1	2	2	1	2	0
Paderborn			1	0	1	0	0	1	0	1

Season	Division	Pos	P	W	D	L	F	A	GD	Pts
2013-14	Bundesliga	13	34	9	9	16	40	57	-17	36
2012-13	Bundesliga	6	34	14	9	11	49	46	+3	51
2011-12	2.Bundesliga	2	34	20	8	6	76	33	+43	68

Over/Under 50%/50% 16th   **Both score** 53%/47% 14th

FREIBURG

Dreisamstadion   www.scfreiburg.com

	2013-14 H	A	Last six seasons at home P	W	D	L	OV	UN	BS	CS
B Munich	D	L	5	0	2	3	2	3	3	1
B Dortmund	L	L	5	1	0	4	3	2	3	0
Schalke	L	L	5	1	1	3	3	2	3	1
B Leverkusen	W	L	5	1	1	3	2	3	1	1
Wolfsburg	L	D	5	3	0	2	4	1	2	2
M'gladbach	W	L	5	5	0	0	3	2	1	4
Mainz	L	L	6	2	1	3	2	4	3	2
Augsburg	L	L	4	3	0	1	1	3	1	3
Hoffenheim	D	D	5	2	2	1	2	3	3	1
Hannover	W	L	5	2	1	2	4	1	5	0
Hertha Berlin	D	D	3	0	2	1	2	1	2	0
W Bremen	W	D	5	1	1	3	5	0	4	0
E Frankfurt	D	W	4	0	3	1	0	4	1	2
Freiburg										
Stuttgart	L	L	5	2	0	3	4	1	3	1
Hamburg	L	D	5	1	2	2	3	2	2	2
Cologne			3	2	1	0	2	1	2	1
Paderborn			-	-	-	-	-	-	-	-

Season	Division	Pos	P	W	D	L	F	A	GD	Pts
2013-14	Bundesliga	14	34	9	9	16	43	61	-18	36
2012-13	Bundesliga	5	34	14	9	11	45	40	+5	51
2011-12	Bundesliga	12	34	10	10	14	45	61	-16	40

Over/Under 56%/44% 13th   **Both score** 56%/44% 8th

HAMBURG

Volksparkstadion — www.hsv.de

	2013-14 H	A	Last six seasons at home P	W	D	L	OV	UN	BS	CS
B Munich	L	L	6	2	2	2	2	4	2	3
B Dortmund	W	L	6	4	1	1	5	1	5	1
Schalke	L	D	6	2	2	2	5	1	5	0
B Leverkusen	W	L	6	2	2	2	3	3	4	1
Wolfsburg	L	D	6	0	3	3	3	3	6	0
M'gladbach	L	L	6	2	1	3	1	5	2	2
Mainz	L	L	5	1	1	3	2	3	2	2
Augsburg	L	L	3	0	1	2	0	3	1	0
Hoffenheim	L	L	6	4	1	1	2	4	2	4
Hannover	W	L	6	4	2	0	2	4	2	4
Hertha Berlin	L	L	4	1	2	1	2	2	2	1
W Bremen	L	L	6	4	0	2	5	1	4	1
E Frankfurt	D	D	5	2	2	1	0	5	1	3
Freiburg	D	W	5	1	1	3	1	4	2	1
Stuttgart	D	L	6	3	1	2	4	2	3	1
Hamburg										
Cologne			4	2	0	2	3	1	3	0
Paderborn			-	-	-	-	-	-	-	-

Season	Division	Pos	P	W	D	L	F	A	GD	Pts
2013-14	Bundesliga	16	34	7	6	21	51	75	-24	27
2012-13	Bundesliga	7	34	14	6	14	42	53	-11	48
2011-12	Bundesliga	15	34	8	12	14	35	57	-22	36

Over/Under 74%/26% 3rd **Both score** 62%/38% 5th

HANNOVER

Niedersachenstadion — www.hannover96.de

	2013-14 H	A	Last six seasons at home P	W	D	L	OV	UN	BS	CS
B Munich	L	L	6	3	0	3	5	1	3	1
B Dortmund	L	L	6	1	3	2	4	2	4	0
Schalke	L	L	6	3	2	1	4	2	4	1
B Leverkusen	D	L	6	2	4	0	2	4	3	3
Wolfsburg	W	W	6	4	0	2	2	4	1	3
M'gladbach	W	L	6	4	0	2	5	1	5	0
Mainz	W	L	5	2	3	0	2	3	4	1
Augsburg	W	D	3	2	1	0	2	1	2	1
Hoffenheim	L	L	6	3	0	3	3	3	3	2
Hannover										
Hertha Berlin	D	W	4	1	2	1	1	3	2	1
W Bremen	L	L	6	3	1	2	5	1	6	0
E Frankfurt	W	W	5	3	2	0	2	3	3	2
Freiburg	W	L	5	3	1	1	4	1	3	2
Stuttgart	D	L	6	3	3	0	3	3	3	3
Hamburg	L	L	6	4	2	0	5	1	5	1
Cologne			4	3	0	1	4	0	4	0
Paderborn			-	-	-	-	-	-	-	-

Season	Division	Pos	P	W	D	L	F	A	GD	Pts
2013-14	Bundesliga	10	34	12	6	16	46	59	-13	42
2012-13	Bundesliga	9	34	13	6	15	60	62	-2	45
2011-12	Bundesliga	7	34	12	12	10	41	45	-4	48

Over/Under 62%/38% 5th **Both score** 56%/44% 8th

HERTHA BERLIN

Olympiastadion — www.herthabsc.de

	2013-14 H	A	Last six seasons at home P	W	D	L	OV	UN	BS	CS
B Munich	L	L	4	1	0	3	4	0	3	0
B Dortmund	L	W	4	0	1	3	2	2	1	1
Schalke	L	L	4	0	1	3	1	3	1	1
B Leverkusen	L	L	4	1	2	1	2	2	2	1
Wolfsburg	L	L	4	0	2	2	3	1	3	1
M'gladbach	W	L	4	2	1	1	2	2	2	2
Mainz	W	D	3	1	2	0	1	2	1	1
Augsburg	D	D	3	1	2	0	2	1	2	1
Hoffenheim	D	W	4	2	1	1	1	3	2	1
Hannover	L	D	4	2	0	2	2	2	0	2
Hertha Berlin										
W Bremen	W	L	4	3	0	1	3	1	3	1
E Frankfurt	W	L	3	2	0	1	3	0	3	0
Freiburg	D	D	3	0	1	2	2	1	1	1
Stuttgart	L	W	4	2	0	2	1	3	1	1
Hamburg	W	W	4	2	0	2	3	1	3	1
Cologne			4	2	1	1	2	2	2	1
Paderborn			2	1	1	0	1	1	1	1

Season	Division	Pos	P	W	D	L	F	A	GD	Pts
2013-14	Bundesliga	11	34	11	8	15	40	48	-8	41
2012-13	2.Bundesliga	1	34	22	10	2	65	28	+37	76
2011-12	Bundesliga	16	34	7	10	17	38	64	-26	31

Over/Under 47%/53% 17th **Both score** 47%/53% 16th

HOFFENHEIM

Rhein-Neckar Arena — www.achtzehn99.de

	2013-14 H	A	Last six seasons at home P	W	D	L	OV	UN	BS	CS
B Munich	L	D	6	0	3	3	3	3	4	1
B Dortmund	D	L	6	3	1	2	4	2	4	2
Schalke	D	L	6	2	4	0	4	2	4	2
B Leverkusen	L	W	6	0	1	5	5	1	4	0
Wolfsburg	W	L	6	3	0	3	6	0	6	0
M'gladbach	W	D	6	4	2	0	3	3	3	3
Mainz	L	D	5	0	2	3	2	3	3	1
Augsburg	W	L	3	1	2	0	1	2	1	2
Hoffenheim										
Hannover	W	W	6	4	2	0	5	1	4	2
Hertha Berlin	D	W	4	1	1	2	2	2	3	0
W Bremen	D	L	6	1	2	3	4	2	4	1
E Frankfurt	D	W	5	2	2	1	2	3	2	2
Freiburg	D	D	5	1	3	1	2	3	4	0
Stuttgart	W	L	6	1	2	3	3	3	4	1
Hamburg	W	W	4	1	1	5	1	2	4	1
Cologne			4	1	2	1	0	4	2	1
Paderborn			-	-	-	-	-	-	-	-

Season	Division	Pos	P	W	D	L	F	A	GD	Pts
2013-14	Bundesliga	9	34	11	11	12	72	70	+2	44
2012-13	Bundesliga	16	34	8	7	19	42	67	-25	31
2011-12	Bundesliga	11	34	10	11	13	41	47	-6	41

Over/Under 82%/18% 1st **Both score** 79%/21% 1st

LEVERKUSEN

BayArena www.bayer04.de

	2013-14 H	2013-14 A	Last six seasons at home P	W	D	L	OV	UN	BS	CS
B Munich	D	L	6	1	3	2	1	5	4	1
B Dortmund	D	W	6	0	3	3	4	2	5	1
Schalke	L	L	6	3	0	3	2	4	2	2
B Leverkusen										
Wolfsburg	W	L	6	5	1	0	4	2	4	2
M'gladbach	W	W	6	3	1	2	5	1	5	1
Mainz	L	W	5	2	1	2	3	2	3	0
Augsburg	W	W	3	3	0	0	3	0	3	0
Hoffenheim	L	W	6	5	0	1	4	2	3	3
Hannover	W	D	6	6	0	0	3	3	1	5
Hertha Berlin	W	W	4	1	2	1	2	2	3	0
W Bremen	W	L	6	3	3	0	2	4	3	3
E Frankfurt	L	W	5	3	1	1	3	2	3	1
Freiburg	W	L	5	3	1	1	3	2	3	1
Stuttgart	W	W	6	4	1	1	6	0	5	1
Hamburg	W	L	6	3	2	1	5	1	5	1
Cologne			4	2	1	1	2	2	2	2
Paderborn										

Season	Division	Pos	P	W	D	L	F	A	GD	Pts
2013-14	Bundesliga	4	34	19	4	11	60	41	+19	61
2012-13	Bundesliga	3	34	19	8	7	65	39	+26	65
2011-12	Bundesliga	5	34	15	9	10	52	44	+8	54

Over/Under 59%/41% 10th **Both score** 65%/35% 4th

MAINZ

Coface Arena www.mainz05.de

	2013-14 H	2013-14 A	Last six seasons at home P	W	D	L	OV	UN	BS	CS
B Munich	L	L	5	2	0	3	4	1	3	0
B Dortmund	L	L	5	1	0	4	3	2	3	1
Schalke	L	D	5	0	2	3	2	3	2	1
B Leverkusen	L	W	5	2	1	2	2	3	2	2
Wolfsburg	L	L	5	1	2	2	0	5	1	2
M'gladbach	D	L	5	2	1	2	2	3	1	3
Mainz										
Augsburg	W	L	4	2	1	1	1	3	1	2
Hoffenheim	D	W	5	3	1	1	5	0	3	1
Hannover	W	L	5	3	1	1	1	4	2	2
Hertha Berlin	D	L	3	1	1	1	2	1	3	0
W Bremen	W	W	5	1	2	2	3	2	4	1
E Frankfurt	W	L	4	2	2	0	2	2	1	3
Freiburg	W	W	6	3	2	1	3	3	3	3
Stuttgart	W	W	5	4	1	0	3	2	4	1
Hamburg	W	W	5	1	2	2	3	2	3	1
Cologne			3	3	0	0	1	2	0	3
Paderborn										

Season	Division	Pos	P	W	D	L	F	A	GD	Pts
2013-14	Bundesliga	7	34	16	5	13	52	54	-2	53
2012-13	Bundesliga	13	34	10	12	12	42	44	-2	42
2011-12	Bundesliga	13	34	9	12	13	47	51	-4	39

Over/Under 59%/41% 10th **Both score** 56%/44% 8th

MONCHENGLADBACH

Stadion im Borussia-Park www.borussia.de

	2013-14 H	2013-14 A	Last six seasons at home P	W	D	L	OV	UN	BS	CS
B Munich	L	L	6	1	3	2	4	2	5	0
B Dortmund	W	W	6	2	3	1	0	6	3	2
Schalke	W	W	6	5	0	1	3	3	2	3
B Leverkusen	L	L	6	0	3	3	4	2	5	0
Wolfsburg	D	L	6	2	2	2	4	2	4	1
M'gladbach										
Mainz	W	D	5	4	0	1	2	3	2	3
Augsburg	L	D	3	1	1	1	1	2	1	2
Hoffenheim	D	L	6	2	2	2	4	2	5	1
Hannover	W	L	6	5	0	1	5	1	4	2
Hertha Berlin	W	L	4	2	1	1	2	2	1	2
W Bremen	W	W	6	4	1	1	5	1	5	1
E Frankfurt	W	L	5	3	0	2	3	2	2	2
Freiburg	W	L	5	2	3	0	0	5	2	3
Stuttgart	D	W	6	0	3	3	3	3	5	1
Hamburg	W	W	6	3	2	1	4	2	5	1
Cologne			4	2	1	1	3	1	2	2
Paderborn			-	-	-	-	-	-	-	-

Season	Division	Pos	P	W	D	L	F	A	GD	Pts
2013-14	Bundesliga	6	34	16	7	11	59	43	+16	55
2012-13	Bundesliga	8	34	12	11	11	45	49	-4	47
2011-12	Bundesliga	4	34	17	9	8	49	24	+25	60

Over/Under 59%/41% 10th **Both score** 62%/38% 5th

PADERBORN

Benteler-Arena www.scpaderborn07.de

	2013-14 H	2013-14 A	Last six seasons at home P	W	D	L	OV	UN	BS	CS
B Munich			-	-	-	-	-	-	-	-
B Dortmund			-	-	-	-	-	-	-	-
Schalke			-	-	-	-	-	-	-	-
B Leverkusen			-	-	-	-	-	-	-	-
Wolfsburg			-	-	-	-	-	-	-	-
M'gladbach			-	-	-	-	-	-	-	-
Mainz			-	-	-	-	-	-	-	-
Augsburg			2	0	2	0	1	1	2	0
Hoffenheim			-	-	-	-	-	-	-	-
Hannover			-	-	-	-	-	-	-	-
Hertha Berlin			2	1	0	1	0	2	0	1
W Bremen			-	-	-	-	-	-	-	-
E Frankfurt			1	1	0	0	1	0	1	0
Freiburg			-	-	-	-	-	-	-	-
Stuttgart			-	-	-	-	-	-	-	-
Hamburg			-	-	-	-	-	-	-	-
Cologne	D	W	2	0	1	1	1	1	2	0
Paderborn										

Season	Division	Pos	P	W	D	L	F	A	GD	Pts
2013-14	2.Bundesliga	2	34	18	8	8	63	48	+15	62
2012-13	2.Bundesliga	12	34	11	9	14	45	45	0	42
2011-12	2.Bundesliga	5	34	17	10	7	51	42	+9	61

Over/Under 65%/35% 1st **Both score** 59%/41% 4th

SCHALKE 04

Veltins-Arena   www.schalke04.de

	2013-14 H	A	Last six seasons at home P	W	D	L	OV	UN	BS	CS
B Munich	L	L	6	1	0	5	3	3	2	1
B Dortmund	L	D	6	2	1	3	5	1	6	0
Schalke										
B Leverkusen	W	W	6	2	2	2	3	3	3	2
Wolfsburg	W	L	6	4	1	1	5	1	3	3
M'gladbach	L	L	6	3	2	1	3	3	4	1
Mainz	D	W	5	2	2	1	2	3	2	3
Augsburg	W	W	3	3	0	0	3	0	3	0
Hoffenheim	W	D	6	4	0	2	4	2	2	3
Hannover	W	L	6	5	0	1	4	2	2	4
Hertha Berlin	W		4	4	0	0	1	3	0	4
W Bremen	W	D	6	5	0	1	4	2	2	3
E Frankfurt	W	D	5	4	1	0	1	4	2	3
Freiburg	W	W	5	3	0	2	2	3	2	2
Stuttgart	W	L	6	3	1	2	6	0	5	1
Hamburg	D	W	6	2	2	2	5	1	5	0
Cologne			4	4	0	0	2	2	1	3
Paderborn			-	-	-	-	-	-	-	-

Season	Division	Pos	P	W	D	L	F	A	GD	Pts
2013-14	Bundesliga	3	34	19	7	8	63	43	+20	64
2012-13	Bundesliga	4	34	16	7	11	58	50	+8	55
2011-12	Bundesliga	3	34	20	4	10	74	44	+30	64

Over/Under 62%/38% 5th   **Both score** 50%/50% 15th

STUTTGART

Mercedes-Benz Arena   www.vfb.de

	2013-14 H	A	Last six seasons at home P	W	D	L	OV	UN	BS	CS
B Munich	L	L	6	0	2	4	4	2	4	1
B Dortmund	L	L	6	2	1	3	5	1	6	0
Schalke	W	L	6	5	0	1	4	2	3	3
B Leverkusen	L	L	6	1	1	4	3	3	3	0
Wolfsburg	L	L	6	3	1	2	4	2	5	0
M'gladbach	L	D	6	4	0	2	3	3	1	3
Mainz	L	L	5	2	2	1	4	1	4	1
Augsburg	L	L	3	2	0	1	3	0	3	0
Hoffenheim	W	L	6	3	2	1	4	2	4	1
Hannover	W	D	6	5	0	1	4	2	3	3
Hertha Berlin	L	W	4	2	1	1	2	2	2	2
W Bremen	D	D	6	3	1	2	4	2	4	1
E Frankfurt	D	L	5	3	1	1	2	2	4	1
Freiburg	W	W	5	4	0	1	3	2	3	1
Stuttgart										
Hamburg	W	D	6	3	0	3	3	3	2	3
Cologne			4	0	1	3	2	2	2	0
Paderborn			-	-	-	-	-	-	-	-

Season	Division	Pos	P	W	D	L	F	A	GD	Pts
2013-14	Bundesliga	15	34	8	8	18	49	62	-13	32
2012-13	Bundesliga	12	34	12	7	15	37	55	-18	43
2011-12	Bundesliga	6	34	15	8	11	63	46	+17	53

Over/Under 62%/38% 5th   **Both score** 71%/29% 3rd

WERDER BREMEN

Weserstadion   www.werder.de

	2013-14 H	A	Last six seasons at home P	W	D	L	OV	UN	BS	CS
B Munich	L	L	6	0	1	5	4	2	3	1
B Dortmund	L	L	6	1	2	3	3	3	3	1
Schalke	D	L	6	0	3	3	1	5	4	0
B Leverkusen	W	L	6	1	3	2	3	3	4	1
Wolfsburg	L	L	6	2	1	3	5	1	4	0
M'gladbach	D	L	6	2	4	0	3	3	4	2
Mainz	L	L	5	2	0	3	4	1	2	1
Augsburg	W	L	3	1	1	1	0	3	1	1
Hoffenheim	W	D	6	4	2	0	4	2	5	1
Hannover	W	W	6	4	2	0	3	3	3	3
Hertha Berlin	W	L	4	4	0	0	3	1	3	1
W Bremen										
E Frankfurt	L	D	5	1	2	2	3	2	2	2
Freiburg	D	L	5	3	1	1	4	1	3	2
Stuttgart	D	D	6	2	4	0	3	3	4	2
Hamburg	W	W	6	5	1	0	1	5	2	4
Cologne			4	4	0	0	3	1	3	1
Paderborn			-	-	-	-	-	-	-	-

Season	Division	Pos	P	W	D	L	F	A	GD	Pts
2013-14	Bundesliga	12	34	10	9	15	42	66	-24	39
2012-13	Bundesliga	14	34	8	10	16	50	66	-16	34
2011-12	Bundesliga	9	34	11	9	14	49	58	-9	42

Over/Under 56%/44% 13th   **Both score** 56%/44% 8th

WOLFSBURG

Volkswagen Arena   www.vfl-wolfsburg.de

	2013-14 H	A	Last six seasons at home P	W	D	L	OV	UN	BS	CS
B Munich	L	L	6	1	1	4	3	3	4	0
B Dortmund	W	L	6	2	1	3	6	0	4	1
Schalke	W	L	6	4	1	1	6	0	5	1
B Leverkusen	W	L	6	4	0	2	6	0	6	0
Wolfsburg										
M'gladbach	W	D	6	5	1	0	5	1	4	2
Mainz	W	L	5	1	2	2	4	1	3	1
Augsburg	D	W	3	0	2	1	1	2	3	0
Hoffenheim	W	L	6	3	2	1	6	0	4	2
Hannover	L	L	6	4	0	2	5	1	4	1
Hertha Berlin	W	W	4	2	0	2	3	1	3	1
W Bremen	W	W	6	3	2	1	4	2	4	2
E Frankfurt	W	W	5	2	2	1	3	2	4	0
Freiburg	D	W	5	2	2	1	4	1	4	0
Stuttgart	W	W	6	6	0	0	2	4	2	4
Hamburg	D	W	6	2	2	2	3	3	4	1
Cologne			4	3	0	1	3	1	3	1
Paderborn			-	-	-	-	-	-	-	-

Season	Division	Pos	P	W	D	L	F	A	GD	Pts
2013-14	Bundesliga	5	34	18	6	10	63	50	+13	60
2012-13	Bundesliga	11	34	10	13	11	47	52	-5	43
2011-12	Bundesliga	8	34	13	6	15	47	60	-13	44

Over/Under 74%/26% 3rd   **Both score** 74%/26% 2nd

League table 2013-14

Pos	H	A		P	W	D	L	F	A	W	D	L	F	A	GD	Pts
					Home					**Away**						
1	1	1	B Munich	34	15	1	1	48	15	14	2	1	46	8	+71	90 (C)
2	5	2	B Dortmund	34	11	2	4	41	19	11	3	3	39	19	+42	71
3	2	4	Schalke	34	12	2	3	37	16	7	5	5	26	27	+20	64
4	6	3	B Leverkusen	34	10	3	4	35	22	9	1	7	25	19	+19	61
5	4	5	Wolfsburg	34	11	3	3	37	22	7	3	7	26	28	+13	60
6	3	9	M'gladbach	34	11	3	3	38	17	5	4	8	21	26	+16	55
7	7	8	Mainz	34	10	3	4	28	17	6	2	9	24	37	-2	53
8	8	6	Augsburg	34	9	3	5	27	22	6	4	7	20	25	0	52
9	10	10	Hoffenheim	34	7	6	4	43	31	4	5	8	29	39	+2	44
10	9	15	Hannover	34	8	5	4	27	25	4	1	12	19	34	-13	42
11	13	7	Hertha Berlin	34	6	3	8	20	24	5	5	7	20	24	-8	41
12	11	12	W Bremen	34	6	6	5	21	30	4	3	10	21	36	-24	39
13	14	11	E Frankfurt	34	5	5	7	22	24	4	4	9	18	33	-17	36
14	12	13	Freiburg	34	6	4	7	25	30	3	5	9	18	31	-18	36
15	15	14	Stuttgart	34	5	4	8	28	28	3	4	10	21	34	-13	32
16	17	17	Hamburg	34	5	3	9	24	34	2	3	12	27	41	-24	27
17	18	16	Nuremberg	34	3	5	9	16	32	2	6	9	21	38	-33	26 (R)
18	16	18	Braunschweig	34	5	3	9	18	24	1	4	12	11	36	-31	25 (R)

Results 2013-14

	Augsburg	B Munich	Braunschweig	B Dortmund	E Frankfurt	Freiburg	Hamburg	Hannover	Hertha Berlin	Hoffenheim	B Leverkusen	Mainz	M'gladbach	Nuremberg	Schalke	Stuttgart	W Bremen	Wolfsburg
Augsburg		1-0	4-1	0-4	2-1	2-1	3-1	1-1	0-0	2-0	1-3	2-1	2-2	0-1	1-2	2-1	3-1	1-2
B Munich	3-0		2-0	0-3	5-0	4-0	3-1	2-0	3-2	3-3	2-1	4-1	3-1	2-0	5-1	1-0	5-2	1-0
Braunschweig	0-1	0-2		1-2	0-2	0-1	4-2	3-0	0-2	1-0	1-0	3-1	1-1	1-1	2-3	0-4	0-1	1-1
B Dortmund	2-2	0-3	2-1		4-0	5-0	6-2	1-0	1-2	3-2	0-1	4-2	1-2	3-0	0-0	6-1	1-0	2-1
E Frankfurt	1-1	0-1	3-0	1-2		1-4	2-2	2-3	1-0	1-2	0-2	2-0	1-0	1-1	3-3	2-1	0-0	1-2
Freiburg	2-4	1-1	2-0	0-1	1-1		0-3	2-1	1-1	1-1	3-2	1-2	4-2	3-2	0-2	1-3	3-1	0-3
Hamburg	0-1	1-1	4-0	3-0	1-1	1-1		3-1	0-3	1-5	2-1	2-3	0-2	2-1	0-3	3-3	0-1	1-0
Hannover	2-1	0-4	0-0	0-3	2-0	3-2	2-1		1-1	1-4	1-1	4-1	3-1	3-3	2-1	0-0	1-2	2-0
Hertha Berlin	0-0	1-3	2-0	0-4	6-1	0-0	1-0	0-3		1-1	0-1	3-1	1-0	1-3	0-2	0-1	3-2	1-2
Hoffenheim	2-0	1-2	3-1	2-2	0-0	3-3	3-0	3-1	2-3		1-2	2-4	2-1	2-2	3-3	4-1	4-4	6-2
B Leverkusen	2-1	1-1	1-1	2-2	0-1	3-1	5-3	2-0	2-1	2-3		0-1	4-2	3-0	1-2	2-1	2-1	3-1
Mainz	3-0	0-2	2-0	1-3	1-0	2-0	3-2	2-0	1-1	2-2	1-4		0-0	2-0	0-1	3-2	3-0	2-0
M'gladbach	1-2	0-2	4-1	2-0	4-1	1-0	3-1	3-0	3-0	2-2	0-1	3-1		3-1	1-1	4-1	2-2	
Nuremberg	0-1	0-2	2-1	1-1	2-5	0-3	0-5	0-2	2-2	4-0	1-4	1-1	0-2		0-0	2-0	0-2	1-1
Schalke	4-1	0-4	3-1	1-3	2-0	2-0	3-3	2-0	2-0	4-0	2-0	0-0	0-1	4-1		3-0	3-1	2-1
Stuttgart	1-4	1-2	2-2	2-3	1-1	2-0	1-0	4-2	1-2	6-2	0-1	1-2	0-2	1-1	3-1		1-1	1-2
W Bremen	1-0	0-7	0-0	1-5	0-3	0-0	1-0	3-2	2-0	3-1	1-0	2-3	1-1	3-3	1-1	1-1		1-3
Wolfsburg	1-1	1-6	0-2	2-1	2-1	2-2	1-1	1-3	2-0	2-1	3-1	3-0	3-1	4-1	4-0	3-1	3-0	

Over 2.5 goals

	H	A	%
Hoffenheim	15	13	82%
B Dortmund	13	14	79%
Hamburg	12	13	74%
Wolfsburg	13	12	74%
Augsburg, B Munich,			62%
Hannover, Schalke, Stuttgart			

Under 2.5 goals

	H	A	%
Braunschweig	11	8	56%
Hertha Berlin	9	9	53%
E Frankfurt	8	9	50%
Nurnberg	10	6	47%
Freiburg, W Bremen			44%

Both to score

	H	A	%
Hoffenheim	14	13	79%
Wolfsburg	12	13	74%
Stuttgart	13	11	71%
B Leverkusen	13	9	65%
M'gladbach,			62%
Augsburg, Hamburg			

Both not to score

	H	A	%
Braunschweig	10	9	56%
B Munich	9	10	56%
Hertha Berlin	10	8	53%
Schalke	10	7	50%
E Frankfurt	7	9	47%

YOUR BUNDESLIGA BUDDY

SOCCERBASE.COM
BET SMARTER THIS SEASON

ALMERIA

Los Juegos Mediterraneos www.udalmeriasad.com

	2013-14 H	2013-14 A	P	W	D	L	OV	UN	BS	CS
Atl Madrid	W	L	4	2	2	0	1	3	2	2
Barcelona	L	L	4	0	1	3	2	2	1	0
Real Madrid	L	L	4	0	2	2	2	2	3	0
Ath Bilbao	D	L	4	1	1	2	3	1	3	1
Seville	L	L	4	0	0	4	2	2	2	0
Villarreal	L	L	5	2	2	1	3	2	3	2
Sociedad	W	L	2	1	1	0	2	0	2	0
Valencia	D	W	4	0	2	2	4	0	2	0
Celta Vigo	L	L	2	1	0	1	1	1	1	1
Levante	D	L	2	0	1	1	1	1	1	0
Malaga	D	L	4	2	2	0	0	4	1	3
R Vallecano	L	L	1	0	0	1	0	1	0	0
Getafe	W	D	4	3	0	1	2	2	2	2
Espanyol	D	W	4	1	1	2	2	2	1	1
Granada	W	W	1	1	0	0	0	0	0	1
Elche	D	L	3	1	1	1	2	1	2	0
Almeria										
Eibar			-	-	-	-	-	-	-	-
Deportivo			4	1	2	1	0	4	2	1
Cordoba			2	2	0	0	2	0	1	1

Season	Division	Pos	P	W	D	L	F	A	GD	Pts
2013-14	Primera Liga	17	38	11	7	20	43	71	-28	40
2012-13	Liga Segunda	3	42	22	8	12	72	50	+22	74
2011-12	Liga Segunda	7	42	18	16	8	63	43	+20	70

Over/Under 58%/42% 7th **Both score** 47%/53% 10th

ATHLETIC BILBAO

San Mames www.athletic-club.net

	2013-14 H	2013-14 A	P	W	D	L	OV	UN	BS	CS
Atl Madrid	L	L	6	3	0	3	5	1	3	3
Barcelona	W	L	6	1	3	2	3	3	4	1
Real Madrid	D	L	6	1	1	4	4	2	2	1
Ath Bilbao										
Seville	W	D	6	4	0	2	4	2	3	2
Villarreal	W	L	5	2	1	2	2	3	3	1
Sociedad	D	L	4	2	1	1	2	2	3	1
Valencia	D	D	6	2	1	3	4	2	4	1
Celta Vigo	W	D	2	2	0	0	1	1	1	1
Levante	W	L	4	3	0	1	3	1	2	1
Malaga	W	W	6	3	0	3	3	3	3	3
R Vallecano	W	W	3	1	1	1	2	1	3	0
Getafe	W	W	6	2	2	2	3	3	2	3
Espanyol	L	L	6	2	2	2	4	2	4	1
Granada	W	L	3	2	0	1	1	2	0	2
Elche	D	D	1	0	1	0	1	0	1	0
Almeria	W	D	4	3	0	1	3	1	3	1
Eibar			-	-	-	-	-	-	-	-
Deportivo			4	1	1	2	1	3	2	1
Cordoba			-	-	-	-	-	-	-	-

Season	Division	Pos	P	W	D	L	F	A	GD	Pts
2013-14	Primera Liga	4	38	20	10	8	66	39	+27	70
2012-13	Primera Liga	12	38	12	9	17	44	65	-21	45
2011-12	Primera Liga	10	38	12	13	13	49	52	-3	49

Over/Under 53%/47% 9th **Both score** 61%/39% 2nd

ATLETICO MADRID

Vicente Calderon www.clubatleticodemadrid.com

	2013-14 H	2013-14 A	P	W	D	L	OV	UN	BS	CS
Atl Madrid										
Barcelona	D	D	6	2	1	3	5	1	5	1
Real Madrid	D	W	6	0	1	5	6	0	6	0
Ath Bilbao	W	W	6	4	0	2	3	3	2	3
Seville	D	W	6	2	3	1	3	3	3	2
Villarreal	W	D	5	4	0	1	4	1	3	2
Sociedad	W	W	4	2	1	1	2	2	1	2
Valencia	W	W	6	3	2	1	3	3	3	3
Celta Vigo	W	W	2	2	0	0	1	1	1	1
Levante	W	L	4	4	0	0	1	3	3	1
Malaga	D	W	6	3	1	2	4	2	3	1
R Vallecano	W	W	3	3	0	0	3	0	2	1
Getafe	W	W	6	4	1	1	3	3	1	4
Espanyol	W	L	6	5	0	1	4	2	3	3
Granada	W	W	3	3	0	0	1	2	0	3
Elche	W	W	1	1	0	0	0	1	0	1
Almeria	W	L	4	2	2	0	3	1	3	1
Eibar			-	-	-	-	-	-	-	-
Deportivo			4	4	0	0	3	1	1	3
Cordoba			-	-	-	-	-	-	-	-

Season	Division	Pos	P	W	D	L	F	A	GD	Pts
2013-14	Primera Liga	1	38	28	6	4	77	26	+51	90
2012-13	Primera Liga	3	38	23	7	8	65	31	+34	76
2011-12	Primera Liga	5	38	15	11	12	53	46	+7	56

Over/Under 45%/55% 15th **Both score** 37%/63% 16th

BARCELONA

Camp Nou www.fcbarcelona.cat

	2013-14 H	2013-14 A	P	W	D	L	OV	UN	BS	CS
Atl Madrid	D	D	6	5	1	0	5	1	4	2
Barcelona										
Real Madrid	W	W	6	4	1	1	4	2	3	3
Ath Bilbao	W	L	6	6	0	0	4	2	4	2
Seville	W	W	6	5	1	0	5	1	2	4
Villarreal	W	W	5	3	2	0	4	1	4	1
Sociedad	W	L	4	4	0	0	4	0	3	1
Valencia	L	W	6	5	0	1	5	1	3	3
Celta Vigo	W	W	2	2	0	0	2	0	1	1
Levante	W	D	4	4	0	0	1	1	1	3
Malaga	W	W	6	6	0	0	6	0	4	2
R Vallecano	W	W	3	3	0	0	3	0	1	2
Getafe	D	W	6	4	2	0	5	1	5	1
Espanyol	W	W	6	5	0	1	3	3	1	5
Granada	W	L	3	3	0	0	2	1	1	2
Elche	W	D	1	1	0	0	1	0	0	1
Almeria	W	W	4	4	0	0	3	1	2	2
Eibar			-	-	-	-	-	-	-	-
Deportivo			4	3	1	0	2	2	0	4
Cordoba			-	-	-	-	-	-	-	-

Season	Division	Pos	P	W	D	L	F	A	GD	Pts
2013-14	Primera Liga	2	38	27	6	5	100	33	+67	87
2012-13	Primera Liga	1	38	32	4	2	115	40	+75	100
2011-12	Primera Liga	2	38	28	7	3	114	29	+85	91

Over/Under 68%/32% 2nd **Both score** 50%/50% 9th

CELTA VIGO

Balaidos — www.celta vigo.net

	2013-14 H	A	Last six seasons at home P	W	D	L	OV	UN	BS	CS
Atl Madrid	L	L	2	0	0	2	1	1	1	0
Barcelona	L	L	2	0	1	1	2	0	1	0
Real Madrid	W	L	2	1	0	1	1	1	1	1
Ath Bilbao	D	L	2	0	2	0	0	2	1	1
Seville	W	W	2	2	0	0	0	2	0	2
Villarreal	D	W	1	0	1	0	0	1	0	1
Sociedad	D	L	4	0	3	1	1	3	2	1
Valencia	W	L	2	1	0	1	1	1	1	0
Celta Vigo										
Levante	L	W	4	0	3	1	1	3	3	0
Malaga	L	W	2	0	0	2	0	2	0	0
R Vallecano	L	L	5	0	3	2	0	5	0	3
Getafe	D	L	2	1	1	0	1	1	2	0
Espanyol	D	L	2	1	1	0	1	1	1	1
Granada	D	W	3	1	2	0	1	2	3	0
Elche	L	L	5	1	2	2	4	1	4	0
Almeria	W	W	2	2	0	0	2	0	2	0
Eibar			1	0	0	1	1	0	1	0
Deportivo			2	0	1	1	1	1	2	0
Cordoba			4	3	1	0	1	3	1	3

Season	Division	Pos	P	W	D	L	F	A	GD	Pts
2013-14	Primera Liga	9	38	14	7	17	49	54	-5	49
2012-13	Primera Liga	17	38	10	7	21	37	52	-15	37
2011-12	Liga Segunda	2	42	26	7	9	83	37	+46	85

Over/Under 50%/50% 11th **Both score** 42%/58% 14th

CORDOBA

Estadio Nuevo Arcangel — www.cordobacf.com

	2013-14 H	A	Last six seasons at home P	W	D	L	OV	UN	BS	CS
Atl Madrid			-	-	-	-	-	-	-	-
Barcelona			-	-	-	-	-	-	-	-
Real Madrid			-	-	-	-	-	-	-	-
Ath Bilbao			-	-	-	-	-	-	-	-
Seville			-	-	-	-	-	-	-	-
Villarreal			1	0	0	1	0	1	0	0
Sociedad			2	1	1	0	1	1	1	1
Valencia			-	-	-	-	-	-	-	-
Celta Vigo			4	1	2	1	1	3	1	3
Levante			2	2	0	0	2	0	2	0
Malaga			-	-	-	-	-	-	-	-
R Vallecano			3	0	1	2	1	2	1	1
Getafe			-	-	-	-	-	-	-	-
Espanyol			-	-	-	-	-	-	-	-
Granada			1	0	1	0	0	1	1	0
Elche			5	2	2	1	0	5	1	3
Almeria			2	1	1	0	1	1	2	0
Eibar	L	L	2	0	1	1	0	2	1	0
Deportivo	L	W	2	0	0	2	0	2	0	0
Cordoba										

Season	Division	Pos	P	W	D	L	F	A	GD	Pts
2013-14	Liga Segunda	7	42	16	13	13	46	43	+3	61
2012-13	Liga Segunda	14	42	15	9	18	55	55	0	54
2011-12	Liga Segunda	6	42	20	11	11	52	43	+9	71

Over/Under 33%/67% 20th **Both score** 45%/55% 10th

DEPORTIVO LA CORUNA

Estadio Municipal de Riazor — www.canaldeportivo.com

	2013-14 H	A	Last six seasons at home P	W	D	L	OV	UN	BS	CS
Atl Madrid			4	1	1	2	2	2	2	1
Barcelona			4	0	1	3	3	1	3	0
Real Madrid			4	1	1	2	3	1	3	1
Ath Bilbao			4	3	1	0	3	1	4	0
Seville			4	1	1	2	2	2	2	1
Villarreal			3	3	0	0	1	2	0	3
Sociedad			2	1	0	1	1	1	1	0
Valencia			4	0	2	2	1	3	2	1
Celta Vigo			2	2	0	0	1	1	1	1
Levante			2	0	0	2	0	2	0	0
Malaga			4	4	0	0	1	3	0	4
R Vallecano			1	0	1	0	0	1	0	1
Getafe			4	0	3	1	2	2	4	0
Espanyol			4	3	0	1	2	2	1	3
Granada			1	0	0	1	1	0	0	0
Elche			1	1	0	0	1	0	1	0
Almeria			4	2	1	1	1	3	1	2
Eibar	D	L	1	0	1	0	0	1	1	0
Deportivo										
Cordoba	L	W	2	1	0	1	0	2	0	1

Season	Division	Pos	P	W	D	L	F	A	GD	Pts
2013-14	Liga Segunda	2	42	19	12	11	48	36	+12	69
2012-13	Primera Liga	19	38	8	11	19	47	70	-23	35
2011-12	Liga Segunda	1	42	29	4	9	76	45	+31	91

Over/Under 33%/67% 20th **Both score** 38%/62% 18th

EIBAR

Municipal de Ipurua — www.sdeibar.com

	2013-14 H	A	Last six seasons at home P	W	D	L	OV	UN	BS	CS
Atl Madrid			-	-	-	-	-	-	-	-
Barcelona			-	-	-	-	-	-	-	-
Real Madrid			-	-	-	-	-	-	-	-
Ath Bilbao			-	-	-	-	-	-	-	-
Seville			-	-	-	-	-	-	-	-
Villarreal			-	-	-	-	-	-	-	-
Sociedad			1	0	1	0	0	1	1	0
Valencia			-	-	-	-	-	-	-	-
Celta Vigo			1	0	1	0	0	1	0	1
Levante			1	0	1	0	0	1	0	1
Malaga			-	-	-	-	-	-	-	-
R Vallecano			1	0	0	1	0	1	0	0
Getafe			-	-	-	-	-	-	-	-
Espanyol			-	-	-	-	-	-	-	-
Granada			-	-	-	-	-	-	-	-
Elche			1	0	0	1	1	0	1	0
Almeria			-	-	-	-	-	-	-	-
Eibar										
Deportivo	W	D	1	1	0	0	1	0	1	0
Cordoba	W	W	2	2	0	0	0	2	0	2

Season	Division	Pos	P	W	D	L	F	A	GD	Pts
2013-14	Liga Segunda	1	42	19	14	9	49	28	+21	71
2012-13	Segunda B	2	38	21	10	7	59	28	+31	73
2011-12	Segunda B	3	38	17	15	6	46	35	+11	66

Over/Under 29%/71% 22nd **Both score** 33%/67% 21st

ELCHE

Estadio Martinez Valero www.elchecf.es

	2013-14		Last six seasons at home							
---	H	A	P	W	D	L	OV	UN	BS	CS
Atl Madrid	L	L	1	0	0	1	0	1	0	0
Barcelona	D	L	1	0	1	0	0	1	0	1
Real Madrid	L	L	1	0	0	1	1	0	1	0
Ath Bilbao	D	D	1	0	1	0	0	1	0	0
Seville	D	L	1	0	1	0	0	1	1	0
Villarreal	L	D	2	1	0	1	0	2	0	1
Sociedad	D	L	3	1	1	1	2	1	3	0
Valencia	W	L	1	1	0	0	1	0	1	0
Celta Vigo	W	W	5	2	1	2	1	4	2	2
Levante	D	L	3	0	2	1	0	3	1	1
Malaga	L	W	1	0	0	1	0	1	0	0
R Vallecano	W	L	4	2	2	0	1	3	2	2
Getafe	W	D	1	1	0	0	0	1	0	1
Espanyol										
Granada	L	L	2	0	1	1	0	2	0	1
Elche										
Almeria	W	D	3	2	0	1	0	2	1	2
Eibar			1	0	0	1	0	1	0	0
Deportivo			1	1	0	0	1	0	1	0
Cordoba			5	3	1	1	3	2	2	2

Season	Division	Pos	P	W	D	L	F	A	GD	Pts
2013-14	Primera Liga	16	38	9	13	16	30	50	-20	40
2012-13	Liga Segunda	1	42	23	13	6	54	27	+27	82
2011-12	Liga Segunda	11	42	17	6	19	56	58	-2	57

Over/Under 42%/58% 16th **Both score** 45%/55% 12th

ESPANYOL

Cornella-El Prat www.rcdespanyol.com

	2013-14		Last six seasons at home							
---	H	A	P	W	D	L	OV	UN	BS	CS
Atl Madrid	W	L	6	3	1	2	4	2	3	2
Barcelona	L	L	6	0	2	4	2	4	3	1
Real Madrid	L	L	6	0	1	5	2	4	1	0
Ath Bilbao	W	W	6	5	1	0	4	2	4	2
Seville	L	L	6	1	2	3	3	3	4	1
Villarreal	L	L	5	0	3	2	1	4	1	3
Sociedad	L	L	4	1	2	1	4	0	4	0
Valencia	W	D	6	3	2	1	5	1	3	2
Celta Vigo	W	D	2	2	0	0	0	2	0	2
Levante	D	L	4	2	1	1	3	1	3	1
Malaga	D	W	6	3	2	1	4	2	3	4
R Vallecano	D	W	3	2	1	0	3	0	3	0
Getafe	L	D	6	2	1	3	1	5	2	1
Espanyol										
Granada	W	W	3	2	0	1	1	2	0	2
Elche	W	L	1	1	0	0	1	0	1	0
Almeria	L	D	4	2	1	1	2	2	2	2
Eibar	-	-	-	-	-	-	-	-	-	-
Deportivo			4	4	0	0	1	3	1	3
Cordoba	-	-	-	-	-	-	-	-	-	-

Season	Division	Pos	P	W	D	L	F	A	GD	Pts
2013-14	Primera Liga	14	38	11	9	18	41	51	-10	42
2012-13	Primera Liga	13	38	11	11	16	43	52	-9	44
2011-12	Primera Liga	14	38	12	10	16	46	56	-10	46

Over/Under 53%/47% 9th **Both score** 53%/47% 5th

GETAFE

Coliseum Alfonso Perez www.getafecf.com

	2013-14		Last six seasons at home							
---	H	A	P	W	D	L	OV	UN	BS	CS
Atl Madrid	L	L	6	2	2	2	2	4	3	2
Barcelona	L	D	6	1	0	5	3	3	3	1
Real Madrid	L	L	6	2	0	4	5	1	4	0
Ath Bilbao	L	L	6	2	3	1	1	5	2	3
Seville	W	L	6	4	1	1	2	4	3	2
Villarreal	L	W	5	2	1	2	2	3	1	3
Sociedad	D	L	4	2	1	1	3	1	2	1
Valencia	L	W	6	2	0	4	4	2	3	0
Celta Vigo	W	D	2	2	0	0	1	1	1	1
Levante	W	W	4	2	1	1	1	3	2	1
Malaga	W	L	6	3	0	3	3	3	3	2
R Vallecano	L	W	3	0	0	3	1	2	1	0
Getafe										
Espanyol	D	W	6	0	4	2	1	5	4	1
Granada	D	W	3	1	2	0	2	1	2	1
Elche	D	L	1	0	1	0	0	1	1	0
Almeria	D	L	4	1	3	0	3	1	3	1
Eibar	-	-	-	-	-	-	-	-	-	-
Deportivo			4	2	0	2	3	1	3	0
Cordoba	-	-	-	-	-	-	-	-	-	-

Season	Division	Pos	P	W	D	L	F	A	GD	Pts
2013-14	Primera Liga	13	38	11	9	18	35	54	-19	42
2012-13	Primera Liga	10	38	13	8	17	43	57	-14	47
2011-12	Primera Liga	11	38	12	11	15	40	51	-11	47

Over/Under 34%/66% 19th **Both score** 32%/68% 19th

GRANADA

Nuevo Los Carmenes www.granadacf.es

	2013-14		Last six seasons at home							
---	H	A	P	W	D	L	OV	UN	BS	CS
Atl Madrid	L	L	3	0	1	2	1	2	1	1
Barcelona	W	L	3	1	0	2	1	2	1	1
Real Madrid	L	L	3	0	2	1	2	1	2	1
Ath Bilbao	W	L	3	1	1	1	2	1	2	1
Seville	W	L	3	0	1	2	2	1	2	0
Villarreal	W	L	2	2	0	0	0	2	0	2
Sociedad	L	D	3	1	1	1	2	1	2	1
Valencia	L	L	3	0	0	3	1	2	1	0
Celta Vigo	L	L	3	1	1	1	2	1	3	0
Levante	L	W	3	1	1	1	1	2	2	0
Malaga	W	L	3	3	0	0	2	1	2	1
R Vallecano	L	W	4	1	1	2	2	2	2	1
Getafe	L	L	3	2	0	1	0	3	0	2
Espanyol	L	L	3	1	1	1	1	2	1	1
Granada										
Elche	W	W	2	1	1	0	1	1	1	1
Almeria	L	L	1	0	0	1	0	1	0	0
Eibar	-	-	-	-	-	-	-	-	-	-
Deportivo			1	0	1	0	0	1	1	0
Cordoba			1	0	1	0	0	1	1	0

Season	Division	Pos	P	W	D	L	F	A	GD	Pts
2013-14	Primera Liga	15	38	12	5	21	32	56	-24	41
2012-13	Primera Liga	15	38	11	9	18	37	54	-17	42
2011-12	Primera Liga	17	38	12	6	20	35	56	-21	42

Over/Under 42%/58% 16th **Both score** 29%/71% 20th

LEVANTE

Ciutat de Valencia www.levanteud.com

	2013-14 H	A	P	W	D	L	OV	UN	BS	CS
Atl Madrid	W	L	4	3	1	0	0	4	1	3
Barcelona	D	L	4	0	2	2	2	2	3	0
Real Madrid	L	L	4	1	1	2	2	2	2	2
Ath Bilbao	L	L	4	2	0	2	4	0	3	1
Seville	D	W	4	2	1	1	1	3	1	3
Villarreal	L	L	3	1	0	2	2	1	1	1
Sociedad	D	D	6	4	1	1	3	3	3	2
Valencia	W	L	4	2	0	2	0	4	0	2
Celta Vigo	L	W	4	1	0	3	1	3	1	1
Levante										
Malaga	W	L	4	3	0	1	3	1	2	2
R Vallecano	D	W	5	2	1	2	3	2	3	2
Getafe	D	L	4	1	2	1	1	3	1	3
Espanyol	W	D	4	4	0	0	3	1	2	2
Granada	L	W	3	2	0	1	2	1	2	0
Elche	W	D	3	3	0	0	2	1	2	1
Almeria	W	D	2	2	0	0	2	0	2	2
Eibar			1	1	0	0	0	1	0	1
Deportivo			2	0	0	2	2	0	1	0
Cordoba			2	1	1	0	1	1	0	2

Season	Division	Pos	P	W	D	L	F	A	GD	Pts
2013-14	Primera Liga	10	38	12	12	14	35	43	-8	48
2012-13	Primera Liga	11	38	12	10	16	40	57	-17	46
2011-12	Primera Liga	6	38	16	7	15	54	50	+4	55

Over/Under 34%/66% 19th **Both score** 34%/66% 17th

MALAGA

La Rosaleda www.malagacf.es

	2013-14 H	A	P	W	D	L	OV	UN	BS	CS
Atl Madrid	L	D	6	1	3	2	2	4	1	3
Barcelona	L	L	6	0	0	6	4	2	4	0
Real Madrid	L	L	6	1	1	4	3	3	3	0
Ath Bilbao	L	L	6	2	3	1	1	5	3	3
Seville	W	D	6	2	2	2	5	1	5	1
Villarreal	W	D	5	3	1	1	3	2	3	2
Sociedad	W	D	4	0	1	3	2	2	3	2
Valencia	D	L	6	2	1	3	2	4	1	3
Celta Vigo	L	W	2	0	1	1	1	1	1	0
Levante	W	L	4	4	0	0	1	3	1	3
Malaga										
R Vallecano	W	L	3	2	0	1	3	0	2	1
Getafe	W	D	6	5	1	0	4	2	4	2
Espanyol	W	D	6	4	0	2	4	2	3	2
Granada	W	L	3	3	0	0	3	0	1	2
Elche	L	W	1	0	0	1	0	1	0	0
Almeria	W	D	4	3	0	1	3	1	3	1
Eibar			-	-	-	-	-	-	-	-
Deportivo			4	1	3	0	1	3	2	2
Cordoba			-	-	-	-	-	-	-	-

Season	Division	Pos	P	W	D	L	F	A	GD	Pts
2013-14	Primera Liga	11	38	12	9	17	39	46	-7	45
2012-13	Primera Liga	6	38	16	9	13	53	50	+3	57
2011-12	Primera Liga	4	38	17	7	14	54	53	+1	58

Over/Under 37%/63% 18th **Both score** 34%/66% 17th

REAL MADRID

Santiago Bernabeu www.realmadrid.com

	2013-14 H	A	P	W	D	L	OV	UN	BS	CS
Atl Madrid	L	D	6	4	1	1	2	4	3	2
Barcelona	L	L	6	1	1	4	4	2	5	0
Real Madrid										
Ath Bilbao	W	D	6	6	0	0	6	0	6	0
Seville	W	L	6	5	0	1	5	1	4	2
Villarreal	W	D	5	5	0	0	4	1	3	2
Sociedad	W	W	4	4	0	0	4	0	4	0
Valencia	D	W	6	3	3	0	1	5	2	4
Celta Vigo	W	L	2	2	0	0	1	1	2	2
Levante	W	W	4	4	0	0	3	1	2	2
Malaga	W	W	6	5	1	0	3	3	3	3
R Vallecano	W	W	3	3	0	0	2	1	1	2
Getafe	W	W	6	6	0	0	5	1	3	3
Espanyol	W	W	6	4	2	0	6	0	3	3
Granada	W	W	3	3	0	0	2	1	1	2
Elche	W	W	1	1	0	0	1	0	0	1
Almeria	W	W	4	4	0	0	4	0	2	2
Eibar			-	-	-	-	-	-	-	-
Deportivo			4	4	0	0	3	1	3	1
Cordoba			-	-	-	-	-	-	-	-

Season	Division	Pos	P	W	D	L	F	A	GD	Pts
2013-14	Primera Liga	3	38	27	6	5	104	38	+66	87
2012-13	Primera Liga	2	38	26	7	5	103	42	+61	85
2011-12	Primera Liga	1	38	32	4	2	121	32	+89	100

Over/Under 76%/24% 1st **Both score** 53%/47% 5th

SEVILLE

Ramon Sanchez Pizjuan www.Sevillefc.es

	2013-14 H	A	P	W	D	L	OV	UN	BS	CS
Atl Madrid	L	D	6	3	1	2	3	3	4	1
Barcelona	L	L	6	0	1	5	4	2	5	0
Real Madrid	W	L	6	3	0	3	5	1	5	1
Ath Bilbao	D	L	6	3	2	1	4	2	4	2
Seville										
Villarreal	D	W	5	3	1	1	3	2	3	2
Sociedad	W	D	4	3	0	1	2	2	2	2
Valencia	W	D	6	4	2	0	2	4	2	4
Celta Vigo	L	L	2	1	0	1	1	1	1	0
Levante	L	D	4	1	2	1	2	2	3	1
Malaga	D	L	6	1	3	2	3	3	3	1
R Vallecano	W	W	3	3	0	0	3	0	3	0
Getafe	W	L	6	3	0	3	5	1	3	2
Espanyol	W	L	6	3	2	1	3	3	2	4
Granada	W	W	3	2	0	1	3	0	1	2
Elche	W	D	1	1	0	0	1	0	1	0
Almeria	W	W	4	3	0	1	3	1	3	1
Eibar			-	-	-	-	-	-	-	-
Deportivo			4	2	2	0	1	3	2	2
Cordoba			-	-	-	-	-	-	-	-

Season	Division	Pos	P	W	D	L	F	A	GD	Pts
2013-14	Primera Liga	5	38	18	9	11	69	52	+17	63
2012-13	Primera Liga	9	38	14	8	16	58	54	+4	50
2011-12	Primera Liga	9	38	13	11	14	48	47	+1	50

Over/Under 66%/34% 4th **Both score** 68%/32% 1st

Anoeta — www.realsociedad.com

	2013-14 H	A	P	W	D	L	OV	UN	BS	CS
Atl Madrid	L	L	4	0	0	4	3	1	2	0
Barcelona	W	L	4	3	1	0	4	0	4	0
Real Madrid	L	L	4	0	1	3	3	1	2	0
Ath Bilbao	W	D	4	3	0	1	1	3	1	3
Seville	D	L	4	2	1	1	2	2	3	1
Villarreal	L	L	3	1	1	1	1	2	2	1
Sociedad										
Valencia	W	W	4	3	0	1	2	2	2	2
Celta Vigo	W	D	4	3	1	0	3	1	3	1
Levante	D	D	6	1	4	1	2	4	5	1
Malaga	D	W	4	2	1	1	2	2	2	1
R Vallecano	L	L	5	3	1	1	3	2	2	3
Getafe	W	D	4	1	3	0	0	4	2	2
Espanyol	W	W	4	2	1	1	1	3	1	2
Granada	D	W	3	1	2	0	1	2	2	1
Elche	W	D	3	1	1	1	1	2	0	2
Almeria	W	L	2	2	0	0	1	1	0	2
Eibar			1	0	1	0	0	1	0	1
Deportivo			2	1	1	0	1	1	1	1
Cordoba			2	1	0	1	0	2	0	1

Season	Division	Pos	P	W	D	L	F	A	GD	Pts
2013-14	Primera Liga	7	38	16	11	11	62	55	+7	59
2012-13	Primera Liga	4	38	18	12	8	70	49	+21	66
2011-12	Primera Liga	12	38	12	11	15	46	52	-6	47

Over/Under 58%/42% 7th **Both score** 58%/42% 4th

Mestalla — www.valenciafc.com

	2013-14 H	A	P	W	D	L	OV	UN	BS	CS
Atl Madrid	L	L	6	3	2	1	2	4	3	2
Barcelona	L	W	6	0	4	2	3	3	4	1
Real Madrid	L	L	6	1	0	5	6	0	4	1
Ath Bilbao	D	D	6	4	2	0	2	4	4	2
Seville	W	D	6	4	0	2	3	3	3	2
Villarreal	W	L	5	4	1	0	4	1	3	2
Sociedad	L	L	4	1	0	3	3	1	2	0
Valencia										
Celta Vigo	W	L	2	2	0	0	2	0	2	0
Levante	W	L	4	1	3	0	1	3	2	2
Malaga	W	D	6	5	1	0	2	4	3	3
R Vallecano	W	L	3	2	0	1	1	2	1	1
Getafe	L	W	6	5	0	1	5	1	5	1
Espanyol	D	W	6	5	1	0	5	1	5	1
Granada	W	W	3	3	0	0	1	2	1	2
Elche	W	L	1	1	0	0	1	0	1	0
Almeria	L	D	4	3	0	1	3	1	3	1
Eibar			-	-	-	-	-	-	-	-
Deportivo			4	3	1	0	2	2	2	2
Cordoba			-	-	-	-	-	-	-	-

Season	Division	Pos	P	W	D	L	F	A	GD	Pts
2013-14	Primera Liga	8	38	13	10	15	51	53	-2	49
2012-13	Primera Liga	5	38	19	8	11	67	54	+13	65
2011-12	Primera Liga	3	38	17	10	11	59	44	+15	61

Over/Under 61%/39% 5th **Both score** 61%/39% 2nd

Campo de Vallecas — www.rayovallecano.es

	2013-14 H	A	P	W	D	L	OV	UN	BS	CS
Atl Madrid	L	L	3	1	0	2	2	1	2	0
Barcelona	L	L	3	0	0	3	3	0	0	0
Real Madrid	L	L	3	0	0	3	1	2	1	0
Ath Bilbao	L	L	3	0	1	2	3	0	2	0
Seville	L	L	3	1	1	1	1	2	1	1
Villarreal	L	L	2	0	0	2	1	1	1	0
Sociedad	W	W	5	3	1	1	3	2	2	2
Valencia	W	L	3	1	0	2	2	1	1	1
Celta Vigo	W	W	5	3	0	2	5	0	4	1
Levante	L	D	5	1	2	2	3	2	2	3
Malaga	W	L	3	2	0	1	2	1	2	1
R Vallecano										
Getafe	L	W	3	2	0	1	2	1	2	1
Espanyol	L	D	3	1	0	2	1	2	1	1
Granada	L	W	4	2	1	1	0	4	1	2
Elche	W	L	4	1	0	3	3	1	2	1
Almeria	W	W	1	1	0	0	1	0	1	0
Eibar			1	1	0	0	1	0	1	0
Deportivo			1	1	0	0	1	0	1	0
Cordoba			3	3	0	0	3	0	2	1

Season	Division	Pos	P	W	D	L	F	A	GD	Pts
2013-14	Primera Liga	12	38	13	4	21	46	80	-34	43
2012-13	Primera Liga	8	38	16	5	17	50	66	-16	53
2011-12	Primera Liga	15	38	13	4	21	53	73	-20	43

Over/Under 68%/32% 2nd **Both score** 42%/58% 14th

El Madrigal — www.villarrealcf.es

	2013-14 H	A	P	W	D	L	OV	UN	BS	CS
Atl Madrid	D	L	5	2	2	1	2	3	3	1
Barcelona	L	L	5	0	1	4	3	2	3	1
Real Madrid	D	L	5	1	2	2	3	2	4	0
Ath Bilbao	D	L	5	3	2	0	3	2	4	1
Seville	L	D	5	2	1	2	3	2	2	2
Villarreal										
Sociedad	W	W	3	2	1	0	2	1	3	0
Valencia	W	W	5	3	2	0	3	2	4	1
Celta Vigo	L	D	1	0	0	1	0	1	0	0
Levante	W	W	3	1	0	2	1	2	0	1
Malaga	D	L	5	2	2	1	2	3	4	0
R Vallecano	W	W	2	2	0	0	1	1	0	2
Getafe	L	W	5	2	1	2	4	1	4	0
Espanyol	W	W	5	3	2	0	2	3	1	4
Granada	W	L	2	2	0	0	2	0	1	1
Elche	D	W	2	0	1	1	1	1	2	0
Almeria	W	W	5	4	1	0	1	4	2	3
Eibar			-	-	-	-	-	-	-	-
Deportivo			3	3	0	0	0	3	0	3
Cordoba			1	1	0	0	0	1	0	1

Season	Division	Pos	P	W	D	L	F	A	GD	Pts
2013-14	Primera Liga	6	38	17	8	13	60	44	+16	59
2012-13	Liga Segunda	2	42	21	14	7	68	38	+30	77
2011-12	Primera Liga	18	38	9	14	15	39	53	-14	41

Over/Under 50%/50% 11th **Both score** 53%/47% 5th

League table 2013-14

Pos	H	A		P	Home W	D	L	F	A	Away W	D	L	F	A	GD	Pts
1	3	1	Atl Madrid	38	15	4	0	49	10	13	2	4	28	16	+51	90 (C)
2	1	3	Barcelona	38	16	2	1	64	15	11	4	4	36	18	+67	87
3	2	2	Real Madrid	38	16	1	2	63	17	11	5	3	41	21	+66	87
4	4	4	Ath Bilbao	38	13	4	2	42	18	7	6	6	24	21	+27	70
5	5	6	Seville	38	11	4	4	40	21	7	5	7	29	31	+17	63
6	7	5	Villarreal	38	9	6	4	36	21	8	2	9	24	23	+16	59
7	6	8	Sociedad	38	11	4	4	38	19	5	7	7	24	36	+7	59
8	8	15	Valencia	38	10	3	6	35	24	3	7	9	16	29	-2	49
9	14	7	Celta Vigo	38	6	7	6	23	23	8	0	11	26	31	-5	49
10	10	9	Levante	38	7	6	6	19	16	5	6	8	16	27	-8	48
11	11	10	Malaga	38	8	2	9	24	21	4	7	8	15	25	-7	45
12	17	12	R Vallecano	38	8	0	11	28	36	5	4	10	18	44	-34	43
13	15	13	Getafe	38	6	6	7	20	24	5	3	11	15	30	-19	42
14	12	14	Espanyol	38	7	5	7	23	22	4	4	11	18	29	-10	42
15	19	11	Granada	38	7	1	11	18	22	5	4	10	14	34	-24	41
16	13	18	Elche	38	6	8	5	13	12	3	5	11	17	38	-20	40
17	16	16	Almeria	38	6	6	7	26	31	5	1	13	17	40	-28	40
18	18	17	Osasuna	38	6	5	8	20	25	4	4	11	12	37	-30	39 (R)
19	9	19	Valladolid	38	6	9	4	20	17	1	6	12	18	43	-22	36 (R)
20	20	20	Betis	38	5	3	11	19	31	1	4	14	17	47	-42	25 (R)

Results 2013-14

	Almeria	Ath Bilbao	Atl Madrid	Barcelona	Betis	Celta Vigo	Elche	Espanyol	Getafe	Granada	Levante	Malaga	Osasuna	Real Madrid	Seville	Sociedad	Valencia	Valladolid	R Vallecano	Villarreal
Almeria		0-0	2-0	0-2	3-2	2-4	2-2	0-0	1-0	3-0	2-2	0-0	1-2	0-5	1-3	4-3	2-2	1-0	0-1	2-3
Ath Bilbao	6-1		1-2	1-0	2-1	3-2	2-2	1-2	1-0	4-0	2-1	3-0	2-0	1-1	3-1	1-1	1-1	4-2	2-1	2-0
Atl Madrid	4-2	2-0		0-0	5-0	2-1	2-0	1-0	7-0	1-0	3-2	1-1	2-1	2-2	1-1	4-0	3-0	3-0	5-0	1-0
Barcelona	4-1	2-1	1-1		3-1	3-0	4-0	1-0	2-2	4-0	7-0	3-0	7-0	2-1	3-2	4-1	2-3	4-1	6-0	2-1
Betis	0-1	0-2	0-2	1-4		1-2	1-2	2-0	2-0	0-0	0-0	1-2	1-2	0-5	0-2	0-1	3-1	4-3	2-2	1-0
Celta Vigo	3-1	0-0	0-2	0-3	4-2		0-1	2-2	1-1	1-1	0-1	0-2	1-1	2-0	1-0	2-2	2-1	4-1	0-2	0-0
Elche	1-0	0-0	0-2	0-0	0-0	1-0		2-1	1-0	0-1	1-1	0-1	0-0	1-2	1-1	1-1	2-1	0-0	2-0	0-1
Espanyol	1-2	3-2	1-0	0-1	0-0	1-0	3-1		0-2	1-0	0-0	1-1	0-1	1-3	1-2	3-1	4-2	2-2	1-2
Getafe	2-2	0-1	0-2	2-5	3-1	2-0	1-1	0-0		3-3	1-0	1-0	0-3	1-0	2-2	0-1	0-0	0-1	0-1
Granada	0-2	2-0	1-2	1-0	1-0	1-2	1-0	0-1	0-2		0-2	3-1	0-0	0-1	1-2	1-3	0-1	4-0	0-3	2-0
Levante	1-0	1-2	2-0	1-1	1-3	0-1	2-1	3-0	0-0	0-1		1-0	2-0	2-3	0-0	0-0	2-0	1-1	0-0	0-3
Malaga	2-0	1-2	0-1	0-1	3-2	0-5	0-1	1-2	1-0	4-1	1-0		0-1	0-1	3-2	0-1	0-0	1-1	5-0	2-0
Osasuna	0-1	1-5	3-0	0-0	2-1	0-2	2-1	1-0	2-0	1-2	0-1	0-2		2-2	1-2	1-1	1-1	0-0	3-1	0-3
Real Madrid	4-0	3-1	0-1	3-4	2-1	3-0	3-0	3-1	4-1	2-0	3-0	2-0	4-0		7-3	5-1	2-2	4-0	5-0	4-2
Seville	2-1	1-1	1-3	1-4	4-0	0-1	3-0	4-0	2-3	2-2	2-1	2-1		1-0	0-0	4-1	4-1	0-0
Sociedad	3-0	2-0	1-2	3-1	5-1	4-3	4-0	2-1	2-0	1-1	0-0	0-0	5-0	0-4	1-1		1-0	1-0	2-3	1-2
Valencia	1-2	1-1	0-1	2-3	5-0	2-1	2-1	2-2	1-3	2-1	2-0	1-0	3-0	2-3	3-1	1-2		2-2	1-0	2-1
Valladolid	1-0	1-2	0-2	1-0	0-0	3-0	2-2	1-0	1-0	0-1	1-1	2-2	0-1	1-1	2-2	2-2	0-0		1-1	1-0
R Vallecano	3-1	0-3	2-4	0-4	3-1	3-0	3-0	1-4	1-2	0-2	1-2	4-1	1-0	2-3	0-1	1-0	1-0	0-3		2-5
Villarreal	2-0	1-1	1-1	2-3	1-1	0-2	1-1	2-1	0-2	3-0	1-0	1-1	3-1	2-2	1-2	5-1	4-1	2-1	4-0	

Over 2.5 goals top five	H	A	%
Real Madrid	16	13	76%
Barcelona	17	9	68%
Vallecano	14	12	68%
Seville	14	11	66%
Valencia, Betis			61%

Under 2.5 goals top five	H	A	%
Levante	13	12	66%
Getafe	12	13	66%
Malaga	12	13	63%
Elche	16	6	58%
Granada	12	10	58%

Both to score top five	H	A	%
Seville	12	14	68%
Ath Bilbao	13	10	61%
Valencia	13	10	61%
Sociedad	9	13	58%
Villarreal	13	7	53%

Both not to score top five	H	A	%
Granada	14	13	71%
Getafe	12	14	68%
Levante	13	12	66%
Malaga	13	12	66%
Atl Madrid	12	12	63%

BASTIA

Stade Armand Cesari — www.sc-bastia.net

	2013-14 H	A	Last six seasons at home P	W	D	L	OV	UN	BS	CS
Paris St-G	L	L	2	0	0	2	2	0	0	0
Monaco	L	L	2	0	1	1	0	2	1	0
Lille	D	L	2	0	1	1	1	1	2	0
St-Etienne	L	D	2	0	0	2	1	1	0	0
Lyon	L	L	2	1	0	1	2	0	2	0
Marseille	D	L	2	0	1	1	1	1	1	1
Bordeaux	W	L	2	2	0	0	1	1	1	1
Lorient	W	D	2	2	0	0	2	0	2	0
Toulouse	W	W	2	1	1	0	1	1	1	1
Bastia										
Reims	W	L	4	3	1	0	2	2	2	2
Rennes	W	L	2	1	0	1	0	2	0	1
Nantes	D	L	3	1	2	0	1	2	2	1
Evian	W	L	2	1	1	0	0	2	0	2
Montpellier	D	W	3	2	1	0	1	2	1	2
Guingamp	W	D	4	3	1	0	3	1	3	1
Nice	W	L	2	1	0	1	0	2	0	1
Metz			3	2	0	1	2	1	1	2
Lens			2	0	1	1	1	1	1	0
Caen			1	0	0	1	1	0	1	0

Season	Division	Pos	P	W	D	L	F	A	GD	Pts
2013-14	Ligue 1	10	38	13	10	15	42	56	-14	49
2012-13	Ligue 1	12	38	13	8	17	50	66	-16	47
2011-12	Ligue 2	1	38	21	8	9	61	36	+25	71

Over/Under 47%/53% 6th **Both score** 47%/53% 13th

BORDEAUX

Stade Chaban-Delmas — www.girondins.com

	2013-14 H	A	Last six seasons at home P	W	D	L	OV	UN	BS	CS
Paris St-G	L	L	6	3	1	2	1	5	1	3
Monaco	L	D	4	2	0	2	0	4	0	2
Lille	W	L	6	2	4	0	2	4	5	1
St-Etienne	W	L	6	3	2	1	2	4	3	3
Lyon	L	D	6	3	1	2	3	3	2	3
Marseille	D	D	6	2	4	0	1	5	5	1
Bordeaux										
Lorient	W	D	6	5	1	0	2	4	3	3
Toulouse	L	D	6	4	0	2	2	4	2	3
Bastia	W	L	2	2	0	0	2	0	2	0
Reims	D	L	2	0	2	0	0	2	0	2
Rennes	D	D	6	3	3	0	1	5	2	4
Nantes	L	D	2	1	0	1	1	1	0	1
Evian	W	D	3	2	1	0	2	1	2	1
Montpellier	W	D	5	3	2	0	2	3	3	2
Guingamp	W	W	1	1	0	0	1	0	1	0
Nice	D	W	6	3	2	1	3	3	4	2
Metz			-	-	-	-	-	-	-	-
Lens			2	1	1	0	2	0	2	0
Caen			3	2	0	1	2	1	2	1

Season	Division	Pos	P	W	D	L	F	A	GD	Pts
2013-14	Ligue 1	7	38	13	14	11	49	43	+6	53
2012-13	Ligue 1	7	38	13	16	9	40	34	+6	55
2011-12	Ligue 1	5	38	16	13	9	53	41	+12	61

Over/Under 37%/63% 16th **Both score** 55%/45% 6th

CAEN

Stade Michel D'Ornano — www.smcaen.fr

	2013-14 H	A	Last six seasons at home P	W	D	L	OV	UN	BS	CS
Paris St-G			3	0	1	2	2	1	2	0
Monaco			3	1	2	0	2	1	1	2
Lille			3	0	0	3	2	1	2	0
St-Etienne			3	2	0	1	1	2	1	2
Lyon			3	2	0	1	2	1	1	1
Marseille			3	0	1	2	2	1	2	0
Bordeaux			3	1	1	1	0	3	0	2
Lorient			3	1	1	1	0	3	1	1
Toulouse			3	0	2	1	0	3	1	1
Bastia			1	1	0	0	0	1	0	1
Reims			-	-	-	-	-	-	-	-
Rennes			3	1	1	1	0	3	1	1
Nantes			3	2	0	1	1	2	0	2
Evian			1	0	1	0	1	0	1	0
Montpellier			2	1	0	1	1	1	1	1
Guingamp			2	1	0	1	1	1	1	1
Nice			3	0	3	0	0	3	2	1
Metz	L	L	2	0	0	2	0	2	0	0
Lens	W	L	3	1	2	0	0	3	1	2
Caen										

Season	Division	Pos	P	W	D	L	F	A	GD	Pts
2013-14	Ligue 2	3	38	18	10	10	65	44	+21	64
2012-13	Ligue 2	4	38	17	12	9	48	28	+20	63
2011-12	Ligue 1	18	38	9	11	18	39	59	-20	38

Over/Under 61%/39% 3rd **Both score** 71%/29% 1st

EVIAN

Parc des Sports — www.etgfc.com

	2013-14 H	A	Last six seasons at home P	W	D	L	OV	UN	BS	CS
Paris St-G	W	L	3	1	1	1	1	2	1	1
Monaco	W	D	1	1	0	0	0	1	0	1
Lille	D	L	3	0	1	2	2	1	1	0
St-Etienne	L	L	3	0	1	2	3	0	3	0
Lyon	W	L	3	1	1	1	2	1	3	0
Marseille	L	L	3	1	1	1	1	2	2	1
Bordeaux	D	L	3	0	2	1	1	2	2	1
Lorient	L	D	3	1	1	1	2	1	2	0
Toulouse	W	L	3	2	0	1	3	0	2	0
Bastia	W	L	2	2	0	0	2	0	1	1
Reims	D	L	3	0	2	1	2	1	3	0
Rennes	L	D	3	1	0	2	3	0	3	0
Nantes	W	L	2	2	0	0	1	1	0	2
Evian										
Montpellier	D	D	3	1	1	1	2	1	2	0
Guingamp	L	W	1	0	0	1	1	0	1	0
Nice	W	L	3	3	0	0	1	2	0	3
Metz			1	1	0	0	1	0	1	0
Lens			-	-	-	-	-	-	-	-
Caen			1	0	0	1	1	0	1	0

Season	Division	Pos	P	W	D	L	F	A	GD	Pts
2013-14	Ligue 1	14	38	11	11	16	39	51	-12	44
2012-13	Ligue 1	16	38	10	10	18	46	53	-7	40
2011-12	Ligue 1	9	38	13	11	14	54	55	-1	50

Over/Under 45%/55% 10th **Both score** 53%/47% 10th

GUINGAMP

Stade du Roudourou   www.eaguingamp.com

	2013-14 H	A	Last six seasons at home P	W	D	L	OV	UN	BS	CS
Paris St-G	D	L	1	0	1	0	0	1	1	0
Monaco	L	D	3	1	0	2	2	1	1	1
Lille	D	L	1	0	1	0	0	1	0	1
St-Etienne	D	L	1	0	1	0	0	1	0	1
Lyon	L	L	1	0	0	1	0	1	0	0
Marseille	L	L	1	0	0	1	1	0	1	0
Bordeaux	L	L	1	0	0	1	0	1	0	0
Lorient	W	L	1	1	0	0	0	1	0	1
Toulouse	W	D	1	1	0	0	0	1	0	1
Bastia	D	L	4	1	3	0	1	3	4	0
Reims	L	D	3	0	0	3	2	1	2	0
Rennes	W	W	1	1	0	0	0	1	0	1
Nantes	W	L	4	4	0	0	1	3	1	3
Evian	L	W	1	0	0	1	0	1	0	0
Montpellier	L	D	2	0	0	2	1	1	1	0
Guingamp										
Nice	W	L	1	1	0	0	0	1	0	1
Metz			3	1	0	2	1	2	1	0
Lens			3	2	1	0	2	1	0	3
Caen			2	1	1	0	0	2	0	2

Season	Division	Pos	P	W	D	L	F	A	GD	Pts
2013-14	Ligue 1	16	38	11	9	18	34	42	-8	42
2012-13	Ligue 2	2	38	20	10	8	63	38	+25	70
2011-12	Ligue 2	7	38	15	10	13	46	43	+3	55

Over/Under 24%/76% 20th **Both score** 39%/61% 17th

LENS

Stade Felix Bollaert-Delelis   www.rclens.fr

	2013-14 H	A	Last six seasons at home P	W	D	L	OV	UN	BS	CS
Paris St-G			2	0	1	1	0	2	1	0
Monaco			4	1	2	1	4	0	2	1
Lille			2	0	1	1	1	1	2	0
St-Etienne			2	2	0	0	1	1	1	1
Lyon			2	0	0	2	1	1	1	0
Marseille			2	1	1	0	2	0	1	1
Bordeaux			2	2	0	0	1	1	1	1
Lorient			2	0	1	1	1	1	2	0
Toulouse			2	0	0	2	0	2	0	0
Bastia			2	1	0	1	1	1	1	1
Reims			2	1	0	1	0	2	0	1
Rennes			2	0	2	0	1	1	1	1
Nantes			2	1	0	1	1	1	1	1
Evian			-	-	-	-	-	-	-	-
Montpellier			3	1	0	2	0	3	0	1
Guingamp			3	1	1	1	0	3	1	1
Nice			2	2	0	0	0	2	0	2
Metz	W	W	3	1	0	2	1	2	1	0
Lens										
Caen	W	L	3	2	1	0	0	2	1	2

Season	Division	Pos	P	W	D	L	F	A	GD	Pts
2013-14	Ligue 2	2	38	17	14	7	58	40	+18	65
2012-13	Ligue 2	12	38	9	18	11	39	53	-14	45
2011-12	Ligue 2	12	38	12	12	14	42	48	-6	48

Over/Under 39%/61% 15th **Both score** 55%/45% 8th

LILLE

Stade Pierre Mauroy   www.losc.fr

	2013-14 H	A	Last six seasons at home P	W	D	L	OV	UN	BS	CS
Paris St-G	L	D	6	2	2	2	4	2	4	2
Monaco	W	D	4	4	0	0	3	1	2	2
Lille										
St-Etienne	W	L	6	4	2	0	3	3	2	4
Lyon	W	D	6	3	3	0	4	2	4	2
Marseille	W	D	6	3	1	2	4	2	4	2
Bordeaux	W	L	6	4	1	1	4	2	5	1
Lorient	W	W	6	3	2	1	3	3	4	2
Toulouse	W	D	6	4	2	0	1	5	3	3
Bastia	W	D	2	1	1	0	1	1	1	1
Reims	L	L	2	1	0	1	2	0	1	1
Rennes	D	L	6	4	2	0	1	5	2	4
Nantes	D	W	2	1	1	0	0	2	0	2
Evian	W	D	3	1	1	1	2	1	2	1
Montpellier	W	W	5	4	0	1	3	2	3	1
Guingamp	W	D	1	1	0	0	0	1	0	1
Nice	L	L	6	0	4	2	1	5	4	0
Metz			-	-	-	-	-	-	-	-
Lens			2	2	0	0	0	2	0	2
Caen			3	2	1	0	3	0	2	1

Season	Division	Pos	P	W	D	L	F	A	GD	Pts
2013-14	Ligue 1	3	38	20	11	7	46	26	+20	71
2012-13	Ligue 1	6	38	16	14	8	59	40	+19	62
2011-12	Ligue 1	3	38	21	11	6	72	39	+33	74

Over/Under 32%/68% 18th **Both score** 34%/66% 19th

LORIENT

Stade du Moustoir   www.fclweb.fr

	2013-14 H	A	Last six seasons at home P	W	D	L	OV	UN	BS	CS
Paris St-G	L	L	6	0	2	4	2	4	4	0
Monaco	D	L	4	1	3	0	2	4	4	0
Lille	L	L	6	3	1	2	3	3	4	1
St-Etienne	W	L	6	5	1	0	4	2	2	4
Lyon	D	W	6	1	3	2	2	4	3	2
Marseille	L	L	6	1	1	4	4	2	4	2
Bordeaux	D	L	6	2	2	2	4	2	4	1
Lorient										
Toulouse	L	L	6	2	3	1	1	5	2	4
Bastia	D	L	2	1	1	0	1	1	2	0
Reims	D	D	2	0	2	0	1	1	1	1
Rennes	W	D	6	2	2	2	2	4	3	2
Nantes	W	L	2	2	0	0	0	2	0	2
Evian	D	W	3	1	1	1	2	2	2	0
Montpellier	D	W	5	2	3	0	4	1	4	1
Guingamp	W	L	1	1	0	0	0	1	0	1
Nice	W	W	6	3	1	2	3	3	3	2
Metz			-	-	-	-	-	-	-	-
Lens			2	2	0	0	1	1	0	2
Caen			3	0	1	2	0	3	1	1

Season	Division	Pos	P	W	D	L	F	A	GD	Pts
2013-14	Ligue 1	8	38	13	10	15	48	53	-5	49
2012-13	Ligue 1	8	38	14	11	13	57	58	-1	53
2011-12	Ligue 1	17	38	14	7	17	53	55	-2	49

Over/Under 42%/58% 11th **Both score** 47%/53% 13th

LYON

Stade de Gerland — www.olweb.fr

	2013-14 H	2013-14 A	P	W	D	L	OV	UN	BS	CS
			Last six seasons at home							
Paris St-G	W	L	6	2	3	1	3	3	3	2
Monaco	L	L	4	1	2	1	3	1	2	2
Lille	D	D	6	2	3	1	4	2	5	1
St-Etienne	L	W	6	1	3	2	1	5	4	1
Lyon										
Marseille	D	L	6	2	4	0	3	3	3	3
Bordeaux	D	W	6	2	2	2	2	4	3	1
Lorient	L	D	6	4	1	1	3	3	3	2
Toulouse	D	D	6	5	1	0	4	2	4	2
Bastia	W	W	2	2	0	0	2	0	2	0
Reims	L	W	2	1	0	1	1	1	0	1
Rennes	D	L	6	1	4	1	1	5	4	2
Nantes	W	W	2	2	0	0	2	0	1	1
Evian	W	L	3	2	1	0	2	1	1	2
Montpellier	D	L	5	3	1	1	3	2	3	2
Guingamp	W	W	1	1	0	0	0	1	0	1
Nice	W	W	6	5	0	1	4	2	2	4
Metz			-	-	-	-	-	-	-	-
Lens			2	2	0	0	1	1	0	2
Caen			3	1	1	1	2	1	2	1

Season	Division	Pos	P	W	D	L	F	A	GD	Pts
2013-14	Ligue 1	5	38	17	10	11	56	44	+12	61
2012-13	Ligue 1	3	38	19	10	9	61	38	+23	67
2011-12	Ligue 1	4	38	19	7	12	64	51	+13	64

Over/Under 55%/45% 2nd   **Both score** 55%/45% 6th

MARSEILLE

Stade Velodrome — www.om.net

	2013-14 H	2013-14 A	P	W	D	L	OV	UN	BS	CS
			Last six seasons at home							
Paris St-G	L	L	6	3	1	2	5	1	4	2
Monaco	L	L	4	0	2	2	3	1	3	1
Lille	D	D	6	3	2	1	2	4	2	4
St-Etienne	W	D	6	5	1	0	3	3	3	3
Lyon	W	D	6	2	2	2	5	1	6	0
Marseille										
Bordeaux	D	D	6	3	3	0	2	4	2	4
Lorient	W	W	6	3	1	2	3	3	3	2
Toulouse	D	D	6	1	4	1	4	2	5	0
Bastia	W	W	2	2	0	0	2	0	1	1
Reims	L	D	2	0	1	1	1	1	1	1
Rennes	L	D	6	3	1	2	3	3	2	2
Nantes	L	D	2	1	0	1	0	2	0	1
Evian	W	W	3	3	0	0	3	0	0	3
Montpellier	W	W	5	4	0	1	4	1	3	2
Guingamp	W	W	1	1	0	0	0	1	0	1
Nice	L	L	6	4	1	1	4	2	4	1
Metz			-	-	-	-	-	-	-	-
Lens			2	1	1	0	0	2	1	1
Caen			3	1	1	1	2	1	3	0

Season	Division	Pos	P	W	D	L	F	A	GD	Pts
2013-14	Ligue 1	6	38	16	12	10	53	40	+13	60
2012-13	Ligue 1	2	38	21	8	9	42	36	+6	71
2011-12	Ligue 1	10	38	12	12	14	45	41	+4	48

Over/Under 42%/58% 11th   **Both score** 58%/42% 3rd

METZ

Stade Saint-Symphorien — www.fcmetz.com

	2013-14 H	2013-14 A	P	W	D	L	OV	UN	BS	CS
			Last six seasons at home							
Paris St-G			-	-	-	-	-	-	-	-
Monaco			1	0	0	1	0	1	0	0
Lille			-	-	-	-	-	-	-	-
St-Etienne			-	-	-	-	-	-	-	-
Lyon			-	-	-	-	-	-	-	-
Marseille			-	-	-	-	-	-	-	-
Bordeaux			-	-	-	-	-	-	-	-
Lorient			-	-	-	-	-	-	-	-
Toulouse			-	-	-	-	-	-	-	-
Bastia			3	1	1	1	0	3	0	2
Reims			3	1	2	0	0	3	0	3
Rennes			-	-	-	-	-	-	-	-
Nantes			3	0	2	1	1	2	2	1
Evian			1	0	0	1	0	1	0	0
Montpellier			1	1	0	0	1	0	1	0
Guingamp			3	2	0	1	1	2	1	2
Nice			-	-	-	-	-	-	-	-
Metz										
Lens	L	L	3	1	0	2	1	2	1	1
Caen	W	W	2	1	0	1	2	0	2	0

Season	Division	Pos	P	W	D	L	F	A	GD	Pts
2013-14	Ligue 2	1	38	22	10	6	55	28	+27	76
2012-13	National	2	38	20	10	8	62	37	+25	70
2011-12	Ligue 2	18	38	10	12	16	30	44	-14	42

Over/Under 39%/61% 15th   **Both score** 34%/66% 21st

MONACO

Stade Louis II — www.asm-fc.com

	2013-14 H	2013-14 A	P	W	D	L	OV	UN	BS	CS
			Last six seasons at home							
Paris St-G	D	D	4	2	2	0	0	4	2	2
Monaco										
Lille	D	L	4	1	1	2	1	3	1	1
St-Etienne	W	L	4	1	1	2	3	1	3	0
Lyon	W	L	4	1	1	2	1	3	2	0
Marseille	W	W	4	1	1	2	1	3	1	2
Bordeaux	D	W	4	0	3	1	2	2	3	1
Lorient	W	W	4	4	0	0	1	3	1	3
Toulouse	D	D	4	2	2	0	1	3	1	3
Bastia	W	W	2	1	0	1	1	1	0	1
Reims	W	D	2	1	0	1	2	0	2	0
Rennes	W	W	4	4	0	0	1	3	1	3
Nantes	W	W	4	2	0	2	3	1	3	0
Evian	D	L	1	0	1	0	0	1	1	0
Montpellier	W	D	3	2	1	0	2	1	1	2
Guingamp	D	W	3	1	2	0	1	2	2	1
Nice	W	W	4	2	1	1	2	2	2	0
Metz			1	0	0	1	0	1	0	0
Lens			4	2	2	0	2	2	3	1
Caen			3	0	2	1	1	2	2	0

Season	Division	Pos	P	W	D	L	F	A	GD	Pts
2013-14	Ligue 1	2	38	23	11	4	63	31	+32	80
2012-13	Ligue 2	1	38	21	13	4	64	33	+31	76
2011-12	Ligue 2	8	38	13	13	12	41	48	-7	52

Over/Under 39%/61% 15th   **Both score** 55%/45% 6th

MONTPELLIER

Stade de la Mosson — www.mhscfoot.com

	2013-14 H	A	P	W	D	L	OV	UN	BS	CS
Paris St-G	D	L	5	0	4	1	1	4	4	0
Monaco	D	L	3	0	2	1	0	3	1	1
Lille	L	L	5	3	1	1	0	5	0	4
St-Etienne	L	L	5	2	1	2	2	3	3	1
Lyon	W	D	5	2	0	3	3	2	3	1
Marseille	L	L	5	2	0	3	3	2	3	2
Bordeaux	D	L	5	3	1	1	0	5	1	3
Lorient	L	D	5	4	0	1	3	2	2	2
Toulouse	W	D	5	2	3	0	1	4	4	1
Bastia	L	D	3	2	0	1	2	1	1	1
Reims	D	W	3	1	2	0	2	1	2	1
Rennes	D	D	5	3	1	1	2	3	1	3
Nantes	D	L	1	0	1	0	0	1	1	0
Evian	D	D	3	0	2	1	3	0	3	0
Montpellier										
Guingamp	D	W	2	0	2	0	0	2	1	1
Nice	W	D	5	4	1	0	2	3	3	2
Metz			1	0	0	1	1	0	1	0
Lens			3	1	0	2	1	2	1	1
Caen			2	1	1	0	1	1	0	2

Season	Division	Pos	P	W	D	L	F	A	GD	Pts
2013-14	Ligue 1	15	38	8	18	12	45	53	-8	42
2012-13	Ligue 1	9	38	15	7	16	54	51	+3	52
2011-12	Ligue 1	1	38	25	7	6	68	34	+34	82

Over/Under 37%/63% 16th   **Both score** 58%/42% 3rd

NANTES

Stade de la Beaujoire-Louis Fonteneau — www.fcnantes.com

	2013-14 H	A	P	W	D	L	OV	UN	BS	CS
Paris St-G	L	L	2	0	0	2	2	0	2	0
Monaco	L	L	4	1	2	1	1	3	2	1
Lille	L	D	2	0	0	2	0	2	0	0
St-Etienne	L	L	2	1	0	1	1	1	1	1
Lyon	L	L	2	1	0	1	2	0	2	0
Marseille	D	W	2	0	2	0	0	2	2	0
Bordeaux	D	W	2	0	1	1	1	1	1	1
Lorient	W	L	2	1	1	0	0	2	1	1
Toulouse	L	D	2	0	1	1	1	1	2	0
Bastia	W	D	3	2	0	1	2	1	1	1
Reims	D	D	3	1	2	0	0	3	1	2
Rennes	L	W	2	0	1	1	1	1	1	0
Nantes										
Evian	W	L	2	1	0	1	1	1	0	1
Montpellier	W	D	1	1	0	0	1	0	1	0
Guingamp	W	L	4	2	1	1	1	3	1	2
Nice	W	D	2	2	0	0	0	2	0	2
Metz			3	0	3	0	2	1	2	2
Lens			2	2	0	0	1	1	0	2
Caen			3	1	1	1	2	1	3	0

Season	Division	Pos	P	W	D	L	F	A	GD	Pts
2013-14	Ligue 1	13	38	12	10	16	38	43	-5	46
2012-13	Ligue 2	3	38	19	12	7	54	29	+25	69
2011-12	Ligue 2	9	38	14	9	15	51	42	+9	51

Over/Under 42%/58% 11th   **Both score** 39%/61% 17th

NICE

Allianz Riviera — www.ogcnice.com

	2013-14 H	A	P	W	D	L	OV	UN	BS	CS
Paris St-G	L	L	6	3	1	2	2	4	1	3
Monaco	L	L	4	1	1	2	3	1	2	1
Lille	W	W	6	1	2	3	1	5	2	1
St-Etienne	L	L	6	2	2	2	2	4	4	0
Lyon	L	L	6	1	2	3	4	2	5	0
Marseille	W	W	6	2	1	3	1	5	2	2
Bordeaux	L	D	6	2	2	2	4	2	4	1
Lorient	L	L	6	4	1	1	1	5	2	4
Toulouse	L	L	6	3	1	2	0	6	1	3
Bastia	W	L	2	1	1	0	1	1	1	1
Reims	W	W	2	2	0	0	0	2	0	2
Rennes	W	D	6	3	1	2	4	2	3	2
Nantes	D	L	2	1	1	0	1	1	1	1
Evian	W	L	3	2	1	0	2	1	3	0
Montpellier	D	L	5	1	1	3	2	3	1	1
Guingamp	W	L	1	1	0	0	0	1	0	1
Nice										
Metz			-	-	-	-	-	-	-	-
Lens			2	0	2	0	0	2	0	2
Caen			3	1	1	1	2	1	1	1

Season	Division	Pos	P	W	D	L	F	A	GD	Pts
2013-14	Ligue 1	17	38	12	6	20	30	44	-14	42
2012-13	Ligue 1	4	38	15	10	10	57	46	+11	64
2011-12	Ligue 1	13	38	10	12	16	39	46	-7	42

Over/Under 32%/68% 18th   **Both score** 26%/74% 20th

PARIS SAINT-GERMAIN

Parc des Princes — www.psg.fr

	2013-14 H	A	P	W	D	L	OV	UN	BS	CS
Paris St-G										
Monaco	D	D	4	0	3	1	1	3	2	1
Lille	D	W	6	3	3	0	3	3	2	4
St-Etienne	W	D	6	5	0	1	4	2	3	3
Lyon	W	L	6	5	1	0	1	5	1	5
Marseille	W	W	6	4	0	2	4	2	3	2
Bordeaux	W	W	6	3	2	1	2	4	3	3
Lorient	W	W	6	2	2	2	4	2	2	2
Toulouse	W	W	6	5	0	1	2	4	2	3
Bastia	W	W	2	2	0	0	2	0	1	1
Reims	W	W	2	2	0	0	1	1	0	2
Rennes	L	W	6	1	2	3	3	3	3	2
Nantes	W	W	2	2	0	0	1	1	0	2
Evian	W	L	3	3	0	0	2	1	1	2
Montpellier	W	D	5	2	2	1	4	1	3	2
Guingamp	W	D	1	1	0	0	0	1	0	1
Nice	W	W	6	4	1	1	4	2	3	2
Metz			-	-	-	-	-	-	-	-
Lens			2	0	2	0	0	2	0	2
Caen			3	3	0	0	2	1	2	1

Season	Division	Pos	P	W	D	L	F	A	GD	Pts
2013-14	Ligue 1	1	38	27	8	3	84	23	+61	89
2012-13	Ligue 1	1	38	25	8	5	69	23	+46	83
2011-12	Ligue 1	2	38	21	16	1	75	41	+34	79

Over/Under 53%/47% 4th   **Both score** 42%/58% 16th

REIMS

Stade Auguste-Delaune II   www.stade-de-reims.com

	2013-14 H	A	P	W	D	L	OV	UN	BS	CS
Paris St-G	L	L	2	1	0	1	1	1	0	1
Monaco	D	L	2	1	1	0	0	2	1	1
Lille	W	W	2	1	1	0	1	1	2	0
St-Etienne	D	L	2	0	2	0	1	1	2	0
Lyon	L	W	2	1	0	1	0	2	0	1
Marseille	D	W	2	0	1	1	0	2	1	0
Bordeaux	W	D	2	1	1	0	0	2	0	2
Lorient	D	D	2	1	1	0	0	2	1	1
Toulouse	L	L	2	0	1	1	1	1	2	0
Bastia	W	L	4	3	0	1	2	2	2	2
Reims										
Rennes	L	L	2	1	0	1	1	1	1	1
Nantes	D	D	3	2	1	0	2	1	2	1
Evian	W	D	3	1	0	2	2	1	2	1
Montpellier	L	D	3	1	0	2	3	0	2	0
Guingamp	D	W	3	1	2	0	1	2	2	1
Nice	W	L	2	2	0	0	1	1	1	1
Metz			3	1	2	0	2	1	2	1
Lens			2	0	1	1	1	1	2	0
Caen			-	-	-	-	-	-	-	-

Season	Division	Pos	P	W	D	L	F	A	GD	Pts
2013-14	Ligue 1	11	38	12	12	14	44	52	-8	48
2012-13	Ligue 1	14	38	10	13	15	33	42	-9	43
2011-12	Ligue 2	2	38	18	11	9	54	37	+17	65

Over/Under 47%/53% 6th   **Both score** 55%/45% 6th

RENNES

Stade de la Route de Lorient   www.staderennais.com

	2013-14 H	A	P	W	D	L	OV	UN	BS	CS
Paris St-G	L	W	6	3	1	2	1	5	2	3
Monaco	L	L	4	3	0	1	1	3	1	2
Lille	D	D	6	2	3	1	2	4	4	2
St-Etienne	W	D	6	3	3	0	2	4	3	3
Lyon	W	D	6	2	2	2	2	4	3	2
Marseille	D	W	6	0	4	2	3	3	5	0
Bordeaux	D	W	6	2	2	2	2	4	3	2
Lorient	W	L	6	3	1	2	3	3	4	2
Toulouse	L	W	6	3	1	2	3	3	3	2
Bastia	W	L	2	2	0	0	2	0	1	1
Reims	W	W	2	2	0	0	1	1	1	1
Rennes										
Nantes	L	W	2	0	1	1	1	1	1	1
Evian	W	W	3	1	1	1	1	2	1	1
Montpellier	D	D	5	2	1	2	3	2	2	1
Guingamp	L	L	1	0	0	1	0	1	0	0
Nice	D	L	6	3	2	1	3	3	2	3
Metz			-	-	-	-	-	-	-	-
Lens			2	1	1	0	0	2	1	1
Caen			3	2	1	0	1	2	2	1

Season	Division	Pos	P	W	D	L	F	A	GD	Pts
2013-14	Ligue 1	12	38	11	13	14	47	45	+2	46
2012-13	Ligue 1	13	38	13	7	18	48	59	-11	46
2011-12	Ligue 1	6	38	17	9	12	53	44	+9	60

Over/Under 50%/50% 5th   **Both score** 53%/47% 10th

SAINT-ETIENNE

Stade Geoffroy-Guichard   www.asse.fr

	2013-14 H	A	P	W	D	L	OV	UN	BS	CS
Paris St-G	D	L	6	1	4	1	2	4	3	2
Monaco	W	L	4	3	1	0	1	3	1	3
Lille	W	L	6	2	1	3	4	2	5	1
St-Etienne										
Lyon	L	W	6	0	0	6	2	4	2	0
Marseille	D	L	6	1	4	1	1	5	2	3
Bordeaux	W	L	6	2	3	1	4	2	5	1
Lorient	W	L	6	2	0	4	4	2	4	0
Toulouse	L	D	6	1	3	2	4	2	5	0
Bastia	D	W	2	1	1	0	2	0	1	1
Reims	W	D	2	1	1	0	1	1	0	2
Rennes	D	L	6	2	2	2	3	3	1	4
Nantes	W	W	2	2	0	0	1	1	1	1
Evian	D	W	3	2	0	1	0	3	0	2
Montpellier	W	W	5	4	1	0	2	3	2	3
Guingamp	W	D	1	1	0	0	0	1	0	1
Nice	D	W	6	1	1	4	2	4	2	1
Metz			-	-	-	-	-	-	-	-
Lens			2	1	0	1	2	0	2	0
Caen			3	2	1	0	1	2	2	1

Season	Division	Pos	P	W	D	L	F	A	GD	Pts
2013-14	Ligue 1	4	38	20	9	9	56	34	+22	69
2012-13	Ligue 1	5	38	16	15	7	60	32	+28	63
2011-12	Ligue 1	7	38	16	9	13	49	45	+4	57

Over/Under 47%/53% 6th   **Both score** 47%/53% 13th

TOULOUSE

Stadium Municipal   www.tfc.info

	2013-14 H	A	P	W	D	L	OV	UN	BS	CS
Paris St-G	L	L	6	2	0	4	4	2	3	1
Monaco	L	D	4	1	2	1	0	4	0	3
Lille	L	L	6	1	3	2	2	4	3	2
St-Etienne	D	W	6	3	1	2	3	3	3	1
Lyon	D	D	6	3	3	0	2	4	0	6
Marseille	D	D	6	0	4	2	0	6	2	2
Bordeaux	D	W	6	3	2	1	3	3	3	3
Lorient	W	W	6	2	2	2	1	5	2	2
Toulouse										
Bastia	L	L	2	0	1	1	1	1	1	1
Reims	W	W	2	1	1	0	1	1	2	0
Rennes	L	W	6	2	2	2	4	2	3	2
Nantes	D	W	2	1	1	0	0	2	1	1
Evian	D	L	3	1	2	0	1	2	2	1
Montpellier	D	L	5	1	1	3	0	5	1	1
Guingamp	D	L	1	0	1	0	0	1	0	1
Nice	W	W	6	1	3	2	2	4	3	2
Metz			-	-	-	-	-	-	-	-
Lens			2	1	1	0	0	2	1	1
Caen			3	2	0	1	0	3	0	2

Season	Division	Pos	P	W	D	L	F	A	GD	Pts
2013-14	Ligue 1	9	38	12	13	13	46	53	-7	49
2012-13	Ligue 1	10	38	13	12	13	49	47	+2	51
2011-12	Ligue 1	8	38	15	11	12	37	34	+3	56

Over/Under 47%/53% 6th   **Both score** 61%/39% 2nd

League table 2013-14

Pos	H	A		P	Home					Away					GD	Pts
					W	D	L	F	A	W	D	L	F	A		
1	1	1	Paris St-G.	38	15	3	1	51	7	12	5	2	33	16	+61	89 (C)
2	2	2	Monaco	38	12	6	1	32	14	11	5	3	31	17	+32	80
3	3	4	Lille	38	13	3	3	25	10	7	8	4	21	16	+20	71
4	4	5	St-Etienne	38	12	5	2	36	15	8	4	7	20	19	+22	69
5	9	3	Lyon	38	8	7	4	30	15	9	3	7	26	29	+12	61
6	7	6	Marseille	38	10	3	6	30	20	6	9	4	23	20	+13	60
7	6	11	Bordeaux	38	10	4	5	31	20	3	10	6	18	23	+6	53
8	10	12	Lorient	38	8	7	4	29	25	5	3	11	19	28	-5	49
9	17	7	Toulouse	38	5	9	5	23	26	7	4	8	23	27	-7	49
10	5	16	Bastia	38	10	5	4	24	18	3	5	11	18	38	-14	49
11	14	10	Reims	38	7	6	6	26	26	5	6	8	18	26	-8	48
12	18	8	Rennes	38	5	8	6	24	23	6	5	8	23	22	+2	46
13	15	9	Nantes	38	7	4	8	19	19	5	6	8	19	24	-5	46
14	13	14	Evian	38	7	6	6	25	24	4	5	10	14	27	-12	44
15	16	13	Montpellier	38	5	9	5	22	19	3	9	7	23	34	-8	42
16	12	15	Guingamp	38	8	4	7	21	16	3	5	11	13	26	-8	42
17	8	18	Nice	38	10	2	7	22	16	2	4	13	8	28	-14	42
18	11	19	Sochaux	38	8	6	5	20	18	2	4	13	17	43	-24	40 (R)
19	19	17	Valenciennes	38	4	5	10	23	31	3	3	13	14	34	-28	29 (R)
20	20	20	Ajaccio	38	3	6	10	23	33	1	5	13	14	39	-35	23 (R)

Results 2013-14

	Ajaccio	Bastia	Bordeaux	Evian	Guingamp	Lille	Lorient	Lyon	Marseille	Monaco	Montpellier	Nantes	Nice	Paris St-G	Reims	Rennes	Sochaux	St-Etienne	Toulouse	Valenciennes
Ajaccio		1-1	1-1	2-3	1-2	2-3	1-2	2-1	1-3	1-4	1-1	0-1	0-0	1-2	2-1	3-1	1-1	0-1	2-2	1-3
Bastia	2-1		1-0	2-0	3-2	1-1	4-1	1-3	0-0	0-2	0-0	0-0	1-0	0-3	2-0	1-0	2-2	0-2	2-1	2-0
Bordeaux	4-0	1-0		2-1	5-1	1-0	3-2	1-2	1-1	0-2	2-0	0-3	1-1	0-2	0-0	2-2	4-1	2-0	0-1	2-1
Evian	1-1	2-1	1-1		1-2	2-2	0-4	2-1	1-2	1-0	2-2	2-0	2-0	1-1	1-2	1-1	1-2	2-1	0-1	0-1
Guingamp	2-1	1-1	0-1	0-1		0-0	2-0	0-1	1-3	0-2	1-2	1-0	1-0	1-1	1-2	2-0	5-1	0-0	2-0	1-0
Lille	3-0	2-1	2-1	3-0	1-0		1-0	0-0	1-0	2-0	2-0	0-0	0-2	1-3	1-2	1-1	2-0	1-0	1-0	1-0
Lorient	1-0	1-1	3-3	1-1	2-0	1-4		2-2	0-2	2-2	4-4	2-1	3-0	0-1	0-0	2-0	2-1	1-0	1-3	1-0
Lyon	3-1	4-1	1-1	3-0	2-0	0-0	0-1		2-2	2-3	0-0	3-1	4-0	1-0	0-1	0-0	2-0	1-2	1-1	1-1
Marseille	3-1	3-0	2-2	2-0	1-0	0-0	1-0	4-2		1-2	2-0	0-1	1-2	2-3	0-1	2-1	2-1	2-2	2-2	2-1
Monaco	1-0	3-0	1-1	1-1	1-1	1-1	1-0	2-1	2-0		4-1	3-1	1-0	1-1	3-2	2-0	2-1	2-1	0-0	1-2
Montpellier	2-0	0-2	1-1	1-1	1-1	0-1	0-2	5-1	2-3	1-1		1-1	3-1	1-1	0-0	0-0	2-1	0-1	2-1	0-0
Nantes	2-2	2-0+	0-0	3-0	1-0	0-1	1-0	1-2	1-1	0-1	2-1		2-0	1-2	0-0	0-3	1-0	1-3	1-2	2-1
Nice	2-0	2-0	1-2	3-1	1-0	1-0	1-2	0-1	1-0	0-3	2-2	0-0		0-1	1-0	2-1	1-0	0-1	0-2	4-0
Paris St-G	1-1	4-0	2-0	1-0	2-0	2-2	4-0	4-0	2-0	1-1	4-0	5-0	3-1		3-0	1-2	5-0	2-0	2-0	3-0
Reims	4-1	4-2	1-0	1-0	1-1	2-1	1-1	0-2	1-1	1-1	2-4	0-0	1-0	0-3		1-3	0-1	2-2	1-2	3-1
Rennes	2-0	3-0	1-1	0-0	0-2	0-0	1-1	2-0	1-1	0-1	2-2	1-3	0-0	1-3	2-1		1-2	3-1	2-3	2-2
Sochaux	0-0	1-1	2-0	0-3	1-0	0-2	0-0	1-3	1-1	2-2	0-2	1-0	0-2	1-1	0-2	2-1		0-0	2-0	2-0
St-Etienne	3-1	2-2	2-1	1-0	1-0	2-0	3-2	1-2	1-1	2-0	2-0	2-0	1-1	2-2	4-0	0-0	3-1		1-2	3-0
Toulouse	1-1	1-3	1-1	1-1	0-0	1-2	1-0	0-0	1-1	0-2	1-1	1-1	1-0	2-4	3-2	0-5	5-1	0-0		3-1
Valenciennes	2-3	3-2	0-1	0-1	1-1	0-1	1-1	1-2	0-1	1-2	1-1	2-6	2-1	0-1	1-1	2-1	2-2	1-3	3-0	

+Result officially recorded as 0-0 after Nantes were docked points for fielding an ineligible player

Over 2.5 goals	H	A	%		Under 2.5 goals	H	A	%		Both to score	H	A	%		Both not to score	H	A	%
Ajaccio	12	10	58%		Guingamp	14	15	76%		Ajaccio	16	11	71%		Nice	14	14	74%
Lyon	8	13	55%		Lille	13	13	68%		Toulouse	12	11	61%		Lille	14	11	66%
Valenciennes	10	11	55%		Nice	12	14	68%		Montpellier	11	11	58%		Guingamp	12	11	61%
Paris St-G	11	9	53%		Bordeaux	10	14	63%		Marseille	10	12	58%		Nantes	11	12	61%
Rennes	9	10	50%		Montpellier	14	10	63%		Valenciennes	13	9	58%		Paris SG	14	8	58%

Uefa Association Coefficients 2013-14

Pos	Change	Country	09-10	10-11	11-12	12-13	13-14	Pts	Change
1		Spain	17.928	18.214	20.857	17.714	23.000	97.713	+9.688
2		England	17.928	18.357	15.250	16.428	16.785	84.748	+1.785
3		Germany	18.083	15.666	15.250	17.928	14.714	81.641	+2.027
4		Italy	15.428	11.571	11.357	14.416	14.166	66.938	+2.791
5		Portugal	10.000	18.800	11.833	11.750	9.916	62.299	+3.131
6		France	15.000	10.750	10.500	11.750	8.500	56.500	-2.500
7	-1	Russia	6.166	10.916	9.750	9.750	10.416	46.998	+0.666
8	-1	Holland	9.416	11.166	13.600	4.214	5.916	44.312	-0.417
9	+2	Ukraine	5.800	10.083	7.750	9.500	7.833	40.966	-8.792
10	-1	Belgium	8.700	4.600	10.100	6.500	6.400	36.300	+1.900
11	+1	Turkey	7.600	4.600	5.100	10.200	6.700	34.200	-0.300
12		Greece	7.900	7.600	7.600	4.400	6.100	33.600	-0.400
13		Switzerland	5.750	5.900	6.000	8.375	7.200	33.225	+4.300
14	-2	Austria	9.375	4.375	7.125	2.250	7.800	30.925	+5.550
15	-2	Czech Republic	4.100	3.500	5.250	8.500	8.000	29.350	+5.625
16	-2	Romania	6.083	3.166	4.333	6.800	6.875	27.257	+4.233
17	-2	Israel	7.250	4.625	6.000	3.250	5.750	26.875	+4.000
18	+4	Cyprus	4.250	3.125	9.125	4.000	2.750	23.250	-3.583
19	+4	Denmark	4.400	6.700	3.100	3.300	3.800	21.300	-4.400
20	-2	Croatia	3.000	4.125	3.750	4.375	4.375	19.625	+0.042
21		Poland	2.125	4.500	6.625	2.500	3.125	18.875	-1.875
22	+2	Belarus	3.375	5.875	3.125	4.500	1.750	18.625	-2.250
23	-1	Scotland	2.666	3.600	2.750	4.300	3.250	16.566	+1.375
24	+1	Sweden	2.500	2.600	2.900	5.125	3.200	16.325	+0.700
25	-3	Bulgaria	3.125	4.625	1.500	0.750	5.625	15.625	+3.375
26	-1	Norway	2.100	2.375	2.300	4.900	2.600	14.275	+0.100
27	+2	Serbia	3.000	3.500	2.125	3.000	2.500	14.125	-0.500
28	-1	Hungary	2.750	2.750	2.250	3.000	0.875	11.625	-0.125
29	-1	Slovenia	1.375	1.500	2.250	3.250	2.625	11.000	+1.292
30	+4	Slovakia	2.500	3.000	2.375	1.500	1.625	11.000	-3.208
31	-4	Moldova	2.125	2.125	0.500	2.250	3.375	10.375	+2.709
32		Azerbaijan	1.500	2.000	1.375	3.000	2.500	10.375	+1.834
33	+2	Georgia	1.750	1.875	2.875	1.500	1.875	9.875	+0.709
34	-4	Kazakhstan	1.250	0.875	1.625	1.375	3.125	8.250	+2.292
35	+1	Bosnia-Hz	1.750	1.875	1.125	1.250	1.500	7.500	-0.333
36	+3	Finland	1.375	1.800	1.500	2.000	0.500	7.175	-1.333
37	-3	Iceland	1.250	0.375	1.375	1.250	2.500	6.750	+1.334
38	-1	Latvia	2.250	0.500	0.625	1.250	1.625	6.250	+0.459
39	-2	Montenegro	1.125	1.750	0.500	1.375	1.250	6.000	+0.750
40	-3	Albania	1.000	0.875	0.875	0.750	2.000	5.500	+1.334
41	+4	Lithuania	1.250	0.625	1.000	1.125	1.250	5.250	-1.250
42		Macedonia	0.500	1.375	1.625	1.250	0.500	5.250	=
43	+7	Rep of Ireland	1.375	1.000	1.500	1.000	0.250	5.125	-2.250
44	-2	Luxembourg	0.250	0.625	1.125	1.375	1.500	4.875	+1.500
45	+1	Malta	0.750	1.500	0.833	0.875	0.875	4.833	+0.875
46	+1	Liechtenstein	1.000	0.500	2.000	0.000	1.000	4.500	+1.000
47		N Ireland	0.125	1.125	0.500	1.000	0.875	3.625	+0.542
48		Wales	0.250	0.875	0.625	0.500	0.750	3.000	+0.417
49	-1	Armenia	0.500	0.250	0.125	0.875	1.125	2.875	+1.125
50	+1	Estonia	0.875	0.250	0.375	0.375	1.000	2.875	+0.667
51		Faroe Islands	0.000	0.250	0.500	0.500	0.875	2.125	+0.542
52		San Marino	0.500	0.166	0.000	0.000	0.333	0.999	+0.333
53		Andorra	0.500	0.000	0.000	0.000	0.333	0.833	+0.333

Uefa's country coefficients are calculated from performances of each FA's clubs in the last five Europa League and Champions League seasons. They are used to allocate places in Uefa's club competitions and determine seedings.

Two points are awarded for a win and one for a draw, and half that in qualifying matches. An extra point is awarded for every round from the last 16 of the Champions League and the quarter-finals of the Europa League. Four extra points are given for reaching the group stage of the Champions League and four more for the knockout rounds.

The country coefficient is the sum of the average points for each nation in each of the last five seasons. England's clubs have averaged 17.928, 18.357, 15.25, 16.428 and 16.785 over the last five campaigns – add them togehter and you get 84.748, England's country coefficient.

Portuguese league table 2013-14 (top eight only)

		P	W	D	L	F	A	D	Pts
1	Benfica	30	23	5	2	58	18	+40	74
2	Sporting Lisbon	30	20	7	3	54	20	+34	67
3	Porto	30	19	4	7	57	25	+32	61
4	Estoril	30	15	9	6	42	26	+16	54
5	Nacional	30	11	12	7	43	33	+10	45
6	Maritimo	30	11	8	11	40	44	-4	41
7	Vitoria Setubal	30	10	9	11	41	41	0	39
8	Braga	30	10	7	13	39	37	+2	37

Russian league table 2013-14 (top eight only)

		P	W	D	L	F	A	D	Pts
1	CSKA Moscow	30	20	4	6	49	26	+23	64
2	Zenit	30	19	6	5	65	33	+32	63
3	Lok. Moscow	30	17	8	5	51	23	+28	59
4	Din. Moscow	30	15	7	8	55	39	+16	52
5	FK Krasnodar	30	15	5	10	46	39	+7	50
6	Spartak Moscow	30	15	5	10	46	36	+10	50
7	R. Rostov	30	10	9	11	40	40	0	39
8	Amkar Perm	30	9	11	10	36	37	-1	38

Dutch league table 2013-14 (top eight only)

		P	W	D	L	F	A	D	Pts
1	Ajax	34	20	11	3	69	28	+41	71
2	Feyenoord	34	20	7	7	76	40	+36	67
3	FC Twente	34	17	12	5	72	37	+35	63
4	PSV Eindhoven	34	18	5	11	60	45	+15	59
5	Heerenveen	34	16	9	9	72	51	+21	57
6	Vitesse Arn	35	15	10	10	66	53	+13	55
7	FC Groningen	35	15	9	11	61	54	+7	54
8	AZ Alkmaar	34	13	8	13	54	50	+4	47

Ukrainian league table 2013-14 (top eight only)

		P	W	D	L	F	A	D	Pts
1	Shakhtar	28	21	2	5	62	23	+39	65
2	Dnipro	28	18	5	5	56	28	+28	59
3	Metalist	28	16	9	3	54	29	+25	57
4	Dynamo Kiev	28	16	5	7	55	33	+22	53
5	Ch. Odessa	28	12	10	6	30	22	+8	46
6	Metalurg D	28	12	7	9	45	42	+3	43
7	Zorya	28	11	9	8	35	30	+5	42
8	Vorskla Poltava	28	10	10	8	36	38	-2	40

Belgian league table 2013-14 (top eight only)

		P	W	D	L	F	A	D	Pts
1	Standard Liege	30	20	7	3	59	17	+42	67
2	FC Bruges	30	19	6	5	54	28	+26	63
3	Anderlecht	30	18	3	9	61	31	+30	57
4	Waregem	30	14	11	5	51	38	+13	53
5	Lokeren	30	15	6	9	48	31	+17	51
6	Genk	30	14	3	13	42	39	+3	45
7	Gent	30	12	8	10	39	37	+2	44
8	Kortrikj	30	10	9	11	42	44	-2	39

Turkish league table 2013-14 (top eight only)

		P	W	D	L	F	A	D	Pts
1	Fenerbahce	33	22	5	6	71	33	+38	71
2	Galatasaray	34	18	11	5	59	32	+27	65
3	Besiktas	34	17	11	6	53	33	+20	62
4	Trabzonspor	33	14	11	8	53	38	+15	53
5	Sivasspor	34	16	5	13	60	55	+5	53
6	Kasimpasa	34	13	12	9	56	39	+17	51
7	Kardemir	34	13	11	10	33	34	-1	50
8	Bursaspor	34	12	10	12	40	46	-6	46

Benfica's Jorge Jesus watches his players work

Greek league table 2013-14 (top eight only)

		P	W	D	L	F	A	D	Pts
1	Olympiakos	34	28	2	4	88	19	+69	86
2	PAOK Salonika	34	21	6	7	68	37	+31	69
3	Atromitos	34	19	9	6	54	25	+29	66
4	Panathinaikos	34	20	6	8	57	28	+29	66
5	Asteras T	34	16	10	8	46	35	+11	58
6	OFI Crete	34	11	11	12	30	39	-9	44
7	Ergotelis	34	11	11	12	39	40	-1	44
8	Levadiakos	34	13	3	18	42	61	-19	42

Swiss league table 2013-14 (top eight only)

		P	W	D	L	F	A	D	Pts
1	Basle	36	19	15	2	70	34	+36	72
2	Grasshoppers	36	19	8	9	67	43	+24	65
3	Young Boys	36	17	8	11	59	50	+9	59
4	Lucerne	36	15	6	15	48	54	-6	51
5	FC Zurich	36	14	8	14	51	52	-1	50
6	Thun	36	13	9	14	57	53	+4	48
7	St Gallen	36	11	12	13	37	47	-10	45
8	FC Sion	36	12	7	17	38	45	-7	43

Austrian league table 2013-14 (top eight only)

		P	W	D	L	F	A	D	Pts
1	RB Salzburg	36	25	5	6	110	35	+75	80
2	Rapid Vienna	36	17	11	8	63	40	+23	62
3	SV Grodig	36	15	9	12	68	71	-3	54
4	Austria Vienna	36	14	11	11	58	44	+14	53
5	Sturm Graz	36	13	9	14	55	55	0	48
6	Ried	36	10	13	13	55	66	-11	43
7	Wolfsberger	36	11	8	17	50	63	-13	41
8	Wiener Neustadt	36	10	9	17	43	84	-41	39

Czech league table 2013-14 (top eight only)

		P	W	D	L	F	A	D	Pts
1	Sparta Prague	30	25	4	1	78	19	+59	79
2	Viktoria Plzen	30	19	9	2	64	21	+43	66
3	Mlada Boleslav	30	14	8	8	54	38	+16	50
4	Slovan Liberec	30	14	6	10	37	46	-9	48
5	Teplice	30	13	7	10	51	35	+16	46
6	Synot	30	11	7	12	43	40	+3	40
7	Dukla Prague	30	10	8	12	35	37	-2	38
8	Vysocina Jihlava	30	10	7	13	45	50	-5	37

Romanian league table 2013-14 (top eight only)

		P	W	D	L	F	A	D	Pts
1	Steaua	34	22	11	1	71	20	+51	77
2	Astra Giurgiu	34	22	6	6	70	28	+42	72
3	Petrolul Ploiesti	34	18	14	2	53	20	+33	68
4	Din. Bucharest	34	17	8	9	52	34	+18	59
5	CFR Cluj	34	13	12	9	44	33	+11	51
6	Pandurii	34	14	8	12	59	39	+20	50
7	FC Vaslui	34	15	6	13	38	32	+6	43 *
8	Botosani	34	12	7	15	36	52	-16	43

UEFA RESULTS 2013-14

First qualifying round

Tuesday July 2 2013
Bala Town.....(1) 1-0 (0) Levadia Tallinn
Metalurg S....(0) 0-1 (0).. FK Qarabag
Sliema W. .....(0) 1-1 (1)..........Khazar
Trans Narva ..(0) 0-3 (1)............ Gefle

Wednesday July 3 2013
IF Fuglafjordur (0) 0-2 (0)......... Linfield

Thursday July 4 2013
Airbus UK .....(0) 1-1 (0)...... Ventspils
Astana..........(0) 0-1 (1) Botev Plovdiv
Breidablik .....(3) 4-0 (0)FC Santa Coloma
Celik Zenica ..(1) 1-4 (2)........ Honved
Chikhura Sach. (0) 0-0 (0)...........Vaduz
Crusaders .....(1) 1-2 (1)....Rosenborg
Domzale ....(0) 0-1 (0) Astra Giurgiu
Drogheda .....(0) 0-0 (0)......... Malmo
FC Tiraspol....(0) 0-1 (0)..Skonto Riga
FK Suduva.....(1) 2-2 (2)........Turnovo
Flora Tallinn ..(1) 1-1 (0)........... Kukesi
Gand Kapan..(0) 1-2 (0)......... Aktobe
Hibernians ....(0) 1-4 (2) Vojvodina NS
IBV Vestmann(1) 1-1 (0). HB Torshavn
Inter Baku.....(1) 1-1 (0)....Mariehamn
Jeunesse Esch(1) 2-0 (0)..... TPS Turku
KF Laci..........(0) 0-1 (0).. Differdange
KR Reykjavik .(0) 0-0 (0).......Glentoran
Kruoja...........(0) 0-3 (0) Dinamo Minsk
La Fiorita .....(0) 0-3 (1).......Valletta
Levski Sofia...(0) 0-0 (0)...........Irtysh
Milsami Orhei(1) 1-0 (0)F91 Dudelange
Prestatyn .....(1) 1-2 (1). Metalurgs L.
Rudar Pljevlja(1) 1-0 (0).......FC Mika
Sarajevo ....(1) 1-0 (0)...... Libertas
Teteks ....(0) 1-1 (0)Pyunik Yerevan
Teuta ....(1) 3-1 (1)..........Dacia
Torpedo Kutaisi (0) 0-3 (0) ....Zilina
Tromso..........(1) 1-2 (0)...... NK Celje
UE Santa.......(1) 1-3 (0) Zrinjski Mostar
Videoton.......(2) 2-1 (1) Mladost Pod.
Vikingur (FIs).(0) 1-1 (1)...... FC Inter
Zalgiris Vilnius (1) 2-2 (0)....St Patrick's

Second legs

Tuesday July 9 2013
Differdange...(0) 2-1 (1)..........KF Laci
   Agg: 3-1 Differdange
FC Mika ....(1) 1-1 (0)Rudar Pljevlja
   Agg: 2-1 Rudar Pljevlja
TPS Turku......(1) 2-1 (0)Jeunesse Esch
   Agg: 3-2 Jeuness Esch

Wednesday July 10 2013
Linfield ....(1) 3-0 (0) IF Fuglafjordur
   Agg: 5-0 Linfield

Thursday July 11 2013
Aktobe..........(1) 2-1 (1). Gand Kapan
   Agg: 4-2 Aktobe

Astra Giurgiu (0) 2-0 (0).......Domzale
   Agg: 3-0 Astra Giurgiu
Botev Plovdiv(0) 5-0 (0)..........Astana
   Agg: 6-0 Botev Plovdiv
Dacia ....(1) 2-0 (0)...........Teuta
   Agg: 3-3. Dacia away goals
Dinamo Minsk.(4) 5-0 (0).......... Kruoja
   Agg: 8-0 Dinamo Minsk
F91 Dudelange(0) 0-0 (0)Milsami Orhei
   Agg: 1-0 Milsami Orhei
FC Inter.........(0) 0-1 (0) Vikingur (FIs)
   Agg: 2-1 Vikingur
FC Santa Coloma(0)0-0 (0).....Breidablik
   Agg: 4-0 Bredablik
FK Qarabag....(0) 1-0 (0).. Metalurg S.
   Agg: 2-0 FK Qarabag
Gefle.............(1) 5-1 (0).. Trans Narva
   Agg: 8-1 Gefle
Glentoran .....(0) 0-3 (1).KR Reykjavik
   Agg: 3-0 KR Reykjavik
HB Torshavn..(0) 0-1 (0)IBV Vestmann
   Agg: 2-1 IBV Vestmann
Honved.........(3) 9-0 (0)..Celik Zenica
   Agg: 13-1 Honved
Irtysh ....(2) 2-0 (0).. Levski Sofia
   Agg: 2-0 Irtysh
Khazar ....(1) 1-0 (0).....Sliema W.
   Agg: 2-1 Khazar
Kukesi............(0) 0-0 (0)..Flora Tallinn
   Agg: 1-1. Kukesi away goals
Levadia Tallinn(2) 3-1 (0).... Bala Town
   Agg: 3-2 Levadia
Libertas.........(1) 1-2 (2).......Sarajevo
   Agg: 3-1 Sarajevo
Malmo..........(1) 2-0 (0).....Drogheda
   Agg: 2-0 Malmo
Mariehamn ...(0) 0-2 (1).... Inter Baku
   Agg: 3-1 Inter Baku
Metalurgs L. .(1) 1-2 (0)......Prestatyn
   AET Agg: 3-3. Prestatyn 4-3 pens
Mladost Pod. (0) 1-0 (0)...... Videoton
   Agg: 2-2. Mladost Pod. away goals
NK Celje........(0) 0-2 (2)........ Tromso
   Agg: 3-2 Tromso
Pyunik Yerevan(0) 1-0 (0)..........Teteks
   Agg: 2-1 Pyunik Yerevan
Rosenborg ....(2) 7-2 (0)....Crusaders
   Agg: 9-3 Rosenborg
Skonto Riga ..(0) 0-1 (0)... FC Tiraspol
   AET Agg: 1-1. Skonto 4-2 pens
St Patrick's ....(0) 1-2 (1) Zalgiris Vilnius
   Agg: 4-3 Zalgiris Vilnius
Turnovo ....(0) 2-2 (1).... FK Suduva
   Agg: 4-4 Turnovo 5-4 pens
Vaduz ....(1) 1-1 (1)Chikhura Sach.
   Agg: 1-1. Chikhura Sach. away goals
Valletta ....(0) 1-0 (0)...... La Fiorita
   Agg: 4-0 Valletta
Ventspils.......(0) 0-0 (0).....Airbus UK
   Agg: 1-1. Ventspils away goals
Vojvodina NS (1) 3-2 (1)....Hibernians
   Agg: 7-3 Vojvodina NS
Zilina ....(2) 3-3 (1)Torpedo Kutaisi
   Agg: 6-3 Zilina

Zrinjski Mostar(0) 1-0 (0)...... UE Santa
   Agg: 4-1 Zrinjski Mostar

Second qualifying round

Tuesday July 16 2013
Levadia Tallinn(0) 0-0 (0)........Pandurii

Thursday July 18 2013
Anorthosis Fam. (2) 3-0 (0)............ Gefle
Astra Giurgiu (1) 1-1 (0)Omonia Nicosia
Beroe Stara...(1) 1-4 (2).....H Tel Aviv
Breidablik .....(0) 0-0 (0)... Sturm Graz
Ch. Odessa ...(0) 2-0 (0)...........Dacia
Crvena Zvezda (1) 2-0 (0)IBV Vestmann
Differdange...(1) 2-1 (1).... FC Utrecht
Dila...............(0) 3-0 (0)........ Aalborg
Dinamo Minsk.(0) 1-2 (2) Loko. Zagreb
FK Qarabag...(1) 2-1 (1).Piast Gliwice
Hajduk Split ..(1) 2-1 (1)........Turnovo
Hodd............(1) 1-0 (0)........ Aktobe
Honka...........(1) 1-3 (1). Lech Poznan
IFK Goth'burg(0) 0-0 (0)Dukla Trencin
Irtysh ....(2) 3-2 (0)NK Siroki Brijeg
Jagodina.......(0) 2-3 (2).......... Rubin
KR Reykjavik .(1) 1-3 (1)Standard Liege
Kukesi............(2) 3-2 (2)....... Sarajevo
M. Haifa ....(1) 2-0 (0)...........Khazar
Malmo...........(2) 2-0 (0)..... Hibernian
Mladost Pod. (0) 2-2 (1)........ Senica
O. Ljubljana ..(2) 3-1 (0)...........Zilina
Petrolul Ploiesti(1) 3-0 (0) Vikingur (FIs)
Rijeka ....(2) 5-0 (0)...... Prestatyn
Rosenborg ....(0) 0-1 (1).St Johnstone
Shakhtyor .....(1) 1-1 (0)Milsami Orhei
Skonto Riga ..(1) 2-1 (1) Slovan Liberec
Slask Wroclaw (2) 4-0 (0)Rudar Pljevlja
Sparta Prague(1) 2-2 (0).........Hacken
Stromsgodset(0) 2-2 (1).......Debrecen
Thun.............(2) 2-0 (0) Chikhura Sach.
Trabzonspor..(3) 4-2 (2).....Derry City
Tromso..........(1) 2-0 (0)..... Inter Baku
Valletta ....(1) 1-1 (1).... FC Minsk
Ventspils.......(1) 1-0 (0)Jeunesse Esch
Vojvodina NS (1) 2-0 (0) .... Honved
Xanthi...........(0) 0-1 (1)......... Linfield
Zalgiris Vilnius (0) 2-0 (0)Pyunik Yerevan
Zrinjski Mostar(1) 1-1 (0)Botev Plovdiv

Second legs

Thursday July 25 2013
Aalborg ....(0) 0-0 (0).............. Dila
   Agg: 3-0 Dila
Aktobe...........(1) 2-0 (0)...........Hodd
   Agg: 2-1 Aktobe
Botev Plovdiv(0) 2-0 (0) Zrinjski Mostar
   Agg: 3-1 Botev Plovdiv
Chikhura Sach.(1) 1-3 (1)............ Thun
   Agg: 5-1 Thun
Dacia ....(1) 2-1 (1)... Ch. Odessa
   Agg: 3-2 Ch. Odessa
Debrecen ......(0) 0-3 (1)Stromsgodset
   Agg: 5-2 Stromsgodset

Drogheda and Malmo take to the field at Dublin's Tallaght Stadium for their first-round qualifier

Derry City .....(0) 0-3 (0). Trabzonspor
Agg: 7-2 Trabzonspor

Dukla Trencin(1) 2-1 (0)IFK Goth'burg
Agg: 2-1 Dukla Trencin

FC Minsk.......(0) 2-0 (0).........Valletta
Agg: 3-1 FC Minsk

FC Utrecht.....(1) 3-3 (1).. Differdange
Agg: 5-4 Differdange

Gefle.............(1) 4-0 (0)Anorthosis Fam.
Agg: 4-3 Gefle

H Tel Aviv .....(1) 2-2 (1)...Beroe Stara
Agg: 6-3 H Tel Aviv

Hacken ....(0) 1-0 (0)Sparta Prague
Agg: 3-2 Hacken

Hibernian......(0) 0-7 (4).........Malmo
Agg: 9-0 Malmo

Honved.........(1) 1-3 (2)Vojvodina NS
Agg: 5-1 Vojvodina NS

IBV Vestmann(0) 0-0 (0) Crvena Zvezda
Agg: 2-0 Crvena Zvezda

Inter Baku......(0) 0-0 (0) .... Tromso
Agg: 2-1 Tromso

Jeunesse Esch(1) 1-4 (1)...... Ventspils
Agg: 5-1 Ventspils

Khazar ....(0) 0-8 (6)....... M. Haifa
Agg: 10-0 M. Haifa

Lech Poznan..(2) 2-1 (1).......... Honka
Agg: 5-2 Lech Poznan

Linfield ....(0) 1-2 (1).......... Xanthi
AET Agg: 2-2 Xanthi away goals

Loko. Zagreb.(0) 2-3 (1) Dinamo Minsk
Agg: 4-4. Dinamo Minsk away goals

Milsami Orhei(1) 1-1 (1).....Shakhtyor
AET Agg 2-2. Milsami Orhei 4-2 pens

NK Siroki Brijeg(1) 2-0 (0)............Irtysh
Agg: 4-3 NK Siroki Brijeg

Omonia Nicosia(0)1-2 (1) Astra Giurgiu
Agg: 3-2 Astra Giurgiu

Pandurii ....(3) 4-0 (0)Levadia Tallinn
Agg: 4-0 Pandurii

Piast Gliwice .(2) 2-2 (1).. FK Qarabag
AET Agg: 4-3 FK Qarabag

Prestatyn ......(0) 0-3 (2)........... Rijeka
Agg: 8-0 Rijeka

Pyunik Yerevan(0) 1-1 (0) Zalgiris Vilnius
Agg: 3-1 Zalgiris Vilnius

Rubin............(0) 1-0 (0)...... Jagodina
Agg: 4-2 Rubin

Rudar Pljevlja(0) 2-2 (2) Slask Wroclaw
Agg: 6-2 Slask Wroclaw

Sarajevo ....(0) 0-0 (0)........... Kukesi
Agg: 3-2 Kukesi

Senica...........(0) 0-1 (1) Mladost Pod.
Agg: 3-2 Mladost Pod.

Slovan Liberec.(1) 1-0 (0)..Skonto Riga
Agg: 2-2. Slovan Liberec away goals

St Johnstone .(1) 1-1 (1)....Rosenborg
Agg: 2-1 St Johnstone

Standard Liege(1) 3-1 (0).KR Reykjavik
Agg: 6-2 Standard Liege

Sturm Graz....(0) 0-1 (1).....Breidablik
Agg: 1-0 Breidablik

Turnovo ....(0) 1-1 (0)..Hajduk Split
Agg: 3-2 Hajduk Split

Vikingur (FIs).(0) 0-4 (2)Petrolul Ploiesti
Agg: 7-0 Petrolul Ploiesti

Zilina ....(1) 2-0 (0)..O. Ljubljana
Agg: 3-3. Zilina away goals

Third qualifying round

Thursday August 1 2013

Aktobe..........(0) 1-0 (0).....Breidablik

Asteras T. ......(1) 1-1 (1) Rapid Vienna

Botev Plovdiv(0) 1-1 (0).......Stuttgart

Ch. Odessa ...(2) 3-1 (1) Crvena Zvezda

Dinamo Minsk.(0) 0-1 (1) . Trabzonspor

Dukla Trencin(0) 1-3 (1) Astra Giurgiu

Estoril ....(0) 0-0 (0)Hap Ramat Gan

FC Minsk.......(0) 0-1 (0).St Johnstone

FK Qarabag...(0) 1-0 (0)........... Gefle

Hacken ....(0) 1-2 (1)............ Thun

Hajduk Split ..(0) 0-1 (1).............. Dila

Jablonec ....(1) 2-1 (1)Stromsgodset

Kukesi...........(1) 2-0 (0)..Metalurg D.

Motherwell...(0) 0-2 (0)....... Kuban K

NK Siroki Brijeg(0) 1-3 (3)........Udinese

Pandurii ....(1) 1-1 (1)....H Tel Aviv

Petrolul Ploiesti(0) 1-1 (0)..Vitesse Arn.

Randers Freja(0) 1-2 (2)........... Rubin

Rijeka ....(1) 2-1 (0)............Zilina

Seville...........(1) 3-0 (0) Mladost Pod.

Slask Wroclaw (0) 1-0 (0).....FC Bruges

Slovan Liberec.(0) 2-1 (1)...... FC Zurich

St-Etienne .....(2) 3-0 (0)Milsami Orhei

Swansea ....(1) 4-0 (0) .... Malmo

Tromso..........(0) 1-0 (0).. Differdange

Ventspils ....(0) 0-0 (0) .... M. Haifa

Vojvodina NS(0) 2-2 (1).....Bursaspor

Xanthi...........(1) 1-2 (1)Standard Liege

Zalgiris Vilnius (1) 1-0 (0). Lech Poznan

Second legs

Thursday August 8 2013

Astra Giurgiu (0) 2-2 (0)Dukla Trencin
Agg: 5-3 Astra Giurgiu

Breidablik .....(1) 1-0 (0)......... Aktobe
AET Agg: 1-1. Aktobe 2-1 pens

Bursaspor .....(0) 0-3 (2) Vojvodina NS
Agg: 5-2 Vojvodina NS

Crvena Zvezda (0) 0-0 (0)...Ch. Odessa
Agg: 3-1 Ch. Odessa

Differdange...(0) 1-0 (0)......... Tromso
AET Agg: 1-1. Tromso 4-3 pens

Dila...............(0) 1-0 (0)..Hajduk Split
Agg: 2-0 Dila

FC Bruges .....(0) 3-3 (1) Slask Wroclaw
Agg: 4-3 Slask Wroclaw

FC Zurich ......(1) 1-2 (0) Slovan Liberec
Agg: 4-2 Slovan Liberec

Gefle.............(0) 0-2 (1).. FK Qarabag
Agg: 3-0 FK Qarabag

H Tel Aviv .....(1) 1-2 (1)........Pandurii
     Agg: 3-2 Pandurii
Hap Ramat Gan(0)0-1 (1)...........Estoril
     Agg: 1-0 Estoril
Kuban K........(0) 1-0 (0).. Motherwell
     Agg: 3-0 Kuban K
Lech Poznan..(0) 2-1 (1) Zagiris Vilnius
     Agg: 2-2. Zagiris Vilnius away goals
M. Haifa ....(2) 3-0 (0) ...... Ventspils
     Agg: 3-0 M. Haifa
Malmo..........(0) 0-0 (0) ...... Swansea
     Agg: 4-0 Swansea
Metalurg D. ..(1) 1-0 (0) .... Kukesi
     Agg: 2-1 Kukesi
Milsami Orhei(0) 0-3 (2) .....St-Etienne
     Agg: 6-0 St-Etienne
Mladost Pod. (0) 1-6 (5) .... Seville
     Agg: 9-1 Seville
Rapid Vienna (1) 3-1 (0) ......Asteras T.
     Agg: 4-2 Rapid Vienna
Rubin............(1) 2-0 (0)Randers Freja
     Agg: 4-1 Rubin
St Johnstone .(0) 0-1 (0) ...... FC Minsk
     AET Agg: 1-1. FC Minsk 3-2 pens
Standard Liege(0) 2-1 (0) .... Xanthi
     Agg: 4-2 Standard Liege
Stromsgodset(0) 1-3 (1) ....Jablonec
     Agg: 5-2 Jablonec
Stuttgart ....(0) 0-0 (0)Botev Plovdiv
     Agg: 1-1. Stuttgart away goals
Thun.............(0) 1-0 (0).........Hacken
     Agg: 3-1 Thun
Trabzonspor..(0) 0-0 (0) Dinamo Minsk
     Agg: 1-0 Trabzonspor
Udinese ....(1) 4-0 (0)NK Siroki Brijeg
     Agg: 7-1 Udinese
Vitesse Arn. ..(0) 1-2 (1)Petrolul Ploiesti
     Agg: 3-2 Petrolul Pluiesti
Zilina ....(0) 1-1 (0) .... Rijeka
     Agg: 3-2 Rijeka

Playoffs

Thursday August 22 2013

Aktobe..........(1) 2-3 (1) Dynamo Kiev
Ap Limassol ..(0) 2-0 (0) .... Nice
Atromitos .....(0) 1-3 (0) .. AZ Alkmaar
Ch. Odessa ...(0) 1-0 (0).. Skenderbeu
Dinamo Tbilisi.(0) 0-5 (2) ....Tottenham
Elfsborg ....(0) 1-1 (1)Nordsjaelland
Esbjerg ....(1) 4-3 (2) .....St-Etienne
Estoril ....(2) 2-0 (0) ....Pasching
FC Minsk.......(0) 0-2 (0)Standard Liege
FK Qarabag....(0) 0-2 (1) ....E Frankfurt
Grasshoppers(0) 1-2 (1) ......Fiorentina
Hafnarfjordur(0) 0-2 (1) .... Genk
Jablonec ....(1) 1-2 (1) ..... Real Betis
Kuban K........(0) 1-0 (0)..... Feyenoord
Kukesi...........(0) 0-2 (1) . Trabzonspor
M. Haifa ....(1) 2-0 (0) Astra Giurgiu
Molde............(0) 0-2 (0) .... Rubin
Nomme Kalju(0) 1-3 (2) ....Dnipro
Pandurii ....(0) 0-1 (0) .... Braga
Partizan ....(1) 1-0 (0) .... Thun
RB Salzburg ..(3) 5-0 (0) Zalgiris Vilnius
Rapid Vienna (1) 1-0 (0) .... Dila
Rijeka ....(0) 2-1 (0) ....Stuttgart
Seville...........(1) 4-1 (1) Slask Wroclaw
St Gallen ....(0) 1-1 (1)Spartak Moscow

Swansea ....(3) 5-1 (0)Petrolul Ploiesti
Tromso..........(0) 2-1 (1) ....Besiktas
Udinese ....(1) 1-3 (1) Slovan Liberec
Vojvodina NS (0) 1-1 (1) ......FC Sheriff
Waregem......(1) 1-1 (0)Apoel Nicosia

Second legs

Thursday August 29 2013

Apoel Nicosia(0) 1-2 (1) ..... Waregem
     Agg: 3-2 Waregem
Astra Giurgiu (1) 1-1 (1) ....M. Haifa
     Agg: 3-1 M. Haifa
Besiktas ....(0) 2-0 (0) .... Tromso
     Agg: 3-2 Besiktas
Braga............(0) 0-2 (1) ....Pandurii
     AET Agg: 2-1 Panduri
Dila...............(0) 0-3 (1) Rapid Vienna
     Agg: 4-0 Rapid Vienna
Dnipro ....(1) 2-0 (0)Nomme Kalju
     Agg: 5-1 Dninpro
Dynamo Kiev (3) 5-1 (1) .... Aktobe
     Agg: 8-3 Dynamo Kiev
E Frankfurt....(1) 2-1 (0).. FK Qarabag
     Agg: 4-1 E Frankfurt
FC Sheriff......(0) 2-1 (0)Vojvodina NS
     Agg: 3-2 FC Sheriff
Feyenoord ....(1) 1-2 (1) .... Kuban K
     Agg: 3-1 Kuban K
Fiorentina .....(0) 0-1 (1)Grasshoppers
     Agg: 2-2. Fiorentina away goals
Genk.............(1) 5-2 (1)Hafnarfjordur
     Agg: 7-2 Genk
Nice..............(1) 1-0 (0)..Ap Limassol
     Agg: 2-1 Ap Limassol
Nordsjaelland(0) 0-1 (0) ....Elfsborg
     Agg: 2-1 Elfsborg
Pasching ....(0) 1-2 (1) ....Estoril
     Agg: 4-1 Estoril
Petrolul Ploiesti(0) 2-1 (0) ...... Swansea
     Agg: 6-3 Swansea

Real Betis......(2) 6-0 (0) ....Jablonec
     Agg: 8-1 Real Betis
Rubin............(1) 3-0 (0) .... Molde
     Agg: 5-0 Rubin
Skenderbeu ..(1) 1-0 (0)...Ch. Odessa
     AET Agg: 1-1. Ch. Odessa 7-6 pens
Slask Wroclaw (0) 0-5 (2) .... Seville
     Agg: 9-1 Seville
Slovan Liberec.(1) 1-1 (1) ....Udinese
     Agg: 4-2 Slovan Liberec
Spartak Moscow(1)2-4(3) ...... St Gallen
     Agg: 5-3 St Gallen
St-Etienne .....(0) 0-1 (0) ....Esbjerg
     Agg: 5-3 Esbjerg
Standard Liege(3) 3-1 (1)......FC Minsk
     Agg: 5-1 Standard Liege
Stuttgart ....(1) 2-2 (1) ....Rijeka
     Agg: 4-3 Rijeka
Thun.............(1) 3-0 (0) ....Partizan
     Agg: 3-1 Thun
Tottenham ....(2) 3-0 (0) Dinamo Tbilisi
     Agg: 8-0 Tottenham
Trabzonspor..(1) 3-1 (1) .... Kukesi
     Agg: 5-1 Trabzonspor
Zalgiris Vilnius (0) 0-2 (0)..RB Salzburg
     Agg: 7-0 RB Salzburg

Friday August 30 2013

AZ Alkmaar...(0) 0-2 (0) .....Atromitos
     Agg: 3-3. AZ Alkmaar away goals

Group A

	P	W	D	L	F	A	D	Pts
Valencia	6	4	1	1	12	7	5	13
Swansea	6	2	2	2	6	4	2	8
Kuban K	6	1	3	2	7	7	0	6
St Gallen	6	2	0	4	6	13	-7	6

Thursday September 19 2013

St Gallen.......(0) 2-0 (0) .... Kuban K
Valencia........(0) 0-3 (1) ...... Swansea

Wilfried Bony fires first in Swansea's 3-0 win over Valencia

Thursday October 3 2013
Kuban K........(0) 0-2 (0)....... Valencia
Swansea.......(0) 1-0 (0)...... St Gallen

Thursday October 24 2013
Swansea.......(0) 1-1 (0)....... Kuban K
Valencia........(4) 5-1 (0)...... St Gallen

Thursday November 7 2013
Kuban K........(0) 1-1 (1)...... Swansea
St Gallen.......(1) 2-3 (1)....... Valencia

Thursday November 28 2013
Kuban K........(1) 4-0 (0)...... St Gallen
Swansea.......(0) 0-1 (1)....... Valencia

Thursday December 12 2013
St Gallen.......(0) 1-0 (0)...... Swansea
Valencia........(0) 1-1 (0)...... Kuban K

Group B

	P	W	D	L	F	A	D	Pts
Ludogorets	6	5	1	0	11	2	9	16
Ch. Odessa	6	3	1	2	6	6	0	10
PSV Eindhoven	6	2	1	3	4	5	-1	7
Dyn. Zagreb	6	0	1	5	3	11	-8	1

Thursday September 19 2013
Dyn. Zagreb..(1) 1-2 (0)...Ch. Odessa
PSV Eindhoven(0) 0-2 (0)...Ludogorets

Thursday October 3 2013
Ch. Odessa ...(0) 0-2 (1)PSV Eindhoven
Ludogorets ...(2) 3-0 (0). Dyn. Zagreb

Thursday October 24 2013
Ch. Odessa ...(0) 0-1 (1)...Ludogorets
Dyn. Zagreb..(0) 0-0 (0)PSV Eindhoven

Thursday November 7 2013
Ludogorets ...(0) 1-1 (0)...Ch. Odessa
PSV Eindhoven(1) 2-0 (0). Dyn. Zagreb

Thursday November 28 2013
Ch. Odessa ...(0) 2-1 (1). Dyn. Zagreb
Ludogorets ...(1) 2-0 (0)PSV Eindhoven

Thursday December 12 2013
Dyn. Zagreb..(1) 1-2 (1)...Ludogorets
PSV Eindhoven(0) 0-1 (0)...Ch. Odessa

Group C

	P	W	D	L	F	A	D	Pts
RB Salzburg	6	6	0	0	15	3	12	18
Esbjerg	6	4	0	2	8	8	0	12
Elfsborg	6	1	1	4	5	10	-5	4
Standard Liege	6	0	1	5	6	13	-7	1

Thursday September 19 2013
RB Salzburg ..(2) 4-0 (0)........Elfsborg
Standard Liege(0) 1-2 (0).........Esbjerg

Thursday October 3 2013
Elfsborg ....(1) 1-1 (0)Standard Liege
Esbjerg ....(0) 1-2 (2)..RB Salzburg

Thursday October 24 2013
Elfsborg ....(0) 1-2 (1).........Esbjerg
RB Salzburg ..(0) 2-1 (0)Standard Liege

Thursday November 7 2013
Esbjerg ....(0) 1-0 (0)........Elfsborg
Standard Liege(0) 1-3 (2)..RB Salzburg

Thursday November 28 2013
Elfsborg ....(0) 0-1 (1)..RB Salzburg
Esbjerg ....(1) 2-1 (0)Standard Liege

Thursday December 12 2013
RB Salzburg ..(1) 3-0 (0).........Esbjerg
Standard Liege(1) 1-3 (1)........Elfsborg

Group D

	P	W	D	L	F	A	D	Pts
Rubin	6	4	2	0	14	4	10	14
NK Maribor	6	2	1	3	9	12	-3	7
Waregem	6	2	1	3	4	10	-6	7
Wigan	6	1	2	3	6	7	-1	5

Thursday September 19 2013
NK Maribor...(1) 2-5 (2)........... Rubin
Waregem......(0) 0-0 (0).......... Wigan

Thursday October 3 2013
Rubin............(0) 4-0 (0)..... Waregem
Wigan...........(2) 3-1 (0).. NK Maribor

Thursday October 24 2013
Waregem......(1) 1-3 (2).. NK Maribor
Wigan...........(1) 1-1 (1)......... Rubin

Thursday November 7 2013
Rubin............(1) 1-0 (0).......... Wigan
NK Maribor...(0) 0-1 (1)..... Waregem

Thursday November 28 2013
Rubin............(1) 1-1 (0).. NK Maribor
Wigan...........(1) 1-2 (1)..... Waregem

Thursday December 12 2013
NK Maribor...(1) 2-1 (1).......... Wigan
Waregem......(0) 0-2 (0).......... Rubin

Group E

	P	W	D	L	F	A	D	Pts
Fiorentina	6	5	1	0	12	3	9	16
Dnipro	6	4	0	2	11	5	6	12
Pacos Ferreira	6	0	3	3	1	8	-7	3
Pandurii	6	0	2	4	3	11	-8	2

Thursday September 19 2013
Fiorentina .....(1) 3-0 (0)Pacos Ferreira
Pandurii ....(0) 0-1 (1)..........Dnipro

Thursday October 3 2013
Dnipro ....(0) 1-2 (0).....Fiorentina
Pacos Ferreira(0) 1-1 (1)........Pandurii

Thursday October 24 2013
Fiorentina .....(2) 3-0 (0)........Pandurii
Pacos Ferreira(0) 0-2 (0)..........Dnipro

Thursday November 7 2013
Pandurii ....(1) 1-2 (0).....Fiorentina
Dnipro ....(1) 2-0 (0)Pacos Ferreira

Thursday November 28 2013
Dnipro ....(1) 4-1 (0).......Pandurii
Pacos Ferreira(0) 0-0 (0).....Fiorentina

Thursday December 12 2013
Fiorentina .....(1) 2-1 (1)..........Dnipro
Pandurii ....(0) 0-0 (0)Pacos Ferreira

Group F

	P	W	D	L	F	A	D	Pts
E Frankfurt	6	5	0	1	13	4	9	15
M. Tel Aviv	6	3	2	1	7	5	2	11
Apoel Nicosia	6	1	2	3	3	8	-5	5
Bordeaux	6	1	0	5	4	10	-6	3

Thursday September 19 2013
E Frankfurt....(2) 3-0 (0)......Bordeaux
M. Tel Aviv....(0) 0-0 (0)Apoel Nicosia

Thursday October 3 2013
Apoel Nicosia(0) 0-3 (1)....E Frankfurt
Bordeaux ......(0) 1-2 (0)... M. Tel Aviv

Thursday October 24 2013
Bordeaux ......(1) 2-1 (1)Apoel Nicosia
E Frankfurt....(1) 2-0 (0)... M. Tel Aviv

Thursday November 7 2013
Apoel Nicosia(1) 2-1 (1)......Bordeaux
M. Tel Aviv....(3) 4-2 (0)....E Frankfurt

Thursday November 28 2013
Apoel Nicosia(0) 0-0 (0)... M. Tel Aviv
Bordeaux ......(0) 0-1 (0)....E Frankfurt

Thursday December 12 2013
E Frankfurt....(0) 2-0 (0)Apoel Nicosia
M. Tel Aviv....(0) 1-0 (0)......Bordeaux

Salzburg's Jonatan Soriano scored eight Europa League goals

Group G

	P	W	D	L	F	A	D	Pts
Genk	6	4	2	0	10	5	5	14
Dynamo Kiev	6	3	1	2	11	7	4	10
Rapid Vienna	6	1	3	2	8	10	-2	6
Thun	6	1	0	5	3	10	-7	3

Thursday September 19 2013
Dynamo Kiev (0) 0-1 (0) .... Genk
Thun ....(1) 1-0 (0) Rapid Vienna

Thursday October 3 2013
Rapid Vienna (0) 2-2 (2) Dynamo Kiev
Genk.............(0) 2-1 (0) .... Thun

Thursday October 24 2013
Dynamo Kiev (1) 3-0 (0) .... Thun
Genk.............(1) 1-1 (0) Rapid Vienna

Thursday November 7 2013
Rapid Vienna (2) 2-2 (1) .... Genk
Thun ....(0) 0-2 (1) Dynamo Kiev

Thursday November 28 2013
Genk.............(3) 3-1 (1) Dynamo Kiev
Rapid Vienna (1) 2-1 (0) .... Thun

Thursday December 12 2013
Dynamo Kiev (2) 3-1 (1) Rapid Vienna
Thun ....(0) 0-1 (0) .... Genk

Group H

	P	W	D	L	F	A	D	Pts
Seville	6	3	3	0	9	4	5	12
Slovan Liberec	6	2	3	1	9	8	1	9
Freiburg	6	1	3	2	5	8	-3	6
Estoril	6	0	3	5	8	13	-3	3

Thursday September 19 2013
Freiburg........(2) 2-2 (0) Slovan Liberec
Estoril ....(0) 1-2 (0) .... Seville

Thursday October 3 2013
Seville...........(0) 2-0 (0) ....Freiburg
Slovan Liberec.(1) 2-1 (1) ....Estoril

Thursday October 24 2013
Freiburg ....(1) 1-1 (0) ....Estoril
Slovan Liberec.(1) 1-1 (0) .... Seville

Thursday November 7 2013
Estoril ....(0) 0-0 (0) ....Freiburg
Seville...........(1) 1-1 (0) Slovan Liberec

Thursday November 28 2013
Seville...........(1) 1-1 (0) ....Estoril
Slovan Liberec.(0) 1-2 (1) ....Freiburg

Thursday December 12 2013
Estoril ....(0) 1-2 (1) Slovan Liberec
Freiburg ....(0) 0-2 (1) .... Seville

Group I

	P	W	D	L	F	A	D	Pts
Lyon	6	3	3	0	6	3	3	12
Real Betis	6	2	3	1	3	2	1	9
V Guimaraes	6	1	2	3	6	5	1	5
Rijeka	6	0	4	2	2	7	-5	4

Thursday September 19 2013
Real Betis......(0) 0-0 (0) ....Lyon
V Guimaraes .(1) 4-0 (0) .... Rijeka

Thursday October 3 2013
Lyon ....(0) 1-1 (1).V Guimaraes
Rijeka ....(1) 1-1 (1)..... Real Betis

Thursday October 24 2013
Lyon ....(0) 1-0 (0) ....Rijeka
Real Betis......(0) 1-0 (0).V Guimaraes

Thursday November 7 2013
Rijeka ....(1) 1-1 (1) ....Lyon
V Guimaraes .(0) 0-1 (0)..... Real Betis

Thursday November 28 2013
Lyon ....(0) 1-0 (0) ..... Real Betis
Rijeka ....(0) 0-0 (0).V Guimaraes

Thursday December 12 2013
Real Betis......(0) 0-0 (0) ....Rijeka
V Guimaraes .(1) 1-2 (0) ....Lyon

Group J

	P	W	D	L	F	A	D	Pts
Trabzonspor	6	4	2	0	13	6	7	14
Lazio	6	3	3	0	8	4	4	12
Ap Limassol	6	1	1	4	5	10	-5	4
Legia Warsaw	6	1	0	5	2	8	-6	3

Thursday September 19 2013
Ap Limassol ..(1) 1-2 (1). Trabzonspor
Lazio.............(0) 1-0 (0).Legia Warsaw

Thursday October 3 2013
Legia Warsaw .(0) 0-1 (0)..Ap Limassol
Trabzonspor..(3) 3-3 (1) .... Lazio

Thursday October 24 2013
Ap Limassol ..(0) 0-0 (0) .... Lazio
Trabzonspor..(1) 2-0 (0).Legia Warsaw

Thursday November 7 2013
Lazio.............(2) 2-1 (1)..Ap Limassol
Legia Warsaw .(0) 0-2 (0). Trabzonspor

Thursday November 28 2013
Legia Warsaw .(0) 0-2 (1) .... Lazio
Trabzonspor..(2) 4-2 (0) .Ap Limassol

Thursday December 12 2013
Ap Limassol ..(0) 0-2 (1).Legia Warsaw
Lazio.............(0) 0-0 (0). Trabzonspor

Group K

	P	W	D	L	F	A	D	Pts
Tottenham	6	6	0	0	15	2	13	18
Anzhi	6	2	2	2	4	7	-3	8
FC Sheriff	6	1	3	2	5	6	-1	6
Tromso	6	0	1	5	1	10	-9	1

Thursday September 19 2013
FC Sheriff ......(0) 0-0 (0)............Anzhi
Tottenham ....(2) 3-0 (0) .... Tromso

Thursday October 3 2013
Anzhi.............(0) 0-2 (2) ....Tottenham
Tromso..........(0) 1-1 (0)....FC Sheriff

Thursday October 24 2013
Anzhi.............(1) 1-0 (0).......... Tromso
FC Sheriff ......(0) 0-2 (1)....Tottenham

Thursday November 7 2013
Tottenham ....(0) 2-1 (0)......FC Sheriff
Tromso..........(0) 0-1 (0)............Anzhi

Thursday November 28 2013
Anzhi............(0) 1-1 (0)....FC Sheriff
Tromso..........(0) 0-2 (0)....Tottenham

Thursday December 12 2013
FC Sheriff ......(2) 2-0 (0) .... Tromso
Tottenham ...(2) 4-1 (1)............Anzhi

Group L

	P	W	D	L	F	A	D	Pts
AZ Alkmaar	6	3	3	0	8	4	4	12
PAOK Salonika	6	3	3	0	10	6	4	12
M. Haifa	6	1	2	3	6	9	-3	5
S Karagandy	6	0	2	4	5	10	-5	2

Thursday September 19 2013
M. Haifa ....(0) 0-1 (0).. AZ Alkmaar
PAOK Salonika (0) 2-1 (0).S Karagandy

Thursday October 3 2013
AZ Alkmaar...(0) 1-1 (0) PAOK Salonika
S Karagandy .(2) 2-2 (2) ....M. Haifa

Thursday October 24 2013
PAOK Salonika (2) 3-2 (2).......M. Haifa
S Karagandy .(1) 1-1 (1).. AZ Alkmaar

Thursday November 7 2013
AZ Alkmaar...(0) 1-0 (0).S Karagandy
M. Haifa ....(0) 0-0 (0) PAOK Salonika

Thursday November 28 2013
AZ Alkmaar...(1) 2-0 (0).......M. Haifa
S Karagandy .(0) 0-2 (0) PAOK Salonika

Thursday December 12 2013
M. Haifa ....(0) 2-1 (1).S Karagandy
PAOK Salonika (1) 2-2 (1).. AZ Alkmaar

Last 32

Thursday February 20 2014
Ajax..............(0) 0-3 (3)..RB Salzburg
Anzhi.............(0) 0-0 (0) .... Genk
Ch. Odessa ...(0) 0-0 (0) .... Lyon
Dnipro...........(0) 1-0 (0)....Tottenham
Dynamo Kiev (0) 0-2 (0) .... Valencia
Esbjerg ....(1) 1-3 (3) .....Fiorentina
Juventus ....(1) 2-0 (0). Trabzonspor
Lazio.............(0) 0-1 (1) ...Ludogorets
M. Tel Aviv....(0) 0-0 (0) .... Basle
NK Maribor...(1) 2-2 (0) .... Seville
PAOK Salonika (0) 0-1 (0) .... Benfica
Porto.............(1) 2-2 (0)....E Frankfurt
Real Betis......(1) 1-1 (0) .... Rubin
Slovan Liberec.(0) 0-1 (0).. AZ Alkmaar
Swansea.......(0) 0-0 (0) .... Napoli
Viktoria Plzen.(1) 1-1 (0).......Shakhtar

Second legs

Thursday February 27 2014
AZ Alkmaar...(1) 1-1 (0) Slovan Liberec
Agg: 2-1 AZ Alkmaar
Basle ....(1) 3-0 (0).. M. Tel Aviv
Agg: 3-0 Basle
Benfica ....(0) 3-0 (0) PAOK Salonika
Agg: 4-0 Benfica
E Frankfurt....(1) 3-3 (0) .... Porto
Agg: 5-5. Porto away goals
Fiorentina .....(0) 1-1 (0) .... Esbjerg
Agg: 4-2 Fiorentina

Seville keeper Beto in action during the penalty shootout that decided the Europa League final

Genk.............(0) 0-2 (0)............Anzhi
Agg: 2-0 Anzhi
Ludogorets ...(0) 3-3 (1)............ Lazio
Agg: 4-3 Ludogorets
Lyon ....(0) 1-0 (0)...Ch. Odessa
Agg: 1-0 Lyon
Napoli ....(1) 3-1 (1)...... Swansea
Agg: 3-1 Napoli
RB Salzburg ..(0) 3-1 (0)..............Ajax
Agg: 6-1 RB Salzburg
Rubin.............(0) 0-2 (1)..... Real Betis
Agg: 3-1 Real Betis
Seville...........(1) 2-1 (0).. NK Maribor
Agg: 4-3 Seville
Shakhtar ....(0) 1-2 (2)Viktoria Plzen
Agg: 3-2 Viktoria Plzen
Tottenham ....(0) 3-1 (0)..........Dnipro
Agg: 3-2 Tottenham
Trabzonspor..(0) 0-2 (2).......Juventus
Agg: 4-0 Juventus
Valencia........(0) 0-0 (0) Dynamo Kiev
Agg: 2-0 Valencia

Last 16
Thursday March 13 2014
AZ Alkmaar...(1) 1-0 (0)............Anzhi
Basle ....(0) 0-0 (0)..RB Salzburg
Juventus ....(1) 1-1 (0).....Fiorentina
Ludogorets ...(0) 0-3 (2)....... Valencia

Lyon ....(1) 4-1 (1)Viktoria Plzen
Porto.............(0) 1-0 (0).......... Napoli
Seville...........(0) 0-2 (1)..... Real Betis
Tottenham ....(0) 1-3 (1).........Benfica
Second legs
Thursday March 20 2014
Anzhi............(0) 0-0 (0).. AZ Alkmaar
Agg: 1-0 AZ Alkmaar
Benfica ....(1) 2-2 (0)....Tottenham
Agg: 5-3 Benfica
Fiorentina .....(0) 0-1 (0).......Juventus
Agg: 2-1 Juventus
Napoli ....(1) 2-2 (0)............ Porto
Agg: 3-2 Porto
RB Salzburg ..(1) 1-2 (0)............ Basle
Agg: 2-1 Basle
Real Betis......(0) 0-2 (1).......... Seville
AET Agg: 2-2. Seville 4-3 pens
Valencia........(0) 1-0 (0)...Ludogorets
Agg: 4-0 Valencia
Viktoria Plzen(0) 2-1 (1)..............Lyon
Agg: 5-3 Lyon

Quarter-finals
Thursday April 3 2014
AZ Alkmaar...(0) 0-1 (0).......Benfica
Basle ....(2) 3-0 (0)....... Valencia
Lyon ....(0) 0-1 (0).......Juventus

Porto.............(1) 1-0 (0)......... Seville
Second legs
Thursday April 10 2014
Benfica ....(1) 2-0 (0).. AZ Alkmaar
Agg: 3-0 Benfica
Juventus ....(1) 2-1 (1).............Lyon
Agg: 3-1 Juventus
Seville...........(3) 4-1 (0)............ Porto
Agg: 4-2 Seville
Valencia........(2) 5-0 (0)............ Basle
AET Agg: 5-3 Valencia

Semi-finals
Thursday April 24 2014
Seville...........(2) 2-0 (0)....... Valencia
Benfica ....(1) 2-1 (0).......Juventus
Second legs
Thursday 1 May 2014
Valencia........(2) 3-1 (0).......... Seville
Agg: 3-3. Seville away goals
Juventus ....(0) 0-0 (0).........Benfica
Agg: 2-1 Benfica

Final
Thursday April 24 2014
Seville...........(0) 0-0 (0).........Benfica
AET: Seville 4-2 pens

CHAMPIONS LEAGUE

First qualifying round

Tuesday July 2 2013
FC Lusitans ...(2) 2-2 (0)..EB Streymur
Shirak Gumri.(1) 3-0 (0).....Tre Penne

Second legs

Tuesday July 9 2013
EB Streymur..(2) 5-1 (0)...FC Lusitans
    Agg: 7-3 EB Streymur
Tre Penne......(1) 1-0 (0) Shirak Gumri
    Agg: 3-1 Shirak

Second qualifying round

Tuesday July 16 2013
BATE Borisov (0) 0-1 (0).S Karagandy
Birkirkara ......(0) 0-0 (0).. NK Maribor
Dinamo Tbilisi.(2) 6-1 (1)..EB Streymur
Ekranas.........(0) 0-1 (1)Hafnarfjordur
FC Sheriff......(1) 1-1 (0)....... Sutjeska
Fola Esch ......(0) 0-5 (0). Dyn. Zagreb
Steaua ....(3) 3-0 (0)Vardar Skopje
Viktoria Plzen(0) 4-3 (0)....Zeljeznicar

Wednesday July 17 2013
Cliftonville ....(0) 0-3 (2)............Celtic
Elfsborg ....(1) 7-1 (0)..FC Daugava
Gyori ETO .....(0) 0-2 (0)... M. Tel Aviv
HJK Helsinki..(0) 0-0 (0)Nomme Kalju
Neftchi Baku.(0) 0-0 (0).. Skenderbeu
S. Bratislava..(0) 2-1 (0)... Ludogorets
Shirak Gumri.(0) 1-1 (0)........Partizan
Sligo Rovers..(0) 0-1 (1).......... Molde
The New Saints(1) 1-3 (0).Legia Warsaw

Second legs

Tuesday July 23 2013
Celtic ....(1) 2-0 (0)....Cliftonville
    Agg: 5-0 Celtic
Dyn. Zagreb..(0) 1-0 (0)......Fola Esch
    Agg: 6-0 Dyn. Zagreb
EB Streymur..(1) 1-3 (2) Dinamo Tbilisi
    Agg: 9-2 Dinamo Tbilisi
FC Daugava ..(0) 0-4 (1)........Elfsborg
    Agg: 11-1 Elfsborg
Hafnarfjordur(1) 2-1 (1)........ Ekranas
    Agg: 3-1 Hafnarfjordur
M. Tel Aviv....(1) 2-1 (0).....Gyori ETO
    Agg: 4-1 M. Tel Aviv
Molde...........(1) 2-0 (0). Sligo Rovers
    Agg: 3-0 Molde
Nomme Kalju(2) 2-1 (0)..HJK Helsinki
    Agg: 2-1 Nomme Kalkju
S Karagandy .(0) 1-0 (0) BATE Borisov
    Agg: 2-0 S Karagandy
Skenderbeu ..(0) 1-0 (0) Neftchi Baku
    AET 0-0 90 mins. Agg: 1-0 Skenderbeu
Sutjeska........(0) 0-5 (1)......FC Sheriff
    Agg: 6-1 Sheriff
Vardar Skopje(1) 1-2 (1)..........Steaua
    Agg: 5-1 Steaua
Zeljeznicar ....(1) 1-2 (2)Viktoria Plzen
    Agg: 6-4 Viktoria Plzen

Wednesday July 24 2013
Legia Warsaw .(0) 1-0 (0)The New Saints
    Agg: 4-1 Legia Warsaw

Who? The draw for the first and second qualifying rounds

Ludogorets ...(2) 3-0 (0). S. Bratislava
    Agg: 4-2 Ludogorets
NK Maribor...(1) 2-0 (0)......Birkirkara
    Agg: 2-0 NK Maribor
Partizan ....(0) 0-0 (0) Shirak Gumri
    Agg: 1-1. Partizan away goals

Third qualifying round

Tuesday July 30 2013
Aus. Vienna ...(1) 1-0 (0)Hafnarfjordur
Basle ....(1) 1-0 (0)... M. Tel Aviv
Dinamo Tbilisi.(0) 0-2 (0)..........Steaua
Dyn. Zagreb..(0) 1-0 (0)......FC Sheriff
Lyon ....(0) 1-0 (0)Grasshoppers
Nomme Kalju(0) 0-4 (1)Viktoria Plzen
Nordsjaelland(0) 0-1 (0)............Zenit
PAOK Salonika (0) 0-2 (1)........Metalist
PSV Eindhoven(0) 2-0 (0)..... Waregem
S Karagandy .(1) 3-0 (0).. Skenderbeu

Wednesday July 31 2013
Apoel Nicosia(1) 1-1 (0).. NK Maribor
Celtic ....(0) 1-0 (0)........Elfsborg
Ludogorets ...(0) 2-1 (0)........Partizan
Molde...........(1) 1-1 (0).Legia Warsaw
RB Salzburg ..(0) 1-1 (0)...Fenerbahce

Second legs

Tuesday August 6 2013
Fenerbahce...(3) 3-1 (1)..RB Salzburg
    Agg: 4-2 Fenerbahce
Grasshoppers(0) 0-1 (0).............Lyon
    Agg: 2-0 Lyon
M. Tel Aviv....(2) 3-3 (3)............Basle
    Agg: 4-3 Basle
NK Maribor....(0) 0-0 (0)Apoel Nicosia
    Agg: 1-1. NK Maribor away goals
Partizan ....(0) 0-1 (0)... Ludogorets
    Agg: 3-1 Ludogorets
Skenderbeu ..(3) 3-2 (1).S Karagandy
    Agg: 5-3 S Karagandy
Steaua ....(1) 1-1 (0) Dinamo Tbilisi
    Agg: 3-1 Steaua

Wednesday August 7 2013
Elfsborg ....(0) 0-0 (0)............Celtic
    Agg: 1-0 Celtic
FC Sheriff ......(0) 0-3 (2). Dyn. Zagreb
    Agg: 4-0 Dyn. Zagreb
Hafnarfjordur(0) 0-0 (0)..Aus. Vienna
    Agg: 1-0 Aus. Vienna
Legia Warsaw .(0) 0-0 (0).......... Molde
    Agg: 1-1. Legia away goals

Efe Ambrose heads home for Celtic against Belfast's Cliftonville

KNOW YOUR OPPONENT

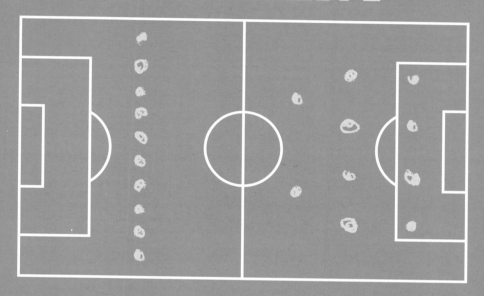

KNOW THE SCORE

BET SMARTER THIS SEASON USING OUR UP-TO-DATE AND EASY-TO-USE
DATABASE OF STATS FOR EVERY TEAM, PLAYER, GROUND AND REFEREE

SOCCERBASE.COM

BET SMARTER THIS SEASON

RESULTS | FIXTURES | STATS | TIPS | NEWS | BETTING

Metalist ....(0) 1-1 (0) PAOK Salonika
Agg: 3-1 Metalist
Viktoria Plzen(2) 6-2 (1)Nomme Kalju
Agg: 10-2 Viktoria Plzen
Waregem......(0) 0-3 (0)PSV Eindhoven
Agg: 5-0 PSV Eindhoven
Zenit............(1) 5-0 (0)Nordsjaelland
Agg: 6-0 Zenit

Playoffs

Tuesday August 20 2013
Lyon ....(0) 0-2 (1)..... Sociedad
PSV Eindhoven(0) 1-1 (1)........... Milan
Pacos Ferreira(0) 1-4 (1).............Zenit
S Karagandy .(1) 2-0 (0)............Celtic
Viktoria Plzen(1) 3-1 (0).. NK Maribor

Wednesday August 21 2013
Dyn. Zagreb..(0) 0-2 (0)..Aus. Vienna
Fenerbahce...(0) 0-3 (0).........Arsenal
Ludogorets ...(1) 2-4 (1)........... Basle
Schalke ....(1) 1-1 (0) PAOK Salonika
Steaua ....(1) 1-1 (0).Legia Warsaw

Second legs

Tuesday August 27 2013
Arsenal ....(1) 2-0 (0)...Fenerbahce
Agg: 5-0 Arsenal
Aus. Vienna ..(1) 2-3 (2). Dyn. Zagreb
Agg: 4-3 Aus. Vienna
Basle ....(1) 2-0 (0)... Ludogorets
Agg: 6-2 Basle
Legia Warsaw .(1) 2-2 (2)..........Steaua
Agg: 3-3. Steaua away goals
PAOK Salonika (0) 2-3 (1).........Schalke
Agg: 4-3 Schalke

Wednesday August 28 2013
Celtic ....(1) 3-0 (0).S Karagandy
Agg: 3-2 Celtic
Milan............(1) 3-0 (0)PSV Eindhoven
Agg: 4-1 Milan
NK Maribor...(0) 0-1 (1)Viktoria Plzen
Agg: 4-1 Viktoria Plzen
Sociedad.......(0) 2-0 (0)............. Lyon
Agg: 4-0 Sociedad
Zenit............(1) 4-2 (0)Pacos Ferreira
Agg: 8-3 Zenit

Clockwise from left: there's no stopping Toni Kroos's free kick against Arsenal, Vladimir Weiss grabs a beauty against PSG, Diego scored one of the goals of the season in the away leg of Atletico's quarter-final against Barcelona, Hulk celebrates a screamer for Zenit against 2013 finalists Dortmund, PSG's Javier Pastore jinks his way onto the scoresheet against Chelsea

Group A

	P	W	D	L	F	A	D	Pts
Man Utd	6	4	2	0	12	3	9	14
B Leverkusen	6	3	1	2	9	10	-1	10
Shakhtar	6	2	2	2	7	6	1	8
Sociedad	6	0	1	5	1	10	-9	1

Tuesday September 17 2013
Man Utd ....(1) 4-2 (0) B Leverkusen
Sociedad.......(0) 0-2 (0).......Shakhtar

Wednesday October 2 2013
B Leverkusen (1) 2-1 (0)...... Sociedad
Shakhtar ....(0) 1-1 (1).......Man Utd

Wednesday October 23 2013
B Leverkusen (1) 4-0 (0).......Shakhtar
Man Utd ....(1) 1-0 (0)...... Sociedad

Tuesday November 5 2013
Shakhtar ....(0) 0-0 (0) B Leverkusen
Sociedad.......(0) 0-0 (0).......Man Utd

Wednesday November 27 2013
B Leverkusen (0) 0-5 (2).......Man Utd
Shakhtar.......(1) 4-0 (0)...... Sociedad

Tuesday December 10 2013
Man Utd ....(0) 1-0 (0).......Shakhtar
Sociedad.......(0) 0-1 (0) B Leverkusen

Group B

	P	W	D	L	F	A	D	Pts
Real Madrid	6	5	1	0	20	5	15	16
Galatasaray	6	2	1	3	8	14	-6	7
Juventus	6	1	3	2	9	9	0	6
FC Copenhagen	6	1	1	4	4	13	-9	4

Tuesday September 17 2013
Galatasaray ..(0) 1-6 (1). Real Madrid
FC Copenhagen(1)1-1 (0).......Juventus

Wednesday October 2 2013
Juventus ....(0) 2-2 (1)...Galatasaray
Real Madrid..(1) 4-0 (0)FC Copenhagen

Wednesday October 23 2013
Real Madrid..(2) 2-1 (1).......Juventus
Galatasaray ..(3) 3-1 (0)FC Copenhagen

Tuesday November 5 2013
FC Copenhagen(1)1-0 (0).. Galatasaray
Juventus ....(1) 2-2 (0). Real Madrid

Wednesday November 27 2013
Juventus ....(1) 3-1 (0)FC Copenhagen
Real Madrid..(1) 4-1 (1).. Galatasaray

Tuesday December 10 2013
FC Copenhagen(0)0-2 (1). Real Madrid

Wednesday December 11 2013
Galatasaray ..(0) 1-0 (0).......Juventus

Group C

	P	W	D	L	F	A	D	Pts
Paris St-G.	6	4	1	1	16	5	11	13
Olympiakos	6	3	1	2	10	8	2	10
Benfica	6	3	1	2	8	8	0	10
Anderlecht	6	0	1	5	4	17	-13	1

Tuesday September 17 2013
Benfica ....(2) 2-0 (0)....Anderlecht
Olympiakos...(1) 1-4 (1).... Paris St-G.

Wednesday October 2 2013
Anderlecht ....(0) 0-3 (1).. Olympiakos
Paris St-G......(3) 3-0 (0).........Benfica

Wednesday October 23 2013
Anderlecht ....(0) 0-5 (3).... Paris St-G.
Benfica ....(0) 1-1 (1).. Olympiakos

Tuesday November 5 2013
Olympiakos...(1) 1-0 (0).........Benfica
Paris St-G......(0) 1-1 (0)....Anderlecht

Wednesday November 27 2013
Anderlecht....(1) 2-3 (1).........Benfica
Paris St-G......(1) 2-1 (0).. Olympiakos

Tuesday December 10 2013
Benfica ....(1) 2-1 (1).... Paris St-G.
Olympiakos...(1) 3-1 (1)....Anderlecht

Group D

	P	W	D	L	F	A	D	Pts
B Munich	6	5	0	1	17	5	12	15
Man City	6	5	0	1	18	10	8	15
Viktoria Plzen	6	1	0	5	6	17	-11	3
CSKA Mosc.	6	1	0	5	8	17	-9	3

Tuesday September 17 2013
B Munich ......(2) 3-0 (0)..CSKA Mosc.
Viktoria Plzen(0) 0-3 (0)...... Man City

Wednesday October 2 2013
CSKA Mosc...(2) 3-2 (1)Viktoria Plzen
Man City.......(0) 1-3 (1)......B Munich

Wednesday October 23 2013
CSKA Mosc...(1) 1-2 (2)...... Man City
B Munich ......(2) 5-0 (0)Viktoria Plzen

Tuesday November 5 2013
Man City.......(3) 5-2 (1)..CSKA Mosc.
Viktoria Plzen(0) 0-1 (0)......B Munich

Wednesday November 27 2013
CSKA Mosc. ..(0) 1-3 (1)......B Munich
Man City.......(1) 4-2 (1)Viktoria Plzen

Tuesday December 10 2013
B Munich ......(2) 2-3 (1)...... Man City
Viktoria Plzen(0) 2-1 (0)..CSKA Mosc.

Group E

	P	W	D	L	F	A	D	Pts
Chelsea	6	4	0	2	12	3	9	12
Schalke	6	3	1	2	6	6	0	10
Basle	6	2	2	2	5	6	-1	8
Steaua	6	0	3	3	2	10	-8	3

Wednesday September 18 2013
Chelsea.........(1) 1-2 (0)............Basle
Schalke ....(0) 3-0 (0)..........Steaua

Tuesday October 1 2013
Basle ....(0) 0-1 (0).........Schalke
Steaua ....(0) 0-4 (2)........ Chelsea

Tuesday October 22 2013
Schalke ....(0) 0-3 (1).......... Chelsea
Steaua ....(0) 1-1 (0)............Basle

Wednesday November 6 2013
Basle ....(0) 1-1 (1)..........Steaua
Chelsea.........(1) 3-0 (0).........Schalke

Tuesday November 26 2013
Basle ....(0) 1-0 (0)........ Chelsea
Steaua ....(0) 0-0 (0).........Schalke

Wednesday December 11 2013
Chelsea.........(1) 1-0 (0)..........Steaua
Schalke ....(0) 2-0 (0)............ Basle

Group F

	P	W	D	L	F	A	D	Pts
B Dortmund	6	4	0	2	11	6	5	12
Arsenal	6	4	0	2	8	5	3	12
Napoli	6	4	0	2	10	9	1	12
Marseille	6	0	0	6	5	14	-9	0

Wednesday September 18 2013
Marseille.......(0) 1-2 (0).........Arsenal
Napoli ....(1) 2-1 (0)..B Dortmund

Tuesday October 1 2013
Arsenal ....(2) 2-0 (0).......... Napoli
B Dortmund ..(1) 3-0 (0)...... Marseille

Tuesday October 22 2013
Arsenal ....(1) 1-2 (1)..B Dortmund
Marseille.......(0) 1-2 (1)...... Napoli

Wednesday November 6 2013
B Dortmund ..(0) 0-1 (0).........Arsenal
Napoli ....(2) 3-2 (1)...... Marseille

Tuesday November 26 2013
Arsenal ....(1) 2-0 (0) ..... Marseille
B Dortmund ..(1) 3-1 (0) .... Napoli

Wednesday December 11 2013
Marseille.......(1) 1-2 (1)..B Dortmund
Napoli ....(0) 2-0 (0).........Arsenal

Group G

	P	W	D	L	F	A	D	Pts
Atl Madrid	6	5	1	0	15	3	12	16
Zenit	6	1	3	2	5	9	-4	6
Porto	6	1	2	3	4	7	-3	5
Aus. Vienna	6	1	2	3	5	10	-5	5

Wednesday September 18 2013
Atl Madrid ....(1) 3-1 (0) ....Zenit
Aus. Vienna ..(0) 0-1 (0) .... Porto

Tuesday October 1 2013
Porto.............(1) 1-2 (0)....Atl Madrid
Zenit.............(0) 0-0 (0)..Aus. Vienna

Tuesday October 22 2013
Aus. Vienna ..(0) 0-3 (2)....Atl Madrid
Porto.............(0) 0-1 (0).............Zenit

Wednesday November 6 2013
Atl Madrid ....(3) 4-0 (0)..Aus. Vienna
Zenit.............(1) 1-1 (1)............ Porto

Tuesday November 26 2013
Porto.............(1) 1-1 (1)..Aus. Vienna
Zenit.............(0) 1-1 (0)....Atl Madrid

Wednesday December 11 2013
Atl Madrid ....(2) 2-0 (0) .... Porto
Aus. Vienna ..(1) 4-1 (1).............Zenit

Group H

	P	W	D	L	F	A	D	Pts
Barcelona	6	4	1	1	16	5	11	13
Milan	6	2	3	1	8	5	3	9
Ajax	6	2	2	2	5	8	-3	8
Celtic	6	1	0	5	3	14	-11	3

Wednesday September 18 2013
Barcelona .....(1) 4-0 (0) ....Ajax
Milan............(0) 2-0 (0) ....Celtic

Tuesday October 1 2013
Ajax..............(0) 1-1 (0) .... Milan
Celtic.............(0) 0-1 (0) ..... Barcelona

Tuesday October 22 2013
Celtic ....(1) 2-1 (0) ....Ajax
Milan............(1) 1-1 (1) ..... Barcelona

Wednesday November 6 2013
Ajax..............(0) 1-0 (0)............Celtic
Barcelona .....(2) 3-1 (1) .... Milan

Tuesday November 26 2013
Ajax..............(2) 2-1 (0) ..... Barcelona
Celtic ....(0) 0-3 (1) .... Milan

Wednesday December 11 2013
Barcelona .....(3) 6-1 (0) ....Celtic
Milan............(0) 0-0 (0) ....Ajax

Last 16

Tuesday February 18 2014
B Leverkusen (0) 0-4 (3).... Paris St-G.
Man City.......(0) 0-2 (0) ..... Barcelona

Wednesday February 19 2014
Arsenal ....(0) 0-2 (0)......B Munich
Milan............(0) 0-1 (0)....Atl Madrid

Tuesday February 25 2014
Olympiakos...(1) 2-0 (0).......Man Utd
Zenit.............(0) 2-4 (2)..B Dortmund

Wednesday February 26 2014
Galatasaray ..(0) 1-1 (1)........ Chelsea
Schalke ....(0) 1-6 (2). Real Madrid

Second legs

Tuesday March 11 2014
Atl Madrid ....(2) 4-1 (1)........... Milan
Agg: 5-1 Atl Madrid
B Munich ......(0) 1-1 (0).........Arsenal
Agg: 3-1 B Munich

Wednesday March 12 2014
Barcelona .....(0) 2-1 (0) ..... Man City
Agg: 4-1 Barcelona
Paris St-G......(1) 2-1 (1) B Leverkusen
Agg: 6-1 Paris St-G

Tuesday March 18 2014
Chelsea.........(2) 2-0 (0).. Galatasaray
Agg: 3-1 Chelsea
Real Madrid ..(1) 3-1 (1).........Schalke
Agg: 9-2 Real Madrid

Wednesday March 19 2014
B Dortmund ..(1) 1-2 (1)............Zenit
Agg: 5-4 B Dortmund
Man Utd ....(2) 3-0 (0).. Olympiakos
Agg: 3-2 Man Utd

Quarter-finals

Tuesday April 1 2014
Barcelona .....(0) 1-1 (0)....Atl Madrid
Man Utd ....(0) 1-1 (0)......B Munich

Wednesday April 2 2014
Paris St-G......(1) 3-1 (0) .... Chelsea
Real Madrid ..(2) 3-0 (0)..B Dortmund

Second legs

Tuesday April 8 2014
B Dortmund ..(2) 2-0 (0). Real Madrid
Agg: 3-2 Real Madrid
Chelsea.........(1) 2-0 (0).... Paris St-G.
Agg: 3-3. Chelsea away goals

Wednesday April 9 2014
Atl Madrid ....(1) 1-0 (0) ..... Barcelona
Agg: 2-1 Atl Madrid
B Munich ......(0) 3-1 (0).......Man Utd
Agg: 4-2 B Munich

Semi-finals

Tuesday April 22 2014
Atl Madrid ....(0) 0-0 (0) .... Chelsea

Wednesday April 23 2014
Real Madrid ..(1) 1-0 (0) ......B Munich

Second legs

Tuesday April 29 2014
B Munich ......(0) 0-4 (3). Real Madrid
Agg: 5-0 Real Madrid

Wednesday April 30 2014
Chelsea.........(1) 1-3 (1)....Atl Madrid
Agg: 3-1 Atl Madrid

Final

Saturday May 24 2014
Real Madrid ..(0) 4-1 (0)....Atl Madrid
AET 1-1 90 mins

Gareth Bale heads Real Madrid into the lead as they finally win their tenth European Cup

EURO 2016 QUALIFYING FIXTURES

Sunday September 7

Group D
Georgia v Rep of Ireland
Germany v Scotland
Gibraltar v Poland

Group F
Faroe Islands v Finland
Greece v Romania
Hungary v N Ireland

Group I
Denmark v Armenia
Portugal v Albania

Monday September 8

Group C
Luxembourg v Belarus
Spain v Macedonia
Ukraine v Slovakia

Group E
Estonia v Slovenia
San Marino v Lithuania
Switzerland v England

Group G
Austria v Sweden
Montenegro v Moldova
Russia v Liechtenstein

Tuesday September 9

Group A
Czech Republic v Holland
Iceland v Turkey
Kazakhstan v Latvia

Group B
Andorra v Wales
Bosnia-Hz v Cyprus
Israel v Belgium

Group H
Azerbaijan v Bulgaria
Croatia v Malta
Norway v Italy

Thursday October 9

Group C
Belarus v Ukraine
Macedonia v Luxembourg
Slovakia v Spain

Group E
England v San Marino
Lithuania v Estonia
Slovenia v Switzerland

Group G
Liechtenstein v Montenegro
Moldova v Austria
Sweden v Russia

Friday October 10

Group A
Holland v Kazakhstan

Latvia v Iceland
Turkey v Czech Republic

Group B
Belgium v Andorra
Cyprus v Israel
Wales v Bosnia-Hz

Group H
Bulgaria v Croatia
Italy v Azerbaijan
Malta v Norway

Saturday October 11

Group D
Poland v Germany
Rep of Ireland v Gibraltar
Scotland v Georgia

Group F
Finland v Greece
N Ireland v Faroe Islands
Romania v Hungary

Group I
Albania v Denmark
Armenia v Serbia

Sunday October 12

Group C
Belarus v Slovakia
Luxembourg v Spain
Ukraine v Macedonia

Group E
Estonia v England
Lithuania v Slovenia

Group G
Austria v Montenegro
Russia v Moldova
Sweden v Liechtenstein

Monday October 13

Group A
Iceland v Holland
Kazakhstan v Czech Rep
Latvia v Turkey

Group B
Andorra v Israel
Bosnia-Hz v Belgium
Wales v Cyprus

Group H
Croatia v Azerbaijan
Malta v Italy
Norway v Bulgaria

Tuesday October 14

Group D
Germany v Rep of Ireland
Gibraltar v Georgia
Poland v Scotland

Group E
San Marino v Switzerland

Group F
Faroe Islands v Hungary
Finland v Romania
Greece v N Ireland

Group I
Denmark v Portugal
Serbia v Albania

Friday November 14

Group D
Georgia v Poland
Germany v Gibraltar
Scotland v Rep of Ireland

Group F
Greece v Faroe Islands
Hungary v Finland
Romania v N Ireland

Group I
Portugal v Armenia
Serbia v Denmark

Saturday November 15

Group C
Luxembourg v Ukraine
Macedonia v Slovakia
Spain v Belarus

Group E
England v Slovenia
San Marino v Estonia
Switzerland v Lithuania

Group G
Austria v Russia
Moldova v Liechtenstein
Montenegro v Sweden

Sunday November 16

Group A
Czech Republic v Iceland
Holland v Latvia
Turkey v Kazakhstan

Group B
Belgium v Wales
Cyprus v Andorra
Israel v Bosnia-Hz

Group H
Azerbaijan v Norway
Bulgaria v Malta
Italy v Croatia

Friday March 27

Group C
Macedonia v Belarus
Slovakia v Luxembourg
Spain v Ukraine

Group E
England v Lithuania
Slovenia v San Marino
Switzerland v Estonia

Group G
Liechtenstein v Austria
Moldova v Sweden
Montenegro v Russia

Saturday March 28

Group A
Czech Republic v Latvia
Kazakhstan v Iceland
Holland v Turkey

Group B
Andorra v Bosnia-Hz
Belgium v Cyprus
Israel v Wales

Group H
Azerbaijan v Malta
Bulgaria v Italy
Croatia v Norway

Sunday March 29

Group D
Georgia v Germany
Rep of Ireland v Poland
Scotland v Gibraltar

Group F
Hungary v Greece
N Ireland v Finland
Romania v Faroe Islands

Group I
Albania v Armenia
Portugal v Serbia

Friday June 12

Group A
Iceland v Czech Republic
Kazakhstan v Turkey
Latvia v Holland

Group B
Andorra v Cyprus
Bosnia-Hz v Israel
Wales v Belgium

Group H
Croatia v Italy
Malta v Bulgaria
Norway v Azerbaijan

Saturday June 13

Group D
Gibraltar v Germany
Poland v Georgia
Rep of Ireland v Scotland

Group F
Faroe Islands v Greece
Finland v Hungary
N Ireland v Romania

Group I
Armenia v Portugal
Denmark v Serbia

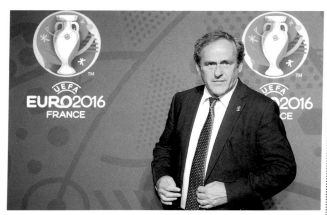

Michel Platini attends the logo and slogan launch for Euro 2016

Sunday June 14

Group C
Belarus v Spain
Slovakia v Macedonia
Ukraine v Luxembourg

Group E
Estonia v San Marino
Lithuania v Switzerland
Slovenia v England

Group G
Liechtenstein v Moldova
Russia v Austria
Sweden v Montenegro

Thursday September 3

Group A
Czech Rep v Kazakhstan
Holland v Iceland
Turkey v Latvia

Group B
Belgium v Bosnia-Hz
Cyprus v Wales
Israel v Andorra

Group H
Azerbaijan v Croatia
Bulgaria v Norway
Italy v Malta

Friday September 4

Group D
Georgia v Scotland
Germany v Poland
Gibraltar v Rep of Ireland

Group F
Faroe Islands v N Ireland
Greece v Finland
Hungary v Romania

Group I
Denmark v Albania
Serbia v Armenia

Saturday September 5

Group C
Luxembourg v Macedonia
Spain v Slovakia
Ukraine v Belarus

Group E
Estonia v Lithuania
San Marino v England
Switzerland v Slovenia

Group G
Austria v Moldova
Montenegro v Liechtenstein
Russia v Sweden

Sunday September 6

Group A
Iceland v Kazakhstan
Latvia v Czech Republic
Turkey v Holland

Group B
Bosnia-Hz v Andorra
Cyprus v Belgium
Wales v Israel

Group H
Italy v Bulgaria
Malta v Azerbaijan
Norway v Croatia

Monday September 7

Group D
Poland v Gibraltar
Rep of Ireland v Georgia
Scotland v Germany

Group F
Finland v Faroe Islands
N Ireland v Hungary
Romania v Greece

Group I
Albania v Portugal
Armenia v Denmark

Tuesday September 8

Group C
Belarus v Luxembourg
Macedonia v Spain
Slovakia v Ukraine

Group E
England v Switzerland
Lithuania v San Marino
Slovenia v Estonia

Group G
Liechtenstein v Russia
Moldova v Montenegro
Sweden v Austria

Thursday October 8

Group D
Georgia v Gibraltar
Rep of Ireland v Germany
Scotland v Poland

Group F
Hungary v Faroe Islands
N Ireland v Greece
Romania v Finland

Group I
Albania v Serbia
Portugal v Denmark

Friday October 9

Group C
Macedonia v Ukraine
Slovakia v Belarus
Spain v Luxembourg

Group E
England v Estonia
Slovenia v Lithuania
Switzerland v San Marino

Group G
Liechtenstein v Sweden
Moldova v Russia
Montenegro v Austria

Saturday October 10

Group A
Czech Republic v Turkey
Iceland v Latvia
Kazakhstan v Holland

Group B
Andorra v Belgium
Bosnia-Hz v Wales
Israel v Cyprus

Group H
Azerbaijan v Italy
Croatia v Bulgaria
Norway v Malta

Sunday October 11

Group D
Germany v Georgia
Gibraltar v Scotland
Poland v Rep of Ireland

Group F
Faroe Islands v Romania
Finland v N Ireland
Greece v Hungary

Group I
Armenia v Albania
Serbia v Portugal

Monday October 12

Group C
Belarus v Macedonia
Luxembourg v Slovakia
Ukraine v Spain

Group E
Estonia v Switzerland
Lithuania v England
San Marino v Slovenia

Group G
Austria v Liechtenstein
Russia v Montenegro
Sweden v Moldova

Tuesday October 13

Group A
Latvia v Kazakhstan
Holland v Czech Republic
Turkey v Iceland

Group B
Belgium v Israel
Cyprus v Bosnia-Hz
Wales v Andorra

Group H
Bulgaria v Azerbaijan
Italy v Norway
Malta v Croatia

Key dates

March 2015
Ticket sales begin

December 12 2015
Final tournament draw

June 10-July 10 2016
Euro 2016 finals (France)

Euro 2016 winner

	b365	BFred	Coral	Hills	Lads	Power
Germany	7-2	3	7-2	3	10-3	3
Spain	5	9-2	4	4	10-3	5
France	6	5	11-2	5	6	9-2
Belgium	10	10	12	10	12	10
Holland	9	10	10	10	10	11
Italy	10	10	10	11	11	11
England	14	14	12	12	12	14
Portugal	16	16	16	16	12	16
Russia	25	25	22	20	20	22
Croatia	50	40	28	50	33	40
Switzerland	50	50	40	66	50	40
Serbia	100	80	66	80	66	66
Turkey	80	50	66	50	66	50
Czech Rep	100	80	80	100	66	66
Denmark	80	50	66	50	50	70
Sweden	125	66	80	66	66	66
Bosnia-Hz	100	100	100	100	66	100
Greece	100	100	150	100	80	100
Ukraine	100	100	150	150	100	100
Poland	150	100	100	150	100	66
Rep of Ireland	250	200	200	250	150	150
Norway	250	100	200	200	100	100
Scotland	500	250	500	500	150	150
Wales	500	250	400	250	150	500
N Ireland	2500	1000	500	1000	1000	500

Win or each-way. Others available

The World Cup winners are Euro 2016 favourites

Euro 2016 Group A winner

	b365	BFred	Coral	Hills	Lads	Power
Holland	1-4	2-7	1-4	1-4	2-7	2-5
Turkey	6	11-2	11-2	5	11-2	9-2
Czech Rep	7	8	8	7	7	11-2
Iceland	50	33	16	40	18	16
Latvia	250	100	250	100	66	100
Kazakhstan	1000	1000	1000	750	1000	500

Win only

Euro 2016 Group B winner

	b365	BFred	Coral	Hills	Lads	Power
Belgium	2-7	4-11	4-9	2-5	1-3	2-5
Bosnia-Hz	3	11-4	9-4	11-4	3	21-10
Israel	25	20	20	16	20	20
Wales	50	16	14	14	14	22
Cyprus	200	80	100	100	100	150
Andorra	5000	5000	5000	2000	1000	500

Win only

Euro 2016 Group C winner

	b365	BFred	Coral	Hills	Lads	Power
Spain	1-12	1-14	1-12	1-14	1-16	1-20
Ukraine	7	9	7	8	9	9
Slovakia	25	14	14	20	16	22
Belarus	250	100	150	125	80	250
Macedonia	500	100	150	200	350	500
Luxembourg	5000	500	2500	2000	1500	500

Win only

Euro 2016 Group D winner

	b365	BFred	Coral	Hills	Lads	Power
Germany	1-10	1-9	1-9	1-7	1-8	1-6
Poland	9	8	9	8	10	8
Rep of Ireland	16	12	16	14	14	9
Scotland	40	33	16	14	14	14
Georgia	500	500	250	200	100	275
Gibraltar	10000	5000	5000	2500	750	500

Win only

Euro 2016 Group E winner

	b365	BFred	Coral	Hills	Lads	Power
England	2-7	2-5	8-15	4-9	4-11	4-11
Switzerland	3	5-2	2	9-4	3	13-5
Slovenia	16	10	15-2	7	10	9
Estonia	250	100	100	100	50	50
Lithuania	250	250	100	300	100	200
San Marino	5000	5000	5000	2500	1000	500

Win only

Euro 2016 Group F winner

	b365	BFred	Coral	Hills	Lads	Power
Greece	5-4	11-10	Evs	5-6	11-10	11-10
Romania	2	11-4	11-4	11-4	5-2	2
Hungary	4	7-2	4	4	4	7-2
Finland	10	9	8	8	8	15-2
N Ireland	33	25	22	25	20	33
Faroe Islands	2500	5000	1000	1000	500	500

Win only

Euro 2016 Group G winner

	b365	BFred	Coral	Hills	Lads	Power
Russia	4-5	Evs	6-5	5-6	8-11	10-11
Sweden	2	13-8	9-5	2	2	15-8
Austria	15-2	8	9-2	7	9	6
Montenegro	10	8	7	9	9	6
Moldova	750	150	200	100	125	150
Liechtenstein	5000	5000	1000	1000	750	500

Win only

Euro 2016 Group H winner

	b365	BFred	Coral	Hills	Lads	Power
Italy	2-5	2-5	2-5	2-5	2-5	4-11
Croatia	3	3	3	7-2	3	3
Norway	14	10	12	10	10	9
Bulgaria	16	14	12	14	14	18
Azerbaijan	250	1000	500	500	200	500
Malta	5000	2500	2500	1000	1000	500

Win only

Euro 2016 Group I winner

	b365	BFred	Coral	Hills	Lads	Power
Portugal	8-15	8-15	8-13	1-2	1-2	1-2
Denmark	3	11-4	7-2	3	3	3
Serbia	6	6	7-2	7	6	6
Armenia	20	25	16	12	14	11
Albania	500	500	150	500	500	500

Win only

BRAZIL 2014 WORLD CUP RESULTS

Group A

	P	W	D	L	F	A	D	Pts
Brazil	3	2	1	0	7	2	5	7
Mexico	3	2	1	0	4	1	3	7
Croatia	3	1	0	2	6	6	0	3
Cameroon	3	0	0	3	1	9	-8	0

Thursday June 12 2014
Brazil ....(1) 3-1 (1) .... Croatia
Friday June 13 2014
Chile ....(2) 3-1 (1) ......Australia
Tuesday June 17 2014
Brazil ....(0) 0-0 (0) .... Mexico
Wednesday June 18 2014
Cameroon ......(0) 0-4 (1) .... Croatia
Monday June 23 2014
Brazil ....(2) 4-1 (1) .... Cameroon
Croatia..........(0) 1-3 (0) .... Mexico

Group B

	P	W	D	L	F	A	D	Pts
Holland	3	3	0	0	10	3	7	9
Chile	3	2	0	1	5	3	2	6
Spain	3	1	0	2	4	7	-3	3
Australia	3	0	0	3	3	9	-6	0

Friday June 13 2014
Mexico..........(0) 1-0 (0) .... Cameroon
Spain ....(1) 1-5 (1) .... Holland
Wednesday June 18 2014
Australia ......(1) 2-3 (1) .... Holland
Spain ....(0) 0-2 (2) .... Chile
Monday June 23 2014
Australia ......(0) 0-3 (1) ....Spain
Holland..........(0) 2-0 (0) .... Chile

Group C

	P	W	D	L	F	A	D	Pts
Colombia	3	3	0	0	9	2	7	9
Greece	3	1	1	1	2	4	-2	4
Ivory Coast	3	1	0	2	4	5	-1	3
Japan	3	0	1	2	2	6	-4	1

Saturday June 14 2014
Colombia ......(1) 3-0 (0) ......Greece
Sunday June 15 2014
Ivory Coast ...(0) 2-1 (1) .... Japan
Thursday June 19 2014
Colombia ......(0) 2-1 (0) ...Ivory Coast
Japan.............(0) 0-0 (0) ....Greece
Tuesday June 24 2014
Greece ....(1) 2-1 (0) ...Ivory Coast
Japan.............(1) 1-4 (1) ......Colombia

Group D

	P	W	D	L	F	A	D	Pts
Costa Rica	3	2	1	0	4	1	3	7
Uruguay	3	2	0	1	4	4	0	6
Italy	3	1	0	2	2	3	-1	3
England	3	0	1	2	2	4	-2	1

Saturday June 14 2014
England ....(1) 1-2 (1) ....Italy
Uruguay ....(1) 1-3 (0) .... Costa Rica

Thursday June 19 2014
Uruguay ....(1) 2-1 (0) ....England
Friday June 20 2014
Italy ....(0) 0-1 (1) .... Costa Rica
Tuesday June 24 2014
Costa Rica.....(0) 0-0 (0) ....England
Italy ....(0) 0-1 (0) .... Uruguay

Group E

	P	W	D	L	F	A	D	Pts
France	3	2	1	0	8	2	6	7
Switzerland	3	2	0	1	7	6	1	6
Ecuador	3	1	1	1	3	3	0	4
Honduras	3	0	0	3	1	8	-7	0

Sunday June 15 2014
France............(1) 3-0 (0) ..... Honduras
Switzerland...(0) 2-1 (1) ....Ecuador
Friday June 20 2014
Honduras......(1) 1-2 (1) ....Ecuador
Switzerland...(0) 2-5 (3) .... France
Wednesday June 25 2014
Ecuador ....(0) 0-0 (0) .... France
Honduras......(0) 0-3 (2) .. Switzerland

Group F

	P	W	D	L	F	A	D	Pts
Argentina	3	3	0	0	6	3	3	9
Nigeria	3	1	1	1	3	3	0	4
Bosnia-Hz	3	1	0	2	4	4	0	3
Iran	3	0	1	2	1	4	-3	1

Sunday June 15 2014
Argentina .....(1) 2-1 (0) .... Bosnia-Hz.
Monday June 16 2014
Iran................(0) 0-0 (0) .... Nigeria
Saturday June 21 2014
Argentina .....(0) 1-0 (0) .... Iran
Nigeria ....(1) 1-0 (0) .... Bosnia-Hz.
Wednesday June 25 2014
Bosnia-Hz. ....(1) 3-1 (0) .... Iran
Nigeria ....(2) 2-3 (2) ..... Argentina

Group G

	P	W	D	L	F	A	D	Pts
Germany	3	2	1	0	7	2	5	7
USA	3	1	1	1	4	4	0	4
Portugal	3	1	1	1	4	7	-3	4
Ghana	3	0	1	2	4	6	-2	1

Monday June 16 2014
Germany.......(3) 4-0 (0) .... Portugal
Ghana...........(0) 1-2 (1) ....USA
Saturday June 21 2014
Germany.......(0) 2-2 (0) .... Ghana
Sunday June 22 2014
USA ....(0) 2-2 (1) .... Portugal
Thursday June 26 2014
Algeria...........(0) 1-1 (0) .... Russia
South Korea..(0) 0-1 (0) ....Belgium

Group H

	P	W	D	L	F	A	D	Pts
Belgium	3	3	0	0	4	1	3	9
Algeria	3	1	1	1	6	5	1	4
Russia	3	0	2	1	2	3	-1	2
S Korea	3	0	1	2	3	6	-3	1

Tuesday June 17 2014
Belgium ....(0) 2-1 (1) .... Algeria
Russia............(0) 1-1 (0). South Korea
Sunday June 22 2014
Belgium ....(0) 1-0 (0) .... Russia
South Korea ..(0) 2-4 (3) .... Algeria
Thursday June 26 2014
Portugal........(1) 2-1 (0) .... Ghana
USA ....(0) 0-1 (0) ..... Germany

Last 16

Saturday June 28 2014
Brazil ....(1) 1-1 (1) .... Chile
AET 1-1 90 mins. Brazil 3-2 pens
Colombia ......(1) 2-0 (0) ...... Uruguay
Sunday June 29 2014
Costa Rica.....(0) 1-1 (0) ....Greece
AET 1-1 90 mins. Costa Rica 5-3 pens
Holland..........(0) 2-1 (0) .... Mexico
Monday June 30 2014
France............(0) 2-0 (0) .... Nigeria
Germany.......(0) 2-1 (0) .... Algeria
AET 0-0 90 mins
Tuesday July 1 2014
Argentina .....(0) 1-0 (0) .. Switzerland
AET 0-0 90 mins
Belgium ....(0) 2-1 (0) ....USA
AET 0-0 90 mins

Quarter-finals

Friday July 4 2014
France............(0) 0-1 (1) ...... Germany
Brazil ....(1) 2-1 (0) ......Colombia
Saturday July 5 2014
Argentina .....(1) 1-0 (0) ....Belgium
Holland..........(0) 0-0 (0) .... Costa Rica
AET Holland 4-3 pens

Semi-finals

Tuesday July 8 2014
Brazil ....(0) 1-7 (5) ...... Germany
Wednesday July 9 2014
Holland..........(0) 0-0 (0) ..... Argentina
AET Argentina 4-2 pens

3rd/4th place playoff

Saturday July 12 2014
Brazil ....(0) 0-3 (2) .... Holland

Final

Sunday July 13 2014
Germany.......(0) 1-0 (0) ..... Argentina
AET 0-0 90 mins

To the right of each fixture are results for the corresponding league match in each of the last six seasons. The most recent result – 2013-14 – is on the right. The results cover matches in the Premier League, Championship, League 1, League 2, Conference. Scottish Premiership, Scottish Championship, Scottish League One and Scottish League Two.

Where Scottish clubs have met more than once at the same venue in the same season, results are separated by an oblique stroke with the most recent to the right. The Scottish Premier League will split into top- and bottom-six sections later in the season. These fixtures cover the period until the split. Please note that TV coverage and postponements will cause alterations to the fixture list.

	2008-09	2009-10	2010-11	2011-12	2012-13	2013-14
Friday August 8th, 2014						
Championship						
Blackburn v Cardiff	-	-	-	-	1-4	-
Saturday August 9th, 2014						
Championship						
Brentford v Charlton	-	1-1	2-1	0-1	-	-
Brighton v Sheff Wed	-	-	2-0	-	3-0	1-1
Derby v Rotherham	-	-	-	-	-	-
Huddersfield v Bournemouth	-	-	2-2	0-1	-	5-1
Ipswich v Fulham	-	-	-	-	-	-
Middlesbro v Birmingham	-	-	-	3-1	0-1	3-1
Millwall v Leeds	3-1	2-1	3-2	0-1	1-0	2-0
Nottm Forest v Blackpool	0-0	0-1	-	0-0	1-1	0-1
Watford v Bolton	-	-	-	-	2-1	0-1
Wigan v Reading	-	-	-	-	3-2	3-0
League 1						
Barnsley v Crawley Town	-	-	-	-	-	-
Bradford v Coventry	-	-	-	-	-	3-3
Colchester v Oldham	2-2	1-0	1-0	4-1	0-2	0-1
Fleetwood Town v Crewe	-	-	-	-	-	-
Leyton Orient v Chesterfield	-	-	-	1-1	-	-
MK Dons v Gillingham	-	2-0	-	-	-	0-1
Port Vale v Walsall	-	-	-	-	-	1-0
Preston v Notts Co	-	-	-	2-0	0-0	2-0
Rochdale v Peterborough	-	-	2-2	-	-	-
Sheff Utd v Bristol City	3-0	2-0	3-2	-	-	3-0
Swindon v Scunthorpe	4-2	-	-	-	1-1	-
Yeovil v Doncaster	-	-	-	-	2-1	1-0
League 2						
Accrington v Southend	-	-	3-1	1-2	1-1	1-1
AFC Wimbledon v Shrewsbury	-	-	-	3-1	-	-
Bury v Cheltenham	-	0-1	2-3	-	-	4-1
Cambridge U v Plymouth	-	-	-	-	-	-
Carlisle v Luton	-	-	-	-	-	-
Dag & Red v Morecambe	0-2	1-1	-	1-2	1-2	1-1
Exeter v Portsmouth	-	-	-	-	-	1-1
Newport Co v Wycombe	-	-	-	-	-	2-0
Northampton v Mansfield	-	-	-	-	-	1-1
Oxford v Burton	2-1	-	3-0	2-2	1-1	1-2
Stevenage v Hartlepool	-	-	-	2-2	1-0	-
Tranmere v York	-	-	-	-	-	-

Results cover matches from Premier League to Conference and Scottish Premiership to League Two

	2008-09	2009-10	2010-11	2011-12	2012-13	2013-14
Conference						
Aldershot v Altrincham	-	-	-	-	-	-
Alfreton v Woking	-	-	-	-	0-3	3-1
Bristol Rovers v Grimsby	-	-	-	-	-	-
Chester v Barnet	5-1	-	-	-	-	2-1
Dartford v Wrexham	-	-	-	-	2-1	1-5
Dover v Halifax	-	-	-	-	-	-
Gateshead v Torquay	-	-	-	-	-	-
Lincoln v Kidderminster	-	-	-	0-1	1-0	2-0
Macclesfield v Braintree	-	-	-	-	2-1	0-1
Nuneaton v Eastleigh	-	-	-	-	-	-
Southport v Forest Green	-	-	4-0	1-3	1-2	2-0
Welling v Telford	-	-	-	-	-	-
Scottish Premiership						
Aberdeen v Dundee Utd	0-1/2-2	0-2/2-2	1-1	3-1/3-1	2-2	1-0/1-1
Celtic v Partick	-	-	-	-	-	1-0
Dundee v Kilmarnock	-	-	-	-	0-0/2-3	-
Hamilton v Inverness CT	1-0	-	1-3/1-2	-	-	-
Motherwell v St Mirren	2-1/0-2	2-0	3-1/0-1	1-1	1-1/2-2	3-0
Ross County v St Johnstone	1-2/2-2	-	-	-	1-2/1-0	1-0
Scottish Championship						
Cowdenbeath v Falkirk	-	-	0-0/1-2	-	1-1/4-1	1-0/0-2
Hibernian v Livingston	-	-	-	-	-	-
Queen of Sth v Alloa	-	-	-	-	1-0/0-0	0-0/3-1
Raith v Dumbarton	-	-	-	-	2-2/3-2	2-1/1-3
Scottish League One						
Ayr v Morton	-	0-2/2-0	-	0-1/0-0	-	-
Dunfermline v Brechin	-	-	-	-	-	3-1/2-1
Peterhead v Stirling	1-1/1-1	3-2/1-1	-	-	2-2/0-0	3-1/0-4
Stenh'semuir v Airdrieonians	-	-	1-3/1-0	1-1/0-3	-	1-1/1-2
Stranraer v Forfar	-	1-0/2-0	-	-	4-1/0-3	0-4/3-1
Scottish League Two						
Albion v Annan	0-1/2-1	0-0/1-0	0-0/0-0	-	-	2-0/0-2
Berwick v Arbroath	-	-	4-1/0-4	-	-	-
Elgin v East Fife	-	-	-	-	-	-
Montrose v East Stirling	3-0/0-2	0-3/0-1	0-2/3-0	2-1/3-1	3-1/2-2	2-0/2-0
Queen's Park v Clyde	-	-	0-1/4-0	3-0/3-0	1-0/4-1	1-1/1-3

Sunday August 10th, 2014

	2008-09	2009-10	2010-11	2011-12	2012-13	2013-14
Championship						
Wolves v Norwich	3-3	-	-	2-2	-	-
Scottish Championship						
Rangers v Hearts	2-0/2-2/2-0	1-1/2-0	1-0/4-0	1-1/1-2	-	-

Tuesday August 12th, 2014

	2008-09	2009-10	2010-11	2011-12	2012-13	2013-14
Conference						
Altrincham v Lincoln	-	-	-	-	-	-
Barnet v Bristol Rovers	-	-	-	2-0	1-1	-
Braintree v Dover	-	-	-	-	-	-
Forest Green v Chester	-	-	-	-	-	3-0
Grimsby v Nuneaton	-	-	-	-	0-0	1-2
Halifax v Southport	-	-	-	-	-	1-0
Kidderminster v Alfreton	-	-	-	3-1	3-1	1-3
Telford v Macclesfield	-	-	-	-	0-2	-
Torquay v Welling	-	-	-	-	-	-
Woking v Dartford	-	-	-	-	1-0	3-0
Wrexham v Gateshead	-	0-0	2-7	2-1	1-1	3-2

Results cover matches from Premier League to Conference and Scottish Premiership to League Two

Wednesday August 13th, 2014

Scottish Premiership

	2008-09	2009-10	2010-11	2011-12	2012-13	2013-14
Dundee Utd v Motherwell	0-4	0-1/3-0	2-0/4-0	1-3/1-1	1-2/1-3	2-2/3-1/5-1
Inverness CT v Dundee	-	1-1/1-0	-	-	4-1	-
Kilmarnock v Aberdeen	1-2	1-1/2-0	2-0	2-0/1-1	1-3/1-1	0-1
Partick v Ross County	0-1/0-2	0-0/2-1	1-1/1-1	0-1/0-1	-	3-3/2-3
St Johnstone v Celtic	-	1-4	0-3/0-1	0-2	2-1/1-1	0-1/3-3
St Mirren v Hamilton	1-0/0-1	0-2/0-0	2-2/3-1/0-1	-	-	-

Thursday August 14th, 2014

Conference

	2008-09	2009-10	2010-11	2011-12	2012-13	2013-14
Eastleigh v Aldershot	-	-	-	-	-	-

Friday August 15th, 2014

Scottish Championship

	2008-09	2009-10	2010-11	2011-12	2012-13	2013-14
Falkirk v Rangers	0-1/0-1	1-3	-	-	-	-

Saturday August 16th, 2014

Premier League

	2008-09	2009-10	2010-11	2011-12	2012-13	2013-14
Arsenal v Crystal Palace	-	-	-	-	-	2-0
Burnley v Chelsea	-	1-2	-	-	-	-
Leicester v Everton	-	-	-	-	-	-
Liverpool v Southampton	-	-	-	-	1-0	0-1
Man Utd v Swansea	-	-	-	2-0	2-1	2-0
Newcastle v Man City	2-2	-	1-3	0-2	1-3	0-2
QPR v Hull	-	-	1-1	-	-	-
Stoke v Aston Villa	3-2	0-0	2-1	0-0	1-3	2-1
West Brom v Sunderland	3-0	-	1-0	4-0	2-1	3-0
West Ham v Tottenham	0-2	1-2	1-0	-	2-3	2-0

Championship

	2008-09	2009-10	2010-11	2011-12	2012-13	2013-14
Birmingham v Brighton	-	-	-	0-0	2-2	0-1
Blackpool v Blackburn	-	-	1-2	-	2-0	2-2
Bolton v Nottm Forest	-	-	-	-	2-2	1-1
Bournemouth v Brentford	0-1	-	3-1	1-0	2-2	-
Cardiff v Huddersfield	-	-	-	-	1-0	-
Charlton v Wigan	-	-	-	-	-	0-0
Fulham v Millwall	-	-	-	-	-	-
Leeds v Middlesbro	-	-	1-1	0-1	2-1	2-1
Norwich v Watford	2-0	-	2-3	-	-	-
Reading v Ipswich	0-1	1-1	1-0	1-0	-	2-1
Rotherham v Wolves	-	-	-	-	-	3-3
Sheff Wed v Derby	0-1	0-0	-	-	2-2	0-1

League 1

	2008-09	2009-10	2010-11	2011-12	2012-13	2013-14
Bristol City v Colchester	-	-	-	-	-	1-1
Chesterfield v Rochdale	3-0	2-0	-	2-1	1-1	2-2
Coventry v Sheff Utd	1-2	3-2	0-0	-	1-1	3-2
Crawley Town v Swindon	-	-	-	0-3	1-1	0-0
Crewe v Barnsley	-	-	-	-	-	-
Doncaster v Port Vale	-	-	-	-	-	-
Gillingham v Yeovil	-	1-0	-	-	-	-
Notts Co v Fleetwood Town	-	-	-	-	-	-
Oldham v Leyton Orient	1-1	2-0	1-1	0-1	2-0	1-1
Peterborough v MK Dons	0-0	-	2-1	-	-	2-1
Scunthorpe v Preston	-	3-1	0-3	1-1	2-3	-
Walsall v Bradford	-	-	-	-	-	0-2

Results cover matches from Premier League to Conference and Scottish Premiership to League Two

	2008-09	2009-10	2010-11	2011-12	2012-13	2013-14
League 2						
Burton v Dag & Red	-	0-1	-	1-1	3-2	1-1
Cheltenham v Accrington	-	1-1	1-2	4-1	0-3	1-2
Hartlepool v Bury	-	-	-	3-0	2-0	0-3
Luton v AFC Wimbledon	-	1-2	3-0	-	-	-
Mansfield v Oxford	1-3	2-1	-	-	-	1-3
Morecambe v Newport Co	-	-	-	-	-	4-1
Plymouth v Exeter	-	-	2-0	-	1-0	1-2
Portsmouth v Cambridge U	-	-	-	-	-	-
Shrewsbury v Tranmere	-	-	-	-	1-1	0-1
Southend v Stevenage	-	-	1-0	-	-	-
Wycombe v Carlisle	-	0-0	-	1-1	-	-
York v Northampton	-	-	-	-	1-1	1-0
Conference						
Altrincham v Bristol Rovers	-	-	-	-	-	-
Barnet v Lincoln	3-2	1-2	4-2	-	-	1-1
Braintree v Chester	-	-	-	-	-	3-0
Eastleigh v Gateshead	-	-	-	-	-	-
Forest Green v Alfreton	-	-	-	4-1	1-1	3-1
Grimsby v Dover	-	-	-	-	-	-
Halifax v Welling	-	-	-	-	-	3-0
Kidderminster v Dartford	-	-	-	-	5-1	1-2
Telford v Aldershot	-	-	-	-	-	-
Torquay v Southport	-	-	-	-	-	-
Woking v Macclesfield	-	-	-	-	5-4	3-2
Wrexham v Nuneaton	-	-	-	-	6-1	3-0
Scottish Premiership						
Aberdeen v St Mirren	2-0	1-0/2-1	2-0/0-1	2-2/0-0	0-0/0-0	2-0
Celtic v Dundee Utd	2-2/2-1	1-1/1-0	1-1/4-1	5-1/2-1	4-0/6-2	1-1/3-1
Dundee v Partick	0-0/4-0	2-0/1-0	2-1/3-2	0-1/0-3	-	-
Hamilton v St Johnstone	-	0-2/1-0	1-2/0-0	-	-	-
Motherwell v Inverness CT	3-2/2-2	-	0-0	3-0/0-1	4-1/3-0	2-0/2-1
Ross County v Kilmarnock	-	-	-	-	0-0/0-1	1-2/2-1
Scottish Championship						
Alloa v Raith	1-1/0-0	-	-	-	-	1-0/0-1
Dumbarton v Queen of Sth	-	-	-	-	-	0-1/0-3
Livingston v Cowdenbeath	-	-	-	-	1-1/3-0	5-1/1-0
Scottish League One						
Airdrieonians v Peterhead	-	-	2-2/1-0	-	-	-
Brechin v Stenh'semuir	-	1-0/2-2	0-0/3-1	2-0/1-0	7-2/1-2	0-1/1-3
Forfar v Dunfermline	-	-	-	-	-	4-0/2-4
Morton v Stranraer	-	-	-	-	-	-
Stirling v Ayr	2-2/2-0	-	-	-	-	-
Scottish League Two						
Annan v Queen's Park	-	3-1/0-2	2-1/1-2	5-2/2-3	2-3/2-0	3-2/1-1
Arbroath v Albion	-	-	1-1/3-0	6-2/6-1	2-1/2-1	-
Clyde v Montrose	-	-	2-0/1-1	1-0/1-2	1-2/1-0	0-3/1-1
East Fife v Berwick	-	-	-	-	-	-
East Stirling v Elgin	5-2/1-0	1-1/2-0	0-2/2-1	1-1/2-2	1-4/3-2	3-0/3-0

Tuesday August 19th, 2014

	2008-09	2009-10	2010-11	2011-12	2012-13	2013-14
Championship						
Birmingham v Ipswich	2-1	-	-	2-1	0-1	1-1
Blackpool v Brentford	-	-	-	-	-	-
Bolton v Middlesbro	4-1	-	-	-	2-1	2-2

Results cover matches from Premier League to Conference and Scottish Premiership to League Two

	2008-09	2009-10	2010-11	2011-12	2012-13	2013-14
Bournemouth v Nottm Forest	-	-	-	-	-	4-1
Cardiff v Wigan	-	-	-	-	-	-
Charlton v Derby	2-2	-	-	-	1-1	0-2
Leeds v Brighton	3-1	1-1	-	1-2	1-2	2-1
Norwich v Blackburn	-	-	-	3-3	-	-
Reading v Huddersfield	-	-	-	-	-	1-1
Rotherham v Watford	-	-	-	-	-	-
Sheff Wed v Millwall	-	-	-	-	3-2	2-2

League 1						
Bristol City v Leyton Orient	-	-	-	-	-	2-2
Chesterfield v MK Dons	-	-	-	1-1	-	-
Coventry v Barnsley	1-1	3-1	3-0	1-0	-	-
Crawley Town v Bradford	-	-	-	3-1	-	1-0
Crewe v Rochdale	-	2-2	-	-	-	-
Doncaster v Preston	0-2	1-1	1-1	-	1-3	-
Gillingham v Swindon	-	5-0	-	3-1	-	2-0
Notts Co v Colchester	-	-	2-0	4-1	3-1	2-0
Oldham v Port Vale	-	-	-	-	-	3-1
Peterborough v Sheff Utd	-	1-0	-	-	-	0-0
Scunthorpe v Fleetwood Town	-	-	-	-	-	0-0
Walsall v Yeovil	2-0	0-1	0-1	1-1	2-2	-

League 2						
Burton v Exeter	-	-	-	-	4-2	1-1
Cheltenham v Carlisle	1-1	-	-	-	-	-
Hartlepool v Dag & Red	-	-	0-1	-	-	2-1
Luton v Bury	1-2	-	-	-	-	-
Mansfield v Newport Co	-	-	3-3	5-0	3-4	2-1
Morecambe v Oxford	-	-	0-3	0-0	1-1	1-1
Plymouth v Stevenage	-	-	-	-	-	-
Portsmouth v Northampton	-	-	-	-	-	0-0
Shrewsbury v Accrington	2-0	0-1	0-0	1-0	-	-
Southend v AFC Wimbledon	-	-	-	2-0	1-3	0-1
Wycombe v Tranmere	-	0-1	-	2-1	-	-
York v Cambridge U	0-0	2-2	0-0	2-2	-	-

Sunday August 17th, 2014

Scottish Championship						
Hearts v Hibernian	0-0/0-1	0-0/2-1	1-0	2-0/2-0	0-0/1-2	1-0/2-0

Wednesday August 20th, 2014

Championship						
Fulham v Wolves	-	0-0	2-1	5-0	-	-

Saturday August 23rd, 2014

Premier League						
Aston Villa v Newcastle	1-0	-	1-0	1-1	1-2	1-2
Chelsea v Leicester	-	-	-	-	-	-
Crystal Palace v West Ham	-	-	-	2-2	-	1-0
Everton v Arsenal	1-1	1-6	1-2	0-1	1-1	3-0
Hull v Stoke	1-2	2-1	-	-	-	0-0
Man City v Liverpool	2-3	0-0	3-0	3-0	2-2	2-1
Southampton v West Brom	-	-	-	-	0-3	1-0
Sunderland v Man Utd	1-2	0-1	0-0	0-1	0-1	1-2
Swansea v Burnley	1-1	-	1-0	-	-	-
Tottenham v QPR	-	-	-	3-1	2-1	-

Results cover matches from Premier League to Conference and Scottish Premiership to League Two

Championship						
Blackburn v Bournemouth	-	-	-	-	-	0-1
Brentford v Birmingham	-	-	-	-	-	-
Brighton v Bolton	-	-	-	-	1-1	3-1
Derby v Fulham	-	-	-	-	-	-
Huddersfield v Charlton	-	1-1	3-1	1-0	0-1	2-1
Ipswich v Norwich	3-2	-	1-5	-	-	-
Middlesbro v Sheff Wed	-	1-0	-	-	3-1	1-1
Millwall v Rotherham	-	-	-	-	-	-
Nottm Forest v Reading	0-0	2-1	3-4	1-0	-	2-3
Watford v Leeds	-	-	0-1	1-1	1-2	3-0
Wigan v Blackpool	-	-	0-4	-	-	0-2
Wolves v Cardiff	2-2	-	-	-	1-2	-

League 1						
Barnsley v Gillingham	-	-	-	-	-	-
Bradford v Peterborough	-	-	-	-	-	1-0
Colchester v Doncaster	-	-	-	-	1-2	-
Fleetwood Town v Chesterfield	-	-	-	-	1-3	1-1
Leyton Orient v Walsall	0-1	2-0	0-0	1-1	2-1	1-1
MK Dons v Coventry	-	-	-	-	2-3	1-3
Port Vale v Notts Co	1-2	2-1	-	-	-	2-1
Preston v Oldham	-	-	-	3-3	2-0	2-1
Rochdale v Bristol City	-	-	-	-	-	-
Sheff Utd v Crawley Town	-	-	-	-	0-2	1-1
Swindon v Crewe	0-0	-	-	3-0	4-1	5-0
Yeovil v Scunthorpe	1-2	-	-	2-2	3-0	-

League 2						
Accrington v Luton	0-0	-	-	-	-	-
AFC Wimbledon v Hartlepool	-	-	-	-	-	2-1
Bury v Plymouth	-	-	-	-	-	4-0
Cambridge U v Morecambe	-	-	-	-	-	-
Carlisle v Southend	2-1	2-1	-	-	-	-
Dag & Red v Mansfield	-	-	-	-	-	0-0
Exeter v York	-	-	-	-	1-1	2-1
Newport Co v Burton	-	-	-	-	-	1-1
Northampton v Shrewsbury	-	2-0	2-3	2-7	-	-
Oxford v Portsmouth	-	-	-	-	-	0-0
Stevenage v Wycombe	-	-	0-2	1-1	-	-
Tranmere v Cheltenham	2-0	-	-	-	-	-

Conference						
Aldershot v Forest Green	-	-	-	-	-	2-2
Alfreton v Wrexham	-	-	-	1-4	1-2	1-0
Bristol Rovers v Telford	-	-	-	-	-	-
Chester v Halifax	-	-	-	-	-	2-1
Dartford v Torquay	-	-	-	-	-	-
Dover v Eastleigh	-	-	-	-	-	1-2
Gateshead v Grimsby	-	-	0-0	1-0	1-1	1-2
Lincoln v Braintree	-	-	-	3-3	3-0	2-0
Macclesfield v Kidderminster	-	-	-	-	1-0	1-1
Nuneaton v Barnet	-	-	-	-	-	0-1
Southport v Altrincham	-	-	1-0	-	-	-
Welling v Woking	-	-	-	-	-	3-0

Scottish Premiership						
Dundee Utd v Ross County	-	-	-	-	0-0/1-1	1-0
Inverness CT v Celtic	1-2/0-0	-	0-1/3-2	0-2	2-4/1-3	0-1
Kilmarnock v Motherwell	1-0/0-0	0-3	0-1/3-1	0-0/2-0	1-2/2-0	0-2
Partick v Hamilton	-	-	-	1-1/2-0	4-0/1-0	-

Results cover matches from Premier League to Conference and Scottish Premiership to League Two

	2008-09	2009-10	2010-11	2011-12	2012-13	2013-14
St Johnstone v Aberdeen	-	1-0/1-1	0-1/0-0	1-2	1-2/3-1	0-2
St Mirren v Dundee	-	-	-	-	3-1/1-2	-

Scottish Championship						
Cowdenbeath v Alloa	-	1-1/1-1	-	-	-	0-2/2-2
Hibernian v Falkirk	3-2/0-0	2-0	-	-	-	-
Queen of Sth v Livingston	6-1/3-3	-	-	0-2/0-4	-	2-2/2-0
Raith v Hearts	-	-	-	-	-	-
Rangers v Dumbarton	-	-	-	-	-	-

Scottish League One						
Ayr v Forfar	-	-	0-1/3-1	-	2-3/2-1	2-0/2-3
Dunfermline v Airdrieonians	0-0/1-1	2-0/2-0	-	-	1-3/1-2	2-1/0-1
Peterhead v Morton	-	-	-	-	-	-
Stenh'semuir v Stirling	-	1-2/1-3	-	4-0/4-0	-	-
Stranraer v Brechin	1-2/0-3	-	-	-	0-2/3-2	3-0/1-2

Scottish League Two						
Albion v East Fife	-	-	-	0-3/1-1	0-3/1-1	-
Berwick v East Stirling	2-1/1-2	0-1/2-2	3-0/1-1	4-2/0-2	3-0/2-0	2-0/1-0
Elgin v Clyde	-	-	0-1/0-1	0-3/1-1	2-1/4-2	1-0/3-1
Montrose v Annan	1-1/0-3	0-0/1-2	1-1/0-1	2-3/1-1	0-0/5-1	0-2/2-1
Queen's Park v Arbroath	1-2/0-1	-	5-2/1-1	-	-	-

Monday August 25th, 2014

Conference						
Altrincham v Gateshead	-	3-2	1-1	-	-	-
Barnet v Dartford	-	-	-	-	-	1-0
Braintree v Nuneaton	-	-	-	-	2-2	2-1
Eastleigh v Welling	-	-	-	-	-	-
Forest Green v Bristol Rovers	-	-	-	-	-	-
Grimsby v Alfreton	-	-	-	5-2	4-2	3-1
Halifax v Lincoln	-	-	-	-	-	5-1
Kidderminster v Chester	-	-	-	-	-	3-1
Telford v Southport	-	-	-	0-1	1-3	-
Torquay v Aldershot	-	1-1	0-1	1-0	4-3	-
Woking v Dover	-	-	-	-	-	-
Wrexham v Macclesfield	-	-	-	-	0-0	1-0

Saturday August 30th, 2014

Premier League						
Aston Villa v Hull	1-0	3-0	-	-	-	3-1
Burnley v Man Utd	-	1-0	-	-	-	-
Everton v Chelsea	0-0	2-1	1-0	2-0	1-2	1-0
Leicester v Arsenal	-	-	-	-	-	-
Man City v Stoke	3-0	2-0	3-0	3-0	3-0	1-0
Newcastle v Crystal Palace	-	2-0	-	-	-	1-0
QPR v Sunderland	-	-	-	2-3	3-1	-
Swansea v West Brom	-	0-2	-	3-0	3-1	1-2
Tottenham v Liverpool	2-1	2-1	2-1	4-0	2-1	0-5
West Ham v Southampton	-	-	-	1-1	4-1	3-1

Championship						
Brighton v Charlton	-	0-2	1-1	-	0-0	3-0
Derby v Ipswich	0-1	1-3	1-2	0-0	0-1	4-4
Fulham v Cardiff	-	-	-	-	-	1-2
Leeds v Bolton	-	-	-	-	1-0	1-5
Middlesbro v Reading	-	1-1	3-1	0-2	-	3-0
Millwall v Blackpool	-	-	-	2-2	0-2	3-1
Norwich v Bournemouth	-	-	-	-	-	-
Rotherham v Brentford	0-0	-	-	-	-	3-0

Results cover matches from Premier League to Conference and Scottish Premiership to League Two

	2008-09	2009-10	2010-11	2011-12	2012-13	2013-14
Sheff Wed v Nottm Forest	1-0	1-1	-	-	0-1	0-1
Watford v Huddersfield	-	-	-	-	4-0	1-4
Wigan v Birmingham	-	2-3	2-1	-	-	0-0
Wolves v Blackburn	-	1-1	2-3	0-2	1-1	-
League 1						
Colchester v Peterborough	0-1	-	2-1	-	-	1-0
Doncaster v Oldham	-	-	-	-	1-0	-
Fleetwood Town v Leyton Orient	-	-	-	-	-	-
Gillingham v Crewe	-	-	1-3	3-4	-	1-3
MK Dons v Crawley Town	-	-	-	-	0-0	0-2
Notts Co v Bristol City	-	-	-	-	-	1-1
Port Vale v Chesterfield	0-1	1-2	1-1	-	0-2	-
Preston v Sheff Utd	0-0	2-1	3-1	2-4	0-1	0-0
Rochdale v Bradford	3-0	1-3	-	-	0-0	-
Scunthorpe v Walsall	1-1	-	-	0-1	1-1	-
Swindon v Coventry	-	-	-	-	2-2	2-1
Yeovil v Barnsley	-	-	-	-	-	1-4
League 2						
AFC Wimbledon v Stevenage	-	0-3	-	-	-	-
Bury v Accrington	1-0	0-2	3-0	-	-	3-0
Cambridge U v Carlisle	-	-	-	-	-	-
Cheltenham v Hartlepool	2-0	-	-	-	-	2-2
Mansfield v Burton	0-2	-	-	-	-	0-0
Northampton v Exeter	-	-	-	-	3-0	1-2
Oxford v Dag & Red	-	-	-	2-1	2-3	2-1
Plymouth v Southend	-	-	-	2-2	1-1	1-1
Portsmouth v Newport Co	-	-	-	-	-	0-2
Shrewsbury v Luton	3-0	-	-	-	-	-
Tranmere v Morecambe	-	-	-	-	-	-
York v Wycombe	-	-	-	-	1-3	2-0
Conference						
Aldershot v Grimsby	2-2	1-1	-	-	-	0-3
Alfreton v Braintree	-	-	-	0-1	1-1	3-1
Bristol Rovers v Halifax	-	-	-	-	-	-
Dartford v Telford	-	-	-	-	1-4	-
Dover v Kidderminster	-	-	-	-	-	-
Gateshead v Chester	-	-	-	-	-	3-2
Lincoln v Torquay	-	0-0	0-2	-	-	-
Macclesfield v Eastleigh	-	-	-	-	-	-
Nuneaton v Altrincham	-	-	-	-	-	-
Southport v Barnet	-	-	-	-	-	1-1
Welling v Forest Green	-	-	-	-	-	5-2
Wrexham v Woking	1-1	-	-	-	3-1	2-0
Scottish Premiership						
Aberdeen v Partick	-	-	-	-	-	4-0
Hamilton v Ross County	-	-	-	5-1/0-2	-	-
Inverness CT v Kilmarnock	3-1/2-1	-	1-3	2-1/1-1	1-1/1-1	2-1
Motherwell v St Johnstone	-	1-3	4-0	0-3/3-2/5-1	1-1/3-2	4-0/2-1
St Mirren v Dundee Utd	0-2	0-0/1-2	1-1/1-1	2-2	0-1/0-0	4-1
Scottish Championship						
Alloa v Hibernian	-	-	-	-	-	-
Cowdenbeath v Raith	-	-	1-2/0-3	-	4-4/1-1	3-4/1-0
Dumbarton v Livingston	-	-	1-2/0-3	-	3-4/0-3	1-2/2-2
Hearts v Falkirk	2-1	0-0/3-2	-	-	-	-
Rangers v Queen of Sth	-	-	-	-	-	-

Results cover matches from Premier League to Conference and Scottish Premiership to League Two

	2008-09	2009-10	2010-11	2011-12	2012-13	2013-14
Scottish League One						
Airdrieonians v Stirling	-	-	-	1-1/4-1	-	-
Brechin v Peterhead	2-2/1-1	3-0/1-2	4-2/3-1	-	-	-
Forfar v Morton	-	-	-	-	-	-
Stenh'semuir v Ayr	-	-	3-1/2-1	-	1-1/4-0	1-1/1-1
Stranraer v Dunfermline	-	-	-	-	-	1-2/3-1
Scottish League Two						
Albion v Queen's Park	-	0-1/1-0	2-1/1-2	-	-	2-1/1-0
Annan v Elgin	5-0/6-0	0-2/3-3	0-1/2-2	1-1/1-1	2-0/2-2	2-1/2-0
Arbroath v Montrose	-	-	4-0/4-1	-	-	-
Clyde v Berwick	-	-	1-4/2-0	1-4/2-2	2-1/2-1	1-0/3-3
East Fife v East Stirling	-	-	-	-	-	-

Sunday August 31th, 2014

Scottish Premiership						
Dundee v Celtic	-	-	-	-	0-2	-

Saturday September 6th, 2014

League 1						
Barnsley v Doncaster	4-1	0-1	2-2	2-0	-	0-0
Bradford v Yeovil	-	-	-	-	-	-
Bristol City v Scunthorpe	-	1-1	2-0	-	-	-
Chesterfield v Swindon	-	-	-	-	-	-
Coventry v Gillingham	-	-	-	-	-	2-1
Crawley Town v Rochdale	-	-	-	-	-	-
Crewe v Notts Co	-	0-1	-	-	1-2	1-3
Leyton Orient v Preston	-	-	-	2-1	2-0	0-1
Oldham v Fleetwood Town	-	-	-	-	-	-
Peterborough v Port Vale	-	-	-	-	-	0-0
Sheff Utd v MK Dons	-	-	-	2-1	0-0	0-1
Walsall v Colchester	2-0	1-0	0-1	3-1	1-0	0-1
League 2						
Accrington v Tranmere	-	-	-	-	-	-
Carlisle v AFC Wimbledon	-	-	-	-	-	-
Dag & Red v Northampton	-	0-1	-	0-1	0-1	0-3
Exeter v Mansfield	-	-	-	-	-	0-1
Hartlepool v Shrewsbury	-	-	-	-	2-2	-
Luton v Plymouth	-	-	-	-	-	-
Morecambe v Cheltenham	-	1-0	1-1	3-1	0-0	0-1
Newport Co v Cambridge U	-	-	1-1	0-1	6-2	-
Southend v Oxford	-	-	2-1	2-1	1-0	3-0
Stevenage v York	3-3	1-0	-	-	-	-
Wycombe v Bury	2-1	-	1-0	0-2	-	1-2
Conference						
Altrincham v Dartford	-	-	-	-	-	-
Barnet v Alfreton	-	-	-	-	-	1-0
Braintree v Bristol Rovers	-	-	-	-	-	-
Chester v Macclesfield	0-2	-	-	-	-	2-1
Eastleigh v Southport	-	-	-	-	-	-
Forest Green v Wrexham	2-3	0-2	3-0	1-0	0-0	1-1
Grimsby v Welling	-	-	-	-	-	1-1
Halifax v Aldershot	-	-	-	-	-	4-0
Kidderminster v Gateshead	-	3-2	2-1	2-3	1-1	3-1
Telford v Dover	-	-	-	-	-	-
Torquay v Nuneaton	-	-	-	-	-	-
Woking v Lincoln	-	-	-	-	1-1	0-0

Results cover matches from Premier League to Conference and Scottish Premiership to League Two

Sunday September 7th, 2014

League 2	2008-09	2009-10	2010-11	2011-12	2012-13	2013-14
Burton v Portsmouth	-	-	-	-	-	1-2

Tuesday September 9th, 2014

Conference	2008-09	2009-10	2010-11	2011-12	2012-13	2013-14
Aldershot v Woking	-	-	-	-	-	2-1
Alfreton v Altrincham	-	-	-	-	-	-
Bristol Rovers v Wrexham	-	-	-	-	-	-
Chester v Torquay	-	-	-	-	-	-
Dartford v Eastleigh	-	-	-	-	-	-
Dover v Barnet	-	-	-	-	-	-
Gateshead v Telford	-	-	-	3-0	1-1	-
Lincoln v Grimsby	1-1	0-0	-	1-2	1-4	0-2
Macclesfield v Halifax	-	-	-	-	-	2-2
Nuneaton v Forest Green	-	-	-	-	1-1	1-1
Southport v Kidderminster	-	-	2-2	1-2	1-3	1-2
Welling v Braintree	-	-	-	-	-	0-2

Saturday September 13th, 2014

Premier League	2008-09	2009-10	2010-11	2011-12	2012-13	2013-14
Arsenal v Man City	2-0	0-0	0-0	1-0	0-2	1-1
Chelsea v Swansea	-	-	-	4-1	2-0	1-0
Crystal Palace v Burnley	0-0	-	0-0	2-0	4-3	-
Hull v West Ham	1-0	3-3	-	0-2	-	1-0
Liverpool v Aston Villa	5-0	1-3	3-0	1-1	1-3	2-2
Man Utd v QPR	-	-	-	2-0	3-1	-
Southampton v Newcastle	-	-	-	-	2-0	4-0
Stoke v Leicester	-	-	-	-	-	-
Sunderland v Tottenham	1-1	3-1	1-2	0-0	1-2	1-2
West Brom v Everton	1-2	-	1-0	0-1	2-0	1-1

Championship	2008-09	2009-10	2010-11	2011-12	2012-13	2013-14
Birmingham v Leeds	-	-	-	1-0	1-0	1-3
Blackburn v Wigan	2-0	2-1	2-1	0-1	-	4-3
Blackpool v Wolves	2-2	-	2-1	-	1-2	-
Bolton v Sheff Wed	-	-	-	-	0-1	1-1
Bournemouth v Rotherham	0-0	1-0	-	-	-	-
Brentford v Brighton	-	0-0	0-1	-	-	-
Cardiff v Norwich	2-2	-	3-1	-	-	2-1
Charlton v Watford	2-3	-	-	-	1-2	3-1
Huddersfield v Middlesbro	-	-	-	-	2-1	2-2
Ipswich v Millwall	-	-	2-0	0-3	3-0	3-0
Reading v Fulham	-	-	-	-	3-3	-

League 1	2008-09	2009-10	2010-11	2011-12	2012-13	2013-14
Barnsley v MK Dons	-	-	-	-	-	-
Bradford v Swindon	-	-	-	0-0	-	1-1
Bristol City v Doncaster	4-1	2-5	1-0	2-1	-	-
Chesterfield v Scunthorpe	-	-	-	1-4	-	1-1
Coventry v Yeovil	-	-	-	-	0-1	-
Crawley Town v Fleetwood	-	-	1-1	-	-	-
Crewe v Port Vale	-	1-2	2-1	1-1	-	1-2
Leyton Orient v Colchester	2-1	0-1	4-2	0-1	0-2	2-1
Oldham v Gillingham	-	1-0	-	-	-	1-0
Peterborough v Notts Co	-	-	2-3	-	-	4-3
Sheff Utd v Rochdale	-	-	-	3-0	-	-
Walsall v Preston	-	-	-	1-0	3-1	0-3

Results cover matches from Premier League to Conference and Scottish Premiership to League Two

	2008-09	2009-10	2010-11	2011-12	2012-13	2013-14
League 2						
Accrington v AFC Wimbledon	-	-	-	2-1	4-0	3-2
Burton v York	2-1	-	-	-	3-1	1-1
Carlisle v Bury	-	-	-	4-1	2-1	-
Dag & Red v Cambridge U	-	-	-	-	-	-
Exeter v Oxford	-	-	-	-	1-3	0-0
Hartlepool v Tranmere	2-1	1-0	1-1	0-2	0-2	-
Luton v Cheltenham	-	-	-	-	-	-
Morecambe v Plymouth	-	-	-	2-2	2-3	2-1
Newport Co v Northampton	-	-	-	-	-	1-2
Southend v Portsmouth	-	-	-	-	-	2-1
Stevenage v Shrewsbury	-	-	1-1	-	1-1	1-3
Wycombe v Mansfield	-	-	-	-	-	0-1
Conference						
Altrincham v Eastleigh	-	-	-	-	-	-
Braintree v Kidderminster	-	-	-	1-4	1-1	0-1
Dover v Macclesfield	-	-	-	-	-	-
Forest Green v Halifax	-	-	-	-	-	2-1
Gateshead v Dartford	-	-	-	-	2-0	2-0
Grimsby v Torquay	-	0-3	-	-	-	-
Lincoln v Bristol Rovers	-	-	-	-	-	-
Nuneaton v Aldershot	-	-	-	-	-	2-1
Southport v Alfreton	-	-	-	2-1	0-2	2-1
Telford v Barnet	-	-	-	-	-	-
Woking v Chester	-	-	-	-	-	0-1
Wrexham v Welling	-	-	-	-	-	2-1
Scottish Premiership						
Celtic v Aberdeen	3-2/2-0	3-0	9-0/1-0	2-1	1-0/4-3	3-1/5-2
Dundee Utd v Hamilton	1-1	1-1/0-2	2-1	-	-	-
Kilmarnock v St Mirren	0-1/2-1	1-2/1-1	2-1/2-0	2-1/0-2	3-1/1-1/1-3	2-1/1-0
Partick v Inverness CT	-	2-1/0-1	-	-	-	0-0
Ross County v Motherwell	-	-	-	-	0-0/3-0	1-2
St Johnstone v Dundee	2-0/0-0	-	-	-	1-0	-
Scottish Championship						
Dumbarton v Hearts	-	-	-	-	-	-
Falkirk v Queen of Sth	-	-	3-1/0-3	1-0/3-0	-	2-1/1-0
Hibernian v Cowdenbeath	-	-	-	-	-	-
Livingston v Alloa	-	-	3-3/4-0	-	-	3-2/2-0
Raith v Rangers	-	-	-	-	-	-
Scottish League One						
Ayr v Stranraer	3-2/5-0	-	-	-	2-1/2-1	3-6/5-0
Dunfermline v Stenh'semuir	-	-	-	-	-	3-2/0-0
Forfar v Peterhead	-	-	1-1/2-1	-	-	-
Morton v Airdrieonians	2-0/0-0	1-0/2-1	-	-	2-0/5-2	-
Stirling v Brechin	1-2/2-3	1-0/6-2	-	1-0/2-3	-	-
Scottish League Two						
Annan v Berwick	1-2/1-1	1-1/0-1	1-1/2-3	2-2/1-1	3-2/2-2	3-2/4-0
Arbroath v East Fife	0-1/0-2	0-1/2-2	-	3-0/2-2	2-0/1-0	2-2/2-1
East Stirling v Clyde	-	-	0-0/2-0	1-1/0-1	3-0/3-0	0-1/2-4
Montrose v Albion	1-2/1-0	0-0/0-0	0-2/0-2	-	-	2-1/2-1
Queen's Park v Elgin	-	0-3/0-1	1-1/1-0	6-0/1-3	1-1/0-1	3-3/2-0

Sunday September 14th, 2014

	2008-09	2009-10	2010-11	2011-12	2012-13	2013-14
Championship						
Nottm Forest v Derby	1-3	3-2	5-2	1-2	0-1	1-0

Results cover matches from Premier League to Conference and Scottish Premiership to League Two

Tuesday September 16th, 2014

Championship

	2008-09	2009-10	2010-11	2011-12	2012-13	2013-14
Birmingham v Sheff Wed	3-1	-	-	-	0-0	4-1
Blackburn v Derby	-	-	-	-	2-0	1-1
Blackpool v Watford	0-2	3-2	-	0-0	2-2	1-0
Bolton v Rotherham	-	-	-	-	-	-
Bournemouth v Leeds	-	-	-	-	-	4-1
Brentford v Norwich	-	2-1	-	-	-	-
Cardiff v Middlesbro	-	1-0	0-3	2-3	1-0	-
Charlton v Wolves	1-3	-	-	-	2-1	-
Huddersfield v Wigan	-	-	-	-	-	1-0
Ipswich v Brighton	-	-	-	3-1	0-3	2-0
Reading v Millwall	-	-	2-1	2-2	-	1-1

League 1

	2008-09	2009-10	2010-11	2011-12	2012-13	2013-14
Colchester v Sheff Utd	-	-	-	1-1	1-1	0-1
Doncaster v Crawley Town	-	-	-	-	0-1	-
Fleetwood Town v Barnsley	-	-	-	-	-	-
Gillingham v Peterborough	-	-	-	-	-	2-2
MK Dons v Bradford	-	-	-	-	-	2-3
Notts Co v Leyton Orient	-	-	3-2	1-2	1-1	0-0
Port Vale v Bristol City	-	-	-	-	-	1-1
Preston v Chesterfield	-	-	-	0-0	-	-
Rochdale v Walsall	-	-	3-2	3-3	-	-
Scunthorpe v Coventry	-	1-0	0-2	-	1-2	-
Swindon v Oldham	2-0	4-2	0-2	-	1-1	0-1
Yeovil v Crewe	3-2	-	-	-	1-0	-

League 2

	2008-09	2009-10	2010-11	2011-12	2012-13	2013-14
AFC Wimbledon v Burton	-	-	-	4-0	1-1	3-1
Bury v Stevenage	-	-	3-0	1-2	2-0	-
Cambridge U v Exeter	-	-	-	-	-	-
Cheltenham v Southend	0-0	-	0-2	3-0	1-3	1-2
Mansfield v Morecambe	-	-	-	-	-	1-2
Northampton v Hartlepool	1-0	-	-	-	-	2-0
Oxford v Accrington	-	-	0-0	1-1	5-0	1-2
Plymouth v Wycombe	-	-	-	-	0-1	0-3
Portsmouth v Dag & Red	-	-	-	-	-	1-0
Shrewsbury v Carlisle	-	-	-	-	2-1	2-2
Tranmere v Newport Co	-	-	-	-	-	-
York v Luton	-	0-0	1-0	3-0	-	-

Conference

	2008-09	2009-10	2010-11	2011-12	2012-13	2013-14
Aldershot v Braintree	-	-	-	-	-	2-1
Alfreton v Telford	-	-	-	0-0	1-1	-
Barnet v Wrexham	-	-	-	-	-	1-1
Bristol Rovers v Nuneaton	-	-	-	-	-	-
Chester v Southport	-	-	-	-	-	2-2
Dartford v Dover	-	-	-	-	-	-
Eastleigh v Forest Green	-	-	-	-	-	-
Halifax v Grimsby	-	-	-	-	-	4-0
Kidderminster v Altrincham	4-0	3-0	2-1	-	-	-
Macclesfield v Gateshead	-	-	-	-	0-4	0-2
Torquay v Woking	2-1	-	-	-	-	-
Welling v Lincoln	-	-	-	-	-	1-0

Wednesday September 17th, 2014

Championship

	2008-09	2009-10	2010-11	2011-12	2012-13	2013-14
Nottm Forest v Fulham	-	-	-	-	-	-

Results cover matches from Premier League to Conference and Scottish Premiership to League Two

Saturday September 20th, 2014

Premier League	2008-09	2009-10	2010-11	2011-12	2012-13	2013-14
Aston Villa v Arsenal	2-2	0-0	2-4	1-2	0-0	1-2
Burnley v Sunderland	-	3-1	-	-	-	-
Everton v Crystal Palace	-	-	-	-	-	2-3
Leicester v Man Utd	-	-	-	-	-	-
Man City v Chelsea	1-3	2-1	1-0	2-1	2-0	0-1
Newcastle v Hull	1-2	-	-	-	-	2-3
QPR v Stoke	-	-	-	1-0	0-2	-
Swansea v Southampton	3-0	-	-	-	0-0	0-1
Tottenham v West Brom	1-0	-	2-2	1-0	1-1	1-1
West Ham v Liverpool	0-3	2-3	3-1	-	2-3	1-2

Championship						
Brighton v Blackpool	-	-	-	2-2	6-1	1-1
Derby v Cardiff	1-1	2-0	1-2	0-3	1-1	-
Fulham v Blackburn	1-2	3-0	3-2	1-1	-	-
Leeds v Huddersfield	1-2	2-2	-	-	1-2	5-1
Middlesbro v Brentford	-	-	-	-	-	-
Millwall v Nottm Forest	-	-	0-0	2-0	0-1	2-2
Norwich v Birmingham	1-1	-	-	-	-	-
Rotherham v Charlton	-	-	-	-	-	-
Sheff Wed v Reading	1-2	0-2	-	-	-	5-2
Watford v Bournemouth	-	-	-	-	-	6-1
Wigan v Ipswich	-	-	-	-	-	2-0
Wolves v Bolton	-	2-1	2-3	2-3	2-2	-

League 1						
Colchester v Bradford	-	-	-	-	-	0-2
Doncaster v Chesterfield	-	-	-	-	-	-
Fleetwood Town v Bristol City	-	-	-	-	-	-
Gillingham v Walsall	-	0-0	-	-	-	2-2
MK Dons v Crewe	2-2	-	-	-	1-0	1-0
Notts Co v Oldham	-	-	0-2	1-0	1-0	3-2
Port Vale v Barnsley	-	-	-	-	-	-
Preston v Crawley Town	-	-	-	-	1-2	1-0
Rochdale v Coventry	-	-	-	-	-	-
Scunthorpe v Leyton Orient	2-1	-	-	2-3	2-1	-
Swindon v Sheff Utd	-	-	-	-	0-0	2-1
Yeovil v Peterborough	0-1	-	0-2	-	-	-

League 2						
AFC Wimbledon v Morecambe	-	-	-	1-1	2-0	0-3
Bury v Burton	-	3-0	1-0	-	-	0-0
Cambridge U v Luton	-	3-4	0-0	1-1	2-2	1-1
Cheltenham v Dag & Red	-	1-1	-	2-1	2-0	2-3
Mansfield v Carlisle	-	-	-	-	-	-
Northampton v Accrington	-	4-0	0-0	0-0	2-0	1-0
Oxford v Stevenage	1-1	2-1	1-2	-	-	-
Plymouth v Hartlepool	-	-	0-1	-	-	1-1
Portsmouth v Wycombe	-	-	-	-	-	2-2
Shrewsbury v Newport Co	-	-	-	-	-	-
Tranmere v Exeter	-	3-1	4-0	2-0	-	-
York v Southend	-	-	-	-	2-1	0-0

Conference						
Aldershot v Lincoln	2-0	3-1	2-2	-	-	2-3
Alfreton v Nuneaton	-	-	-	-	0-3	1-1
Barnet v Altrincham	-	-	-	-	-	-

Results cover matches from Premier League to Conference and Scottish Premiership to League Two

	2008-09	2009-10	2010-11	2011-12	2012-13	2013-14
Bristol Rovers v Woking	-	-	-	-	-	-
Chester v Wrexham	-	-	-	-	-	0-0
Dartford v Forest Green	-	-	-	-	0-1	0-1
Eastleigh v Braintree	-	-	-	-	-	-
Halifax v Telford	-	-	-	-	-	-
Kidderminster v Grimsby	-	-	3-2	1-1	0-0	0-1
Macclesfield v Southport	-	-	-	-	2-2	2-2
Torquay v Dover	-	-	-	-	-	-
Welling v Gateshead	-	-	-	-	-	2-0

Scottish Premiership						
Aberdeen v Ross County	-	-	-	-	0-0/0-1	1-0
Celtic v Motherwell	2-0	0-0/2-1/4-0	1-0/4-0	4-0/1-0	1-0	2-0/3-0
Dundee v Dundee Utd	-	-	-	-	0-3	-
Hamilton v Kilmarnock	1-0/2-1	0-0/3-0	2-2/1-1	-	-	-
Inverness CT v St Johnstone	-	-	1-1/2-0	0-1	1-1/0-0	1-0/2-0
Partick v St Mirren	-	-	-	-	-	0-3/1-1

Scottish Championship						
Alloa v Rangers	-	-	-	-	-	-
Falkirk v Dumbarton	-	-	-	-	3-4/1-3	1-2/2-0
Hearts v Cowdenbeath	-	-	-	-	-	-
Livingston v Raith	-	-	-	1-1/4-0	2-1/2-3	3-0/2-0
Queen of Sth v Hibernian	-	-	-	-	-	-

Scottish League One						
Airdrieonians v Stranraer	-	-	-	-	-	3-2/1-1
Brechin v Ayr	0-1/1-0	-	0-3/1-0	-	2-1/2-1	1-1/2-1
Morton v Dunfermline	1-1/2-1	0-2/1-2	2-1/0-2	-	4-2/0-1	-
Peterhead v Stenh'semuir	-	2-2/0-1	2-2/0-3	-	-	-
Stirling v Forfar	-	-	-	2-4/2-2	-	-
Scottish League Two						
Berwick v Albion	0-3/1-1	2-0/1-2	1-6/2-2	-	-	2-1/3-1
Clyde v Arbroath	-	1-0/0-2	1-1/0-3	-	-	-
East Fife v Queen's Park	1-2/4-2	-	-	-	-	-
East Stirling v Annan	2-1/1-1	1-3/3-1	1-5/2-0	1-0/0-4	2-2/1-2	1-1/2-1
Elgin v Montrose	1-2/1-0	0-1/5-2	3-2/1-0	3-1/2-1	6-1/3-2	3-3/2-3

Saturday September 27th, 2014

Premier League						
Arsenal v Tottenham	4-4	3-0	2-3	5-2	5-2	1-0
Chelsea v Aston Villa	2-0	7-1	3-3	1-3	8-0	2-1
Crystal Palace v Leicester	-	0-1	3-2	1-2	2-2	-
Hull v Man City	2-2	2-1	-	-	-	0-2
Liverpool v Everton	1-1	1-0	2-2	3-0	0-0	4-0
Man Utd v West Ham	2-0	3-0	3-0	-	1-0	3-1
Southampton v QPR	0-0	-	-	-	1-2	-
Stoke v Newcastle	1-1	-	4-0	1-3	2-1	1-0
Sunderland v Swansea	-	-	-	2-0	0-0	1-3
West Brom v Burnley	-	-	-	-	-	-

Championship						
Birmingham v Fulham	-	1-0	0-2	-	-	-
Blackburn v Watford	-	-	-	-	1-0	1-0
Blackpool v Norwich	2-0	-	-	-	-	-
Bolton v Derby	-	-	-	-	2-0	2-2
Bournemouth v Wigan	-	-	-	-	-	1-0
Brentford v Leeds	-	0-0	-	-	-	-
Cardiff v Sheff Wed	2-0	3-2	-	-	1-0	-
Charlton v Middlesbro	-	-	-	-	1-4	0-1

Results cover matches from Premier League to Conference and Scottish Premiership to League Two

	2008-09	2009-10	2010-11	2011-12	2012-13	2013-14
Huddersfield v Millwall	1-2	1-0	-	-	3-0	1-0
Ipswich v Rotherham	-	-	-	-	-	-
Nottm Forest v Brighton	-	-	-	1-1	2-2	1-2
Reading v Wolves	1-0	-	-	-	-	-
League 1						
Barnsley v Swindon	-	-	-	-	-	-
Bradford v Port Vale	0-1	0-0	0-2	1-1	0-1	1-0
Bristol City v MK Dons	-	-	-	-	-	2-2
Chesterfield v Notts Co	3-1	2-1	-	1-3	-	-
Coventry v Preston	0-0	1-1	1-2	-	1-1	4-4
Crawley Town v Yeovil	-	-	-	-	0-1	-
Crewe v Colchester	2-0	-	-	-	3-2	0-0
Leyton Orient v Rochdale	-	-	2-1	2-1	-	-
Oldham v Scunthorpe	3-0	-	-	1-2	1-1	-
Peterborough v Fleetwood Town	-	-	-	-	-	-
Sheff Utd v Gillingham	-	-	-	-	-	1-2
Walsall v Doncaster	-	-	-	-	0-3	-
League 2						
Accrington v Plymouth	-	-	-	0-4	1-1	1-1
Burton v Cheltenham	-	5-6	2-0	0-2	3-1	2-1
Carlisle v Tranmere	1-2	3-0	2-0	0-0	0-3	4-1
Dag & Red v York	-	-	-	-	0-1	2-0
Exeter v Bury	0-0	-	-	3-2	-	2-2
Hartlepool v Portsmouth	-	-	-	-	0-0	0-0
Luton v Oxford	-	2-1	-	-	-	-
Morecambe v Northampton	-	2-4	1-2	1-2	1-1	1-1
Newport Co v AFC Wimbledon	-	-	3-3	-	-	1-2
Southend v Shrewsbury	-	-	0-2	3-0	-	-
Stevenage v Mansfield	3-2	3-1	-	-	-	-
Wycombe v Cambridge U	-	-	-	-	-	-
Conference						
Altrincham v Welling	-	-	-	-	-	-
Braintree v Halifax	-	-	-	-	-	1-0
Dover v Alfreton	-	-	-	-	-	-
Forest Green v Barnet	-	-	-	-	-	1-2
Gateshead v Aldershot	-	-	-	-	-	0-0
Grimsby v Chester	1-3	-	-	-	-	2-1
Lincoln v Macclesfield	1-0	0-0	2-1	-	2-3	1-0
Nuneaton v Dartford	-	-	-	-	1-0	3-1
Southport v Bristol Rovers	-	-	-	-	-	-
Telford v Torquay	-	-	-	-	-	-
Woking v Kidderminster	1-5	-	-	-	2-2	1-0
Wrexham v Eastleigh	-	-	-	-	-	-
Scottish Premiership						
Aberdeen v Inverness CT	0-2/1-0	-	1-2/1-0	2-1/0-1	2-3	1-0/0-1
Dundee Utd v St Johnstone	-	3-3	1-0/2-0	0-0	1-1/0-1	4-0/0-1
Kilmarnock v Partick	-	-	-	-	-	2-1/1-2
Motherwell v Hamilton	2-0/1-0	1-0	0-1/1-0	-	-	-
Ross County v Dundee	1-2/1-1	0-1/1-1	0-3/0-1	1-1/3-0	1-1	-
St Mirren v Celtic	1-3	0-2/4-0	0-1	0-2/0-2	0-5/1-1	0-4
Scottish Championship						
Cowdenbeath v Queen of Sth	-	-	1-3/2-2	-	-	0-2/1-1
Dumbarton v Alloa	-	1-3/3-1	4-1/2-2	-	-	1-1/4-1
Hearts v Livingston	-	-	-	-	-	-
Raith v Falkirk	-	-	2-1/1-2	1-0/2-2	2-1/0-0	1-1/2-4
Rangers v Hibernian	1-0	1-1/3-0	0-3	1-0/4-0	-	-

Results cover matches from Premier League to Conference and Scottish Premiership to League Two

	2008-09	2009-10	2010-11	2011-12	2012-13	2013-14
Scottish League One						
Ayr v Airdrieonians	-	1-1/1-4	1-0/3-1	-	-	2-2/3-0
Dunfermline v Peterhead	-	-	-	-	-	-
Forfar v Brechin	-	-	1-1/2-1	0-0/4-1	1-0/1-4	2-0/1-1
Stenh'semuir v Morton	-	-	-	-	-	-
Stranraer v Stirling	1-0/2-8	-	-	-	-	-
Scottish League Two						
Albion v East Stirling	0-2/0-2	3-0/2-1	1-0/2-0	-	-	3-2/2-1
Arbroath v Elgin	-	-	2-0/3-5	-	-	-
Clyde v Annan	-	-	0-2/0-2	0-0/1-1	2-1/2-3	2-1/0-3
Montrose v East Fife	-	-	-	-	-	-
Queen's Park v Berwick	-	2-0/2-3	0-2/1-0	1-1/2-2	1-1/2-1	0-4/1-3

Tuesday September 30th, 2014

	2008-09	2009-10	2010-11	2011-12	2012-13	2013-14
Championship						
Brighton v Cardiff	-	-	-	2-2	0-0	-
Derby v Bournemouth	-	-	-	-	-	1-0
Leeds v Reading	-	-	0-0	0-1	-	2-4
Middlesbro v Blackpool	-	0-3	-	2-2	4-2	1-1
Millwall v Birmingham	-	-	-	0-6	3-3	2-3
Norwich v Charlton	1-0	2-2	-	-	-	-
Rotherham v Blackburn	-	-	-	-	-	-
Sheff Wed v Ipswich	0-0	0-1	-	-	1-1	1-1
Watford v Brentford	-	-	-	-	-	-
Wigan v Nottm Forest	-	-	-	-	-	2-1
Wolves v Huddersfield	-	-	-	-	1-3	-
Conference						
Alfreton v Halifax	-	-	-	-	-	3-0
Altrincham v Macclesfield	-	-	-	-	-	-
Braintree v Barnet	-	-	-	-	-	0-3
Dover v Aldershot	-	-	-	-	-	-
Eastleigh v Bristol Rovers	-	-	-	-	-	-
Forest Green v Torquay	1-2	-	-	-	-	-
Grimsby v Southport	-	-	1-1	0-1	2-2	0-0
Lincoln v Gateshead	-	-	-	1-0	1-1	0-1
Telford v Chester	-	-	-	-	-	-
Welling v Dartford	-	-	-	-	-	1-1
Woking v Nuneaton	-	-	-	-	6-1	2-0
Wrexham v Kidderminster	0-1	2-2	2-2	2-0	1-2	0-0

Wednesday October 1st, 2014

	2008-09	2009-10	2010-11	2011-12	2012-13	2013-14
Championship						
Fulham v Bolton	2-1	1-1	3-0	2-0	-	-

Saturday October 4th, 2014

	2008-09	2009-10	2010-11	2011-12	2012-13	2013-14
Premier League						
Aston Villa v Man City	4-2	1-1	1-0	0-1	0-1	3-2
Chelsea v Arsenal	1-2	2-0	2-0	3-5	2-1	6-0
Hull v Crystal Palace	-	-	1-1	0-1	0-0	0-1
Leicester v Burnley	-	-	4-0	0-0	2-1	1-1
Liverpool v West Brom	3-0	-	1-0	0-1	0-2	4-1
Man Utd v Everton	1-0	3-0	1-0	4-4	2-0	0-1
Sunderland v Stoke	2-0	0-0	2-0	4-0	1-1	1-0
Swansea v Newcastle	-	1-1	-	0-2	1-0	3-0
Tottenham v Southampton	-	-	-	-	1-0	3-2
West Ham v QPR	-	-	-	-	1-1	-

Results cover matches from Premier League to Conference and Scottish Premiership to League Two

	2008-09	2009-10	2010-11	2011-12	2012-13	2013-14
Championship						
Blackburn v Huddersfield	-	-	-	-	1-0	0-0
Blackpool v Cardiff	1-1	1-1	-	1-1	1-2	-
Bolton v Bournemouth	-	-	-	-	-	2-2
Brentford v Reading	-	-	-	-	-	-
Charlton v Birmingham	0-0	-	-	-	1-1	0-2
Derby v Millwall	-	-	0-0	3-0	1-0	0-1
Leeds v Sheff Wed	-	-	-	-	2-1	1-1
Middlesbro v Fulham	0-0	-	-	-	-	-
Norwich v Rotherham	-	-	-	-	-	-
Nottm Forest v Ipswich	1-1	3-0	2-0	3-2	1-0	0-0
Watford v Brighton	-	-	-	1-0	0-1	2-0
Wolves v Wigan	-	0-2	1-2	3-1	-	-
League 1						
Bradford v Crewe	-	2-3	1-5	3-0	-	3-3
Chesterfield v Sheff Utd	-	-	-	0-1	-	-
Coventry v Crawley Town	-	-	-	-	3-1	2-2
Fleetwood Town v Port Vale	-	-	-	-	2-5	-
Leyton Orient v Swindon	1-2	0-0	3-0	-	0-0	2-0
Notts Co v Gillingham	0-1	-	-	-	-	3-1
Peterborough v Oldham	2-2	-	5-2	-	-	2-1
Preston v Colchester	-	-	-	2-4	0-0	1-1
Rochdale v Barnsley	-	-	-	-	-	-
Scunthorpe v Doncaster	-	2-2	1-3	-	2-3	-
Walsall v Bristol City	-	-	-	-	-	0-1
Yeovil v MK Dons	0-0	1-0	1-0	0-1	2-1	-
League 2						
Burton v Cambridge U	3-1	-	-	-	-	-
Bury v Tranmere	-	-	-	2-0	0-1	-
Cheltenham v AFC Wimbledon	-	-	-	0-0	2-1	1-0
Dag & Red v Exeter	1-2	-	1-1	-	1-1	1-1
Hartlepool v Carlisle	2-2	4-1	0-4	4-0	1-2	-
Mansfield v Accrington	-	-	-	-	-	2-3
Oxford v Newport Co	-	-	-	-	-	0-0
Plymouth v Shrewsbury	-	-	-	1-0	-	-
Southend v Morecambe	-	-	2-3	1-1	0-1	1-3
Stevenage v Luton	-	0-1	-	-	-	-
Wycombe v Northampton	-	-	2-2	-	0-0	1-1
York v Portsmouth	-	-	-	-	-	4-2
Conference						
Aldershot v Alfreton	-	-	-	-	-	2-3
Barnet v Eastleigh	-	-	-	-	-	-
Bristol Rovers v Dover	-	-	-	-	-	-
Chester v Welling	-	-	-	-	-	1-3
Dartford v Grimsby	-	-	-	-	1-2	1-0
Gateshead v Braintree	-	-	-	2-2	1-2	1-0
Halifax v Altrincham	-	-	-	-	-	-
Kidderminster v Telford	-	-	-	2-2	1-0	-
Macclesfield v Forest Green	-	-	-	-	1-2	1-2
Nuneaton v Lincoln	-	-	-	-	1-0	2-2
Southport v Woking	-	-	-	-	1-2	1-1
Torquay v Wrexham	1-1	-	-	-	-	-
Scottish Premiership						
Celtic v Hamilton	4-0/4-0	2-0	3-1/2-0	-	-	-
Dundee v Aberdeen	-	-	-	-	1-3/1-1	-
Inverness CT v Ross County	-	1-3/3-0	-	-	3-1/2-1	1-2

Results cover matches from Premier League to Conference and Scottish Premiership to League Two

	2008-09	2009-10	2010-11	2011-12	2012-13	2013-14
Kilmarnock v Dundee Utd	2-0	0-2/4-4	1-2/1-1	1-1	3-1/2-3	1-4
Partick v Motherwell	-	-	-	-	-	1-5
St Johnstone v St Mirren	-	1-0/2-2	2-1/0-0	0-1	2-1/1-0	2-0

Scottish Championship						
Dumbarton v Cowdenbeath	2-1/1-1	0-3/2-1	-	0-4/0-2	0-3/2-2	0-0/5-1
Falkirk v Alloa	-	-	-	-	-	0-0/3-1
Hibernian v Raith	-	-	-	-	-	-
Livingston v Rangers	-	-	-	-	-	-
Queen of Sth v Hearts	-	-	-	-	-	-

Scottish League One						
Airdrieonians v Forfar	-	-	2-0/3-1	4-4/3-0	-	0-2/5-1
Brechin v Morton	-	-	-	-	-	-
Peterhead v Ayr	3-0/2-3	-	2-4/1-2	-	-	-
Stenh'semuir v Stranraer	-	-	-	-	0-0/1-2	1-0/1-1
Stirling v Dunfermline	-	-	1-5/1-1	-	-	-

Tuesday October 7th, 2014

Conference						
Bristol Rovers v Dartford	-	-	-	-	-	-
Chester v Aldershot	0-1	-	-	-	-	1-1
Gateshead v Alfreton	-	-	-	2-0	2-0	3-0
Grimsby v Altrincham	-	-	0-1	-	-	-
Halifax v Wrexham	-	-	-	-	-	3-2
Kidderminster v Welling	-	-	-	-	-	2-0
Macclesfield v Barnet	2-1	1-1	1-1	0-0	-	2-0
Nuneaton v Dover	-	-	-	-	-	-
Southport v Lincoln	-	-	-	2-2	4-2	0-1
Telford v Forest Green	-	-	-	2-0	1-2	-

Saturday October 11th, 2014

League 1						
Barnsley v Bradford	-	-	-	-	-	-
Bristol City v Chesterfield	-	-	-	-	-	-
Colchester v Fleetwood Town	-	-	-	-	-	-
Crawley Town v Peterborough	-	-	-	-	-	1-0
Crewe v Coventry	-	-	-	-	1-0	1-2
Doncaster v Notts Co	-	-	-	-	0-1	-
Gillingham v Scunthorpe	-	-	-	-	-	-
MK Dons v Rochdale	-	-	1-1	3-1	-	-
Oldham v Walsall	3-2	1-0	1-1	2-1	1-1	0-1
Port Vale v Yeovil	-	-	-	-	-	-
Sheff Utd v Leyton Orient	-	-	-	3-1	0-0	1-1
Swindon v Preston	-	-	-	-	1-1	1-0

League 2						
Accrington v Dag & Red	0-0	0-1	-	3-0	0-2	1-2
AFC Wimbledon v Bury	-	-	-	-	-	0-1
Cambridge U v Oxford	1-1	1-1	-	-	-	-
Carlisle v Stevenage	-	-	-	1-0	2-1	0-0
Exeter v Hartlepool	-	3-1	1-2	0-0	-	0-3
Luton v Southend	-	-	-	-	-	-
Morecambe v Wycombe	0-0	-	0-3	-	0-1	1-1
Newport Co v York	-	-	4-0	2-1	-	3-0
Northampton v Burton	-	1-1	2-3	2-3	1-0	1-0
Portsmouth v Mansfield	-	-	-	-	-	1-1
Shrewsbury v Cheltenham	-	0-0	1-1	2-0	-	-
Tranmere v Plymouth	-	-	1-0	-	-	-

Results cover matches from Premier League to Conference and Scottish Premiership to League Two

	2008-09	2009-10	2010-11	2011-12	2012-13	2013-14
Conference						
Aldershot v Bristol Rovers	-	-	-	1-0	2-2	-
Alfreton v Torquay	-	-	-	-	-	-
Altrincham v Woking	1-0	-	-	-	-	-
Barnet v Kidderminster	-	-	-	-	-	1-0
Braintree v Southport	-	-	-	0-0	1-3	1-0
Dartford v Macclesfield	-	-	-	-	2-0	2-1
Dover v Chester	-	-	-	-	-	-
Eastleigh v Halifax	-	-	-	-	-	-
Forest Green v Gateshead	-	1-0	1-1	2-1	1-0	1-0
Lincoln v Telford	-	-	-	1-1	3-2	-
Welling v Nuneaton	-	-	-	-	-	1-2
Wrexham v Grimsby	-	-	2-0	2-2	0-0	0-1
Scottish Championship						
Alloa v Hearts	-	-	-	-	-	-
Cowdenbeath v Rangers	-	-	-	-	-	-
Falkirk v Livingston	-	-	-	4-3/2-5	1-2/2-0	4-1/1-1
Hibernian v Dumbarton	-	-	-	-	-	-
Raith v Queen of Sth	-	1-0/0-0	0-1/0-1	0-2/3-1	-	2-1/3-2
Scottish League One						
Airdrieonians v Brechin	-	-	1-1/2-2	2-3/4-1	-	3-1/2-1
Ayr v Dunfermline	-	1-0/1-2	-	-	-	2-4/1-1
Forfar v Stenh'semuir	1-0/4-4	-	1-1/2-0	2-3/1-2	3-2/3-3	1-2/3-0
Morton v Stirling	-	-	0-0/2-0	-	-	-
Stranraer v Peterhead	0-3/0-1	-	-	2-1/0-3	-	-
Scottish League Two						
Annan v Arbroath	-	-	1-2/3-0	-	-	-
Berwick v Montrose	3-2/0-1	2-0/0-2	1-0/0-1	1-2/2-2	1-4/4-0	1-1/5-0
East Fife v Clyde	-	1-0/1-1	-	-	-	-
East Stirling v Queen's Park	-	1-0/0-3	0-1/3-2	1-3/1-2	0-2/0-2	1-1/1-4
Elgin v Albion	1-6/1-0	0-2/3-1	2-2/1-1	-	-	1-2/1-1

Saturday October 18th, 2014

	2008-09	2009-10	2010-11	2011-12	2012-13	2013-14
Premier League						
Arsenal v Hull	1-2	3-0	-	-	-	2-0
Burnley v West Ham	-	2-1	-	2-2	-	-
Crystal Palace v Chelsea	-	-	-	-	-	1-0
Everton v Aston Villa	2-3	1-1	2-2	2-2	3-3	2-1
Man City v Tottenham	1-2	0-1	1-0	3-2	2-1	6-0
Newcastle v Leicester	-	1-0	-	-	-	-
QPR v Liverpool	-	-	-	3-2	0-3	-
Southampton v Sunderland	-	-	-	-	0-1	1-1
Stoke v Swansea	-	-	-	2-0	2-0	1-1
West Brom v Man Utd	0-5	-	1-2	1-2	5-5	0-3
Championship						
Birmingham v Bolton	-	1-2	2-1	-	2-1	1-2
Bournemouth v Charlton	-	-	2-2	0-1	-	2-1
Brighton v Middlesbro	-	-	-	1-1	0-1	0-2
Cardiff v Nottm Forest	2-0	1-1	0-2	1-0	3-0	-
Fulham v Norwich	-	-	-	2-1	5-0	1-0
Huddersfield v Blackpool	-	-	-	-	1-1	1-1
Ipswich v Blackburn	-	-	-	-	1-1	3-1
Millwall v Wolves	-	-	-	-	0-2	-
Reading v Derby	3-0	4-1	2-1	2-2	-	0-0
Rotherham v Leeds	-	-	-	-	-	-
Sheff Wed v Watford	2-0	2-1	-	-	1-4	1-4
Wigan v Brentford	-	-	-	-	-	-

Results cover matches from Premier League to Conference and Scottish Premiership to League Two

	2008-09	2009-10	2010-11	2011-12	2012-13	2013-14
League 1						
Bradford v Sheff Utd	-	-	-	-	-	2-0
Chesterfield v Oldham	-	-	-	1-1	-	-
Coventry v Bristol City	0-3	1-1	1-4	1-0	-	5-4
Fleetwood Town v Doncaster	-	-	-	-	-	-
Leyton Orient v MK Dons	1-2	1-2	2-2	0-3	2-0	2-1
Notts Co v Crawley Town	-	-	-	-	1-1	1-0
Peterborough v Barnsley	-	1-2	-	3-4	2-1	-
Preston v Port Vale	-	-	-	-	-	3-2
Rochdale v Gillingham	0-1	-	-	-	1-1	-
Scunthorpe v Colchester	3-0	-	-	1-1	1-0	-
Walsall v Crewe	1-1	-	-	-	2-2	1-1
Yeovil v Swindon	1-0	0-1	3-3	-	0-2	-
League 2						
Burton v Morecambe	-	5-2	3-2	3-2	3-2	0-1
Bury v Portsmouth	-	-	-	-	2-0	4-4
Cheltenham v Northampton	0-1	2-2	1-0	2-2	1-0	1-1
Dag & Red v Newport Co	-	-	-	-	-	1-1
Hartlepool v Luton	-	-	-	-	-	-
Mansfield v Cambridge U	1-1	2-1	1-0	1-2	3-1	-
Oxford v Tranmere	-	-	-	-	-	-
Plymouth v Carlisle	-	-	1-1	-	-	-
Southend v Exeter	-	0-0	-	-	2-1	2-3
Stevenage v Accrington	-	-	2-2	-	-	-
Wycombe v AFC Wimbledon	-	-	-	-	0-1	0-3
York v Shrewsbury	-	-	-	-	-	-
Conference						
Altrincham v Braintree	-	-	-	-	-	-
Bristol Rovers v Forest Green	-	-	-	-	-	-
Chester v Alfreton	-	-	-	-	-	0-1
Dartford v Aldershot	-	-	-	-	-	1-1
Eastleigh v Nuneaton	-	-	-	-	-	-
Gateshead v Barnet	-	-	-	-	-	1-2
Halifax v Kidderminster	-	-	-	-	-	1-1
Lincoln v Wrexham	-	-	-	1-2	1-2	2-0
Macclesfield v Dover	-	-	-	-	-	-
Southport v Welling	-	-	-	-	-	2-2
Torquay v Grimsby	-	0-2	-	-	-	-
Woking v Telford	-	-	-	-	5-2	-
Scottish Premiership						
Dundee Utd v Partick	-	-	-	-	-	4-1
Hamilton v Aberdeen	2-0	0-3/1-1	0-1/1-1	-	-	-
Motherwell v Dundee	-	-	-	-	1-1	-
Ross County v Celtic	-	-	-	-	1-1/3-2/1-1	1-4
St Johnstone v Kilmarnock	-	0-1	0-3/0-0	2-0	2-1/2-0	3-1
St Mirren v Inverness CT	2-0/1-2	-	1-2/3-3	1-2/0-1	2-2/2-1	0-0
Scottish Championship						
Alloa v Cowdenbeath	-	2-1/3-1	-	-	-	3-1/0-1
Hearts v Dumbarton	-	-	-	-	-	-
Livingston v Hibernian	-	-	-	-	-	-
Queen of Sth v Falkirk	-	-	1-5/0-1	1-5/0-0	-	2-0/1-2
Rangers v Raith	-	-	-	-	-	-

Results cover matches from Premier League to Conference and Scottish Premiership to League Two

	2008-09	2009-10	2010-11	2011-12	2012-13	2013-14
Scottish League One						
Brechin v Stranraer	1-0/2-1	-	-	-	3-0/2-2	1-1/1-3
Dunfermline v Forfar	-	-	-	-	-	1-1/0-0
Morton v Ayr	-	1-0/2-1	-	4-1/3-1	-	-
Peterhead v Airdrieonians	-	-	5-1/2-4	-	-	-
Stirling v Stenh'semuir	-	0-0/1-1	-	2-2/3-1	-	-
Scottish League Two						
Albion v Clyde	-	-	3-1/1-1	-	-	3-0/1-0
Arbroath v East Stirling	-	-	2-0/3-5	-	-	-
Berwick v Elgin	1-1/2-1	2-0/2-1	6-2/4-0	1-1/3-3	0-0/2-1	2-3/2-3
East Fife v Annan	-	-	-	-	-	-
Queen's Park v Montrose	-	3-2/3-0	1-0/4-1	3-1/5-0	2-2/1-2	0-1/1-1

Tuesday October 21st, 2014

	2008-09	2009-10	2010-11	2011-12	2012-13	2013-14
Championship						
Blackburn v Birmingham	-	2-1	1-1	-	1-1	2-3
Blackpool v Derby	3-2	0-0	-	0-1	2-1	1-3
Bournemouth v Reading	-	-	-	-	-	3-1
Brentford v Sheff Wed	-	-	1-0	1-2	-	-
Cardiff v Ipswich	0-3	1-2	0-2	2-2	0-0	-
Charlton v Bolton	-	-	-	-	3-2	0-0
Huddersfield v Brighton	2-2	7-1	2-1	-	1-2	1-1
Norwich v Leeds	-	1-0	1-1	-	-	-
Rotherham v Fulham	-	-	-	-	-	-
Watford v Nottm Forest	2-1	0-0	1-1	0-1	2-0	1-1
Wigan v Millwall	-	-	-	-	-	0-1
Wolves v Middlesbro	-	-	-	-	3-2	-
League 1						
Barnsley v Notts Co	-	-	-	-	-	-
Bristol City v Bradford	-	-	-	-	-	2-2
Colchester v Chesterfield	-	-	-	1-2	-	-
Crawley Town v Walsall	-	-	-	-	2-2	0-0
Crewe v Peterborough	1-1	-	-	-	-	2-2
Doncaster v Leyton Orient	-	-	-	-	2-0	-
Gillingham v Preston	-	-	-	-	-	1-2
MK Dons v Fleetwood Town	-	-	-	-	-	-
Oldham v Coventry	-	-	-	-	0-1	0-0
Port Vale v Scunthorpe	-	-	-	-	-	-
Sheff Utd v Yeovil	-	-	-	4-0	0-2	-
Swindon v Rochdale	-	-	1-1	-	-	-
League 2						
Accrington v Hartlepool	-	-	-	-	-	0-0
AFC Wimbledon v Plymouth	-	-	-	1-2	1-1	1-1
Cambridge U v Cheltenham	-	-	-	-	-	-
Carlisle v Burton	-	-	-	-	-	-
Exeter v Wycombe	1-0	1-1	-	1-3	3-2	0-1
Luton v Dag & Red	2-1	-	-	-	-	-
Morecambe v York	-	-	-	-	2-2	0-0
Newport Co v Southend	-	-	-	-	-	3-1
Northampton v Oxford	-	-	2-1	2-1	1-0	3-1
Portsmouth v Stevenage	-	-	-	-	0-0	-
Shrewsbury v Bury	1-0	1-1	0-3	-	0-0	-
Tranmere v Mansfield	-	-	-	-	-	-
Conference						
Barnet v Braintree	-	-	-	-	-	1-1

Results cover matches from Premier League to Conference and Scottish Premiership to League Two

Saturday October 25th, 2014

Premier League	2008-09	2009-10	2010-11	2011-12	2012-13	2013-14
Burnley v Everton	-	1-0	-	-	-	-
Liverpool v Hull	2-2	6-1	-	-	-	2-0
Man Utd v Chelsea	3-0	1-2	2-1	3-1	0-1	0-0
QPR v Aston Villa	-	-	-	1-1	1-1	-
Southampton v Stoke	-	-	-	-	1-1	2-2
Sunderland v Arsenal	1-1	1-0	1-1	1-2	0-1	1-3
Swansea v Leicester	-	1-0	2-0	-	-	-
Tottenham v Newcastle	1-0	-	2-0	5-0	2-1	0-1
West Brom v Crystal Palace	-	0-1	-	-	-	2-0
West Ham v Man City	1-0	1-1	1-3	-	0-0	1-3

Championship	2008-09	2009-10	2010-11	2011-12	2012-13	2013-14
Birmingham v Bournemouth	-	-	-	-	-	2-4
Bolton v Brentford	-	-	-	-	-	-
Brighton v Rotherham	-	-	-	-	-	-
Derby v Wigan	-	-	-	-	-	0-1
Fulham v Charlton	-	-	-	-	-	-
Ipswich v Huddersfield	-	-	-	-	2-2	2-1
Leeds v Wolves	-	-	-	-	1-0	-
Middlesbro v Watford	-	0-1	2-1	1-0	1-2	2-2
Millwall v Cardiff	-	-	3-3	0-0	0-2	-
Nottm Forest v Blackburn	-	-	-	-	0-0	4-1
Reading v Blackpool	1-0	2-1	-	3-1	-	5-1
Sheff Wed v Norwich	3-2	-	-	-	-	-

League 1	2008-09	2009-10	2010-11	2011-12	2012-13	2013-14
Barnsley v Bristol City	0-0	2-3	4-2	1-2	1-0	-
Coventry v Peterborough	-	3-2	-	2-2	-	4-2
Crewe v Sheff Utd	-	-	-	-	1-0	3-0
Doncaster v MK Dons	-	-	-	-	0-0	-
Gillingham v Crawley Town	-	-	-	0-1	-	1-0
Oldham v Bradford	-	-	-	-	-	1-1
Port Vale v Leyton Orient	-	-	-	-	-	0-2
Preston v Fleetwood Town	-	-	-	-	-	-
Scunthorpe v Notts Co	-	-	-	0-0	2-2	-
Swindon v Colchester	1-3	1-1	2-1	-	0-1	0-0
Walsall v Chesterfield	-	-	-	3-2	-	-
Yeovil v Rochdale	-	-	0-1	3-1	-	-

League 2	2008-09	2009-10	2010-11	2011-12	2012-13	2013-14
AFC Wimbledon v Tranmere	-	-	-	-	-	-
Cambridge U v Hartlepool	-	-	-	-	-	-
Carlisle v Oxford	-	-	-	-	-	-
Luton v Northampton	-	-	-	-	-	-
Morecambe v Exeter	1-1	-	-	-	0-3	2-0
Newport Co v Accrington	-	-	-	-	-	4-1
Plymouth v Cheltenham	-	-	-	1-2	2-0	1-1
Shrewsbury v Portsmouth	-	-	-	-	3-2	-
Southend v Bury	-	-	1-1	-	-	0-0
Stevenage v Burton	4-1	-	2-1	-	-	-
Wycombe v Dag & Red	2-1	-	-	-	1-0	2-0
York v Mansfield	1-1	3-0	2-1	2-2	-	1-2

Scottish Premiership	2008-09	2009-10	2010-11	2011-12	2012-13	2013-14
Aberdeen v Motherwell	2-0	0-0/0-3	1-2	1-2	3-3/0-0	0-1/0-1
Celtic v Kilmarnock	3-0	3-0/3-1	1-1	2-1	0-2/4-1	4-0
Dundee v Hamilton	-	-	-	0-1/2-2	-	0-0/1-0

Results cover matches from Premier League to Conference and Scottish Premiership to League Two

	2008-09	2009-10	2010-11	2011-12	2012-13	2013-14
Inverness CT v Dundee Utd	1-3	-	0-2	2-3	4-0/0-0/1-2	1-1/1-1
Partick v St Johnstone	4-0/0-0	-	-	-	-	0-1
St Mirren v Ross County	-	-	-	-	5-4/1-4	2-1/1-0

Scottish Championship						
Dumbarton v Rangers	-	-	-	-	-	-
Falkirk v Cowdenbeath	-	-	5-1/2-0	-	2-0/4-0	4-0/5-0
Hibernian v Hearts	1-1/1-0	1-1/1-2	0-2/2-2	1-3	1-1/0-0	2-1/1-2
Livingston v Queen of Sth	2-0/2-2	-	-	2-2/2-2	-	3-3/1-2
Raith v Alloa	4-1/3-1	-	-	-	-	4-2/1-1

Scottish League One						
Ayr v Brechin	1-1/4-2	-	0-2/2-0	-	3-0/1-2	2-2/1-3
Dunfermline v Morton	0-1/2-1	3-1/4-1	2-0/1-3	-	2-2/1-4	-
Forfar v Stranraer	-	1-0/2-0	-	-	4-0/3-1	1-2/1-0
Stenh'semuir v Peterhead	-	2-0/1-1	3-1/4-2	-	-	-
Stirling v Airdrieonians	-	-	-	1-4/0-2	-	-

Scottish League Two						
Albion v Berwick	2-0/2-1	2-1/4-1	2-2/0-1	-	-	0-2/0-3
Annan v East Stirling	2-1/4-0	0-1/1-0	3-1/2-1	3-0/2-2	5-2/1-2	1-2/2-3
Clyde v Elgin	-	-	1-1/3-3	1-2/0-2	2-2/1-1	2-1/4-0
Montrose v Arbroath	-	-	3-0/0-5	-	-	-
Queen's Park v East Fife	0-0/3-1	-	-	-	-	-

Saturday November 1st, 2014

Premier League						
Arsenal v Burnley	-	3-1	-	-	-	-
Aston Villa v Tottenham	1-2	1-1	1-2	1-1	0-4	0-2
Chelsea v QPR	-	-	-	6-1	0-1	-
Crystal Palace v Sunderland	-	-	-	-	-	3-1
Everton v Swansea	-	-	-	1-0	0-0	3-2
Hull v Southampton	-	-	-	0-2	-	0-1
Leicester v West Brom	-	1-2	-	-	-	-
Man City v Man Utd	0-1	0-1	0-0	1-0	2-3	4-1
Newcastle v Liverpool	1-5	-	3-1	2-0	0-6	2-2
Stoke v West Ham	0-1	2-1	1-1	-	0-1	3-1

Championship						
Blackburn v Reading	-	-	-	-	-	0-0
Blackpool v Ipswich	0-1	1-0	-	2-0	6-0	2-3
Bournemouth v Brighton	-	-	1-0	-	-	1-1
Brentford v Derby	-	-	-	-	-	-
Cardiff v Leeds	-	-	2-1	1-1	2-1	-
Charlton v Sheff Wed	1-2	-	1-0	1-1	1-2	1-1
Huddersfield v Nottm Forest	-	-	-	-	1-1	0-3
Norwich v Bolton	-	-	-	2-0	-	-
Rotherham v Middlesbro	-	-	-	-	-	-
Watford v Millwall	-	-	1-0	2-1	0-0	4-0
Wigan v Fulham	0-0	1-1	1-1	0-2	1-2	-
Wolves v Birmingham	1-1	0-1	1-0	-	1-0	-

League 1						
Bradford v Doncaster	-	-	-	-	-	-
Bristol City v Oldham	-	-	-	-	-	1-1
Chesterfield v Yeovil	-	-	-	2-2	-	-
Colchester v Port Vale	-	-	-	-	-	1-0
Crawley Town v Crewe	-	-	-	1-1	2-0	1-2
Fleetwood Town v Gillingham	-	-	-	-	2-2	-
Leyton Orient v Coventry	-	-	-	-	0-1	2-0

Results cover matches from Premier League to Conference and Scottish Premiership to League Two

	2008-09	2009-10	2010-11	2011-12	2012-13	2013-14
MK Dons v Swindon	1-2	2-1	2-1	-	2-0	1-1
Notts Co v Walsall	-	-	1-1	2-1	0-1	1-5
Peterborough v Scunthorpe	2-1	3-0	-	-	-	-
Rochdale v Preston	-	-	-	1-1	-	-
Sheff Utd v Barnsley	2-1	0-0	2-2	-	-	-

League 2						
Accrington v Morecambe	1-0	3-2	1-1	1-1	2-0	5-1
Burton v Plymouth	-	-	-	2-1	1-0	1-0
Bury v Cambridge U	-	-	-	-	-	-
Cheltenham v York	-	-	-	-	1-1	2-2
Dag & Red v Shrewsbury	1-2	5-0	-	0-2	-	-
Exeter v Luton	0-1	-	-	-	-	-
Hartlepool v Newport Co	-	-	-	-	-	3-0
Mansfield v Southend	-	-	-	-	-	2-1
Northampton v AFC Wimbledon	-	-	-	1-0	2-0	2-2
Oxford v Wycombe	-	-	2-2	-	0-1	2-2
Portsmouth v Carlisle	-	-	-	-	1-1	-
Tranmere v Stevenage	-	-	-	3-0	3-1	0-0

Conference						
Aldershot v Gateshead	-	-	-	-	-	1-2
Altrincham v Alfreton	-	-	-	-	-	-
Braintree v Woking	-	-	-	-	1-1	2-0
Eastleigh v Chester	-	-	-	-	-	-
Forest Green v Lincoln	-	-	-	0-2	3-0	4-1
Grimsby v Dartford	-	-	-	-	0-2	5-2
Kidderminster v Torquay	1-0	-	-	-	-	-
Nuneaton v Macclesfield	-	-	-	-	3-3	1-0
Southport v Dover	-	-	-	-	-	-
Telford v Bristol Rovers	-	-	-	-	-	-
Welling v Barnet	-	-	-	-	-	1-1
Wrexham v Halifax	-	-	-	-	-	0-0

Scottish Premiership						
Celtic v Inverness CT	1-0	-	2-2	2-0/1-0	0-1/4-1	2-2/5-0/6-0
Dundee Utd v St Mirren	2-0/3-2	3-2	1-2	1-1/0-0	3-4	4-0/3-2
Hamilton v Partick	-	-	-	1-0/2-2	1-0/0-2	-
Kilmarnock v Dundee	-	-	-	-	0-0/1-2	-
Ross County v Aberdeen	-	-	-	-	2-1	1-0/1-1
St Johnstone v Motherwell	-	2-2/1-2	0-2/1-0	0-3	1-3/2-0	2-0/3-0

Tuesday November 4th, 2014

Championship						
Birmingham v Watford	3-2	-	-	3-0	0-4	0-1
Bolton v Cardiff	-	-	-	-	2-1	-
Brighton v Wigan	-	-	-	-	-	1-2
Derby v Huddersfield	-	-	-	-	3-0	3-1
Ipswich v Wolves	0-2	-	-	-	0-2	-
Leeds v Charlton	-	0-0	-	-	1-1	0-1
Middlesbro v Norwich	-	-	1-1	-	-	-
Millwall v Blackburn	-	-	-	-	1-2	2-2
Reading v Rotherham	-	-	-	-	-	-
Sheff Wed v Bournemouth	-	-	1-1	3-0	-	1-2

Conference						
Braintree v Grimsby	-	-	-	5-0	2-0	0-0
Lincoln v Altrincham	-	-	-	-	-	-

Results cover matches from Premier League to Conference and Scottish Premiership to League Two

Wednesday November 5th, 2014

Championship

	2008-09	2009-10	2010-11	2011-12	2012-13	2013-14
Fulham v Blackpool	-	-	3-0	-	-	-
Nottm Forest v Brentford	-	-	-	-	-	-

Saturday November 8th, 2014

Premier League

	2008-09	2009-10	2010-11	2011-12	2012-13	2013-14
Burnley v Hull	-	2-0	4-0	1-0	0-1	-
Liverpool v Chelsea	2-0	0-2	2-0	4-1	2-2	0-2
Man Utd v Crystal Palace	-	-	-	-	-	2-0
QPR v Man City	-	-	-	2-3	0-0	-
Southampton v Leicester	-	-	-	0-2	-	-
Sunderland v Everton	0-2	1-1	2-2	1-1	1-0	0-1
Swansea v Arsenal	-	-	-	3-2	0-2	1-2
Tottenham v Stoke	3-1	0-1	3-2	1-1	0-0	3-0
West Brom v Newcastle	2-3	1-1	3-1	1-3	1-1	1-0
West Ham v Aston Villa	0-1	2-1	1-2	-	1-0	0-0

Championship

	2008-09	2009-10	2010-11	2011-12	2012-13	2013-14
Birmingham v Cardiff	1-1	-	-	1-1	0-1	-
Bolton v Wigan	0-1	4-0	1-1	1-2	-	1-1
Brighton v Blackburn	-	-	-	-	1-1	3-0
Derby v Wolves	2-3	-	-	-	0-0	-
Fulham v Huddersfield	-	-	-	-	-	-
Ipswich v Watford	0-0	1-1	0-3	1-2	0-2	1-1
Leeds v Blackpool	-	-	-	0-5	2-0	2-0
Middlesbro v Bournemouth	-	-	-	-	-	3-3
Millwall v Brentford	-	1-1	-	-	-	-
Nottm Forest v Norwich	1-2	-	1-1	-	-	-
Reading v Charlton	2-2	-	-	-	-	1-0
Sheff Wed v Rotherham	-	-	-	-	-	-

Scottish Premiership

	2008-09	2009-10	2010-11	2011-12	2012-13	2013-14
Aberdeen v Celtic	4-2/1-3	1-3/4-4	0-3	0-1/1-1	0-2	0-2/2-1
Dundee v St Johnstone	1-1/0-1	-	-	-	1-3/2-2	-
Inverness CT v Hamilton	0-1/1-1/1-1	-	0-1/1-1	-	-	-
Kilmarnock v Ross County	-	-	-	-	3-0	2-0/2-2
Motherwell v Dundee Utd	1-1/2-1	2-2/2-3	2-1/2-1	0-0/0-2	0-1/0-1	0-4
St Mirren v Partick	-	-	-	-	-	1-2/0-0

Scottish Championship

	2008-09	2009-10	2010-11	2011-12	2012-13	2013-14
Alloa v Livingston	-	-	2-2/1-3	-	-	1-0/0-3
Cowdenbeath v Hibernian	-	-	-	-	-	-
Hearts v Raith	-	-	-	-	-	-
Queen of Sth v Dumbarton	-	-	-	-	-	1-2/3-1
Rangers v Falkirk	3-1	4-1/3-0	-	-	-	-

Scottish League One

	2008-09	2009-10	2010-11	2011-12	2012-13	2013-14
Airdrieonians v Stenh'semuir	-	-	1-0/2-2	5-2/0-3	-	0-1/1-1
Brechin v Stirling	2-1/1-2	1-0/1-1	-	1-3/1-2	-	-
Morton v Forfar	-	-	-	-	-	-
Peterhead v Dunfermline	-	-	-	-	-	-
Stranraer v Ayr	1-3/1-4	-	-	-	2-0/0-1	1-1/4-0

Scottish League Two

	2008-09	2009-10	2010-11	2011-12	2012-13	2013-14
Arbroath v Queen's Park	1-1/3-0	-	1-0/2-2	-	-	-
East Fife v Albion	-	-	-	2-0/1-2	1-2/2-0	-
East Stirling v Berwick	1-0/0-4	1-0/3-2	0-0/1-0	1-3/2-1	0-1/0-3	1-0/1-1
Elgin v Annan	1-2/0-1	1-1/1-0	2-0/2-3	3-0/1-2	2-2/3-1	2-3/2-3
Montrose v Clyde	-	-	8-1/3-1	4-0/5-0	2-3/1-1	0-2/0-2

Results cover matches from Premier League to Conference and Scottish Premiership to League Two

Jose Mourinho won't be welcome at Anfield after pooping the party last season

Tuesday November 11th, 2014

Conference	2008-09	2009-10	2010-11	2011-12	2012-13	2013-14
Alfreton v Bristol Rovers	-	-	-	-	-	-
Barnet v Torquay	-	1-1	0-3	0-1	1-0	-
Dartford v Welling	-	-	-	-	-	1-2
Dover v Braintree	-	-	-	-	-	-
Forest Green v Eastleigh	-	-	-	-	-	-
Gateshead v Lincoln	-	-	-	3-3	1-1	3-1
Grimsby v Halifax	-	-	-	-	-	0-1
Kidderminster v Aldershot	-	-	-	-	-	0-0
Macclesfield v Chester	3-1	-	-	-	-	3-2
Telford v Altrincham	-	-	-	-	-	3-1
Woking v Wrexham	1-1	-	-	-	2-0	2-1

Saturday November 15th, 2014

League 1	2008-09	2009-10	2010-11	2011-12	2012-13	2013-14
Barnsley v Colchester	-	-	-	-	-	-
Coventry v Notts Co	-	-	-	-	1-2	3-0
Crewe v Chesterfield	-	0-1	2-0	-	-	-
Doncaster v Sheff Utd	0-2	1-1	2-0	-	2-2	-
Gillingham v Leyton Orient	-	1-1	-	-	-	1-2
Oldham v Crawley Town	-	-	-	-	2-1	1-0
Port Vale v Rochdale	2-1	1-1	-	-	2-2	-
Preston v Bradford	-	-	-	-	-	2-2
Scunthorpe v MK Dons	0-1	-	-	0-3	0-3	-
Swindon v Bristol City	-	-	-	-	-	3-2
Walsall v Peterborough	1-2	-	1-3	-	-	2-0
Yeovil v Fleetwood Town	-	-	-	-	-	-

League 2	2008-09	2009-10	2010-11	2011-12	2012-13	2013-14
AFC Wimbledon v Dag & Red	-	-	-	2-1	2-2	1-1
Cambridge U v Northampton	-	-	-	-	-	-
Carlisle v Accrington	-	-	-	-	-	-
Luton v Tranmere	-	-	-	-	-	-
Morecambe v Bury	0-0	3-0	1-4	-	-	0-0
Newport Co v Exeter	-	-	-	-	-	1-1
Plymouth v Portsmouth	-	-	-	-	-	1-1
Shrewsbury v Mansfield	-	-	-	-	-	-
Southend v Hartlepool	3-2	3-2	-	-	-	1-1
Stevenage v Cheltenham	-	-	4-0	-	-	-
Wycombe v Burton	-	-	4-1	-	3-0	1-2
York v Oxford	0-0	1-1	-	-	3-1	0-0

Conference	2008-09	2009-10	2010-11	2011-12	2012-13	2013-14
Aldershot v Nuneaton	-	-	-	-	-	2-2
Alfreton v Dover	-	-	-	-	-	-
Altrincham v Grimsby	-	-	2-2	-	-	-
Barnet v Telford	-	-	-	-	-	-
Braintree v Wrexham	-	-	-	0-0	1-5	3-0
Bristol Rovers v Kidderminster	-	-	-	-	-	-
Chester v Gateshead	-	-	-	-	-	1-1
Dartford v Southport	-	-	-	-	2-2	1-0
Eastleigh v Lincoln	-	-	-	-	-	-
Halifax v Woking	-	-	-	-	-	3-4
Torquay v Forest Green	3-3	-	-	-	-	-
Welling v Macclesfield	-	-	-	-	-	1-0

Results cover matches from Premier League to Conference and Scottish Premiership to League Two

	2008-09	2009-10	2010-11	2011-12	2012-13	2013-14
Scottish Championship						
Falkirk v Hearts	2-1/0-0	0-1	-	-	-	-
Hibernian v Queen of Sth	-	-	-	-	-	-
Livingston v Dumbarton	-	-	2-0/1-1	-	5-0/2-3	1-3/1-2
Raith v Cowdenbeath	-	-	2-1/2-2	-	2-2/0-1	3-3/1-2
Rangers v Alloa	-	-	-	-	-	-
Scottish League One						
Airdrieonians v Morton	5-0/1-0	2-4/3-0	-	-	2-3/0-4	-
Ayr v Peterhead	2-0/0-0	-	1-1/2-2	-	-	-
Brechin v Forfar	-	-	0-0/0-1	0-1/2-1	4-1/3-4	2-1/1-5
Stenh'semuir v Dunfermline	-	-	-	-	-	4-5/1-2
Stirling v Stranraer	3-2/1-2	-	-	-	-	-
Scottish League Two						
Albion v Arbroath	-	-	0-2/3-0	1-0/1-1	4-0/0-1	-
Annan v Montrose	1-2/2-1	2-0/0-0	2-2/2-1	2-1/1-2	2-1/1-1	2-1/1-0
Berwick v East Fife	-	-	-	-	-	-
Clyde v East Stirling	-	-	1-2/2-0	7-1/3-0	2-1/2-0	1-2/1-0
Elgin v Queen's Park	-	0-1/0-1	4-2/0-1	2-0/1-1	0-4/3-5	3-2/1-1

Saturday November 22nd, 2014

	2008-09	2009-10	2010-11	2011-12	2012-13	2013-14
Premier League						
Arsenal v Man Utd	2-1	1-3	1-0	1-2	1-1	0-0
Aston Villa v Southampton	-	-	-	-	0-1	0-0
Chelsea v West Brom	2-0	-	6-0	2-1	1-0	2-2
Crystal Palace v Liverpool	-	-	-	-	-	3-3
Everton v West Ham	3-1	2-2	2-2	-	2-0	1-0
Hull v Tottenham	1-2	1-5	-	-	-	1-1
Leicester v Sunderland	-	-	-	-	-	-
Man City v Swansea	-	-	-	4-0	1-0	3-0
Newcastle v QPR	-	1-1	-	1-0	1-0	-
Stoke v Burnley	-	2-0	-	-	-	-
Championship						
Blackburn v Leeds	-	-	-	-	0-0	1-0
Blackpool v Bolton	-	-	4-3	-	2-2	0-0
Bournemouth v Ipswich	-	-	-	-	-	1-1
Brentford v Fulham	-	-	-	-	-	-
Cardiff v Reading	2-2	0-0	2-2	3-1	-	-
Charlton v Millwall	-	4-4	-	-	0-2	0-1
Huddersfield v Sheff Wed	-	-	1-0	0-2	0-0	0-2
Norwich v Brighton	-	4-1	-	-	-	-
Rotherham v Birmingham	-	-	-	-	-	-
Watford v Derby	3-1	0-1	3-0	0-1	2-1	2-3
Wigan v Middlesbro	0-1	-	-	-	-	2-2
Wolves v Nottm Forest	5-1	-	-	-	1-2	-
League 1						
Bradford v Gillingham	2-2	-	1-0	2-2	0-1	1-1
Bristol City v Preston	1-1	4-2	1-1	-	-	1-1
Chesterfield v Barnsley	-	-	-	-	-	-
Colchester v Coventry	-	-	-	-	1-3	2-1
Crawley Town v Scunthorpe	-	-	-	-	3-0	-
Fleetwood Town v Walsall	-	-	-	-	-	-
Leyton Orient v Crewe	1-0	-	-	-	1-1	2-0
MK Dons v Port Vale	-	-	-	-	-	3-0
Notts Co v Yeovil	-	-	4-0	3-1	1-2	-
Peterborough v Swindon	2-2	-	5-4	-	-	1-0
Rochdale v Doncaster	-	-	-	-	-	-
Sheff Utd v Oldham	-	-	-	2-3	1-1	1-1

Results cover matches from Premier League to Conference and Scottish Premiership to League Two

	2008-09	2009-10	2010-11	2011-12	2012-13	2013-14
League 2						
Accrington v Cambridge U	-	-	-	-	-	-
Burton v Luton	-	-	-	-	-	-
Bury v Newport Co	-	-	-	-	-	0-0
Cheltenham v Wycombe	-	-	1-2	-	4-0	1-1
Dag & Red v Carlisle	-	-	3-0	-	-	-
Exeter v Shrewsbury	0-1	-	-	-	-	-
Hartlepool v York	-	-	-	-	-	2-0
Mansfield v Plymouth	-	-	-	-	-	0-1
Northampton v Stevenage	-	-	2-0	-	-	-
Oxford v AFC Wimbledon	-	2-0	-	1-0	3-2	2-1
Portsmouth v Morecambe	-	-	-	-	-	3-0
Tranmere v Southend	2-2	2-0	-	-	-	-
Conference						
Aldershot v Eastleigh	-	-	-	-	-	-
Chester v Bristol Rovers	-	-	-	-	-	-
Dover v Forest Green	-	-	-	-	-	-
Grimsby v Kidderminster	-	-	3-3	1-2	1-3	3-1
Lincoln v Dartford	-	-	-	-	2-1	0-0
Macclesfield v Alfreton	-	-	-	-	1-2	0-1
Nuneaton v Southport	-	-	-	-	0-1	3-1
Telford v Braintree	-	-	-	1-0	3-0	-
Torquay v Gateshead	-	-	-	-	-	-
Welling v Halifax	-	-	-	-	-	0-1
Woking v Barnet	-	-	-	-	-	0-0
Wrexham v Altrincham	0-1	1-1	2-1	-	-	-
Scottish Premiership						
Celtic v Dundee	-	-	-	-	2-0/5-0	-
Dundee Utd v Kilmarnock	0-2/0-0	0-0	1-1/4-2	1-1/4-0	3-3	1-0/3-2
Hamilton v St Mirren	1-2/0-0	1-0/0-0	0-0	-	-	-
Inverness CT v Motherwell	1-2/1-2	-	1-2/3-0	2-3	1-5/4-3	2-0/1-2
Partick v Aberdeen	-	-	-	-	-	0-3/3-1
St Johnstone v Ross County	2-1/0-0	-	-	-	1-1/2-2	4-0/0-1
Scottish Championship						
Alloa v Falkirk	-	-	-	-	-	0-0/3-0
Cowdenbeath v Livingston	-	-	-	-	1-1/2-2	2-3/4-0
Dumbarton v Hibernian	-	-	-	-	-	-
Hearts v Rangers	2-1	1-2/1-4	1-2/1-0	0-2/0-3	-	-
Queen of Sth v Raith	-	1-1/3-0	1-3/0-2	1-3/1-0	-	0-1/1-0
Scottish League One						
Dunfermline v Stirling	-	-	3-0/4-1	-	-	-
Forfar v Ayr	-	-	4-1/3-2	-	2-1/2-1	0-1/4-2
Morton v Stenh'semuir	-	-	-	-	-	-
Peterhead v Brechin	5-1/0-1	1-0/0-3	0-5/1-1	-	-	-
Stranraer v Airdrieonians	-	-	-	-	-	3-1/1-1
Scottish League Two						
Arbroath v Clyde	-	0-3/2-0	3-2/2-0	-	-	-
Berwick v Annan	3-0/1-1	2-1/0-2	2-2/2-3	0-1/1-3	3-1/0-2	4-2/1-4
East Fife v Elgin	-	-	-	-	-	-
East Stirling v Montrose	5-0/2-1	1-0/2-3	2-1/1-2	1-0/3-1	2-2/1-2	2-2/1-2
Queen's Park v Albion	-	0-1/1-0	0-1/2-1	-	-	1-1/4-0

Tuesday November 25th, 2014

	2008-09	2009-10	2010-11	2011-12	2012-13	2013-14
Conference						
Braintree v Welling	-	-	-	-	-	2-3
Bristol Rovers v Barnet	-	-	-	0-2	2-1	-

Results cover matches from Premier League to Conference and Scottish Premiership to League Two

	2008-09	2009-10	2010-11	2011-12	2012-13	2013-14
Dartford v Chester	-	-	-	-	-	0-1
Dover v Nuneaton	-	-	-	-	-	-
Grimsby v Woking	-	-	-	-	5-1	2-2
Kidderminster v Wrexham	1-0	2-0	1-0	0-1	2-0	3-1
Macclesfield v Torquay	-	2-1	3-3	1-2	-	-
Southport v Aldershot	-	-	-	-	-	1-0

Saturday November 29th, 2014

Premier League						
Burnley v Aston Villa	-	1-1	-	-	-	-
Liverpool v Stoke	0-0	4-0	2-0	0-0	0-0	1-0
Man Utd v Hull	4-3	4-0	-	-	-	3-1
QPR v Leicester	-	1-2	1-0	-	-	0-1
Southampton v Man City	-	-	-	-	3-1	1-1
Sunderland v Chelsea	2-3	1-3	2-4	1-2	1-3	3-4
Swansea v Crystal Palace	1-3	0-0	3-0	-	-	1-1
Tottenham v Everton	0-1	2-1	1-1	2-0	2-2	1-0
West Brom v Arsenal	1-3	-	2-2	2-3	1-2	1-1
West Ham v Newcastle	3-1	-	1-2	-	0-0	1-3

Championship						
Birmingham v Nottm Forest	2-0	-	-	1-2	2-1	0-0
Bolton v Huddersfield	-	-	-	-	1-0	0-1
Bournemouth v Millwall	-	-	-	-	-	5-2
Brentford v Wolves	-	-	-	-	-	0-3
Brighton v Fulham	-	-	-	-	-	-
Charlton v Ipswich	2-1	-	-	-	1-2	0-1
Leeds v Derby	-	-	1-2	0-2	1-2	1-1
Middlesbro v Blackburn	0-0	-	-	-	1-0	0-0
Norwich v Reading	0-2	-	2-1	-	2-1	-
Rotherham v Blackpool	-	-	-	-	-	-
Sheff Wed v Wigan	-	-	-	-	-	0-3
Watford v Cardiff	2-2	0-4	4-1	1-1	0-0	-

League 1						
Barnsley v Scunthorpe	-	1-1	2-1	-	-	-
Bradford v Leyton Orient	-	-	-	-	-	1-1
Coventry v Walsall	-	-	-	-	5-1	2-1
Crawley Town v Chesterfield	-	-	-	-	-	-
Crewe v Doncaster	-	-	-	-	1-2	-
Gillingham v Port Vale	1-0	-	3-0	1-1	1-2	3-2
MK Dons v Colchester	1-1	2-1	1-1	1-0	5-1	0-0
Peterborough v Bristol City	-	0-1	-	3-0	1-2	1-2
Rochdale v Oldham	-	-	1-1	3-2	-	-
Sheff Utd v Notts Co	-	-	-	2-1	1-1	2-1
Swindon v Fleetwood Town	-	-	-	-	-	-
Yeovil v Preston	-	-	-	2-1	3-1	-

League 2						
Accrington v Exeter	2-1	-	-	-	0-3	2-3
AFC Wimbledon v Cambridge U	-	0-0	3-0	-	-	-
Bury v Dag & Red	2-2	0-0	-	-	-	1-1
Carlisle v Newport Co	-	-	-	-	-	-
Cheltenham v Oxford	-	-	1-1	0-0	2-1	2-2
Hartlepool v Wycombe	-	1-1	-	1-3	-	1-2
Luton v Mansfield	-	4-1	2-0	0-0	2-3	-
Plymouth v York	-	-	-	-	2-0	0-4
Shrewsbury v Burton	-	3-1	3-0	1-0	-	-
Southend v Northampton	1-0	-	1-1	2-2	1-2	2-0
Stevenage v Morecambe	-	-	2-0	-	-	-
Tranmere v Portsmouth	-	-	-	-	2-2	-

Results cover matches from Premier League to Conference and Scottish Premiership to League Two

	2008-09	2009-10	2010-11	2011-12	2012-13	2013-14
Conference						
Altrincham v Kidderminster	2-2	3-2	1-2	-	-	-
Barnet v Macclesfield	1-3	1-2	1-0	2-1	-	1-2
Bristol Rovers v Welling	-	-	-	-	-	-
Forest Green v Dartford	-	-	-	-	2-3	1-0
Gateshead v Dover	-	-	-	-	-	-
Halifax v Alfreton	-	-	-	-	-	2-0
Lincoln v Southport	-	-	-	2-0	1-0	1-0
Nuneaton v Chester	-	-	-	-	-	1-0
Telford v Grimsby	-	-	-	0-0	1-2	-
Torquay v Eastleigh	-	-	-	-	-	-
Woking v Braintree	-	-	-	-	1-4	1-0
Wrexham v Aldershot	-	-	-	-	-	2-1
Scottish League Two						
Annan v Albion	2-4/1-1	0-0/1-2	4-1/2-2	-	-	1-1/2-0
Clyde v Queen's Park	-	-	2-3/0-2	0-2/1-2	0-3/2-3	3-0/1-2
East Stirling v East Fife	-	-	-	-	-	-
Elgin v Arbroath	-	-	3-5/3-2	-	-	-
Montrose v Berwick	1-1/1-1	1-3/1-1	1-1/1-1	3-5/1-1	3-1/1-3	1-1/0-0

Tuesday December 2nd, 2014

	2008-09	2009-10	2010-11	2011-12	2012-13	2013-14
Premier League						
Arsenal v Southampton	-	-	-	-	6-1	2-0
Burnley v Newcastle	-	-	-	-	-	-
Crystal Palace v Aston Villa	-	-	-	-	-	1-0
Leicester v Liverpool	-	-	-	-	-	-
Man Utd v Stoke	5-0	4-0	2-1	2-0	4-2	3-2
Swansea v QPR	0-0	2-0	0-0	1-1	4-1	-
West Brom v West Ham	3-2	-	3-3	-	0-0	1-0
Conference						
Alfreton v Gateshead	-	-	-	1-1	3-2	1-1
Chester v Telford	-	-	-	-	-	-
Dover v Torquay	-	-	-	-	-	-
Eastleigh v Dartford	-	-	-	-	-	-
Halifax v Forest Green	-	-	-	-	-	1-0
Kidderminster v Nuneaton	-	-	-	-	1-0	0-0
Woking v Altrincham	1-2	-	-	-	-	-
Wrexham v Bristol Rovers	-	-	-	-	-	-

Wednesday December 3rd, 2014

	2008-09	2009-10	2010-11	2011-12	2012-13	2013-14
Premier League						
Chelsea v Tottenham	1-1	3-0	2-1	0-0	2-2	4-0
Everton v Hull	2-0	5-1	-	-	-	2-1
Sunderland v Man City	0-3	1-1	1-0	1-0	1-0	1-0

Saturday December 6th, 2014

	2008-09	2009-10	2010-11	2011-12	2012-13	2013-14
Premier League						
Aston Villa v Leicester	-	-	-	-	-	-
Hull v West Brom	2-2	-	-	-	-	2-0
Liverpool v Sunderland	2-0	3-0	2-2	1-1	3-0	2-1
Man City v Everton	0-1	0-2	1-2	2-0	1-1	3-1
Newcastle v Chelsea	0-2	-	1-1	0-3	3-2	2-0
QPR v Burnley	1-2	-	1-1	-	-	3-3
Southampton v Man Utd	-	-	-	-	2-3	1-1
Stoke v Arsenal	2-1	1-3	3-1	1-1	0-0	1-0
Tottenham v Crystal Palace	-	-	-	-	-	2-0
West Ham v Swansea	-	-	-	-	1-0	2-0

Results cover matches from Premier League to Conference and Scottish Premiership to League Two

	2008-09	2009-10	2010-11	2011-12	2012-13	2013-14
Championship						
Blackburn v Sheff Wed	-	-	-	-	1-0	0-0
Blackpool v Birmingham	2-0	-	1-2	2-2	1-1	1-2
Cardiff v Rotherham	-	-	-	-	-	-
Derby v Brighton	-	-	-	0-1	0-0	1-0
Fulham v Watford	-	-	-	-	-	-
Huddersfield v Brentford	-	0-0	4-4	3-2	-	-
Ipswich v Leeds	-	-	2-1	2-1	3-0	1-2
Millwall v Middlesbro	-	-	2-3	1-3	3-1	0-2
Nottm Forest v Charlton	0-0	-	-	-	2-1	0-1
Reading v Bolton	-	-	-	-	-	7-1
Wigan v Norwich	-	-	-	1-1	1-0	-
Wolves v Bournemouth	-	-	-	-	-	-
Conference						
Aldershot v Kidderminster	-	-	-	-	-	0-0
Chester v Lincoln	0-2	-	-	-	-	3-3
Dartford v Halifax	-	-	-	-	-	1-2
Dover v Wrexham	-	-	-	-	-	-
Eastleigh v Grimsby	-	-	-	-	-	-
Forest Green v Altrincham	1-3	4-3	1-0	-	-	-
Gateshead v Woking	-	-	-	-	2-1	0-2
Macclesfield v Telford	-	-	-	-	2-1	-
Nuneaton v Alfreton	-	-	-	-	1-0	3-0
Southport v Braintree	-	-	-	0-4	0-2	0-4
Torquay v Barnet	-	0-1	1-1	1-0	3-2	-
Welling v Bristol Rovers	-	-	-	-	-	-
Scottish Premiership						
Aberdeen v Hamilton	1-2/1-0	1-2/1-3	4-0/1-0	-	-	-
Dundee v Inverness CT	-	2-2/2-2	-	-	1-4/1-1	-
Motherwell v Celtic	2-4/1-1	2-3	0-1/2-0	1-2/0-3	0-2/2-1/3-1	0-5/3-3
Partick v Kilmarnock	-	-	-	-	-	1-1/1-1
Ross County v Dundee Utd	-	-	-	-	1-2/1-0	2-4/3-0
St Mirren v St Johnstone	-	1-1/1-1	1-2/0-0	0-0/0-3	1-1	4-3/0-1
Scottish Championship						
Alloa v Dumbarton	-	1-3/1-2	0-0/2-3	-	-	1-2/1-5
Falkirk v Hibernian	1-1	1-3/1-3	-	-	-	-
Hearts v Queen of Sth	-	-	-	-	-	-
Raith v Livingston	-	-	-	0-1/0-3	0-0/0-2	1-0/2-4
Rangers v Cowdenbeath	-	-	-	-	-	-
Scottish League One						
Brechin v Airdrieonians	-	-	3-1/1-2	1-1/1-1	-	4-3/1-1
Dunfermline v Ayr	-	3-1/0-1	-	-	-	5-1/3-0
Stenh'semuir v Forfar	1-1/0-1	-	3-0/0-1	2-3/1-2	0-4/2-0	1-1/4-1
Stirling v Peterhead	0-0/2-1	2-1/2-0	-	-	1-0/0-1	2-0/1-2
Stranraer v Morton	-	-	-	-	-	-
Scottish League Two						
Albion v Elgin	2-1/0-3	1-1/1-2	3-1/2-0	-	-	0-0/5-2
Arbroath v Annan	-	-	0-2/2-1	-	-	-
Berwick v Clyde	-	-	2-1/1-1	0-2/3-0	2-1/3-3	0-1/3-0
East Fife v Montrose	-	-	-	-	-	-
Queen's Park v East Stirling	-	1-0/2-0	2-0/2-0	2-0/5-1	1-2/5-1	1-3/0-0

Tuesday December 9th, 2014

	2008-09	2009-10	2010-11	2011-12	2012-13	2013-14
Conference						
Aldershot v Macclesfield	1-1	0-0	0-0	1-2	-	1-0
Alfreton v Eastleigh	-	-	-	-	-	-

Results cover matches from Premier League to Conference and Scottish Premiership to League Two

	2008-09	2009-10	2010-11	2011-12	2012-13	2013-14
Forest Green v Woking	0-2	-	-	-	3-1	2-2
Gateshead v Southport	-	-	1-0	2-3	2-2	2-2
Lincoln v Nuneaton	-	-	-	-	2-1	1-2
Telford v Welling	-	-	-	-	-	-
Torquay v Halifax	-	-	-	-	-	-

Saturday December 13th, 2014

Premier League	2008-09	2009-10	2010-11	2011-12	2012-13	2013-14
Arsenal v Newcastle	3-0	-	0-1	2-1	7-3	3-0
Burnley v Southampton	3-2	-	-	1-1	-	-
Chelsea v Hull	0-0	2-1	-	-	-	2-0
Crystal Palace v Stoke	-	-	-	-	-	1-0
Everton v QPR	-	-	-	0-1	2-0	-
Leicester v Man City	-	-	-	-	-	-
Man Utd v Liverpool	1-4	2-1	3-2	2-1	2-1	0-3
Sunderland v West Ham	0-1	2-2	1-0	-	3-0	1-2
Swansea v Tottenham	-	-	-	1-1	1-2	1-3
West Brom v Aston Villa	1-2	-	2-1	0-0	2-2	2-2

Championship	2008-09	2009-10	2010-11	2011-12	2012-13	2013-14
Birmingham v Reading	1-3	-	-	2-0	-	1-2
Bolton v Ipswich	-	-	-	-	1-2	1-1
Bournemouth v Cardiff	-	-	-	-	-	-
Brentford v Blackburn	-	-	-	-	-	-
Brighton v Millwall	4-1	0-1	-	2-2	2-2	1-1
Charlton v Blackpool	2-2	-	-	-	2-1	0-0
Leeds v Fulham	-	-	-	-	-	-
Middlesbro v Derby	-	2-0	2-1	2-0	2-2	1-0
Norwich v Huddersfield	-	3-0	-	-	-	-
Rotherham v Nottm Forest	-	-	-	-	-	-
Sheff Wed v Wolves	0-1	-	-	-	0-0	-
Watford v Wigan	-	-	-	-	-	1-0

League 1	2008-09	2009-10	2010-11	2011-12	2012-13	2013-14
Bristol City v Crawley Town	-	-	-	-	-	2-0
Chesterfield v Bradford	0-2	1-1	2-2	-	2-2	-
Colchester v Rochdale	-	-	1-0	0-0	-	-
Doncaster v Gillingham	-	-	-	-	-	-
Fleetwood Town v Sheff Utd	-	-	-	-	-	-
Leyton Orient v Peterborough	2-3	-	2-1	-	-	1-2
Notts Co v Swindon	-	-	1-0	-	1-0	2-0
Oldham v Yeovil	0-2	0-0	0-0	1-2	1-0	-
Port Vale v Coventry	-	-	-	-	-	3-2
Preston v MK Dons	-	-	-	1-1	0-0	2-2
Scunthorpe v Crewe	3-0	-	-	-	1-2	-
Walsall v Barnsley	-	-	-	-	-	-

League 2	2008-09	2009-10	2010-11	2011-12	2012-13	2013-14
Burton v Hartlepool	-	-	-	-	-	3-0
Cambridge U v Shrewsbury	-	-	-	-	-	-
Dag & Red v Tranmere	-	-	2-2	-	-	-
Exeter v Carlisle	-	2-3	2-1	0-0	-	-
Mansfield v Cheltenham	-	-	-	-	-	0-2
Morecambe v Luton	1-2	-	-	-	-	-
Newport Co v Stevenage	-	-	-	-	-	-
Northampton v Plymouth	-	-	-	0-0	1-0	0-2
Oxford v Bury	-	-	1-2	-	-	2-1
Portsmouth v Accrington	-	-	-	-	-	1-0
Wycombe v Southend	-	1-1	3-1	-	1-2	2-1
York v AFC Wimbledon	-	5-0	4-1	-	0-3	0-2

Results cover matches from Premier League to Conference and Scottish Premiership to League Two

	2008-09	2009-10	2010-11	2011-12	2012-13	2013-14
Scottish Premiership						
Celtic v St Mirren	1-0/7-0	3-1	4-0/1-0	5-0	2-0	1-0/3-0
Dundee Utd v Aberdeen	2-1/1-1	0-1	3-1/3-1	1-2	1-1/1-0	1-2/1-3
Hamilton v Dundee	-	-	-	1-6/3-1	-	0-3/1-1
Inverness CT v Partick	-	2-3/2-1	-	-	-	1-2/1-0
Kilmarnock v St Johnstone	-	2-1/3-2/1-2	1-1	1-2/0-0	1-2	0-0/1-2
Motherwell v Ross County	-	-	-	-	3-2/2-0	3-1/2-1
Scottish Championship						
Cowdenbeath v Hearts	-	-	-	-	-	-
Dumbarton v Raith	-	-	-	-	4-2/1-2	2-4/3-3
Hibernian v Alloa	-	-	-	-	-	-
Livingston v Falkirk	-	-	-	1-1/1-2	2-1/1-2	0-3/0-1
Queen of Sth v Rangers	-	-	-	-	-	-
Scottish League One						
Airdrieonians v Dunfermline	1-3/1-1	1-1/0-1	-	-	1-2/3-3	0-3/2-0
Ayr v Stenh'semuir	-	-	2-0/4-3	-	1-1/1-2	4-3/2-3
Forfar v Stirling	-	-	-	2-2/4-3	-	-
Morton v Brechin	-	-	-	-	-	-
Peterhead v Stranraer	4-0/1-0	-	-	1-3/1-1	-	-
Scottish League Two						
Annan v East Fife	-	-	-	-	-	-
Clyde v Albion	-	-	1-2/0-1	-	-	2-2/4-0
East Stirling v Arbroath	-	-	1-3/2-5	-	-	-
Elgin v Berwick	0-2/2-0	3-3/1-5	1-2/3-2	4-1/4-0	3-1/1-2	2-0/1-3
Montrose v Queen's Park	-	1-2/1-2	1-2/0-2	0-1/3-1	1-1/1-2	1-2/1-0

Saturday December 20th, 2014

	2008-09	2009-10	2010-11	2011-12	2012-13	2013-14
Premier League						
Aston Villa v Man Utd	0-0	1-1	2-2	0-1	2-3	0-3
Hull v Swansea	-	-	2-0	-	-	1-0
Liverpool v Arsenal	4-4	1-2	1-1	1-2	0-2	5-1
Man City v Crystal Palace	-	-	-	-	-	1-0
Newcastle v Sunderland	1-1	-	5-1	1-1	0-3	0-3
QPR v West Brom	-	3-1	-	1-1	1-2	-
Southampton v Everton	-	-	-	-	0-0	2-0
Stoke v Chelsea	0-2	1-2	1-1	0-0	0-4	3-2
Tottenham v Burnley	-	5-0	-	-	-	-
West Ham v Leicester	-	-	-	3-2	-	-
Championship						
Blackburn v Charlton	-	-	-	-	1-2	0-1
Blackpool v Bournemouth	-	-	-	-	-	0-1
Cardiff v Brentford	-	-	-	-	-	-
Derby v Norwich	3-1	-	1-2	-	-	-
Fulham v Sheff Wed	-	-	-	-	-	-
Huddersfield v Birmingham	-	-	-	-	1-1	1-3
Ipswich v Middlesbro	-	1-1	3-3	1-1	4-0	3-1
Millwall v Bolton	-	-	-	-	2-1	1-1
Nottm Forest v Leeds	-	-	1-1	0-4	4-2	2-1
Reading v Watford	4-0	1-1	1-1	0-2	-	3-3
Wigan v Rotherham	-	-	-	-	-	-
Wolves v Brighton	-	-	-	-	3-3	-
League 1						
Barnsley v Leyton Orient	-	-	-	-	-	-
Bradford v Scunthorpe	-	-	-	-	-	-
Coventry v Fleetwood Town	-	-	-	-	-	-

Results cover matches from Premier League to Conference and Scottish Premiership to League Two

	2008-09	2009-10	2010-11	2011-12	2012-13	2013-14
Crawley Town v Port Vale	-	-	-	3-2	-	0-3
Crewe v Bristol City	-	-	-	-	-	1-0
Gillingham v Chesterfield	2-1	-	0-2	-	1-1	-
MK Dons v Oldham	6-2	0-0	0-0	5-0	2-0	2-1
Peterborough v Preston	-	0-1	-	-	-	2-0
Rochdale v Notts Co	3-0	2-1	1-0	0-1	-	-
Sheff Utd v Walsall	-	-	-	3-2	1-0	1-1
Swindon v Doncaster	-	-	-	-	1-1	-
Yeovil v Colchester	0-2	0-1	4-2	3-2	3-1	-

League 2						
Accrington v Wycombe	0-1	-	1-1	-	0-2	1-1
AFC Wimbledon v Mansfield	-	2-0	2-1	-	-	0-0
Bury v York	-	-	-	-	-	2-1
Carlisle v Northampton	1-1	-	-	-	-	-
Cheltenham v Portsmouth	-	-	-	-	-	2-2
Hartlepool v Oxford	-	-	-	-	-	1-3
Luton v Newport Co	-	-	1-1	2-0	2-2	-
Plymouth v Dag & Red	-	-	2-1	0-0	0-0	2-1
Shrewsbury v Morecambe	0-0	2-3	1-3	2-0	-	-
Southend v Burton	-	-	1-1	0-1	0-1	1-0
Stevenage v Exeter	-	-	-	0-0	-	-
Tranmere v Cambridge U	-	-	-	-	-	-

Conference						
Alfreton v Macclesfield	-	-	-	-	1-2	0-1
Altrincham v Dover	-	-	-	-	-	-
Barnet v Chester	3-1	-	-	-	-	3-0
Braintree v Torquay	-	-	-	-	-	-
Bristol Rovers v Gateshead	-	-	-	-	-	-
Grimsby v Forest Green	-	-	1-1	2-1	1-0	3-1
Halifax v Nuneaton	-	-	-	-	-	2-2
Kidderminster v Lincoln	-	-	-	1-1	3-0	4-1
Telford v Eastleigh	-	-	-	-	-	-
Welling v Aldershot	-	-	-	-	-	1-0
Woking v Southport	-	-	-	-	2-3	2-0
Wrexham v Dartford	-	-	-	-	2-2	1-2

Scottish Premiership						
Aberdeen v Kilmarnock	1-0/0-0	1-0/1-2	0-1/5-0	2-2/0-0	0-2/1-0	2-1/2-1
Dundee Utd v Celtic	1-1/2-2	2-1/0-2	1-2/1-3	0-1/1-0	2-2/0-4	0-1/0-2
Partick v Dundee	0-0/1-1	0-2/0-1	1-0/0-0	0-1/0-0	-	-
Ross County v Hamilton	-	-	-	1-0/5-1	-	-
St Johnstone v Inverness CT	-	-	1-0/0-3	2-0/0-0	0-0/1-0	4-0/0-1
St Mirren v Motherwell	0-0/1-3	3-3/0-0	1-1	0-1/0-0	2-1	0-1/3-2

Scottish Championship						
Dumbarton v Falkirk	-	-	-	-	0-2/0-2	1-1/2-1
Hearts v Alloa	-	-	-	-	-	-
Queen of Sth v Cowdenbeath	-	-	3-0/2-2	-	-	1-1/2-1
Raith v Hibernian	-	-	-	-	-	-
Rangers v Livingston	-	-	-	-	-	-

Scottish League One						
Ayr v Stirling	1-1/3-1	-	-	-	-	-
Dunfermline v Stranraer	-	-	-	-	-	3-1/3-2
Forfar v Airdrieonians	-	-	1-2/1-2	3-2/2-3	-	3-3/1-1
Morton v Peterhead	-	-	-	-	-	-
Stenh'semuir v Brechin	-	1-1/1-2	0-0/1-3	1-1/2-1	3-1/3-3	3-2/4-2

Results cover matches from Premier League to Conference and Scottish Premiership to League Two

Scottish League Two						
Albion v Montrose	0-1/0-1	0-0/1-0	3-1/0-2	-	-	0-2/1-0
Arbroath v Berwick	-	-	3-2/2-1	-	-	-
Clyde v East Fife	-	1-3/2-1	-	-	-	-
Elgin v East Stirling	0-4/0-2	1-2/0-1	0-2/2-0	2-0/3-1	3-4/3-2	0-1/5-0
Queen's Park v Annan	-	0-0/3-2	3-0/0-1	0-0/2-0	2-2/2-2	2-5/0-1

Friday December 26th, 2014

Premier League						
Arsenal v QPR	-	-	-	1-0	1-0	-
Burnley v Liverpool	-	0-4	-	-	-	-
Chelsea v West Ham	1-1	4-1	3-0	-	2-0	0-0
Crystal Palace v Southampton	3-0	-	-	0-2	-	0-1
Everton v Stoke	3-1	1-1	1-0	0-1	1-0	4-0
Leicester v Tottenham	-	-	-	-	-	-
Man Utd v Newcastle	1-1	-	3-0	1-1	4-3	0-1
Sunderland v Hull	1-0	4-1	-	-	-	0-2
Swansea v Aston Villa	-	-	-	0-0	2-2	4-1
West Brom v Man City	2-1	-	0-2	0-0	1-2	2-3

Championship						
Birmingham v Derby	1-0	-	-	2-2	3-1	3-3
Bolton v Blackburn	0-0	0-2	2-1	2-1	1-0	4-0
Bournemouth v Fulham	-	-	-	-	-	-
Brentford v Ipswich	-	-	-	-	-	-
Brighton v Reading	-	-	-	0-1	-	1-1
Charlton v Cardiff	2-2	-	-	-	5-4	-
Leeds v Wigan	-	-	-	-	-	2-0
Middlesbro v Nottm Forest	-	1-1	1-1	2-1	1-0	1-1
Norwich v Millwall	-	2-0	2-1	-	-	-
Rotherham v Huddersfield	-	-	-	-	-	-
Sheff Wed v Blackpool	1-1	2-0	-	-	0-2	2-0
Watford v Wolves	2-3	-	-	-	2-1	-

League 1						
Bristol City v Yeovil	-	-	-	-	-	-
Chesterfield v Peterborough	-	-	-	-	-	-
Colchester v Gillingham	-	2-1	-	-	-	3-0
Doncaster v Coventry	1-0	0-0	1-1	1-1	1-4	-
Fleetwood Town v Bradford	-	-	-	-	2-2	-
Leyton Orient v Crawley Town	-	-	-	-	0-1	2-3
Notts Co v MK Dons	-	-	2-0	1-1	1-2	1-3
Oldham v Crewe	1-1	-	-	-	1-2	1-1
Port Vale v Sheff Utd	-	-	-	-	-	1-2
Preston v Barnsley	2-1	1-4	1-2	-	-	-
Scunthorpe v Rochdale	-	-	-	1-0	-	3-0
Walsall v Swindon	2-1	1-1	1-2	-	0-2	1-1

League 2						
Burton v Tranmere	-	-	-	-	-	-
Cambridge U v Southend	-	-	-	-	-	-
Dag & Red v Stevenage	-	-	-	-	-	-
Exeter v Cheltenham	-	-	-	-	0-1	1-1
Mansfield v Hartlepool	-	-	-	-	-	1-4
Morecambe v Carlisle	-	-	-	-	-	-
Newport Co v Plymouth	-	-	-	-	-	1-2
Northampton v Bury	-	1-1	2-4	-	-	0-3
Oxford v Shrewsbury	-	-	3-1	2-0	-	-
Portsmouth v AFC Wimbledon	-	-	-	-	-	1-0
Wycombe v Luton	0-0	-	-	-	-	-
York v Accrington	-	-	-	-	1-1	1-1

Results cover matches from Premier League to Conference and Scottish Premiership to League Two

Conference

	2008-09	2009-10	2010-11	2011-12	2012-13	2013-14
Aldershot v Barnet	1-1	4-0	1-0	4-1	1-0	3-3
Chester v Altrincham	-	-	-	-	-	-
Dartford v Braintree	-	-	-	-	0-0	0-2
Dover v Welling	-	-	-	-	-	-
Eastleigh v Woking	-	-	-	-	-	-
Forest Green v Kidderminster	2-2	1-1	1-1	1-1	0-1	1-1
Gateshead v Halifax	-	-	-	-	-	1-1
Lincoln v Alfreton	-	-	-	0-1	1-2	4-1
Macclesfield v Grimsby	1-0	0-0	-	-	1-3	1-1
Nuneaton v Telford	-	-	-	-	3-1	-
Southport v Wrexham	-	-	0-1	0-0	1-4	1-2
Torquay v Bristol Rovers	-	-	-	2-2	3-3	1-1

Saturday December 27th, 2014

Scottish Premiership

	2008-09	2009-10	2010-11	2011-12	2012-13	2013-14
Celtic v Ross County	-	-	-	-	4-0	2-1/1-1
Dundee v St Mirren	-	-	-	-	0-2/2-1	-
Inverness CT v Aberdeen	0-3	-	2-0/0-2	2-1/0-2	1-1/3-0	3-4/0-0
Kilmarnock v Hamilton	1-0/0-1	3-0/1-2	3-0	-	-	-
Motherwell v Partick	-	-	-	-	-	1-0/4-3
St Johnstone v Dundee Utd	-	2-3/0-1	0-0	3-3/1-5/0-2	0-0/1-1	3-0/2-0

Scottish Championship

	2008-09	2009-10	2010-11	2011-12	2012-13	2013-14
Alloa v Queen of Sth	-	-	-	-	1-0/1-2	0-3/0-1
Cowdenbeath v Dumbarton	2-0/0-0	2-1/0-0	-	0-0/4-1	0-1/2-3	3-2/2-4
Falkirk v Raith	-	-	0-0/2-1	2-0/2-3	0-2/1-1	3-1/2-1
Hibernian v Rangers	0-3/2-3/1-1	1-4/0-1	0-3/0-2	0-2	-	-
Livingston v Hearts	-	-	-	-	-	-

Scottish League One

	2008-09	2009-10	2010-11	2011-12	2012-13	2013-14
Airdrieonians v Ayr	-	3-1/1-1	2-2/0-5	-	-	0-1/3-0
Brechin v Dunfermline	-	-	-	-	-	1-1/3-2
Peterhead v Forfar	-	-	1-2/1-1	-	-	-
Stirling v Morton	-	-	0-1/3-2	-	-	-
Stranraer v Stenh'semuir	-	-	-	-	1-1/1-1	1-0/1-1

Scottish League Two

	2008-09	2009-10	2010-11	2011-12	2012-13	2013-14
Annan v Clyde	-	-	0-2/1-0	1-0/1-0	1-3/0-1	1-2/0-1
Berwick v Queen's Park	-	1-0/1-1	1-1/3-1	2-0/1-4	2-0/4-1	4-0/1-0
East Fife v Arbroath	3-2/0-0	1-1/3-1	-	2-2/1-3	2-1/0-1	2-1/1-0
East Stirling v Albion	1-0/0-1	2-0/3-1	0-0/1-2	-	-	1-4/1-1
Montrose v Elgin	1-0/3-1	1-1/0-4	0-1/1-0	3-0/2-3	2-2/4-1	3-3/0-3

Sunday December 28th, 2014

Premier League

	2008-09	2009-10	2010-11	2011-12	2012-13	2013-14
Aston Villa v Sunderland	2-1	1-1	0-1	0-0	6-1	0-0
Hull v Leicester	-	-	0-1	2-1	0-0	-
Liverpool v Swansea	-	-	-	0-0	5-0	4-3
Man City v Burnley	-	3-3	-	-	-	-
Newcastle v Everton	0-0	-	1-2	2-1	1-2	0-3
QPR v Crystal Palace	0-0	1-1	2-1	-	-	-
Southampton v Chelsea	-	-	-	-	2-1	0-3
Stoke v West Brom	1-0	-	1-1	1-2	0-0	0-0
Tottenham v Man Utd	0-0	1-3	0-0	1-3	1-1	2-2
West Ham v Arsenal	0-2	2-2	0-3	-	1-3	1-3

Championship

	2008-09	2009-10	2010-11	2011-12	2012-13	2013-14
Blackburn v Middlesbro	1-1	-	-	-	1-2	1-0
Blackpool v Rotherham	-	-	-	-	-	-
Cardiff v Watford	2-1	3-1	4-2	1-1	2-1	-

Results cover matches from Premier League to Conference and Scottish Premiership to League Two

	2008-09	2009-10	2010-11	2011-12	2012-13	2013-14
Derby v Leeds	-	-	2-1	1-0	3-1	3-1
Fulham v Brighton	-	-	-	-	-	-
Huddersfield v Bolton	-	-	-	-	2-2	0-1
Ipswich v Charlton	1-1	-	-	-	1-2	1-1
Millwall v Bournemouth	-	-	-	-	-	1-0
Nottm Forest v Birmingham	1-1	-	-	1-3	2-2	1-0
Reading v Norwich	2-0	-	3-3	-	0-0	-
Wigan v Sheff Wed	-	-	-	-	-	1-0
Wolves v Brentford	-	-	-	-	-	0-0

League 1						
Barnsley v Oldham	-	-	-	-	-	-
Bradford v Notts Co	2-1	0-0	-	-	-	1-1
Coventry v Chesterfield	-	-	-	-	-	-
Crawley Town v Colchester	-	-	-	-	3-0	1-0
Crewe v Preston	-	-	-	-	1-0	2-1
Gillingham v Bristol City	-	-	-	-	-	1-1
MK Dons v Walsall	0-1	1-0	1-1	0-1	2-4	1-0
Peterborough v Doncaster	-	1-2	-	1-2	-	-
Rochdale v Fleetwood Town	-	-	-	-	0-0	1-2
Sheff Utd v Scunthorpe	-	0-1	0-4	2-1	3-0	-
Swindon v Port Vale	-	-	-	5-0	-	5-2
Yeovil v Leyton Orient	0-0	3-3	2-1	2-2	3-0	-

League 2						
Accrington v Burton	-	0-2	3-1	2-1	3-3	0-1
AFC Wimbledon v Exeter	-	-	-	-	2-2	2-1
Bury v Mansfield	-	-	-	-	-	0-0
Carlisle v York	-	-	-	-	-	-
Cheltenham v Newport Co	-	-	-	-	-	0-0
Hartlepool v Morecambe	-	-	-	-	-	2-1
Luton v Portsmouth	-	-	-	-	-	-
Plymouth v Oxford	-	-	-	1-1	0-1	0-2
Shrewsbury v Wycombe	0-1	-	1-1	-	-	-
Southend v Dag & Red	-	-	-	1-1	3-1	0-1
Stevenage v Cambridge U	2-1	4-1	-	-	-	-
Tranmere v Northampton	4-1	-	-	-	-	-

Conference						
Alfreton v Dartford	-	-	-	-	3-2	2-1
Altrincham v Nuneaton	-	-	-	-	-	-
Barnet v Dover	-	-	-	-	-	-
Braintree v Eastleigh	-	-	-	-	-	-
Bristol Rovers v Macclesfield	-	-	-	0-0	-	-
Grimsby v Lincoln	5-1	2-2	-	3-1	1-1	1-1
Halifax v Chester	-	-	-	-	-	2-1
Kidderminster v Southport	-	-	3-4	2-0	2-2	1-1
Telford v Gateshead	-	-	-	1-2	0-0	-
Welling v Torquay	-	-	-	-	-	-
Woking v Aldershot	-	-	-	-	-	1-2
Wrexham v Forest Green	1-1	1-0	2-1	1-2	2-1	2-0

Thursday January 1st, 2015

Premier League						
Aston Villa v Crystal Palace	-	-	-	-	-	0-1
Hull v Everton	2-2	3-2	-	-	-	0-2
Liverpool v Leicester	-	-	-	-	-	-
Man City v Sunderland	1-0	4-3	5-0	3-3	3-0	2-2
Newcastle v Burnley	-	-	-	-	-	-
QPR v Swansea	1-0	1-1	4-0	3-0	0-5	-

Results cover matches from Premier League to Conference and Scottish Premiership to League Two

	2008-09	2009-10	2010-11	2011-12	2012-13	2013-14
Southampton v Arsenal	-	-	-	-	1-1	2-2
Stoke v Man Utd	0-1	0-2	1-2	1-1	0-2	2-1
Tottenham v Chelsea	1-0	2-1	1-1	1-1	2-4	1-1
West Ham v West Brom	0-0	-	2-2	-	3-1	3-3

Conference						
Alfreton v Lincoln	-	-	-	1-3	0-2	1-1
Altrincham v Chester	-	-	-	-	-	-
Barnet v Aldershot	0-3	3-0	1-2	2-1	0-1	1-3
Braintree v Dartford	-	-	-	-	0-2	1-0
Bristol Rovers v Torquay	-	-	-	1-2	3-2	1-2
Grimsby v Macclesfield	0-0	1-1	-	-	0-1	2-3
Halifax v Gateshead	-	-	-	-	-	3-3
Kidderminster v Forest Green	1-1	2-1	1-0	1-0	0-1	4-1
Telford v Nuneaton	-	-	-	-	0-3	-
Welling v Dover	-	-	-	-	-	-
Woking v Eastleigh	-	-	-	-	-	-
Wrexham v Southport	-	-	2-1	2-0	2-2	1-0

Scottish Premiership						
Aberdeen v St Johnstone	-	2-1/1-3	0-1/0-2	0-0/0-0	2-0	0-0/1-0-1-1
Dundee Utd v Dundee	-	-	-	-	3-0/1-1	-
Hamilton v Motherwell	2-0/0-3	2-2/0-0	0-0	-	-	
Partick v Celtic	-	-	-	-	-	1-2/1-5
Ross County v Inverness CT	-	2-1/0-0	-	-	0-0/1-0	0-3/1-2
St Mirren v Kilmarnock	0-0/1-1	1-0/1-0	0-2	3-0/4-2	1-1	1-1/2-0

Saturday January 3rd, 2015

League 1						
Bristol City v Peterborough	-	1-1	-	1-2	4-2	0-3
Chesterfield v Crawley Town	-	-	-	-	-	-
Colchester v MK Dons	0-3	2-0	1-3	1-5	0-2	3-1
Doncaster v Crewe	-	-	-	-	0-2	-
Fleetwood Town v Swindon	-	-	-	-	-	-
Leyton Orient v Bradford	-	-	-	-	-	0-1
Notts Co v Sheff Utd	-	-	-	2-5	1-1	2-1
Oldham v Rochdale	-	-	1-2	2-0	-	-
Port Vale v Gillingham	1-3	-	0-0	2-1	0-2	2-1
Preston v Yeovil	-	-	-	4-3	3-2	-
Scunthorpe v Barnsley	-	2-1	0-0	-	-	-
Walsall v Coventry	-	-	-	-	4-0	0-1

League 2						
Burton v Shrewsbury	-	1-1	0-0	1-1	-	-
Cambridge U v AFC Wimbledon	-	2-2	1-2	-	-	-
Dag & Red v Bury	1-3	3-1	-	-	-	2-1
Exeter v Accrington	2-1	-	-	-	2-0	0-1
Mansfield v Luton	-	0-0	0-0	1-1	2-2	-
Morecambe v Stevenage	-	-	0-0	-	-	-
Newport Co v Carlisle	-	-	-	-	-	-
Northampton v Southend	2-3	-	2-1	2-5	3-3	2-1
Oxford v Cheltenham	-	-	1-1	1-3	1-0	1-1
Portsmouth v Tranmere	-	-	-	-	1-0	-
Wycombe v Hartlepool	-	2-0	-	5-0	-	2-1
York v Plymouth	-	-	-	-	2-0	1-1

Scottish Championship						
Cowdenbeath v Raith	-	-	1-2/0-3	-	4-4/1-1	3-4/1-0
Falkirk v Alloa	-	-	-	-	-	0-0/3-1
Hearts v Hibernian	0-0/0-1	0-0/2-1	1-0	2-0/2-0	0-0/1-2	1-0/2-0

Results cover matches from Premier League to Conference and Scottish Premiership to League Two

	2008-09	2009-10	2010-11	2011-12	2012-13	2013-14
Queen of Sth v Livingston	6-1/3-3	-	-	0-2/0-4	-	2-2/2-0
Rangers v Dumbarton	-	-	-	-	-	-

Scottish League One						
Ayr v Stranraer	3-2/5-0	-	-	-	2-1/2-1	3-6/5-0
Dunfermline v Peterhead	-	-	-	-	-	-
Forfar v Brechin	-	-	1-1/2-1	0-0/4-1	1-0/1-4	2-0/1-1
Morton v Airdrieonians	2-0/0-0	1-0/2-1	-	-	2-0/5-2	-
Stenh'semuir v Stirling	-	1-2/1-3	-	4-0/4-0	-	-

Scottish League Two						
Albion v Annan	0-1/2-1	0-0/1-0	0-0/0-0	-	-	2-0/0-2
Arbroath v Montrose	-	-	4-0/4-1	-	-	-
Berwick v East Stirling	2-1/1-2	0-1/2-2	3-0/1-1	4-2/0-2	3-0/2-0	2-0/1-0
Elgin v East Fife	-	-	-	-	-	-
Queen's Park v Clyde	-	-	0-1/4-0	3-0/3-0	1-0/4-1	1-1/1-3

Sunday January 4th, 2015

Conference						
Aldershot v Telford	-	-	-	-	-	-
Chester v Braintree	-	-	-	-	-	0-2
Dartford v Kidderminster	-	-	-	-	1-0	3-0
Dover v Grimsby	-	-	-	-	-	-
Eastleigh v Altrincham	-	-	-	-	-	-
Forest Green v Welling	-	-	-	-	-	0-0
Gateshead v Wrexham	-	1-0	0-1	1-4	0-1	0-3
Lincoln v Barnet	2-0	1-0	1-0	-	-	3-3
Macclesfield v Woking	-	-	-	-	0-0	3-2
Nuneaton v Bristol Rovers	-	-	-	-	-	-
Southport v Halifax	-	-	-	-	-	2-1
Torquay v Alfreton	-	-	-	-	-	-

Scottish Premiership						
Dundee v Ross County	1-2/2-0	2-0/0-1	0-0/2-0	1-2/1-1	0-1/0-2	-
Inverness CT v St Mirren	1-2/2-1	-	1-2/1-0	2-1/0-0	2-2	3-0/2-2
Kilmarnock v Celtic	1-3/1-2	1-0	1-2/0-4/0-2	3-3/0-6	1-3	2-5/0-3
Motherwell v Aberdeen	0-1/1-1	1-1	1-1/2-1	1-0/1-0	4-1	1-3/2-2
Partick v Dundee Utd	-	-	-	-	-	0-0/1-1
St Johnstone v Hamilton	-	1-1/2-3	2-0/1-0	-	-	-

Saturday January 10th, 2015

Premier League						
Arsenal v Stoke	4-1	2-0	1-0	3-1	1-0	3-1
Burnley v QPR	1-0	-	0-0	-	-	2-0
Chelsea v Newcastle	0-0	-	2-2	0-2	2-0	3-0
Crystal Palace v Tottenham	-	-	-	-	-	0-1
Everton v Man City	1-2	2-0	2-1	1-0	2-0	2-3
Leicester v Aston Villa	-	-	-	-	-	-
Man Utd v Southampton	-	-	-	-	2-1	1-1
Sunderland v Liverpool	0-1	1-0	0-2	1-0	1-1	1-3
Swansea v West Ham	-	-	-	-	3-0	0-0
West Brom v Hull	0-3	-	-	-	-	1-1

Championship						
Birmingham v Wigan	-	1-0	0-0	-	-	0-1
Blackburn v Wolves	-	3-1	3-0	1-2	0-1	-
Blackpool v Millwall	-	-	-	1-0	2-1	1-0
Bolton v Leeds	-	-	-	-	2-2	0-1
Bournemouth v Norwich	-	-	-	-	-	-

Results cover matches from Premier League to Conference and Scottish Premiership to League Two

	2008-09	2009-10	2010-11	2011-12	2012-13	2013-14
Brentford v Rotherham	0-0	-	-	-	-	0-1
Cardiff v Fulham	-	-	-	-	-	3-1
Charlton v Brighton	-	1-2	0-4	-	2-2	3-2
Huddersfield v Watford	-	-	-	-	2-3	1-2
Ipswich v Derby	2-0	1-0	0-2	1-0	1-2	2-1
Nottm Forest v Sheff Wed	2-1	2-1	-	-	1-0	3-3
Reading v Middlesbro	-	0-2	5-2	0-0	-	2-0

League 1						
Barnsley v Yeovil	-	-	-	-	-	1-1
Bradford v Rochdale	2-0	0-3	-	-	2-4	-
Bristol City v Notts Co	-	-	-	-	-	2-1
Chesterfield v Port Vale	2-1	0-5	2-0	-	2-2	-
Coventry v Swindon	-	-	-	-	1-2	1-2
Crawley Town v MK Dons	-	-	-	-	2-0	0-2
Crewe v Gillingham	-	-	1-1	1-2	-	0-3
Leyton Orient v Fleetwood Town	-	-	-	-	-	-
Oldham v Doncaster	-	-	-	-	1-2	-
Peterborough v Colchester	2-1	-	1-1	-	-	2-0
Sheff Utd v Preston	1-0	1-0	1-0	2-1	0-0	0-1
Walsall v Scunthorpe	2-1	-	-	-	2-2	1-4	-

League 2						
Accrington v Bury	1-2	2-4	1-0	-	-	0-0
Burton v Mansfield	1-0	-	-	-	-	1-0
Carlisle v Cambridge U	-	-	-	-	-	-
Dag & Red v Oxford	-	-	-	0-1	0-1	1-0
Exeter v Northampton	-	-	-	-	3-0	0-1
Hartlepool v Cheltenham	4-1	-	-	-	-	0-1
Luton v Shrewsbury	3-1	-	-	-	-	-
Morecambe v Tranmere	-	-	-	-	-	-
Newport Co v Portsmouth	-	-	-	-	-	1-2
Southend v Plymouth	-	-	-	2-0	0-2	1-0
Stevenage v AFC Wimbledon	-	0-0	-	-	-	-
Wycombe v York	-	-	-	-	4-0	1-1

Scottish Premiership						
Celtic v St Johnstone	-	5-2/3-0	2-0	0-1/2-0/1-0	1-1/4-0	2-1/3-0
Dundee v Motherwell	-	-	-	-	1-2/0-3	-
Hamilton v Dundee Utd	3-1/0-1	0-1	0-1/1-1	-	-	-
Kilmarnock v Inverness CT	1-2/1-0	-	1-2/1-1	3-6/4-3	1-2	1-2/2-0
Ross County v Partick	1-0/0-2	2-2/1-2	0-2/0-0	2-2/3-0	-	1-3/1-1
St Mirren v Aberdeen	0-1/1-1	1-0/0-1	2-1/3-2	1-0/1-1	1-4/0-0	1-1/0-1

Scottish Championship						
Alloa v Rangers	-	-	-	-	-	-
Dumbarton v Hearts	-	-	-	-	-	-
Hibernian v Falkirk	3-2/0-0	2-0	-	-	-	-
Livingston v Cowdenbeath	-	-	-	-	1-1/3-0	5-1/1-0
Raith v Queen of Sth	-	1-0/0-0	0-1/0-1	0-2/3-1	-	2-1/3-2

Scottish League One						
Airdrieonians v Peterhead	-	-	2-2/1-0	-	-	-
Brechin v Ayr	0-1/1-0	-	0-3/1-0	-	2-1/2-1	1-1/2-1
Stenh'semuir v Morton	-	-	-	-	-	-
Stirling v Dunfermline	-	-	1-5/1-1	-	-	-
Stranraer v Forfar	-	1-0/2-0	-	-	4-1/0-3	0-4/3-1

Scottish League Two						
Annan v Elgin	5-0/6-0	0-2/3-3	0-1/2-2	1-1/1-1	2-0/2-2	2-1/2-0
Arbroath v Albion	-	-	1-1/3-0	6-2/6-1	2-1/2-1	-

Results cover matches from Premier League to Conference and Scottish Premiership to League Two

	2008-09	2009-10	2010-11	2011-12	2012-13	2013-14
Clyde v Berwick	-	-	1-4/2-0	1-4/2-2	2-1/2-1	1-0/3-3
East Fife v Queen's Park	1-2/4-2	-	-	-	-	-
Montrose v East Stirling	3-0/0-2	0-3/0-1	0-2/3-0	2-1/3-1	3-1/2-2	2-0/2-0

Saturday January 17th, 2015

Premier League						
Aston Villa v Liverpool	0-0	0-1	1-0	0-2	1-2	0-1
Burnley v Crystal Palace	4-2	-	1-0	1-1	1-0	-
Everton v West Brom	2-0	-	1-4	2-0	2-1	0-0
Leicester v Stoke	-	-	-	-	-	-
Man City v Arsenal	3-0	4-2	0-3	1-0	1-1	6-3
Newcastle v Southampton	-	-	-	-	4-2	1-1
QPR v Man Utd	-	-	-	0-2	0-2	-
Swansea v Chelsea	-	-	-	1-1	1-1	0-1
Tottenham v Sunderland	1-2	2-0	1-1	1-0	1-0	5-1
West Ham v Hull	2-0	3-0	-	2-1	-	2-1

Championship						
Brighton v Brentford	-	3-0	1-0	-	-	-
Derby v Nottm Forest	1-1	1-0	0-1	1-0	1-1	5-0
Fulham v Reading	-	-	-	-	2-4	-
Leeds v Birmingham	-	-	-	1-4	0-1	4-0
Middlesbro v Huddersfield	-	-	-	-	3-0	1-1
Millwall v Ipswich	-	-	2-1	4-1	0-0	1-0
Norwich v Cardiff	2-0	-	1-1	-	-	0-0
Rotherham v Bournemouth	1-0	1-3	-	-	-	-
Sheff Wed v Bolton	-	-	-	-	1-2	1-3
Watford v Charlton	1-0	-	-	-	3-4	1-1
Wigan v Blackburn	3-0	1-1	4-3	3-3	-	2-1
Wolves v Blackpool	2-0	-	4-0	-	1-2	-

League 1						
Colchester v Walsall	0-2	2-1	2-0	1-0	2-0	1-1
Doncaster v Barnsley	0-1	0-1	0-2	2-0	-	2-2
Fleetwood Town v Oldham	-	-	-	-	-	-
Gillingham v Coventry	-	-	-	-	-	4-2
MK Dons v Sheff Utd	-	-	-	1-0	1-0	0-1
Notts Co v Crewe	-	2-0	-	-	1-1	4-0
Port Vale v Peterborough	-	-	-	-	-	0-1
Preston v Leyton Orient	-	-	-	0-2	0-0	1-1
Rochdale v Crawley Town	-	-	-	-	-	-
Scunthorpe v Bristol City	-	3-0	0-2	-	-	-
Swindon v Chesterfield	-	-	-	-	-	-
Yeovil v Bradford	-	-	-	-	-	-

League 2						
AFC Wimbledon v Carlisle	-	-	-	-	-	-
Bury v Wycombe	0-0	-	1-3	1-4	-	1-0
Cambridge U v Newport Co	-	-	0-1	1-1	0-0	-
Cheltenham v Morecambe	-	2-0	1-1	1-2	2-0	3-0
Mansfield v Exeter	-	-	-	-	-	0-0
Northampton v Dag & Red	-	1-0	-	2-1	3-1	2-2
Oxford v Southend	-	-	0-2	0-2	2-0	0-2
Plymouth v Luton	-	-	-	-	-	-
Portsmouth v Burton	-	-	-	-	-	0-0
Shrewsbury v Hartlepool	-	-	-	-	1-1	-
Tranmere v Accrington	-	-	-	-	-	-
York v Stevenage	0-2	1-1	-	-	-	-

Results cover matches from Premier League to Conference and Scottish Premiership to League Two

Conference					
Altrincham v Torquay	0-1	-	-	-	-	-
Braintree v Forest Green	-	-	-	1-5	3-1	1-1
Dover v Dartford	-	-	-	-	-	-
Grimsby v Barnet	0-1	2-0	-	-	-	2-1
Halifax v Eastleigh	-	-	-	-	-	-
Kidderminster v Macclesfield	-	-	-	-	3-0	2-1
Lincoln v Aldershot	0-2	1-0	0-3	-	-	0-1
Nuneaton v Gateshead	-	-	-	-	0-1	1-4
Southport v Chester	-	-	-	-	-	0-0
Welling v Alfreton	-	-	-	-	-	1-2
Woking v Bristol Rovers	-	-	-	-	-	-
Wrexham v Telford	-	-	-	4-0	4-1	-

Scottish Premiership					
Aberdeen v Dundee	-	-	-	-	2-0/1-0	-
Dundee Utd v Inverness CT	2-1/1-1	-	0-4/1-0	3-1/3-0	4-4	0-1/2-1
Hamilton v Celtic	1-2	1-2/0-1	1-1	-	-	-
Motherwell v Kilmarnock	0-2/1-2	3-1/1-0	0-1/1-1	0-0	2-2	2-1/1-2
Ross County v St Mirren	-	-	-	-	0-0	3-0/2-1
St Johnstone v Partick	3-0/1-1	-	-	-	-	1-1/1-1

Scottish Championship					
Falkirk v Queen of Sth	-	-	3-1/0-3	1-0/3-0	-	2-1/1-0
Hibernian v Cowdenbeath	-	-	-	-	-	-
Livingston v Alloa	-	-	3-3/4-0	-	-	3-2/2-0
Raith v Dumbarton	-	-	-	-	2-2/3-2	2-1/1-3
Rangers v Hearts	2-0/2-2/2-0	1-1/2-0	1-0/4-0	1-1/1-2	-	-

Scottish League One					
Ayr v Morton	-	0-2/2-0	-	0-1/0-0	-	-
Dunfermline v Airdrieonians	0-0/1-1	2-0/2-0	-	-	1-3/1-2	2-1/0-1
Forfar v Stenh'semuir	1-0/4-4	-	1-1/2-0	2-3/1-2	3-2/3-3	1-2/3-0
Peterhead v Stirling	1-1/1-1	3-2/1-1	-	-	2-2/0-0	3-1/0-4
Stranraer v Brechin	1-2/0-3	-	-	-	0-2/3-2	3-0/1-2

Scottish League Two					
Albion v East Fife	-	-	-	0-3/1-1	0-3/1-1	-
Berwick v Montrose	3-2/0-1	2-0/0-2	1-0/0-1	1-2/2-2	1-4/4-0	1-1/5-0
East Stirling v Annan	2-1/1-1	1-3/3-1	1-5/2-0	1-0/0-4	2-2/1-2	1-1/2-1
Elgin v Clyde	-	-	0-1/0-1	0-3/1-1	2-1/4-2	1-0/3-1
Queen's Park v Arbroath	1-2/0-1	-	5-2/1-1	-	-	-

Wednesday January 21st, 2015

Scottish Premiership					
Aberdeen v Ross County	-	-	-	-	0-0/0-1	1-0
Celtic v Motherwell	2-0	0-0/2-1/4-0	1-0/4-0	4-0/1-0	1-0	2-0/3-0
Dundee v Kilmarnock	-	-	-	-	0-0/2-3	-
Inverness CT v St Johnstone	-	-	1-1/2-0	0-1	1-1/0-0	1-0/2-0
Partick v Hamilton	-	-	-	1-1/2-0	4-0/1-0	-
St Mirren v Dundee Utd	0-2	0-0/1-2	1-1/1-1	2-2	0-1/0-0	4-1

Saturday January 24th, 2015

Championship					
Brighton v Ipswich	-	-	-	3-0	1-1	0-2
Derby v Blackburn	-	-	-	-	1-1	1-1
Fulham v Nottm Forest	-	-	-	-	-	-
Leeds v Bournemouth	-	-	-	-	-	2-1
Middlesbro v Cardiff	-	0-1	1-0	0-2	2-1	-

Results cover matches from Premier League to Conference and Scottish Premiership to League Two

	2008-09	2009-10	2010-11	2011-12	2012-13	2013-14
Millwall v Reading	-	-	0-0	1-2	-	0-3
Norwich v Brentford	-	1-0	-	-	-	-
Rotherham v Bolton	-	-	-	-	-	-
Sheff Wed v Birmingham	1-1	-	-	-	3-2	4-1
Watford v Blackpool	3-4	2-2	-	0-2	1-2	4-0
Wigan v Huddersfield	-	-	-	-	-	2-1
Wolves v Charlton	2-1	-	-	-	1-1	-

League 1

	2008-09	2009-10	2010-11	2011-12	2012-13	2013-14
Colchester v Leyton Orient	1-0	1-0	3-2	1-1	2-1	1-2
Doncaster v Bristol City	1-0	1-0	1-1	1-1	-	-
Fleetwood v Crawley Town	-	-	1-2	-	-	-
Gillingham v Oldham	-	1-0	-	-	-	0-1
MK Dons v Barnsley	-	-	-	-	-	-
Notts Co v Peterborough	-	-	0-1	-	-	2-4
Port Vale v Crewe	-	0-1	2-1	1-1	-	1-3
Preston v Walsall	-	-	-	0-0	1-3	2-1
Rochdale v Sheff Utd	-	-	-	2-5	-	-
Scunthorpe v Chesterfield	-	-	-	2-2	-	1-1
Swindon v Bradford	-	-	-	0-0	-	1-0
Yeovil v Coventry	-	-	-	-	1-1	-

League 2

	2008-09	2009-10	2010-11	2011-12	2012-13	2013-14
AFC Wimbledon v Accrington	-	-	-	0-2	1-2	1-1
Bury v Carlisle	-	-	-	0-2	1-1	-
Cambridge U v Dag & Red	-	-	-	-	-	-
Cheltenham v Luton	-	-	-	-	-	-
Mansfield v Wycombe	-	-	-	-	-	2-2
Northampton v Newport Co	-	-	-	-	-	3-1
Oxford v Exeter	-	-	-	-	2-4	0-0
Plymouth v Morecambe	-	-	-	1-1	2-1	5-0
Portsmouth v Southend	-	-	-	-	-	1-2
Shrewsbury v Stevenage	-	-	1-0	-	2-1	1-0
Tranmere v Hartlepool	1-0	0-0	0-1	1-1	0-1	-
York v Burton	1-3	-	-	-	3-0	0-0

Conference

	2008-09	2009-10	2010-11	2011-12	2012-13	2013-14
Aldershot v Dover	-	-	-	-	-	-
Alfreton v Forest Green	-	-	-	1-6	2-1	3-2
Barnet v Southport	-	-	-	-	-	1-0
Bristol Rovers v Braintree	-	-	-	-	-	-
Chester v Kidderminster	-	-	-	-	-	0-0
Dartford v Woking	-	-	-	-	4-1	5-1
Eastleigh v Wrexham	-	-	-	-	-	-
Gateshead v Welling	-	-	-	-	-	1-1
Macclesfield v Altrincham	-	-	-	-	-	-
Nuneaton v Grimsby	-	-	-	-	1-0	0-1
Telford v Halifax	-	-	-	-	-	-
Torquay v Lincoln	-	2-3	2-0	-	-	-

Scottish Premiership

	2008-09	2009-10	2010-11	2011-12	2012-13	2013-14
Dundee Utd v Motherwell	0-4	0-1/3-0	2-0/4-0	1-3/1-1	1-2/1-3	2-2/3-1/5-1
Hamilton v Inverness CT	1-0	-	1-3/1-2	-	-	-
Kilmarnock v Partick	-	-	-	-	-	2-1/1-2
Ross County v Celtic	-	-	-	-	1-1/3-2/1-1	1-4
St Johnstone v Aberdeen	-	1-0/1-1	0-1/0-0	1-2	1-2/3-1	0-2
St Mirren v Dundee	-	-	-	-	3-1/1-2	-

Results cover matches from Premier League to Conference and Scottish Premiership to League Two

	2008-09	2009-10	2010-11	2011-12	2012-13	2013-14
Scottish Championship						
Alloa v Raith	1-1/0-0	-	-	-	-	1-0/0-1
Cowdenbeath v Rangers	-	-	-	-	-	-
Dumbarton v Livingston	-	-	1-2/0-3	-	3-4/0-3	1-2/2-2
Hearts v Falkirk	2-1	0-0/3-2	-	-	-	-
Queen of Sth v Hibernian	-	-	-	-	-	-
Scottish League One						
Airdrieonians v Stranraer	-	-	-	-	-	3-2/1-1
Brechin v Peterhead	2-2/1-1	3-0/1-2	4-2/3-1	-	-	-
Morton v Dunfermline	1-1/2-1	0-2/1-2	2-1/0-2	-	4-2/0-1	-
Stenh'semuir v Ayr	-	-	3-1/2-1	-	1-1/4-0	1-1/1-1
Stirling v Forfar	-	-	-	2-4/2-2	-	-
Scottish League Two						
Annan v Berwick	1-2/1-1	1-1/0-1	1-1/2-3	2-2/1-1	3-2/2-2	3-2/4-0
Clyde v Arbroath	-	1-0/0-2	1-1/0-3	-	-	-
East Fife v East Stirling	-	-	-	-	-	-
Montrose v Albion	1-2/1-0	0-0/0-0	0-2/0-2	-	-	2-1/2-1
Queen's Park v Elgin	-	0-3/0-1	1-1/1-0	6-0/1-3	1-1/0-1	3-3/2-0

Saturday January 31st, 2015

	2008-09	2009-10	2010-11	2011-12	2012-13	2013-14
Premier League						
Arsenal v Aston Villa	0-2	3-0	1-2	3-0	2-1	1-3
Chelsea v Man City	1-0	2-4	2-0	2-1	0-0	2-1
Crystal Palace v Everton	-	-	-	-	-	0-0
Hull v Newcastle	1-1	-	-	-	-	1-4
Liverpool v West Ham	0-0	3-0	3-0	-	0-0	4-1
Man Utd v Leicester	-	-	-	-	-	-
Southampton v Swansea	2-2	-	-	-	1-1	2-0
Stoke v QPR	-	-	-	2-3	1-0	-
Sunderland v Burnley	-	2-1	-	-	-	-
West Brom v Tottenham	2-0	-	1-1	1-3	0-1	3-3
Championship						
Birmingham v Norwich	1-1	-	-	-	-	-
Blackburn v Fulham	1-0	2-0	1-1	3-1	-	-
Blackpool v Brighton	-	-	-	3-1	1-1	0-1
Bolton v Wolves	-	1-0	1-0	1-1	2-0	-
Bournemouth v Watford	-	-	-	-	-	1-1
Brentford v Middlesbro	-	-	-	-	-	-
Cardiff v Derby	4-1	6-1	4-1	2-0	1-1	-
Charlton v Rotherham	-	-	-	-	-	-
Huddersfield v Leeds	1-0	2-2	-	-	2-4	3-2
Ipswich v Wigan	-	-	-	-	-	1-3
Nottm Forest v Millwall	-	-	1-1	3-1	1-4	1-2
Reading v Sheff Wed	6-0	5-0	-	-	-	0-2
League 1						
Barnsley v Port Vale	-	-	-	-	-	-
Bradford v Colchester	-	-	-	-	-	2-2
Bristol City v Fleetwood Town	-	-	-	-	-	-
Chesterfield v Doncaster	-	-	-	-	-	-
Coventry v Rochdale	-	-	-	-	-	-
Crawley Town v Preston	-	-	-	-	1-0	2-2
Crewe v MK Dons	2-2	-	-	-	2-1	2-0
Leyton Orient v Scunthorpe	2-2	-	-	1-3	1-3	-
Oldham v Notts Co	-	-	3-0	3-2	2-2	1-1
Peterborough v Yeovil	1-3	-	2-2	-	-	-
Sheff Utd v Swindon	-	-	-	-	2-0	1-0
Walsall v Gillingham	-	0-0	-	-	-	1-1

Results cover matches from Premier League to Conference and Scottish Premiership to League Two

	2008-09	2009-10	2010-11	2011-12	2012-13	2013-14
League 2						
Accrington v Northampton	-	0-3	3-1	2-1	2-4	0-1
Burton v Bury	-	0-0	1-3	-	-	2-2
Carlisle v Mansfield	-	-	-	-	-	-
Dag & Red v Cheltenham	-	0-2	-	0-5	1-0	1-2
Exeter v Tranmere	-	2-1	1-1	3-0	-	-
Hartlepool v Plymouth	-	-	2-0	-	-	1-0
Luton v Cambridge U	-	2-2	2-0	0-1	3-2	0-0
Morecambe v AFC Wimbledon	-	-	-	1-2	3-1	1-1
Newport Co v Shrewsbury	-	-	-	-	-	-
Southend v York	-	-	-	-	0-0	2-1
Stevenage v Oxford	1-1	1-0	0-0	-	-	-
Wycombe v Portsmouth	-	-	-	-	-	0-1
Conference						
Altrincham v Aldershot	-	-	-	-	-	-
Braintree v Macclesfield	-	-	-	-	0-3	0-1
Dartford v Bristol Rovers	-	-	-	-	-	-
Forest Green v Nuneaton	-	-	-	-	1-0	1-0
Grimsby v Telford	-	-	-	2-0	1-0	-
Halifax v Barnet	-	-	-	-	-	2-1
Kidderminster v Eastleigh	-	-	-	-	-	-
Lincoln v Dover	-	-	-	-	-	-
Southport v Gateshead	-	-	5-1	1-3	2-1	2-1
Welling v Chester	-	-	-	-	-	2-0
Woking v Alfreton	-	-	-	-	1-2	2-1
Wrexham v Torquay	1-1	-	-	-	-	-
Scottish Premiership						
Aberdeen v Dundee Utd	0-1/2-2	0-2/2-2	1-1	3-1/3-1	2-2	1-0/1-1
Celtic v Kilmarnock	3-0	3-0/3-1	1-1	2-1	0-2/4-1	4-0
Dundee v Hamilton	-	-	-	0-1/2-2	-	0-0/1-0
Inverness CT v Ross County	-	1-3/3-0	-	-	3-1/2-1	1-2
Motherwell v St Johnstone	-	1-3	4-0	0-3/3-2/5-1	1-1/3-2	4-0/2-1
Partick v St Mirren	-	-	-	-	-	0-3/1-1
Scottish Championship						
Alloa v Hearts	-	-	-	-	-	-
Cowdenbeath v Queen of Sth	-	-	1-3/2-2	-	-	0-2/1-1
Falkirk v Dumbarton	-	-	-	-	3-4/1-3	1-2/2-0
Hibernian v Raith	-	-	-	-	-	-
Livingston v Rangers	-	-	-	-	-	-
Scottish League One						
Airdrieonians v Brechin	-	-	1-1/2-2	2-3/4-1	-	3-1/2-1
Ayr v Dunfermline	-	1-0/1-2	-	-	-	2-4/1-1
Forfar v Morton	-	-	-	-	-	-
Peterhead v Stenh'semuir	-	2-2/0-1	2-2/0-3	-	-	-
Stranraer v Stirling	1-0/2-8	-	-	-	-	-
Scottish League Two						
Albion v Queen's Park	-	0-1/1-0	2-1/1-2	-	-	2-1/1-0
Arbroath v East Fife	0-1/0-2	0-1/2-2	-	3-0/2-2	2-0/1-0	2-2/2-1
Berwick v Elgin	1-1/2-1	2-0/2-1	6-2/4-0	1-1/3-3	0-0/2-1	2-3/2-3
East Stirling v Clyde	-	-	0-0/2-0	1-1/0-1	3-0/3-0	0-1/2-4
Montrose v Annan	1-1/0-3	0-0/1-2	1-1/0-1	2-3/1-1	0-0/5-1	0-2/2-1

Saturday February 7th, 2015

Premier League						
Aston Villa v Chelsea	0-1	2-1	0-0	2-4	1-2	1-0
Burnley v West Brom	-	-	-	-	-	-

Results cover matches from Premier League to Conference and Scottish Premiership to League Two

	2008-09	2009-10	2010-11	2011-12	2012-13	2013-14
Everton v Liverpool	0-2	0-2	2-0	0-2	2-2	3-3
Leicester v Crystal Palace	-	2-0	1-1	3-0	1-2	-
Man City v Hull	5-1	1-1	-	-	-	2-0
Newcastle v Stoke	2-2	-	1-2	3-0	2-1	5-1
QPR v Southampton	4-1	-	-	-	1-3	-
Swansea v Sunderland	-	-	-	0-0	2-2	4-0
Tottenham v Arsenal	0-0	2-1	3-3	2-1	2-1	0-1
West Ham v Man Utd	0-1	0-4	2-4	-	2-2	0-2

Championship						
Brighton v Nottm Forest	-	-	-	1-0	0-0	1-3
Derby v Bolton	-	-	-	-	1-1	0-0
Fulham v Birmingham	-	2-1	1-1	-	-	-
Leeds v Brentford	-	1-1	-	-	-	-
Middlesbro v Charlton	-	-	-	-	2-2	1-0
Millwall v Huddersfield	2-1	3-1	-	-	4-0	0-1
Norwich v Blackpool	1-1	-	-	-	-	-
Rotherham v Ipswich	-	-	-	-	-	-
Sheff Wed v Cardiff	1-0	3-1	-	-	0-2	-
Watford v Blackburn	-	-	-	-	4-0	3-3
Wigan v Bournemouth	-	-	-	-	-	3-0
Wolves v Reading	0-3	-	-	-	-	-

League 1						
Colchester v Crewe	0-1	-	-	-	1-2	1-2
Doncaster v Walsall	-	-	-	-	1-2	-
Fleetwood Town v Peterborough	-	-	-	-	-	-
Gillingham v Sheff Utd	-	-	-	-	-	0-1
MK Dons v Bristol City	-	-	-	-	-	2-2
Notts Co v Chesterfield	0-1	1-0	-	1-0	-	-
Port Vale v Bradford	0-2	2-1	2-1	3-2	0-0	2-1
Preston v Coventry	2-1	3-2	2-1	-	2-2	1-1
Rochdale v Leyton Orient	-	-	1-1	0-2	-	-
Scunthorpe v Oldham	2-0	-	-	1-2	2-2	-
Swindon v Barnsley	-	-	-	-	-	-
Yeovil v Crawley Town	-	-	-	-	2-2	-

League 2						
AFC Wimbledon v Newport Co	-	-	2-2	-	-	2-2
Bury v Exeter	0-1	-	-	2-0	-	2-0
Cambridge U v Wycombe	-	-	-	-	-	-
Cheltenham v Burton	-	0-1	2-1	2-0	1-0	2-2
Mansfield v Stevenage	2-1	2-3	-	-	-	-
Northampton v Morecambe	-	2-0	3-3	0-2	3-0	0-0
Oxford v Luton	-	2-0	-	-	-	-
Plymouth v Accrington	-	-	-	2-2	0-0	0-0
Portsmouth v Hartlepool	-	-	-	-	1-3	1-0
Shrewsbury v Southend	-	-	1-1	2-1	-	-
Tranmere v Carlisle	4-1	0-0	2-1	1-2	0-1	0-0
York v Dag & Red	-	-	-	-	3-2	3-1

Conference						
Aldershot v Halifax	-	-	-	-	-	2-2
Alfreton v Southport	-	-	-	0-0	3-3	2-1
Barnet v Woking	-	-	-	-	-	1-3
Bristol Rovers v Lincoln	-	-	-	-	-	-
Chester v Dartford	-	-	-	-	-	0-0
Dover v Altrincham	-	-	-	-	-	-
Eastleigh v Telford	-	-	-	-	-	-
Forest Green v Grimsby	-	-	3-3	0-1	0-1	2-1

Results cover matches from Premier League to Conference and Scottish Premiership to League Two

	2008-09	2009-10	2010-11	2011-12	2012-13	2013-14
Gateshead v Kidderminster	-	0-2	2-2	2-1	2-0	3-1
Macclesfield v Welling	-	-	-	-	-	2-1
Nuneaton v Wrexham	-	-	-	-	0-0	2-0
Torquay v Braintree	-	-	-	-	-	-

Scottish League One						
Ayr v Airdrieonians	-	1-1/1-4	1-0/3-1	-	-	2-2/3-0
Dunfermline v Brechin	-	-	-	-	-	3-1/2-1
Forfar v Peterhead	-	-	1-1/2-1	-	-	-
Morton v Stirling	-	-	0-0/2-0	-	-	-
Stenh'semuir v Stranraer	-	-	-	-	0-0/1-2	1-0/1-1

Scottish League Two						
Arbroath v East Stirling	-	-	2-0/3-5	-	-	-
Clyde v Annan	-	-	0-2/0-2	0-0/1-1	2-1/2-3	2-1/0-3
East Fife v Berwick	-	-	-	-	-	-
Elgin v Albion	1-6/1-0	0-2/3-1	2-2/1-1	-	-	1-2/1-1
Queen's Park v Montrose	-	3-2/3-0	1-0/4-1	3-1/5-0	2-2/1-2	0-1/1-1

Tuesday February 10th, 2015

Premier League						
Arsenal v Leicester	-	-	-	-	-	-
Crystal Palace v Newcastle	-	0-2	-	-	-	0-3
Hull v Aston Villa	0-1	0-2	-	-	-	0-0
Liverpool v Tottenham	3-1	2-0	0-2	0-0	3-2	4-0
Man Utd v Burnley	-	3-0	-	-	-	-
Southampton v West Ham	-	-	-	1-0	1-1	0-0
West Brom v Swansea	-	0-1	-	1-2	2-1	0-2

Championship						
Birmingham v Millwall	-	-	-	3-0	1-1	4-0
Blackburn v Rotherham	-	-	-	-	-	-
Blackpool v Middlesbro	-	2-0	-	3-0	4-1	0-2
Bolton v Fulham	1-3	0-0	0-0	0-3	-	-
Bournemouth v Derby	-	-	-	-	-	0-1
Brentford v Watford	-	-	-	-	-	-
Cardiff v Brighton	-	-	-	1-3	0-2	-
Charlton v Norwich	4-2	0-1	-	-	-	-
Huddersfield v Wolves	-	-	-	-	2-1	-
Ipswich v Sheff Wed	1-1	0-0	-	-	0-3	2-1
Reading v Leeds	-	-	0-0	2-0	-	1-0

League 1						
Barnsley v Fleetwood Town	-	-	-	-	-	-
Bradford v MK Dons	-	-	-	-	-	1-0
Bristol City v Port Vale	-	-	-	-	-	5-0
Chesterfield v Preston	-	-	-	0-2	-	-
Coventry v Scunthorpe	-	2-1	1-1	-	1-2	-
Crawley Town v Doncaster	-	-	-	-	1-1	-
Crewe v Yeovil	2-0	-	-	-	0-1	-
Leyton Orient v Notts Co	-	-	2-0	0-3	2-1	5-1
Oldham v Swindon	0-0	2-2	2-0	-	0-2	2-1
Peterborough v Gillingham	-	-	-	-	-	2-0
Sheff Utd v Colchester	-	-	-	3-0	3-0	1-1
Walsall v Rochdale	-	-	0-0	0-0	-	-

League 2						
Accrington v Oxford	-	-	0-0	0-2	0-3	0-0
Burton v AFC Wimbledon	-	-	-	3-2	6-2	1-1
Carlisle v Shrewsbury	-	-	-	-	2-2	0-0
Dag & Red v Portsmouth	-	-	-	-	-	1-4

Results cover matches from Premier League to Conference and Scottish Premiership to League Two

	2008-09	2009-10	2010-11	2011-12	2012-13	2013-14
Exeter v Cambridge U	-	-	-	-	-	-
Hartlepool v Northampton	2-0	-	-	-	-	2-0
Luton v York	-	1-1	5-0	1-2	-	-
Morecambe v Mansfield	-	-	-	-	-	0-1
Newport Co v Tranmere	-	-	-	-	-	-
Southend v Cheltenham	2-0	-	1-2	4-0	1-2	1-1
Stevenage v Bury	-	-	3-3	3-0	2-2	-
Wycombe v Plymouth	-	-	-	-	1-1	0-1

Conference						
Southport v Eastleigh	-	-	-	-	-	-

Wednesday February 11th, 2015

Premier League						
Chelsea v Everton	0-0	3-3	1-1	3-1	2-1	1-0
Stoke v Man City	1-0	1-1	1-1	1-1	1-1	0-0
Sunderland v QPR	-	-	-	3-1	0-0	-

Championship						
Nottm Forest v Wigan	-	-	-	-	-	1-4

Saturday February 14th, 2015

Championship						
Birmingham v Middlesbro	-	-	-	3-0	3-2	2-2
Blackpool v Nottm Forest	1-1	3-1	-	1-2	2-2	1-1
Bolton v Watford	-	-	-	-	2-1	2-0
Bournemouth v Huddersfield	-	-	1-1	2-0	-	2-1
Cardiff v Blackburn	-	-	-	-	3-0	-
Charlton v Brentford	-	2-0	0-1	2-0	-	-
Fulham v Ipswich	-	-	-	-	-	-
Leeds v Millwall	2-0	0-2	3-1	2-0	1-0	2-1
Norwich v Wolves	5-2	-	-	2-1	-	-
Reading v Wigan	-	-	-	-	0-3	1-2
Rotherham v Derby	-	-	-	-	-	-
Sheff Wed v Brighton	-	-	1-0	-	3-1	1-0

League 1						
Bristol City v Sheff Utd	0-0	2-3	3-0	-	-	0-1
Chesterfield v Leyton Orient	-	-	-	0-0	-	-
Coventry v Bradford	-	-	-	-	-	0-0
Crawley Town v Barnsley	-	-	-	-	-	-
Crewe v Fleetwood Town	-	-	-	-	-	-
Doncaster v Yeovil	-	-	-	-	1-1	2-1
Gillingham v MK Dons	-	2-2	-	-	-	3-2
Notts Co v Preston	-	-	-	0-0	0-1	0-1
Oldham v Colchester	0-1	2-2	0-0	1-1	1-1	0-2
Peterborough v Rochdale	-	-	2-1	-	-	-
Scunthorpe v Swindon	3-3	-	-	-	3-1	-
Walsall v Port Vale	-	-	-	-	-	0-2

League 2						
Burton v Oxford	0-1	-	0-0	1-1	4-0	0-2
Cheltenham v Bury	-	5-2	0-2	-	-	2-1
Hartlepool v Stevenage	-	-	-	0-0	0-2	-
Luton v Carlisle	-	-	-	-	-	-
Mansfield v Northampton	-	-	-	-	-	3-0
Morecambe v Dag & Red	1-2	1-0	-	1-2	2-1	2-2
Plymouth v Cambridge U	-	-	-	-	-	-
Portsmouth v Exeter	-	-	-	-	-	3-2
Shrewsbury v AFC Wimbledon	-	-	-	0-0	-	-

Results cover matches from Premier League to Conference and Scottish Premiership to League Two

	2008-09	2009-10	2010-11	2011-12	2012-13	2013-14
Southend v Accrington	-	-	1-1	2-2	0-1	1-0
Wycombe v Newport Co	-	-	-	-	-	0-1
York v Tranmere	-	-	-	-	-	-

Conference						
Aldershot v Welling	-	-	-	-	-	3-1
Altrincham v Forest Green	2-5	2-2	2-1	-	-	-
Braintree v Alfreton	-	-	-	1-2	2-1	3-1
Eastleigh v Torquay	-	-	-	-	-	-
Gateshead v Nuneaton	-	-	-	-	0-2	2-1
Grimsby v Bristol Rovers	-	-	-	-	-	-
Halifax v Dover	-	-	-	-	-	-
Kidderminster v Woking	3-0	-	-	-	2-2	2-0
Lincoln v Chester	1-1	-	-	-	-	1-1
Southport v Macclesfield	-	-	-	-	3-2	4-1
Telford v Dartford	-	-	-	-	0-2	-
Wrexham v Barnet	-	-	-	-	-	0-1

Scottish Premiership						
Dundee v Partick	0-0/4-0	2-0/1-0	2-1/3-2	0-1/0-3	-	-
Hamilton v Aberdeen	2-0	0-3/1-1	0-1/1-1	-	-	-
Kilmarnock v Dundee Utd	2-0	0-2/4-4	1-2/1-1	1-1	3-1/2-3	1-4
Ross County v Motherwell	-	-	-	-	0-0/3-0	1-2
St Johnstone v Celtic	-	1-4	0-3/0-1	0-2	2-1/1-1	0-1/3-3
St Mirren v Inverness CT	2-0/1-2	-	1-2/3-3	1-2/0-1	2-2/2-1	0-0

Scottish Championship						
Dumbarton v Cowdenbeath	2-1/1-1	0-3/2-1	-	0-4/0-2	0-3/2-2	0-0/5-1
Hearts v Livingston	-	-	-	-	-	-
Queen of Sth v Alloa	-	-	-	-	1-0/0-0	0-0/3-1
Raith v Falkirk	-	-	2-1/1-2	1-0/2-2	2-1/0-0	1-1/2-4
Rangers v Hibernian	1-0	1-1/3-0	0-3	1-0/4-0	-	-

Scottish League One						
Airdrieonians v Forfar	-	-	2-0/3-1	4-4/3-0	-	0-2/5-1
Brechin v Morton	-	-	-	-	-	-
Dunfermline v Stenh'semuir	-	-	-	-	-	3-2/0-0
Stirling v Ayr	2-2/2-0	-	-	-	-	-
Stranraer v Peterhead	0-3/0-1	-	-	2-1/0-3	-	-

Scottish League Two						
Albion v Clyde	-	-	3-1/1-1	-	-	3-0/1-0
Annan v Queen's Park	-	3-1/0-2	2-1/1-2	5-2/2-3	2-3/2-0	3-2/1-1
Berwick v Arbroath	-	-	4-1/0-4	-	-	-
East Stirling v Elgin	5-2/1-0	1-1/2-0	0-2/2-1	1-1/2-2	1-4/3-2	3-0/3-0
Montrose v East Fife	-	-	-	-	-	-

Saturday February 21st, 2015

Premier League						
Aston Villa v Stoke	2-2	1-0	1-1	1-1	0-0	1-4
Chelsea v Burnley	-	3-0	-	-	-	-
Crystal Palace v Arsenal	-	-	-	-	-	0-2
Everton v Leicester	-	-	-	-	-	-
Hull v QPR	-	-	0-0	-	-	-
Man City v Newcastle	2-1	-	2-1	3-1	4-0	4-0
Southampton v Liverpool	-	-	-	-	3-1	0-3
Sunderland v West Brom	4-0	-	2-3	2-2	2-4	2-0
Swansea v Man Utd	-	-	-	0-1	1-1	1-4
Tottenham v West Ham	1-0	2-0	0-0	-	3-1	0-3

Results cover matches from Premier League to Conference and Scottish Premiership to League Two

	2008-09	2009-10	2010-11	2011-12	2012-13	2013-14
Championship						
Blackburn v Blackpool	-	-	2-2	-	1-1	2-0
Brentford v Bournemouth	2-0	-	1-1	1-1	0-0	-
Brighton v Birmingham	-	-	-	1-1	0-1	1-0
Derby v Sheff Wed	3-0	3-0	-	-	2-2	3-0
Huddersfield v Cardiff	-	-	-	-	0-0	-
Ipswich v Reading	2-0	2-1	1-3	2-3	-	2-0
Middlesbro v Leeds	-	-	1-2	0-2	1-0	0-0
Millwall v Fulham	-	-	-	-	-	-
Nottm Forest v Bolton	-	-	-	-	1-1	3-0
Watford v Norwich	2-1	-	2-2	-	-	-
Wigan v Charlton	-	-	-	-	-	2-1
Wolves v Rotherham	-	-	-	-	-	6-4
League 1						
Barnsley v Crewe	-	-	-	-	-	-
Bradford v Walsall	-	-	-	-	-	0-2
Colchester v Bristol City	-	-	-	-	-	2-2
Fleetwood Town v Notts Co	-	-	-	-	-	-
Leyton Orient v Oldham	2-1	1-2	1-0	1-3	1-1	1-1
MK Dons v Peterborough	1-2	-	1-0	-	-	0-2
Port Vale v Doncaster	-	-	-	-	-	-
Preston v Scunthorpe	-	3-2	2-3	0-0	3-0	-
Rochdale v Chesterfield	2-1	2-3	-	1-1	1-1	2-2
Sheff Utd v Coventry	1-1	1-0	0-1	-	1-2	2-1
Swindon v Crawley Town	-	-	-	3-0	3-0	1-1
Yeovil v Gillingham	-	0-0	-	-	-	-
League 2						
Accrington v Cheltenham	-	4-0	2-4	0-1	2-2	0-1
AFC Wimbledon v Luton	-	1-1	0-0	-	-	-
Bury v Hartlepool	-	-	-	1-2	2-1	1-0
Cambridge U v Portsmouth	-	-	-	-	-	-
Carlisle v Wycombe	-	1-0	-	2-2	-	-
Dag & Red v Burton	-	2-1	-	1-1	1-1	2-0
Exeter v Plymouth	-	-	1-0	-	1-1	3-1
Newport Co v Morecambe	-	-	-	-	-	2-3
Northampton v York	-	-	-	-	0-2	0-2
Oxford v Mansfield	1-0	2-0	-	-	-	3-0
Stevenage v Southend	-	-	1-1	-	-	-
Tranmere v Shrewsbury	-	-	-	-	0-2	2-1
Conference						
Alfreton v Aldershot	-	-	-	-	-	1-4
Barnet v Grimsby	3-3	3-0	-	-	-	2-1
Bristol Rovers v Altrincham	-	-	-	-	-	-
Chester v Eastleigh	-	-	-	-	-	-
Dartford v Gateshead	-	-	-	-	3-0	0-1
Dover v Southport	-	-	-	-	-	-
Forest Green v Telford	-	-	-	2-1	0-0	-
Halifax v Braintree	-	-	-	-	-	0-0
Macclesfield v Lincoln	1-2	0-1	1-1	-	2-1	3-1
Nuneaton v Kidderminster	-	-	-	-	0-1	2-1
Welling v Wrexham	-	-	-	-	-	1-1
Woking v Torquay	2-2	-	-	-	-	-
Scottish Premiership						
Aberdeen v St Mirren	2-0	1-0/2-1	2-0/0-1	2-2/0-0	0-0/0-0	2-0
Celtic v Hamilton	4-0/4-0	2-0	3-1/2-0	-	-	-
Dundee Utd v St Johnstone	-	3-3	1-0/2-0	0-0	1-1/0-1	4-0/0-1
Inverness CT v Kilmarnock	3-1/2-1	-	1-3	2-1/1-1	1-1/1-1	2-1

Results cover matches from Premier League to Conference and Scottish Premiership to League Two

	2008-09	2009-10	2010-11	2011-12	2012-13	2013-14
Motherwell v Dundee	-	-	-	-	1-1	-
Partick v Ross County	0-1/0-2	0-0/2-1	1-1/1-1	0-1/0-1	-	3-3/2-3

Scottish Championship						
Cowdenbeath v Alloa	-	1-1/1-1	-	-	-	0-2/2-2
Falkirk v Livingston	-	-	-	4-3/2-5	1-2/2-0	4-1/1-1
Hibernian v Dumbarton	-	-	-	-	-	-
Queen of Sth v Hearts	-	-	-	-	-	-
Raith v Rangers	-	-	-	-	-	-

Scottish League One						
Forfar v Dunfermline	-	-	-	-	-	4-0/2-4
Morton v Stranraer	-	-	-	-	-	-
Peterhead v Ayr	3-0/2-3	-	2-4/1-2	-	-	-
Stenh'semuir v Airdrieonians	-	-	1-3/1-0	1-1/0-3	-	1-1/1-2
Stirling v Brechin	1-2/2-3	1-0/6-2	-	1-0/2-3	-	-

Scottish League Two						
Albion v East Stirling	0-2/0-2	3-0/2-1	1-0/2-0	-	-	3-2/2-1
Annan v Arbroath	-	-	1-2/3-0	-	-	-
East Fife v Clyde	-	1-0/1-1	-	-	-	-
Elgin v Montrose	1-2/1-0	0-1/5-2	3-2/1-0	3-1/2-1	6-1/3-2	3-3/2-3
Queen's Park v Berwick	-	2-0/2-3	0-2/1-0	1-1/2-2	1-1/2-1	0-4/1-3

Tuesday February 24th, 2015

Championship						
Blackburn v Norwich	-	-	-	2-0	-	-
Brentford v Blackpool	-	-	-	-	-	-
Brighton v Leeds	0-2	0-3	-	3-3	2-2	1-0
Derby v Charlton	1-0	-	-	-	3-2	3-0
Huddersfield v Reading	-	-	-	-	-	0-1
Ipswich v Birmingham	0-1	-	-	1-1	3-1	1-0
Middlesbro v Bolton	1-3	-	-	-	2-1	1-0
Millwall v Sheff Wed	-	-	-	-	1-2	1-1
Watford v Rotherham	-	-	-	-	-	-
Wigan v Cardiff	-	-	-	-	-	-
Wolves v Fulham	-	2-1	1-1	2-0	-	-

Wednesday February 25th, 2015

Championship						
Nottm Forest v Bournemouth	-	-	-	-	-	1-1

Saturday February 28th, 2015

Premier League						
Arsenal v Everton	3-1	2-2	2-1	1-0	0-0	1-1
Burnley v Swansea	0-2	-	2-1	-	-	-
Leicester v Chelsea	-	-	-	-	-	-
Liverpool v Man City	1-1	2-2	3-0	1-1	2-2	3-2
Man Utd v Sunderland	1-0	2-2	2-0	1-0	3-1	0-1
Newcastle v Aston Villa	2-0	-	6-0	2-1	1-1	1-0
QPR v Tottenham	-	-	-	1-0	0-0	-
Stoke v Hull	1-1	2-0	-	-	-	1-0
West Brom v Southampton	-	-	-	-	2-0	0-1
West Ham v Crystal Palace	-	-	-	0-0	-	0-1

Championship						
Birmingham v Brentford	-	-	-	-	-	-
Blackpool v Wigan	-	-	1-3	-	-	1-0
Bolton v Brighton	-	-	-	-	1-0	0-2

Results cover matches from Premier League to Conference and Scottish Premiership to League Two

	2008-09	2009-10	2010-11	2011-12	2012-13	2013-14
Bournemouth v Blackburn	-	-	-	-	-	1-3
Cardiff v Wolves	1-2	-	-	-	3-1	-
Charlton v Huddersfield	-	2-1	0-1	2-0	1-1	0-0
Fulham v Derby	-	-	-	-	-	-
Leeds v Watford	-	-	2-2	0-2	1-6	3-3
Norwich v Ipswich	2-0	-	4-1	-	-	-
Reading v Nottm Forest	0-1	0-0	1-1	1-0	-	1-1
Rotherham v Millwall	-	-	-	-	-	-
Sheff Wed v Middlesbro	-	1-3	-	-	2-0	1-0

League 1						
Bristol City v Rochdale	-	-	-	-	-	-
Chesterfield v Fleetwood Town	-	-	-	-	1-2	2-1
Coventry v MK Dons	-	-	-	-	1-1	1-2
Crawley Town v Sheff Utd	-	-	-	-	0-2	0-2
Crewe v Swindon	1-0	-	-	2-0	2-1	1-1
Doncaster v Colchester	-	-	-	-	1-0	-
Gillingham v Barnsley	-	-	-	-	-	-
Notts Co v Port Vale	4-2	3-1	-	-	-	4-2
Oldham v Preston	-	-	-	1-1	3-1	1-3
Peterborough v Bradford	-	-	-	-	-	2-1
Scunthorpe v Yeovil	2-0	-	-	2-1	0-4	-
Walsall v Leyton Orient	0-2	2-2	0-2	1-0	1-2	1-1

League 2						
Burton v Newport Co	-	-	-	-	-	1-0
Cheltenham v Tranmere	1-0	-	-	-	-	-
Hartlepool v AFC Wimbledon	-	-	-	-	-	3-1
Luton v Accrington	1-2	-	-	-	-	-
Mansfield v Dag & Red	-	-	-	-	-	3-0
Morecambe v Cambridge U	-	-	-	-	-	-
Plymouth v Bury	-	-	-	-	-	2-1
Portsmouth v Oxford	-	-	-	-	-	1-4
Shrewsbury v Northampton	-	3-0	3-1	1-1	-	-
Southend v Carlisle	3-0	2-2	-	-	-	-
Wycombe v Stevenage	-	-	0-1	0-1	-	-
York v Exeter	-	-	-	-	1-2	2-1

Conference						
Aldershot v Dartford	-	-	-	-	-	3-0
Altrincham v Barnet	-	-	-	-	-	-
Eastleigh v Macclesfield	-	-	-	-	-	-
Forest Green v Southport	-	-	0-0	2-3	0-1	3-1
Gateshead v Bristol Rovers	-	-	-	-	-	-
Grimsby v Braintree	-	-	-	1-1	3-0	1-0
Kidderminster v Halifax	-	-	-	-	-	2-0
Lincoln v Woking	-	-	-	-	0-2	2-2
Nuneaton v Welling	-	-	-	-	-	2-0
Telford v Alfreton	-	-	-	1-0	0-0	-
Torquay v Chester	-	-	-	-	-	-
Wrexham v Dover	-	-	-	-	-	-

Scottish Premiership						
Celtic v Aberdeen	3-2/2-0	3-0	9-0/1-0	2-1	1-0/4-3	3-1/5-2
Dundee Utd v Partick	-	-	-	-	-	4-1
Motherwell v Inverness CT	3-2/2-2	-	0-0	3-0/0-1	4-1/3-0	2-0/2-1
Ross County v Dundee	1-2/1-1	0-1/1-1	0-3/0-1	1-1/3-0	1-1	-
St Johnstone v Kilmarnock	-	0-1	0-3/0-0	2-0	2-1/2-0	3-1
St Mirren v Hamilton	1-0/0-1	0-2/0-0	2-2/3-1/0-1	-	-	-

Results cover matches from Premier League to Conference and Scottish Premiership to League Two

	2008-09	2009-10	2010-11	2011-12	2012-13	2013-14
Scottish Championship						
Alloa v Hibernian	-	-	-	-	-	-
Dumbarton v Queen of Sth	-	-	-	-	-	0-1/0-3
Falkirk v Rangers	0-1/0-1	1-3	-	-	-	-
Hearts v Cowdenbeath	-	-	-	-	-	-
Livingston v Raith	-	-	-	1-1/4-0	2-1/2-3	3-0/2-0
Scottish League One						
Airdrieonians v Stirling	-	-	-	1-1/4-1	-	-
Ayr v Forfar	-	-	0-1/3-1	-	2-3/2-1	2-0/2-3
Brechin v Stenh'semuir	-	1-0/2-2	0-0/3-1	2-0/1-0	7-2/1-2	0-1/1-3
Peterhead v Morton	-	-	-	-	-	-
Stranraer v Dunfermline	-	-	-	-	-	1-2/3-1
Scottish League Two						
Arbroath v Elgin	-	-	2-0/3-5	-	-	-
Berwick v Albion	0-3/1-1	2-0/1-2	1-6/2-2	-	-	2-1/3-1
Clyde v Montrose	-	-	2-0/1-1	1-0/1-2	1-2/1-0	0-3/1-1
East Fife v Annan	-	-	-	-	-	-
East Stirling v Queen's Park	-	1-0/0-3	0-1/3-2	1-3/1-2	0-2/0-2	1-1/1-4

Tuesday March 3rd, 2015

	2008-09	2009-10	2010-11	2011-12	2012-13	2013-14
Premier League						
Aston Villa v West Brom	2-1	-	2-1	1-2	1-1	4-3
Hull v Sunderland	1-4	0-1	-	-	-	1-0
Liverpool v Burnley	-	4-0	-	-	-	-
QPR v Arsenal	-	-	-	2-1	0-1	-
Southampton v Crystal Palace	1-0	-	-	2-0	-	2-0
West Ham v Chelsea	0-1	1-1	1-3	-	3-1	0-3
Championship						
Birmingham v Blackpool	0-1	-	2-0	3-0	1-1	1-1
Bolton v Reading	-	-	-	-	-	1-1
Bournemouth v Wolves	-	-	-	-	-	-
Brentford v Huddersfield	-	3-0	0-1	0-4	-	-
Brighton v Derby	-	-	-	2-0	2-1	1-2
Charlton v Nottm Forest	0-2	-	-	-	0-2	1-1
Leeds v Ipswich	-	-	0-0	3-1	2-0	1-1
Middlesbro v Millwall	-	-	0-1	1-1	1-2	1-2
Norwich v Wigan	-	-	-	1-1	2-1	-
Rotherham v Cardiff	-	-	-	-	-	-
Sheff Wed v Blackburn	-	-	-	-	3-2	3-3
Watford v Fulham	-	-	-	-	-	-
League 1						
Barnsley v Coventry	1-2	0-2	2-1	2-0	-	-
Bradford v Crawley Town	-	-	-	1-2	-	2-1
Colchester v Notts Co	-	-	2-1	4-2	0-2	0-4
Fleetwood Town v Scunthorpe	-	-	-	-	-	0-1
Leyton Orient v Bristol City	-	-	-	-	-	1-3
MK Dons v Chesterfield	-	-	-	6-2	-	-
Port Vale v Oldham	-	-	-	-	-	1-0
Preston v Doncaster	1-0	1-1	0-2	-	0-3	-
Rochdale v Crewe	-	2-0	-	-	-	-
Sheff Utd v Peterborough	-	1-0	-	-	-	2-0
Swindon v Gillingham	-	3-1	-	2-0	-	2-2
Yeovil v Walsall	1-1	1-3	1-1	2-1	0-0	-

Results cover matches from Premier League to Conference and Scottish Premiership to League Two

	2008-09	2009-10	2010-11	2011-12	2012-13	2013-14
League 2						
Accrington v Shrewsbury	2-1	1-3	1-3	1-1	-	-
AFC Wimbledon v Southend	-	-	-	1-4	0-4	0-1
Bury v Luton	1-2	-	-	-	-	-
Cambridge U v York	1-0	0-1	2-1	0-1	-	-
Carlisle v Cheltenham	1-0	-	-	-	-	-
Dag & Red v Hartlepool	-	-	1-1	-	-	0-2
Exeter v Burton	-	-	-	-	3-0	0-1
Newport Co v Mansfield	-	-	1-0	1-0	2-0	1-1
Northampton v Portsmouth	-	-	-	-	-	0-1
Oxford v Morecambe	-	-	4-0	1-2	1-1	3-0
Stevenage v Plymouth	-	-	-	-	-	-
Tranmere v Wycombe	-	0-3	-	2-0	-	-

Wednesday March 4th, 2015

	2008-09	2009-10	2010-11	2011-12	2012-13	2013-14
Premier League						
Man City v Leicester	-	-	-	-	-	-
Newcastle v Man Utd	1-2	-	0-0	3-0	0-3	0-4
Stoke v Everton	2-3	0-0	2-0	1-1	1-1	1-1
Tottenham v Swansea	-	-	-	3-1	1-0	1-0

Saturday March 7th, 2015

	2008-09	2009-10	2010-11	2011-12	2012-13	2013-14
Championship						
Blackburn v Bolton	2-2	3-0	1-0	1-2	1-2	4-1
Blackpool v Sheff Wed	0-2	1-2	-	-	0-0	2-0
Cardiff v Charlton	2-0	-	-	-	0-0	-
Derby v Birmingham	1-1	-	-	2-1	3-2	1-1
Fulham v Bournemouth	-	-	-	-	-	-
Huddersfield v Rotherham	-	-	-	-	-	-
Ipswich v Brentford	-	-	-	-	-	-
Millwall v Norwich	-	2-1	1-1	-	-	-
Nottm Forest v Middlesbro	-	1-0	1-0	2-0	0-0	2-2
Reading v Brighton	-	-	-	3-0	-	0-0
Wigan v Leeds	-	-	-	-	-	1-0
Wolves v Watford	3-1	-	-	-	1-1	-
League 1						
Barnsley v Walsall	-	-	-	-	-	-
Bradford v Chesterfield	3-2	3-0	0-1	-	0-0	-
Coventry v Port Vale	-	-	-	-	-	2-2
Crawley Town v Bristol City	-	-	-	-	-	1-1
Crewe v Scunthorpe	3-2	-	-	-	1-0	-
Gillingham v Doncaster	-	-	-	-	-	-
MK Dons v Preston	-	-	-	0-1	1-1	0-0
Peterborough v Leyton Orient	3-0	-	2-2	-	-	1-3
Rochdale v Colchester	-	-	1-2	2-2	-	-
Sheff Utd v Fleetwood Town	-	-	-	-	-	-
Swindon v Notts Co	-	-	1-2	-	0-0	2-0
Yeovil v Oldham	2-2	3-0	1-1	3-1	4-1	-
League 2						
Accrington v Portsmouth	-	-	-	-	-	2-2
AFC Wimbledon v York	-	0-1	1-0	-	3-2	0-1
Bury v Oxford	-	-	3-0	-	-	1-1
Carlisle v Exeter	-	0-1	2-2	4-1	-	-
Cheltenham v Mansfield	-	-	-	-	-	1-2
Hartlepool v Burton	-	-	-	-	-	1-1

Results cover matches from Premier League to Conference and Scottish Premiership to League Two

	2008-09	2009-10	2010-11	2011-12	2012-13	2013-14
Luton v Morecambe	1-1	-	-	-	-	-
Plymouth v Northampton	-	-	-	4-1	3-2	1-0
Shrewsbury v Cambridge U	-	-	-	-	-	-
Southend v Wycombe	-	1-1	3-2	-	1-0	1-1
Stevenage v Newport Co	-	-	-	-	-	-
Tranmere v Dag & Red	-	-	2-0	-	-	-
Conference						
Alfreton v Kidderminster	-	-	-	0-2	1-1	3-1
Barnet v Forest Green	-	-	-	-	-	2-1
Braintree v Gateshead	-	-	-	3-1	2-1	0-0
Bristol Rovers v Eastleigh	-	-	-	-	-	-
Dover v Lincoln	-	-	-	-	-	-
Halifax v Dartford	-	-	-	-	-	2-0
Macclesfield v Aldershot	4-2	1-1	2-0	0-1	-	1-1
Southport v Nuneaton	-	-	-	-	3-1	1-0
Torquay v Telford	-	-	-	-	-	-
Welling v Altrincham	-	-	-	-	-	-
Woking v Grimsby	-	-	-	-	0-1	1-2
Wrexham v Chester	-	-	-	-	-	0-2
Scottish Championship						
Cowdenbeath v Falkirk	-	-	0-0/1-2	-	1-1/4-1	1-0/0-2
Dumbarton v Alloa	-	1-3/3-1	4-1/2-2	-	-	1-1/4-1
Hibernian v Livingston	-	-	-	-	-	-
Raith v Hearts	-	-	-	-	-	-
Rangers v Queen of Sth	-	-	-	-	-	-
Scottish League One						
Brechin v Airdrieonians	-	-	3-1/1-2	1-1/1-1	-	4-3/1-1
Dunfermline v Ayr	-	3-1/0-1	-	-	-	5-1/3-0
Morton v Forfar	-	-	-	-	-	-
Stenh'semuir v Peterhead	-	2-0/1-1	3-1/4-2	-	-	-
Stirling v Stranraer	3-2/1-2	-	-	-	-	-
Scottish League Two						
Annan v Albion	2-4/1-1	0-0/1-2	4-1/2-2	-	-	1-1/2-0
Clyde v East Stirling	-	-	1-2/2-0	7-1/3-0	2-1/2-0	1-2/1-0
Elgin v Berwick	0-2/2-0	3-3/1-5	1-2/3-2	4-1/4-0	3-1/1-2	2-0/1-3
Montrose v Arbroath	-	-	3-0/0-5	-	-	-
Queen's Park v East Fife	0-0/3-1	-	-	-	-	-

Saturday March 14th, 2015

	2008-09	2009-10	2010-11	2011-12	2012-13	2013-14
Premier League						
Arsenal v West Ham	0-0	2-0	1-0	-	5-1	3-1
Burnley v Man City	-	1-6	-	-	-	-
Chelsea v Southampton	-	-	-	-	2-2	3-1
Crystal Palace v QPR	0-0	0-2	1-2	-	-	-
Everton v Newcastle	2-2	-	0-1	3-1	2-2	3-2
Leicester v Hull	-	-	1-1	2-1	3-1	-
Man Utd v Tottenham	5-2	3-1	2-0	3-0	2-3	1-2
Sunderland v Aston Villa	1-2	0-2	1-0	2-2	0-1	0-1
Swansea v Liverpool	-	-	-	1-0	0-0	2-2
West Brom v Stoke	0-2	-	0-3	0-1	0-1	1-2
Championship						
Birmingham v Huddersfield	-	-	-	-	0-1	1-2
Bolton v Millwall	-	-	-	-	1-1	3-1
Bournemouth v Blackpool	-	-	-	-	-	1-2

Results cover matches from Premier League to Conference and Scottish Premiership to League Two

	2008-09	2009-10	2010-11	2011-12	2012-13	2013-14
Brentford v Cardiff	-	-	-	-	-	-
Brighton v Wolves	-	-	-	-	2-0	-
Charlton v Blackburn	-	-	-	-	1-1	1-3
Leeds v Nottm Forest	-	-	4-1	3-7	2-1	0-2
Middlesbro v Ipswich	-	3-1	1-3	0-0	2-0	2-0
Norwich v Derby	1-2	-	3-2	-	-	-
Rotherham v Wigan	-	-	-	-	-	-
Sheff Wed v Fulham	-	-	-	-	-	-
Watford v Reading	2-2	3-0	1-1	1-2	-	0-1

League 1						
Bristol City v Gillingham	-	-	-	-	-	2-1
Chesterfield v Coventry	-	-	-	-	-	-
Colchester v Crawley Town	-	-	-	-	1-1	1-1
Doncaster v Peterborough	-	3-1	-	1-1	-	-
Fleetwood Town v Rochdale	-	-	-	-	0-3	0-0
Leyton Orient v Yeovil	0-1	2-0	1-5	2-2	4-1	-
Notts Co v Bradford	3-1	5-0	-	-	-	3-0
Oldham v Barnsley	-	-	-	-	-	-
Port Vale v Swindon	-	-	-	0-2	-	2-3
Preston v Crewe	-	-	-	-	1-3	0-2
Scunthorpe v Sheff Utd	-	3-1	3-2	1-1	1-1	-
Walsall v MK Dons	0-3	2-1	1-2	0-2	1-0	0-3

League 2						
Burton v Accrington	-	0-2	1-1	0-2	1-0	2-1
Cambridge U v Stevenage	1-1	1-3	-	-	-	-
Dag & Red v Southend	-	-	-	2-3	0-3	1-1
Exeter v AFC Wimbledon	-	-	-	-	2-0	2-0
Mansfield v Bury	-	-	-	-	-	1-4
Morecambe v Hartlepool	-	-	-	-	-	1-2
Newport Co v Cheltenham	-	-	-	-	-	0-1
Northampton v Tranmere	1-1	-	-	-	-	-
Oxford v Plymouth	-	-	-	5-1	2-1	2-3
Portsmouth v Luton	-	-	-	-	-	-
Wycombe v Shrewsbury	1-1	-	2-2	-	-	-
York v Carlisle	-	-	-	-	-	-

Conference						
Aldershot v Southport	-	-	-	-	-	5-1
Altrincham v Wrexham	1-1	1-3	0-0	-	-	-
Chester v Grimsby	1-1	-	-	-	-	0-0
Dartford v Alfreton	-	-	-	-	5-1	1-0
Eastleigh v Barnet	-	-	-	-	-	-
Forest Green v Braintree	-	-	-	0-2	4-1	0-2
Gateshead v Macclesfield	-	-	-	-	2-2	2-2
Halifax v Bristol Rovers	-	-	-	-	-	-
Kidderminster v Dover	-	-	-	-	-	-
Lincoln v Welling	-	-	-	-	-	1-2
Nuneaton v Torquay	-	-	-	-	-	-
Telford v Woking	-	-	-	-	1-0	-

Scottish Premiership						
Aberdeen v Motherwell	2-0	0-0/0-3	1-2	1-2	3-3/0-0	0-1/0-1
Dundee v Celtic	-	-	-	-	0-2	-
Hamilton v Ross County	-	-	-	5-1/0-2	-	-
Inverness CT v Dundee Utd	1-3	-	0-2	2-3	4-0/0-0/1-2	1-1/1-1
Kilmarnock v St Mirren	0-1/2-1	1-2/1-1	2-1/2-0	2-1/0-2	3-1/1-1/1-3	2-1/1-0
Partick v St Johnstone	4-0/0-0	-	-	-	-	0-1

Results cover matches from Premier League to Conference and Scottish Premiership to League Two

Scottish Championship						
Alloa v Falkirk	-	-	-	-	-	0-0/3-0
Cowdenbeath v Hibernian	-	-	-	-	-	-
Hearts v Dumbarton	-	-	-	-	-	-
Queen of Sth v Raith	-	1-1/3-0	1-3/0-2	1-3/1-0	-	0-1/1-0
Rangers v Livingston	-	-	-	-	-	-

Scottish League One						
Airdrieonians v Morton	5-0/1-0	2-4/3-0	-	-	2-3/0-4	-
Ayr v Stenh'semuir	-	-	2-0/4-3	-	1-1/1-2	4-3/2-3
Dunfermline v Stirling	-	-	3-0/4-1	-	-	-
Forfar v Stranraer	-	1-0/2-0	-	-	4-0/3-1	1-2/1-0
Peterhead v Brechin	5-1/0-1	1-0/0-3	0-5/1-1	-	-	-

Scottish League Two						
Albion v Montrose	0-1/0-1	0-0/1-0	3-1/0-2	-	-	0-2/1-0
Arbroath v Clyde	-	0-3/2-0	3-2/2-0	-	-	-
Berwick v Annan	3-0/1-1	2-1/0-2	2-2/2-3	0-1/1-3	3-1/0-2	4-2/1-4
East Stirling v East Fife	-	-	-	-	-	-
Elgin v Queen's Park	-	0-1/0-1	4-2/0-1	2-0/1-1	0-4/3-5	3-2/1-1

Tuesday March 17th, 2015

Championship						
Blackburn v Brentford	-	-	-	-	-	-
Blackpool v Charlton	2-0	-	-	-	0-2	0-3
Cardiff v Bournemouth	-	-	-	-	-	-
Derby v Middlesbro	-	2-2	3-1	0-1	3-1	2-1
Huddersfield v Norwich	-	1-3	-	-	-	-
Ipswich v Bolton	-	-	-	-	1-0	1-0
Millwall v Brighton	0-1	1-1	-	1-1	1-2	0-1
Reading v Birmingham	1-2	-	-	1-0	-	2-0
Wigan v Watford	-	-	-	-	-	2-1
Wolves v Sheff Wed	4-1	-	-	-	1-0	-

League 1						
Bristol City v Crewe	-	-	-	-	-	0-0
Chesterfield v Gillingham	0-1	-	3-1	-	0-1	-
Colchester v Yeovil	1-0	2-1	0-0	2-2	2-0	-
Doncaster v Swindon	-	-	-	-	1-0	-
Fleetwood Town v Coventry	-	-	-	-	-	-
Leyton Orient v Barnsley	-	-	-	-	-	-
Notts Co v Rochdale	1-2	1-0	1-2	2-0	-	-
Oldham v MK Dons	2-0	2-1	1-2	2-1	3-1	1-2
Port Vale v Crawley Town	-	-	-	2-2	-	2-1
Preston v Peterborough	-	2-0	-	-	-	3-1
Scunthorpe v Bradford	-	-	-	-	-	-
Walsall v Sheff Utd	-	-	-	3-2	1-1	2-1

League 2						
Burton v Southend	-	-	3-1	0-2	2-0	0-1
Cambridge U v Tranmere	-	-	-	-	-	-
Dag & Red v Plymouth	-	-	0-1	2-3	0-0	1-2
Exeter v Stevenage	-	-	-	1-1	-	-
Mansfield v AFC Wimbledon	-	0-1	2-5	-	-	1-0
Morecambe v Shrewsbury	1-0	1-1	1-0	0-1	-	-
Newport Co v Luton	-	-	1-1	0-1	5-2	-
Northampton v Carlisle	1-0	-	-	-	-	-
Oxford v Hartlepool	-	-	-	-	-	1-0
Portsmouth v Cheltenham	-	-	-	-	-	0-0
Wycombe v Accrington	2-1	-	1-2	-	0-1	0-0
York v Bury	-	-	-	-	-	1-0

Results cover matches from Premier League to Conference and Scottish Premiership to League Two

Wednesday March 18th, 2015

Championship

	2008-09	2009-10	2010-11	2011-12	2012-13	2013-14
Fulham v Leeds	-	-	-	-	-	-
Nottm Forest v Rotherham	-	-	-	-	-	-

Saturday March 21st, 2015

Premier League

	2008-09	2009-10	2010-11	2011-12	2012-13	2013-14
Aston Villa v Swansea	-	-	-	0-2	2-0	1-1
Hull v Chelsea	0-3	1-1	-	-	-	0-2
Liverpool v Man Utd	2-1	2-0	3-1	1-1	1-2	1-0
Man City v West Brom	4-2	-	3-0	4-0	1-0	3-1
Newcastle v Arsenal	1-3	-	4-4	0-0	0-1	0-1
QPR v Everton	-	-	-	1-1	1-1	-
Southampton v Burnley	2-2	-	-	2-0	-	-
Stoke v Crystal Palace	-	-	-	-	-	2-1
Tottenham v Leicester	-	-	-	-	-	-
West Ham v Sunderland	2-0	1-0	0-3	-	1-1	0-0

Championship

	2008-09	2009-10	2010-11	2011-12	2012-13	2013-14
Blackburn v Brighton	-	-	-	-	1-1	3-3
Blackpool v Leeds	-	-	-	1-0	2-1	1-1
Bournemouth v Middlesbro	-	-	-	-	-	0-0
Brentford v Millwall	-	2-2	-	-	-	-
Cardiff v Birmingham	1-2	-	-	1-0	2-1	-
Charlton v Reading	4-2	-	-	-	-	0-1
Huddersfield v Fulham	-	-	-	-	-	-
Norwich v Nottm Forest	2-3	-	2-1	-	-	-
Rotherham v Sheff Wed	-	-	-	-	-	-
Watford v Ipswich	2-1	2-1	2-1	2-1	0-1	3-1
Wigan v Bolton	0-0	0-0	1-1	1-3	-	3-2
Wolves v Derby	3-0	-	-	-	1-1	-

League 1

	2008-09	2009-10	2010-11	2011-12	2012-13	2013-14
Barnsley v Preston	1-1	0-3	2-0	-	-	-
Bradford v Fleetwood Town	-	-	-	-	1-0	-
Coventry v Doncaster	1-0	1-0	2-1	0-2	1-0	-
Crawley Town v Leyton Orient	-	-	-	-	1-0	2-1
Crewe v Oldham	0-3	-	-	-	0-2	1-1
Gillingham v Colchester	-	0-0	-	-	-	0-1
MK Dons v Notts Co	-	-	2-1	3-0	1-1	3-1
Peterborough v Chesterfield	-	-	-	-	-	-
Rochdale v Scunthorpe	-	-	-	1-0	-	0-4
Sheff Utd v Port Vale	-	-	-	-	-	2-1
Swindon v Walsall	3-2	1-1	0-0	-	2-2	1-3
Yeovil v Bristol City	-	-	-	-	-	-

League 2

	2008-09	2009-10	2010-11	2011-12	2012-13	2013-14
Accrington v York	-	-	-	-	0-1	1-1
AFC Wimbledon v Portsmouth	-	-	-	-	-	4-0
Bury v Northampton	-	2-2	1-1	-	-	1-1
Carlisle v Morecambe	-	-	-	-	-	-
Cheltenham v Exeter	-	-	-	-	3-0	1-0
Hartlepool v Mansfield	-	-	-	-	-	2-4
Luton v Wycombe	0-1	-	-	-	-	-
Plymouth v Newport Co	-	-	-	-	-	0-0
Shrewsbury v Oxford	-	-	3-0	2-2	-	-
Southend v Cambridge U	-	-	-	-	-	-
Stevenage v Dag & Red	-	-	-	-	-	-
Tranmere v Burton	-	-	-	-	-	-

Results cover matches from Premier League to Conference and Scottish Premiership to League Two

	2008-09	2009-10	2010-11	2011-12	2012-13	2013-14
Conference						
Alfreton v Chester	-	-	-	-	-	0-1
Altrincham v Halifax	-	-	-	-	-	-
Barnet v Welling	-	-	-	-	-	0-0
Braintree v Telford	-	-	-	2-1	3-2	-
Bristol Rovers v Aldershot	-	-	-	0-1	2-2	-
Dover v Gateshead	-	-	-	-	-	-
Grimsby v Eastleigh	-	-	-	-	-	-
Macclesfield v Nuneaton	-	-	-	-	0-0	0-1
Southport v Dartford	-	-	-	-	2-2	3-0
Torquay v Kidderminster	0-1	-	-	-	-	-
Woking v Forest Green	0-1	-	-	-	2-0	2-1
Wrexham v Lincoln	-	-	-	2-0	2-4	0-1
Scottish Premiership						
Celtic v Dundee Utd	2-2/2-1	1-1/1-0	1-1/4-1	5-1/2-1	4-0/6-2	1-1/3-1
Dundee v Aberdeen	-	-	-	-	1-3/1-1	-
Motherwell v Hamilton	2-0/1-0	1-0	0-1/1-0	-	-	-
Partick v Inverness CT	-	2-1/0-1	-	-	-	0-0
Ross County v Kilmarnock	-	-	-	-	0-0/0-1	1-2/2-1
St Johnstone v St Mirren	-	1-0/2-2	2-1/0-0	0-1	2-1/1-0	2-0
Scottish Championship						
Falkirk v Hearts	2-1/0-0	0-1	-	-	-	-
Hibernian v Rangers	0-3/2-3/1-1	1-4/0-1	0-3/0-2	0-2	-	-
Livingston v Dumbarton	-	-	2-0/1-1	-	5-0/2-3	1-3/1-2
Queen of Sth v Cowdenbeath	-	-	3-0/2-2	-	-	1-1/2-1
Raith v Alloa	4-1/3-1	-	-	-	-	4-2/1-1
Scottish League One						
Brechin v Forfar	-	-	0-0/0-1	0-1/2-1	4-1/3-4	2-1/1-5
Morton v Ayr	-	1-0/2-1	-	4-1/3-1	-	-
Stenh'semuir v Dunfermline	-	-	-	-	-	4-5/1-2
Stirling v Peterhead	0-0/2-1	2-1/2-0	-	-	1-0/0-1	2-0/1-2
Stranraer v Airdrieonians	-	-	-	-	-	3-1/1-1
Scottish League Two						
Annan v East Stirling	2-1/4-0	0-1/1-0	3-1/2-1	3-0/2-2	5-2/1-2	1-2/2-3
Clyde v Elgin	-	-	1-1/3-3	1-2/0-2	2-2/1-1	2-1/4-0
East Fife v Arbroath	3-2/0-0	1-1/3-1	-	2-2/1-3	2-1/0-1	2-1/1-0
Montrose v Berwick	1-1/1-1	1-3/1-1	1-1/1-1	3-5/1-1	3-1/1-3	1-1/0-0
Queen's Park v Albion	-	0-1/1-0	0-1/2-1	-	-	1-1/4-0

Saturday March 28th, 2015

	2008-09	2009-10	2010-11	2011-12	2012-13	2013-14
League 1						
Bradford v Oldham	-	-	-	-	-	2-3
Bristol City v Barnsley	2-0	5-3	3-3	2-0	5-3	-
Chesterfield v Walsall	-	-	-	1-1	-	-
Colchester v Swindon	3-2	3-0	2-1	-	0-1	1-2
Crawley Town v Gillingham	-	-	-	1-2	-	3-2
Fleetwood Town v Preston	-	-	-	-	-	-
Leyton Orient v Port Vale	-	-	-	-	-	3-2
MK Dons v Doncaster	-	-	-	-	3-0	-
Notts Co v Scunthorpe	-	-	-	3-2	1-0	-
Peterborough v Coventry	-	0-1	-	1-0	-	1-0
Rochdale v Yeovil	-	-	0-1	0-0	-	-
Sheff Utd v Crewe	-	-	-	-	3-3	3-1

Results cover matches from Premier League to Conference and Scottish Premiership to League Two

League 2

	2008-09	2009-10	2010-11	2011-12	2012-13	2013-14
Accrington v Newport Co	-	-	-	-	-	3-3
Burton v Stevenage	2-0	-	0-2	-	-	-
Bury v Southend	-	-	1-0	-	-	1-1
Cheltenham v Plymouth	-	-	-	2-1	2-1	1-3
Dag & Red v Wycombe	0-1	-	-	-	3-0	2-0
Exeter v Morecambe	2-2	-	-	-	0-3	1-1
Hartlepool v Cambridge U	-	-	-	-	-	-
Mansfield v York	1-0	0-1	5-0	1-1	-	0-1
Northampton v Luton	-	-	-	-	-	-
Oxford v Carlisle	-	-	-	-	-	-
Portsmouth v Shrewsbury	-	-	-	-	3-1	-
Tranmere v AFC Wimbledon	-	-	-	-	-	-

Conference

	2008-09	2009-10	2010-11	2011-12	2012-13	2013-14
Aldershot v Wrexham	-	-	-	-	-	2-0
Alfreton v Barnet	-	-	-	-	-	3-1
Chester v Woking	-	-	-	-	-	0-2
Dartford v Altrincham	-	-	-	-	-	-
Dover v Telford	-	-	-	-	-	-
Gateshead v Eastleigh	-	-	-	-	-	-
Kidderminster v Braintree	-	-	-	5-4	2-1	2-2
Lincoln v Forest Green	-	-	-	1-1	1-2	2-1
Macclesfield v Bristol Rovers	-	-	-	0-0	-	-
Nuneaton v Halifax	-	-	-	-	-	-
Southport v Torquay	-	-	-	-	-	0-1
Welling v Grimsby	-	-	-	-	-	1-0

Scottish Championship

	2008-09	2009-10	2010-11	2011-12	2012-13	2013-14
Alloa v Livingston	-	-	2-2/1-3	-	-	1-0/0-3
Dumbarton v Falkirk	-	-	-	-	0-2/0-2	1-1/2-1
Hearts v Queen of Sth	-	-	-	-	-	-
Raith v Hibernian	-	-	-	-	-	-
Rangers v Cowdenbeath	-	-	-	-	-	-

Scottish League One

	2008-09	2009-10	2010-11	2011-12	2012-13	2013-14
Airdrieonians v Stenh'semuir	-	-	1-0/2-2	5-2/0-3	-	0-1/1-1
Ayr v Brechin	1-1/4-2	-	0-2/2-0	-	3-0/1-2	2-2/1-3
Dunfermline v Morton	0-1/2-1	3-1/4-1	2-0/1-3	-	2-2/1-4	-
Forfar v Stirling	-	-	-	2-2/4-3	-	-
Peterhead v Stranraer	4-0/1-0	-	-	1-3/1-1	-	-

Scottish League Two

	2008-09	2009-10	2010-11	2011-12	2012-13	2013-14
Albion v Elgin	2-1/0-3	1-1/1-2	3-1/2-0	-	-	0-0/5-2
Annan v Clyde	-	-	0-2/1-0	1-0/1-0	1-3/0-1	1-2/0-1
Berwick v Queen's Park	-	1-0/1-1	1-1/3-1	2-0/1-4	2-0/4-1	4-0/1-0
East Fife v Montrose	-	-	-	-	-	-
East Stirling v Arbroath	-	-	1-3/2-5	-	-	-

Saturday April 4th, 2015

Premier League

	2008-09	2009-10	2010-11	2011-12	2012-13	2013-14
Arsenal v Liverpool	1-1	1-0	1-1	0-2	2-2	2-0
Burnley v Tottenham	-	4-2	-	-	-	-
Chelsea v Stoke	2-1	7-0	2-0	1-0	1-0	3-0
Crystal Palace v Man City	-	-	-	-	-	0-2
Everton v Southampton	-	-	-	-	3-1	2-1
Leicester v West Ham	-	-	-	1-2	-	-
Man Utd v Aston Villa	3-2	0-1	3-1	4-0	3-0	4-1
Sunderland v Newcastle	2-1	-	1-1	0-1	1-1	2-1
Swansea v Hull	-	-	1-1	-	-	1-1
West Brom v QPR	-	2-2	-	1-0	3-2	-

Results cover matches from Premier League to Conference and Scottish Premiership to League Two

	2008-09	2009-10	2010-11	2011-12	2012-13	2013-14
Championship						
Birmingham v Rotherham	-	-	-	-	-	-
Bolton v Blackpool	-	-	2-2	-	2-2	1-0
Brighton v Norwich	-	1-2	-	-	-	-
Derby v Watford	1-0	2-0	4-1	1-2	5-1	4-2
Fulham v Brentford	-	-	-	-	-	-
Ipswich v Bournemouth	-	-	-	-	-	2-2
Leeds v Blackburn	-	-	-	-	3-3	1-2
Middlesbro v Wigan	0-0	-	-	-	-	0-0
Millwall v Charlton	-	4-0	-	-	0-0	0-0
Nottm Forest v Wolves	0-1	-	-	-	3-1	-
Reading v Cardiff	1-1	0-1	1-1	1-2	-	-
Sheff Wed v Huddersfield	-	-	0-2	4-4	1-3	1-2
League 1						
Barnsley v Sheff Utd	1-2	2-2	1-0	-	-	-
Coventry v Leyton Orient	-	-	-	-	0-1	3-1
Crewe v Crawley Town	-	-	-	1-1	2-0	1-0
Doncaster v Bradford	-	-	-	-	-	-
Gillingham v Fleetwood Town	-	-	-	-	2-2	-
Oldham v Bristol City	-	-	-	-	-	1-1
Port Vale v Colchester	-	-	-	-	-	2-0
Preston v Rochdale	-	-	-	0-1	-	-
Scunthorpe v Peterborough	1-0	4-0	-	-	-	-
Swindon v MK Dons	1-1	0-0	0-1	-	1-0	1-2
Walsall v Notts Co	-	-	0-3	0-1	1-1	1-1
Yeovil v Chesterfield	-	-	-	3-2	-	-
League 2						
AFC Wimbledon v Northampton	-	-	-	0-3	1-1	0-2
Cambridge U v Bury	-	-	-	-	-	-
Carlisle v Portsmouth	-	-	-	-	4-2	-
Luton v Exeter	1-2	-	-	-	-	-
Morecambe v Accrington	1-1	1-2	1-2	1-2	0-0	1-2
Newport Co v Hartlepool	-	-	-	-	-	2-0
Plymouth v Burton	-	-	-	2-1	1-2	0-1
Shrewsbury v Dag & Red	2-1	2-1	-	1-0	-	-
Southend v Mansfield	-	-	-	-	-	3-0
Stevenage v Tranmere	-	-	-	2-1	1-1	3-1
Wycombe v Oxford	-	-	0-0	-	1-3	0-1
York v Cheltenham	-	-	-	-	0-0	0-0
Conference						
Altrincham v Southport	-	-	1-1	-	-	-
Barnet v Nuneaton	-	-	-	-	-	1-1
Braintree v Lincoln	-	-	-	1-0	0-3	0-2
Bristol Rovers v Chester	-	-	-	-	-	-
Eastleigh v Dover	-	-	-	-	-	1-0
Forest Green v Aldershot	-	-	-	-	-	3-1
Grimsby v Gateshead	-	-	2-2	2-0	3-0	2-2
Halifax v Macclesfield	-	-	-	-	-	2-1
Telford v Kidderminster	-	-	-	2-1	0-2	-
Torquay v Dartford	-	-	-	-	-	-
Woking v Welling	-	-	-	-	-	2-4
Wrexham v Alfreton	-	-	-	0-1	1-1	2-3
Scottish Premiership						
Aberdeen v Partick	-	-	-	-	-	4-0
Dundee Utd v Ross County	-	-	-	-	0-0/1-1	1-0
Hamilton v St Johnstone	-	0-2/1-0	1-2/0-0	-	-	-

Results cover matches from Premier League to Conference and Scottish Premiership to League Two

	2008-09	2009-10	2010-11	2011-12	2012-13	2013-14
Inverness CT v Dundee	-	1-1/1-0	-	-	4-1	-
Kilmarnock v Motherwell	1-0/0-0	0-3	0-1/3-1	0-0/2-0	1-2/2-0	0-2
St Mirren v Celtic	1-3	0-2/4-0	0-1	0-2/0-2	0-5/1-1	0-4

Scottish Championship

Cowdenbeath v Dumbarton	2-0/0-0	2-1/0-0	-	0-0/4-1	0-1/2-3	3-2/2-4
Falkirk v Raith	-	-	0-0/2-1	2-0/2-3	0-2/1-1	3-1/2-1
Hibernian v Queen of Sth	-	-	-	-	-	-
Livingston v Hearts	-	-	-	-	-	-
Rangers v Alloa	-	-	-	-	-	-

Scottish League One

Morton v Brechin	-	-	-	-	-	-
Peterhead v Dunfermline	-	-	-	-	-	-
Stenh'semuir v Forfar	1-1/0-1	-	3-0/0-1	2-3/1-2	0-4/2-0	1-1/4-1
Stirling v Airdrieonians	-	-	-	1-4/0-2	-	-
Stranraer v Ayr	1-3/1-4	-	-	-	2-0/0-1	1-1/4-0

Scottish League Two

Albion v Berwick	2-0/2-1	2-1/4-1	2-2/0-1	-	-	0-2/0-3
Arbroath v Annan	-	-	0-2/2-1	-	-	-
Clyde v East Fife	-	1-3/2-1	-	-	-	-
Elgin v East Stirling	0-4/0-2	1-2/0-1	0-2/2-0	2-0/3-1	3-4/3-2	0-1/5-0
Montrose v Queen's Park	-	1-2/1-2	1-2/0-2	0-1/3-1	1-1/1-2	1-2/1-0

Monday April 6th, 2015

Championship

Blackburn v Millwall	-	-	-	-	0-2	3-2
Blackpool v Reading	2-2	2-0	-	1-0	-	1-0
Bournemouth v Birmingham	-	-	-	-	-	0-2
Brentford v Nottm Forest	-	-	-	-	-	-
Cardiff v Bolton	-	-	-	-	1-1	-
Charlton v Fulham	-	-	-	-	-	-
Huddersfield v Ipswich	-	-	-	-	0-0	0-2
Norwich v Sheff Wed	0-1	-	-	-	-	-
Rotherham v Brighton	-	-	-	-	-	-
Watford v Middlesbro	-	1-1	3-1	2-1	1-2	1-0
Wigan v Derby	-	-	-	-	-	1-3
Wolves v Leeds	-	-	-	-	2-2	-

League 1

Bradford v Preston	-	-	-	-	-	0-0
Bristol City v Swindon	-	-	-	-	-	0-0
Chesterfield v Crewe	-	2-3	5-5	-	-	-
Colchester v Barnsley	-	-	-	-	-	-
Crawley Town v Oldham	-	-	-	-	1-1	1-0
Fleetwood Town v Yeovil	-	-	-	-	-	-
Leyton Orient v Gillingham	-	3-1	-	-	-	5-1
MK Dons v Scunthorpe	0-2	-	-	0-0	0-1	-
Notts Co v Coventry	-	-	-	-	2-2	3-0
Peterborough v Walsall	1-0	-	4-1	-	-	0-0
Rochdale v Port Vale	1-0	0-0	-	-	2-2	-
Sheff Utd v Doncaster	0-1	1-1	2-2	-	0-0	-

League 2

Accrington v Carlisle	-	-	-	-	-	-
Burton v Wycombe	-	-	1-2	-	2-0	1-0
Bury v Morecambe	2-1	0-0	1-0	-	-	0-2
Cheltenham v Stevenage	-	-	1-0	-	-	-
Dag & Red v AFC Wimbledon	-	-	-	0-2	0-1	1-0

Results cover matches from Premier League to Conference and Scottish Premiership to League Two

	2008-09	2009-10	2010-11	2011-12	2012-13	2013-14
Exeter v Newport Co	-	-	-	-	-	0-2
Hartlepool v Southend	3-0	3-0	-	-	-	0-1
Mansfield v Shrewsbury	-	-	-	-	-	-
Northampton v Cambridge U	-	-	-	-	-	-
Oxford v York	1-0	2-1	-	-	0-0	0-1
Portsmouth v Plymouth	-	-	-	-	-	3-3
Tranmere v Luton	-	-	-	-	-	-

Conference						
Aldershot v Torquay	-	0-2	1-0	0-1	1-0	-
Alfreton v Grimsby	-	-	-	2-5	0-2	3-3
Chester v Forest Green	-	-	-	-	-	1-2
Dartford v Barnet	-	-	-	-	-	0-2
Dover v Woking	-	-	-	-	-	-
Gateshead v Altrincham	-	1-0	2-0	-	-	-
Kidderminster v Bristol Rovers	-	-	-	-	-	-
Lincoln v Halifax	-	-	-	-	-	3-1
Macclesfield v Wrexham	-	-	-	-	2-0	3-2
Nuneaton v Braintree	-	-	-	-	2-4	1-1
Southport v Telford	-	-	-	3-2	0-3	-
Welling v Eastleigh	-	-	-	-	-	-

Wednesday April 8th, 2015

Scottish Premiership						
Aberdeen v Inverness CT	0-2/1-0	-	1-2/1-0	2-1/0-1	2-3	1-0/0-1
Celtic v Partick	-	-	-	-	-	1-0
Dundee v Dundee Utd	-	-	-	-	0-3	-
Hamilton v Kilmarnock	1-0/2-1	0-0/3-0	2-2/1-1	-	-	-
Motherwell v St Mirren	2-1/0-2	2-0	3-1/0-1	1-1	1-1/2-2	3-0
Ross County v St Johnstone	1-2/2-2	-	-	-	1-2/1-0	1-0

Scottish Championship						
Dumbarton v Hibernian	-	-	-	-	-	-
Hearts v Alloa	-	-	-	-	-	-
Livingston v Falkirk	-	-	-	1-1/1-2	2-1/1-2	0-3/0-1
Queen of Sth v Rangers	-	-	-	-	-	-
Raith v Cowdenbeath	-	-	2-1/2-2	-	2-2/0-1	3-3/1-2

Saturday April 11th, 2015

Premier League						
Burnley v Arsenal	-	1-1	-	-	-	-
Liverpool v Newcastle	3-0	-	3-0	3-1	1-1	2-1
Man Utd v Man City	2-0	4-3	2-1	1-6	1-2	0-3
QPR v Chelsea	-	-	-	1-0	0-0	-
Southampton v Hull	-	-	-	2-1	-	4-1
Sunderland v Crystal Palace	-	-	-	-	-	0-0
Swansea v Everton	-	-	-	0-2	0-3	1-2
Tottenham v Aston Villa	1-2	0-0	2-1	2-0	2-0	3-0
West Brom v Leicester	-	3-0	-	-	-	-
West Ham v Stoke	2-1	0-1	3-0	-	1-1	0-1

Championship						
Birmingham v Wolves	2-0	2-1	1-1	-	2-3	-
Bolton v Norwich	-	-	-	1-2	-	-
Brighton v Bournemouth	-	-	1-1	-	-	1-1
Derby v Brentford	-	-	-	-	-	-
Fulham v Wigan	2-0	2-1	2-0	2-1	1-1	-
Ipswich v Blackpool	1-1	3-1	-	2-2	1-0	0-0

Results cover matches from Premier League to Conference and Scottish Premiership to League Two

Can Louis van Gaal help United silence their noisy neighbours?

	2008-09	2009-10	2010-11	2011-12	2012-13	2013-14
Leeds v Cardiff	-	-	0-4	1-1	0-1	-
Middlesbro v Rotherham	-	-	-	-	-	-
Millwall v Watford	-	-	1-6	0-2	1-0	2-2
Nottm Forest v Huddersfield	-	-	-	-	6-1	1-0
Reading v Blackburn	-	-	-	-	-	0-1
Sheff Wed v Charlton	4-1	-	2-2	0-1	2-0	2-3

League 1

	2008-09	2009-10	2010-11	2011-12	2012-13	2013-14
Barnsley v Chesterfield	-	-	-	-	-	-
Coventry v Colchester	-	-	-	-	2-2	2-0
Crewe v Leyton Orient	0-2	-	-	-	1-1	1-2
Doncaster v Rochdale	-	-	-	-	-	-
Gillingham v Bradford	0-2	-	2-0	0-0	3-1	0-1
Oldham v Sheff Utd	-	-	-	0-2	0-2	1-1
Port Vale v MK Dons	-	-	-	-	-	1-0
Preston v Bristol City	2-0	2-2	0-4	-	-	1-0
Scunthorpe v Crawley Town	-	-	-	-	2-1	-
Swindon v Peterborough	2-2	-	1-1	-	-	2-1
Walsall v Fleetwood Town	-	-	-	-	-	-
Yeovil v Notts Co	-	-	2-1	1-0	0-0	-

League 2

	2008-09	2009-10	2010-11	2011-12	2012-13	2013-14
AFC Wimbledon v Oxford	-	0-1	-	0-2	0-3	0-2
Cambridge U v Accrington	-	-	-	-	-	-
Carlisle v Dag & Red	-	-	0-2	-	-	-
Luton v Burton	-	-	-	-	-	-
Morecambe v Portsmouth	-	-	-	-	-	2-2
Newport Co v Bury	-	-	-	-	-	0-0
Plymouth v Mansfield	-	-	-	-	-	1-1
Shrewsbury v Exeter	1-1	-	-	-	-	-
Southend v Tranmere	2-1	1-1	-	-	-	-
Stevenage v Northampton	-	-	0-1	-	-	-
Wycombe v Cheltenham	-	-	2-1	-	1-1	1-2
York v Hartlepool	-	-	-	-	-	0-0

Conference

	2008-09	2009-10	2010-11	2011-12	2012-13	2013-14
Barnet v Halifax	-	-	-	-	-	0-4
Braintree v Aldershot	-	-	-	-	-	1-0
Bristol Rovers v Southport	-	-	-	-	-	-
Chester v Dover	-	-	-	-	-	-
Dartford v Nuneaton	-	-	-	-	0-1	1-2
Eastleigh v Alfreton	-	-	-	-	-	-
Forest Green v Macclesfield	-	-	-	-	1-1	2-3
Grimsby v Wrexham	-	-	2-1	1-3	1-0	3-1
Telford v Lincoln	-	-	-	1-2	1-1	-
Torquay v Altrincham	3-1	-	-	-	-	-
Welling v Kidderminster	-	-	-	-	-	1-2
Woking v Gateshead	-	-	-	-	2-1	1-2

Scottish Premiership

	2008-09	2009-10	2010-11	2011-12	2012-13	2013-14
Dundee Utd v Hamilton	1-1	1-1/0-2	2-1	-	-	-
Inverness CT v Celtic	1-2/0-0	-	0-1/3-2	0-2	2-4/1-3	0-1
Kilmarnock v Aberdeen	1-2	1-1/2-0	2-0	2-0/1-1	1-3/1-1	0-1
Partick v Motherwell	-	-	-	-	-	1-5
St Johnstone v Dundee	2-0/0-0	-	-	-	1-0	-
St Mirren v Ross County	-	-	-	-	5-4/1-4	2-1/1-0

Scottish Championship

	2008-09	2009-10	2010-11	2011-12	2012-13	2013-14
Alloa v Dumbarton	-	1-3/1-2	0-0/2-3	-	-	1-2/1-5
Cowdenbeath v Livingston	-	-	-	-	1-1/2-2	2-3/4-0

Results cover matches from Premier League to Conference and Scottish Premiership to League Two

	2008-09	2009-10	2010-11	2011-12	2012-13	2013-14
Hibernian v Hearts	1-1/1-0	1-1/1-2	0-2/2-2	1-3	1-1/0-0	2-1/1-2
Queen of Sth v Falkirk	-	-	1-5/0-1	1-5/0-0	-	2-0/1-2
Rangers v Raith	-	-	-	-	-	-

Scottish League One						
Ayr v Peterhead	2-0/0-0	-	1-1/2-2	-	-	-
Brechin v Stirling	2-1/1-2	1-0/1-1	-	1-3/1-2	-	-
Dunfermline v Stranraer	-	-	-	-	-	3-1/3-2
Forfar v Airdrieonians	-	-	1-2/1-2	3-2/2-3	-	3-3/1-1
Morton v Stenh'semuir	-	-	-	-	-	-

Scottish League Two						
Berwick v Clyde	-	-	2-1/1-1	0-2/3-0	2-1/3-3	0-1/3-0
East Fife v Albion	-	-	-	2-0/1-2	1-2/2-0	-
East Stirling v Montrose	5-0/2-1	1-0/2-3	2-1/1-2	1-0/3-1	2-2/1-2	2-2/1-2
Elgin v Arbroath	-	-	3-5/3-2	-	-	-
Queen's Park v Annan	-	0-0/3-2	3-0/0-1	0-0/2-0	2-2/2-2	2-5/0-1

Tuesday April 14th, 2015

Championship						
Birmingham v Blackburn	-	2-1	2-1	-	1-1	2-4
Bolton v Charlton	-	-	-	-	2-0	1-1
Brighton v Huddersfield	0-1	0-0	2-3	-	4-1	0-0
Derby v Blackpool	4-1	0-2	-	2-1	4-1	5-1
Ipswich v Cardiff	1-2	2-0	2-0	3-0	1-2	-
Leeds v Norwich	-	2-1	2-2	-	-	-
Middlesbro v Wolves	-	-	-	-	2-0	-
Millwall v Wigan	-	-	-	-	-	2-1
Reading v Bournemouth	-	-	-	-	-	1-2
Sheff Wed v Brentford	-	-	1-3	0-0	-	-

League 1						
Bradford v Bristol City	-	-	-	-	-	1-1
Chesterfield v Colchester	-	-	-	0-1	-	-
Coventry v Oldham	-	-	-	-	2-1	1-1
Fleetwood Town v MK Dons	-	-	-	-	-	-
Leyton Orient v Doncaster	-	-	-	-	0-2	-
Notts Co v Barnsley	-	-	-	-	-	-
Peterborough v Crewe	4-2	-	-	-	-	4-2
Preston v Gillingham	-	-	-	-	-	3-1
Rochdale v Swindon	-	-	3-3	-	-	-
Scunthorpe v Port Vale	-	-	-	-	-	-
Walsall v Crawley Town	-	-	-	-	2-2	1-2
Yeovil v Sheff Utd	-	-	-	0-1	0-1	-

League 2						
Burton v Carlisle	-	-	-	-	-	-
Bury v Shrewsbury	2-1	1-0	1-0	-	2-2	-
Cheltenham v Cambridge U	-	-	-	-	-	-
Dag & Red v Luton	2-1	-	-	-	-	-
Hartlepool v Accrington	-	-	-	-	-	2-1
Mansfield v Tranmere	-	-	-	-	-	-
Oxford v Northampton	-	-	3-1	2-0	2-1	2-0
Plymouth v AFC Wimbledon	-	-	-	0-2	1-2	1-2
Southend v Newport Co	-	-	-	-	-	0-0
Stevenage v Portsmouth	-	-	-	-	2-1	-
Wycombe v Exeter	1-1	2-2	-	3-1	0-1	1-1
York v Morecambe	-	-	-	-	1-4	1-0

Results cover matches from Premier League to Conference and Scottish Premiership to League Two

Wednesday April 15th, 2015

Championship

	2008-09	2009-10	2010-11	2011-12	2012-13	2013-14
Fulham v Rotherham	-	-	-	-	-	-
Nottm Forest v Watford	3-2	2-4	1-0	1-1	0-3	4-2

Saturday April 18th, 2015

Premier League

	2008-09	2009-10	2010-11	2011-12	2012-13	2013-14
Arsenal v Sunderland	0-0	2-0	0-0	2-1	0-0	4-1
Aston Villa v QPR	-	-	-	2-2	3-2	-
Chelsea v Man Utd	1-1	1-0	2-1	3-3	2-3	3-1
Crystal Palace v West Brom	-	1-1	-	-	-	3-1
Everton v Burnley	-	2-0	-	-	-	-
Hull v Liverpool	1-3	0-0	-	-	-	3-1
Leicester v Swansea	-	2-1	2-1	-	-	-
Man City v West Ham	3-0	3-1	2-1	-	2-1	2-0
Newcastle v Tottenham	2-1	-	1-1	2-2	2-1	0-4
Stoke v Southampton	-	-	-	-	3-3	1-1

Championship

	2008-09	2009-10	2010-11	2011-12	2012-13	2013-14
Blackburn v Nottm Forest	-	-	-	-	3-0	0-1
Blackpool v Fulham	-	-	2-2	-	-	-
Bournemouth v Sheff Wed	-	-	0-0	2-0	-	2-4
Brentford v Bolton	-	-	-	-	-	-
Cardiff v Millwall	-	-	2-1	0-0	1-0	-
Charlton v Leeds	-	1-0	-	-	2-1	2-4
Huddersfield v Derby	-	-	-	-	1-0	1-1
Norwich v Middlesbro	-	-	1-0	-	-	-
Rotherham v Reading	-	-	-	-	-	-
Watford v Birmingham	0-1	-	-	2-2	2-0	1-0
Wigan v Brighton	-	-	-	-	-	0-1
Wolves v Ipswich	0-0	-	-	-	0-2	-

League 1

	2008-09	2009-10	2010-11	2011-12	2012-13	2013-14
Barnsley v Peterborough	-	2-2	-	1-0	0-2	-
Bristol City v Coventry	2-0	1-1	1-2	3-1	-	1-2
Colchester v Scunthorpe	0-0	-	-	1-1	1-2	-
Crawley Town v Notts Co	-	-	-	-	0-0	1-0
Crewe v Walsall	2-1	-	-	-	2-0	0-3
Doncaster v Fleetwood Town	-	-	-	-	-	-
Gillingham v Rochdale	1-1	-	-	-	1-2	-
MK Dons v Leyton Orient	1-2	1-0	2-3	4-1	1-0	1-3
Oldham v Chesterfield	-	-	-	5-2	-	-
Port Vale v Preston	-	-	-	-	-	0-2
Sheff Utd v Bradford	-	-	-	-	-	2-2
Swindon v Yeovil	2-3	3-1	0-1	-	4-1	-

League 2

	2008-09	2009-10	2010-11	2011-12	2012-13	2013-14
Accrington v Stevenage	-	-	1-0	-	-	-
AFC Wimbledon v Wycombe	-	-	-	-	2-2	1-0
Cambridge U v Mansfield	2-1	3-2	1-5	1-2	4-1	-
Carlisle v Plymouth	-	-	1-1	-	-	-
Exeter v Southend	-	1-0	-	-	3-0	0-2
Luton v Hartlepool	-	-	-	-	-	-
Morecambe v Burton	-	3-2	2-1	2-2	0-0	0-1
Newport Co v Dag & Red	-	-	-	-	-	1-2
Northampton v Cheltenham	4-2	2-1	1-1	2-3	2-3	1-1
Portsmouth v Bury	-	-	-	-	2-0	1-0
Shrewsbury v York	-	-	-	-	-	-
Tranmere v Oxford	-	-	-	-	-	-

Results cover matches from Premier League to Conference and Scottish Premiership to League Two

	2008-09	2009-10	2010-11	2011-12	2012-13	2013-14
Conference						
Aldershot v Chester	2-2	-	-	-	-	2-0
Alfreton v Welling	-	-	-	-	-	2-2
Altrincham v Telford	-	-	-	-	-	1-1
Dover v Bristol Rovers	-	-	-	-	-	-
Gateshead v Forest Green	-	3-1	1-1	1-0	1-1	1-1
Halifax v Torquay	-	-	-	-	-	-
Kidderminster v Barnet	-	-	-	-	-	1-0
Lincoln v Eastleigh	-	-	-	-	-	-
Macclesfield v Dartford	-	-	-	-	2-0	3-1
Nuneaton v Woking	-	-	-	-	0-0	0-2
Southport v Grimsby	-	-	2-2	1-2	1-1	2-1
Wrexham v Braintree	-	-	-	5-1	1-1	2-3
Scottish Championship						
Alloa v Queen of Sth	-	-	-	-	1-0/1-2	0-3/0-1
Dumbarton v Rangers	-	-	-	-	-	-
Falkirk v Cowdenbeath	-	-	5-1/2-0	-	2-0/4-0	4-0/5-0
Hearts v Raith	-	-	-	-	-	-
Livingston v Hibernian	-	-	-	-	-	-
Scottish League One						
Airdrieonians v Ayr	-	3-1/1-1	2-2/0-5	-	-	0-1/3-0
Brechin v Dunfermline	-	-	-	-	-	1-1/3-2
Peterhead v Forfar	-	-	1-2/1-1	-	-	-
Stirling v Morton	-	-	0-1/3-2	-	-	-
Stranraer v Stenh'semuir	-	-	-	-	1-1/1-1	1-0/1-1
Scottish League Two						
Annan v East Fife	-	-	-	-	-	-
Arbroath v Queen's Park	1-1/3-0	-	1-0/2-2	-	-	-
Clyde v Albion	-	-	1-2/0-1	-	-	2-2/4-0
East Stirling v Berwick	1-0/0-4	1-0/3-2	0-0/1-0	1-3/2-1	0-1/0-3	1-0/1-1
Montrose v Elgin	1-0/3-1	1-1/0-4	0-1/1-0	3-0/2-3	2-2/4-1	3-3/0-3

Saturday April 25th, 2015

	2008-09	2009-10	2010-11	2011-12	2012-13	2013-14
Premier League						
Arsenal v Chelsea	1-4	0-3	3-1	0-0	1-2	0-0
Burnley v Leicester	-	-	3-0	1-3	0-1	0-2
Crystal Palace v Hull	-	-	0-0	0-0	4-2	1-0
Everton v Man Utd	1-1	3-1	3-3	0-1	1-0	2-0
Man City v Aston Villa	2-0	3-1	4-0	4-1	5-0	4-0
Newcastle v Swansea	-	3-0	-	0-0	1-2	1-2
QPR v West Ham	-	-	-	-	1-2	-
Southampton v Tottenham	-	-	-	-	1-2	2-3
Stoke v Sunderland	1-0	1-0	3-2	0-1	0-0	2-0
West Brom v Liverpool	0-2	-	2-1	0-2	3-0	1-1
Championship						
Birmingham v Charlton	3-2	-	-	-	1-1	0-1
Bournemouth v Bolton	-	-	-	-	-	0-2
Brighton v Watford	-	-	-	2-2	1-3	1-1
Cardiff v Blackpool	2-0	1-1	-	1-3	3-0	-
Fulham v Middlesbro	3-0	-	-	-	-	-
Huddersfield v Blackburn	-	-	-	-	2-2	2-4
Ipswich v Nottm Forest	2-1	1-1	0-1	1-3	3-1	1-1
Millwall v Derby	-	-	2-0	0-0	2-1	1-5
Reading v Brentford	-	-	-	-	-	-
Rotherham v Norwich	-	-	-	-	-	-
Sheff Wed v Leeds	-	-	-	-	1-1	6-0
Wigan v Wolves	-	0-1	2-0	3-2	-	-

Results cover matches from Premier League to Conference and Scottish Premiership to League Two

	2008-09	2009-10	2010-11	2011-12	2012-13	2013-14
League 1						
Bradford v Barnsley	-	-	-	-	-	-
Chesterfield v Bristol City	-	-	-	-	-	-
Coventry v Crewe	-	-	-	-	1-2	2-2
Fleetwood Town v Colchester	-	-	-	-	-	-
Leyton Orient v Sheff Utd	-	-	-	1-1	0-1	1-1
Notts Co v Doncaster	-	-	-	-	0-2	-
Peterborough v Crawley Town	-	-	-	-	-	0-2
Preston v Swindon	-	-	-	-	4-1	2-1
Rochdale v MK Dons	-	-	1-4	1-2	-	-
Scunthorpe v Gillingham	-	-	-	-	-	-
Walsall v Oldham	1-2	3-0	1-1	0-1	3-1	1-0
Yeovil v Port Vale	-	-	-	-	-	-
League 2						
Burton v Northampton	-	3-2	1-1	0-1	3-3	1-0
Bury v AFC Wimbledon	-	-	-	-	-	1-1
Cheltenham v Shrewsbury	-	1-2	0-1	0-0	-	-
Dag & Red v Accrington	0-0	3-1	-	2-1	1-1	0-0
Hartlepool v Exeter	-	1-1	2-3	2-0	-	0-2
Mansfield v Portsmouth	-	-	-	-	-	2-2
Oxford v Cambridge U	3-1	0-0	-	-	-	-
Plymouth v Tranmere	-	-	1-3	-	-	-
Southend v Luton	-	-	-	-	-	-
Stevenage v Carlisle	-	-	-	1-0	1-1	1-3
Wycombe v Morecambe	1-1	-	2-0	-	2-2	1-0
York v Newport Co	-	-	2-1	1-1	-	1-0
Conference						
Barnet v Gateshead	-	-	-	-	-	0-1
Braintree v Altrincham	-	-	-	-	-	-
Bristol Rovers v Alfreton	-	-	-	-	-	-
Chester v Nuneaton	-	-	-	-	-	3-3
Dartford v Lincoln	-	-	-	-	2-4	1-2
Eastleigh v Kidderminster	-	-	-	-	-	-
Forest Green v Dover	-	-	-	-	-	-
Grimsby v Aldershot	1-0	1-2	-	-	-	1-1
Telford v Wrexham	-	-	-	0-2	0-2	-
Torquay v Macclesfield	-	1-0	1-3	3-0	-	-
Welling v Southport	-	-	-	-	-	4-3
Woking v Halifax	-	-	-	-	-	0-0
Scottish Championship						
Cowdenbeath v Hearts	-	-	-	-	-	-
Hibernian v Alloa	-	-	-	-	-	-
Queen of Sth v Dumbarton	-	-	-	-	-	1-2/3-1
Raith v Livingston	-	-	-	0-1/0-3	0-0/0-2	1-0/2-4
Rangers v Falkirk	3-1	4-1/3-0	-	-	-	-
Scottish League One						
Ayr v Stirling	1-1/3-1	-	-	-	-	-
Dunfermline v Forfar	-	-	-	-	-	1-1/0-0
Peterhead v Airdrieonians	-	-	5-1/2-4	-	-	-
Stenh'semuir v Brechin	-	1-1/1-2	0-0/1-3	1-1/2-1	3-1/3-3	3-2/4-2
Stranraer v Morton	-	-	-	-	-	-
Scottish League Two						
Albion v Arbroath	-	-	0-2/3-0	1-0/1-1	4-0/0-1	-
Berwick v East Fife	-	-	-	-	-	-

Results cover matches from Premier League to Conference and Scottish Premiership to League Two

	2008-09	2009-10	2010-11	2011-12	2012-13	2013-14
Elgin v Annan	1-2/0-1	1-1/1-0	2-0/2-3	3-0/1-2	2-2/3-1	2-3/2-3
Montrose v Clyde	-	-	8-1/3-1	4-0/5-0	2-3/1-1	0-2/0-2
Queen's Park v East Stirling	-	1-0/2-0	2-0/2-0	2-0/5-1	1-2/5-1	1-3/0-0

Saturday May 2nd, 2015

Premier League						
Aston Villa v Everton	3-3	2-2	1-0	1-1	1-3	0-2
Chelsea v Crystal Palace	-	-	-	-	-	2-1
Hull v Arsenal	1-3	1-2	-	-	-	0-3
Leicester v Newcastle	-	0-0	-	-	-	-
Liverpool v QPR	-	-	-	1-0	1-0	-
Man Utd v West Brom	4-0	-	2-2	2-0	2-0	1-2
Sunderland v Southampton	-	-	-	-	1-1	2-2
Swansea v Stoke	-	-	-	2-0	3-1	3-3
Tottenham v Man City	2-1	3-0	0-0	1-5	3-1	1-5
West Ham v Burnley	-	5-3	-	1-2	-	-

Championship						
Blackburn v Ipswich	-	-	-	-	1-0	2-0
Blackpool v Huddersfield	-	-	-	-	1-3	1-0
Bolton v Birmingham	-	2-1	2-2	-	3-1	2-2
Brentford v Wigan	-	-	-	-	-	-
Charlton v Bournemouth	-	-	1-0	3-0	-	1-0
Derby v Reading	0-2	2-1	1-2	0-1	-	1-3
Leeds v Rotherham	-	-	-	-	-	-
Middlesbro v Brighton	-	-	-	1-0	0-2	0-1
Norwich v Fulham	-	-	-	1-1	0-0	1-2
Nottm Forest v Cardiff	0-1	0-0	2-1	0-1	3-1	-
Watford v Sheff Wed	2-2	4-1	-	-	2-1	0-1
Wolves v Millwall	-	-	-	-	0-1	-

League 1						
Barnsley v Rochdale	-	-	-	-	-	-
Bristol City v Walsall	-	-	-	-	-	1-0
Colchester v Preston	-	-	-	3-0	1-0	1-2
Crawley Town v Coventry	-	-	-	-	2-0	3-2
Crewe v Bradford	-	0-1	2-1	1-0	-	0-0
Doncaster v Scunthorpe	-	4-3	3-0	-	4-0	-
Gillingham v Notts Co	2-2	-	-	-	-	2-1
MK Dons v Yeovil	3-0	2-2	3-2	0-1	1-0	-
Oldham v Peterborough	1-2	-	0-5	-	-	5-4
Port Vale v Fleetwood Town	-	-	-	-	0-2	-
Sheff Utd v Chesterfield	-	-	-	4-1	-	-
Swindon v Leyton Orient	0-1	3-2	2-2	-	0-1	1-3

League 2						
Accrington v Mansfield	-	-	-	-	-	1-1
AFC Wimbledon v Cheltenham	-	-	-	4-1	1-2	4-3
Cambridge U v Burton	2-0	-	-	-	-	-
Carlisle v Hartlepool	0-1	3-2	1-0	1-2	3-0	-
Exeter v Dag & Red	2-1	-	2-1	-	0-1	2-2
Luton v Stevenage	-	0-1	-	-	-	-
Morecambe v Southend	-	-	2-1	1-0	1-0	2-1
Newport Co v Oxford	-	-	-	-	-	3-2
Northampton v Wycombe	-	-	1-1	-	3-1	1-4
Portsmouth v York	-	-	-	-	-	0-1
Shrewsbury v Plymouth	-	-	-	1-1	-	-
Tranmere v Bury	-	-	-	2-0	3-0	-

Results cover matches from Premier League to Conference and Scottish Premiership to League Two

	2008-09	2009-10	2010-11	2011-12	2012-13	2013-14
Scottish Championship						
Alloa v Cowdenbeath	-	2-1/3-1	-	-	-	3-1/0-1
Dumbarton v Raith	-	-	-	-	4-2/1-2	2-4/3-3
Falkirk v Hibernian	1-1	1-3/1-3	-	-	-	-
Hearts v Rangers	2-1	1-2/1-4	1-2/1-0	0-2/0-3	-	-
Livingston v Queen of Sth	2-0/2-2	-	-	2-2/2-2	-	3-3/1-2
Scottish League One						
Airdrieonians v Dunfermline	1-3/1-1	1-1/0-1	-	-	1-2/3-3	0-3/2-0
Brechin v Stranraer	1-0/2-1	-	-	-	3-0/2-2	1-1/1-3
Forfar v Ayr	-	-	4-1/3-2	-	2-1/2-1	0-1/4-2
Morton v Peterhead	-	-	-	-	-	-
Stirling v Stenh'semuir	-	0-0/1-1	-	2-2/3-1	-	-
Scottish League Two						
Annan v Montrose	1-2/2-1	2-0/0-0	2-2/2-1	2-1/1-2	2-1/1-1	2-1/1-0
Arbroath v Berwick	-	-	3-2/2-1	-	-	-
Clyde v Queen's Park	-	-	2-3/0-2	0-2/1-2	0-3/2-3	3-0/1-2
East Fife v Elgin	-	-	-	-	-	-
East Stirling v Albion	1-0/0-1	2-0/3-1	0-0/1-2	-	-	1-4/1-1

Saturday May 9th, 2015

	2008-09	2009-10	2010-11	2011-12	2012-13	2013-14
Premier League						
Arsenal v Swansea	-	-	-	1-0	0-2	2-2
Aston Villa v West Ham	1-1	0-0	3-0	-	2-1	0-2
Chelsea v Liverpool	0-1	2-0	0-1	1-2	1-1	2-1
Crystal Palace v Man Utd	-	-	-	-	-	0-2
Everton v Sunderland	3-0	2-0	2-0	4-0	2-1	0-1
Hull v Burnley	-	1-4	0-1	2-3	0-1	-
Leicester v Southampton	-	-	-	3-2	-	-
Man City v QPR	-	-	-	3-2	3-1	-
Newcastle v West Brom	2-1	2-2	3-3	2-3	2-1	2-1
Stoke v Tottenham	2-1	1-2	1-2	2-1	1-2	0-1

Saturday May 16th, 2015

	2008-09	2009-10	2010-11	2011-12	2012-13	2013-14
Premier League						
Burnley v Stoke	-	1-1	-	-	-	-
Liverpool v Crystal Palace	-	-	-	-	-	3-1
Man Utd v Arsenal	0-0	2-1	1-0	8-2	2-1	1-0
QPR v Newcastle	-	0-1	-	0-0	1-2	-
Southampton v Aston Villa	-	-	-	-	4-1	2-3
Sunderland v Leicester	-	-	-	-	-	-
Swansea v Man City	-	-	-	1-0	0-0	2-3
Tottenham v Hull	0-1	0-0	-	-	-	1-0
West Brom v Chelsea	0-3	-	1-3	1-0	2-1	1-1
West Ham v Everton	1-3	1-2	1-1	-	1-2	2-3

Sunday May 24th, 2015

	2008-09	2009-10	2010-11	2011-12	2012-13	2013-14
Premier League						
Arsenal v West Brom	1-0	-	2-3	3-0	2-0	1-0
Aston Villa v Burnley	-	5-2	-	-	-	-
Chelsea v Sunderland	5-0	7-2	0-3	1-0	2-1	1-2
Crystal Palace v Swansea	2-0	0-1	0-3	-	-	0-2
Everton v Tottenham	0-0	2-2	2-1	1-0	2-1	0-0
Hull v Man Utd	0-1	1-3	-	-	-	2-3
Leicester v QPR	-	4-0	0-2	-	-	1-0
Man City v Southampton	-	-	-	-	3-2	4-1
Newcastle v West Ham	2-2	-	5-0	-	0-1	0-0
Stoke v Liverpool	0-0	1-1	2-0	1-0	3-1	3-5

Results cover matches from Premier League to Conference and Scottish Premiership to League Two

PREMIER LEAGUE

Sunderland	+23.95	Arsenal	+2.12
C Palace	+16.44	West Ham	+1.91
Newcastle	+11.93	Southampton	-0.74
Stoke	+9.10	Hull	-4.35
Chelsea	+8.83	Man Utd	-6.48
Everton	+7.15	Cardiff	-6.85
Aston Villa	+7.10	West Brom	-9.91
Liverpool	+6.47	Fulham	-10.55
Tottenham	+4.83	Norwich	-12.23
Man City	+3.33	Swansea	-13.06

Sunderland were a profitable team to follow

CHAMPIONSHIP

Leicester	+18.07	Millwall	-4.08
Burnley	+15.29	Doncaster	-4.62
Derby	+10.70	Middlesbro	-4.71
Reading	+4.40	Leeds	-5.28
Wigan	+3.57	Huddersfield	-5.57
Brighton	+2.56	Blackpool	-7.60
QPR	+2.08	Bolton	-8.12
Bournemouth	+1.62	Nottm Forest	-8.40
Blackburn	+0.31	Barnsley	-11.26
Ipswich	-1.39	Birmingham	-11.85
Sheff Wed	-2.84	Yeovil	-12.50
Charlton	-2.88	Watford	-14.28

LEAGUE 1

Wolves	+13.12	Crawley	-2.66
Rotherham	+13.03	MK Dons	-2.82
Brentford	+9.29	Bradford	-4.15
Leyton Orient	+7.58	Sheff Utd	-5.50
Port Vale	+6.25	Coventry	-5.81
Gillingham	+4.70	Notts Co	-6.80
Preston	+4.52	Carlisle	-7.38
Peterborough	+3.54	Walsall	-7.52
Tranmere	+1.70	Stevenage	-8.73
Colchester	+1.13	Oldham	-9.18
Crewe	-0.63	Bristol C	-9.74
Swindon	-0.96	Shrewsbury	-18.45

LEAGUE 2

Rochdale	+6.55	AFC W'bledon	-1.38
Scunthorpe	+6.27	Morecambe	-3.02
Southend	+4.72	Torquay	-3.26
Accrington	+4.46	Oxford	-4.95
Fleetwood	+3.97	Northampton	-5.56
Mansfield	+3.85	Newport Co	-8.15
Burton	+3.10	Cheltenham	-9.18
York	+3.04	Portsmouth	-9.96
Dag & Red	+2.59	Hartlepool	-10.20
Plymouth	+2.27	Wycombe	-11.20
Chesterfield	+1.59	Bury	-11.93
Exeter	+0.07	Bristol R	-13.25

SCOTTISH PREMIERSHIP

Motherwell	+12.16	Ross County	-0.38
Aberdeen	+11.20	St Mirren	-4.75
Celtic	+4.87	Dundee Utd	-5.99
Hearts	+2.73	Kilmarnock	-7.26
Inverness CT	+1.46	Partick	-11.98
St Johnstone	+0.87	Hibernian	-16.28

SCOTTISH CHAMPIONSHIP

Dumbarton	+16.23	Alloa	+0.57
Cowdenbeath	+11.09	Queen of Sth	+0.18
Falkirk	+7.32	Livingston	-0.38
Dundee	+5.68	Raith	-10.06
Hamilton	+1.32	Morton	-14.39

SCOTTISH LEAGUE ONE

Rangers	+3.97	Forfar	-1.65
Airdrieonians	+3.95	Stenh'semuir	-4.08
Dunfermline	+2.00	Ayr	-4.70
Stranraer	-0.30	Brechin	-4.96
East Fife	-1.35	Arbroath	-6.98

SCOTTISH LEAGUE TWO

Clyde	+13.86	Montrose	-1.51
Peterhead	+9.08	Berwick	-3.43
East Stirling	+7.75	Elgin City	-8.47
Stirling	+7.12	Albion	-9.07
Annan	+6.75	Queen's Park	-16.00

Multiple bets

Selections	2	3	4	5	6	7
Doubles	1	3	6	10	15	21
Trebles	-	1	4	10	20	35
Fourfolds	-	-	1	5	15	35
Fivefolds	-	-	-	1	6	21
Sixfolds	-	-	-	-	1	7
Sevenfolds	-	-	-	-	-	1
Full cover	3	7	15	31	63	127

All profit & loss figures to £1 level stake at best odds

WINNERS & LOSERS 2013-14

PREMIER LEAGUE

Champions	Manchester City
Champions League	Liverpool
	Chelsea
	Arsenal
Europa League	Everton
	Tottenham
Relegated	Norwich
	Fulham
	Cardiff

CHAMPIONSHIP

Champions	Leicester
Promoted	Burnley
Playoff winners	QPR
Relegated	Doncaster
	Barnsley
	Yeovil

LEAGUE 1

Champions	Wolves
Promoted	Brentford
Playoff winners	Rotherham
Relegated	Tranmere
	Carlisle
	Shrewsbury
	Stevenage

LEAGUE 2

Champions	Chesterfield
Promoted	Scunthorpe
	Rochdale
Playoff winners	Fleetwood
Relegated	Bristol Rovers
	Torquay

Manchester United bag the Community Shield

Manchester City take the Premier League title

CONFERENCE PREMIER

Champions	Luton
Playoff winners	Cambridge
Relegated	Tamworth
	Hyde
Expelled	Salisbury
	Hereford

CONFERENCE NORTH

Champions	Telford
Playoff winners	Altrincham
Relegated	Histon
	Workington
Resigned	Vauxhall Motors

CONFERENCE SOUTH

Champions	Eastleigh
Playoff winners	Dover
Relegated	Tonbridge
	Dorchester

COMMUNITY SHIELD

Winners	Manchester United
Beaten finalists	Wigan

Clockwise from top left: Real Madrid, St Johnstone, Seville and Celtic all get the party started

FA CUP

Winners	Arsenal
Beaten finalists	Hull

LEAGUE CUP

Winners	Manchester City
Beaten finalists	Sunderland

FOOTBALL LEAGUE TROPHY

Winners	Peterborough
Beaten finalists	Chesterfield

FA TROPHY

Winners	Cambridge
Beaten finalists	Gosport

SCOTTISH PREMIERSHIP

Champions	Celtic
Europa League	Motherwell
	Aberdeen
Relegated	Hibernian
	Hearts

SCOTTISH CHAMPIONSHIP

Champions	Dundee
Promoted	Hamilton
Relegated	Morton

SCOTTISH LEAGUE ONE

Champions	Rangers
Relegated	East Fife
	Arbroath

SCOTTISH LEAGUE TWO

Champions	Peterhead
Promoted	Stirling Albion

SCOTTISH CUP

Winners	St Johnstone
Beaten finalists	Dundee United

SCOTTISH LEAGUE CUP

Winners	Aberdeen
Beaten finalists	Inverness

SCOTTISH CHALLENGE CUP

Winners	Raith Rovers
Beaten finalists	Rangers

CHAMPIONS LEAGUE

Winners	Real Madrid
Beaten finalists	Atletico Madrid

EUROPA LEAGUE

Winners	Seville
Beaten finalists	Benfica

INDEX OF TEAMS

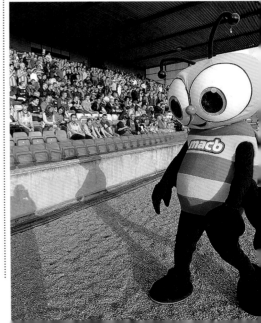

*Partick mascot Jaggy Macbee gets to work
before Thistle kick off their 2013-14 campaign*

Odds of recent champions

Premier League		Best odds
2013-14	Manchester City	23-10
2012-13	Manchester United	13-5
2011-12	Manchester City	9-2
Championship		**Best odds**
2013-14	Leicester City	14-1
2012-13	Cardiff City	12-1
2011-12	Reading	18-1
League 1		**Best odds**
2013-14	Wolves	4-1
2012-13	Doncaster Rovers	14-1
2011-12	Charlton Athletic	9-1
League 2		**Best odds**
2013-14	Chesterfield	8-1
2012-13	Gillingham	22-1
2011-12	Swindon Town	12-1
Conference		**Best odds**
2013-14	Luton Town	9-2
2012-13	Mansfield Town	5-1
2011-12	Fleetwood Town	5-1
Scottish Premiership		**Best odds**
2013-14	Celtic	1-40
2012-13	Celtic	1-25
2011-12	Celtic	5-6
Scottish Championship		**Best odds**
2013-14	Dundee	15-8
2012-13	Partick Thistle	5-1
2011-12	Ross County	11-1
Scottish League One		**Best odds**
2013-14	Rangers	1-12
2012-13	Queen of the South	7-2
2011-12	Cowdenbeath	13-2
Scottish League Two		**Best odds**
2013-14	Peterhead	15-8
2012-13	Rangers	1-20
2011-12	Alloa Athletic	5-2

Odds conversion

Odds-on		Fractional	Odds-against	
As %	Decimal		Decimal	As %
50.00%	2.00	Evens	2.00	50.00%
52.38%	1.91	11-10	2.10	47.62%
54.55%	1.83	6-5	2.20	45.45%
55.56%	1.80	5-4	2.25	44.44%
57.89%	1.73	11-8	2.38	42.11%
60.00%	1.67	6-4	2.50	40.00%
61.90%	1.62	13-8	2.63	38.10%
63.64%	1.57	7-4	2.75	36.36%
65.22%	1.53	15-8	2.88	34.78%
66.67%	1.50	2-1	3.00	33.33%
69.23%	1.44	9-4	3.25	30.77%
71.43%	1.40	5-2	3.50	28.57%
72.22%	1.38	13-5	3.60	27.78%
73.33%	1.36	11-4	3.75	26.67%
73.68%	1.36	14-5	3.80	26.32%
75.00%	1.33	3-1	4.00	25.00%
76.92%	1.30	10-3	4.33	23.08%
77.78%	1.29	7-2	4.50	22.22%
80.00%	1.25	4-1	5.00	20.00%
81.82%	1.22	9-2	5.50	18.18%
83.33%	1.20	5-1	6.00	16.67%
84.62%	1.18	11-2	6.50	15.38%
85.71%	1.17	6-1	7.00	14.29%

Correct scores 2013-14

	Prem	Chmp	Lg1	Lg2	Conf	SCP	SCh	SLg1	SLg2
1-0	45	61	59	57	63	21	15	6	14
2-0	36	36	44	35	43	19	20	13	14
2-1	20	45	50	43	48	22	13	15	20
3-0	13	23	14	26	28	11	7	12	8
3-1	19	19	24	18	29	7	11	8	6
3-2	8	10	21	10	19	3	4	9	4
4-0	11	6	6	4	6	7	3	2	9
4-1	13	9	7	6	10	4	4	3	1
4-2	2	2	6	2	2	1	1	3	1
4-3	2	1	1	2	3	2	1	2	0
0-0	27	40	39	56	39	13	10	3	5
1-1	28	74	69	83	56	25	20	25	22
2-2	17	30	27	30	28	7	4	4	8
3-3	6	11	6	3	8	5	4	2	4
4-4	0	1	1	1	0	0	0	0	1
0-1	30	58	49	53	46	19	16	11	7
0-2	18	22	20	33	24	13	9	7	11
1-2	21	33	37	43	41	18	11	16	12
0-3	16	13	15	13	10	4	7	5	4
1-3	13	19	20	10	6	6	2	7	7
2-3	11	7	9	8	9	2	1	5	9
0-4	3	1	4	4	3	4	0	4	2
1-4	5	6	1	6	3	2	1	1	4
2-4	1	6	4	2	2	3	6	3	2
3-4	1	0	3	0	4	1	3	2	0
Other	14	19	16	4	22	9	7	12	5

Home win/draw/away win percentages 2013-14

	Prem	Chmp	Lg1	Lg2	Conf	SCP	SCh	SLg1	SLg2
Home	47	41	44	38	48	45	47	44	44
Draw	21	28	26	31	24	22	21	19	22
Away	32	30	30	31	28	33	32	37	33

Over & under percentages 2013-14

	Prem	Chmp	Lg1	Lg2	Conf	SCP	SCh	SLg1	SLg2
<1.5	27	29	27	30	27	23	23	11	14
>1.5	73	71	73	70	73	77	77	89	86
<2.5	48	53	51	57	49	48	50	36	41
>2.5	52	47	49	43	51	52	50	64	59
<3.5	67	73	72	80	72	72	71	63	65
>3.5	33	27	28	20	28	28	29	37	35

Asian handicaps

Giving up handicap			Receiving handicap	
Result of bet	Result of game	Handicap	Result of game	Result of bet
Win	Win	**0**	Win	Win
No bet	Draw	**Scratch**	Draw	No bet
Lose	Lose		Lose	Lose
Win	Win	**0,0.5**	Win	Win
Lose half	Draw	**0.25**	Draw	Win half
Lose	Lose		Lose	Lose
Win	Win	**0.5**	Win	Win
Lose	Draw		Draw	Win
Lose	Lose		Lose	Lose
Win	Win by 2+	**0.5,1**	Lose by 2+	Lose
Win half	Win by 1	**0.75**	Lose by 1	Lose half
Lose	Draw		Draw	Win
Lose	Lose		Win	Win
Win	Win by 2+	**1**	Lose by 2+	Lose
Return stake	Win by 1		Lose by 1	Return stake
Lose	Draw		Draw	Win
Lose	Lose		Win	Win